020450

TRENDS IN BRITISH SOCIETY SINCE 1900

9

'00

WITHDRAWN FROM STOCK

D0266910

Trends in British Society since 1900

A GUIDE TO THE CHANGING SOCIAL STRUCTURE OF BRITAIN

Edited by
A. H. Halsey

MACMILLAN

© A. H. Halsey 1972

All rights reserved. No part of this publication
may be reproduced or transmitted, in any form
or by any means, without permission

First edition 1972
Reprinted 1974

Published by
THE MACMILLAN PRESS LTD
London and Basingstoke
Associated companies in New York Dublin
Melbourne Johannesburg and Madras

SBN (paperback) 333 17722 3

Printed in Great Britain by
REDWOOD BURN LIMITED
Trowbridge & Esher

THE LIBRARY
West Surrey College of Art and Design

The paperback edition of this book is sold
subject to the condition that it shall not, by way
of trade or otherwise, be lent, resold, hired out,
or otherwise circulated without the publisher's
prior consent, in any form of binding or cover
other than that in which it is published and
without a similar condition including this
condition being imposed on the subsequent
purchaser.

309.142
HAL

20450

Contents

List of Tables

Table

Table

List of Contributors

ROBERT BACON, Fellow of Lincoln College, Oxford.

GEORGE SAYER BAIN, Deputy Director, Industrial Relations Research Unit, University of Warwick.

DAVID BUTLER, Fellow of Nuffield College, Oxford.

JULIET CHEETHAM, Lecturer in Applied Social Studies, Department of Social and Administrative Studies, University of Oxford.

ROBERT CURRIE, Fellow of Wadham College, Oxford.

ALAN GILBERT, Nuffield College, Oxford.

A. H. HALSEY, Head of Department of Social and Administrative Studies, University of Oxford, and Fellow of Nuffield College.

KATHLEEN JONES, Professor of Social Administration, University of York.

KENNETH MACDONALD, Senior Research Officer, Nuffield College, Oxford.

JULIA PARKER, Lecturer in Social Administration, Department of Social and Administrative Studies, University of Oxford.

JOHN PIMLOTT, W.E.A. Tutor Organiser in Industrial Relations.

JOHN RIDGE, Lecturer in Sociology, Department of Social and Administrative Studies, University of Oxford, and Fellow of Linacre College.

CONSTANCE ROLLETT, Department of Social and Administrative Studies, University of Oxford.

JOHN SHEEHAN, Lecturer in Economics, University College, Dublin.

JOHN VAIZEY, Professor of Economics, Brunel University.

NIGEL WALKER, University Reader in Criminology, Fellow of Nuffield College, Oxford.

BRUCE WOOD, Lecturer in Government, University of Manchester.

Preface

In one or another guise, courses on the changing social structure of modern or twentieth-century Britain are staples of undergraduate courses in sociology and a familiar feature of university extra-mural and other adult education lectures and classes in the social studies. Moreover a much wider and varied group of politicians, lawyers, teachers, administrators, social workers and people interested in public affairs need access to a convenient compilation of British social facts.

Such a compilation appeared from official sources in 1970 as *Social Trends*,[1] a parallel and companion to *Economic Trends* and a first shot at what we may hope and expect to be an improving annual record of social indicators. This product of the statistical reforms and developments begun by Claus Moser and his colleagues at the Central Statistical Office will greatly ease the accessibility of numerical measures of the changing social structure of Britain. But it has two limitations. The first of these is that it covers the relatively short period since 1951. There are good reasons for this, and the hazards of our attempt in this book to trace changes over the course of the whole of the twentieth century will quickly become apparent to the reader. None the less the attempt has been made here, and the student can use it either as a more or less tentative measure of more long-run changes or as the necessary longer perspective for evaluating the significance of more recent trends.

The second limitation of *Social Trends* relates to the coverage of facets of social structure. The present book is rather wider, dealing for example with religious affiliation and social mobility, and taking advantage of unofficial as well as official statistics. Part of the gap, however, may be temporary and in any case the two sources should be used to complement each other.

Independently David Butler had pointed out to me that there was a case for producing a volume parallel to his own *British Political Facts*, and my colleagues in the Department of Social and Administrative Studies, Nuffield College, the Faculty of Social Studies at Oxford and elsewhere have collaborated in putting together the present volume. I am indebted to them for their patient work and all the more so because they agreed that royalties from the book should be donated to a social

[1] *Social Trends*, no. 1, 1970, Central Statistical Office (HMSO, London, 1970).

science research fund. We all owe a special debt to Mrs Constance Rollett, who acted as research assistant in preparing most of the material and who, together with Mrs Julia Parker, undertook a good deal of the editing. I would also like to acknowledge the cheerful and efficient secretarial services provided by Mrs Jenny Norman.

Inevitably readers will find errors, omissions and dispensable inclusions. I shall be glad to hear of them and to take account of them when the time comes for a revised edition.

A. H. HALSEY

Acknowledgements

The author and publishers wish to thank the following, who have kindly given permission for the use of copyright material: the Baptist Union for the tables from *The Baptist Handbook*; George Bell & Sons for the table from *The Aged in the Welfare State* by Peter Townsend and Dorothy Wedderburn (1965); Basil Blackwell & Mott Ltd for *Monograph No. 5, Oxford University Institute of Statistics* by H. F. Lydall and the article from *1961 Bulletin* by H. F. Lydall and D. G. Tipping; British Broadcasting Corporation for material from *The People's Activities 1965* and the Audience Research Department; *British Journal of Sociology* for the tables from *Trend of Class Differentials in Educational Opportunity in England and Wales* by A. Little and J. Westergaard; British Tourist Authority for the tables from *The Digest of Tourist Statistics 1969*; Cambridge University Press for the tables from *Demography* by Peter R. Cox, *The Wealth of the Nation: The National Balance Sheet of the U.K. 1957–61* by J. R. Revell, *Occupation and Pay in Great Britain* by Guy Routh, *Wages and Income in the U.K. since 1860* by A. L. Bowley and *Abstract of British Historical Statistics* by B. R. Mitchell and Phyllis Deane; the Clarendon Press for the tables from 'Wage Rates in Five Countries 1860–1959' by E. H. Phelps Brown from *Oxford Economic Papers*, vol. 2 (1950) and *A Survey of Social Conditions in England and Wales* by A. M. Carr-Saunders, D. Caradog Jones and C. A. Moser (1958); Crosby Lockwood & Son Ltd for the extract from William A. Belson, *The Impact of Television*; Episcopal Church in Scotland for the tables from *Scottish Episcopal Church Year Book and Directory* and *Annual Report of the Representative Church Council 1901–68*; Eyre & Spottiswoode Ltd for the tables from *Parliamentary Representation 1944* and *Election and Electors 1955* by J. F. S. Ross; Heinemann Educational Books Ltd for the tables from *Divorce in England* by O. R. McGregor, *English Hospital Statistics* by Robert Pinker, *A History of the Nursing Profession* by Brian Abel-Smith, *Crime in England and Wales* by F. H. McClintock and N. H. Avison, and *The Police: A Study in Manpower* by J. P. Martin and G. L. Wilson (ed. L. Radzinowicz); Humanities Press Inc. for an extract from *The Changing Social Structure of England and Wales 1871–1951* by D. C. Marsh and *Parity and Prestige in English Secondary Education* by O. Banks; the Institute of Race Relations for the tables from *The Dependants of the Coloured Commonwealth Population of England and Wales* by David Eversley and Fred Sukdeo, 1969, copyright © Institute of Race Relations 1969 and *Institute of Race Relations Facts Paper: Colour and Immigration in the U.K. 1969*, published by the Institute of Race Relations, London, copyright © Institute of Race Relations 1969; the Library Association for the extracts from *A Century of Public Libraries 1850–1950* and *Statistics of Public Libraries in Great Britain and Northern Ireland*; Longman Group Ltd for the tables from *Population* by R. K. Kelsall and *The Public Schools* by G. Kalton; MacGibbon & Kee Ltd for the tables from *The British Political Élite* by W. L. Guttsman; Oxford University Press for the tables from *Colour and Citizenship* by E. J. B. Rose *et al.*; Political and Economic Planning for the use of the table from *The British Film Industry 1952* and *1958*; Population Studies for the use of the table from 'Inter-generation Differences in Occupation', *Population Studies*, vol. xi (1958) by Dr Bernard Benjamin; Reader's Digest Association Ltd for the table from *Products and People, 1963*; Religious Society of Friends for the figures from *Society of Friends: Minutes of London Yearly Meeting* and data covering the period 1901–68; Routledge & Kegan Paul Ltd for the tables from *The Changing Social Structure of England and Wales 1871–1961* by D. C. Marsh, *Parity and Prestige in English Secondary Education: A Study in Educational Sociology* by Olive Banks, and *Relative Deprivation and Social Justice* by W. G. Runciman; Routledge & Kegan Paul Ltd and Augustus M. Kelley Publishers for the extract from *A History of the Labour Party from 1914* by G. D. H. Cole; Royal Geographical Society for the extracts from *The Geographical Cycle* by W. M. Davis and *The Cycle of Mountain Glaciation* by W. H. Hobbs; Royal Statistical Society for the tables from 'The Long-Term Trend in the Size Distribution of Income' from *Journal of the Royal Statistical Society*, series 4, part i, by H. F. Lydall; the Salvation Army for the table from *Salvation Army Year Book*; Town and Country Planning Association and the International Textbook Company Ltd for the table from 'The New Towns' by F. J. Osborn and A. Whittick, from Jan–Feb 1968 issue of *Town and Country Planning*, the journal of the Town and Country Planning Association; The Committee of Vice-Chancellors and Principals of the Universities of the United Kingdom for the tables from *Report on an Enquiry into Admissions to Universities 1955–56, Association of Universities of the British Commonwealth* by R. K. Kelsall; University of Keele for the tables from *National Recreation Study*, 1967; University of Wales Press for the tables from *The House of Commons 1837–1901*, *The House of Commons 1900–11* and Vallentine, Mitchell & Co. Ltd for the table from *The Jewish Year Book;* Watch Tower Bible and Tract Society for the table from *Yearbook of Jehovah's Witnesses*.

The publishers have made every effort to trace the copyright-holders, but if they have inadvertently overlooked any, they will be pleased to make the necessary arrangement at the first opportunity.

I The Study of British Society

A. H. HALSEY

'Let us', the English pragmatist is fond of saying, 'start with the facts.' He stands in a tradition of social arithmetic which goes back to the second half of the seventeenth century and which has made an enormous contribution to the numerical description of social problems. From this point of view a book of statistical tables indicating trends in a wide variety of aspects of social life in Britain during a century in which rapid changes are in train needs no further justification. But we need to be clear what purposes can be served by such a book. It cannot claim to be either a history or a sociology of twentieth-century Britain. The question is rather to what use such material can be put by sociologists.

FACTS AND STATISTICS

The facts, it is sometimes held, especially in the form of numbers, speak for themselves. But neither life nor sociology are so happily simple as that. Facts are given significance or meaning only in the context of some prior theory or interpretation, whether explicit or implicit. The statistics about trends in British society in the twentieth century which are collected together in this book suffer the same constraint – a theory of social structure and social change must underlie them. To describe is also, however imperfectly, to explain. Statistical compilations of the kind made here can all too easily inform the student only to deceive. They may appear, or even purport, to 'speak for themselves': but this is never completely and often very far from so for two broad reasons. There may be difficulties about the meaning of the numbers which arise from the manner of their collection and classification. Or, more fundamentally, the chosen collection may reflect a partial or distorted view of what is significant in social structure and change.

The first type of difficulty is the lesser: it can, admittedly laboriously, be avoided by careful description of the sources and of the method of collection and definition of the data. Thus one aim of each of the following chapters is to guide students in the use of the statistical sources and to point out the dangers in interpreting statistics which are typically collected for administrative purposes rather than to answer questions in the social sciences. Illustrations of this kind of difficulty recur in every chapter. Classifications may change, as for example in the occupational classifications used by the Registrar-General in successive censuses. Or the administrative basis of data collection may change, as for example in the statistical series on unemployment, the basis of which has shifted during the century with the extension of unemployment legislation.[1]

The second type of difficulty, which merges into the first, is more intractable. It arises if we reverse the logical procedure implied by a table of bare social statistics (i.e. to infer a conception of change from the facts) and start instead from a conception of social structure and deduce what facts should be collected.

At the outset, however, the student must expect disappointment. Sociologists must rely to a considerable degree on data collected by other men for other purposes. A recurring problem is one which arises particularly in interpreting data relevant to social policy and the provision of welfare services. This is the difficulty of gaining from the statistics any idea of quality or adequacy. Obviously any analysis of health or welfare services or of housing should include some statement about how far the standard or amount of the service supplied meets the need for it. But for the most part the figures are concerned only with supply; independent measures of need which would be required to judge adequacy are virtually non-existent. In Chaps 10, 11 and 12 we are looking at the growth or decline of various public services but for the most part we are not able to relate them to the needs they are designed to meet.

In the face of theoretically inadequate statistics the social scientist may, of course, resort to the academic sociological survey which can be designed in explicit relation to theory.[2] The direct sociological investigation is a powerful tool[3] and 'panel' or longitudinal studies in which a cohort of respondents is followed over a long period of time[4]

---

[1] See Chap. 4, pp. 102–4.
[2] A recent example is J. H. Goldthorpe, D. Lockwood, F. Bechhofer and J. Platt, *The Affluent Worker*, 3 vols (C.U.P. 1969). This interview survey was designed to test the theory of embourgeoisement.
[3] For a short introduction to its methods see E. Grebenik and C. A. Moser, 'Statistical Surveys' in A. T. Welford *et al.*, *Society: Problems of Methods of Study* (Routledge 1962). For a more extended exposition of survey methods see C. A. Moser, *Survey Methods in Social Investigation* (Heinemann 1958).
[4] See for example the follow-up investigations carried out under the auspices of the Population Investigation Committee and directed by Dr J. W. B. Douglas and the follow-up study undertaken by the Scottish Council for Research in Education into the trend of intelligence. See especially the introduction by D. V. Glass to J. W. B. Douglas, *The Home and the School* (MacGibbon & Kee 1964).

can yield information on trends: but such studies do not constitute more than a tiny fraction of the numerical data available, the bulk of which is collected and published by governmental agencies. The measurement of social mobility is a case in point which is dealt with in Chap. 5. To answer questions concerning the rate of mobility, reliance has to be placed on the results of direct sociological inquiry with the resulting difficulty that trends are difficult to establish without exact repetition of a given study at later points in time. Theoretically informed statistical studies are rarely repeated by sociologists, partly for reasons of academic organisation (systematic storage of survey data is only just beginning) and partly because theoretical interest in the social sciences and definitions of concepts are influenced as much by fashion as by cumulation.

In practice therefore the problem remains largely that of adapting to social science ends statistics which, from the point of view of the sociologist, are a by-product of administrative and organisational activity. The authors of this book have had to wrestle with this problem in every chapter. One example is Bruce Wood's attempt (in Chap. 9) to use a sociological definition of urbanism in addition to the legal definition in terms of local government boundaries. Thus, in order to bring into focus the increasing interdependence of town and country he has to use such indicators as the journey to work, shops and centres of entertainment. Another example recurs frequently in the analysis of stratification. When the sociologist attempts to use the census for analysis of any aspect of the British system of stratification he finds a host of tables using 'social class' or 'socio-economic group' as a variable. But frequently he wants to ask questions which pre-suppose distinction between class, status and power and between the 'subjective' and 'objective' character of stratified social relationships. The Registrar-General's tables may not yield answers. Thus, in a review of one of the best known books of British social arithmetic[1] and referring to three tables on 'industrial status', 'type of income', and 'social class' derived from the census, John Rex makes the plaintive comment that 'It is figures like this which drive the theoretically oriented sociologist to something like despair. Is the classification of the population into status groups meant solely as a statistical exercise, or are these classifications meant to refer to groups who might act as groups, or who might be thought of by their fellows as sharing a common way of life and meriting a characteristic degree of esteem? Clearly there does seem to be some claim that these represent real groups rather than statistical classifications. The . . . table . . . is said to be a classification according to "social class". But the implications of this term are left open to be filled in by the reader according to his

[1] A. M. Carr Saunders, D. Caradog Jones and C. A. Moser, *A Survey of Social Conditions in England and Wales* (O.U.P. 1958).

own ideological preconceptions. Surely it would be more valuable if statisticians, who continually claim to be using sociological concepts, were to find out what groupings were of real sociological importance and then seek to describe these, rather than the groupings which are of little importance, but which happen to be easily measurable.'[1]

What is a Society?

But what groups are of sociological importance? What kind of a notion of structure and change would be adequate to prescribe the scope and character of statistics to be collected, either officially or academically? This question is the first to confront anyone who tries to devise a book like this one but there is little agreement amongst sociologists about the definition of their own subject. As T. B. Bottomore has put it, 'The fundamental conception, or directing idea, in sociology is that of *social structure*'[2] but 'while many useful distinctions have been made, an adequate classification of societies, social groups and social relationships has still not appeared'.[3] Bottomore's reference is, in principle, to the analysis of all societies. Our problem here however is to devise a descriptive framework for one particular advanced industrial society – Britain.[4] This immediately raises the problem of what *is* a society? What are the limits in time and space which are in practice to be used meaningfully in order to specify British society as a more or less circumscribed network of social relationships. The time span must be arbitrary since neither evolution nor revolution ever totally transform all the institutions of a society, its language, its kinship structure, its economy. We have chosen to confine our attention to the twentieth century but for particular reasons we might just as reasonably have begun with, say, the first census in 1801 or the Education Act of 1870 or the beginning of the first world war in 1914. Though there would be general agreement that Britain in 1700 was a different society in respect of its fundamental institutions and culture from Britain in 1970 – the former being classified as pre-industrial or agricultural and the latter as industrially advanced – there could be no agreement as to a unique date for the transition. Again the partial social integration of England, Scotland, Wales and Northern Ireland as well as the regions within them raises the same question in relation to population. The main focus of this book

---

[1] In E. Butterworth and D. Weir (eds), *The Sociology of Modern Britain* (Collins: Fontana 1970) pp. 203–4.

[2] T. B. Bottomore, *Sociology – A Guide to Problems and Literature* (Allen & Unwin 1962) p. 20.

[3] *Ibid.*, p. 36.

[4] Bottomore's text is an excellent introduction to the study of society. His purpose is to review the literature but the structure of his book also provides the framework we seek for statistical description of a given society.

is on England and Wales, each author having decided himself whether it would make more sense to use Great Britain or the United Kingdom as the aggregate unit for analysis in the light of his knowledge of national variations in the structure of the social relationships with which he is concerned and in the light of the availability of statistics. Already then, though we may begin with the intention of defining the data collection in terms of sociological concepts, there will be ambiguities in theory and obstacles in practice which result in more or less unsatisfactory compromise.

These problems of delimiting a society in both time and space might well be held to distort the picture induced from the statistics in this book. The period in question is one in which the relations between Britain and the rest of the world have changed radically; and the consequences are not only external but ramify throughout the indigenous structure of British life. During the century Britain has lost a vast empire which once 'meant that India and Africa and parts of the Middle and Far East were also in a sense the lower strata of British society, the peak of which was the destined inheritance of the successful survivors of institutional discipline. . . . The dissolution of the Empire and increasing real independence of the English-speaking dominions have contracted the size of the society over which the British elite – and British society as a whole – were superordinated.'[1] The Leninist thesis concerning export of exploitation by imperial countries cannot be tested merely by trend statistics on the material conditions of British manual workers. Neither the pattern of migration shown in Chap. 2, nor the course of immigration treated more fully in Chap. 11, nor the changes in distribution of life chances between the social strata shown in the chapters on housing, health and welfare can more than partially and incompletely express the changes in class structure which have accompanied the transition of British society to its post-imperial position.

The distortion which might arise from this 'boundary' ambiguity has another aspect. To look at the trends of economic growth (Chap. 3), advancing division of labour (Chap. 4), decreasing family size (Chap. 2), expanding urbanism (Chap. 9), developing education (Chaps 6 and 7), and so on suggests a model of the evolution of industrial or post-industrial society. Theories of convergence, determined by a 'logic of industrialism' which is more or less independent of the political and cultural peculiarities of particular nations, have become widely received in sociological literature since the second world war.[2] In the absence of *comparative*

[1] Edward Shils, 'Background to Policies: Britain Awake' in P. Hall (ed.), *Labour's New Frontiers* (André Deutsch 1964).

[2] See for example Clark Kerr *et al.*, *Industrialism and Industrial Man* (Harvard U.P. 1960), and for criticism of this general thesis see J. H. Goldthorpe, 'Social Stratifica-

statistics, the student may therefore be tempted to use this book as a compilation of twentieth-century trends in Industrial Society, only writ small. In other words the meaning of the British trends and the unique constellation of forces for change which have impinged on this country cannot be properly gauged until the immense task of compiling exactly comparable statistics for other countries is also undertaken.

There is another severe limitation of the currently available statistics from which we have drawn. It is related both to the protest by John Rex referred to earlier – that statisticians do not use sociological concepts – and also to Edmund Leach's comment on the position taken by Meyer Fortes:

> The anthropologist's focus of interest is not in the [social structure] as such but in 'the way it works' – that is in the perception of the way in which living human beings, who are all the time being born, growing older, and dying, *pass through* an ordered system of offices.[1]

Official statistics, quite apart from their deficiencies as a record of objective experience, also seldom offer data on the subjective experience of actors in social systems. The census and most surveys undertaken for Royal Commissions eschew 'opinion'.

A particular example may be taken from the sociology of higher education. An appendix of the Robbins Report[2] was devoted to the study of the changing career structure of the university teaching professions and in it C. A. Moser offered the first sociographic description of these professions – their ranks and discipline, their career possibilities and patterns. It was a meticulous numerical account of the situation of teachers in the British universities in 1962. Given its purpose as part of a public inquiry, it could not be expected to provide a comprehensive sociological account of these professions. This was subsequently undertaken[3] using the same sample of respondents and the later study provided related survey evidence of the opinions and perceptions and collective self-conceptions of university teachers. But the two surveys together could not exhaust the sociology of these professions because many of the relevant sociological questions required comparable information at different points of time in the evolution of university teaching. The Higher Education Research Unit at the London School

tion in Industrial Society', in Reinhard Bendix and Seymour Martin Lipset, *Class Status and Power: Social Stratification in Comparative Perspective*, 2nd ed. (Free Press: The Macmillan Co., N.Y. 1966), pp. 648–60.

[1] E. R. Leach, 'Social Structure' in *International Encyclopaedia of Social Sciences* (Free Press: The Macmillan Co., N.Y. 1968), Vol. 14, p. 485. In this article Leach gives a succinct account of the history and current usage of the term social structure.

[2] *Committee on Higher Education Report, Appendix III*, Cmnd 2154 III (HMSO 1963).

[3] A. H. Halsey and Martin Trow, *The British Academics* (Faber 1971).

of Economics has repeated some of the survey questions after a five-year interval and thus will add still further to our knowledge of the changing character of the academic professions. Replicated surveys (or panel studies) yield trends. But again the theorist may be thwarted in that the surveys may not bear directly on the questions he wishes to put. In this sense the survey is never more than historical evidence, albeit precise and quantified, to be used like any other historical evidence as a servant which may not be adequate to its theoretical master.[1]

The central term social structure has no single usage. It derives from biology as an organismic analogy. Among British anthropologists the term was defined by Radcliffe-Brown, in a way synonymous with the term social organisation, to include the whole network of social relationships in a society. Other anthropologists and sociologists have also used the term with empirical reference but more narrowly. If a society is a bounded network of social relationships, social structure is the relatively enduring and sanctioned set of relations within the network.[2] This definition again has the problem of time buried within it. It excludes the more ephemeral and fleeting of social interactions and emphasises the complex of *institutions* which constitute the more or less permanent structure of a society. Institutions are enduring, organised and sanctioned structures of relationships between individuals and groups, for example marriage or property.[3] But the definition of enduring is ambiguous. It may refer to regularities in the life cycle in which individual members of the population move through sequences of positions or it may refer to stability in the pattern of behaviour and sanctioning involved in the institution.

It is moreover useful in defining social structure to include reference to the group formations as well as to the patterns of relationship involved, not only because of John Rex's plea but also because the approach to institutions is often to define them as made up of social roles and thereby to focus attention on individual actions. Though the difference is largely one of emphasis, many sociologists state the view

[1] In his attempt to answer the question of what has been the relation between institutionalised inequalities and awareness or resentment of them in twentieth-century Britain, W. G. Runciman used the results of a national sample survey in 1962 in combination with non-survey evidence from the social history of England since 1918. Use of the two types of material, as he argues, 'should be seen as the connected parts of a single argument; the difference between them is one of style, not of kind', *Relative Deprivation and Social Justice* (Routledge 1966), p. 8.

[2] Some writers, for example Lévi-Strauss, have a quite different usage, referring to general models of social structure rather than directly to actual social relationships.

[3] Thus Weber defined the institution of property as made up of relations of exclusion between individuals and groups in respect of objects having exchangeable value in society.

that to concentrate on the roles which make up institutions (which in turn and in interaction make up social structure) is to distract attention from larger groups or collectivities such as social classes or religious denominations, which may occupy a significant place in a society, characterising and changing it in ways which are not fully appreciable if social behaviour is reduced to the acts or sum of the acts of individuals.

It should be added that those, particularly anthropologists, who work in the Radcliffe-Brown tradition link structure closely to function and are interested as much in the working of institutions as in their form: but in either case 'a full description of the social structure would entail an analysis of all of the offices and corporations in the system – a task which would be plainly impossible but which can be carried out piece-meal in a partial way'.[1] The statistical series which comprised this book cannot be expected to achieve the impossible: they are indeed piece-meal and partial. In the context of the whole field of analysis of social structure and change they offer no more than a useful addition to other kinds of sociological, anthropological and historical evidence. They have, as we have pointed out, limitations derived from the non-socio-logical purposes for which the bulk of them were initially assembled, they have shortcomings of reliability, validity and consistency and, above all, they may defy or at least resist adaptation as indicators or measures of sociological concepts.

What then can be expected of them? It would seem reasonable to expect them to cover the essential institutional framework of the society for the chosen period. The functional prerequisites of society are such that certain institutions and groups are easily identifiable in all societies. We may list these minimum requirements as five institutional systems.[2]

A system of *production*.
A system of *reproduction*.
A system of *authority and power*.
A system of *ritual*.
A system of *communication*.

All societies must produce goods and services and reproduce appropriate social personalities in order to maintain themselves. Hence the necessity for a division of labour, work organisations and familial and educational institutions. These two systems of production and reproduction together form the basis of social arrangements for the distribution of life chances which 'work' through a system of power and authority. At least in societies with a complex division of labour, life chances are distributed unequally and the society is composed of groups which are stratified by class, status and power. Social cohesion is then further reinforced

---

[1] E. R. Leach, *loc. cit.*, p. 484.   [2] Cf. T. B. Bottomore, *op. cit.*, p. 111.

through ritual institutions serving to assert and reassert values and to offer social recognition to personal events such as birth or marriage. Finally society presupposes communication and hence requires institutions of language and organisations for storing and transmitting information.

Each of these elements has to be covered in the following chapters, but according to the special form of social structure which has emerged in modern Britain. It is at this point that our own emphases and interpretations have entered. We have paid little attention to the institutions of language. The British population is almost universally literate in a common language though in earlier centuries dialects and illiteracy would have to be taken into account, and in any case it is open to debate how far the existence of the Welsh language, of class-linked linguistic structure and usages and of non-English-speaking communities among recent immigrants can be disregarded. Chap. 2 is concerned with those aspects of social structure which determine the reproductive character of the society. The productive system is dealt with in Chaps 3 and 4. Having thus outlined the twin bases of stratification we go on to examine social mobility in Chap. 5. Chaps 6 and 7 on schools and higher education are concerned with the formation of social personalities. Chap. 8 on the electorate and the House of Commons, as well as Chap. 9 on urbanisation and local government, may be seen as statistics on the distribution of power and authority. We then look at three aspects of the distribution of life chances – housing (Chap. 10), health (Chap. 11), and welfare (Chap. 12) in the context of the so-called welfare state. Chap. 13 on religion deals in part with the system of ritual, but Chap. 14 on immigration, Chap. 15 on crime and Chap. 16 on leisure may also be thought of as concerned with those institutions which maintain social cohesion. However this classification of the content of chapters is somewhat arbitrary since all groupings and institutions tend to have multiple functions; for example churches and chapels are also part of the system of communication, the economy, the socialisation process and the distribution of authority and power.

The trends shown in these chapters may now be briefly summarised in terms of the fundamental elements of social structure to which we have referred.

THE PRODUCTIVE SYSTEM

Though we have already characterised twentieth-century Britain as a contracting society because of its transition from the position of a dominant imperial power, it is nonetheless important to note the expansion of its productive system. The Gross National Product has risen since 1900 from £1846m. to £36,815m. in 1968. This increase in available

THE LIBRARY
West Surrey College of Art and Design

goods and services has, of course, to be discounted in terms of inflation and population increase and cannot in any case be wholly satisfactory to the sociologist because of the methods used in calculating it. It excludes a wide range of social exchanges (e.g. between friends and spouses) which are not defined as 'economic' and it includes economic exchanges such that, for example, the employment of more warders to guard more prisoners would count as economic progress and a reduction in the staff of tuberculosis clinics would count as economic regression. Nonetheless the amelioration of material conditions must be taken as a central fact of this century and especially of the period since the second world war in Britain as in other advanced industrial countries, which account for roughly a third of the world's population. Hence the interest of trends shown in Chap. 3 concerning the distribution of national income and wealth which gives us an indication of changes in the structure of classes and status groups. Again there are difficulties in interpreting the data, for example the probability that tax avoidance is positively correlated with income and therefore inequality may be underestimated. Inequality remains the outstanding feature of both income and especially wealth distributions. The trends have been slowly towards less inequality of income: but the richest one per cent of the population still owned 42 per cent of total wealth in 1951–6 (compared with 65·5 per cent in 1911–12) and most capital redistribution in the meantime took place within the middle and upper classes.

The changing class structure appears from another point of view in Chap. 4, where the development of the division of labour is traced. Income distribution statistics in Chap. 3 show a steady rise throughout the century in the share going to the salariat and this now can be seen as a growth of 176 per cent in the white collar labour force between 1911 and 1966. White collar workers are not yet, as in the U.S.A., in a majority, but they are approaching 40 per cent, and within their ranks the growing number of scientific and technical workers (for example the number of laboratory assistants went up by 2,160 per cent between 1921 and 1966) reflects the development of an increasingly complex division of labour on the basis of an increasingly scientific and capital-intensive technology. The productive life of the working class has been gradually transformed in the process. Hours of work have been reduced (from 54 to 44·5 per week between 1900 and 1968) and unemployment has changed its character from that of a fundamental deprivation of a national class to a problem of small minorities and localities. The working man also figures less prominently on the work scene for the double reason of extended education and increased longevity. Meanwhile corporate organisation of working men in occupational or industrial unions has increased sevenfold since the beginning of the century – increasing the proportion of actual to potential male union membership (or density) from 16·7 per cent to 51·9 per cent in 1968.[1] The interests of groups included in the productive process have thus become highly organised. This should not, however, be interpreted as evidence for growing proletarian solidarity. The most dramatic recent rises of unionisation have been among white collar workers and the interests of 'the proletariat' have become divided by a complex of competing occupational groups within the broad stratum of manual workers. Perhaps the most telling reflection of advancing material affluence in statistics concerning working class living standards is that of the progressive shift of the definition of a 'cost of living' from its narrow and normative focus on the 'necessities of life' towards a retail price index reflecting the consumption patterns of the general population. These patterns have changed, especially since the war, towards greater emphasis on the purchase of leisure, private transport and consumer durables.

The trends in women's participation in paid employment are the opposite of those of men. Women have contributed especially to the growth of white collar employment. This is all the more remarkable in the light of developments in the institution of marriage and of increased longevity which might have been expected to produce reverse results. Indeed, especially since 1951, the increasing participation of married women is the most outstanding factor in the changing balance between employment and non-employment – a fact which raises many questions about the changing structure of family life and particularly for the Parsonian analysis of the relation between marriage, kinship and economy in advanced industrial society.[2]

THE REPRODUCTIVE SYSTEM

As a reproductive system, British society has also expanded in this century. The population of England and Wales has grown by 45 per cent and that of Scotland by 16 per cent. Industrially advanced countries share some basic similarities of demographic history and, apart from the special features of international migration associated with Britain's colonial past, there seems to be nothing especially remarkable about the British record. Fertility declined from the beginning of the

[1] But note the lower density of trade union membership among women (3·2 per cent in 1900 rising to 21·6 per cent in 1968). Men and women together show a trend from 12·7 per cent in 1900 to 42·5 per cent in 1968.

[2] Parsons denies evidence for a trend to homogeneity of sex roles and stresses the complementality or non-competing character of women's employment compared with men – 'The American Family' in T. Parsons and R. Bales, *Family Socialisation and Interaction Processes* (Free Press: The Macmillan Co., N.Y. 1955). But see also Norman Dennis's 'Secondary Group Relations and the Pre-eminence of the Family', *Int. J. Comp. Sociol.*, **3**, no. 3 (1962), 80–90.

century until the second world war and, subsequently, fluctuated at a higher level than that to which it had declined in the nineteen-thirties. Mortality declined throughout. Marriage rates rose: the age of marriage fell: family size has decreased and divorce has become more common. The details are set out in Chap. 2 but, it may be noted, they are just as unclear as a guide to changes in the quality of marital and family life as are income statistics a measure of the quality of material existence.

The trends in marriage, fertility and longevity suggest an increasingly uniform pattern of sexual and family experience in the society as a whole – spinsterhood, membership of a large family or early death or bereavement have become increasingly rare. Nevertheless it should be noted that differential experience in those respects continues to mark off the social classes from each other. Later marriage remains more common among the better off. Fertility differentials diminished between 1931 but were still present in the figures for 1961.

Another aspect of the demographic trends, which appears again later in the discussion of urbanisation in Chap. 9, is the emergence of families and households which are not only smaller but more mobile. As many as 30 per cent. of the British population moved house in the five years preceding the 1961 census, though the bulk of this movement was local. The net result of internal migration during the century has been a faster rate of population growth in the South-East, South-West and Midlands compared with the North of England, Scotland and Wales. Throughout the century Scotland has exported part of its natural increase, i.e. has 'reproduced' Englishmen, Americans, Canadians and Australians. At the same time, it emerges from Chap. 9, while nineteenth-century industrialisation had urbanised the society, there has been a more recent trend to 'reproduce' a more mobile and suburban style of life, which adds another facet to the attenuation of working-class life from its earlier attachment to the work place. The working-class community as a dormitory annexe to the industrial factory has become less visible and more fluid in this century. This loosening of local occupationally homogeneous and single-class communities by increased mobility is also indicated by the trends in the issue of motor-car licences.[1] Before the second world war the development of urbanisation was mainly an outcome of market forces. Since that time state planning has superimposed itself on the earlier pattern: half a million people have been moved to new towns or other planned 'overspill' developments outside the conurbations and this deliberate policy of suburbanisation shows no sign of slackening.

Nor is mobility restricted to movement within regions and localities. Part of the imperial legacy was a net loss of population overseas up to

[1] See Table 9.9, p. 280.

about 1931, a continuous interchange throughout the century and a large influx of immigrants, especially between the end of the war and 1962, when the Commonwealth Immigration Act put severe restriction on entry. The more recent immigrations must certainly be regarded as working against the trend towards a more homogeneous society.[1] At the same time the new immigrant communities have contributed disproportionately to the lower-paid manual strata and have hence introduced a new complication into the changing structure of class, status and mobility.

Mobility has yet another dimension – what the sociologists call social mobility normally refers to either intra-generational or inter-generational movement between occupations carrying different degrees of prestige. In Chap. 5 the burden of the argument is to reinforce extreme caution in any statement about trends on the basis of existing data. Such evidence as there is does not preclude the interpretation that mobility between generations has somewhat increased during the century, i.e. that Britain has become a more open society in this sense. But what is more remarkable is that the strong emphasis on egalitarian social policies in education and the social services, which have dominated public thinking in the twentieth century, have not led to unequivocal evidence of greater fluidity of movement between the classes.

This is not to deny that the educational system has come to occupy a greater role as the agency of selection for different places in the hierarchy. But it re-emphasises the crucial influence of family background over the educational performance of children. The basic strategy for the equalisation of educational opportunity has been educational expansion. Children from all social origins have taken advantage of the developing opportunities for secondary and more recently for higher education. But despite this raising of the general standard, class differences in educational attainment have remained fairly constant. Too much, in any case, must not be made of the tendency towards a more meritocratic class system. This interpretation exaggerates the selective role of the educational system. The point is well illustrated in Table 6.26 which, besides showing the clear class gradient in opportunities for entry into higher education, also shows that nearly two-thirds of the children born in 1940–1 into middle-class homes and with I.Q.s of 130 or more at age eleven received no higher education.

The State has increasingly intervened in the distribution of life chances in this century, not only through taxation and education but also in other fields of social policy which are dealt with below in the chapters on housing, health and welfare. Exchequer subsidies to housing

[1] For a good account of the impact on one British town see John Brown, *The Unmelting Pot: An English Town and its Immigrants* (Macmillan 1970).

rose from £0·20m. in 1919–20 to £92·4m. in 1966–7. The costs of the
health and welfare services rose from £406m. to £1490m. between
1949–50 and 1967–8. In consequence, just as there is more education,
so there is more health, housing and welfare. But the impact of these
expansions in state activity on the pattern of class differences in life
chances is similarly unclear. Certainly crude mortality rates have
dropped (from 15·9 to 11·9 per thousand between 1901–10 and 1968)
and infant mortality has dropped from 154 per thousand to 18 per
thousand over the same period. But the Registrar-General's Class V has
had consistently higher death rates than the other classes throughout
as well as higher rates of morbidity (measured by the consultation rate).
The trends have been well summarised by T. Arie:

> The relationship between health and 'social class' remains close
> though not always simple. Certainly there are diseases of the rich
> as well as diseases of the poor, but the burden of the latter is still
> heavy in our prosperous society; in the crucial area of birth and
> infancy some of the gaps between the classes have scarcely changed
> in our time. We know that many of the diseases of poverty can be
> effectively attacked by remedying the privations from which they
> arise. But the 'new diseases' (e.g. coronary heart disease and lung
> cancer) pose problems which are vastly more complicated, being
> due apparently to a multiplicity of causes, rooted in many aspects
> of human life and running across our conventional lines of social
> stratification.[1]

There has been a diminution in the amount of overcrowding over
the course of the century: 16 per cent of householders were living at a
density of more than one and a half persons per room in 1921, but only
one per cent in 1966. Amenities have also improved: 37 per cent of
households lacked baths in 1951 and 15 per cent in 1966. The fact that
there has been an increase in the number of unfit dwellings between
1960 and 1967 from 62,000 to 1,836,000 is more an illustration of rising
norms than of deteriorating objective conditions. On the other hand the
increased mobility of the population to which we have referred is also
reflected in the fact that the number of adults and children in public
accommodation as a result of homelessness trebled between 1950 and
1968.

An increasing proportion of the Gross National Product is paid in
welfare cash benefits (0·2 per cent in 1900 and 7·9 per cent in 1967),
though with a backward movement between 1930 and 1960.

[1] T. Arie, 'Class and Disease', *New Society*, 27 Jan 1966.

POWER AND AUTHORITY

The great institutional centres of power in Britain, as in most advanced industrial societies, are in politics and the economy. We have already commented on the slow reduction of economic inequality shown by the trends in Chaps 3 and 4. Two aspects of the distribution of political power are dealt with in Chap. 8 – the electorate and its voting behaviour in Parliamentary elections and the social composition of Parliament.

This century has seen the completion of universal enfranchisement which was begun with the 1832 Reform Bill. By 1900 the electoral roll included 58 per cent of adult males. By 1950 plural voting had gone and some 95 per cent of adult men and women were on the roll. In 1969 the franchise was extended to 18-year-olds. But the enfranchisement of the whole population has not created enormous discontinuities in the political power structure. The pattern of party support is, of course, class related; but the Conservative Party has continued to attract a quarter of the votes of the unskilled and one-third of the skilled workers down to the present day. Meanwhile Conservative M.P.s, and even more the members of Conservative cabinets, remain dominantly upper and middle class. They are recruited overwhelmingly from the public schools (80 per cent in 1966). The rise of the Labour Party permitted entry of working-class leaders and trade unionists into government. But it too has recruited increasingly from the professional classes and about a fifth of its post-war M.P.s were educated in the public schools. By 1966 one-half of the Labour M.P.s were university graduates.

British conservatism and traditional deference are nowhere better illustrated than in these indications of the voting behaviour of a highly proletarianised society and the social composition of its political rulers. The figures by themselves offer more questions than answers. As Peter Worsley has commented:

> Simple 'objective' classification of occupations, then, or of the distribution of power, does not take us very far in explaining the success of British conservatism in attracting one third of the trade union vote even to this date. Counting heads is essential in order to establish some primary facts about who people are, but even in order to know what to count at this level, we operate with (often implicit) theoretical assumptions. To get any further, to explore deeper levels of behaviour, we have to move beyond this kind of classificatory activity into the field of 'political culture'.[1]

[1] P. Worsley, 'The Analysis of Power and Politics' in E. Butterworth and D. Weir, *op. cit.*, p. 254.

In the final section of Chap. 9 Bruce Wood discusses a further aspect of the distribution of political power, by focusing attention on the structure of local government. An analysis of the available data reveals that, despite the continued pre-eminence of the restrictive century-old basic principle of separate government for town and country, the structure of local government has been subject to a large amount of modification. The 1963 London Government Act, by creating the vast Greater London Council and 32 new London Boroughs, probably offers the clearest example of this process of modification, But, *in toto*, earlier changes were at least as dramatic. After all, no fewer than 350 county districts 'disappeared' in one decade (the 1930s), and from 1888–1970 the creation of 25 new county boroughs, coupled with more than 300 boundary extensions, has meant the transfer of over 750,000 acres and $4\frac{1}{2}$ million people from the county to the county borough system of government.

Large though it may be, this rate of change would probably have been far higher but for two restrictive factors. First, there is the principle of an urban-rural dichotomy in local government. Secondly, successive governments have not been prepared to legislate for anything which could be termed 'radical' change (London, possibly, apart). Modification there has been, but most of it has been directed at keeping up with the trends in urbanisation, discussed earlier in this chapter. As the 'bricks-and-mortar' approach to urbanisation has been superseded by the 'socio-geographic' concept, so too has the principle of an urban-rural dichotomy in local administration been increasingly questioned. The Redcliffe-Maud Report is the most recent, and possibly most compelling, example of this.

SOCIAL COHESION

Arrangements for the maintenance of order and cohesiveness in society are part and parcel of all of the major institutions. But we can single out the chapters on crime, on religion and on immigration in order to throw light on particular trends and problems. The sociologist will examine the statistics on crime and punishment to seek a measure of the level of adherence to or respect for the legitimacy of the social order. The statistics, as Nigel Walker shows, are difficult to interpret. An increasingly complex society generates, on the one hand, a more elaborate code of formal rules and therefore raises the potential of the population to offend against them, and, on the other hand, also generates a more complex system of social control and crime detection. Thus Walker quotes Lady Wootton's comment that 'the internal combustion engine has revolutionalised [*sic*] the business of our criminal courts'. On the other hand, although the number of men and women employed by the police forces have more than doubled since 1900, the actual man hours worked per thousand of the population has remained at more or less the same level throughout the century.

As a general measure of trends in criminality, Table 15.9 records the history of recorded indictable offences. This table takes the average annual frequency for the years 1901–5 as the base and frequencies for later years are given as a percentage of that base. The picture then emerges that the frequency of murder has changed very little while the frequency of attempts at burglaries and other 'breaking and entering' crimes has increased 42-fold. These figures however do not take account of the rise in the number of potential offenders and of potential victims arising from increases both in population and affluence. As Walker argues, probably the least inaccurate basis for a general comparison of reported offence frequencies and potential offenders is the number of males between their fifteenth and fiftieth birthdays, and the extent to which their indictable offences have increased since the turn of the century is elevenfold.

On the side of punishment there are again difficulties in interpreting the statistics. The daily average prison population rose from 17,435 in 1901 to 35,009 in 1967. Prison has become used less readily as punishment. Even in the Higher Courts the percentage of offenders imprisoned has fallen from over 90 per cent to under 54 per cent. The clear-up rate for property offences is low and getting lower while for offences against the person it is high but also declining.

The trends in religion assembled in Chap. 13 throw light on social cohesion from another point of view. In general there has been a decline in organised religion in both absolute and relative terms as indicated by the rise of civil marriages and the reduction in membership of religious organisations. The protestant denominations (i.e. not including the Church of England) now have only 12 per cent adherence among those aged fifteen or over compared with 20 per cent at the beginning of the century. Nevertheless the decline has not been a steady one and differs between regions and churches. Ireland stands out as an important religious sub-culture within the British Isles. According to the census no less than 97 per cent of the Irish claimed religious adherence in 1961. In 1900 there were 1,945,000 Church of England communicants on Easter Day, and by 1966 this total had fallen by 46,000. The Presbyterian churches have resisted decline rather better than the Church of England. Robert Currie and Alan Gilbert suggest that the relative success of the Church of Scotland may be due to its nationalist appeal. Yet the appeal to a national community has not greatly helped the Presbyterian Church of Wales (the Calvinist Methodists), whose membership has been in continuous decline for the past forty years.

In general it is difficult to assess the course of participation in national and community rituals. The rise of television to near saturation point in access has undoubtedly introduced a new element into popular consciousness. It should also be noted from Chap. 16 that while participation in sports has undoubtedly increased, attendance at sporting events which, at least in part, serve community ritual functions, has declined.

Finally we may glance at another aspect of national integration which has become an important preoccupation in recent years – the immigrant communities. The British Isles, as is well known, are thought of as having had a somewhat isolated and homogeneous ethnic and cultural character. In the first thirty years of the century 96 per cent of the total population of England and Wales were born in Britain, and this high proportion has declined to 94 per cent in 1951 and 93 per cent in 1961. Nevertheless the influx of immigrants from the so-called 'new Commonwealth' has attracted a great deal of attention during the nineteen-fifties and sixties.[1] Since 1955 some 800,000 coloured people have settled in Britain. It has been estimated that by 1978 one in six of the school leavers in Birmingham will be coloured. Present evidence indicates that tension between white and coloured adolescents will increase, and that coloured youngsters will experience considerable discrimination in obtaining employment. The culture of the migrant homelands will be less important: simple distinctions of colour will be more important, and a great deal will depend on the degree to which the coloured communities become integrated occupationally and residentially into the mainstream of the social structure. So far coloured immigrants have tended to concentrate in the conurbations and in unskilled labour, though there have also been some trends towards dispersal and the sharp reduction of the numbers entering with vouchers (3500 in 1969) has involved the recruitment of relatively more skilled and professional people. The coloured immigrant population multiplied four times between 1931 and 1961 from just over 100,000 to over 400,000. In mid-1968 the total number of immigrants and British-born coloureds was estimated at 1,113,000.

Policy-makers are now forced to recognise that the older assimilationist approach ended with the restrictions introduced by the 1962 Act which had the paradoxical consequence of increasing the flow of Indian and Pakistani families to settle permanently in place of the groups of male temporary workers intending to return to their homelands. These developments have underlined the assumption of the older assimilative theory that the coloured population was a homogeneous collection of individuals. This was never a fact. Distinctions have to be drawn not

[1] For a comprehensive account of the recent history of race relations in Britain see E. J. B. Rose's *Colour and Citizenship* (O.U.P. 1969).

only between different nationalities and ethnic groups but also within these between castes, classes and occupations and between individuals, families and types of community group. The pattern of group formation among the British coloureds is changing rapidly and in different directions among West Indians, Pakistanis and Cypriots as well as between the first and second generation of immigrants. At the same time the terms of assimilation have been transformed. The assimilative readiness of Britain as a host society is no longer that of a homogeneous culture. In this context it might be useful to refer to these changes as the 'Americanisation' of British society and thus to draw attention on the one hand to the declining social homogeneity of the British population, its less certain use of informal sanctions through tacit understandings, its growing impersonality, its mobility and its aspirations towards privatised affluence, and on the other hand to the relevance, however uncertain, of the American experience of urban ghettoes, cultural pluralism and black separatism. At root the coloured communities raise in a relatively dramatic form the basic problem of social inequality and social integration in modern Britain. There is overwhelming evidence that the coloured population suffers discrimination on grounds of colour, in employment, housing, leisure activities and over the whole range of social relationships. Differences in power and advantage, whether based on colour or on any other socially evaluated attribute, tend to be generalised and to be transmitted between generations. They therefore form systems of social stratification which are highly resistant to change. The citizenship status of the coloured Briton underlies and emphasises the continuing problem of maintaining the legitimacy of a conservative and stratified society.

2 Population and Family

CONSTANCE ROLLETT
AND JULIA PARKER

Of the two sections in this chapter, the first is concerned with the broad outlines of the population structure; with total size, with growth through natural increase and migration both for the whole country and for the regions, with the age and sex composition of the population and with movement within as well as into and out of particular areas. The second section concentrates on the more 'personal' aspects – on the way in which the population 'arranges' itself. We examine marital status, rates of marriage and divorce, fertility and family and household size.

SOURCES OF INFORMATION

The two primary sources for information on the population of Great Britain are the census tables and the Registrar-General's reports. The *Annual Abstract of Statistics* (a series beginning 1840 and called until 1938 *The Statistical Abstract of the United Kingdom*) reprints a great deal of information from both the census and the Registrar-General's reports along with other statistics collected by the government.

We have also used a number of secondary sources. Kelsall[1] provides an introduction to the study of the population of Britain with a discussion of the sources of information and of the main trends, and some tables. Information from the 1961 census is included, but the 1966 census reports had not been issued at the time of writing. Cox[2] deals with all aspects of demography as an academic discipline using population data from Britain and other countries, as illustrative material. Two older books by Marsh[3] and Carr-Saunders, Caradog Jones and Moser[4] both published in 1958, deal more extensively with trends in social conditions and social structure, and we have adapted or simply brought up to date a number of their tables.

Both these latter books deal primarily with England and Wales and

[1] R. K. Kelsall, *Population* (Longmans 1967).

[2] Peter R. Cox, *Demography*, 4th ed. (C.U.P. 1970).

[3] D. C. Marsh, *The Changing Social Structure of England and Wales 1871–1951*, rev. ed. (Routledge 1965).

[4] A. M. Carr-Saunders, D. Caradog Jones and C. A. Moser, *A Survey of Social Conditions in England and Wales* (O.U.P. 1958).

there seems to be a lack of secondary sources giving data for Great Britain as a whole. Kelsall argues that where only a broad picture is required, figures for England and Wales alone can be used, since England and Wales accounted for 70 per cent of the population of Great Britain in 1961.[1] However since the population of Scotland does show some distinctive features and since some of the later chapters have used information compiled for the whole of Great Britain we have added Scottish statistics to those for England and Wales wherever possible.

We shall refer below to particular problems in the use of census material but Benjamin deals with general problems of the collection of data and the definition of terms.[2] There are no problems about the basic statistics – the numbers of people counted on the census day and their age and sex. We have used the secondary sources or the census figures given in issues of the *Annual Abstract of Statistics* to calculate the size of the various age and sex groups. The Registrar-General's *Statistical Review for England and Wales* and *Annual Report for Scotland* give historical tables of birth and death rates which we have used.

The migration balance for the two countries (Table 2.3) and for the regions (Tables 2.9–2.11) shown in our tables is simply the difference between the natural increase and the actual increase for a given period. Kelsall discusses the inadequacy of overseas migration figures and the difficulty of obtaining reasonably accurate figures for the traffic in both directions.[3] There are obvious problems in separating migrants from tourists and for this reason migration figures are based only on movement by the long sea routes up to January 1964. Since that date information has been obtained from a stratified sample of passengers entering and leaving the United Kingdom on both air and sea routes (other than to and from Eire). The cumulative effects of overseas migration are shown, to a certain extent, for the first generation migrants, by the question on birthplace which has been on the census schedule since the beginning of our period.[4]

The same drawbacks apply to the data on internal migration. Useful though the net figures undoubtedly are,[5] regional planning of roads, housing, leisure facilities and so on also requires knowledge of gross movement. The 1961 census for the first time included a question to the 10 per cent sample on change of usual address within one year of the census date, ignoring intermediate changes of address. This question

[1] R. K. Kelsall, *op. cit.*, p. 15.
[2] B. Benjamin, *The Population Census*, Social Science Research Council: Reviews of Current Research, no. 7 (Heinemann 1970).
[3] R. K. Kelsall, *op. cit.*, chap. 6.
[4] See Chap. 14, p.p 492–3
[5] R. K. Kelsall, *op. cit.*, p. 31.

was repeated in 1966 with the addition that respondents were also asked about a change of address within five years of the census date. Our Table 2.8 shows total gross movements within and between England and Wales and Scotland but there are also tabulations showing place of origin of immigrants into a region and the destination of emigrants leaving the region. The migrant population is also analysed in terms of age, sex, marital condition, occupation, industry and socio-economic group.

The basic problem in presenting trends in regional population growth or decline is that of changes in the regional boundaries. We have tried to overcome this to some extent by giving tables for the two periods with consistent boundaries separately. We have also attempted to put figures for the two periods together by amalgamating regions (Tables 2.11 and 2.12) but while this gives the broad nature of the trends, much detail is lost because of the size of the regions used. For the same reason only rough comparisons can be made between regional densities in 1931 and 1968 (Table 2.13).

The figures on marital condition (Tables 2.14–2.18) can be drawn straight from census data, though the divorced are not separated from the widowed in 1900, presumably because the numbers were so small. Divorced and widowed persons are not distinguished in the information reprinted in the *Annual Abstract of Statistics* so that it is necessary to refer to the census documents.

Marriage rates, birth rates, divorces and divorce rates are obtained from information published by the Registrar-General. But it is difficult to construct Scottish tables comparable with those for England and Wales either because of differences in the methods of presentation of data or because of lack of raw data for Scotland. For instance, for marriage rates per 1000 unmarried persons aged 15 and over, the *Statistical Review* gives a historical table with five-year period rates up to 1965. *The Annual Report for Scotland* has no such table. For our table we have taken the raw data (number of marriages in a year) and expressed it per 1000 unmarried persons in census years or other years for which population data are easily available. This is the reason why Scottish figures in our tables are frequently given as rates for a single year rather than for periods.

Census data on size of family units (Table 2.32), and family units with different types of structure (Table 2.31) are comparable for England and Wales and Scotland, but only exists for 1961 and 1966. Benjamin has a full account of the difference between the concept of household and family in the census data.[1] As he points out, census procedure involves the enumerator distributing schedules to all the inhabited build-

[1] B. Benjamin, *op. cit.*, section g.

ings in his area, so that it is natural to move from the concept of house to that of household to that of family. The first censuses used only one schedule per building, not distinguishing between several households living in the same building, and this was still the case in 1901. In 1911 the concept 'private family' was first used (see Chap. 10). In fact this was the equivalent of the term 'private household' in use since 1951 and distinguished groups of people sharing housekeeping arrangements, whether related or not. Consequently our table on the size of households starts in 1911 for England and Wales. For Scotland, however, it starts in 1951 as the published tabulations for Scotland up to that date show only the number of persons in each house rather than in each household. The census of 1961 was the first when the additional tabulations on the size and structure of family units based on census questions about degrees of family relationships were published. Table 2.40 shows the relationship between family units and households for 1966. Most non-family households are one-person households, so that if these latter are ignored, we have some idea of the relative distribution of family size before 1961.

Fertility statistics are complex because a great deal of information must be analysed in a variety of ways to assess changes in family building habits over time, and between the different social classes. The chief items of information are the number of children born to a woman, the age of the mother at birth, the age of the mother at marriage, the calendar year of marriage and the duration of marriage. From these can be derived the ultimate size of the family and the spread of fertility over the duration of married life. There are three primary sources of fertility data. The first is the population tables of the Registrar-General's reports which currently give average family size by age at marriage, marriage duration, and year of marriage (for recent years only). The second source is the Family Census of 1946 conducted by Professors Glass and Grebenik for the Royal Commission on Population. Thirdly there is census material both in the ordinary census schedule and in the special inquiries into fertility made in 1911, 1951 and 1961. No fertility inquiry was made in 1966. Our tables are taken from Cox[1] and the 1961 fertility tables for England and Wales and Scotland.

There are two main problems in the use of fertility data. One is that ultimate family size cannot be known until the end of the child-bearing period, so that either figures have to be restricted to the experience of earlier generations or an element of speculation must be introduced to demonstrate recent trends.[2] We have preferred to avoid speculation and show only completed families. The second problem arises in attempting to compare differences in social class fertility for periods

---

[1] Peter R. Cox, *op. cit.*   [2] Peter R. Cox, *op. cit.*, p. 103.

before and after 1961.[1] The socio-economic groups are not easy to match with the five social classes; also the mean family size is given for a wide variety of ages at marriage and duration of marriage and the graduation of social class differentials is not uniform throughout all the groupings. Both Kelsall and Cox, however, compare some 1961 figures for individual groups with earlier figures and find a continuation of the pattern of class differentials.

POPULATION GROWTH – NATURAL INCREASE AND MIGRATION
The population of England and Wales increased by 45 per cent between 1901 and 1966 but that of Scotland by only 16 per cent (Table 2.1). The most rapid rate of increase in both countries was at the beginning of the century though the Scottish rate was lower. The 1921 census showed a considerable drop in the rate in both countries, which continued in England and Wales during the nineteen-thirties and early forties but rose in the fifties falling again after the 1961 census. The Scottish population actually declined in the twenties and again between 1961 and 1966.

Some explanation for these population changes is found in Tables 2.2 and 2.3. From the beginning of the century until 1940 the birth rate fell, but then recovered slightly; the rate has subsequently fluctuated but remains somewhat higher than that of the thirties. There has been a fairly constant but slower decline in the death rate. The rate of natural increase in the late nineteen-thirties dropped to a quarter that of the 1901–5 period but in the sixties it has risen to a half.

Before looking at the balance of natural increase and migration, the influence of the two world wars on population growth (which is not fully shown in the tables) should be noted. Losses directly attributable to the 1914–18 war are estimated by Cox[2] for England and Wales as 1,300,000 (550,000 military losses, 150,000 excess civilian deaths due to lowered resistance to disease and 600,000 birth losses due to separation of married couples). Total population loss for England and Wales has been estimated at seven million including loss of births because of the premature deaths of marriageable men and women. The second world war had much less effect on population; for the whole of Britain, military casualties were approximately 252,000 and civilian casualties due to enemy action 60,000. There was probably little loss of births or excess of civilian deaths.

Table 2.3 shows the excess of births over deaths and the net balance of migration for the intercensal periods. England and Wales experienced a fairly large net loss until about 1931, principally because of emigration

[1] R. K. Kelsall, op. cit., p. 56. Peter R. Cox, op. cit., p. 359.
[2] Peter R. Cox, op. cit., p. 319.

to Commonwealth countries and the United States of America. This was reversed however in the following thirty years. There was a gain from Scotland and Ireland throughout the period, from European refugees in the thirties, and from Commonwealth immigrants in the post-war period. This was in spite of the resumption of outward emigration to the U.S.A., Australia and Canada after the end of the war (reaching 200,000 per year from the United Kingdom in the peak years 1952 and 1957)[1] so that the net increase conceals large movements in both directions. The 1962 Commonwealth Immigrants Act restricted immigration (see Chap. 14) and reduced the inward balance for the United Kingdom from 1962, though England and Wales continued to show a fairly large inward balance with continuing immigration from Scotland and Ireland. Scotland shows a consistent loss through migration, much larger in relation to the size of the population than the movements in the population of England and Wales. Scottish emigration was both to England and Wales and the U.S.A., Canada and Australia, the peak years being 1911–31.

POPULATION STRUCTURE – AGE AND SEX

The proportion of the population of Great Britain in the youngest age group declined between 1901 and 1931 but has subsequently hardly changed (Table 2.4). The teenage group declined slightly until 1951 but has since risen. There has been a steady decline (of about 7 per cent) in the proportion of 'young marrieds' (20–39 group). The proportion of older people has correspondingly increased, though since 1951 the 40–59 group has remained almost the same in England and Wales, and declined in Scotland. The 60–64 group and the 65–75 group have doubled their representation in the population and there were about three times as many over seventy-fives in the population in 1966 as in 1901. So far as the 'burden of dependency' is concerned, however, the doubling of the elderly population has been balanced by the decline in the proportion of the young (Table 2.5). Total dependants formed 35·4 per cent of the population in 1966 compared with 37 per cent in 1901 in England and Wales and slightly higher proportions in Scotland. The proportion of the population of working age, though declining since 1931, is still slightly higher than in 1901 (but see Chap. 4 for rates of participation in economic activity). However the fact that the working population is older than it was at the beginning of the century, and the elderly make up half the number of dependants instead of one-sixth, has changed the situation in a way which calls for considerable readjustment, particularly in the social services.

In both countries there have been more females than males at each

[1] R. K. Kelsall, *op. cit.*, p. 30.

census despite the fact that more boys are born than girls (Table 2.6) – a reflection of the greater mortality of males through natural causes and wars. In 1901 females predominated in every age group in England and Wales; however the decline in infantile and youthful mortality has resulted in more males in the lowest age groups, starting with the 0–14 group in 1931 and shifting to older groups so that in 1966 there were more males than females in all groups under 40.

The Scottish experience has been somewhat different; in 1901 there were more males than females in the lowest age groups and in 1966 there were still more females than males in the 20–39 age group. This is probably explained by a higher male to female birth ratio in Scotland (for the 1901–5 period there were 1042 males born per 1000 females in Scotland and 1037 males per 1000 females in England and Wales) and the slightly slower decline in the death rate in Scotland.

The preponderance of females among older people has increased with every census, most markedly in England and Wales where there were twice as many women as men aged 75 or more in 1966. Table 2.7 also shows in more detail that the shift to an increasing proportion aged 75 and over among the whole elderly group has been much stronger among women than men.

POPULATION MOVEMENT

Table 2.8 is a rough guide to the amount of movement within England and Wales and Scotland, and between England and Wales and Scotland, within one and five years of the 1966 census. All immigrants into the areas in the same periods are also shown. The table fails to take into account people who have moved more than once during the one or five year period, and also children less than one year or five years old. Nevertheless it does show that almost 10 per cent of the population had moved within the areas within one year of the census and approximately 30 per cent within five years. In England and Wales about half the movement was within a single local authority area and in Scotland about two-thirds of the movement was local. Only 1 per cent of the population had moved into the areas during the year preceding the census and between 2 per cent and 3 per cent during the preceding five years. The proportion of Scots moving into England and Wales was much greater than the reverse movement, leaving Scotland with a very small positive migration balance (difference between the immigrants and emigrants shown in the table) if immigrants from all areas are included and a negative balance if only movement between England and Wales and Scotland is considered.

Tables 2.9 and 2.10, however, give only the net intercensal regional population changes according to the boundaries in use during the periods shown. Between 1921 and 1931 the South East gained most by migration, Greater London growing by 3 per cent. In the period between 1951 and 1961 the population of the South East increased dramatically through migration, though Greater London was losing population at about the same rate. In the 1961–6 period, however, the South West was the fastest growing area and Greater London was losing more than 80,000 people a year. The latest population changes between 1967 and 1968 in the *Abstract of Regional Statistics* (not illustrated because of further boundary changes in 1966) show the largest annual increase by migration in the South West, followed by East Anglia and the East Midlands; the largest loss in Scotland followed by the North West, York and Humberside, the North, West Midlands and Wales.

Table 2.11 attempts to show trends over the whole period as accurately as is permitted by changes in the standard regions. It is clear that the South East, South West and Midlands have been growing at a much faster rate than the Northern region, Wales and Scotland, but the amalgamation of regions blurs more detailed trends. The results of the inter-regional population changes and the proportion of the total population living in the various regions, using the same amalgamated regions as for Table 2.11, appear in Table 2.12.

Regional densities have been calculated from the acreages and population estimates in use at the dates shown (Table 2.13). There has been a general increase in density between 1931 and 1951, but the South East and North West stand out as being much the most densely populated of the regions (Greater London being a conurbation).

THE FAMILY – MARITAL STATUS

The marital condition of the population from 1900 to 1966 is shown in Tables 2.14–2.18. The proportion who are married has risen substantially since the beginning of the century and there has been a corresponding decrease in the proportion of single people (Table 2.14). There has also been a rise in the proportion of widows as opposed to widowers – reflecting greater female longevity (Tables 2.15 and 2.16). A higher proportion of both men and women who are widowed now are over 65 than in 1931; a natural result of the fact that both sexes now live longer (Table 2.17). Analysis by age group shows a particularly marked trend to more marriages among younger people: only a quarter of women aged 20–24 were married in 1901 but more than half of them in 1966. There was a substantial though less pronounced trend to more marriages among those between 25 and 29, and also among men in their twenties (Table 2.18).

The greater popularity of marriage is also evident in the increasing marriage rate – higher for both sexes in the first years of the nineteen-sixties than at the beginning of the century (Table 2.19) and again it is the younger men and women among whom the increase is most marked (Table 2.20). It is notable that remarriage rates among divorced, but not among widowed, persons are much higher both for men and for women than the rate for first marriages (Table 2.21) – a reflection no doubt of the fact that the object of many divorces is to allow one or other of the partners to marry again. Table 2.22 presents an analysis of married men by age and social class which underlines the later marriage habits of the higher social groups.

Trends in divorce have to be analysed with caution; the figures represent the difficulty or ease of obtaining a divorce as well as instability in marriages. Petitions for divorce are a surer guide than decrees made absolute, as McGregor points out,[1] since the latter may be affected by changes in procedure designed to expedite the settlement of outstanding cases, thus distorting the figures for particular years. The increase in the number of petitions through the first half of the century is shown in Table 2.23 but these figures in themselves are not very helpful since they need to be related to the population 'at risk' and this is done in Table 2.24. The trend to more petitions for divorce is still marked though much less dramatic. The majority of petitions result in decrees absolute so that the number of marriages ending in divorce is very similar to the number of petitions filed (Table 2.25). If we try to relate divorce to duration of marriage official statistics are misleading for they record petitions for divorce or divorces made absolute rather than the point at which a marriage in fact breaks down. As the latter may precede the former by several years, marriages of only a few years' duration may be relatively more vulnerable than the statistics (Tables 2.26 and 2.27) suggest.[1] Also, although divorce appears more common in childless marriages and although the risk appears to decrease as size of family increases (Table 2.28), the available statistics do not permit any certain conclusions.[3]

FERTILITY AND FAMILY SIZE

Trends in fertility since 1900 appear in Table 2.29. The decrease evident since the beginning of the century was halted in the nineteen-forties and the early sixties show a clear increase. The proportion of illegitimate births dropped till the nineteen-thirties but has since risen

[1] O. R. McGregor, *Divorce in England* (Heinemann 1957), esp. chaps 1 and 2.
[2] For a discussion of the inadequacies of the official statistics see Robert Chester, 'The duration of marriage to divorce', *British Journal of Sociology*, Vol. XXII, No. 2, June 1971.
[3] Robert Chester, 'Is there a relationship between childlessness and marriage breakdown?', *Journal of Biosocial Science*, 1972, Vol. 4.

quite sharply. Until recently the highest birth rate occurred among women aged 25–29 though this has now been exceeded by the 20–24-year-olds (Table 2.30). It is in this latter group and among women of 15–19 that the increase in the birth rate since 1939 is particularly marked–a reflection of the trend to marry younger.

Tables 2.31 and 2.32 analyse families by type and size. The most usual type of family is one headed by a married couple with the man aged under 45, though the proportion of families with only one parent increased slightly between 1961 and 1966. Two-person households are the most usual, though the proportion of those with more than five persons has risen slightly since 1961.

If we consider the size of completed families in relation to the date of the first marriage, there emerges a clear move towards smaller families for the later marriages (Table 2.33). More than half of all marriages contracted in 1940, compared with a third of those contracted between 1900 and 1909, resulted in one or two children and a rather higher proportion of those of the later date were childless. All the larger family sizes showed a proportionate decline over the period. When family size is analysed by date of marriage and age at marriage the decrease in family size is again apparent, affecting all women, regardless of the age at which they marry, though, as would be expected, throughout the period women marrying younger have had larger families (Table 2.34). Similarly marriages of longest duration contain the most children though this seems to reflect the habits of an earlier generation rather than the longer period of 'exposure to risk' (Table 2.35).

An analysis of family size by date of marriage and social class shows a trend to smaller families for both manual and non-manual workers but a persistent tendency for the latter to have fewer children than the former (Tables 2.36 and 2.37). But the social class differences in fertility diminished between 1931 and 1951 (Table 2.38). Figures for 1961 do not allow direct comparison with the earlier years, since the social categories changed, but suggest a continuing tendency for the higher socio-economic groups to have fewer children (Table 2.39).

Households are distinguished from families in that they may consist of unrelated persons or may on the other hand contain several family units. Table 2.40 shows one-fifth of all households without any family in 1966, the great majority made up of one family and a handful comprising two or more. Like families, households have tended to become smaller. Since 1911 the proportion of households of up to three persons has increased while that of households containing four or more has decreased (Table 2.41). Nearly 70 per cent of the population is now to be found in households of four or fewer persons compared with only 39 per cent in 1911. When households are analysed by social class it is clear that the higher social classes tend to form smaller households (Table 2.42) with fewer children (Table 2.43).

ADDITIONAL REFERENCES

Benjamin, B., *Demographic Analysis* (Allen & Unwin 1968).

SOURCES OF TABLES

Central Statistical Office
  Abstract of Regional Statistics, no. 5, 1969.
  Annual Abstract of Statistics, no. 84, 1935–46; no. 96, 1967; no. 105,
    1968; no. 106, 1969.
General Register Office
  Census 1911: Summary Tables, England and Wales.
               Scotland, Vol. 2: Summary Tables.
  Census 1921: General Report, England and Wales.
               General Report: Scotland.
  Census 1931: General Report, England and Wales.
               General Report, Scotland.
  Census 1951: General Report, Vol. III: Scotland.
               Housing Report, England and Wales.
  Census 1961: Age, Marital and General Tables, England and Wales.
               Household Composition Tables, England and Wales.
               Fertility Tables, England and Wales.
               Housing and Household Report, Scotland.
               Fertility Report, Scotland.
               Age, Marital Condition and General Tables, Scotland.
  Sample census 1966: Household Composition Tables, Scotland.
               Migration Tables, Part I: Scotland.
               Household Composition Tables, Part I: England and
                 Wales.
               Great Britain, Summary Tables.
  Registrar-General's *Annual Report for Scotland*, 1900 to date.
  Registrar-General's *Statistical Review of England and Wales*, 1921 to
    date.
  National Register of the United Kingdom, 1939.
  Royal Commission on Marriage and Divorce, Chairmen Simon and Hender-
    son, Cmd 9678 (HMSO 1956).

TABLE 2.1

Population Growth 1901–1966, England and Wales and Scotland

Year	Population	Increase since previous census	Mean annual rate intercensal increase (a)
ENGLAND AND WALES			
1901	32,527,843	+3,525,318	+1·22
1911	36,070,492	+3,542,649	+1·09
1921	37,886,699	+1,816,207	+0·50
1931	39,952,377	+2,065,678	+0·55
1951	43,757,888	+2,297,888	+0·29
1961	46,104,548	+2,346,660	+0·54
1966	47,135,510	+1,030,962	+0·22
SCOTLAND			
1901	4,472,103	+446,456	+1·11
1911	4,760,904	+288,801	+0·65
1921	4,882,497	+121,593	+0·26
1931	4,842,980	−39,517	−0.08
1951	5,096,415	+253,435	+0·26
1961	5,178,490	+82,075	+0·16
1966	5,168,300	−10,190	−0.04

Note (a) The percentage change over the intervening period divided by the number of intervening years.

Sources: R. K. Kelsall, *Population* (Longmans 1967), p. 16.
  1966 Census figures from *Annual Abstract of Statistics*, no. 105, 1968.

TABLE 2.2

Birth and Death Rates and Natural Increase 1901–1968, England and Wales and Scotland (per 1000 population)

Period or year	England and Wales			Scotland		
	Births	Deaths	Natural increase	Births	Deaths	Natural increase
1901–5	28·2	16·0	12·2	29·2	17·0	12·2
1906–10	26·3	14·7	11·6	27·6	16·1	11·4
1911–15	23·6	14·3	9·3	25·4	15·7	9·7
1916–20	20·0	14·4	5·6	22·8	15·0	7·8
1921–5	19·9	12·1	7·8	23·0	13·9	9·1
1926–30	16·7	12·1	4·6	20·0	13·6	6·4
1931–5	15·0	12·0	3·0	18·2	13·2	5·0
1936–40	14·7	12·2	2·5	17·6	13·6	4·0
1941–5	15·9	12·8	3·1	17·8	14·1	3·7
1946–50	18·0	11·8	6·2	20·0	12·6	7·4
1951–5	15·3	11·7	3·6	17·9	12·1	5·8
1956–60	16·4	11·6	4·8	19·2	12·2	7·0
1960–5	18·1	11·8	6·3	19·7	12·3	7·4
1966	17·7	11·7	6·0	18·6	12·3	6·3
1967	17·2	11·2	6·0	18·6	11·4	7·2
1968	16·9	11·9	5·0	18·3	12·2	6·1

Sources: Registrar-General's *Statistical Review of England and Wales*, Tables I: **Medical** and II: Population, 1968.
  Annual Report of the Registrar-General, Scotland, Parts I and II.

TABLE 2.3

Natural Increase and Net Gain or Loss by Migration 1901–1966, England and Wales and Scotland (thousands)

	Population at beginning of period	Births	Deaths	Excess of births over deaths	Net gain (+) or loss (−) by migration	Actual increase or decrease (−)
ENGLAND AND WALES						
1901–11	32,528	9290	5246	4044	−501	3543
1911–21	36,070	8281	5845*	2436	−620	1816
1921–31	37,887	6928	4692	2236	−170	2060
1931–51	39,952	13,297	10,249*	3048	+758	3806
1951–61	43,758	7138	5181	1957	+387	2347
1961–6	46,105	4259	2769	1490	+311	1807
SCOTLAND						
1901–11	4472	1306	763	543	−254	289
1911–21	4761	1185	824*	360	−239	122
1921–31	4882	1005	652	352	−392	−40
1931–51	4843	1849	1347*	502	−220	253
1951–61	5096	959	619	339	−282	83
1961–6	5179	529	328	201	−199	+11

Notes: Table as given in *Annual Abstract of Statistics*. Estimated population figures used for 1966 differ slightly from census figures in Table 2.1. * Includes deaths of non-civilians and merchant seamen who died outside the country.

Source: Annual Abstract of Statistics, no. 106, 1969, p. 19.

TABLE 2.4

Age Distribution of the Population 1901–1966, England and Wales and Scotland (thousands)

Age-group (years)	Sex	1901			1931			1951			1961			1966		
		Number	Total	% of total population	Number	Total	% of total population	Number	Total	% of total population	Number	Total	% of total population	Number	Total	% of total population
ENGLAND AND WALES																
0–14	M	5265	10345	32·4	4808	9520	23·8	4949	9692	22·1	5424·0	10,584·5	22·95	5558·0	10,841·0	23·0
	F	5280			4712			4743			5159·5			5283·0		
15–19	M	1608	3247	10·0	1710	3435	8·6	1335	2704	6·8	1622·0	3200·7	6·94	1870·0	3682·0	7·81
	F	1639			1725			1369			1578·7			1811·0		
20–39	M	4993	10,522	32·3	6044	12,709	31·8	6200	12,610	28·8	5998·2	11,950·7	25·92	5905·0	11,730·0	24·89
	F	5529			6665			6410			5952·5			5825·0		
40–59	M	2791	5805	17·8	4520	9668	24·2	5621	11,785	26·9	6060·9	12,414·3	26·93	6018·0	12,321·0	26·14
	F	3014			5148			6164			6353·4			6303·0		
60–64	M	410	890	2·7	778	1657	4·1	939	2143	4·9	1096·8	2458·1	5·33	1260·0	2707·0	5·74
	F	480			879			1204			1361·3			1446·0		
65–74	M	478	1076	3·3	954	2141	5·4	1372	3257	7·4	1418·5	3520·5	7·64	1531·0	3757·0	7·97
	F	598			1187			1885			2102·0			2226·0		
75 and over	M	183	442	1·4	318	821	2·0	600	1567	3·6	683·9	1976·0	4·29	698·0	2099·0	4·45
	F	259			503			967			1292·1			1401·0		
All ages	M	15,729	32,528	100·0	19,133	39,952	100·0	21,016	43,758	100·0	22303·8	46,104·5	100·0	22,841·0	47,135·0	100·0
	F	16,799			20,819			22,742			23800·7			24,295·0		
SCOTLAND																
0–14	M	755	1494	33·4	658	1305	26·9	639·2	1255·1	24·6	685·3	1339·2	25·9	683·1	1332·8	25·8
	F	739			647			615·9			653·9			649·7		
15–19	M	230	456	10·2	219	439	9·1	173·2	361·9	7·1	187·4	374·1	7·2	213·4	419·2	8·1
	F	226			220			188·7			186·7			205·8		
20–39	M	675	1405	31·4	698	1475	30·5	703·3	1458·6	28·6	653·7	1340·0	25·9	618·5	1263·6	24·4
	F	730			777			755·3			686·3			645·1		
40–59	M	369	774	17·3	507	1078	22·3	605·8	1288·3	25·3	628·7	1317·8	25·4	612·9	1288·0	24·9
	F	405			571			682·5			689·1			675·1		
60–64	M	56	126	2·8	92	192	4·0	97·9	224·7	4·4	113·2	259·6	5·0	128·8	281·8	5·5
	F	70			100			126·8			146·4			153·0		
65–74	M	63	151	3·4	114	255	5·3	148·9	343·4	6·7	143·6	358·4	6·9	154·0	386·4	7·5
	F	88			141			194·5			214·8			232·4		
75 and over	M	25	66	1·5	39	100	2·1	65·8	163·5	3·2	70·9	190·5	3·7	68·2	196·5	3·8
	F	41			61			97·7			119·6			128·3		
All ages	M	2174	4472	100·0	2326	4843	100·0	2434·4	5096·5	100·0	2482·7	5179·3	100·0	2478·8	5168·3	100·0
	F	2298			2517			2662·1			2696·6			2689·5		

Sources: D. C. Marsh, *The Changing Social Structure of England and Wales 1871–1951* (Routledge 1958, rev. 1965). *Annual Abstract of Statistics*, no. 84, 1946; no. 96, 1957; no. 105, 1968.

TABLE 2.5

Various Age Groups as a Proportion of the Total Population in 1901, 1931, 1951, 1961 and 1966, England and Wales and Scotland (percentages)

Year	The young 0–14	Persons of working age 15–64	The elderly 65 and over	All ages
ENGLAND AND WALES				
1901	32	63	5	100
1931	24	69	7	100
1951	22	67	11	100
1961	23	65	12	100
1966	23	65	12	100
SCOTLAND				
1901	33	62	·5	100
1931	27	66	7	100
1951	25	65	10	100
1961	26	64	11	100
1966	26	63	11	100

Sources: D. C. Marsh, *op. cit.*
Annual Abstract of Statistics, nos 84 and 105.

TABLE 2.6

Sex Ratios at Selected Censuses 1901–1966, England and Wales and Scotland (females per 1000 males)

Year	All ages	Age-groups						
		0–14	15–19	20–39	40–59	60–64	65–74	75 and over
ENGLAND AND WALES								
1901	1068	1003	1019	1107	1079	1141	1251	1415
1931	1088	980	1088	1103	1139	1130	1244	1581
1951	1082	953	1025	1034	1096	1282	1375	1609
1961	1067	951	973	992	1060	1195	1482	1895
1966	1064	951	968	986	1048	1148	1454	2007
SCOTLAND								
1901	1057	979	983	1081	1098	1250	1397	1640
1931	1082	983	1005	1113	1126	1087	1237	1564
1951	1094	964	1089	1074	1127	1294	1306	1485
1961	1086	954	996	1050	1096	1293	1496	1687
1966	1085	951	964	1043	1104	1188	1509	1881

Sources: D. C. Marsh, *op. cit.*
Annual Abstract of Statistics, nos 84 and 105.

TABLE 2.7

The Proportion of Males and Females Aged 65 and over in each Quinquennial Age-Group at the Censuses of 1901, 1951, 1961 and 1966, England and Wales and Scotland (percentages)

Age-group	1901		1951		1961		1966	
	Male	Female	Male	Female	Male	Female	Male	Female
ENGLAND AND WALES								
65–69	42	40	40	37	40	34	41	34
70–74	30	29	30	29	28	28	28	27
75–79	17	18	19	19	19	20	18	20
80–84	8	9	8	10	10	12	9	12
85 and over	3	4	3	5	3	6	4	7
All 65 and over	100	100	100	100	100	100	100	100
SCOTLAND								
65–69	42	39	39	37	39	36	41	37
70–74	30	30	31	29	28	28	28	28
75–79	17	17	19	19	19	20	17	19
80–84	8	10	8	10	10	11	10	11
85 and over	3	5	3	5	4	5	4	6
All 65 and over	100	100	100	100	100	100	100	100

Sources: D. C. Marsh, *op. cit.*
Annual Abstract of Statistics, nos 84 and 105.

TABLE 2.8

Migration within 1 and within 5 years before the 1966 Census, England and Wales and Scotland (showing in parentheses the proportion of migrants per 1000 resident population) (tens)

Area	Resident population at census	Migrants within a LA area	Migrants between LA areas	Total Migrants	Immigrants from all areas inc. abroad	Immigrants from elsewhere in GB only	Emigrants to areas in GB only	Migration balance inc. immigrants from abroad	within GB only
MIGRANTS WITHIN 1 YEAR									
England and Wales	47,141,15	2,400,02	2,277,97	4,677,99 (99)	366,94 (8)	52,65 (1)	36,98 (1)	—	
Scotland	5,162,68	326,00	154,66	480,66 (93)	58,34 (11)	36,98 (7)	52,65 (10)	5,69 (1)	−15,67 (−3)
MIGRANTS WITHIN 5 YEARS									
England and Wales	47,141,15	7,707,02	6,847,70	14,554,72 (309)	1,056,25 (22)	165,12 (4)	86,55 (2)	—	
Scotland	5,162,68	1,053,59	466,65	1,520,24 (294)	136,84 (27)	86,55 (17)	165,12 (32)	−28,28 (−5)	−78,57 (−15)

Source: Sample Census 1966 *Migration Tables,* part I: England and Wales and Scotland.

TABLE 2.9

Regional Population Changes 1921–1931, England and Wales (thousands)

Region	Estd. popn., middle of 1921	Estd. popn., middle of 1931	Decennial increase or decrease (−) 1921–1931 Total Number	Total Per cent	Births and deaths Number	Births and deaths Per cent	By migration Number	By migration Per cent
England and Wales	37,885	39,988	2103	5·6	2260	6·0	−157	−0·4
South East	12,190	13,502	1312	10·8	679	5·6	633	5·2
Greater London (included in South East)	7536	8238	702	9·3	458	6·1	244	3·2
Northumberland and Durham	2238	2248	10	0·5	217	9·7	−207	−9·2
Northern Rural Belt	1230	1281	51	4·1	87	7·0	−36	−2·9
West Riding	3305	3443	138	4·2	181	5·5	−43	−1·3
Lancashire and Cheshire	6003	6128	125	2·1	280	4·7	−155	−2·6
West Midlands	4307	4540	233	5·4	306	7·1	−72	−1·7
East Midlands	2222	2377	155	7·0	153	6·9	3	0·1
Eastern Counties	1763	1822	59	3·3	99	5·6	−41	−2·3
South West Counties	1970	2057	87	4·4	67	3·4	20	1·0
South Wales	1967	1899	−68	−3·4	169	8·6	−237	−12·0
North and Central Wales	691	691	0	0·0	22	3·2	−22	−3·2

Source: Census 1931, *General Report for England and Wales.*

TABLE 2.10

Regional Population Changes 1951–1966,* England and Wales and Scotland (thousands)

Region	Mid-year estimated population		Average annual change 1951–1961			Mid-year population 1966	Average annual change 1961–1966		
	1951	1961	Natural change	Change in armed forces	Net migration etc.†		Natural change	Change in armed forces	Net migration†
North	3130·3	3249·0	+19·4	-1·8	-5·7	3316·9	+20·7	-0·6	-6·5
Yorks. and Humberside	4488·3	4595·9	+19·2	-1·0	-7·5	4731·2	+27·8	-0·8	+10·1
East Midlands	2913·3	3139·3	+16·0	-0·6	+7·2	3298·6	+23·7	-1·1	+9·3
East Anglia	1387·6	1489·2	+6·5	—	+3·8	1581·7	+8·7	-2·4	+12·2
South East	15,216·4	16,345·5	+66·4	-8·5	+55·0	17,006·3	+110·2	-2·4	+24·4
Greater London (inc. South East)	8208·9	7980·4	+33·3	-1·0	-53·1	7836·2	+52·3	-0·4	-80·8
South West	3247·4	3436·0	+10·5	-4·0	+12·3	3634·8	+16·9	-2·7	+25·6
Wales	2588·8	2635·2	+8·4	-0·8	-3·0	2704·1	+11·5	-0·2	+2·4
West Midlands	4426·1	4760·6	+27·6	-2·1	+8·0	4998·9	+41·1	-1·5	+8·1
North West	6416·8	6545·3	+23·5	-3·0	-7·7	6712·8	+38·0	-0·2	-4·2
England and Wales	43,185·0	46,196·2	+197·5	-21·7	+62·3	47,985·3	+298·5	-12·1	+71·4
Scotland	5102·5	5183·8	+33·9	+2·4	-28·2	5190·8	+38·7	+1·6	-38·8

Source: Abstract of Regional Statistics, no. 5, 1969.
* 1966 boundaries.
† Mainly net migration but also includes excess of demobilisation over recruitment and any revisions in the mid-year estimates of natural increase.

TABLE 2.11

Regional Population Changes 1911–1966, England and Wales and Scotland (thousands)

Region	Increase 1911–1931		Increase 1931–1951		Increase 1951–1966	
	Number	*Per cent*	*Number*	*Per cent*	*Number*	*Per cent*
England and Wales	3928	10·9	3817	7·8	4170	9·5
South East	1799	15·4	1714	12·7	1790	11·8
North	1001	8·3	531	4·1	679	5·0
West Midlands and South West	592	9·9	1077	16·3	960	11·1
East Midlands and East	355	9·2	506	12·1	626	13·3
Wales	169	7·0	− 1	− 0·04	115	4·3
Scotland	82	1·7	253	5·2	72	1·4

Note: The standard regions found in Appendix B of the *General Report for England and Wales*, Census 1931, and the Introduction to the Sample Census Reports of 1966 have been combined so that approximately the same areas are covered in 1951 and 1966 as in 1911 and 1931.

Sources: Census 1931, *General Report for England and Wales*, for 1911 and 1931 figures.
Abstract of Regional Statistics, no. 5, 1969, for figures for 1951 and 1966 on 1966 boundaries.

TABLE 2.12

Geographical Distribution of the Population 1911–1966, Great Britain (thousands)

Area	Census population 1911		Mid-year estimate 1931		Mid-year estimate 1951		Mid-year estimate 1966	
	Number	*Per cent*	*Number*	*Per cent*	*Number*	*Per cent*	*Number*	*Per cent*
South East	11,703	28·7	13,502	30·1	15,216	31·1	17,006	32·0
North	12,099	29·6	13,100	29·2	13,631	27·9	14,310	26·9
West Midlands and South West	6005	14·7	6597	14·7	7674	15·7	8634	16·2
East Midlands and East	3844	9·4	4199	9·4	4705	9·6	5331	10·0
Wales	2421	5·9	2590	5·8	2589	5·3	2704	5·1
England and Wales	36,070	88·3	39,988	89·2	43,815	89·6	47,985	90·2
Scotland	4761	11·7	4843	10·8	5103	10·4	5184	9·8
Great Britain	40,831	100	44,831	100	48,918	100	53,169	100

Note: See note to Table 2.11.

Sources: Census 1931, *General Report for England and Wales*, gives figures for 1911 and 1931 on same boundaries.
Abstract of Regional Statistics, no. 5, 1969, gives regional population for 1951 and 1966 on the 1966 boundaries.

TABLE 2.13

Regional Densities, England and Wales and Scotland (persons per acre)

1931		1968	
England & Wales	1·1	England & Wales	1·3
South East	2·0	North	0·7
Greater London	18·5	Yorks & Humberside	1·4
Northumberland & Durham	1·2	North West	3·4
Northern Rural belt	0·4	West Midlands	1·6
West Riding	1·9	East Midlands	1·1
Lancashire & Cheshire	3·3	East Anglia	0·5
West Midlands	1·1	South East	2·5
East Midlands	1·0	South West	0·6
Eastern Counties	0·4	Wales	0·5
South West Counties	0·4	Scotland	0·3
South Wales	1·0		
North & Central Wales	0·2		
Scotland	0·2		

Sources:

1931. Census 1931, *General Report, England and Wales.*

1968. Calculated from the averages and population estimates in *Abstract of Regional Statistics,* no. 5, 1969.

TABLE 2.14

Marital Status of the Population 1901–1966, England and Wales and Scotland (percentages)

Year	Marital status			
	Single	*Married*	*Widowed*	*Divorced*
ENGLAND AND WALES				
1901	59·7	34·8	5·5	
1921	54·3	39·7	6·0	0·4
1931	50·9	42·8	6·3	0·8
1951	42·1	50·5	7·0	0·5
1961	41·2	51·3	6·9	0·6
1966	41·1	51·2	7·0	0·7
SCOTLAND				
1901	63·9	30·6	5·5	
1921	59·6	34·4	6·0	0·1
1931	57·4	36·4	6·1	0·1
1951	48·8	44·1	6·4	0·4
1961	46·6	46·3	6·8	0·4
1966	45·9	46·7	7·0	0·4

Source: Census tables 1901–66.

TABLE 2.15

Marital Status of the Population by Sex 1901–1966, England and Wales and Scotland (percentages)

Year	Men				Women			
	Single	Married	Widowed	Divorced	Single	Married	Widowed	Divorced
ENGLAND AND WALES								
1901	60·8	35·7	3·5		58·6	34·0	7·4	
1921	55·0	41·4	3·6	0·04	53·5	38·3	8·2	0·04
1931	51·8	44·4	3·7	0·1	50·0	41·3	8·6	0·1
1951	43·8	52·3	3·5	0·4	40·5	48·7	10·2	0·6
1961	43·7	53·0	3·0	0·4	38·8	49·8	10·6	0·7
1966	43·8	52·7	3·0	0·5	38·6	49·8	10·8	0·8
SCOTLAND								
1901	65·6	31·1	3·4		62·4	30·0	7·6	
1921	60·7	35·5	3·8	0·1	58·6	33·3	8·0	0·1
1931	58·3	37·6	4·0	0·1	56·5	35·3	8·1	0·1
1951	49·9	45·7	4·0	0·2	47·4	42·7	9·4	0·4
1961	48·6	47·8	3·3	0·3	44·7	44·8	9·9	0·5
1966	48·2	48·3	3·2	0·3	43·8	45·3	10·4	0·5

Source: Census tables 1901–66.

TABLE 2.16

Marital Status of the Population by Sex 1901–1966, England and Wales and Scotland (numbers per 1000 population Aged 15 and Over)

Year	Men			Women		
	Single	Married	Widowed & divorced	Single	Married	Widowed & divorced
ENGLAND AND WALES						
1901	411	536	53	395	497	108
1911	403	545	52	390	506	104
1921	365	584	51	368	520	112
1931	356	593	51	354	534	112
1951	265	684	51	248	616	136
1961	256	700	45	219	636	145
1966	258	696	46	215	636	149
SCOTLAND						
1901	471	477	51	445	443	112
1911	461	483	58	440	452	108
1921	430	513	56	424	464	114
1931	418	524	57	415	475	110
1951	321	619	57	316	555	127
1961	290	660	50	270	592	138
1966	285	666	49	259	597	144

Sources: A. M. Carr-Saunders, D. Caradog Jones and C. A. Moser, *A Survey of Social Conditions in England and Wales* (O.U.P. 1958).
Annual Abstract of Statistics, nos 84, 96, 105.

TABLE 2.17

**Distribution of the Widowed Population by Age Groups 1931–1966,
England and Wales and Scotland (percentages)**

Year	Widowed males			Widowed females		
	15–44	45–64	65 and over	15–44	45–64	65 and over
ENGLAND AND WALES						
1931	10·0	38·0	52·0	11·0	42·0	47·0
1951	5·0	28·0	67·0	6·0	34·0	60·0
1961	3·1	26·9	69·9	3·1	29·6	66·8
1966	3·0	26·8	70·2	2·6	28·5	69·8
SCOTLAND						
1931	10·2	40·7	49·1	10·9	40·9	48·2
1951	6·1	29·5	64·3	7·0	37·8	55·2
1961	3·3	29·6	67·2	4·0	35·7	60·3
1966	2·9	30·4	66·7	3·5	33·7	62·9

Sources: D. C. Marsh, *op. cit.*
Census tables 1901–66.

TABLE 2.18

Married Persons as a Proportion of the Total by Sex and Age 1901–1966, England and Wales and Scotland (numbers per 1000 of relevant age group)

	MEN						WOMEN					
	15–19	20–24	25–29	30–34	35–39	All ages	15–19	20–24	25–29	30–34	35–39	All ages
ENGLAND AND WALES												
1901	3	173	544	732	802	357	15	272	579	718	752	340
1911	2	142	503	716	794	372	12	242	558	711	752	356
1921	4	177	548	756	818	414	18	270	568	697	740	383
1931	3	138	525	771	847	444	18	257	587	733	755	413
1951	5	237	646	799	851	523	44	480	770	827	831	488
1961	11	309	702	818	856	530	66	577	835	875	875	496
1966	17	330	736	840	862	528	79	584	812	892	890	498
SCOTLAND												
1901	4	121	442	649	737	311	18	233	515	659	697	300
1911	2	129	412	624	722	322	13	216	590	649	683	311
1921	5	145	457	666	744	355	21	242	500	636	686	333
1931	8	117	432	680	778	376	23	227	499	652	698	353
1951	4	198	575	747	810	457	35	394	696	784	792	427
1961	12	295	688	805	836	478	58	516	802	841	835	448
1966	19	321	729	839	857	483	68	537	826	873	859	453

Source: Census tables, England and Wales, 1961 and 1966. Census tables, Scotland, 1901–1966.

TABLE 2.19

Marriage Rates for the Population aged 15 and over 1901–1968, England and Wales and Scotland

Period or single year	Number of marriages per 1000 unmarried persons aged 15 and over (including widowed and divorced)	
	Unmarried males	Unmarried females
ENGLAND AND WALES		
1901–5	52·3	43·7
1911–15	54·6	45·6
1921–5	55·3	42·3
1931–5	55·9	43·6
1941–5	63·2	48·3
1951–5	68·3	51·4
1961–5	66·0	51·1
1968	74·4	58·0
SCOTLAND Year		
1901	42·3	36·1
1911	40·2	34·4
1921	49·7	40·6
1931	41·1	34·9
1939	61·9	45·5
1951	60·5	45·7
1961	66·5	48·7
1968	71·6	53·3

Sources: The Registrar-General's *Statistical Review for England and Wales*, 1968. *Annual Reports* of the Registrar-General, Scotland, and *Annual Abstract of Statistics*.

TABLE 2.20

First Marriage Rates by Sex and Age, 1931 and 1938 to 1968, England and Wales

Period	Marriage rates per 1000 single population in each age group									Marriage rate per 1000 population over 15
	15–19	20–24	25–29	30–34	35–39	40–44	45–49	50–54	55 and over	
BACHELORS										
1931	3·3	72·3	152·2	111·5	62·7	33·8	20·4	12·2	5·4	56·0
1938	3.2	87·0	176·8	127·5	68·8	37·7	23·4	13·2	4·8	64·8
1939–50	6·4	112·1	175·6	128·3	75·8	42·1	25·1	15·3	5·1	71·2
1951–5	6·7	131·8	174·4	107·3	60·7	35·6	21·7	14·1	5·1	70·8
1956–60	11·0	153·1	187·4	105·7	55·4	31·1	21·0	12·0	4·8	73·6
1961–5	13·8	158·6	182·3	88·2	46·8	26·7	17·2	11·1	4·5	68·5
1961	13.0	159·2	182·4	91·8	48·4	28·5	17·9	11·8	4·7	70·4
1962	12·8	158·3	180·6	90·4	47·7	26·9	17·9	11·5	4·6	68·1
1963	13·4	156·6	180·3	88·7	46·7	26·6	17·3	11·2	4·6	67·1
1964	13·9	157·4	183·1	85·4	45·7	26·3	16·4	10·8	4·4	67·5
1965	15·5	161·5	185·3	84·7	45·5	24·8	16·6	10·4	4·2	69·4
1966*	18·0	167·8	180·3	85·2	44·4	25·6	16·3	11·1	4·5	72·1
1967*	17·8	162·2	173·3	83·7	41·4	24·4	15·9	10·3	4·3	72·1
1968	18·8	170·8	176·2	86·2	41·3	24·7	15·0	10·2	4·0	76·6
SPINSTERS										
1931	17·1	106·8	119·1	57·2	27·0	14·5	9·6	5·9	2·2	51·7
1938	22·6	147·9	154·0	67·2	33·1	16·8	10·7	6·2	2·0	61·4
1939–50	36·8	191·1	153·3	72·8	36·5	20·4	12·6	7·5	2·0	69·5
1951–5	43·9	231·9	157·2	75·1	38·6	21·2	12·8	7·9	2·1	71·9
1956–60	56·6	264·8	169·9	80·7	37·2	22·6	12·7	7·8	2·2	77·4
1961–5	59·0	257·5	157·7	73·5	38·6	22·0	13·4	8·2	2·2	76·1
1961	59·8	261·2	162·9	74·7	38·0	21·2	13·6	8·0	2·2	76·2
1962	58·0	258·2	159·4	74·3	38·7	22·0	12·9	8·2	2·2	74·7
1963	57·6	253·2	157·4	74·2	38·6	22·4	13·6	8·1	2·2	74·6
1964	58·2	255·4	155·1	73·0	38·6	22·4	13·4	8·5	2·2	76·0
1965	61·4	259·5	153·7	70·8	39·1	22·0	13·7	8·2	2·2	78·8
1966*	66·2	260·2	147·8	72·0	40·9	21·3	14·0	8·2	2·2	81·8
1967*	63·9	250·2	146·2	69·4	37·8	21·6	14·3	8·6	2·1	82·5
1968	67·1	260·9	152·7	68·9	37·3	20·7	14·6	8·8	2·1	88·2

* Revised rates.

Source: The Registrar-General's *Statistical Review for England and Wales*, 1966 and 1968, Part II.

TABLE 2.21

Remarriage Rates of Divorced and Widowed Persons by Sex 1951–1966, England and Wales and Scotland

	Numbers of divorced persons marrying per 1000		
	Period or single year	*Men*	*Women*
ENGLAND AND WALES	1951–1955	234	137
	1961	162	96
	1966	182	108
SCOTLAND	1951	242	138
	1961	172	88
	1966	236	113

	Number of widowed persons marrying per 1000		
	Period or single year	*Men*	*Women*
ENGLAND AND WALES	1951–1955	31	8
	1961	29	7
	1966	29	6
SCOTLAND	1951	22	6
	1961	20	5
	1966	19	5

Note: The Scottish figures were obtained by taking the number of marriages in the given years as a proportion of the widowed or divorced population obtained from census data.

Source: The Registrar-General's *Statistical Review for England and Wales,* 1966, Tables of Population, and the Registrar-General's *Annual Report for Scotland,* 1966. *Annual Abstracts of Statistics* for relevant years.

TABLE 2.22

Proportion of Males Married by Age and Social Class 1931, England and Wales (percentages)

Social class	Age group			
	21–24	*25–29*	*30–34*	*35–44*
I	6·3	38·1	71·3	84·4
II	12·9	48·9	77·0	87·8
III	16·3	53·7	79·5	87·8
IV	17·9	54·1	76·9	84·1
V	20·4	54·0	75·4	82·0
All occupied	16·9	53·1	77·9	86·2
All unoccupied	2·5	14·7	29·7	46·9

Source: Peter R. Cox, *op. cit.,* p. 97.

TABLE 2.23

Petitions for Divorce and Decrees Granted 1901–1968, England and Wales and Scotland

Period	Number of petitions filed (annual averages)	Remarks
ENGLAND AND WALES		
1901–1905	812	Working class in practice denied access to divorce court
1911–15	1003	War
1921–5	2848	
1931–5	4784	Divorce procedures became easier
1941–5	16,075	War
1951	38,382	Legal aid scheme, divorce available to all classes
1956	28,426	
1961	31,905	
1968	55,007	

	Period	Average number of decrees of divorce and nullity
SCOTLAND	1901–5	181
	1911–15	264
	1921–5	429
	1931–5	507
	1941–5	1413
	1951	1955
	1956	1891
	1961	1830
	1968	4803

Sources: O. R. McGregor, *op. cit.*, p. 36.
The Registrar-General's *Statistical Review of England and Wales*, 1968.
Registrar-General's *Annual Report for Scotland*, Part II, 1968.

TABLE 2.24

New Petitions filed in England and Wales, Decrees of Divorce and Nullity Granted in Scotland, in relation to the Number of Married Women aged 20 to 49 years, 1931–1968

ENGLAND AND WALES			SCOTLAND		
Period	Number of petitions	Petitions per 1000 married women 20–49	Period	Number	Decrees per 1000 married women 20–49
1931–5	4784	0·80	1931	590	0·98
1941	8305	1·21	1939	879	1·3
1951	38,382	5·23	1951	1955	2·5
1961	31,905	4·25	1961	1830	2·4
1968	55,007	7·4	1968	4803	6·2

Note: The 1939 figure for married women aged 45–9 was estimated by taking half the 45–54 age group from the National Register of the United Kingdom for 1939.
Sources: The Registrar-General's *Statistical Review for England and Wales*, 1962, *Commentary*, and 1968 Tables of Population.

The Registrar-General's *Annual Report for Scotland*, Part II, 1968. The Census Tables. National Register of the United Kingdom 1939.

TABLE 2.25

Approximate Proportion of Marriages Terminated by Divorce 1911–1968, England and Wales and Scotland

Year	Petitions filed	Petitions per 100 marriages contracted annually 5–15 years earlier	Estimated percentage of marriages terminated by divorce
ENGLAND AND WALES			
1911	859	0·3	0·2
1921	2790	1·0	0·8
1937	5750	1·9	1·6
1950	29,096	7·9	7·1
1953	29,845	7·8	7·0
1954	28,347	7·4	6·7
1961	31,905	8·7	
1968	55,007	15·9	

Year	Divorce actions	Divorce actions per 100 marriages contracted annually 5–15 years earlier	Estimated percentage of marriages terminated by divorce
SCOTLAND			
1911	236	0·7	0·7
1921	520	1·6	1·5
1937	643	1·9	1·9
1950	2216	5·2	5·1
1953	2420	5·4	5·2
1954	2271	5·0	4·9
1961	1830	4·3	
1968	4803	11·6	

Note: 1911 to 1954 figures are taken from *Royal Commission on Marriage and Divorce*. 1961 and 1968 figures are calculated from data obtained from the Registrar-General. No estimate is made of percentages of marriages terminated by divorce.

Sources: Royal Commission on Marriage and Divorce, Cmd 9678, 1956.

Registrar-General's *Annual Report for Scotland*, Part II, 1968.

Registrar-General's *Statistical Review for England and Wales*, 1968, Tables of Population.

TABLE 2.26

Matrimonial Petitions 1899–1945 and Petitions made Absolute 1951–1954 and 1968 by Duration of Marriage, England and Wales

Duration of marriage years	1899–1903	1926–1930	1941–1945	1951–1954	1968
1–5	14·7	14·6	15·2	9·9	13·1
5–10	30·4	34·0	31·8	31·3	31·8
10–20	42·5	38·2	37·7	38·1	34·9
20 and over	12·4	13·2	15·3	20·7	20·1

Sources: O. R. McGregor, op. cit., p. 49.
The Registrar-General's Statistical Review for England and Wales, 1968, Tables of Population.

TABLE 2.27

Actions in which Divorces and Separations were Granted by Duration of Marriage 1901–1968, Scotland

Duration of marriage years	1901	1921	1931	1941	1951	1968
1–5	9·0	15·9	9·0	12·9	10·9	15·7
5–10	30·5	22·9	36·7	32·3	38·1	33·4
10–20	41·4	47·9	45·2	38·2	36·4	34·1
20 and over	19·0	13·3	9·0	16·6	14·7	16·8

Source: Royal Commission on Marriage and Divorce, Cmd 9678, 1956.
Annual Abstract of Statistics, no. 84, 1946; no. 96, 1957; no. 105, 1968.

TABLE 2.28

Matrimonial Petitions 1898–1945 and Dissolutions and Annulments of Marriage made Absolute 1951–1968 by Numbers of Children of Marriage, England and Wales (percentages)

Number of children	Annual averages				
	1899 to 1903	1926 to 1930	1941 to 1945	1951 to 1954	1968
None	39·9	40·8	41·0	33·4	26·9
1	23·8	30·9	31·3	32·7	26·5
2	15·6	16·7	16·7	19·1	25·0
3–6	18·4	11·2	10·7	14·1	20·6
7 or more	2·3	0·4	0·3	0·7	1·0

Sources: O. R. McGregor, op. cit.
Registrar-General's Statistical Review for England and Wales, 1968, Tables of Population.

TABLE 2.29

Fertility Trends 1901–1966, England and Wales and Scotland

Period	Average annual crude birth rate per 1000 population	Average annual number of legi-timate births per 1000 mar-ried women	Illegitimate births per 1000 unmarried women 15–44	Approximate average women's reproduction rate	
				gross	net
ENGLAND AND WALES					
1901–5	28·2	230·5	8·4	1·7	1·3
1911–15	23·6	190·7	7·9	1·5	1·2
1921–5	19·9	156·7	6·7	1·3	1·1
1931–5	15·0	115·2	5·5	0·9	0·8
1941–5	15·9	105·4	11·4	1·0	0·9
1951–5	15·3	105·0	10·7	1·1	1·0
1961–5	18·1	125·9	19·1	1·4	1·4
SCOTLAND					
1900–2	29·5	271·8	13·1*		
1910–12	25·8	233·2	13·7†		
1920–2	25·6	226·7	12·5‡		
				year	
1931–5	18·2	159·3	9·6	*1935* 1·1	0·9
1941–5	17·8	136·4	11·8	*1939* 1·1	0·9
1951	17·8	131·5	9·6	*1951* 1·2	1·1
1956	18·6	137·4	9·6	*1956* 1·3	1·2
1961	19·5	145·7	12·1	*1961* 1·4	1·4
1966	18·6	137·2	16·5	*1966* 1·4	1·4

* Figure for 1902.   † Figure for 1912.   ‡ Figure for 1919.
Sources: Peter R. Cox, *op. cit.*, p. 345.
   Census tables 1961, England and Wales.
   Registrar-General's *Annual Reports for Scotland*, for the relevant years.

TABLE 2.30

Birth Rates by Age of Mother 1939, 1954, 1961 and 1968, England and Wales and Scotland (Legitimate and illegitimate live births per 1000 women)

Year	Age of mother						
	15–19	*20–24*	*25–29*	*30–34*	*35–39*	*40–44*	*45–49* •
ENGLAND AND WALES							
1939	16·0	92·7	113·4	81·4	46·6	15·3	1·5
1954	22·7	136·2	139·1	84·9	44·3	12·9	0·8
1961	37·9	173·6	177·5	103·0	47·8	14·1	0·9
1968	49·2	161·4	160·6	88·0	40·5	10·7	0·7
SCOTLAND							
1939	20·9	104·5	128·1	98·2	60·4	19·3	1·5
1954	21·4	144·0	153·3	104·0	58·2	16·2	1·0
1961	33·8	175·4	185·3	112·9	56·8	16·2	0·8
1968	46·6	168·5	176·9	102·3	48·5	12·1	0·7

Sources: A. M. Carr-Saunders *et al.*, *op. cit.*, p. 11.
Annual Abstract of Statistics, no. 106, 1969.

T.

Families by Type of Head and Number of Per

	Married couple with husband aged:				Married spouse absent	Single widowed or divor man aged:		
	under 45	45–64	65 and over	all ages		under 45	45–64	65+
ENGLAND AND WALES								
Families								
1961	41·5	38·5	11·0	91·1	1·9	0·2	0·6	0·6
1966	41·1	37·8	11·9	90·9	—	0·5	0·8	0·6
Persons								
1961	47·1	37·8	7·9	92·8	1·7	0·2	0·5	0·4
1966	48·1	36·2	8·3	92·7	—	0·4	0·7	0·4
SCOTLAND								
Families								
1961	42·1	37·0	9·4	88·5	2·1	0·2	0·9	0·9
1966	41·8	35·9	10·5	88·2	—	0·4	0·9	0·9
Persons								
1961	47·1	37·0	6·8	90·9	1·7	0·2	0·7	0·7
1966	48·9	34·7	7·2	90·8	—	0·3	0·8	0·6

Source: Census 1961 and Sample Census 1966, Household Composition t
England and Wales and Scotland.

nd 1966, England and Wales and Scotland (percentages)

widowed or divorced woman aged:				Families with one parent as percentage of all families	Total families	Total persons in families
45	45–59*	60+†	All ages			
1·9	2·8	5·6	8·9		100 (12,590,62)	—
2·3	3·0	7·3	9·1		100 (12,666,21)	—
1·6	2·0	4·4	7·2		—	100 (39,921,70)
1·8	2·1	5·8	7·3		—	100 (40,527,77)
2·7	3·7	7·5	11·5		100 (1,333,3)	—
3·1	4·2	9·6	11·8		100 (1,306,2)	—
2·2	2·6	5·8	9·1		—	100 (4,527,7)
2·5	2·9	7·5	9·2		—	100 (4,441,3)

* England and Wales in 1961 the age group is 45–64.
† England and Wales in 1961 the age group is 65+.

TABLE 2.32

Families by Size and Number of Persons 1961 and 1966, England and Wales and Scotland (percentages)

	2	3	4	5	6–7	8–9	10 or more	All
ENGLAND AND WALES								
Families								
1961	39·1	26·9	20·6	8·3	4·3	0·7	0·2	100 (12,590,62)
1966	39·7	25·2	20·5	8·7	4·8		1·0	100 (12,661,31)
Persons								
1961	24·6	25·5	26·0	13·0	8·5	1·8	0·6	100 (39,921,70)
1966	24·8	23·6	25·7	13·6	9·3		2·9	100 (40,525,77)
SCOTLAND								
Families								
1961	33·0	26·5	22·2	10·5	6·4	1·2	0·3	100 (1,333,33)
1966	34·8	24·6	21·5	10·7	6·7		1·7	100 (1,306,15)
Persons								
1961	19·4	23·4	26·1	15·5	11·9	2·8	0·9	100 (4,527,72)
1966	20·5	21·7	25·2	15·7	12·5		4·4	100 (4,441,31)

Source: Census 1961 and Sample Census 1966, Household Composition tables, England and Wales and Scotland.

TABLE 2.33

Family Size (number of children) by Date of Marriage, Great Britain (All Women Marrying at Ages Under 45)

Year of first marriage	Number per 1000 of married women with specified numbers of live births					Average no. of children
	0	1 or 2	3 or 4	5 to 9	10 or more	
1900–9	113	335	277	246	29	3·4
1910	122	373	282	200	23	3·0
1920	138	456	258	136	12	2·5
1930	165	511	220	100	4	2·1
1940	170	528	210	90	2	2·0

Source: Peter R. Cox, *op. cit.*, p. 103.

TABLE 2.34

Mean Family Size by Year of Marriage and Age at Marriage, England and Wales and Scotland

Year of marriage	Age of women at marriage					
	Under 20	20–24	25–29	30–34	35–39	All under 45
ENGLAND AND WALES						
1900–9	4·85	3·60	2·62	2·12	1·52	3·53
1911	4·33	3·16	2·30	1·87	1·38	2·96
1921	3·46	2·54	1·87	1·46	1·02	2·32
1931	3·26	2·25	1·60	1·16	0·73	2·01
1941	2·71	2·15	1·68	1·21	0·66	1·98
SCOTLAND						
1900–9	5·98	4·59	3·36	2·63	1·76	4·43
1911	5·40	4·15	2·94	2·19	1·77*	3·76
1921	4·46	3·46	2·44	1·80	1·13	3·02
1931	4·28	3·07	2·12	1·51	0·91	2·66
1941	3·31	2·63	2·01	1·43	0·80	2·29

* Based on small numbers.
Source: Census 1961, Fertility tables, England and Wales and Scotland.

TABLE 2.35

Mean Family Size by Age and Duration of Marriage, England and Wales and Scotland

Age last birthday	Marriage duration (completed years)				All durations
	5	10–14	20–24	50 and over	
ENGLAND AND WALES					
40–44	0·79	1·63	2·43		2·09
45–49	0·38	1·09	1·95		2·03
50–54	0·27*	0·51	1·49		1·95
55–59		0·24	0·97		1·96
60–64			0·51	2·80	2·10
65–69			0·33	4·64	2·31
70–74				3·93	2·57
75–79				3·49	2·86
80 and over				3·46	3·21

Age last birthday	5	10	15	20	25	50–54	All durations
SCOTLAND							
40–44	0·93	1·64	2·18	2·68	3·93		2·48
45–49	0·40	0·96	1·67	2·06	3·02		2·48
50–54	0·03*	0·34	0·94	1·48	2·13		2·45
55–59		0·12*	0·32	0·87	1·56		2·51
60–64			0·11*	0·31	0·94		2·69
65–69				0·25*	0·38*	5·68	2·90
70–74					0·18*	4·93	3·15
75–79						3·78	3·45
80 and over						2·78	3·78

* Based on very small numbers.

Source: Census 1961, Fertility tables, England and Wales and Scotland.

TABLE 2.36

Estimated Average Size of Completed Family by Social Class According to Period of Marriage, 1909 to 1929, Great Britain

Date of marriage	Social class		All persons
	Manual workers	Non-manual workers	
1900–9	3·94	2·79	3·37
1910–14	3·35	2·34	2·90
1915–19	2·91	2·05	2·53
1920–4	2·73	1·89	2·38
1925–9	2·49	1·73	2·19

Source: Peter R. Cox, *op. cit.*, p. 355.

TABLE 2.37

Family Size by Social Class and Date of Marriage, Great Britain
(Women Marrying at Ages Under 45)

Occupational category of husband	Live births per woman married in		Births in 1920–1924 as a percentage of those in 1900–1905
	1900–1909	1920–1924	
NON-MANUAL			
Professional	2·33	1·75	75
Employers	2·64	1·84	70
Own account	2·96	1·95	66
Farmers	3·50	2·31	66
Salaried Employees	2·37	1·65	70
Wage earners	2·89	1·97	68
MANUAL			
Wage earners	3·96	2·70	68
Agricultural workers	3·88	2·71	70
Labourers	4·45	3·35	75
All categories	3·53	2·42	69

Source: A. M. Carr-Saunders *et al., op. cit.,* p. 25.

TABLE 2.38

Indices of Social Class Differences in Fertility of Married Women,
1931 and 1951, England and Wales

Year	I	II	Social class III	IV	V	All classes
1931	79	84	94	108	124	100
1951	90	93	96	110	123	100

Source: Peter R. Cox, *op. cit.,* p. 358.

Mean Family Size by Duration of Marriage and Socio-Eco

ENGLAND AND WALES

Socio-economic group (see below)	Duration of marriage (completed years)						
	2	4	6	8	10–14	20–24	50
1	0·60	1·08	1·45	1·60	1·81	1·79	
2	0·69	1·15	1·44	1·65	1·78	1·80	
3	0·86	1·41	1·82	2·11	2·17	2·04	
4	0·59	1·13	1·52	1·76	1·86	1·84	
5	0·62	1·00	1·42	1·60	1·76	1·76	
6	0·58	1·02	1·32	1·53	1·68	1·72	
7	0·85	1·11	1·42	1·79	1·90	1·86	
8	0·73	1·13	1·40	1·68	1·90	1·92	
9	0·77	1·21	1·54	1·74	2·00	2·06	
10	0·85	1·33	1·61	1·75	2·02	2·11	
11	1·05	1·51	1·83	2·09	2·30	2·30	
12	0·77	1·22	1·55	1·65	1·88	1·81	
13	0·97	1·46	1·90	2·09	2·22	2·30	
14	0·88	1·30	1·57	1·89	1·99	2·01	
15	0·93	1·36	1·65	1·87	2·10	2·29	
16	0·98	1·58	1·92	2·19	2·40	2·39	
17	0·75	1·35	1·57	1·80	2·04	2·06	
18	0·66*	0·89*	1·41*	1·85*	1·92	3·13*	
19	0·88*	1·49*	1·49	1·96*	2·41	2·20	

Figures marked * are based on small numbers only.
Source: Census 1961, Fertility Tables, England and Wales and Scotland.

Socio-economic groups   Census 1961 Classification
1. Employers and managers in central and local government, industry, com
   etc. – large establishments
2. Employers and managers – small establishments
3. Professional workers – self-employed
4. Professional workers – employees
5. Intermediate non-manual workers
6. Junior non-manual workers
7. Personal service workers
8. Foremen and supervisors
9. Skilled manual workers

of Husband 1961 (for women marrying at all ages under 45)

AND onomic group see below)	Duration of marriage (completed years)						
	2	4	6	8	10–14	20–24	50 and over
1	0·67*	1·22	1·52	1·95	1·88	1·83	2·85
2	0·88	1·35	1·59	1·97	2·00	1·97	3·70
3	0·96*	1·55*	2·04	2·31	2·42	2·10	2·22*
4	0·87	1·13	1·61	1·85	2·09	2·04	2·71*
5	0·79	1·10	1·64	1·84	1·95	1·89	2·79*
6	0·70	1·18	1·45	1·71	1·85	1·89	4·24
7	1·04*	1·50*	1·33*	1·92*	2·25	2·21	5·11*
8	0·85*	1·19	1·60	1·77	2·03	2·15	4·10
9	0·86	1·38	1·73	2·06	2·28	2·44	4·96
10	0·99	1·43	1·82	2·09	2·36	2·56	4·76
11	1·13	1·69	2·01	2·31	2·57	2·93	5·56
12	1·21*	1·45	1·90	2·19	2·09	2·25	4·00*
13	1·08	1·63	2·05	2·20	2·36	2·63	4·23
14	0·79*	1·64	2·04	2·00*	2·07	2·30	4·11*
15	1·05	1·53	1·92	2·22	2·40	2·83	4·66
16	0·93	1·58	1·58	1·94	2·09	2·52*	4·50*
17	0·75*	1·56*	3·00*	3·33*	2·47*	2·89*	5·03
18	0·87*	1·27*	1·33*	1·83*	1·75*	3·00*	—
19	2·00*	1·67*	—	—	2·00*	2·28*	4·33*

mi-skilled manual workers
nskilled manual workers
wn account workers (other than professional)
armers – employers and managers
armers – own account
gricultural workers
embers of armed forces
definite
udents
thers not stating a present or former activity

TABLE 240

Proportion of Private Households by Type and Size 1966, England and Wales and Scotland (percentages)

Household type	Number of persons in household										Total households	Total persons
	1	2	3	4	5	6	7	8	9	10 or more		
ENGLAND AND WALES												
No family	78.4	17.9	2.8	0.7	0.2	neg	neg	neg	neg	neg	100 19.3 (2,965,50)	8.2
One family		34.7	26.3	21.9	10.1	4.2	1.3	0.7	0.3	0.2	100 78.9 (12,086,54)	88.3
Two families				28.6	31.8	23.2	8.7	3.9	1.9	1.9	100 1.8 (282,98)	3.4
Three or more families						25.0	16.4	17.5	14.2	27.0	100 neg (4,52)	0.1
Total households	15.1	30.8	21.3	17.9	8.6	3.8	1.3	0.6	0.3	0.2	100 (15,339,54)	—
Total persons	5.2	20.7	21.5	24.1	14.5	7.6	3.2	1.6	0.8	0.9	—	100 (45,606,58)
SCOTLAND												
No family	77.4	17.9	3.7	0.8	0.2	neg	neg	neg	—	—	100 20.1 (321,20)	8.3
One family		30.3	25.3	22.6	12.0	5.6	2.3	1.1	0.5	0.4	100 78.1 (1,247,05)	88.3
Two families				24.5	29.3	24.3	11.4	5.0	2.5	2.9	100 1.8 (28,70)	3.3
Three or more families						10.7	17.9	21.4	12.5	37.5	100 neg (56)	0.1
Total households	15.6	27.3	20.5	18.2	10.0	4.8	2.0	0.9	0.4	0.4	100 (1,595,51)	—
Total persons	5.0	17.5	19.7	23.4	16.0	9.2	4.4	2.4	1.2	1.3	—	100 (4,987,48)

Source: Sample Census 1966, Household Composition tables, England and Wales and Scotland.

TABLE 2.41

Size of Private Households 1911–1966, England and Wales and Scotland (percentages)

Year	Proportion of households of different sizes									Total	Proportion of persons in households of different sizes								
	1	2	3	4	5	6	7	8–9	10 or more		1	2	3	4	5	6	7	8–9	10 or more
ENGLAND AND WALES																			
1911	5·3	16·2	19·3	18·1	14·4	10·4	6·9	6·9	2·5	100/100	1·2	7·4	13·3	16·6	16·6	14·3	11·2	13·2	6·3
1921	6·0	17·7	20·8	18·6	13·9	9·4	6·0	5·7	1·9	100/100	1·5	8·6	15·1	17·9	16·7	13·6	10·1	11·5	5·0
1931	6·7	21·9	24·1	19·4	12·4	7·3	4·1	3·2	0·9	100/100	1·8	11·8	19·4	20·8	16·7	11·8	7·8	7·2	2·7
1951	10·7	27·7	25·3	19·0	9·6	4·3	1·9	1·2	0·3	100/100	3·4	17·3	23·7	23·8	15·0	8·1	4·3	3·1	1·2
1961	11·9	30·2	23·4	19·1	9·1	3·8	1·5	0·9	0·1	100/100	3·9	19·6	22·9	24·8	14·7	7·5	3·4	2·4	0·8
1966	15·1	30·8	21·3	17·9	8·6	3·8	1·3	1·9	0·2	100/100	5·2	20·7	21·5	24·1	14·5	7·6	3·2	2·5	0·9
SCOTLAND																			
1951	11·1	24·1	23·7	18·9	10·8	5·6	2·9	2·1	0·7	100/100	3·3	14·2	21·0	22·3	15·9	10·0	6·0	5·1	2·2
1961	11·8	26·5	22·8	19·7	10·5	5·0	2·1	1·4	0·3	100/100	3·6	16·4	21·1	24·3	16·1	9·3	4·5	3·5	1·2
1966	15·5	27·3	20·5	18·2	10·0	4·8	2·0	1·4	0·4	100/100	5·0	17·5	19·7	23·4	16·0	9·2	4·4	3·6	1·3

Note: 1901–31 census volumes for Scotland give analyses of number of persons by house, not distinguishing separate households sharing a house.

Source: Census 1911. Summary tables, England and Wales. Census 1961 and Sample Census 1966, Household Composition tables, England and Wales. A. M. Carr-Saunders *et al.*, *op. cit.*, p. 35. Census 1951, Vol. III: Scotland. Census 1961 Scotland, Housing and Household tables. Sample Census 1966, Scotland, Household Composition tables.

TABLE 2.42

Private Households by Size and Social Class 1951, Great Britain (percentages)

Social class of head of household	Number of persons						All sizes
	1	2	3	4	5	6 and over	
I	4·2	30·2	27·6	22·3	9·3	6·2	100 (411,400)
II	8·1	29·9	26·9	19·8	9·1	6·2	100 (2,263,100)
III	5·9	27·2	27·1	21·4	10·3	8·0	100 (6,111,000)
IV	8·0	25·1	24·3	20·1	11·4	11·1	100 (2,028,300)
V	7·9	26·6	22·7	18·5	11·2	13·1	100 (1,523,400)
Unclassified	33·0	30·0	17·2	10·0	5·3	4·5	100 (2,144,300)
All classes	10·7	27·6	24·8	19·1	9·6	8·1	100 (14,481,500)

Source: Census 1951, Housing Report, Appendix C2.

TABLE 2.43

Proportion of Households by Socio-Economic Group and Number of Dependent Children, 1966 England and Wales and Scotland (percentages)

Socio-economic group*	Number of children						All households	All children
	0	*1*	*2*	*3*	*4*	*5 or more*		
ENGLAND AND WALES								
All	60·9	16·5	13·6	5·6	2·1	1·3	100·0	100·0
1	51·6	20·3	18·6	6·9	2·0	0·6	4·0	4·7
2	54·6	19·2	17·0	6·5	2·0	0·8	6·2	6·8
3	47·8	15·6	19·8	11·2	4·1	1·5	0·7	1·0
4	44·6	20·8	22·7	8·6	2·5	0·8	3·1	4·4
5	59·9	16·8	15·6	5·4	1·7	0·6	5·1	4·9
6	66·0	16·1	12·2	4·1	1·2	0·5	12·9	10·2
7	79·1	10·8	6·2	2·4	1·0	0·5	2·0	1·0
8	54·1	20·3	15·7	6·3	2·4	1·3	3·6	4·1
9	51·2	20·6	16·7	7·0	2·8	1·8	24·6	30·9
10	59·8	17·2	12·9	5·8	2·3	1·8	13·6	14·4
11	66·7	13·7	9·6	5·0	2·7	2·3	6·8	6·5
12	60·4	16·4	13·5	5·9	2·4	1·5	3·7	3·8
13	54·1	15·7	16·6	9·0	3·2	1·3	0·7	0·9
14	64·5	14·4	11·8	6·0	2·2	1·1	0·9	0·8
15	58·2	17·2	13·7	6·2	2·8	1·9	1·4	1·5
16	24·8	22·8	29·2	14·4	6·0	2·8	0·8	1·8
17	88·9	5·1	3·1	1·5	0·8	0·6	1·2	0·4
18	70·2	13·3	10·0	4·2	1·1	1·2	0·2	0·1
19	93·3	2·6	1·9	1·2	0·6	0·5	8·6	1·7
SCOTLAND								
All	47·8	20·8	17·2	8·2	3·5	2·4	100.0	100·0
1	43·5	21·6	22·2	8·7	2·8	1·1	3·9	4·0
2	48·4	21·0	18·2	8·2	3·0	1·3	5·0	4·7
3	37·9	18·7	22·4	13·9	5·0	2·1	0·8	1·0
4	32·5	23·1	27·6	12·2	3·3	1·3	2·5	3·2
5	40·9	24·0	21·7	9·3	2·9	1·2	3·8	4·1
6	51·6	21·9	16·8	6·4	2·1	1·2	11·0	9·2
7	53·9	23·2	13·0	6·2	2·6	1·1	1·5	1·2
8	46·2	20·6	18·5	8·4	3·7	2·6	4·1	4·2
9	41·2	22·5	19·5	9·7	4·2	2·9	27·9	32·0
10	47·6	21·1	16·3	8·3	3·8	2·9	14·4	14·6
11	51·7	18·6	13·1	7·5	4·6	4·4	8·7	9·0
12	51·3	17·7	16·3	8·9	3·3	2·5	2·1	2·0
13	47·8	18·9	17·1	9·3	4·3	2·5	1·5	1·5
14	55·6	16·3	14·4	7·8	4·1	1·7	1·0	0·9
15	45·4	20·2	17·5	9·3	4·1	3·5	2·7	3·0
16	22·2	23·7	32·1	13·7	5·2	2·9	0·7	1·1
17	85·5	7·4	2·9	1·5	1·6	1·1	1·0	0·3
18	31·9	32·8	25·6	5·0	4·2	0·4	0·2	0·5
19	71·5	14·1	7·2	3·4	2·0	1·8	7·2	3·8

* See note to Table 2.39.

Source: Sample Census 1966, Household Composition tables.

3 The Economic Environment

ROBERT BACON, GEORGE SAYERS BAIN AND JOHN PIMLOTT

Statistics on the level of income and wealth of the economy of the United Kingdom present an overall picture in terms of frequently used concepts. Precise definitions of these concepts, although well known to economists, are not so well known to others and Section 1 of this chapter therefore defines and explains the various statistics and concepts which are used later. Section 2 presents statistics on the national income and its recipients. Section 3 presents statistics on the amounts spent by the various sectors of the economy. Section 4 presents statistics on the distribution of income and Section 5 gives some statistics on wealth in the economy. Section 6 summarises the main trends in the statistics.

DEFINITIONS AND EXPLANATIONS

It is not feasible in a book of this nature to give a full explanation of national income accounting: for this the reader should consult other texts.[1] Nevertheless, a certain minimum acquaintance with economic concepts and the basic framework of national accounting is necessary to understand the series presented in this chapter.

The 'income' of a country
The central concept used in statistics relating to the economy of a country is that of the level of 'national income'. This can be defined in three ways, but the easiest to understand is that of the sum of all individual incomes received in return for currently supplying some good or service – the so-called 'income approach'. More exact definitions of the three approaches follow.
Income approach. A measure of national income is given by the aggregate of all incomes which are created in the current production of goods and services. These are 'factor' incomes. Pensions, family allowances, private gifts, etc., are not included because they do not correspond to the production of a good or service: such incomes are called 'transfer' incomes.

[1] Wilfred Beckerman, *An Introduction to National Income Analysis* (Weidenfeld 1968). Central Statistical Office, *National Accounts Statistics*, ed. Rita Maurice (HMSO 1968).

Not all services which are produced in the economy correspond to a payment (e.g. the services rendered by a housewife) and generally these are not included in any measure of national income.[1]

Expenditure approach. An alternative approach to national income is the aggregate of expenditure on final goods and services. Expenditure on those goods used in the production of some other good is not included. For example: expenditure on a loaf of bread is included while the expenditure on the flour used in making the bread is not (the final price will obviously include the cost of the flour and other inputs – the so-called 'intermediate' goods).

The total amount spent on final goods and services obviously goes to the people who produced them. The incomes of those who make intermediate goods is included in the final value of the products, so that in theory the total expenditure is identically equal to the total of factor incomes.

An allowance is made for those goods which are produced in a certain period but which are not sold in the same period. Since incomes are paid for producing these goods, the total expenditure must be augmented by the additions to stocks and the value of work in progress.

Output approach. Instead of measuring the amount spent on all goods and services, it is conceptually possible to value the final output of every productive enterprise in the economy. These are the goods which will be sold and counted as total expenditure. Hence total output is identically equal to total expenditure and to total income.

The distinction between valuation at 'market prices' and valuation at 'factor cost'

The expenditure approach to the measurement of national income naturally values goods and services at the prices paid by consumers. This will include all taxes on expenditure, as well as subsidies which can be thought of as negative tax rates. Such a valuation is said to be 'at market prices'.

If it were desirable to value the same goods and services as the sum of the factor incomes which had produced them, then the taxes would not have been included – no worker is paid the amount of the tax. Such a valuation, excluding taxes on expenditure, is said to be 'at factor cost'. By allowing separately for the taxes on expenditure, it is possible to switch from one concept to the other.

---

[1] There are one or two special cases where no payment is made but since the service is included in output (see below) a payment is imputed and included. See Central Statistical Office, *op. cit.*

The distinction between valuation at 'constant' prices and
valuation at 'current' prices

So far the discussion of measures of income has been in terms of 'current' prices. The goods sold in a particular year have been valued in terms of the prices for those goods obtaining in that year. Thus the prices used for each type of good will typically change from year to year; and some of the movement in the measure of income over time will be due to changes in prices rather than the number of goods produced. However it is possible to attempt to alleviate this problem by measurement in 'constant' prices. The output of goods in each year could be valued at the prices which obtained for the same goods in a given year. Thus the movement in the aggregate would be caused by movements in the quantities of the individual goods and not the prices charged for them. A figure of 1969 output at 1958 prices would be interpreted in the following fashion: the physical quantity of each type of good produced in 1969 would be valued at the prices charged for the same goods in 1958. These values when aggregated give total output at 1958 prices.

The year chosen for the prices (the 'base year') can make a very large difference to the aggregate series and the interpretation placed upon a series in 'constant' prices must be made with care.[1] It is highly desirable in constructing a constant price series to use only one 'base year', but this is not always possible. Sometimes the first section of a series will be given at constant prices for one year and the second part at constant prices for a different year. In this case the two halves of the series are not strictly comparable. Part of the movement between the two parts of the series will be caused by the different prices. Further, because the series will in general be made up of several items, it is not possible to construct a simple conversion factor that enables the first part of the series to be turned into a constant price series using the second year as a base. Hence in this situation it is usually possible only to make comparisons over the two individual periods.

Depreciation and the difference between gross and net national product

The concept of national income can be seen as an addition to the nation's wealth. In order that it can be exactly identified with an increase in wealth, it is necessary to allow for that part of existing wealth (fixed assets) which was worn out during the given time period. The part of wealth which was worn out during the period is called 'capital consumption' or 'depreciation'. The measurement of depreciation is complex and no details of the method of obtaining estimates are given here.[2]

[1] For a discussion of the problems associated with this index-number problem see Wilfred Beckerman, *op. cit.*
[2] Central Statistical Office, *op. cit.*

Using figures for depreciation, it is possible to convert any of the three measures of income from 'gross' terms (not allowing for depreciation) to 'net' terms (allowing for depreciation). For example,

Gross National Product – Depreciation = Net National Product

National Income identities
In the following sections of the Chapter, the measures of national income are split into component parts. It is necessary to give the exact definitions in terms of component parts.

G.N.P. (income approach) at factor cost is equal to:
Income from employment
Income from self-employment
Gross trading profits of companies
Gross trading profits of public corporations and other public enterprises
Rent
Net property income from abroad
less Stock appreciation

To obtain net national income, depreciation is subtracted from G.N.P. (income approach). It should be noted that this figure for national income will in practice be different from the one reached by the expenditure approach (see below). The difference is the 'residual error'. In the official publication, *National Income and Expenditure*, the difference between the two measures of income is added to the series given above so that the final figures for national income and G.N.P. are identical between the income and expenditure approaches. In the tables presented later in this chapter this adjustment has not been made so that the two approaches give different results.

G.N.P. (expenditure approach) at factor cost is equal to:
Consumers' expenditure
Public authorities' current expenditure on goods and services
Gross domestic fixed capital formation
Value of physical increase in stocks and work in progress
Exports and property income from abroad
less Imports and property income paid abroad
less Taxes on expenditure
Subsidies

To obtain national income (expenditure approach), depreciation is subtracted from this estimate of G.N.P.

STATISTICS: GENERAL DESCRIPTION

Historical period

Wherever possible series are given from 1900 to the latest year available (usually 1968). Some series are incomplete at present: data for the periods of the two world wars is not always available and occasionally does not exist for the earliest part of the period.[1]

Geographical coverage

All series are given for the United Kingdom. Prior to 1921 the data usually include Southern Ireland. This must be taken into account when any comparison is made for the periods before and after the first world war.

Historical consistency of series

It is clearly desirable that each series should be collected on a consistent basis from 1900 to the present day. Unfortunately this has not been possible in practice, although continuing research may improve the internal consistency of some of the series.[2] Wherever the basis of collection of a series has changed, the fact is noted in the discussion on it. The reader should beware of making comparisons between figures collected on a different base, as the change in method could in some cases completely invalidate any direct comparison.

Accuracy of the figures

Even today there are problems involved in collecting and compiling many economic statistics. Most series will be subject to some margin of error. Each year the Central Statistical Office may revise many series for earlier years in the light of new information that has come to hand. The CSO publication *National Accounts Statistics: Sources and Methods* indicates probable margins of error for economic series that are currently being published. These margins may well be much larger for the earlier part of such series, but estimates of the degree of accuracy are probably impossible to obtain.

Sources of the economic statistics

Since 1840 the Government has published an annual *Statistical Abstract* for the U.K. However, until 1946 little material on the series presented in this chapter was given in official publications. It is necessary to rely

[1] Future research may be able to fill in some of the gaps in the statistics. In particular reference should be made to the forthcoming book by C. H. Feinstein, *National Income, Expenditure and Output of the United Kingdom 1855–1965* (C.U.P).

[2] C. H. Feinstein, *op. cit.*

very heavily on the work of a number of individual scholars in building up data on the economy for the pre-1940 period.

One major constraint on the choice of series is that they must be internally consistent for a given period. The individual items must sum to the same as the aggregate of the items and changes in the method or the basis of collection must be reflected in all the series. This constraint has limited the available material to one major secondary source: *The British Economy: Key Statistics 1900–1966* published by the London and Cambridge Economic Service. These figures are taken along with the government publication: *National Income and Expenditure, 1969* (the so-called 'Blue Book') which gives data for the period 1958–68 and thus makes revisions to the latter part of the series published by LCES, who had in fact used an earlier 'Blue Book' for their post-war data.

Precise definitions and discussion of the problem of National Income Accounting are given in the government publication: *National Accounts Statistics: Sources and Methods*, edited by Rita Maurice and published by HMSO (1968).

NATIONAL INCOME AND ITS RECIPIENTS

Until 1941, estimates of national income were based almost entirely on data on individual incomes obtained from the Inland Revenue. The first attempt to obtain such an estimate by a different method, to serve as a check, was made by Clark[1] in 1937, using data on expenditure. Since 1950 it has been possible to obtain entirely independent data for the income and expenditure approaches and this has enabled more precise checks to be made.

As stated above, the main sources for data on incomes are tax returns made by individuals. Since tax assessment includes nearly all income earners (the lower exemption limit in 1965/6–1967/8 was £283 p.a.) this approach should be highly accurate.

In the classification of types of factor income, a broad distinction is made between employment income and profits. The former includes wages, salaries, and the pay of the armed forces. The latter includes all surpluses from trading (surplus is defined as the excess of receipts over operating costs). Rent, although conceptually part of profits, is traditionally treated as a separate factor income. For self-employed people it is not possible to distinguish between employment and profit, so these incomes are treated separately under the heading of income from self-employment.

Supplements to employment income, e.g. employers' contributions to national insurance and superannuation schemes, are also included in income from employment.

[1] C. Clark, *National Income and Outlay* (Macmillan 1938).

Some of the factor incomes received inside the UK are the result of economic activity abroad or property held abroad, and these are added to the factor incomes arising from internal economic activity.

Net national income at factor cost

There is at present no single series available from 1900 to the present constructed on a consistent basis with no gaps. The official figures start at 1946 and are obtainable from the official publications: *National Income and Expenditure*, using the most up-to-date revisions.

For the period 1870–1952, Jeffreys and Walters[1] give a continuous series including data for both World War periods, but this series is not identical to the official series for the post-Second War period and therefore cannot easily be updated on a consistent basis. Feinstein[2] has constructed a series for 1900–63 but this also does not include data for the two war periods.

The series given in Table 3.1 is taken from LCES[3] and is based on Feinstein[2] for the period 1900–38 and the official Blue Book from 1946.[4]

The resulting series which is given in £m. at current prices has to be interpreted with care for two reasons:

(a) The data for the period before 1920 include Great Britain, Northern Ireland *and* Southern Ireland. Southern Ireland is excluded post-1920.

(b) There are two breaks in the consistency of the series. Pre-1914 stockbuilding is not directly estimated and the imputed figure cannot be highly accurate. There is a change in authorship of the series after 1938, as pointed out above. Probably neither of these factors make a very large effect on the resulting series.

For 1946 and 1947 the figures are taken from Feinstein[5] and not from LCES, and from 1958 onwards the figures are taken from the 1969 Blue Book rather than indirectly from LCES because some revisions have been made to the figures for 1958–66 which have become available after the publication of LCES.

[1] J. B. Jeffreys and D. Walters, *National Income and Expenditure of the United Kingdom, 1870–1952*, Income and Wealth series V (International Association for Research in Income and Wealth 1955).

[2] C. H. Feinstein, 'National Income and Expenditure, 1870–1963', *Times Rev. Ind. Technol.*, June 1964 (LCES Bulletin no. 50).

[3] London and Cambridge Economic Service, *The British Economy, Key Statistics, 1900–1966* (afterwards referred to as LCES).

[4] Central Statistical Office, *National Income and Expenditure* (published annually and referred to as the 'Blue Book').

[5] C. H. Feinstein, *loc. cit.*, 1964.

Income from employment
Income from employment is the total of wages, salaries, pay in cash and
kind of H.M. Forces and employers' contributions to national insurance
and national health (included after 1920).

For the period before 1938 Feinstein[1] is the primary source, while for
the period after 1946 the Blue Book is the primary source. LCES is the
secondary source for these figures from 1900 to 1958, while after 1958
the 1969 Blue Book has been used.

The same reservations about the series apply as for national income,
except that it is not necessary to have figures for stockbuilding to estimate income from employment.

Wages and salaries
It is interesting to subdivide the figure of income from employment into
wages and salaries. Feinstein gives such a division (Forces pay being
included in wages) from 1900 to 1963 (omitting the war years). Figures
calculated on a slightly different basis are available from the Blue Book
from 1946.

The series given here in Table 3.1 are from Feinstein 1900–63
and from the Blue Book after 1963. The sum of wages and salaries for
the period 1946–63 do not exactly equal the figure given for income
from employment since the basis of collection is different; however the
error introduced is very small and almost disappears when percentage
shares in national income are given in Table 3.2.

Again it should be noted that there is a break at 1920 with the exclusion of Southern Ireland.

Income from self-employment
The sources for this series are Feinstein for 1900–38 and the Blue Book
from 1946 to 1968. LCES is used as the secondary source from 1900 to
1957 and the Blue Book for 1969 has been used for 1958–68.

The series is subject to the same reservations as that for national
income with the additional point that, for the period prior to 1914,
income from self-employment is aggregated with gross trading profits.

*Gross trading profits of private companies, public corporations, and other
public enterprises*
For the period 1900–38, the primary source is Feinstein while for
1946–68 the source is the Blue Book. Again LCES is used for a secondary
source for the period 1900–57 and the Blue Book for 1969 is used for the
period 1958–68.

For the period 1900–14, total gross trading profits are aggregated

[1] C. H. Feinstein, *loc. cit.*, 1964.

with income from self-employment. After 1920 figures are given separately for private companies, public corporations, and other public enterprises. After 1966 an allowance is made for selective employment tax.

The division between the private and the public sector is affected by nationalisation in 1946–51, the subsequent denationalisation of iron and steel, and road haulage, and the subsidy paid to the British Transport Commission since 1960.

The series are subject to the change of coverage after 1920 mentioned before.

Rent
The sources for rent are the same as for the above series and the same reservations apply.

EXPENDITURE-GENERATING NATIONAL PRODUCT
The second method of obtaining a measure of national income aggregates the individual types of expenditure on the goods and services that are produced in the economy in the current period. There are two main categories of expenditure: current and investment. Investment expenditure adds to the stock of capital and includes items which will be used in the production of other goods and services over several future years, e.g. buildings, plant and machinery. Current expenditure is further divided into consumers' expenditure, public authorities' current expenditure on goods and services, and the value of the physical increase in stocks and work in progress. The last allows for goods produced but not sold during the period (in order to balance the incomes paid to factors for producing these goods). When imports are subtracted and exports added to the total of these expenditures, the resultant figure is said to be gross national product at market prices. Subtraction of total taxes on expenditure gives gross national product at factor cost. Finally subtraction of depreciation gives national income at factor cost. These concepts of national product must be distinguished from those derived by the income approach; theoretically the two approaches should give identical estimates – the difference between the two is referred to as the 'residual error' and is not usually of noticeable size.

G.N.P. at factor cost (expenditure approach)
The estimate of G.N.P. is built up from series on the individual items of expenditure and hence the source for this series must be the same as that for the individual series. For the period 1900–38 Feinstein[1] is the

[1] C. H. Feinstein, *loc. cit.*, 1964.

primary and LCES the secondary source; from 1946 to 1957 LCES is used and from 1958 to 1968 the 1969 Blue Book is used.

The major problems with these series are as before:

(a) The lack of data for the war years.
(b) The major break in consistency at 1920: after this date Southern Ireland is excluded.
(c) The change in authorship at 1938 may lead to some minor inconsistencies.

Consumers' expenditure
This is the total expenditure on goods and services by persons and non-profit making organisations. Business expenditure, since it is in effect a cost of producing the goods sold (and hence included in the price of the goods), is excluded.

The source for this series are as for national income (expenditure approach) and the same breaks in consistency occur.

Public authorities' current expenditure on goods and services
This series is the aggregate of the expenditure by the central government and by local government on goods and services. This excludes any transfer payments and expenditure on fixed assets included in gross domestic capital formation. The sources are the same as for consumers' expenditure.

Gross domestic capital formation
This is the total of expenditure on fixed assets which either extend or replace the existing stock of assets. Such things as buildings, vehicles, plant and machinery are included but expenditure on maintenance and repairs is excluded. A common alternative name for this series is 'gross investment'. The same sources as for consumers' expenditure are used.

General note
The series on consumers' expenditure, public authorities' expenditure, and gross domestic capital formation are all given at current *market prices*; that is, taxes on expenditure are included. The aggregate figure for national income (and G.N.P.) is given at factor cost by means of making an adjustment for expenditure taxes.

Individual items of consumers' expenditure.
Consumers' expenditure can be further disaggregated into expenditure on particular items. This involves very detailed research but some series are available. LCES, drawing on the work of Stone and Rowe and

Prest,[1] present data on six categories. Data on these series post-1946 are available from the Blue Book. For the period 1900–55 Mitchell and Deane[2] give data on a wider selection of items: these are not reproduced, despite the fact that data are given for both sets of war years, because they do not continue to the present day and are given in constant 1938 prices.

The series given are taken from LCES for the period 1900–57 and are in constant 1958 prices (as in the corresponding figure for total consumers' expenditure). All have a break in consistency at 1920 because of the subsequent exclusion of Southern Ireland. There is a less important break at 1938 when the primary source changes. From 1958 to 1968 the figures are taken from the 1969 Blue Book and are given in 1963 prices. This is an important break because, as explained above, there is no simple way to link the two periods. However figures are also given for expenditure on individual items as a percentage of total consumers' expenditure. This will be much less affected by the change of base at 1958.

THE DISTRIBUTION OF INCOME

Previous sections of this chapter have examined movements in the aggregate of all incomes. It is also of interest to see how their distribution has changed over time.

There are two distinct meanings attached to the notion of distribution of incomes. The first, referred to as 'functional' distribution, means the shares of total national income going to wage earners, to profits etc. These shares have been given in Table 3.2. Some analysis of the movement of these shares over time is given in Feinstein.[3] The second meaning is that of the 'size' distribution. This includes all methods attempting to describe the degree of equality or inequality in incomes received. Perfect equality would occur when every person's income was the same; absolute inequality would occur if the total income of the country accrued to one person. There are infinitely many intermediate possibilities and accordingly statisticians have attempted to devise a measure of the degree of equality of incomes. The most common measure is the Gini coefficient (or 'area under the Lorenz curve') which takes a value of zero for perfect equality and unity for absolute inequality and intermediate values for other cases. Such a

[1] J. R. N. Stone and D. Rowe, *The Measurement of Consumers' Expenditure and Behaviour in the United Kingdom 1920–1938*, 2 vols (C.U.P. 1954 and 1966).

[2] B. R. Mitchell and P. Deane, *Abstract of Historical Statistics* (C.U.P. 1962).

[3] C. H. Feinstein, 'The Distribution of Income between Labour and Property', in J. Marchal and B. Ducros (eds), *The Distribution of National Income*, Proceedings of a Conference held by the International Economic Association (Macmillan 1968).

coefficient is awkward to calculate[1] and has no straightforward interpretation. Thus simpler methods of describing the data are often used.
One method examines the percentages of income recipients who have
an income in excess of varying amounts, while another method takes,
say, the top 1 per cent. of income earners and calculates their average
income and repeats this for the top 5 per cent., etc.

Historical coverage of the series
In order to obtain measures of income distribution in the economy, it
is obviously necessary to use data on all the individual incomes. This
is a very substantial task and it is not surprising that there is no continuous series relating to income distribution. The work of individual
scholars and the CSO gives data on a few years in the period.
(*a*) *The Central Statistical Office.* The Blue Books contain a substantial
amount of information about post-second war income distribution:
there are data for 1938, 1949, 1954, 1959, 1962, 1963, 1964, 1966 and
1967. For 1938 the data are less useful because there are no figures on
incomes less than £250 (which were then the great majority). There are
also changes in the ranges of incomes at 1959 for pre-tax incomes and
at 1964 for post-tax incomes and this prevents absolute continuity of the
series.

A more serious limitation on interpretation of this data comes from
possible sources of inaccuracy in data collection, e.g. tax avoidance.
Reference should be made to Chap. 3 of the book by Titmuss[2] before
these figures are used.

A general problem of interpretation of any time series of figures on
income distribution occurs because all money incomes tend to rise over
time, while 'real' incomes (which are measured relative to changes in
the cost-of-living) may rise considerably less fast. People moving from
one income range to a higher range may be no better off because of
inflation. No allowance is made for this in the figures published by the
CSO.

It is also useful to examine the distribution of incomes both pre-
and post-tax. Taxation is likely to make the distribution of incomes more equal and this can be seen by comparing the following
tables.
(*b*) *Lydall*[3] gives the size distribution for income before tax for 1951–2.
The data are given in terms of the average for 1951/52:

[1] M. G. Kendall and A. Stuart, *The Advanced Theory of Statistics*, Vol. I (Charles
Griffin 1958).
[2] R. M. Titmuss, *Income Distribution and Social Change* (Allen & Unwin 1962).
[3] H. F. Lydall, *British Incomes and Savings*, Oxford University Institute of Statistics
Monograph no. 5 (1955).

(c) *Lydall's later work.*[1] Lydall presents the data in a different form. He gives an income figure such that a given percentage of all units earn this sum or more. These figures are first given in current prices and then Lydall constructs a series in 'real' terms (by deflating by a price index). The figures are then given for each percentage group as a figure indexed to 1938. Reference should be made to Lydall[1] for details of this procedure.

Other sources on income distribution

R. J. Nicholson, 'The distribution of personal income', *Lloyds Bank Review*, 1967.

F. W. Paish, 'The Real Incidence of Personal Taxation', *ibid.*, 1957.

D. Seers, *The Levelling of Incomes since 1938* (Blackwell, Oxford, 1951).

THE LEVEL AND SIZE-DISTRIBUTION OF WEALTH

National wealth is defined as the value of physical assets situated within the national boundaries plus the net foreign balance. The total can be looked at in two ways: either categorised by type of asset or by owners of assets. Revell[2] gives the following categories of owners (or sectors):

1. Persons
2. Non-profit-making organisations
3. Banks and savings banks
4. Insurance companies
5. Pension funds
6. Building societies
7. Investment trusts
8. Other financial companies
9. Non-financial companies
10. Public corporations
11. Central Government
12. Local authorities

13. Foreign enterprises (foreign-owned banks, etc.)

The following are the classes of assets and liabilities:

A. Physical assets in the U.K.
    i. Land
    ii. Dwellings and other buildings
    iii. Plant and equipment
    iv. Consumer durables
B. Physical assets overseas
C. Financial assets
D. Liabilities corresponding to certain items above

It should be noted that financial assets are counterbalanced by financial liabilities.

[1] H. F. Lydall, 'The Long Term Trend in the Size Distribution of Income', *J. Roy. Statist. Soc.*, series 4, pt I (1959).

[2] J. R. Revell, *The Wealth of the Nation: the National Balance Sheet of the U.K., 1957–1961* (C.U.P. 1967).

Obviously the amount of data needed to obtain the total of national wealth is immense and it is not surprising that there is no full historical series in the UK.

Revell[1] gives a summary table with data for a few years as well as very detailed data for 1957–61. The historical figures estimate the total stock of physical assets and most types of financial claim.

The distribution of wealth

Given the difficulties of collecting data on aggregate wealth, it is not surprising that there is little information on the distribution of wealth.

The main up-to-date source is Lydall and Tipping.[2] For the period 1951–6 they give figures for Great Britain of people over twenty owning more than £2000 – this obviously excludes some people who would have been included in earlier tables.

For the single year 1954 a more detailed distribution is available giving information on those with smaller wealth. It is possible to compare the degree of inequality of incomes and of wealth for 1954. The Lorenz curves for post-tax income shows a coefficient of inequality of 0·34 while that for net capital shows considerably more inequality with a value of 0·87.

Finally there is rather more limited data spread over the whole period given in Lydall and Tipping[3] and relating to persons over twenty-five in England and Wales. It shows how much of national wealth is owned by the wealthiest 1 per cent, 5 per cent, etc., of the persons considered.

THE MAIN TRENDS IN THE ECONOMIC ENVIRONMENT
National income and its recipients

The series for national income and the factor incomes are to a certain extent limited in their abilities to show long-run trends. The only reliable basis for the figures is that in 'current' prices. Thus the movements of each series over time are caused partly by changes in prices and partly by changes in the quantities involved. Any interpretation of the data which did not recognise this fact could be highly misleading. Also, the longer the period under consideration the larger will be the effects of price changes. Because of this limitation, the discussion of the trends is largely concentrated on the percentage shares of the various components in the total. This will be relatively less affected by price movements.

[1] *Ibid.*
[2] H. F. Lydall and D. G. Tipping, 'The Distribution of Personal Wealth in Britain', *Bulletin of Oxford University Institute of Economics and Statistics*, 1961.
[3] *Ibid.*

Table 3.2 shows some very clear movements in the shares of the different factors in Net National Income.[1] Before 1938 wages were a remarkably constant share of national income. After 1946 (when there was a change in the primary source of the statistics) the share fell from 48·4 per cent in 1946 to 40 per cent in 1968. Salaries grew steadily throughout the period rising from 9·1 per cent in 1900 to 21·9 per cent in 1938. Post-war they rose from 23·4 per cent in 1946 to 35·4 per cent in 1968. Income from self-employment was fairly stable between the wars but then declined slowly in the post-war period. The gross trading profits of private companies rose slowly during the inter-war period, rose further to a peak in 1951 and then declined very slowly. The gross trading profits of public corporations rose slowly throughout the whole period. The share of rent in the national income exhibited a more complex pattern. It was roughly constant before the first war. It fell sharply after the war but then rose slightly in the inter-war period. After the second war it appeared to have fallen again and then grew steadily during the post-war period.

National income and items of expenditure

Again data limitations prevent the presentation of series in 'constant' prices for the aggregate items of expenditure, so attention is focussed on the shares of expenditure in G.N.P. (Table 3.4).[2]

During the period 1900–38, consumers' expenditure remained a fairly constant proportion of G.N.P. After the second war the share fell slowly from 81·7 per cent in 1946 to 73·7 per cent in 1968. Public authorities' current expenditure was roughly constant before 1938 except for a rise just before both wars. After 1946, when it had reached the extremely high figure of 25·7 per cent the share again remained constant but at a much higher level than before. Gross domestic fixed capital formation (investment) grew slowly in the inter-war and post second war periods but had declined in the period 1900–14.

Selected items of consumers' expenditure

Table 3.5 gives the total consumers' expenditure on certain items in constant prices.[3] Movements in these series represent changes in the quantities bought and not changes in prices. Table 3.6 gives the share of each item in total consumers' expenditure. These shares do not total

[1] The total shares shown in Table 3.2 add to more than 100 per cent of Net National Income, since the individual factors sum to G.N.P. (which includes depreciation).

[2] There is a change in the data source at 1946 so that direct comparisons between the two halves of the series cannot be made.

[3] The base year is 1958 for the period 1900–57 and 1963 for the period 1958–68. The two periods cannot be directly compared.

100 per cent. since there is no data on several categories of consumers' purchases.

(*i*) *Food*. Expenditure grew slowly throughout the period 1900–57 and again for the period 1958–68, except that immediately after the first war and during the second war it declined temporarily. The share of expenditure on food was very nearly constant over the period 1900–57. From 1958 the share declined slowly from 25·8 per cent to 22·1 per cent in 1968.

(*ii*) *Alcoholic drink*. Expenditure declined fairly steadily (with minor fluctuations) from 1900 to 1957. From 1958 to 1968 it rose slowly. As a share of total expenditure alcoholic drink declined from 20·8 per cent in 1900 to 6·1 per cent in 1957 but remained constant in the period 1958–68.

(*iii*) *Tobacco*. Expenditure rose steadily between 1900 and 1946, declined slightly in the late 1940s but then rose again slowly from 1950 to 1957 and again from 1958 to 1968. The proportion of total consumers' expenditure spent on tobacco rose slowly from 3·7 per cent in 1900 to 6·7 per cent in 1957 (with some minor deviations in the war years) but declined slowly in the period 1958–68.

(*iv*) *Furniture, electrical and other durable goods*. Expenditure rose steadily during the period 1900–38, rose again from 1946 to 1957[1] and from 1958 to 1968. Similarly the proportion spent rose from 2·5 per cent in 1900 to 4·7 per cent in 1938. After the war the share had fallen to 2·3 per cent in 1946 but rose to 4·5 per cent in 1957. After this the share remained constant.

(*v*) *Cars and motor-cycles*. As expected with a good first introduced at the beginning of the century, the expenditure on cars and motor-cycles grew very fast from virtually nothing in 1900. It declined very sharply during the Second World War and then rose again in the post-war period. The proportion spent on cars and motor-cycles was very small until after the Second World War, but then grew steadily until 1964 when it levelled out at 4 per cent.

(*vi*) *Clothing and footwear*. Expenditure grew very slowly from 1900 until 1957 (with a decline in the war years) and then somewhat faster in the period 1958–68. The share of total expenditure spent on clothing and footwear was roughly constant from 1900–38 at about 10 per cent, declined to 7 per cent in the war years and then slowly grew to reach 9·6 per cent in 1957. In the period 1958–68 it was almost constant at about 9·5 per cent.

The distribution of income and wealth

The tables on income and wealth distribution are compiled to present

[1] There are no data available for this series for the period 1939–45.

information about the inequality of these factors. It must be emphasised that where the tables are given in 'current' prices (money terms), movements over time are partly attributable to the *general* rise in incomes and wealth as well as to any redistribution effects that there may have been. Nevertheless the tables do suggest some trends.

(i) Tables 3.8 and 3.10 show that 'after-tax' incomes are distributed considerably more equally than 'before-tax' incomes. This has possibly become more marked since 1949.

(ii) Table 3.8 suggests that 'pre-tax' incomes have become more evenly distributed in more recent years and Table 3.10 suggests the same trend for 'after-tax' incomes. In order to substantiate these conclusions some simple measure of the equality of distribution would be needed.

(iii) The tables calculated in 'real' terms (Tables 3.14 and 3.15) show more clearly what has happened. The best paid 1 per cent have suffered a decline of 28 per cent in average 'after-tax' income between 1938 and 1949. After this their average income remained constant. The best paid 50 per cent experienced a steady increase in average income over the period 1938–57. This indicates that the less well paid workers of the top 50 per cent had much larger rises in 'real' income than the better paid workers. This table is entirely consistent with the suggestion that the lower paid workers (as a group) caught up, to some extent, with the better paid and that the distribution of 'after-tax' incomes became equal over this period.

(iv) Table 3.19 examines the share of total wealth owned by the wealthiest 1 per cent, 5 per cent etc. for four different periods. It shows that the wealthiest 1 per cent in 1911–13 owned 65·5 per cent and in 1951–6 owned 42 per cent of total wealth. The other groups also show a decline in the shares owned of total wealth, but this is very slight for the wealthiest 20 per cent. These results suggest that there was some redistribution of wealth towards equality but that most of this was within the wealthiest 20 per cent. People with less wealth did not gain over the period in terms of their share of total wealth.

TABLE 3.1

National Income, Gross National Product and Factor Incomes in Current Prices, 1900–1968, United Kingdom (£ million)

1	2	3	4	5	6	7	8	9	10
					Gross Trading Profits:				
Year	Gross National Product at factor cost (income approach)	Net National Income	Income from employment	Income from self-employment	Private companies	Public corporations and other enterprises	Rent	Wages	Salaries
1900	1846	1750	886	—	637	—	219	726	160
1901	1822	1728	884	—	609	—	222	719	165
1902	1833	1740	874	—	627	—	223	705	169
1903	1812	1717	882	—	591	—	227	706	176
1904	1799	1704	866	—	592	—	228	686	180
1905	1874	1776	885	—	634	—	231	700	185
1906	1977	1874	922	—	688	—	233	732	190
1907	2074	1966	979	—	714	—	237	779	200
1908	1981	1875	945	—	647	—	238	736	209
1909	2014	1907	956	—	662	—	238	742	214
1910	2094	1984	996	—	686	—	242	774	222
1911	2188	2076	1033	—	732	—	246	802	231
1912	2302	2181	1076	—	788	—	251	832	244
1913	2392	2265	1114	—	823	—	255	857	257
1914	2335	2209	1132	—	746	—	257	863	269
1921	5019	4662	2869	627	267	25	272	2033	836
1922	4084	3766	2441	635	442	38	291	1660	781
1923	3935	3643	2345	622	478	40	295	1574	771
1924	4044	3757	2405	646	475	38	300	1619	786
1925	4266	3979	2448	635	450	39	305	1643	805
1926	4051	3764	2367	621	404	38	315	1545	822
1927	4264	3981	2532	634	461	47	322	1684	848
1928	4294	4006	2526	645	475	51	329	1665	861
1929	4444	4147	2573	647	499	51	344	1696	877
1930	4445	4149	2513	618	472	53	356	1636	877
1931	4058	3763	2408	576	420	55	366	1549	859
1932	3902	3614	2384	530	373	57	374	1522	862

Table 3.1 continued

1	2	3	4	5	6	7	8	9	10
	Gross National Product at factor cost (income approach)	Net National Income	Income from employment	Income from self-employment	Gross Trading Profits: Private companies	Gross Trading Profits: Public corporations and other enterprises	Rent	Wages	Salaries
Year									
1933	3991	3704	2428	577	428	61	382	1548	880
1934	4262	3975	2533	612	499	64	389	1610	913
1935	4449	4146	2622	623	576	65	404	1677	945
1936	4677	4355	2770	664	656	66	419	1780	990
1937	4961	4599	2929	650	738	68	433	1897	1032
1938	5180	4805	3018	641	690	69	447	1962	1056
1946	8851	7990	5728	1122	1476	106	429	3872	1876
1947	9455	8580	6227	1207	1694	155	472	4135	2082
1948	10,465	9617	6785	1301	1793	220	456	4413	2362
1949	11,201	10,308	7246	1372	1843	258	463	4648	2583
1950	11,760	10,807	7627	1387	2126	335	539	4847	2765
1951	12,939	11,838	8501	1434	2483	337	552	5398	3073
1952	13,990	12,750	9107	1487	2180	317	597	5792	3315
1953	14,842	13,553	9634	1537	2313	384	670	6109	3510
1954	15,810	14,470	10,284	1575	2578	462	736	6523	3741
1955	16,992	15,531	11,244	1659	2894	427	790	7101	4117
1956	18,246	16,662	12,257	1711	2938	467	852	7706	4525
1957	19,247	17,556	12,958	1772	3091	451	911	8032	4814
1958	20,093	18,302	13,470	1786	2983	495	1061	8190	5280
1959	21,192	19,348	14,107	1890	3317	555	1153	8449	5658
1960	22,982	21,049	15,174	2014	3736	718	1244	9018	6156
1961	24,325	22,260	16,407	2117	3643	741	1338	9645	6762
1962	25,518	23,321	17,207	2155	3595	822	1455	10,016	7291
1963	27,202	24,884	18,191	2215	4108	922	1567	10,379	7812
1964	29,473	26,981	19,703	2342	4601	1022	1700	11,210	8493
1965	31,657	28,960	21,261	2527	4778	1091	1865	11,932	9329
1966	33,115	30,178	22,741	2665	4455	1136	2022	12,588	10,153
1967	34,670	31,522	23,615	2772	4637	1231	2183	12,714	10,901
1968	36,815	33,440	25,267	2840	5117	1463	2359	13,402	11,865

TABLE 3.2

**Percentage Shares in Net National Income (Based on Current Prices)
1900–1968, United Kingdom (percentages)**

Year	Wages	Salaries	Income from self-employment	Gross Trading Profits of:		Rent
				Private companies	Public corporations	
1900	41·4	9·1	—	—	—	12·5
1901	41·6	9·5	—	—	—	12·8
1902	40·5	9·7	—	—	—	12·8
1903	41·1	10·2	—	—	—	13·2
1904	40·2	10·5	—	—	—	13·3
1905	39·4	10·4	—	—	—	13·0
1906	39·0	10·1	—	—	—	12·4
1907	39·6	10·1	—	—	—	12·0
1908	39·2	11·1	—	—	—	12·6
1909	38·9	11·2	—	—	—	12·4
1910	39·0	10·6	—	—	—	12·1
1911	38·6	11·1	—	—	—	11·8
1912	38·1	11·1	—	—	—	11·5
1913	37·8	11·3	—	—	—	11·2
1914	39·0	12·1	—	—	—	11·6
1921	43·6	17·9	13·4	5·7	0·5	5·8
1922	44·0	20·7	16·8	11·7	1·0	7·7
1923	43·2	21·1	17·0	13·1	1·0	8·0
1924	43·0	20·9	17·1	12·6	1·0	7·9
1925	41·2	20·2	15·9	11·3	0·9	7·6
1926	41·0	21·8	16·4	10·7	1·0	8·3
1927	42·3	21·3	15·9	11·5	1·1	8·0
1928	41·5	21·4	16·1	11·8	1·2	8·2
1929	40·8	21·1	15·6	12·0	1·2	8·2
1930	39·4	21·1	14·8	11·3	1·2	8·5
1931	41·1	22·8	15·3	11·1	1·4	9·7
1932	42·1	23·8	14·6	10·3	1·5	10·3
1933	41·7	23·7	15·5	11·5	1·6	10·5
1934	40·7	22·9	15·3	12·5	1·6	9·7
1935	40·4	22·7	15·0	13·8	1·5	9·7
1936	40·8	22·7	15·2	15·0	1·5	9·6
1937	41·2	22·4	14·1	16·0	1·4	9·4
1938	40·8	21·9	13·4	14·3	1·4	9·3
1946	48·4	23·4	14·0	18·4	1·3	5·3
1947	48·1	24·2	14·0	19·7	1·8	5·5
1948	45·8	24·5	13·5	18·6	2·2	4·7
1949	45·0	25·0	13·3	17·8	2·5	4·4
1950	44·8	25·5	12·8	19·6	3·0	4·9
1951	45·5	25·9	12·1	20·9	2·8	4·6
1952	45·4	26·0	11·6	17·0	2·4	4·6

Table 3.2 continued

Year	Wages	Salaries	Income from self-employment	Gross Trading Profits of:		Rent
				Private companies	Public corporations	
1953	45·0	25·8	11·3	17·0	2·8	4·9
1954	45·0	25·8	10·8	17·8	3·1	5·0
1955	45·7	26·5	10·6	18·6	2·7	5·0
1956	46·2	27·7	10·2	17·6	2·8	5·1
1957	45·7	27·8	10·0	17·6	2·5	5·1
1958	44·7	28·2	9·7	16·8	2·7	5·7
1959	43·6	29·2	9·7	17·1	2·8	5·9
1960	42·8	29·2	9·5	17·7	3·4	5·9
1961	43·3	30·3	9·5	16·3	3·3	6·0
1962	42·9	31·2	9·2	15·4	3·5	6·2
1963	41·7	31·3	8·9	16·1	3·7	6·2
1964	41·5	31·4	8·6	17·0	3·7	6·3
1965	41·2	32·2	8·7	16·4	3·7	6·4
1966	41·7	33·6	8·8	14·7	3·7	6·7
1967	40·3	34·5	8·7	14·7	3·9	6·9
1968	40·0	35·4	8·4	15·3	4·3	7·0

TABLE 3.3

National Income and Items of Expenditure in Current Prices, 1900–1968, United Kingdom (£ million)

Year	Gross national product at factor cost	Net national income	Consumers' expenditure	Gross domestic capital formation	Public authorities' current expenditure
1900	1970	1874	1647	197	185
1901	1989	1895	1688	195	206
1902	1992	1899	1697	194	195
1903	1962	1867	1710	195	165
1904	1978	1883	1730	184	155
1905	2043	1945	1749	173	153
1906	2109	2006	1778	170	151
1907	2172	2064	1823	150	152
1908	2072	1966	1826	123	154
1909	2144	2037	1844	127	163
1910	2231	2121	1890	131	171
1911	2328	2216	1950	127	174
1912	2409	2288	2019	130	180
1913	2527	2400	2083	155	189
1914	2537	2411	2078	156	320
1921	5128	4471	4406	458	463

Table 3.3 continued

Year	Gross national product at factor cost	Net national income	Consumers' expenditure	Gross domestic capital formation	Public authorities' current expenditure
1922	4378	4060	3923	381	422
1923	4178	3986	3797	334	382
1924	4271	3984	3860	374	391
1925	4549	4262	3965	420	407
1926	4301	4014	3922	401	418
1927	4478	4195	3976	426	423
1928	4532	4244	4031	420	428
1929	4632	4335	4077	442	440
1930	4576	4280	4026	435	448
1931	4191	3896	3896	408	448
1932	4024	3736	3775	347	436
1933	4042	3755	3787	357	435
1934	4295	4011	3895	427	451
1935	4499	4196	4032	456	488
1936	4664	4342	4181	517	540
1937	5010	4648	4386	574	622
1938	5310	4935	4501	592	766
1946	8851	7990	7329	925	2282
1947	9455	8580	7988	1199	1735
1948	10,520	9672	8609	1422	1756
1949	11,136	10,243	8969	1577	1975
1950	11,740	10,787	9461	1700	2062
1951	12,961	11,860	10,215	1889	2423
1952	14,012	12,772	10,766	2106	2883
1953	15,065	13,776	11,475	2359	3025
1954	15,923	14,583	12,160	2552	3108
1955	16,975	15,514	13,107	2829	3171
1956	18,420	16,836	13,821	3103	3428
1957	19,522	17,831	14,582	3381	3585
1958	20,408	18,617	15,296	3492	3750
1959	21,411	19,567	16,106	3736	4001
1960	22,794	20,861	16,909	4120	4248
1961	24,391	22,326	17,810	4619	4589
1962	25,563	23,366	18,906	4731	4920
1963	27,218	24,900	20,125	4916	5184
1964	29,373	26,881	21,493	5854	5512
1965	31,364	28,667	22,865	6303	6043
1966	33,006	30,069	24,236	6707	6572
1967	34,805	31,657	25,339	7262	7246
1968	36,686	33,311	27,065	7798	7702

TABLE 3.4

Shares of Expenditure Items in Gross National Product (Current Prices) 1900–1968, United Kingdom (percentages)

Year	Consumers' expenditure	Public authorities' current expenditure	Gross domestic fixed capital formation
1900	83·6	9·3	10·0
1901	84·8	10·3	9·8
1902	85·1	9·7	9·7
1903	87·1	8·4	9·4
1904	87·4	7·8	9·3
1905	85·6	7·4	8·4
1906	84·3	7·1	8·0
1907	83·9	6·9	6·9
1908	88·1	7·4	5·9
1909	86·0	7·6	5·9
1910	84·7	7·6	5·8
1911	83·7	7·4	5·4
1912	83·8	7·4	5·3
1913	82·4	7·4	6·1
1914	81·8	12·6	6·1
1921	85·9	9·0	8·9
1922	89·6	9·6	8·7
1923	90·8	9·1	7·9
1924	90·3	9·1	8·7
1925	87·1	8·9	9·2
1926	91·1	9·7	9·3
1927	88·7	9·4	9·5
1928	88·9	9·4	9·2
1929	88·0	9·4	9·5
1930	87·9	9·7	9·5
1931	92·9	10·6	9·7
1932	93·8	10·8	8·6
1933	93·6	10·7	8·8
1934	90·6	10·5	9·9
1935	89·6	10·8	10·1
1936	89·6	11·5	11·0
1937	87·5	12·4	11·4
1938	84·7	14·4	11·1
1946	81·7	25·7	10·4
1947	84·4	18·3	12·6
1948	81·8	16·6	13·5
1949	80·5	17·7	14·1
1950	80·5	17·5	14·4
1951	78·8	18·6	14·5
1952	76·8	20·5	15·0
1953	76·1	20·0	15·6

Table 3.4 continued

Year	Consumers' expenditure	Public authorities' current expenditure	Gross domestic fixed capital formation
1954	76·3	19·5	16·0
1955	77·2	18·6	16·6
1956	75·0	18·0	16·8
1957	74·6	18·3	17·3
1958	74·9	18·3	17·1
1959	75·2	18·6	17·4
1960	74·1	18·6	18·0
1961	73·0	18·8	18·9
1962	73·9	19·2	18·5
1963	73·9	19·0	18·0
1964	73·1	18·7	19·9
1965	72·9	19·2	20·0
1966	73·4	19·9	20·3
1967	72·8	20·8	20·8
1968	73·7	20·9	21·2

TABLE 3.5

Selected items of Consumers' Expenditure at Constant 1958 and 1963 Prices, 1900–1968, United Kingdom (£ million)

Year	Total consumers' expenditure	Food	Alcoholic drink	Tobacco	Furniture, electrical and other durables	Cars and motorcycles	Clothing and footwear
1900	9079	2479	1894	345	236	0	916
1901	9191	2510	1879	335	251	0	953
1902	9166	2513	1851	345	243	3	905
1903	9099	2560	1789	354	233	3	870
1904	9180	2606	1746	359	247	7	884
1905	9160	2617	1719	364	247	7	868
1906	9243	2662	1706	369	243	7	876
1907	9326	2676	1712	378	258	7	870
1908	9315	2668	1629	378	254	7	902
1909	9257	2699	1497	369	233	7	934
1910	9318	2682	1491	378	236	14	942
1911	9598	2782	1546	398	243	14	1009
1912	9620	2775	1540	398	251	21	1012
1913	9843	2795	1598	411	293	28	1049
1921	8978	2685	1118	540	308	25	847
1922	9289	2811	981	524	356	39	957
1923	9557	2966	988	513	381	53	967
1924	9795	3015	1035	525	381	74	981
1925	10,016	3034	1041	545	401	95	1001

Table 3.5 continued

Year	Total consumers' expenditure	Food	Alcoholic drink	Tobacco	Furniture, electrical and other durables	Cars and motorcycles	Clothing and footwear
1926	9972	3057	995	549	422	92	1002
1927	10,369	3121	987	570	461	95	1058
1928	10,543	3190	953	594	485	99	1065
1929	10,766	3219	955	613	508	99	1085
1930	10,922	3308	922	627	524	95	1074
1931	11,031	3435	841	627	543	81	1094
1932	10,969	3462	734	615	585	88	1049
1933	11,212	3445	768	633	595	102	1086
1934	11,555	3523	806	654	638	127	1099
1935	11,876	3517	839	684	663	152	1139
1936	12,208	3571	870	723	676	169	1176
1937	12,405	3607	912	761	641	173	1171
1938	12,470	3624	904	795	594	152	1172
1939	12,031	3648	920	822	—	123	1198
1940	10,822	3189	864	802	—	19	1008
1941	10,354	3013	911	883	—	3	750
1942	10,214	3102	852	927	—	2	748
1943	10,033	2997	864	920	—	0	681
1944	10,321	3167	879	919	—	1	761
1945	10,946	3214	975	1009	—	6	777
1946	12,061	3451	869	1051	282	71	926
1947	12,455	3718	872	920	367	84	1043
1948	12,509	3765	832	890	398	71	1156
1949	12,747	3902	805	864	468	91	1248
1950	13,098	4077	816	870	530	94	1293
1951	12,919	4008	843	898	526	90	1171
1952	12,855	3968	835	915	476	124	1153
1953	13,433	4164	849	929	560	215	1182
1954	13,979	4246	845	949	653	271	1267
1955	14,543	4367	879	973	664	354	1359
1956	14,672	4436	899	986	615	282	1413
1957	14,978	4511	914	1012	680	325	1452
1958	16,764	4340	959	1205	763	350	1557
1959	17,477	4423	1021	1231	899	430	1632
1960	18,135	4518	1072	1275	876	494	1750
1961	18,551	4600	1139	1294	885	449	1785
1962	18,955	4646	1141	1246	901	510	1777
1963	19,799	4695	1175	1286	970	733	1845
1964	20,474	4769	1254	1270	1012	853	1910
1965	20,809	4770	1232	1224	1032	810	1986
1966	21,249	4856	1265	1264	1014	807	1987
1967	21,713	4899	1297	1271	1022	876	1982
1968	22,278	4928	1339	1265	1055	935	2059

TABLE 3.6

Selected Items of Consumer Expenditure as Percentages of Total Consumer Expenditure, 1900–1968, United Kingdom

Year	Food	Alcoholic drink	Tobacco	Furniture, electrical and other durables	Cars and motorcycles	Clothing and footwear
1900	27·3	20·8	3·7	2·5	0·00	10·0
1901	27·3	20·4	3·6	2·7	0·00	10·3
1902	27·4	20·1	3·7	2·6	0·03	9·9
1903	28·1	19·6	3·8	2·5	0·03	9·5
1904	28·3	19·0	3·9	2·6	0·07	9·6
1905	28·5	18·7	3·9	2·6	0·07	9·4
1906	28·8	18·4	3·9	2·6	0·07	9·4
1907	28·6	18·3	4·0	2·7	0·07	9·3
1908	28·6	17·4	4·0	2·7	0·07	9·6
1909	29·1	16·1	3·9	2·5	0·07	10·0
1910	28·7	16·0	4·0	2·5	0·15	10·1
1911	28·9	16·1	4·1	2·5	0·14	10·5
1912	28·8	16·0	4·1	2·6	0·20	10·5
1913	28·3	16·2	4·1	2·9	0·2	10·6
1921	29·9	12·4	6·0	3·4	0·2	9·4
1922	30·2	10·5	5·6	3·8	0·4	10·3
1923	31·0	10·3	5·3	3·9	0·5	10·1
1924	30·7	10·5	5·3	3·8	0·7	10·0
1925	30·2	10·3	5·4	4·0	0·9	9·9
1926	30·6	9·9	5·5	4·2	0·9	10·0
1927	30·0	9·5	5·4	4·4	0·9	10·2
1928	30·2	9·0	5·6	4·6	0·9	10·1
1929	29·8	8·8	5·6	4·7	0·9	10·0
1930	30·2	8·4	5·7	4·7	0·8	9·8
1931	31·1	7·6	5·6	4·9	0·7	9·9
1932	31·5	6·6	5·6	5·3	0·8	9·5
1933	30·7	6·8	5·6	5·3	0·9	9·6
1934	30·4	6·9	5·6	5·5	1·0	9·5
1935	29·6	7·0	5·7	5·5	1·2	9·5
1936	29·2	7·1	5·9	5·5	1·3	9·6
1937	29·0	7·3	6·1	5·1	1·3	9·4
1938	29·0	7·2	6·3	4·7	1·2	9·3
1939	30·3	7·6	6·8	—	1·0	9·9
1940	29·4	7·9	7·4	—	0·1	9·3
1941	29·0	8·7	8·5	—	0·0	7·2
1942	30·3	8·3	9·0	—	0·0	7·3
1943	29·8	8·6	9·1	—	0·0	6·7
1944	30·6	8·5	8·9	—	0·0	7·3
1945	29·3	8·9	9·2	—	0·0	7·0

Table 3.6 continued

Year	Food	Alcoholic drink	Tobacco	Furniture, electrical and other durables	Cars and motorcycles	Clothing and footwear
1946	28·6	7·2	8·7	2·3	0·5	7·6
1947	29·8	7·0	7·3	2·9	0·6	8·3
1948	30·0	6·6	7·1	3·1	0·5	9·2
1949	30·6	6·3	6·7	3·6	0·7	9·7
1950	31·1	6·2	6·6	4·0	0·7	9·8
1951	31·0	6·5	7·0	4·0	0·6	9·0
1952	30·8	6·4	7·1	3·7	0·9	8·9
1953	30·9	6·3	6·9	4·2	1·6	8·7
1954	30·3	6·0	6·7	4·6	1·9	9·0
1955	30·0	6·0	7·1	4·9	2·4	9·3
1956	30·2	6·1	6·7	4·1	1·9	9·6
1957	30·1	6·1	6·7	4·5	2·1	9·6
1958	25·8	5·7	7·1	4·5	2·0	9·2
1959	25·3	5·8	7·0	5·1	2·4	9·3
1960	24·9	5·9	7·0	4·8	2·7	9·6
1961	24·7	6·1	6·9	4·7	2·4	9·6
1962	24·5	6·0	6·5	4·7	2·6	9·3
1963	23·7	5·9	6·4	4·8	3·7	9·3
1964	23·2	6·1	6·2	4·9	4·1	9·3
1965	22·9	5·9	5·8	4·9	3·8	9·5
1966	22·8	5·9	5·9	4·7	3·7	9·3
1967	22·5	5·9	5·8	4·7	4·0	9·1
1968	22·1	6·0	5·6	4·7	4·1	9·2

TABLE 3.7

Income Distribution before Tax in 'Money' Terms for Selected Years 1938–1967, United Kingdom (absolute numbers in each group in thousands)

Income range £	1938	1949	1954
−250	n.a.	12,050	8540
250–500	1890	9980	8690
500–750	390	2130	5900
750–1000	149	560	1750
1000–1500	130	400	700
1500–2000	53	150	210
2000–3000	46	118	161
3000–5000	33	68	96
5000–10,000	18	33	41
10,000–20,000	6	9	10
20,000+	2	2	2

£	1959	1962	1963	1964	1966	1967
50–250	5760	5010	4460	4054	2603	2338
250–300	1710	1175	1400	1608	950	940
300–400	2680	2430	2320	2408	2100	1912
400–500	2640	2255	2270	2149	2318	2104
500–600	2710	2200	2140	1957	2235	2068
600–700	2560	2220	2190	1917	1912	1904
700–800	2250	2235	2110	1935	1775	1729
800–1000	2970	3730	3820	3679	3394	3435
1000–1500	2250	4345	4545	5447	6463	6741
1500–2000	445	870	1250	1385	2378	2769
2000–3000	287	410	456	560	1036	1298
3000–5000	156	204	210	253	350	370
5000–10,000	65	92	105	116	145	150
10,000–20,000	14	20	20	27	34	35
20,000+	3	4	4	5	7	7

TABLE 3.8

Income Distribution before Tax in 'Money' Terms: Percentage in each Income Class for Selected Years 1949–1967, United Kingdom

Income range £	1949	1954
250	47·2	32·6
250–500	39·1	33·2
500–750	8·4	22·5
750–1000	2·2	6·7
1000–1500	1·6	2·7
1500–2000	0·59	0·80
2000–3000	0·46	0·61
3000–5000	0·27	0·37
5000–10,000	0·13	0·16
10,000–20,000	0·04	0·04
20,000+	0·01	0·01

£	1959	1962	1963	1964	1966	1967
50–250	21·7	18·4	16·3	14·7	9·4	8·4
250–300	6·5	4·3	5·1	5·8	3·4	3·4
300–400	10·1	8·9	8·5	8·7	7·6	6·9
400–500	10·0	8·3	8·3	7·8	8·4	7·6
500–600	10·2	8·1	7·8	7·1	8·1	7·4
600–700	9·7	8·2	8·0	7·0	6·9	6·8
700–800	8·5	8·2	7·7	7·0	6·4	6·2
800–1000	11·2	13·7	14·0	13·4	12·3	12·4
1000–1500	8·5	16·0	16·6	19·8	23·3	24·3
1500–2000	1·7	3·2	4·6	5·0	8·6	10·0
2000–3000	1·1	1·5	1·7	2·0	3·7	4·7
3000–5000	0·58	0·75	0·77	0·92	1·3	1·3
5000–10,000	0·25	0·34	0·38	0·42	0·52	0·54
10,000–20,000	0·05	0·07	0·07	0·10	0·12	0·13
20,000+	0·01	0·01	0·01	0·02	0·03	0·03

TABLE 3.9

Income Distribution After Tax in 'Money' Terms for Selected Years 1938–1967, United Kingdom (absolute numbers in thousands)

Income range £	1938	1949	1954	1959	1962	1963
−250	n.a.	12,270	8750	6200	5070	4460
250–500	1940	9940	9420	7400	6570	6760
500–750	375	1940	5780	6630	6155	6020
750–1000	132	442	1315	3880	4830	4945
1000–2000	142·2	368·4	701	2052	4145	4620
2000–4000	54·6	84·4	127·4	267	353	408
4000–6000	11·6	5·14	6·41	28	59	73
6000+	6·6	0·06	0·19	3	18	14

£	1964	1966	1967
−250	4054	2603	2338
250–500	6884	6338	5906
500–750	5750	5523	5418
750–1000	4608	4765	4822
1000–2000	5641	7604	8198
2000–3000	355	595	730
3000–5000	160	211	224
5000–10,000	47	60	63
10,000–20,000	1	1	1
20,000+	0	0	0

TABLE 3.10

Income Distribution after Tax in 'Money' Terms: Percentage in each Income Class for Selected Years 1949–1967, United Kingdom

Income range £	1949	1954	1959	1962	1963
−250	48·1	33·3	23·3	18·6	16·3
250–500	39·0	35·9	27·9	24·2	24·8
500–750	7·6	22·0	25·0	22·6	22·1
750–1000	1·7	5·0	14·6	17·8	18·1
1000–2000	1·4	2·7	7·7	15·2	16·9
2000–4000	0·33	0·48	1·0	1·3	1·5
4000–6000	0·02	0·02	0·10	0·21	0·26
6000+	0	0	0	0·06	0·05

£	1964	1966	1967
0–250	14·7	9·4	8·4
250–500	25·0	22·9	21·2
500–750	20·9	19·9	19·5
750–1000	16·8	17·2	17·3
1000–2000	20·5	27·5	29·8
2000–3000	1·3	2·1	2·6
3000–5000	0·58	0·76	0·81
5000–10,000	0·17	0·22	0·23
10,000–20,000	0	0	0
20,000+	0	0	0

TABLE 3.11

**Income Distribution before Tax of Income
Units in Private Households in
Great Britain 1951/1952**

£	1951/1952 %
0–99	7·8
100–199	16·2
200–299	14·2
300–399	20·6
400–499	16·0
500–599	9·8
600–699	5·4
700–799	3·1
800–999	2·9
1000–1499	2·3
1500–1999	0·8
2000+	0·9

The average income of the 22 million units was £424.

TABLE 3.12

**Percentiles of Allocated Income before Tax in Current Prices 1938,
1949, 1954 and 1957, United Kingdom**

	1938	1949	1954	1957
	£	£	£	£
1%	1140	1860	2210	2450
5%	393	765	995	1180
10%	266	565	795	940
20%	185	430	625	792
50%	110	261	382	512

TABLE 3.13

**Percentiles of Allocated Income after Tax in Current Prices 1938,
1949, 1954, 1957, United Kingdom**

	1938	1949	1954	1957
	£	£	£	£
1%	940	1280	1600	1800
5%	380	655	890	1020
10%	263	520	740	850
20%	184	410	610	740
50%	110	250	360	478

TABLE 3.14

Index Numbers of Percentiles of Allocated Income before Tax in Constant Prices 1938, 1949, 1954, and 1957, United Kingdom

	1938	1949	1954	1957
1%	100	86	84	84
5%	100	103	110	117
10%	100	111	127	134
20%	100	122	144	163
50%	100	124	147	177

TABLE 3.15

Index Numbers of Percentiles of Allocated Income after Tax in Constant Prices 1938, 1949, 1954, and 1957, United Kingdom

	1938	1949	1954	1957
1%	100	72	74	75
5%	100	91	102	105
10%	100	104	120	123
20%	100	117	141	153
50%	100	119	139	162

TABLE 3.16

Physical Assets in the United Kingdom in Current Prices for Selected Years 1900–1948 (£ billion)

	1900	1910	1920	1927	1937	1948
Land	1·3	1·1	2·1	1·4	1·4	3·6
Dwellings	1·0	1·0	3·2	2·4	3·3	8·1
Other buildings and works	2·1	2·2	7·4	4·6	4·4	6·9
Plant and equipment	0·6	0·8	2·9	1·6	2·1	4·0
Consumer durables	0·1	0·1	0·3	0·4	0·7	0·9
Stocks	0·7	0·8	3·5	1·8	1·7	5·2
Net foreign balance	2·5	3·8	4·2	4·9	4·9	−0·3
National wealth	8·3	9·8	23·6	17·1	18·3	28·4

In 1957 the total of physical assets in the U.K. was £62·2 billion and in 1961 it was £84·5 billion (current prices).

TABLE 3.17

**Size Distribution of Persons (over 20) Owning
over £2000 Net Capital in Great Britain
(average of 1951–1956)**

£	%
2000–5000	59·4
5000–10,000	21·2
10,000–25,000	13·2
25,000–50,000	4·0
50,000–100,000	1·5
100,000–250,000	0·5
250,000+	0·1

There were 3,010,000 persons with over £2000.

TABLE 3.18

**Distribution of Personal Net Capital in Great
Britain in 1954 (Persons over 20)**

£	Number of persons 000's
0–100	16,000
100–500	10,500
500–1000	3100
1000–2000	2400
2000–5000	1780
5000–10,000	640
10,000–25,000	400
25,000–50,000	120
50,000–100,000	40
100,000+	20

TABLE 3.19

**Percentage of Personal Net Capital Owned by Various Groups of
Population (over 25) in England and Wales for Selected Years
1911–1956**

	1911–1913	1924–1930	1936	1951–1956
1%	65·5	59·5	56·0	42·0
5%	86·0	82·5	81·0	67·5
10%	90·0	89·5	88·0	79·8
20%	—	96·0	94·0	89·0

4 The Labour Force

GEORGE SAYERS BAIN, ROBERT BACON AND JOHN PIMLOTT

Manpower statistics cover a wide field.[1] This chapter concentrates on those aspects which are of particular importance to sociologists: the structure of the occupied population, unemployment, hours of work, wage rates and earnings, the cost-of-living and retail prices, trade union membership, and industrial disputes. Statistics on other aspects of the labour force, such as mobility and turnover and vacancies in industry, are not discussed here partly because of lack of space but mainly because of lack of adequate historical data. The emphasis in the following discussion is generally upon the strengths and weaknesses of the various series rather than upon the trends which they reveal.

THE OCCUPIED POPULATION

The Census of Population is the only source from which a reasonably detailed historical picture of the occupied population or the labour force can be constructed. The first Census was undertaken in 1801,[2] but the various occupational and industrial classification systems used in the Census prior to 1911 are very difficult to rationalise on a consistent basis. Consequently, the following analysis is restricted to the period 1911–66. From the vast amount of information the Census provides on the occupied population, three aspects have been selected as being of particular interest to sociologists: occupational composition, sex composition, and participation rates.

Occupational composition

The most striking characteristic of the occupational structure presented in Table 4.1 is the rapid growth of the white-collar labour force. This growth is both absolute and relative; not only is the total number of white-collar workers increasing, but so also is the proportion of these workers in the labour force as a whole.

[1] For a more complete discussion of the diverse sources of manpower statistics and of their strengths and weaknesses, see *Labour Statistics* (HMSO 1958); Ely Devons, *An Introduction to British Economic Statistics* (C.U.P. 1961), especially chaps 2 and 3; and F. M. M. Lewes, *Statistics of the British Economy* (Allen & Unwin 1967), chap. 2.

[2] See *Census Reports of Great Britain, 1801–1931* (HMSO 1951), for a discussion of each Census prior to 1951.

Between 1911 and 1966 the number of white-collar workers increased by 176 per cent, while the number of manual workers increased by only 5 per cent, having actually decreased in total since 1931. The disparate growth of these two groups is reflected in the increasing relative importance of the white-collar occupations. The white-collar section of the labour force increased from 18·7 per cent to 38·3 per cent of the total between 1911 and 1966 while the manual share decreased from 74·6 per cent to 58·3 per cent. During this same period the remaining section of the labour force, the employers and proprietors, showed a tendency to decline, this decline being balanced to some extent by an increase in the number of managers and administrators.[1]

There are significant differences in the growth of the occupational groups which compose the white-collar labour force. Table 4.1 shows that the clerks have claimed most of the ground yielded by the manual workers. During the period under review, clerical occupations grew by 292 per cent and increased their share of the total labour force from 4·5 per cent to 13·2 per cent. The growth in the proportionate share of the other white-collar occupational groups has been more moderate: the share of shop assistants increased from 5·4 per cent to 6·1 per cent; that of managers and administrators from 3·4 per cent to 6·1 per cent; that of foremen and inspectors from 1·3 per cent to 3·0 per cent; that of lower professionals and technicians from 3·1 per cent to 6·5 per cent; and that of higher professionals from 1 per cent to 3·4 per cent.

The very broad occupational classification of Table 4.1 tends to obscure the extraordinary increase in the number of scientific and technical employees. Although the total number of such workers is relatively small, they are increasing more rapidly than any other component of the white-collar labour force (see Table 4.2). The 1921 Census was the first to consider draughtsmen and laboratory assistants sufficiently important groups to merit a separate classification. By 1966 the number of draughtsmen had increased by 350 per cent,[2] professional

---

[1] This decline in the employer and proprietor group should be interpreted with caution. Although there is a legal distinction between an employer and a manager, in social science the dividing line is more imaginary than real, for an employer becomes a manager as soon as his business is incorporated. The trend towards the incorporation of business enterprises is at least part of the explanation for the decline in employers and proprietors and the increase in managers and administrators. On this point see Guy Routh, *Occupation and Pay in Great Britain* (C.U.P., 1965), pp. 19–21.

[2] The decline in the number of draughtsmen since 1961 should be interpreted with caution. The design function in industry is becoming increasingly specialised and there has been a proliferation of job titles. Examples include planning engineers, methods engineers, and technical authors. It is conceivable that people who may previously have referred to themselves as draughtsmen now refer to themselves by a new job title, and are consequently placed in a different occupational group in the Census.

scientists and engineers by 894 per cent, and laboratory assistants by 2,160 per cent. If these high growth-rates continue, the occupational composition of the future white-collar labour force will be considerably changed.

Sex composition

There has been a considerable shift in the sex composition of the labour force since 1911 as Table 4.3 makes clear. In that year women made up 29.6 per cent. of the labour force, but by 1966 their share had grown to nearly 36 per cent.

The proportion of women among manual workers generally in 1966 was much the same as it had been in 1911, although it fluctuated slightly between these dates. But during this period there has been a decline in the proportion of skilled female manual workers and an increase in the proportion of unskilled females, while the proportion of women in semi-skilled manual jobs has remained fairly constant.

The proportion of women has increased most dramatically in the white-collar occupations, from 29·8 per cent in 1911 to 46·5 per cent in 1966. Although there are relatively few women in the higher professions in the managerial and supervisory grades, by 1951 they formed a majority among the lower professionals,[1] shop assistants, and clerical workers. Table 4.3 indicates that the most significant substitution of women for men occurred among clerical grades during the First World War. Between 1911 and 1921 the number of male clerks increased a little more slowly than the occpuied population while the number of female clerks increased more than three times.

Participation rates[2]

Table 4.4 shows the number of persons in the labour force, and in the total population, who were aged 14 or 15 years and over, as well as the participation rates or the percentage of the population of working age recorded as being in the labour force.[3] There is not room here to examine

[1] The high proportion of women among the lower professionals over the whole period is explained by the preponderance of the traditional female occupations – teaching and nursing – in this occupational group. Likewise, the decline in the proportion of women in this group over the years is largely explained by the influx of men into these 'female' occupations.

[2] The section of the chapter dealing with participation rates has been prepared by Miss Jackie Johns, and the authors are grateful to her for allowing them to use this material.

[3] Participation rates are sometimes computed on the basis of the whole population instead of the population of working age, which is in this context the population 'at risk'. The usefulness of computing on the basis of the whole population lies in calculating the ratio of active to dependent persons in the economy, and in international comparisons where the definition of the population of working age may vary. Since neither of these conditions applies here the more relevant population of working age is used. It should be noted that in British official publications the term 'activity rate' is used instead of the term 'participation rate'.

in detail the various cross-currents underlying changes in participation rates,[1] but a few points may be noted. The overall male participation rate has declined substantially since 1911, and this is probably due to reductions in the proportion of the male population active in the labour force at either end of the age spectrum. In the first place, a larger proportion of young men now tend to remain for longer periods in full-time education or training,[2] and, secondly, larger numbers of older men are surviving to retiring age and leaving the labour force. On the other hand, the figures indicate a *smaller*, but still important, rise in the overall female participation rate over the period. Looking at the total participation rate, however, it is clear that because of the rising proportion of women in the labour force, the increase in the female rate has *offset* the decline in the male rate, so that in 1966 the proportion of the whole population active in the labour force was actually higher than in 1911. The rise between 1961 and 1966 is particularly noticeable; this result is at least in part statistical in origin. It is likely that the 1966 Census corrected the faulty enumeration in the 1961 Census which seems to have produced an inaccurately low response rate among women working part-time in that year.[3]

Given the change in the social position of women during the twentieth century, the participation rates of females are perhaps of greater interest to sociologists than those of males. Consequently, Tables 4.5, 4.6 and 4.7 classify the number of females in the labour force and in the population of working age as well as female participation rates by age and marital status.

To use a simple explanatory model, the size of the female labour force may be considered the result of the interaction of four main factors: the size of the female population, its age structure, its marital composition, and the level of participation rates for each demographic group. There is no fully reliable method of assessing the impact of changes in any one of these variables on the size of the labour force because of the existence of interdependencies between them.[4] However, the use of simple assumptions holding each of these variables constant at their 1911 values, and comparing the resulting labour force with the actual

---

[1] This is an extremely complex subject. Those interested should consult, for example, Wilfred Beckerman and Jane Sutherland, 'Married Women at Work in 1972', *National Institute Economic Review*, no. 23 (February 1963), pp. 56–60.

[2] For details see chaps 6 and 7, below.

[3] It seems probable that many women actually working part-time returned themselves as 'housewives'. There were over half a million fewer women recorded as active in the Census than reported in the labour force by the Ministry of Labour in the same year. See *Census 1961, England and Wales, Industry Tables*, Part I (HMSO 1966), Appendix A, pp. xxiv–xxx.

[4] See Beckerman and Sutherland, *op. cit.*, p. 60.

labour force in 1966, is sufficient to show that the changes in the age and marital structure of the female population would, in the absence of counteracting changes, have had a detrimental impact on the rate of growth of the labour force. But the increase in the overall size of the female population and the very large rises which have taken place in participation rates over the period have had a favourable effect far outweighing this. Indeed, granted the actual changes in the age and marital structure of the female population and its overall rate of growth, if participation rates *had not* risen since 1911, the female labour force would in 1966 have been smaller than in 1911. The result of this assumption is a labour force 4,856,980 strong instead of the observed total of 8,862,650.[1]

The increase in the female labour force has in fact come mainly from the striking rise in the participation rates of married women of all ages in combination with their increase both in absolute terms and as a proportion of the female population as a whole. In 1911 less than 10 per cent. of married women were active in the labour force; in 1966 38 per cent were active. Table 4.7 shows that the greater part of this rise has taken place since 1951. Married women in 1911 made up about 50 per cent of the female population, while by 1966 some 63 per cent of the female population came into this category. But the rise in the percentage of the female labour force made up by married women has been far greater; in 1911 only 14 per cent. were married, but by 1966 this proportion had grown to no less than 57 per cent. The rise in the actual numbers of married women in the labour force between the two dates reaches well over 600 per cent, with certain age groups attaining rates of increase of an even more extravagant order. The increasing participation of married women in the labour force is a phenomenon which has yet to find a full explanation.[2]

[1] The figure is derived simply by applying the 1911 participation rates for each demographic group (see Table 4.3) to the 1966 total population figures for these groups (see Table 4.6). The comparison shows the massive impact of the rise in participation rates.

[2] A considerable amount of research has been carried out into the question of labour force participation among married women, particularly in the United States. See, for example, Jacob Mincer, 'Labor Force Participation of Married Women' in National Bureau of Economic Research, *Aspects of Labor Economics* (Princeton U.P. 1962), pp. 63–105; Clarence D. Long, *The Labor Force Under Changing Income and Employment* (Princeton U.P. 1958). Some of the more recent British studies are the following: Viola Klein: *Britain's Married Women Workers* (Routledge 1965); Alva Myrdal and Viola Klein, *Women's Two Roles, Home and Work* (Routledge 1962); E. M. Harris, *Married Women in Industry* (Institute of Personnel Management 1954); Audrey Hunt, *A Survey of Women's Employment* (HMSO 1968), Government Social Survey, SS 379, vol. I, *Report*, and vol. II, *Tables*; and P. Pinder, *Women at Work* (Political and Economic Planning 1969).

UNEMPLOYMENT
There are two primary sources of information on unemployment in
Britain: the trade unions and the Department of Employment and
Productivity. The trade union material dates from 1851 and is the only
source of information until 1913 when the Labour Department of the
Board of Trade (the predecessor of the Ministry of Labour which was
formed in 1917) began to collect statistics based on the National
Insurance Act of 1911. But since the trade unions operated this Act, they
remained the primary source of information until it was superseded by
the Unemployment Insurance Act of 1920 which was administered by
the Ministry of Labour (now the DEP). This Act began to operate in
1921, but the Department claims 1923 as the first year of really reliable
unemployment statistics.

Table 4.8 is based upon these two sources and gives the percentage
rate of unemployment in the United Kingdom between 1900 and 1968.
The major trends in unemployment over the course of the twentieth
century are fairly well known and little need be said about them. Unemployment was least during the two world wars and was highest during
the inter-war period. Since 1948 there has been relatively little unemployment in general although certain regions of the country have
been quite seriously affected.[1]

But while the trends in unemployment statistics are well known, the
difficulties associated with them are not, and these require considerable
comment. The principal difficulties concern the reliability and internal
consistency of the series.

The reliability of the series is most in doubt prior to 1922 when the
figures were derived from the returns of those unions which operated
unemployment benefit schemes. Since relatively few unions operated
such schemes, and those that did generally restricted their membership
to craftsmen, the resulting unemployment percentages are clearly not
the same as those prevailing among the labour force as a whole. Despite
this limitation, these figures possess considerable utility. First, they are
the only quantitative measure of unemployment available for the
period. Second, although the figures are not a good guide to the *volume*
of unemployment, expert opinion holds that they do give a reasonable
indication of *fluctuations* in unemployment.[2]

The figure for the year 1921 is perhaps the most unreliable. The 1921

[1] Only aggregate unemployment data are discussed here. But the DEP also collects
and classifies unemployment data by region, occupation, industry, age, sex, and
duration. See the *Employment and Productivity Gazette* for more detailed information.
[2] See, for example, the Committee on Industry and Trade, *Survey of Industrial
Relations* (HMSO 1926), pp. 219–20 and 244–5, and W. H. Beveridge, *Full
Employment in a Free Society* (Allen & Unwin 1944), pp. 40–6.

figure in Table 4.8 is based on the 'crude' trade union return of 14.8 per cent. which was adjusted by Hilton to give 12·9 per cent. But other sources give higher estimates. Hines's estimate is 15·56 per cent Routh's is 16·6 per cent, and Beveridge's is 17 per cent.[1] There are at least three reasons for the confusion: First, the introduction of the Unemployment Insurance Act of 1920 which did not produce reliable figures until 1923. Second, the Irish Treaty of 1920 which required the separation of the unemployed in Southern Ireland from those in the rest of the United Kingdom. Third, the largest recorded annual increase in unemployment – from about 400,000 to 2,500,000 – which the 1920 Act had great difficulty coping with. Hilton's estimate for 1921 is given in Table 4.8 partly because it is comparable with the figures given for the earlier years and partly because, unlike some of the other estimates, the manner in which it was derived is clearly shown.

The internal consistency of the series is an even greater problem than its reliability. For the unemployment percentages reflect not only the changing demand for labour but also the changing occupational coverage of the unemployment insurance legislation. The proportion of the labour force covered by the legislation increased from about 20 per cent. in 1920 to over 90 per cent. in the post-1948 period. The legislation was originally confined to those workers who were most susceptible to unemployment but was continuously extended to workers who were less and less likely to be unemployed. In other words, each extension of the coverage of the insurance scheme generally added proportionately more to the number insured than to the number unemployed with a consequent depressing effect on the percentage unemployed. Thus when making historical comparisons, it must be remembered that the unemployment percentages for the period 1920–39 are exaggerated relative to those for the post-1948 period.[2]

The figures possess a high degree of internal consistency since 1948, but they still slightly understate the actual amount of unemployment. All those drawing unemployment benefit are included. But there are a number of groups who are not eligible for unemployment benefit: school leavers, newly-arrived immigrants, and married women who have either opted to pay the lower rate of insurance which does not cover unemployment benefit or who are not insured at all. Registration for these groups is voluntary, and they are likely to register and hence be counted only if they feel that the Employment Exchange may be able to help them. Thus the figures do not, as Lewes has noted, 'measure all

[1] A. G. Hines, 'Trade Unions and Wage Inflation in the United Kingdom, 1893–1961', *Review of Economic Studies*, XXXI (October 1964), pp. 250–1; Routh, *op. cit.*, p. 110; and Beveridge, *op. cit.*, p. 47.

[2] See Devons, *op. cit.*, pp. 72–3, for a more detailed discussion of this point.

spare labour available, but this is necessarily a vague term, since higher pay or more congenial work may well attract some who would prefer to remain 'unemployed' under existing conditions'.[1]

In view of these shortcomings, the official conclusion that 'the series of figures available since 1921 may be regarded as a continuous series of approximately comparable figures and the fluctuations in them as adequate indications of economic change' is perhaps a bit optimistic.[2] But it is probably safe to say that the series is reasonably comparable within each of the periods 1900–21, 1922–47, and 1948 onwards. The problems arise when comparisons are made not within but between these periods. But if any appreciation of the quantitative significance of unemployment over the long-run is to be obtained, such comparisons must be made, albeit with caution and qualification, for no more internally consistent unemployment series is available.

HOURS OF WORK

The only source of detailed regular figures of hours worked is the Department of Employment and Productivity. It provides data for two basic series: normal weekly hours and weekly hours actually worked.

Normal weekly hours

> are those laid down in voluntary collective agreements between organisations of employers and workpeople by Joint Industrial Councils or other similar bodies or in statutory orders under the Wages Councils Acts, the Agricultural Wages Acts and the Catering Wages Act. The hours are the normal weekly hours in respect of which all rates used in the calculations of the index rates of wages are payable and in the case of individual industries are combined in the same proportions as are those rates. Generally for day workers the normal hours are exclusive of mealtimes but for shift workers an allowance for mealtimes is included in the normal number of hours.[3]

Weekly hours worked are the hours actually worked, including overtime and short-time worked as a result of agreement with management, but excluding individual absences due to sickness or voluntary reasons.

Systematic aggregate[4] data on normal weekly hours begin in 1920 while those on weekly hours actually worked begin in 1943 although data are available for the odd year prior to that date. The two series are given in Table 4.9.

The figures are based on a voluntary return and apply only to manual

---

[1] *Op. cit.*, p. 29.   [2] *Labour Statistics, op. cit.*, p. 14.   [3] *Ibid.*, p. 36.
[4] The data are also broken down by sex, age groups, industry, and region. For details, see the *Employment and Productivity Gazette*.

workers. The normal weekly hours series currently covers most industries and services except domestic service, commerce and finance. But the weekly hours actually worked series excludes the following industries: agriculture; coal mining; railways and London Transport; distribution, commerce, and finance; domestic service; catering; and entertainment. The range of industries covered by the two series has varied over time, and this has slightly lessened their internal consistency, although not seriously.

WAGE RATES AND EARNINGS

There are a number of series which relate to the price of labour which differ from one another in several respects. Some refer to wage rates, defined as 'minimum or standard wages fixed by agreements or Acts of Parliament of various kinds'; while others refer to wage earnings which are the remuneration actually received, including overtime and bonus payments. Some deal only with manual workers while others deal with salaried or white-collar workers. Some are given in money terms and others in real terms. Some are expressed in time units of an hour or week while others are given in units of a month or a year. And finally, many of the series are broken down, at least for recent years, by sex, age, occupation, industry, and geographical region. There is room here to deal only with the two basic series: the money weekly wage rates and the money weekly wage earnings of manual workers.[1] These series can be converted into real terms by using the cost-of-living index given in the next section of this chapter.

These two series may move quite closely together, or they may diverge substantially. The reasons for such divergence can best be appreciated by outlining some of the factors which may influence the average level of earnings, but which are not measured in the wage rate index. Devons has done this and it is worth quoting him at some length:

> Earnings are affected by changes in the amount of overtime or short time worked but no account is taken of this in the wage-rate index. . . . The rates on which the wage-rate index is based are usually the minimum agreed in national bargaining and they take no account of local or factory agreements, bonuses or special incentive payments, all of which will influence the figures of average earnings. Earnings on piece-rate may increase, because of improved machinery, better methods of organisation, or greater effort, even though there is no change in rates. Lastly, average

---

[1] For information on the other series see Devons, *op. cit.*, pp. 193–205; Lewes, *op. cit.*, pp. 31–6; *Labour Statistics*, *op. cit.*, chaps 5 and 6; and the *Employment and Productivity Gazette.*

earnings may increase because people move to the more highly paid occupations and industries or because of regrading and more rapid promotion. But since the wage-rate index uses a fixed set of weights in combining the changes in different industries into an average, it takes no account of such movements.[1]

Unfortunately, no official analysis is published of the contribution of each of these factors to the divergence between the movement of rates and earnings.[2]

Using Board of Trade and Ministry of Labour material, fairly reliable wage indices have been constructed for the period 1860 to the present. Table 4.10 gives a weekly wage rate and earnings series for 1900–68. These series are very useful, but they nevertheless possess certain limitations.

Prior to 1938, and especially before 1914, wage rates in many, if not most, industries were in practice very similar to earnings. Consequently, the distinction between the two concepts was not always clearly drawn. Thus for earlier years the indices may show a greater degree of similarity between wage rates and earnings than was actually the case. But since 1938, and especially after 1945, the problems of 'wage drift' and excessive overtime have caused wage rates and earnings to be very clearly distinguished, and the indices in Table 4.10 are quite unambiguous for this period.

The range of occupations and industries covered by the series has been widened from time to time, and, in addition, the weights used in constructing the indices have been periodically adjusted to take account of changes in the relative importance of different industries and occupations. While these and other technical improvements have been desirable in some respects, they have lessened the internal consistency of the series over the whole period. Similarly, there is a certain lack of comparability between the two series as the industries covered are not identical. The only important industries not covered by the wage rate index are domestic service and commerce and finance. In addition to these, the earnings index excludes agriculture, coal mining, railways and London Transport, distribution, catering, and entertainment.

Finally, the reliability of the figures in the immediate post-World War I period is somewhat in doubt. Routh's[3] figures for 1919, 1920, 1921, and 1922 are considerably different from those in Table 4.10:

---

[1] *Op. cit.*, p. 205.

[2] The Ministry of Labour used to estimate the effect on average earnings of the changes in distribution of the labour force by industry, sex and age, but no such estimates have been published since 1948 (see Devons, *ibid.*).

[3] *Op. cit.*, pp. 110–11.

110·0 compared with 121·0, 144·0 compared with 162·0, 150·0 compared with 130·0, and 110·0 compared with 101·0 respectively.

THE COST-OF-LIVING AND RETAIL PRICES

The cost of living and retail price index of the U.K. for 1900–68 is given by Table 4.11. The prices used are those actually charged and as far as possible are adjusted for changes in quality. The major factor affecting the utility of the index is the way in which it has been weighted over the years.

The most frequently quoted source, and the one used in Table 4.11, for the pre-1914 period is Bowley. His index is weighted according to a 1904 Board of Trade survey of working class consumption patterns.[1] In 1914 an official index was started, the weighting of which was largely based on the 1904 family expenditure survey modified to give effect to the estimated distribution of expenditure in 1914. It covered only those goods and services which were regarded as the 'necessities of life', as it was intended to measure the percentage increase in the cost of maintaining a minimum or subsistence standard of living among working class households in 1914. For this reason the series quickly became known as the 'cost-of-living' index. The series continued on this basis until 1947.[2]

Almost from the outset the index was criticised on the grounds that it was based on an excessively narrow and normative definition of the 'necessities of life' and that the weights based on the 1904 family expenditure survey did not reflect current working class consumption patterns. By 1937–8 these criticisms had convinced the Ministry of Labour that the index should be completely revised, and a further expenditure survey of working class families was undertaken. But the outbreak of the Second World War delayed the construction of a new index until 1947.

Despite the chorus of criticism, the fact remains that this index is the only continuous and consistent source of cost-of-living changes for the period 1914–47. And the opinion of most statisticians, including Devons[3] is that except for the years 1939–47, it is a reasonable guide to *movements* in the cost-of-living. Hence it provides the basis for the cost-of-living series given in Table 4.11 for the period 1914–39.

For the period 1939–47 the official index is completely inadequate.[4]

[1] See A. L. Bowley, *Wages and Income in the United Kingdom Since 1860* (C.U.P. 1937), pp. 118–26, for a discussion of how his index was constructed.

[2] For a detailed explanation of this index see *The Cost of Living Index Number: Method of Compilation* (HMSO 1944).

[3] *Op. cit.*, pp. 184–5.

[4] For a discussion of this point see the *Interim Report of the Cost of Living Advisory Committee* (HMSO 1947).

Fortunately, two reliable private estimates have been made by Allen[1] and Seers.[2] Both their series are based on the 1937–8 weights used in the Interim Index of Retail Prices and, although their methods differ slightly, the resulting series are very similar. That constructed by Allen is used in Table 4.11.

In 1947 the Ministry of Labour abandoned the Cost-of-living Index in favour of an interim Index of Retail Prices.[3] The weights used in the new index were based on the consumption patterns revealed by the 1937–8 expenditure survey adjusted to take account of changes in prices between 1937–8 and 1947. In 1952 a revised Interim Index was begun with weights based on estimates mainly from the national income Blue Book of working class patterns of expenditure in 1950 valued at 1952 prices.[4] This index continued until 1956 when it was replaced by the current Index of Retail Prices with weights based on the results of the 1953–4 family expenditure survey adjusted to correspond with the level of prices ruling in 1956. The 1953–4 expenditure survey, unlike those of 1904 and 1937–8, was not restricted to working class households but was based on a random sample of the vast majority of households. Since 1962 the weights have been revised each January on the basis of family expenditure surveys for the three years ended in the previous June, valued at the prices prevailing at the date of revision.[5]

This discussion of the way in which the index has been weighted makes it clear that its basic nature has changed considerably over the years. Until the Second World War it was very much a 'cost-of-living' index. That is, it attempted to measure the cost of maintaining the 1914 subsistence living standard of manual workers. During the post-war period it has attempted to measure changes in the price of things on which people *actually* spend their money rather than merely those things which are necessary to maintain a minimum living standard. Moreover, since 1956 the index has taken into account the expenditure patterns not only of manual workers but also of most white-collar workers. These changes in the way the index has been weighted lessen its comparability over long periods. Even its comparability since 1948 has been somewhat

[1] See a series of articles by R. G. D. Allen in the LCES *Bulletin*, XXV (11 August 1947), pp. 74–6; XXVI (18 February 1948), pp. 18–19; and XXVII (February 1949), pp. 15–17.

[2] D. Seers, *Changes In the Cost of Living and the Distribution of Income Since 1938* (Blackwell, Oxford, 1949), and *The Levelling of Incomes Since 1938* (Blackwell, Oxford, 1949).

[3] For a detailed explanation of this index see the *Interim Index of Retail Prices: Method of Construction and Calculation* (HMSO 1950).

[4] For a detailed explanation of the index see the *Interim Index of Retail Prices: Method of Construction and Calculation*, rev. ed. (HMSO 1952).

[5] For a detailed explanation of this index see the *Method of Construction and Calculation of the Index of Retail Prices*, 3rd ed. (HMSO 1964).

compromised by the frequent changing of weights. It is doubtful, as Lewes has noted, whether any index of this sort can really meaningfully represent long-term price changes when the 'basket of goods' being priced is changing greatly.[1]

In fact, it is doubtful whether any single index, however weighted, can adequately reflect changes in the cost-of-living. Given wide variations in expenditure patterns according to such factors as family size, income level, and social habits, and given variations in the extent to which the prices of different goods and services change, then an index number which measures the average change in the cost-of-living may not be relevant for particular individuals or groups because their pattern of expenditure differs from that assumed in the index. A possible remedy for this difficulty is to have separate indices for different social groups and geographical regions. This possibility has not met with official favour because of the danger of confusion if two or more indices were published.[2]

UNION MEMBERSHIP

The DEP compiles a series covering the membership of most of the unions operating in the U.K. It goes back to 1892 and is given in Table 4.12 for the period 1900–68.[3] The membership figures 'relate to all organisations of employees – including those of salaried and professional workers, as well as those of manual wage earners – which are known to include in their objects that of negotiating with employers with a view to regulating the wages and working conditions of their members'.[4] They thus include all trade unions and staff associations, whether they be registered or unregistered, affiliated or unaffiliated to the TUC, whose headquarters are situated in the U.K. More specifically, they include all unions listed in the *Directory of Employers' Associations, Trade Unions, Joint Organisations, etc., 1960*. The total memberships given in Table 4.12 represent the aggregate of the memberships of individual unions, and persons who are members of more than one union are, therefore, counted more than once in the totals. 'The precise extent of the duplication is not known', but the DEP believe it 'to be relatively insignificant'.[5]

The total figures also include the membership of British unions located

[1] *Op. cit.*, p. 78.

[2] For a discussion of this point see Devons, *op. cit.*, pp. 179–80 and 186–7.

[3] This aggregate series is broken down by industry, but the resulting classification possesses severe shortcomings. See Bain, *op. cit.*, pp. 199–200.

[4] 'Membership of Trade Unions in 1968', *Employment and Productivity Gazette*, 76 (Nov. 1969), p. 1021.

[5] *Ibid.*

in branches in the Irish Republic and overseas as well as serving with
H.M. Forces. Total union membership at the end of 1968 included
51,000 members in the Irish Republic and 9,000 in other branches
outside the United Kingdom. These non-U.K. figures, unlike those of
total union membership are not published on a revised basis, and hence
it is not possible to obtain accurately a series which pertains solely to
membership in the United Kingdom. But the non-U.K. figures are
relatively small and do not significantly affect the totals.

Another shortcoming of the series is that it excludes certain organisations commonly referred to as 'professional associations', which have
similar functions to trade unions. Professional associations which engage
in collective bargaining are generally included in the *Directory* and hence
in the union membership series. But there are certain exceptions. The
most prominent is the British Medical Association which is not included
even though it bargains with the Ministry of Health over the pay and
conditions of general practitioners employed under the National Health
Service. Moreover, collective bargaining is not the only method unions
use to regulate jobs. They also do this, as do some professional associations such as the Law Society which are excluded from the *Directory*,
by means of unilateral regulation. To the extent that such organisations
are excluded, the membership series is understated. But to include them
would result in some double counting and cause the series to be overstated. For it is fairly common practice for people to hold membership
in both a 'trade union' and in a 'professional association' which is
excluded from the membership series.

Similarly, few internal staff associations or staff committees are
covered by the union membership series, regardless of whether or not
they engage in collective bargaining. While it would clearly be advan-
tageous to know more about the nature and extent of such organisations, it is probably just as well that they are not covered. What evidence there is suggests that the vast majority of these organisations are
sponsored, influenced, or dominated by employers.[1] They are therefore more indicative of the behaviour of employers than of employees,
and hence have a fundamentally different nature from the unions
covered by the series. Moreover, many staff associations and committees
do not have to recruit members; in companies in which they exist all
employees often become members automatically. Hence it is difficult
to apply fruitfully to them the concept of 'membership'. However, there
are no doubt some staff associations which are both independent of
employers and required to recruit members and which should therefore be included in the membership series; but as with professional

[1] See G. S. Bain, *The Growth of White Collar Unionism* (Clarendon Press, Oxford,
1970), pp. 132–3.

associations, this would result in some double counting as it is fairly common for people to hold dual membership is 'staff associations' and 'trade unions'.

Of perhaps even greater interest than actual union membership, is the ratio of this to potential union membership, a ratio generally referred to in Britain as the 'density of union membership'.[1] The main difficulty in obtaining historical density figures is that prior to 1948 the Department of Employment and Productivity (then the Ministry of Labour) only collected statistics on the number of 'insured employees' not on all employees.[2] The only source of information on all employees prior to 1948 is the Census of Population. Thus the potential union membership series in Table 4.12 was obtained by taking the total occupied population of the U.K. – excluding employers, self-employed, and members of the armed forces, but including the unemployed – for each Census year, using linear interpolation for intervening years. These figures are fairly comparable with the post-1948 series. For example, the interpolated figures of total union potential for 1948 and 1961 are 20,644,000 and 22,753,000 respectively, while comparable DEP figures are 20,732,000 and 23,111,000.[3]

Finally, Table 4.13 gives the membership of unions affiliated to the TUC and the Labour Party and expresses it as a percentage of total union membership given in Table 4.12.

STRIKES

Detailed statistics on strikes go back a fairly long way. Information about each industrial dispute resulting in a stoppage of work was given in considerable detail in the Board of Trade's annual *Report on Strikes and Lockouts* for each of the years 1888–1913. A monthly article on strikes has been published in the *Ministry of Labour Gazette* (now the *Employment and Productivity Gazette*) from the first issue in 1893; and since 1914 a more detailed annual analysis has also appeared in the *Gazette*. Information covering years back to 1888 about the number of stoppages of work arising out of industrial disputes, duration of the stoppages, the number of workers involved; the aggregate number of working days lost, analyses of causes, and results and methods of settlement has also been

[1] It is also known as the 'percentage organised', 'real membership', 'degree of unionisation', and 'completeness'.

[2] See the above discussion of the unemployment series.

[3] For a discussion of the trends in union membership see Keith Hendell, *Trade Union Membership* (Political and Economic Planning 1962), B. C. Roberts, 'The Trends of Union Membership', *Trade Union Government and Administration in Great Britain* (Bell 1956), Appendix 1; Guy Routh, 'Trade Union Membership', *Industrial Relations: Contemporary Problems and Perspectives*, rev. ed. (Methuen 1968), pp. 35–55; and Bain, *op. cit.*, chap. 3.

published from time to time in *Abstracts of Labour Statistics*.[1] Breakdowns by industry and by geographical area are also available for certain years.

Some of this information for the period 1900–68 is given in Table 4.14 These statistics, like all the others given in this chapter, possess a number of limitations. These are discussed in great detail by Knowles,[2] but it is worth discussing again here the two major difficulties – understatement and ambiguities of classification.

The figures understate the actual number of stoppages because they only relate to those due to disputes connected with terms and conditions of employment. They exclude political strikes and lockouts[3] such as the anti-conscription, anti-war, and anti-'intervention' strikes at the end of the First World War, as well as strikes and lockouts among the armed forces and police even if these are concerned with terms and conditions of employment. But strikes in these categories are rare. A more serious shortcoming is that the figures do not include stoppages involving less than ten workpeople or lasting less than one day, except where the aggregate number of days lost exceed 100. This means that a number of lightning strikes, one- and two-hour demonstration strikes, as well as partial stoppages sometimes referred to as 'running-sore' strikes are excluded. Moreover, all go-slow strikes are excluded 'owing to the lack of precise definition and therefore of the possibility of measurement'.[4]

The strike statistics suffer from several ambiguities of classification. First, it is sometimes difficult to distinguish between a single strike which spreads from one firm or area to others, and a series of sympathetic strikes. Thus comparisons of the number or average size of strikes in particular years may be misleading. Second, the distinction between workers 'directly' and 'indirectly' involved is fairly arbitrary.[5] And finally, the enumeration of working days lost is imprecise because the actual end-date of a strike is often impossible to determine when the strike peters out and there is a gradual return to work.

---

[1] See *Labour Statistics, op. cit.*, p. 45, for detailed information on the early sources of statistics on strikes.

[2] See K. G. J. C. Knowles, *Strikes – A Study In Industrial Conflict* (Blackwell, Oxford, 1954), pp. 299–306. The following discussion relies very heavily upon this source.

[3] The statistics used to distinguish between strikes and lockouts but no longer do so. See *ibid.*, pp. 299–300, on this point.

[4] *Ibid.*, p. 302.

[5] See *ibid.*, pp. 302–3, on this point.

TABLE 4.1

The Occupied Population of Great Britain by Major Occupational Groups, 1911–1966

Occupational groups	Number of persons in major occupational groups, 1911–1966 (thousands)						Major occupational groups as a percentage of total occupied population 1911–1966 (percentages)						Growth indices of major occupational groups, 1911–1966 (1911 = 100)					
	1911	1921	1931	1951	1961	1966	1911	1921	1931	1951	1961	1966	1911	1921	1931	1951	1961	1966
1. Employers and Proprietors	1232	1318	1407	1117	1139	832	6·7	6·8	6·7	5·0	4·7	3·4	100	107	114	91	92	68
2. White-Collar Workers	3433	4094	4841	6948	8478	9461	18·7	21·2	23·0	30·9	35·9	38·3	100	119	141	202	247	276
(a) Managers and Administrators	631	704	770	1245	1268	1514	3·4	3·6	3·7	5·5	5·4	6·1	100	112	122	197	201	240
(b) Higher Professionals	184	196	240	435	718	829	1·0	1·0	1·1	1·9	3·0	3·4	100	107	130	236	390	451
(c) Lower Professionals and Technicians	560	679	728	1059	1418	1604	3·1	3·5	3·5	4·7	6·0	6·5	100	121	130	189	253	286
(d) Foremen and Inspectors	237	279	323	590	682	736	1·3	1·4	1·5	2·6	2·9	3·0	100	118	136	249	288	311
(e) Clerks	832	1256	1404	2341	2994	3262	4·5	6·5	6·7	10·4	12·7	13·2	100	151	169	281	360	392
(f) Salesmen and Shop Assistants	989	980	1376	1278	1398	1516	5·4	5·1	6·5	5·7	5·9	6·1	100	99	139	129	141	153
3. Manual Workers	13,685	13,920	14,776	14,450	14,022	14,393	74·6	72·0	70·3	64·2	59·3	58·3	100	102	108	106	102	105
(a) Skilled	5608	5572	5618	5617	5981	5857	30·5	28·8	26·7	24·9	25·3	23·7	100	99	100	100	107	104
(b) Semi-skilled	6310	5608	6044	6124	6004	6437	34·4	29·0	28·7	27·2	25·4	26·1	100	89	96	97	95	102
(c) Unskilled	1767	2740	3114	2709	2037	2099	9·6	14·2	14·8	12·0	8·6	8·5	100	155	176	153	115	119
4. Total Occupied Population	18,350	19,332	21,024	22,515	23,639	24,686	100·0	100·0	100·0	100·0	100·0	100·0	100	105	115	123	129	135

Note: In the 1966 sample census the employer and managerial status categories given are 'self-employed with and without employees' and 'managers'. In contrast with 1961 this distinguishes employers from managers but it does not distinguish the self-employed (without employees), which in Table I are included in the groups according to the nature of their occupations, from the employers and proprietors. People of both employer and self-employed status are included in the employer and the proprietor occupations (code nos. 144, 145, 150, 152 and 157) and in the higher and lower professional groups in the table, so that no division of the 'self-employed with and without employees' was necessary. For the other groups in the table, however, the 'self-employed with and without employees' were divided into employers and self-employed according to the 1951 ratio of employers to self-employed in these groups. The 'employers' were then added to the 'employers and proprietors' group and the 'self-employed' added to their appropriate groups (skilled, semi-skilled, etc.).

Source: This table is largely based on G. S. Bain, *The Growth of White-Collar Unionism* (Clarendon Press, Oxford, 1970), Table 2.1; Guy Routh, *Occupation and Pay in Great Britain* (C.U.P., 1965), Table 1; and the Census of Population of England and Wales and Scotland for the various years. For a discussion of the way in which the original table was constructed see Bain, *op. cit.*, pp. 189–90. The present table differs from the original in two major respects. First, the table has been brought up-to-date by the inclusion of the 1966 Census which was classified on a similar basis to the 1961 Census. Second, the 'manual workers' group has been sub-divided into 'skilled', 'semi-skilled', and 'unskilled' categories along the lines of Routh's Table I, except that 'salesmen and shop assistants' were subtracted from Routh's 'semi-skilled workers'. The opportunity has also been taken to correct a minor error in the original table.

TABLE 4.2

The Growth of Scientists and Engineers, Draughtsmen, and Laboratory Assistants in Great Britain, 1921–1966

Year	Scientists and Engineers		Draughtsmen		Laboratory Technicians	
	Number	Growth Indices	Number	Growth Indices	Number	Growth Indices
1921	48	100	38	100	5	100
1931	71	148	59	155	11	220
1951	187	390	130	342	69	1380
1961	378	788	181	476	96	1920
1966	483	994	171	450	113	2260

Note: All numbers are in thousands; for growth indices, 1921 = 100.
Also see note to Table 4.1.
Source: This table is largely based on Bain, *op. cit.*, Table 2.2 and the 1966 Census which was classified on a similar basis to the 1961 Census.

TABLE 4.3

The Percentage of Female Workers in Major Occupational Groups in Great Britain, 1911–1966

Occupational Group	1911	1921	1931	1951	1961	1966
1. Employers and Proprietors	18·8	20·5	19·8	20·0	20·4	23·7
2. White-Collar Workers	29·8	37·6	35·8	42·3	44·5	46·5
(a) Managers and Administrators	19·8	17·0	13·0	15·2	15·5	16·7
(b) Higher Professionals	6·0	5·1	7·5	8·3	9·7	9·4
(c) Lower Professionals and Technicians	62·9	59·4	58·8	53·5	50·8	52·1
(d) Foremen and Inspectors	4·2	6·5	8·7	13·4	10·3	11·4
(e) Clerks	21·4	44·6	46·0	60·2	65·2	69·3
(f) Salesmen and Shop Assistants	35·2	43·6	37·2	51·6	54·9	58·7
3. All Manual Workers	30·5	27·9	28·8	26·1	26·0	29·0
(a) Skilled	24·0	21·0	21·3	15·7	13·8	14·7
(b) Semi-Skilled	40·4	40·3	42·9	38·1	39·3	42·6
(c) Unskilled	15·5	16·8	15·0	20·3	22·4	27·5
4. Total Occupied Population	29·6	29·5	29·8	30·8	32·4	35·6

Note: See note to Table 4.1.
Source: This table is largely based on Bain, *op. cit.*, Table 2.3 and the 1966 Census which was classified on a similar basis to the 1961 Census.

TABLE 4.4

The Labour Force, Total Population, and Participation Rates of Great Britain by Sex, 1911–1966

Year	(1) Labour Force 14 or 15 years and over	(2) Total Population 14 or 15 years and over	(3) Participation Rate (1) as a percentage of (2)
MALES			
1911	12,581,092	13,450,587	93·54
1921	13,612,019	14,825,702	91·81
1931	14,789,589	16,341,139	90·51
1951	15,648,877	17,862,356	87·61
1961	16,232,470	18,810,790	86·29
1966	15,993,850	19,029,670	84·05
FEMALES			
1911	5,224,371	14,793,305	35·32
1921	5,672,548	16,827,469	33·71
1931	6,265,100	18,320,397	34·20
1951	6,961,169	20,045,398	34·73
1961	7,781,850	20,758,310	37·49
1966	8,862,650	21,011,080	42·18
TOTAL			
1911	17,805,463	28,243,892	63·04
1921	19,284,567	31,653,171	60·92
1931	21,054,686	34,661,536	60·74
1951	22,610,046	37,907,754	59·64
1961	24,014,320	39,569,100	60·69
1966	25,856,500	40,040,750	64·58

Note: The labour force is here defined as the 'economically active population' and includes not only employees, but those classified as employers or proprietors, the self-employed, members of the armed forces, and persons reported as unemployed or otherwise out of work. Certain amendments have been made to the Census returns in order to increase the comparability of the figures over the period since 1911. In the Census for 1911 the population of working age as then defined covered persons aged 10 years and over; in 1921, those aged 12 years and over; in 1931, those aged 14 years and over; and in 1951, 1961, and 1966, those aged 15 years and over. Children aged from 10 to 14 years have therefore been excluded from the returns for 1911, and children aged 12 and 13 years from the returns for 1921. In that year and in 1931, however, young persons of 14 and 15 years of age were grouped together in the tables and cannot be separated, so that the figures for those years unavoidably contain 14-year-olds and the table must be used bearing this in mind. All other figures quoted refer to persons aged 15 years and over, the population of working age as at present defined.

The labour force figures given here differ slightly from those in Table 4.1, partly because of this age adjustment and partly because the 'inadequately described occupations' were included here but had to be excluded from Table 4.1 because of its occupational classification.

Source: Census of Population of England and Wales and Scotland for the various years.

TABLE 4.5
The Female Labour Force in Great Britain by Age Groups and Marital Status, 1911–1966

Age	Year	Single	Married	Widowed and Divorced	All
14 or 15–24	1911	2,427,509	57,425	1745	2,486,679
	1921	2,681,511	69,816	3602	2,754,929
	1931	2,840,155	101,206	1599	2,942,960
	1951	2,016,410	316,102	2683	2,335,195
	1961	1,837,100	430,650	2280	2,270,030
	1966	1,892,030	505,070	3530	2,400,630
25–34	1911	938,962	217,750	29,952	2,486,679
	1921	926,564	206,292	51,953	1,184,809
	1931	1,018,426	320,477	25,404	1,364,307
	1951	589,016	693,576	48,493	1,331,085
	1961	392,470	818,660	25,060	1,236,190
	1966	311,670	924,900	31,060	1,267,630
35–44	1911	372,360	208,677	87,191	668,228
	1921	426,290	208,833	89,711	724,834
	1931	473,633	248,804	80,202	802,639
	1951	433,753	792,999	101,654	1,328,406
	1961	304,270	1,130,830	87,590	1,522,690
	1966	254,130	1,455,620	86,360	1,796,110
45–54	1911	198,586	143,909	126,656	469,151
	1921	257,739	154,440	119,156	531,335
	1931	314,642	178,225	120,456	613,323
	1951	406,044	618,145	170,344	1,194,533
	1961	354,950	1,055,650	202,850	1,613,450
	1966	272,660	1,405,500	211,840	1,890,000
55 and over	1911	120,208	83,892	209,526	413,626
	1921	177,647	93,932	205,002	476,581
	1931	238,532	104,520	198,792	541,844
	1951	287,624	237,056	247,165	771,845
	1961	330,890	471,750	336,850	1,139,490
	1966	313,010	772,170	423,100	1,508,280
All ages 14 or 15 and over	1911	4,057,625	711,653	455,070	5,224,348
	1921	4,469,751	733,313	469,424	5,672,488
	1931	4,885,388	953,232	426,453	6,265,073
	1951	3,732,847	2,657,878	570,339	6,961,064
	1961	3,219,680	3,907,540	654,630	7,781,850
	1966	3,043,500	5,063,260	755,890	8,862,650

Note: For the years 1911, 1921, 1931, and 1951, the totals given in Tables 4.5 and 4.6 respectively for the female labour force and the female population are slightly different from those given in Table 4.4. This is because it was necessary to exclude persons classified in the Scottish Census for those years under the heading 'Age Not Stated'. In 1911 the Scottish figures for four age groups had to be derived by sub-dividing the groups 25–44 years and 45–64 years according to the ratios observed respectively for the 25–34/35–44 and 45–54/55–64 age groups in the England and Wales Census for the same year. The age divisions shown in the Table were chosen to permit the maximum comparability over the six Censuses with the minimum of statistical manipulations of this kind, since the age classifications used by the Census vary from year to year and also between those for England and Wales and for Scotland in the same year.
Source: Census of Population of England and Wales and Scotland for the various years.

TABLE 4.6

The Female Population in Great Britain by Age Groups and Marital Status, 1911–1966

Age	Year	Single	Married	Widowed and Divorced	All
14 or 15–24	1911	3,324,299	474,512	2985	3,801,796
	1921	3,796,329	550,726	7195	4,354,250
	1931	3,749,888	546,222	2749	4,298,859
	1951	2,383,209	862,571	4006	3,249,786
	1961	2,366,000	1,030,910	3620	3,400,530
	1966	2,570,880	1,160,260	6040	3,737,180
25–34	1911	1,275,551	2,196,990	46,048	3,518,589
	1921	1,215,785	2,199,021	111,945	3,526,751
	1931	1,266,325	2,427,125	46,389	3,739,839
	1951	677,730	2,842,201	71,516	3,591,447
	1961	438,370	2,778,120	36,620	3,253,110
	1966	351,750	2,694,180	47,280	3,093,210
35–44	1911	566,754	2,103,957	143,394	2,814,105
	1921	629,995	2,357,851	198,752	3,186,598
	1931	654,676	2,452,352	177,239	3,284,267
	1951	535,608	3,083,935	159,442	3,778,985
	1961	357,510	3,109,630	122,240	3,589,380
	1966	296,570	2,995,640	116,160	3,408,370
45–54	1911	339,515	1,451,347	275,549	2,066,411
	1921	431,612	1,832,893	295,818	2,560,323
	1931	493,384	2,091,267	338,580	2,923,231
	1951	542,580	2,612,539	315,017	3,470,136
	1961	434,510	2,989,030	304,330	3,727,870
	1966	332,130	2,821,450	292,600	3,446,180
55 and over	1911	347,616	1,166,296	1,078,299	2,592,211
	1921	486,356	1,493,969	1,218,831	3,199,156
	1931	656,614	1,975,096	1,442,421	4,074,131
	1951	969,653	2,826,262	2,158,523	5,954,438
	1961	1,029,740	3,368,790	2,388,890	6,787,420
	1966	1,051,020	3,624,760	2,650,360	7,326,140
All ages 14 or 15 and over	1911	5,853,735	7,393,102	1,546,275	14,793,112
	1921	6,560,077	8,434,460	1,832,541	16,827,078
	1931	6,820,887	9,492,062	2,007,378	18,320,327
	1951	5,108,780	12,227,508	2,708,504	20,044,792
	1961	4,626,130	13,276,480	2,855,700	20,758,310
	1966	4,602,350	13,296,290	3,112,440	21,011,080

Note: See note to Table 4.5.
Source: Census of Population of England and Wales and Scotland for the various years.

TABLE 4.7

Female Participation Rates in Great Britain by Age and Marital Status, 1911–1966 (percentages)

Marital Status	Year	14 or 15–24	25–34	35–44	45–54	55 and over	All ages 14 or 15 and over
Single	1911	73·02	73·61	65·70	55·49	34·58	69·32
	1921	70·63	76·21	67·67	59·72	36·53	68·14
	1931	75·74	80·42	72·35	63·77	36·33	71·62
	1951	84·61	86·91	80·98	74·84	29·66	73·07
	1961	77·65	89·53	85·11	81·69	32·13	69·60
	1966	73·59	88·61	85·69	82·09	29·78	66·13
Married	1911	12·10	9·91	9·92	9·92	7·19	9·63
	1921	12·68	9·38	8·86	8·43	6·29	8·69
	1931	18·53	13·20	10·15	8·52	5·29	10·04
	1951	36·65	24·40	25·71	23·66	8·39	21·74
	1961	41·77	29·47	36·37	35·32	14·00	29·43
	1966	43·53	34·33	48·59	49·81	21·30	38·08
Widowed and Divorced	1911	58·46	65·05	60·81	45·96	19·43	29·43
	1921	50·06	46·41	45·14	40·28	16·82	25·62
	1931	58·17	54·76	45·25	35·58	13·78	21·24
	1951	66·97	67·81	63·76	54·07	11·45	21·06
	1961	62·98	68·43	71·65	66·65	14·10	22·92
	1966	58·44	65·69	74·35	72·40	15·96	24·29
All Females	1911	65·41	33·73	23·75	22·70	15·96	35·32
	1921	63·27	33·59	22·75	20·75	14·90	33·71
	1931	68·46	36·48	24·44	20·98	13·30	34·20
	1951	71·86	37·06	35·15	34·42	12·96	34·73
	1961	66·76	38·00	42·42	43·28	16·79	37·49
	1966	64·24	40·98	52·70	54·84	20·59	42·18

Source: Derived from Tables 4.5 and 4.6.

TABLE 4.8

**The Percentage Rate of Unemployment in the United Kingdom
1900–1968**

Year	Percentage Rate	Year	Percentage Rate	Year	Percentage Rate
1900	2·5	1923	11·7	1946	2·5
1901	3·3	1924	10·3	1947	3·1
1902	4·0	1925	11·3	1948	1·8
1903	4·7	1926	12·5	1949	1·6
1904	6·0	1927	9·7	1950	1·5
1905	5·0	1928	10·8	1951	1·2
1906	3·6	1929	10·4	1952	2·1
1907	3·7	1930	16·0	1953	1·8
1908	7·8	1931	21·3	1954	1·5
1909	7·7	1932	22·1	1955	1·2
1910	4·7	1933	19·9	1956	1·3
1911	3·0	1934	16·7	1957	1·6
1912	3·2	1935	15·5	1958	2·2
1913	2·1	1936	13·1	1959	2·3
1914	3·3	1937	10·8	1960	1·7
1915	1·1	1938	13·5	1961	1·6
1916	0·4	1939	11·6	1962	2·1
1917	0·6	1940	9·7	1963	2·6
1918	0·8	1941	6·6	1964	1·7
1919	2·1	1942	2·4	1965	1·5
1920	2·0	1943	0·8	1966	1·6
1921	12·9	1944	0·7	1967	2·5
1922	14·3	1945	1·2	1968	2·5

Source and Notes: The figures for 1900–12 are the percentage unemployed in certain trade unions and are taken from B. R. Mitchell and P. M. Deane, *Abstract of British Historical Statistics* (C.U.P. 1962); those for 1913–21 are the percentage unemployed in certain trade unions as adjusted by J. Hilton, 'Statistics of Unemployment Derived From the Working of the Unemployment Insurance Acts', *J. Roy. Statist. Soc.*, LXXXVI (March 1923), pp. 154–205, and cited by the LCES, *The British Economy: Key Statistics 1900–1966* (London: Times Newspapers n.d.); those for 1922–47 are the insured unemployed as a percentage of the insured labour force as given by the Ministry of Labour and adjusted by LCES to obtain greater comparability across a period which saw several changes in the coverage of the unemployment insurance legislation; those for 1948–66 are the number registered as unemployed as a percentage of the estimated total number of employees as given by the DEP and cited by the LCES, and those for 1967–68 were supplied by the DEP.

TABLE 4.9

Hours of Work of Manual Workers in the United Kingdom, 1900–1968

Year	Normal Weekly Hours	Weekly Hours Actually Worked	Year	Normal Weekly Hours	Weekly Hours Actually Worked
1900	—	54	1935	47·4	47·8
1901	—	—	1936	47·4	—
1902	—	—	1937	47·2	—
1903	—	—	1938	47·2	46·5
1904	—	—	1939	47·2	—
1905	—	—	1940	47·2	—
1906	—	—	1941	47·2	—
1907	—	—	1942	47·2	—
1908	—	—	1943	47·2	50·0
1909	—	—	1944	47·2	48·6
1910	—	54	1945	47·5	47·4
1911	—	—	1946	46·8	46·2
1912	—	—	1947	44·9	45·2
1913	—	—	1948	44·8	45·3
1914	—	—	1949	44·7	45·4
1915	—	—	1950	44·7	46·1
1916	—	—	1951	44·6	46·3
1917	—	—	1952	44·6	45·9
1918	—	—	1953	44·6	46·3
1919	—	—	1954	44·6	46·7
1920	46·9	—	1955	44·6	47·0
1921	46·9	—	1956	44·6	46·8
1922	47·0	—	1957	44·6	46·6
1923	47·0	—	1958	44·5	46·2
1924	47·1	45·8	1959	44·4	46·6
1925	47·0	—	1960	43·7	46·2
1926	47·6	—	1961	42·8	45·7
1927	47·6	—	1962	42·4	45·3
1928	47·6	—	1963	42·4	45·4
1929	47·6	—	1964	42·2	45·8
1930	47·3	—	1965	41·4	45·3
1931	47·4	—	1966	40·7	44·3
1932	47·6	—	1967	40·5	44·3
1933	47·6	—	1968	40·5	44·5
1934	47·5	—			

Source: The figures for weekly hours worked for 1900 and 1910 are tentative and are supplied by the LCES, *The British Economy, op. cit.*, which unfortunately does not state its source; those for 1924, 1935, 1938, and 1943–50 are from the half-yearly inquiry into earnings, the results of which were published in the *Ministry of Labour Gazette*; those for 1951–68 are from the same inquiry, the results of which were published in *Statistics on Incomes, Prices, Employment and Production*, no. 29 (June 1969), p. 68. The figures of normal weekly hours for 1920–50 are calculated from the *Index of Normal Weekly Hours* using the actual averages available for some years, details of which are given in the *Ministry of Labour Gazette* (September 1957), pp. 330–1; those for 1951–68 are from *Statistics on Incomes, Prices, Employment and Production, loc. cit.*

TABLE 4.10

Index of Money Wage Rates and Earnings of Manual Workers in the United Kingdom, 1900–1968

Year	Weekly Wage Rates	Weekly Wage Earnings	Year	Weekly Wage Rates	Weekly Wage Earnings
1900	49·0	49·0	1935	98·0	100·0
1901	48·0	49·0	1936	100·0	103·0
1902	48·0	48·0	1937	104·0	—
1903	48·0	48·0	1938	106·0	109·0
1904	47·0	46·0	1939	106·0	—
1905	47·0	46·0	1940	119·0	141·0
1906	48·0	48·0	1941	128·0	154·0
1907	48·0	50·0	1942	137·0	174·0
1908	48·0	49·0	1943	144·0	191·0
1909	48·0	49·0	1944	153·0	198·0
1910	48·0	49·0	1945	159·0	196·0
1911	49·0	50·0	1946	172·0	207·0
1912	50·0	51·0	1947	178·0	221·0
1913	52·0	52·0	1948	187·0	239·0
1914	52·0	52·0	1949	193·0	249·0
1915	56·0	56·0	1950	195·9	262·9
1916	61·0	62·0	1951	212·5	289·5
1917	72·0	74·0	1952	229·9	312·3
1918	93·0	99·0	1953	240·7	331·6
1919	121·0	120·0	1954	251·1	353·2
1920	162·0	148·0	1955	268·0	386·0
1921	130·0	142·0	1956	289·2	416·9
1922	101·0	110·0	1957	303·9	436·2
1923	100·0	98·0	1958	314·9	451·2
1924	102·0	102·0	1959	323·2	471·7
1925	102·0	103·0	1960	331·5	502·2
1926	103·0	102·0	1961	345·2	532·7
1927	103·0	103·0	1962	358·0	551·6
1928	101·0	101·0	1963	370·9	574·8
1929	101·0	101·0	1964	388·3	624·5
1930	100·0	100·0	1965	405·2	674·7
1931	99·0	99·0	1966	424·2	714·1
1932	97·0	97·0	1967	440·1	742·3
1933	96·0	96·0	1968	469·2	803·3
1934	96·0	97·0			

Note: 1930 = 100.
Source: The wage-rate figures for 1900–38 are from E. H. Phelps Brown and S. V. Hopkins, 'Wage Rates in Five Countries, 1860–1939', Oxford Economic Papers, New Series, vol. II (O.U.P. 1950), p. 226; those for 1939–49 are from Ministry of Labour data as cited by LCES, The British Economy, op. cit.; and those for 1950–68 are from Statistics on Incomes, Prices, Employment and Production, no. 29, p. 8. The wage earnings figures for 1900–49 are from A. L. Bowley, Wages and Income in the United Kingdom since 1860 (C.U.P. 1937), and by the same author, 'Index Numbers of Wage Rates and Cost of Living', J. Roy. Statist. Soc., series A, 115, pt 4 (1952), pp. 500–6; and those for 1950–68 are from Statistics on Incomes, Prices, Employment and Production, no. 29, p. 8.

TABLE 4.11

The Cost of Living in the United Kingdom, 1900–1968

Year	Index	Year	Index	Year	Index
1900	58·1	1923	112·8	1946	150·8
1901	57·6	1924	115·0	1947	159·0
1902	57·6	1925	111·8	1948	169·8
1903	58·1	1926	110·7	1949	174·9
1904	58·7	1927	105·3	1950	180·5
1905	58·7	1928	105·3	1951	197·1
1906	59·2	1929	104·3	1952	215·0
1907	60·9	1930	100·0	1953	221·8
1908	59·2	1931	92·4	1954	225·9
1909	59·8	1932	90·3	1955	236·0
1910	60·9	1933	89·2	1956	247·8
1911	62·0	1934	89·2	1957	257·0
1912	63·6	1935	92·4	1958	264·6
1913	65·3	1936	94·6	1959	266·0
1914	63·6	1937	100·0	1960	268·8
1915	79·5	1938	98·9	1961	278·0
1916	91·3	1939	101·0	1962	289·8
1917	113·9	1940	114·5	1963	295·7
1918	130·1	1941	124·7	1964	305·4
1919	140·8	1942	132·3	1965	320·0
1920	170·9	1943	138·0	1966	332·5
1921	126·8	1944	140·6	1967	340·5
1922	115·0	1945	145·7	1968	356·6

Note: 1930 = 100.

Source: The cost-of-living index for 1900–39 is derived from Phelps Brown and Hopkins, *op. cit.*, pp. 276 and 281 which, in turn, is based on Bowley's index for 1900–14 and the Ministry of Labour's for 1914–39. For 1940–68, the index is derived from LCES, *The British Economy, op. cit.*, which in turn is based on R. G. D. Allen's estimates for 1940–7 and the Ministry of Labour's for 1947–9. For 1950–68, the index is derived from *Statistics on Incomes, Prices, Employment and Production, loc. cit.*

Source and Notes for Table 4.12

The trade union membership figures are those published annually by the Department of Employment and Productivity in the November issue of the *Employment and Productivity Gazette*. The figures for 1962–8 are provisional and are subject to revision as additional information becomes available. For each year the latest revised figure was used.

The potential union membership figures for 1968 are from the *Employment and Productivity Gazette*, LXXVII (March, 1960), p. 225. Those for 1948–67 were supplied by the DEP from unpublished data and are comparable to the 1968 figures. The pre-1948 figures are from the Census of Population for England and Wales, Scotland, and Northern Ireland (and Southern Ireland prior to 1922) with linear interpolations for the intervening years. All these figures exclude employers, self-employed, and members of the armed forces, but include the unemployed, and they have been rounded off to the nearest thousand. Because the figures have been interpolated and rounded independently, some rounded totals may differ from the sum of the rounded components.

Union Membership in the United Kingdom by Sex, 1900–1968

Year	MALES			FEMALES			TOTAL		
	Actual membership (ooos)	Potential membership (ooos)	Density of membership (%)	Actual membership (ooos)	Potential membership (ooos)	Density of membership (%)	Actual membership (ooos)	Potential membership (ooos)	Density of membership (%)
1900	1869	11,194	16·7	154	4763	3·2	2022	15,957	12·7
1901	1873	11,325	16·5	152	4775	3·2	2025	16,101	12·6
1902	1857	11,433	16·2	156	4833	3·2	2013	16,267	12·4
1903	1838	11,541	15·9	156	4890	3·2	1994	16,433	12·1
1904	1802	11,649	15·5	165	4948	3·3	1967	16,599	11·9
1905	1818	11,757	15·5	180	5005	3·6	1997	16,765	11·9
1906	1999	11,865	16·8	211	5063	4·2	2210	16,932	13·1
1907	2263	11,973	18·9	250	5120	4·9	2513	17,098	14·7
1908	2230	12,080	18·5	255	5178	4·9	2485	17,264	14·4
1909	2214	12,188	18·2	263	5235	5·0	2477	17,430	14·2
1910	2287	12,296	18·6	278	5292	5·3	2565	17,596	14·6
1911	2804	12,404	22·6	335	5350	6·3	3139	17,762	17·7
1912	3027	12,453	24·3	390	5380	7·2	3416	17,841	19·1
1913	3702	12,502	29·6	433	5410	8·0	4135	17,920	23·1
1914	3708	12,551	29·5	437	5440	8·0	4145	17,998	23·0
1915	3867	12,600	30·7	491	5470	9·0	4359	18,077	24·1
1916	4018	12,649	31·8	626	5500	11·4	4644	18,155	25·6
1917	4621	12,698	36·4	878	5530	15·9	5499	18,234	30·2
1918	5324	12,747	41·8	1209	5560	21·7	6533	18,312	35·7
1919	6601	12,796	51·6	1326	5591	23·7	7926	18,391	43·1
1920	7006	12,845	54·5	1342	5621	23·9	8348	18,469	45·2
1921	5627	12,894	43·6	1005	5651	17·8	6633	18,548	35·8
1922	4753	12,334	38·5	872	5470	15·9	5625	17,804	31·6
1923	4607	12,436	37·0	822	5528	14·9	5429	17,965	30·2
1924	4730	12,539	37·7	814	5587	14·7	5544	18,125	30·6
1925	4671	12,641	37·0	835	5645	14·8	5506	18,286	30·1
1926	4407	12,743	34·6	812	5703	14·2	5219	18,446	28·3
1927	4125	12,847	32·1	794	5762	13·8	4919	18,609	26·4
1928	4011	12,950	31·0	795	5821	13·7	4806	18,771	25·6
1929	4056	13,054	31·1	802	5880	13·6	4858	18,934	25·7
1930	4049	13,158	30·8	793	5938	13·4	4842	19,096	25·4
1931	3859	13,261	29·1	765	5997	12·8	4624	19,259	24·0
1932	3698	13,302	27·8	746	6038	12·4	4444	19,340	23·0

Table 4.12 continued

Year	MALES Actual membership (000s)	Potential membership (000s)	Density of membership (%)	FEMALES Actual membership (000s)	Potential membership (000s)	Density of membership (%)	TOTAL Actual membership (000s)	Potential membership (000s)	Density of membership (%)
1933	3661	13,343	27·4	731	6078	12·0	4392	19,422	22·6
1934	3854	13,384	28·8	736	6119	12·0	4590	19,503	23·5
1935	4106	13,425	30·6	761	6159	12·4	4867	19,585	24·9
1936	4495	13,466	33·4	800	6200	12·9	5295	19,666	26·9
1937	4947	13,507	36·6	895	6240	14·3	5842	19,748	29·6
1938	5127	13,548	37·8	926	6281	14·7	6053	19,829	30·5
1939	5288	13,589	38·9	1010	6321	16·0	6298	19,911	31·6
1940	5493	13,630	40·3	1119	6362	17·6	6613	19,992	33·1
1941	5753	13,671	42·1	1412	6402	22·1	7165	20,074	35·7
1942	6151	13,712	44·9	1716	6443	26·6	7866	20,155	39·0
1943	6258	13,753	45·5	1916	6484	29·5	8174	20,237	40·4
1944	6238	13,794	45·2	1848	6524	28·3	8087	20,318	39·8
1945	6237	13,835	45·1	1638	6565	25·0	7875	20,400	38·6
1946	7186	13,876	51·8	1618	6605	24·5	8803	20,481	43·0
1947	7483	13,917	53·8	1662	6646	25·0	9145	20,563	44·5
1948	7691	13,778	55·8	1672	6954	24·0	9363	20,732	45·2
1949	7645	13,828	55·3	1674	6954	24·1	9318	20,782	44·8
1950	7605	13,937	54·6	1684	7118	23·7	9289	21,055	44·1
1951	7742	13,906	55·7	1789	7271	24·6	9530	21,177	45·0
1952	7797	13,966	55·8	1792	7286	24·6	9588	21,252	45·1
1953	7749	14,001	55·3	1778	7351	24·2	9527	21,352	44·6
1954	7756	14,123	54·9	1810	7535	24·0	9566	21,658	44·2
1955	7874	14,224	55·4	1867	7689	24·3	9741	21,913	44·5
1956	7871	14,389	54·7	1907	7791	24·5	9778	22,180	44·1
1957	7935	14,487	54·8	1894	7848	24·1	9829	22,335	44·0
1958	7789	14,512	53·7	1850	7778	23·8	9639	22,290	43·2
1959	7756	14,565	53·3	1868	7864	23·8	9623	22,429	42·9
1960	7884	14,719	53·6	1951	8098	24·1	9835	22,817	43·1
1961	7905	14,869	53·2	1992	8242	24·2	9897	23,111	42·8
1962	7860	15,064	52·2	2027	8368	24·2	9887	23,432	42·2
1963	7859	15,144	51·9	2075	8414	24·7	9934	23,558	42·2
1964	7936	15,163	52·3	2143	8543	25·1	10,079	23,706	42·5
1965	7973	15,243	52·3	2208	8677	25·4	10,181	23,920	42·6
1966	7890	15,200	51·9	2221	8845	25·1	10,111	24,045	42·1
1967	7724	15,056	51·8	2246	8752	25·7	9970	22,808	41·0

TABLE 4.13

Union Membership Affiliated to the TUC and the Labour Party, 1900-1968

Year (a)	Membership affiliated to TUC (000s)	TUC Membership as a proportion of total Union Membership (%)	Union Membership affiliated to Labour Party (000s)	Union Membership affiliated to L.P. as a proportion of total Union Membership (%)
1900	1200	59·3	353	17·4
1901	1400	69·1	455	22·5
1902	1500	74·5	847	42·1
1903	1423	71·4	956	47·9
1904	1541	78·3	855	43·5
1905	1555	77·9	904	45·3
1906	1700	76·9	975	44·1
1907	1777	70·7	1050	41·8
1908	1705	68·6	1127	45·4
1909	1648	66·5	1451	58·6
1910	1662	64·8	1394	54·3
1911	2002	63·8	1502	47·8
1912	2232	65·3	1858	54·4
1913	—(b)	—	—(c)	—
1914	2682	64·7	1572(d)	37·9
1915	2851	65·4	2054	47·1
1916	3082	66·4	2171	46·7
1917	4532	82·4	2415	43·9
1918	5284	80·9	2960	45·3
1919	6505	82·1	3464	43·7
1920	6418	76·9	4318	51·7
1921	5129	77·3	3974	59·9
1922	4369	77·7	3279	58·3
1923	4328	79·7	3120	57·5
1924	4351	78·5	3158	57·0
1925	4366	79·3	3338	60·6
1926	4164	79·8	3352	64·2
1927	3875	78·8	3239	65·8
1928	3673	76·4	2025(e)	44·2
1929	3744	77·1	2044	42·1
1930	3719	76·8	2011	41·5
1931	3613	78·1	2024	43·8
1932	3368	75·8	1960	44·1
1933	3295	75·0	1899	43·2
1934	3389	73·8	1858	40·5
1935	3615	74·3	1913	39·3
1936	4009	75·7	1969	37·2
1937	4461	76·4	2037	34·9
1938	4669	77·1	2158	35·7
1939	4867	77·3	2214	35·2
1940	5079	76·8	2227	33·7
1941	5433	75·8	2231	31·1
1942	6042	76·6	2206	28·0

Table 4.13 continued

Year(a)	Membership affiliated to TUC (000s)	TUC Membership as a proportion of total Union Membership (%)	Union Membership affiliated to Labour Party (000s)	Union Membership affiliated to L.P. as a proportion of total Union Membership (%)
1943	6642	81·3	2237	27·4
1944	6576	81·3	2375	29·4
1945	6671	84·7	2510	31·9
1946	7540	85·7	2635	29·9
1947	7791	85·2	4386(f)	48·0
1948	7937	84·8	4751	50·7
1949	7883	84·6	4946	53·1
1950	7828	84·3	4972	53·5
1951	8020	84·2	4937	51·8
1952	8088	84·4	5072	52·9
1953	8094	85·0	5057	53·1
1954	8107	84·7	5530	57·8
1955	8264	84·8	5606	57·6
1956	8305	84·9	5658	57·9
1957	8337	84·8	5644	57·4
1958	8176	84·8	5628	58·4
1959	8128	84·5	5564	57·8
1960	8299	84·4	5513	56·1
1961	8313	84·0	5550	56·1
1962	8315	84·1	5503	56·5
1963	8326	83·8	5507	55·4
1964	8771	87·0	5502	54·6
1965	8868	87·1	5602	55·0
1966	8787	86·9	5539	54·8
1967	8726	87·5	5540	55·6
1968	8875	88·3	5364	53·3

Notes:
(a) The membership figures published in the TUC's *Annual Report* generally refer to 31 December of the previous year. For example, the figure in the 1969 *Annual Report* refers to 31 December 1968.
(b) No Congress was held in 1914 and hence no affiliation figures for 1913 were published.
(c) 1909–13: figures for 1913 not available for reasons connected with the Osborne Judgement of 1909 which restrained unions from using their funds for political purposes.
(d) 1914–27: the 1913 Trade Union Act partially reversed the Osborne Judgement. Henceforth unions had to establish separate political funds, raised by a specific levy, and objectors were given the right to 'contract-out'.
(e) 1928–46: Trade Disputes Act of 1927 replaced 'contracting-out' with 'contracting-in'.
(f) 1947–68: The 1927 Act was repealed in 1946 and 'contracting-in' was replaced by 'contracting-out'.
Source: The TUC's affiliated membership is taken from its *Annual Report*. Union membership affiliated to the Labour Party was obtained from G. D. H. Cole, *A History of the Labour Party since 1914* (Routledge 1948), p. 480, and for 1947–68 from the Labour Party's *Annual Conference Report 1969*, p. 52.

TABLE 4.14

Stoppages of Work arising from Industrial Disputes in the United Kingdom, 1900–1968

Year	Number of stoppages beginning in year	Number of workers involved in stoppages beginning in year(a) ('000s)			Working days lost in all(b) stoppages in progress in year(c)
		Directly involved	Indirectly involved	Total	
1900	633	132	53	185	3088
1901	631	111	68	179	4130
1902	432	115	140	255	3438
1903	380	93	23	116	2320
1904	346	56	31	87	1464
1905	349	67	25	92	2368
1906	479	158	60	218	3019
1907	585	100	46	146	2148
1908	389	221	72	293	10,785
1909	422	168	129	297	2687
1910	521	384	130	514	9867
1911	872	824	128	952	10,155
1912	834	1232	230	1462	40,890
1913	1459	497	167	664	9804
1914	972	326	121	447	9878
1915	672	401	47	448	2953
1916	532	235	41	276	2446
1917	730	575	297	872	5647
1918	1165	923	193	1116	5875
1919	1352	2401	190	2591	34,969
1920	1607	1779	153	1932	26,568
1921	763	1770	31	1801	85,872
1922	576	512	40	552	19,850
1923	628	343	62	405	10,672
1924	716	558	55	613	8424
1925	603	401	40	441	7952
1926(d)	323	2724	10	2734	162,233
1927	308	90	18	108	1174
1928	302	80	44	124	1388
1929	431	493	40	533	8287
1930	422	286	21	307	4399
1931	420	424	66	490	6983
1932	389	337	42	379	6488
1933	357	114	22	136	1072
1934	471	109	25	134	959
1935	553	230	41	271	1955
1936	818	241	75	316	1829
1937	1129	388	209	597	3413
1938	875	211	63	274	1334
1939	940	246	91	337	1356
1940	922	225	74	299	940
1941	1251	297	63	360	1079
1942	1303	349	107	456	1527
1943	1785	454	103	557	1808
1944	2194	716	105	821	3714
1945	2293	447	84	531	2835
1946	2205	405	121	526	2158

Table 4.14 continued

Year	Number of stoppages beginning in year	Number of workers involved in stoppages beginning in year (a)			Working days lost in all (b) stoppages in progress in year (c)
		Directly involved	Indirectly involved	Total	
1947	1721	489	131	620	2433
1948	1759	324	100	424	1944
1949	1426	313	120	433	1807
1950	1339	269	33	302	1389
1951	1719	336	43	379	1694
1952	1714	303	112	415	1792
1953	1746	1329	41	1370	2184
1954	1989	402	46	448	2457
1955	2419	599	60	659	3781
1956	2648	464	43	507	2083
1957	2859	1275	81	1356	8412
1958	2629	456	67	523	3462
1959	2093	522	123	645	5270
1960	2832	698*	116	814	3024
1961	2686	673	98	771	3046
1962	2449	4297	123	4420	5798
1963	2068	455	135	590	1755
1964	2524	700*	172	872	2277
1965	2354	673	195	868	2925
1966	1937	414*	116	530	2398
1967	2116	552*	180	732	2787
1968 (e)	2378	2074*	182	2256	4690

Notes:

(a) Workers involved in more than one stoppage in any year are counted more than once in the year's total. Workers thrown out of work at the establishments where the disputes occurred, although not themselves party to the disputes, are classified as being 'indirectly involved'.

(b) The figures exclude any loss of time, for example, through shortages of material which may be caused at the establishments by the stoppages which are included in the statistics.

(c) The figures in this column, unlike those in Column 1 of this table which refer only to strikes beginning in the year in question, include stoppages continuing from the previous year. Figures of the number of stoppages *in progress* in a year and the number of workers involved have been compiled since 1919 and can be obtained from the *Employment and Productivity Gazette*.

(d) Including the General Strike, which involved 1,580,000 workers and accounted for the loss of 15,000,000 working days.

(e) Precise comparisons between the number of stoppages in 1968 and the number in earlier years cannot be made due to the changed method of reporting and counting stoppages in the port transport industry following decasualisation. It is estimated that on the previous methods the number of stoppages in the port and inland water transport industry (and so in the total for all industries and services) in 1968 would have been about 30 fewer than those shown.

* Figures exclude workers becoming involved after the end of the year in which the stoppage began.

Source: The figures for the period 1937 to 1968 are from the annual article in the *Employment and Productivity Gazette*. For example, see the *Gazette* for May, 1969, pp. 437-43. The figures for the period 1900 to 1936 are from *Abstract of Labour Statistics*, no. 22 (1922-36), Cmd 5556, p. 127.

5 Social Mobility

KENNETH MACDONALD AND
JOHN RIDGE

The aim of this chapter is to review the credentials of the evidence for trends in social mobility in Britain during this century. We begin with a short prescriptive elaboration of the use of the term 'social mobility', and of a model for empirical study. But this is by way of orientation only, and the emphasis throughout rests on the possibility of detecting trends: neither a general introduction to the analysis of mobility, nor a comprehensive review of the literature on its many aspects is given. As a result, several issues are not mentioned at all, or at best discussed very briefly. This does not mean that they are settled or otherwise unimportant, but simply that they are not particularly relevant to the special problems of trend analysis. For those readers who do require a general introduction, we recommend the articles by Miller (1960) and Duncan (1966) cited in the bibliography (in which all references in this chapter are collected).

Other chapters in this book document recent changes in the pattern of differentiation of British society: e.g. changes in the distribution of crime, in the industrial and occupational structures, or in the distribution of income, housing, health, education or age. We can regard each of these many distributions as one dimension of society, and to each can be related a range of social positions, which differ in terms of the characteristic that defines the dimension. Of course, there is no obvious limit to the number or variety of dimensions that we could choose to study: a major task of the sociologist, on this approach, is to specify his aim of 'understanding society' such that it becomes a guide to which dimensions are relevant and which are not (for a recent discussion, see Runciman, 1968). Similarly, on a given dimension, there are many ways of defining discrete social positions: the method adopted depends on the problem concerned. (Unfortunately, as the rest of the book reveals, the categories imposed by official statistics not only vary over time, but often do not map well on to the dimensions referenced by the analyst.)

CRITERIA OF SOCIAL MOBILITY

Social mobility can be defined as the movement of individuals between social positions. Its analysis is that both of rates and of incidence
of movement between positions: that is, we wish to discover not only the
frequency with which individuals move from A to B, but also the
differences between individuals which explain why some move and
others do not. More generally, we wish to understand how individuals
come to occupy given social positions; the routes they have followed, the
extent to which they have chosen to move or stay, the goals they have
tried to achieve, the success or failure they have experienced, the features
of their situation that have helped or hindered them and so on. Social
mobility, construed in this way, would seem to cover most areas of
sociological enquiry. However, the customary usage is more restricted:
the term normally refers to movement on a socio-economic dimension
which, in practice, is usually represented by an occupational dimension.
A possible justification for this latter restriction is that in modern industrial society occupation is a major determinant of position on other
socio-economic dimensions: for example, occupation is for most people
the only (certainly the main) source of income, and must therefore
affect their behaviour as consumers. But the strength and nature of such
relationships is, of course, an empirical question. An analysis of occupational mobility may well make an important contribution to the development of a more general model of social mobility, but it does not
in itself constitute such a model, though investigators generally employ
an ordering of occupations in terms of status or prestige in an effort
to tighten the link between occupation and social position. One ambiguity in the term 'status' is between status as 'standing' and status as
'location'. The former is meant here, though without any claims as to
the existence of strata; we are not positing a ranking of assumed discrete
groups, and leave it as an empirical question whether orderings on any
dimensions considered define such clusters.

We now give a brief outline of a model of the process of occupational
mobility which can be extended without difficulty to include mobility
on other dimensions. It starts with the observation that at a given point
in time individuals are distributed in certain proportions over the range
of occupations or occupational categories (however defined): this
current distribution is the aggregate result of prior moves by individuals
into their current occupations. The aim is to account for the current
distribution by explaining the individuals' prior moves. This explanation is given by their life-histories, or 'careers': a career is a temporal
sequence of experiences in which the present (at any stage) is dependent
on, and explicable in terms of, the past (i.e. experiences at previous
stages).

THE CHOICE OF WORK

Present occupation is the result of a choice within a range of alternatives. It should be noted that our emphasis on choice or decision-making activity of the individual as the explanatory base for aggregate social activity is mildly heretical. Certainly from the viewpoint of a more decision-oriented discipline sociologists are unhappy with choice (see, for example, A. Campbell *et al.*, *The American Voter*, 1960, Section 1, or B. M. Barry, *Sociologists, Economists and Democracy*, 1970) and it cannot be described as a major preoccupation of the sociological literature. In particular, current quantitative techniques such as path analysis, though they can handle connections between determinate points, are ill-fitted to handling events. Markov techniques for analysing event-sequences do not as yet, even in sophisticated presentations, translate readily into substantive statements. No quantitative analysis of sociological event-centred life history data exists. Consequently our remarks here, which owe more to Homans than Parsons in theoretical orientation, are more programmatic than descriptive. But the programme is one we believe worth following through. (Sørensen, 1970, reports some recent progress; see also Carr-Hill and Macdonald, 1973.)

We must take into account first, factors which affect the range of occupations that the individual considers, and second, factors which influence his choice among them. Past experience may limit alternatives in many ways: a man may be unable to supply the qualifications for a job because he left school at fourteen or left university without a 'good' degree; because he has a criminal record or the wrong accent; because he was a bad timekeeper or a zealous shop-steward in his last job, and so on ad infinitum. But alternatives may be further limited by demand: one cannot choose to enter an occupation in which there are no jobs available. Here we must take into account external factors such as the general economic situation, technological development, and the planning decisions of employers and of central and local government. To simplify, it can be said that supply and demand jointly determine the range of possible choices.

However, the range of choices actually considered is inevitably narrower than this. The most obvious constraint is lack of information: since a man must know of opportunities if he is to consider them, our model must allow for variations in access to information. At this point, we can introduce the concept of the 'local labour market', that is, of geographical limits to the individual's range of perceived opportunities. People tend not to hear about job opportunities outside their area. But this is not really adequate: we want to allow for variations among individuals in the size of their area, and there is no reason to assume that this is solely determined by access to information. Here the earlier distinction between range and choice starts to dissolve, because we must also introduce the possibility of differential costs: that is, that the perceived cost of taking up a perceived opportunity varies with experience and situation. For example, a man who has always lived in a close-knit community may consider the cost of moving elsewhere so great as to rule out jobs that would require such a breaking of ties. Costs are not, however, simply geographically determined: the individual's own priority of needs determines what is to count as a cost. Furthermore, a man may change his priorities from time to time, especially as his 'life-cycle' position changes. A young married man with many dependents may seek to maximise his current earnings: thus he cannot afford to consider available jobs which do not meet this condition, however attractive they may be in other respects. But as his children grow up, and his wife perhaps takes a job herself, his own earnings become less crucial: he may now regard as excessive costs those aspects of his previous jobs (such as frequent overtime work) which were the corollary of maximum earnings. On the other hand, the cost of any change of job may increase with age (if, for instance, pension rights are not transferable).

There is no obvious limit to the number and variety of possible costs, which suggests that building them into the empirical analysis of decisions will be difficult. But, paradoxically, the principle has the appeal of parsimony in explanatory concepts: we can avoid the earlier distinction between restrictions on the range of opportunities and choices within the range by regarding the ultimate decision as the result of the progressive elimination of less feasible opportunities (where differences in cost are one aspect of differences in feasibility).

Clearly this type of model when elaborated becomes very complex, and discussion of it correspondingly lengthy. However our present aim is not to specify details, but rather to suggest the spirit in which we might construct more or less 'basic' versions of the model. Two points deserve emphasis. First, the end-product (the 'working version' of the model) is a set of relationships among variables: this set of relationships is itself a summary description of the process of (in this case) occupational mobility, so there is little chance of finding a single index or statistic which will adequately characterise the process. We will probably feel that any model worked out is already too condensed. Second, the process concerned operates in 'historical time': as noted above, the model must allow for changes in relationships as a result of changes in external factors (that is, actual historical events independent of the 'personal history' of the life cycle). Thus trends, or at least changes, should be an integral part of the model, not the object of separate analysis.

However, it is always possible to concentrate on one part of a model, even on a single relationship, provided that interpretation of the analysis takes into account this simplification. With this caveat, the search for trends is perfectly feasible, if the appropriate data are available. But the reader who has persevered this far is warned that in our view such data are not yet available for Britain.

In the first place, there are few sources of information. Gross data on changes in the occupational structure (though important as parameters of the model) clearly do not in themselves tell us much about the process of mobility, since such aggregate changes are compatible with various patterns of individual movement. For more specific information, official statistics are unhelpful: published results are largely in the form of separate distributions of attributes for various sub-groups of the population (defined by age, sex or region, for example), which do not reveal the pattern of association of attributes for the individuals in the sub-groups. In some cases, it is possible to go behind published figures to the original source data. Natalie Rogoff, in her pioneering study *Recent Trends in Occupational Mobility* (1953), made ingenious use of information recorded on marriage applications in Marion County, Indiana, to obtain interchange tables for two time-points. However, this technique has certain drawbacks: the records do not contain very much information, the quality of the data is problematic, the population sampled is restricted in a variety of ways and is in some respects indeterminate. Miller (1960) discusses some of these difficulties. The information is none the less valuable. In an elegant study Oldman and Illsley (1966) have used birth certificate records to form marriage indices of social status. Historical demographers have begun to exploit the occupational information contained in parish registers of births, marriages and deaths (see, for example, Laslett, 1969): the General Register Office files which contain the same information, and which were started in the mid-nineteenth century, could form the basis for a study similar but superior to Rogoff's, in that the population need not be restricted to those legally resident in a particular locality.

Such an analysis, though at only one time-point, has been reported by Benjamin (1958), who took a sample from the actual schedules returned in the 1951 Census, and then searched the Somerset House records for the birth certificates of the same people. The method is obviously laborious, and liable to error in that more than one certificate may match a single individual as described in the census schedule (for this reason, no attempt was made to match people with the most frequently-occurring surnames). For the cases in which a satisfactory match is achieved, the subject's current occupational position (from the census schedule) can be compared with his 'origin' (his father's occupation as recorded on his birth certificate): Benjamin categorises the occupations in terms of the 'socio-economic groups' of the 1951 Census, stressing that this need not reflect 'status' ('The concept here is of skill and associated material reward rather than of social values', p. 267), and presents the results for 2600 occupied males in the form of a table of current occupation cross-classified by 'origin'. This interesting comparison of birth and maturity which is, as far as we know, unique has been strangely ignored by subsequent writers. The major difficulty of the method is that it requires access to recent census schedules, which is permitted only to staff of the G.R.O.: it is, however, possible that amalgamation of the G.R.O. with the more 'research-oriented' Government Social Survey may lead to further studies of this type in future. For the present, the utility of Benjamin's study for the detection of trends is limited by absence of suitable comparisons. (Macdonald, 1972.)

An advantage of official records is that they allow the accumulation of large samples at low cost; but this is counterbalanced by their major disadvantage: each source covers only a limited range of information, and different sources cannot be linked. At present, special-purpose enquiries are the only method for collecting the type and quantity of information we require: however, for satisfactory analysis of such information large samples are needed, in local as well as national studies. The high costs entailed perhaps help to explain why there have been so few comprehensive studies of mobility.

In many ways the ideal study design is the longitudinal 'follow-up' of a sample of individuals from birth to maturity: since the investigator observes the life-history as it develops, his data is potentially very reliable, and since it is collected on a number of occasions, not all at once, many aspects can be studied in great depth. These are very real advantages, but in practice compromises usually have to be made. It would clearly be prohibitively expensive to organise regular and frequent contacts and carry out extended interviews more or less simultaneously with all the members of a large sample and their parents, if not other relatives. So the sample size has to be somewhat restricted, contacts may be irregular or infrequent, and interviewers may be replaced by postal questionnaires. The effects can be serious. It is obviously desirable to have complete information on a reasonably large and representative final sample: but to allow for the inevitable dropouts, the initial sample must be considerably larger (it is unfortunate that as the life-histories get longer, and the information more valuable, the effective sample shrinks). If contacts are not made frequently, or not followed up when lost, the dropout rate rises and the problem gets worse. If untrained interviewers or postal questionnaires are employed, the reliability and richness of the data are bound to decline. Finally, the study cannot reach maturity before the sample-members do: it is a very long-term investment for its authors. So whatever the advantages of this method, it is unlikely to be applied to the analysis of trends in mobility, since it would involve starting a number of such studies at, say, five-year intervals, all designed and executed in the same way, and all in the end running simultaneously.

Despite the difficulties, an impressive number of longitudinal studies are currently in progress, and in one case recently completed. The last, which is the oldest, is also the most interesting from our point of view since it covers at least the early stages of work experience. Sponsored by the Scottish Council for Research in Education, the '1947 Follow-up' had an initial sample of 1208 Scottish children born in 1936; interviews of varying length were carried out annually by volunteers (including members of the Survey Committee, educational psychologists, and teachers). Some contacts were inevitably lost but strenuous efforts were made to restore them, with the impressive result that the final sample size was 1104 for the 1963 questionnaire (complete information was not available for all of the final sample, of course, since some had been out of touch during parts of the study). The analysis has been brought up to date by Maxwell (1969): he refers to and in part summarises earlier publications. The longest running current study has a larger initial sample (effectively, all the children born in Great Britain in one week of March, 1946): its main contributions to date have been reports on educational selection between Primary and Secondary school (Douglas, 1964), and within and after the Secondary stage (Douglas et al., 1968).

The cross-sectional sample survey can to some extent supply retrospective information on aspects of individuals' life-history. The data will be defective to the extent that people cannot recall the details of their own past experience: there is also the possibility that, with hindsight, informants may 'tidy-up' their history, for example reporting on their past in such a way as to maximise its connection with the present. Miller (1960) includes an excellent discussion of such difficulties, and suggests ways in which the comparability of survey results may be affected. Intelligent design and careful control of the data-collection is obviously vital if distortions are to be kept to a minimum. A scheme for the collection and analysis of life-histories which seems to meet these requirements has been proposed by Balan et al. (1969): similar work is being carried on by a group at Johns Hopkins University (Blum et al., 1969; Sørensen, 1970).

There has only been one large-scale national survey in Britain designed specifically to relate a number of aspects of the mobility process. It was carried out in June and August 1949 by the Government

Social Survey on behalf of the Ministry of Labour and the London School of Economics: the data were divided between the sponsors and analysed separately, by Thomas (G.S.S. 134) and the L.S.E. group (Glass, 1954). There is little overlap between the two reports. Some of the data from the second study has been re-analysed by Miller (1960): he presents the basic mobility table (respondent's occupation cross-classified by reported occupation of father) with the original occupational categories slightly modified to distinguish manual and non-manual occupations. Berent (1952) analyses the information on differential fertility, and relates it to some of the other variables in the L.S.E. study. Lockwood (1958, pp. 107–21) presents a more detailed analysis of the data on clerks, and Kelsall and Mitchell (1959) discuss the data on women's employment (a topic which was not covered in the main report). We have further analysed the date in Ridge (1974).

In 1963 the Ministry of Labour commissioned a further investigation into labour mobility in Britain (Harris and Clausen, 1966): it is similar in aim and design to their part of the 1949 study, and therefore does not cover as wide a range of topics as the combined survey. Unfortunately, even within the area common to both studies there are a number of differences in questionnaire design, coding and analysis which further limit direct comparisons.

More recently, information on some aspects of social mobility for a national sample has been collected in a continuing panel study, which is primarily concerned with voting behaviour (Butler and Stokes, 1969): but again the procedures used do not produce results directly comparable with those of other studies.

This exhausts the relevant national material. The bibliography at the end of this chapter lists some source of additional information (Stacey, 1968, summarises the more important of them).

There are a few studies primarily concerned with trends in specific but crucial aspects of the mobility process.

Little and Westergaard (1964) summarise the available data on changes in the relation of social origin and educational opportunity: Lee (1968) has used Census material in a noble attempt to detect trends in the educational requirements of occupations. In both cases, the findings are negative: but as the authors point out they have had to supplement the data with various assumptions (technical and sub-stantive) which may turn out to be misleading. There are also a number of studies of particular occupational groups (including teachers, Anglican ministers, managers, upland farmers, higher civil servants and affluent manual workers), all providing data on social origins, and some attempting to assess changes in the pattern of recruitment. But as usual the comparability of the data is questionable, and in any case such studies do not (and were not intended to) provide general accounts of occupational mobility or estimates of general trends.

There might at first glance seem to be a fair measure of consistency in occupational prestige coding. For example, many British studies on diverse subjects claim that 'the occupational classification used in this enquiry is derived from that of Hall and Jones (1950)', and a recent official handbook asserts that their scale 'is widely used in this country' (*Comparability in Social Research*, BSA and SSRC, 1969, p. 11). But the historic significance and (in the British context) the continuing uniqueness of the Hall/Jones study should not lead us to overestimate its determining power. The empirical frame for the original scale was a ranking of 30 occupations, industrial categories being weakly represented. Other occupations were then placed within the frame on the judgement of the researchers. This detailed list was not published until 1966.

A thirty-item frame sparsely referencing industrial occupations leaves much room for originality, which is good ground for believing that the claimed derivations are more notional than actual. (Macdonald, 1974.)

In principle, we can detect trends by comparing two or more estimates of a single parameter derived from two or more studies carried out at different times: the value of any study is greatly increased if it forms part of a cumulative series. Our review of the present situation therefore adds a certain poignancy to Glass's observation on completion of the 1949 investigation:

> Not until the results of similar studies in other countries are available, and until repeat studies are done in Britain in the future, will it be possible fully to appreciate the relevance of the present enquiries. (1954, p. 13.)

More specifically,

> It must remain for later investigators, repeating this kind of inquiry in fifteen or twenty years' time, to establish how far the ultimate chances of mobility have been influenced by educational and other developments during the inter-war period, while the net results of the 1944 Education Act will not be fully ascertainable for another forty or fifty years. (*Ibid.*, p. 180.)

'Later investigators' have not yet responded.

DERIVING TREND ESTIMATES

Nevertheless on certain conditions we can derive trend estimates from a single cross-sectional study. The key step is to divide the sample members into cohorts in terms of their age at the time of the survey. If we have collected age-specific information (life-histories), then we can regard the early experience of an old cohort as the equivalent of the recent experience of a young cohort, and attribute any observed differences to secular changes in the mobility process itself. Of course, if we do not have age-specific information, differences between old and young cohorts will be an uninterpretable product of secular changes and age-differences. The 1949 enquiry asked the respondent for the last main occupation of his father, and his own current occupation: thus 'father's occupation' cannot be defined for a single, known point in the respondent's career, while for each cohort 'own occupation' relates to a known, but different, stage. Therefore we cannot use a cohort analysis of the relation between these variables as evidence for secular trends in the relation. This only becomes possible when we have a measure of social origin at some determinate career stage, and a measure of position at some other stage or series of stages. An inevitable limitation is that the number of age-linked occupations is a function of the age of the cohort: consequently, the maximum number of comparisons can be made only for transition between the 'youngest' occupations and, at the limit, no comparison is possible involving any occupation held at an age which only the oldest cohort has attained.

Glass was able to carry out an analysis of this type by using the information primarily collected for the Ministry of Labour on occupation at specific ages. He divides the sample into four 10-year cohorts, and considers changes in the pattern of transition between occupations held at ages 20, 30 and 40. From the comparisons he makes, Glass (1954) finds no evidence of real changes in the patterns of transition (pp. 207-212).

The 'cohort' approach could also be applied, were the data available, to an examination of trends in the parameters of a more complex model, as in the definitive American study (Blau and Duncan, 1967, pp. 107-111). A basic explanatory model of part of the mobility process is constructed, involving only variables which are tied to a fixed age or career-point: a number of parameters can thus be considered simultaneously, and changes in any of them attributed to secular factors, not age-differences (see Ridge, 1974, ch. 2).

Duncan (1965) has also developed an alternative method of assessing trends in the pattern of transition between occupations. 'Origin' still has to be measured at a specific career-stage, but 'destination' can be represented by respondents' current occupations. Briefly, the idea is to use the observed origin distribution of one cohort, and the pattern of transition to current occupation of another cohort, to generate an expected occupational distribution for the first cohort at a time when its members were the same age as those in the second.

For example, suppose we carry out a survey in 1970 on two cohorts, men aged 20 and men aged 30: we may define social origin as 'father's occupation when respondent was aged about 16' (as in Duncan's study). For the first cohort we now construct a table revealing the pattern of movement from origin to destination – that is, to occupation at age 20. If we multiply this table, or transition-matrix, by the origin distribution of the second cohort, we obtain an expected occupational distribution for men aged 20 in 1960. If we can also obtain from the census or elsewhere the actual distribution for men aged 20 in 1960, we can measure the difference between the expected and actual distributions. Any discrepancies must be attributable to changes in the pattern of transition between 1960 and 1970; thus although we did not observe in 1960 the transition matrix for men then aged 20, it could here be inferred that it is different from the matrix for the same age-group 10 years later. This mode of analysis cannot be applied to the 1949 data since the Hall-Jones occupational codes do not translate into those of the census.

The two methods are alternatives in the sense that they use different sources for the actual distributions at earlier points in time. In the first case, the reports by, say, men aged 60 on their occupations at age 20 are taken to represent the distribution we would have observed if we had surveyed a sample of 20-year-olds 40 years ago. In the second case, since retrospective reports are not available, independent contemporary observations are used; it is, of course, essential that their occupational categories be identical to those applied in coding the survey data.

Both methods assume that a current sample of a cohort represents its membership at various times in the past: they do not allow for possible bias due to differential mortality, migration and accuracy of recall.

The first method may have a slight advantage in that any 'cohort bias' will also affect the 'actual' destination distributions, and thus tend to reduce spurious differences between them and the expected distributions. But even if origin and destination errors cancel out completely, we still have to assume that the transition matrices which generate the expected distributions are unbiased or, more precisely, are insensitive to bias in origin distributions. As Duncan (1965) has observed: 'Here, as elsewhere in mobility research, it is easier to appreciate the likelihood of sizeable errors, both random and systematic, than to estimate them or to devise suitable corrections' (p. 492). The quotation is a depressing but fair summary of this chapter.

In a final attempt to produce trend information we might compare available national father/son mobility tables from different studies. Detailed tables exist for 1949, 1951, and 1963 (Glass 1954, p. 183; Benjamin 1958, p. 266; Butler and Stokes, 1969, p. 96). Of these only the 1949 table was specifically constructed as a social mobility table. Bypassing for the moment problems arising from the varying definition of 'fathers' an obvious hindrance is that no two studies employ the same occupational classification. But, it might be argued, each scale references the same dimension while splitting it differently, so some appropriate summary measure might enable us to compare mobility between tables. This we suggest is not so.

The literature on the analysis of straightforward father to son occupational mobility tables is both technical and extensive. (For a way into this discussion see L. A. Goodman, 'How to ransack social mobility tables and other kinds of cross-classification tables', *A.J.S.* (1970), 1–40.) The location of an appropriate summary measure for the association between two variables is itself a vexed question (though habituation has made some indices seem natural); and in the case of mobility tables the problem is compounded by a desire to untangle structural effects. We take one, intuitively interpretable, mode of analysis with the aim of demonstrating that the occupational categories imposed upon the data crucially affect the viability of reading a father/son occupational cross-tabulation as a social mobility table. In particular, we argue that, among available tables, only the 1949 table coded in terms of the Hall-Jones categories can be seen as using occupational categories on a single dimension reflecting social distance.

The technique employed is that of multidimensional scaling, using a computer program and method developed by J. B. Kruskal. (In *Psychometrika*, **29** (1964), 1–27, 115–29, he provides an extremely lucid introduction.) Given a matrix of dissimilarity measures between points, the program attempts to arrange these points within, say, a two-dimensional space so as to satisfy the dissimilarity conditions. A useful, though imprecise, physical analogy is given by a set of objects, each object connected by strings to every other object, the strings being of varying length: problem, move the objects around on the table so that the strings become taut. In the physical case this may be achieved by placing the objects in a straight line (a one-dimensional solution), or may be achieved only by moving some of the objects above the table (a three-dimension solution). As far as data points are concerned we can compare for goodness of fit solutions from one to four (or higher) dimensions. One might verbalise the operation as an attempt to find the dimensionality of a space in terms of which we can describe the points so as to account for the observed dissimilarities between them.

To generate an appropriate matrix we can take the absolute percentage difference between two outflow (or inflow) distributions as an index of their dissimilarity. (See Blau and Duncan (1967, pp. 67ff). It should, incidentally, be noted that their two-dimensional solution (p.70) if rotated to its principal axes provides slightly less support than claimed for a basic prestige dimension in the American data.) The more alike the two percentage distributions, the smaller the index of dissimilarity, and the closer the occupational groups are deemed (on this definition of similarity) to be. This index has the advantage of not presupposing any ranking of the occupational categories.

In the analysis, the 1949 table yielded a perfect one-dimensional solution. The only solution which fitted the 1963 table was a degenerate dichotomy. While the sampling properties of Kruskal's method are unascertained, available evidence suggests that this contrast is significant. (See D. Klahr, 'A Monte-Carlo investigation of the statistical significance of Kruskal's nonmetric scaling procedure', *Psychometrika*, **34**, 1969, 319–50.) We would interpret it by saying that the occupational categories used in the 1949 enquiry, unlike those in the 1963 table, are such that they can be placed on one scale reflecting the social distance between them. The behaviour of the 1951 table is interesting in this regard; it requires (especially in the outflow case) the occupational groups to be arranged in at least two dimensions before the dissimilarity matrix is satisfied. For this phenomenon there are varying descriptions. One might say that the space of social distance between occupational categories is essentially two-dimensioned. We prefer, intuitively and on the evidence of the 1949 table, to suggest that it is possible to construct an occupational categorisation which unidimensionally would yield the distances between the categories; that the 1951 classification does not do so, indicates that it is not describable as a classification of occupations in terms of their social distance.

The occupational classifications in the 1951 and 1963 tables are, from this viewpoint, employing criteria which are not those of the 1949 enquiry.

Before leaving this little exercise there are two points to make. Firstly, the index of social distance may be held to omit important elements, for it says nothing directly about the ease of movement between categories. Nevertheless, the aspect it does locate (similarity of outflow or origin) is not unimportant for social mobility. Secondly, the reader may feel that we have been employing a complicated electronic hammer on an imaginary nut; for is it not obvious that the occupational categorisations derive from varying theoretical bases. We admit the distinctness of the theoretical bases. But in the actual location of the utilised handful of categories, there is a certain amount of slack, and one might be tempted to suppose that the final categories, however derived, were not dissimilar. Accordingly it is of interest to examine the behaviour of these categories in relevant situations (although this requires the assumption that the variations revealed are too striking to belong to the 'real world').

THE EVIDENCE EXAMINED

The existing detailed occupational mobility tables are not comparable. It might, however, be claimed that when collapsed to a straightforward manual/non-manual dichotomy these tables yield useful trend information. Although the dichotomy is neither straightforward (see, e.g., Runciman, 1966, Appendix 3) nor necessarily salient, the four available tables are given.

The classification of three of the tables is determined by the sources; in Table 5.1 (ii) the grouping has been chosen to approximate the non-manual percentage of respondents in Table 5.1 (i).

We have tables for 1949, 1951, 1962, and 1963. Assuming for the moment that manual/non-manual means what it seems, let us see whether obvious trends are indicated.

A puzzling feature of the 1949 table is the stability of the marginals over time. While we recognise fathers are not a cohort, they do at least predate their sons and (see Table 4.1) might thus be expected to be more 'manual'; this trend shows up neatly in the 1951 table. Part explanation is the differing time-point for father's occupation between the two studies (main occupation, contrasted with occupation at respondent's birth). Turning to the 1962 and 1963 tables we note a fair measure of disagreement; again we may attribute this to a variation in question form ('what your father's occupation was' as against 'your father's occupation when you were a child') though this does not seem to have affected the marginals. If we take the two tables, comparable over time, for 1951 and 1963, remembering that we thus equate 'fathers' with 'fathers and fathers-in-law', the most remarkable feature is their similarity. On the other hand, 1949 and 1962, equally comparable on time of father's occupation, present striking contrasts (which are sharpened by locating, so far as one can, the male respondents in the 1962 table – Table 5.1, note c).

Faced with this situation there are too many options. Eliminate one table, and the other three no longer present inconsistencies; elimination can be achieved by locating some slight bias in the achieved sample, claiming that non-response for the specific questions was non-random, etc. Alternatively one can concoct a tale to fit 'the facts'. E.g. the association between occupation and early socialisation has remained steady, but in the early period father's job movement was erratic whereas, more recently, fathers producing white-collar sons tend themselves later to move to white-collar occupations (we are witnessing a three-generation effect from postulated grandfathers, or if you prefer, feedback from successful sons). This little story (and others) can account for all the observed discrepancies between the tables. The criteria for selecting a story to tell, or a table to discard are unclear.

Each table deals with a differently defined population of 'fathers'. In their estimates of transition rates tables separated by one or two years vary as much as those separated by over a decade. We hesitate to take this evidence as supporting any proper statement regarding British trends in social mobility. This is not to say that such trends do not exist.

BIBLIOGRAPHY

(Entries are of two kinds: a selection of items reporting British data and (starred) some methodologically relevant work)

*Balan, J., Browning, H. L., Jelin, E. and Litzler, L. (1969) 'A computerised approach to the processing and analysis of life-histories obtained in sample survey', *Behavioural Science*, **14**, 105–20.

Bell, C. (1968) *Middle Class Families* (Routledge).

Benjamin, B. (1958) 'Inter-generation differences in occupation', *Population Studies*, XI (3), 262–8.

Berent, J. (1952) 'Fertility and Social Mobility', *Population Studies*, **5**, 244–60.

Bishop, T. J. H. (1967) *Winchester and the Public School Elite*, in collaboration with Rupert Wilkinson (Faber & Faber).

*Blau, P. M. and Duncan, O. D. (1967) *The American Occupational Structure* (Wiley, New York).

*Blum, Z. D., Karweit, N. and Sorensen, A. B. (1969) *A Method for he Collection and Analysis of Retrospective Life Histories*, The Johns Hopkins University, Center for the Study of Social Organisation of Schools, Report No. 48.

Butler, D. E. and Stokes, D. (1969) *Political Change in Britain* (Macmillan).

*Carr-Hill, R. A. and Macdonald, K. I. (1973) 'Problems in the analysis of life-histories', *Sociol. Rev. Monograph 19*, 57–95.

Clark, D. G. (1966). *The Industrial Manager: his Background and Career Pattern* (Business Publications Ltd).

Coxon, A. P. M. (1967) 'Patterns of occupational recruitment: the Anglican ministry', *Sociology*, **1**, 73–80.

Douglas, J. W. B. (1964) *The Home and the School* (MacGibbon & Kee).

Douglas, J. W. B., Ross, J. M. and Simpson, H. R. (1968) *All our Future* (Peter Davies).

*Duncan, O. D. (1965) 'The trend of occupational mobility in the United States', *Am. Sociol. Rev.* **30**, 491–8.

*Duncan, O. D. (1966) 'Methodological Issues in the Analysis of Social Mobility' in N. J. Smelser and S. M. Lipset (eds) *Social Structure and Mobility in Economic Development* (Aldine, Chicago).

*Duncan, O. D., Featherman, D. L. and Duncan, B. (1968) *Socioeconomic Background and Occupational Achievement: Extensions of a Basic Model*, Final report, Project No. 5–0074, U.S. Department of Health, Education and Welfare.

Gibson, J. B. (1970) 'Biological aspects of a high socio-economic group. I: IQ, education and social mobility', *J. Biosocial Science*, **2** (1), 1–16.

Glass, D. V. (ed.) (1954) *Social Mobility in Britain* (Routledge).

Halsey, A. H. and Crewe, I. M. (1969) *Social Survey of the Civil Service*, **3** (1) of *The Civil Service*, Evidence submitted to the Committee under the Chairmanship of Lord Fulton, 1966–8 (HMSO).

Halsey, A. H., Floud, Jean and Anderson, C. A. (eds) (1960) *Education, Economy and Society* (Free Press: The Macmillan Co., N.Y.).

Harris, A. and Clausen, R. (1966) *Labour Mobility in Great Britain 1953–1963*, Government Social Survey Report 333 (HMSO).

*Hope, K. (ed.) (1972) *The Analysis of Social Mobility* (O.U.P.).

Hordley, I. and Lee, D. J. (1970) 'The "alternative-route" – social change and opportunity in technical education', *Sociology*, **4**, 23–50.

Jackson, B. and Marsden, D. (1962) *Education and the Working Class* (Routledge).

Kelsall, R. K. (1955) *Higher Civil Servants in Britain from 1870 to the Present Day* (Routledge).

Kelsall, R. K. and Mitchell, S. (1959) 'Married women and employment in England and Wales', *Population Studies*, **13**, 191.

Laslett, P. (1969) 'Historical and Regional Variations in Great Britain' Chap. 19 in M. Dogan and S. Rokkan (eds), *Quantitative Ecological Analysis in the Social Sciences* (M.I.T. Press, Cambridge, Mass.).

Lee, D. J. (1968) 'Class differentials in educational opportunity and promotion from the ranks', *Sociology*, **2**, 293–312.

Little, A. and Westergaard, J. (1964) 'The trend of class differentials in educational opportunity in England and Wales', *Brit. J. Sociol.* xv, 301–15.

Lockwood, D. (1958) *The Black-Coated Worker* (Allen & Unwin).

Macdonald, K. I. (1972) 'MDSCAL and distances between socio-economic groups', in Hope, 1972, 211–34.

Macdonald, K. I. (1974) 'The Hall-Jones scale', in Ridge, 1974, 97–115.

MacKay, D. I. (1969) *Geographical Mobility and the Brain Drain* (Allen & Unwin).

MacPherson, A. F. (1967) Research note, *Scottish Educational Studies*, **1** (1), 65–6.

Maxwell, J. (1969) *Sixteen Years On* (U.L.P.).

Miller, S. M. (1960) 'Comparative Social Mobility', *Current Sociol.*, **9** (1).

Musgrove, F. (1963) *The Migratory Elite* (Heinemann).

Nalson, J. S. (1968) *Mobility of Farm Families* (Manchester U.P.).

Oldman, D. and Illsley, R. (1966) 'Measuring the status of occupations', *Sociol. Rev.* (n.s.), **14**, 53–72.

*Orcutt, G. H., Greenberger, M., Korbel, J. and Rivlin, Alice M. (1961) *Microanalysis of Socioeconomic Systems; A Simulation Study* (Harper Row, N.Y.).

Ridge, J. M. (ed.) (1974) *Mobility in Britain Reconsidered* (O.U.P.).

*Rogoff, Natalie (1953) *Recent Trends in Occupational Mobility* (Free Press: The Macmillan Co., N.Y.).

Runciman, W. G. (1966) *Relative Deprivation and Social Justice* (Routledge).

Runciman, W. G. (1968) 'Class, status and power?', Chap. 3 in J. A. Jackson (ed.) *Social Stratification* (C.U.P.).

Scott, W. H. (1958) 'Fertility and social mobility among teachers', *Population Studies*, **11**, 251–61.

*Sørensen, A. B. (1970) *The Occupational Mobility Process: an Analysis of the Decision to Leave a Job*, Paper presented to the session on Theory, Research and Simulation Studies on Social Mobility, Seventh World Congress of the International Sociological Association, Varna, Bulgaria.

Stacey, B. G. (1968) 'Inter-generation occupational mobility in Britain', *Occupational Psychology*, **42**, 33–48.

Stewart, Rosemary (1956) *Management Succession* (Acton Society Trust).

Thomas, G. (n.d.) *Labour Mobility in Great Britain 1945–1949*, The Social Survey, Report 134: mimeographed.

Wilmott, P. and Young, M. (1960) *Family and Class in a London Suburb* (Routledge).

TABLE 5.1

Intergenerational Mobility between Manual and Non-Manual Occupations

(i) Occupation (males aged 20 or over) by father's main occupation. 1949. England and Wales(a).

Fathers	Sons			Outflow Sons			Inflow Sons	
	A	B	Total	A	B	Total	A	B
A Non-manual	21·5	15·7	37·0	57·9	42·1	100	58·0	24·8
B Manual	15·6	47·3	63·0	24·7	75·3	100	42·0	75·2
Total	37·0	63·0	100 (3498)				100	100

(ii) Occupation (occupied males) by father's occupation at subject's birth. 1951. England and Wales.

Fathers	Sons			Outflow Sons			Inflow Sons	
	A	B	Total	A	B	Total	A	B
A Non-manual	16·3	10·2	26·6	61·5	38·5	100	47·7	15·6
B Manual	17·9	55·5	73·4	24·4	75·6	100	52·3	84·4
Total	34·3	65·7	100 (2534)				100	100

(iii) Occupation (respondent(b) or respondent's husband) by respondent's father's occupation. 1962. England and Wales.

Fathers	Sons or sons-in-law			Outflow Sons or sons-in-law			Inflow(c) Sons or sons-in-law	
	A	B	Total	A	B	Total	A	B
A Non-manual	16·8	7·8	25·6	68·3	31·7	100	47·2	12·1
B Manual	18·8	56·6	75·4	24·9	75·1	100	52·8	87·9
Total	35·6	64·4	100 (1346)				100	100

(iv) Occupation (head of household) by respondent's(d) father.
1963. Great Britain.

Fathers	Sons			Outflow Sons or sons-in-law			Inflow Sons or sons-in-law	
	A	B	Total	A	B	Total	A	B
A Non-manual	18·7	10·8	29·5	63·4	36·6	100	49·9	17·3
B Manual	18·8	51·7	70·5	26·7	73·3	100	50·1	82·7
Total	37·5	62·5	100 (1603)				100	100

Notes:
(a) Miller misidentifies table (i) as being for Great Britain and as being for males 18 and over (cf. Glass, 1954, pp. 180, 181).
(b) Respondents are a sample of electors. For unmarried women the table records their own occupation (*loc. cit.*, p. 151): to be pedantically accurate the subhead should read: 'sons or "head of married daughter's household" or unmarried daughters' since, pace p. 151, 'husband's occupation' is not asked in the questionnaire (pp. 299–313).
(c) From Table 6 (*loc. cit.*) we have the inflow for non-manual men and women separately.

Father	Men	Women
Non-manual	44·2	49·8
Manual	55·8	50·2
Total	100	100

(d) Respondents are a sample of the electorate. Note that in some cases 'father' and 'head of house' may have identical denotation.

Sources:
(i) S. M. Miller, 'Comparative Social Mobility', *Current Sociology*, IX (1960), 71. (A modified version of the table in Glass, 1954, p. 183.)
(ii) B. Benjamin, 'Inter-Generation Differences in Occupation', *Population Studies*, XI (1958), 266. (We have taken SEGs 1, 3–9 as non-manual, and omitted SEG 13.)
(iii) W. G. Runciman, *Relative Deprivation and Social Justice* (Routledge 1966). (We have constructed the present table from Table 6, p. 167 and Table 12, p. 175).
(iv) D. E. Butler and D. Stokes, *Political Change in Britain* (Macmillan 1969), p. 97, fn.

6 Schools

A. H. HALSEY, JOHN SHEEHAN AND JOHN VAIZEY

Socialisation is a sociological and not an administrative concept. The problem therefore arises, in this as in every other aspect of social structure, of translating published official statistics into social indicators. Education has to be thought of sociologically as the organisation of the more formal aspects of socialisation. Throughout the twentieth century formal socialisation has grown in importance in the double sense that it has taken up more of the time of more people at each stage of its development. One result has been an increased production of official statistics which have changed their character in response to changes in the structure of education and to changes in the preoccupations of administrators and policy makers.

We have confined ourselves for the most part to statistics on English and Welsh schools. The Scottish system is distinctive both in its history and its structure.[1] The English system is a complex of deceiving names. Schools may be defined as full-time educational institutions for children up to the statutory leaving age and for those who stay on voluntarily in the same institutions. The following definitions may help the reader to distinguish between the different kinds:

(a) Administratively and financially, schools may be divided into four categories: (i) those maintained by local education authorities who pay for them partly from local rates and partly from general grants provided by the central government; (ii) direct grant schools which receive financial assistance directly from the Department of Education and Science; (iii) independent schools recognised as efficient which have obtained their recognition after inspection by Her Majesty's Inspector of Schools; (iv) voluntary schools, established mainly by religious denominations, which are divided into three types – 'aided', 'controlled' and 'special agreement'.

---

[1] *Education in Scotland in 1963*. A Report of the Secretary of State for Scotland, Cmnd 2307.

'Aided' schools are those for which two-thirds of the managers or governors are appointed by the voluntary body and one-third by the local authority. The authority pays maintenance and running costs and teachers' salaries while the managers are responsible for the exterior of the building, improvements, enlargements and alterations. The central government makes grants of up to 80 per cent. of approved expenditure on listed items. Religious instruction and the appointment of teachers are controlled by the managers or governors. 'Controlled' schools are those for which one-third of the governors and managers are appointed by the voluntary body and two-thirds by the local authority. All costs are borne by the authority which appoints the teachers. Religious instruction follows the agreed syllabus with the addition of two periods of denominational instruction if the parents agree. By 'special agreement', authorities may consent to pay between half to three-quarters of the cost of building a new school or enlarging an existing (usually secondary) voluntary school. The status of the school becomes similar to that of an aided school.

(b) Schools may also be divided according to the age range of their pupils. There are four stages: pre-primary up to age 5; primary from 5 to 11; secondary from 11 until the pupil leaves school; and further education which covers all education and training after full-time schooling ends.

(c) Within the stages, the following types of school may be distinguished: (i) nursery schools, providing education primarily for children below compulsory school age, i.e. under 5; (ii) infants' schools, for children aged 5 to 7; (iii) junior schools for those aged 7 to 11; (iv) secondary modern schools, providing for children aged 11 to 15; (v) secondary technical schools, providing for selected children aged 11 plus; (vi) secondary grammar schools, providing for children aged 11 plus who are selected as capable of a relatively exacting academic schooling; (vii) comprehensive schools, providing education for all secondary pupils in a given district; (viii) all-age-schools containing children of both primary and secondary age; (ix) special schools, either day or boarding, providing education for children who are so seriously handicapped, physically or mentally, that they cannot profit fully from education in normal schools. Some special schools are run by voluntary bodies. They receive some grant from the DES but rely mainly on fees charged to the LEAs for pupils sent to them. Hospital special schools provide for children who are spending a period in hospital.

SOURCES OF USEFUL STATISTICS

Government publications
Annual statistical publications of the Department of Education and Science. From 1900 to 1914 statistics were published separately as parliamentary papers. 1901 figures are taken from *Statistics of Education 1900–1*, Cd 1139, 1902. 1911 figures are taken from *Statistics of Education 1910–1911*, Cd 6551, 1912–13. From 1915 to 1960 statistics were published together with the annual report of the department.

1921, 1931 and 1938 figures are taken from *Education* – the Annual Reports of the Board of Education for the appropriate years, published as parliamentary papers. The 1951 figures are taken from *Education in 1951*, the Annual Report and Statistics of Education of the Ministry of Education, 1951, Cmd 8554.

Since 1961 statistics have been published separately from the annual report, in several parts, and as departmental papers.
1961, 1967 and 1968 figures are taken from the appropriate volumes of *Statistics of Education* for those years.

List 69 and List 71 are selected local authority statistics on education published from 1956 as departmental publications.

15 to 18 – Report of the Central Advisory Council for Education (England) 1959 (Chairman: Sir Geoffrey Crowther).

Half Our Future – Report of the Central Advisory Council for Education (England) 1963 (Chairman: John Newsom).

For a convenient selection of earlier official documents see J. Stuart Maclure, *Educational Documents: England and Wales 1816–1963* (Chapman & Hall 1965).

Higher Education, Appendix 1 (Cmnd 2154–1) and Appendix 2 (B) (Cmnd 2154 11–1) of the Report of the Committee on Higher Education, 1963 (Chairman: Lord Robbins).

Children and their Primary Schools: A report of the Central Advisory Council for Education (England), 2 vols, 1966 (Chairman: Lady Plowden).

Public Schools Commission First Report 1968 (Chairman: Sir John Newsom).

Public Schools Commission Second Report 1970 (Chairman: Professor D. V. Donnison).

Other sources
O. Banks, *Party and Prestige in English Secondary Education* (Routledge 1955).
O. Banks, *The Sociology of Education* (Batsford 1968).

Institute of Municipal Treasurers and Accountants, *Education Statistics*,
   published annually since 1948.
G. Kalton, *The Public Schools*, 2nd ed. (Longmans 1967).
R. K. Kelsall, *Report on an Enquiry into Applications for Admissions to Uni-
   versities 1955–6*, Committee of Vice-Chancellors and Principals of the
   Universities of the United Kingdom, 1957.
A. Little and J. Westergaard, 'Trend of Class Differentials in Educa-
   tional Opportunity in England and Wales' in *Brit. J. Sociol.*, Decem-
   ber 1964.
D. C. Marsh, *The Changing Social Structure of England and Wales 1871–
   1951* (Routledge 1968).
J. Vaizey and J. Sheehan, *Resources for Education* (Allen & Unwin 1968).

For basic data on numbers in school, their ages and the types of school
we have used only the primary sources – the annual statistics published
by the government department responsible for education. However
these are somewhat unsatisfactory for the beginning of our period,
because at that time the idea of financial accountability was dominant
in the collection of government statistics so that only government
financed services were included. The idea that planners and others
need to have information about all types of education has developed
during the period along with the growth in the amount and variety of
educational services so that the scope of the statistics has also increased.

As can be seen from the notes to Table 6.1, in 1901 only numbers in
public elementary schools were counted. By 1911, children in grant-
aided secondary schools and 'recognised efficient' independent schools
were also counted along with all those in maintained schools. However
it was not until 1961 that children in 'other independent' schools were
included so that all children in school were covered by the government
statistics. Trends in the use of private education must be derived from
estimates made in 1921 and 1933 and the later figures.

A minor though difficult problem is that, up to the reorganisation of
education following the 1944 Education Act, figures for grant-aided
secondary schools were given in a less detailed breakdown than those
for public elementary schools, and also in groups which did not correspond to the post-1944 end-on system with the change to secondary
school at 11. No detailed age group breakdowns were given for 'recognised efficient' independent schools before 1951.

There is a lack of data on regional variations in expenditure per pupil
in the Ministry of Education's annual published statistics until the most
recent volumes. However the Institute of Municipal Treasurers and
Accountants has published since 1948 selected statistics including expenditure per pupil for all the county boroughs, and counties with

average expenditure for county boroughs and English and Welsh counties.

Our tables on trends in total educational expenditure and its distribution between the various sections and different items of cost, are taken from the recent book by Vaizey and Sheehan[1] and directly from the education statistics.

The statistics do not give pupil/teacher ratios for the pre-1944 period but we have calculated them from the number of teachers and number of pupils given. Similarly we have calculated the percentage of certificated and uncertificated teachers. Again there is a lack of published information on regional variation until the most recent years.

Information about the number of pupils staying on beyond the statutory school leaving age and the proportion of leavers going on to further education is scanty for the pre-1944 period. The government gives leaving age figures only for those leaving grant-aided secondary schools. Olive Banks[2] gives some figures for the proportion going on to further education from the same schools and also some indication of regional variation in 1925-6. The post-1944 statistics however progressively cover more different schools, though the 1967 statistics still do not include those leaving from 'other independent schools'. Again only the post-war statistics give information of the proportion of children receiving government and local authority financed selective education together with an indication of the regional variation.

The government statistical publications do not include information on class differences in chances of receiving selective education and differential class achievement except for the supplement to the Statistics of Education 1961, which we have used for Tables 6.24 and 6.27. Most of our information is based on surveys undertaken both for private academic research and for government committees. The article by Little and Westergaard[3] summarises the results of several surveys. The social mobility survey reported by Jean Floud (see Notes to Tables 6.21 and 6.22) asked a national sample of people in 1949 about their past educational experience so that the experience of different age cohorts could be compared. The other surveys were concerned with the experience of particular age groups at particular times or with comparatively recent retrospective information. Little and Westergarad discuss the validity of putting together the results of several different studies with slightly differing bases and definitions and conclude that the broad picture is coherent.

Our most recent information representative of a whole age group comes from the survey undertaken for the Robbins Committee in 1960-1961, so that any possible changes in the proportions of the social classes

[1] *Op. cit.*   [2] *Op. cit.*   [3] *Loc. cit.*

in higher education resulting from its recent expansion are not yet clearly documented.

Five basic questions may be asked of the statistics set forth in this chapter:

How many children are there in what kind of schools?
What resources of money, teachers etc. have been spent on them?
What are children's educational attainments?
When did the children leave and for what destinations?
What is the relation between social origin and educational or occupational destination?

Children and Schools

The number of children of school age in Britain has grown throughout the century.[1] Compulsory schooling is from age 5. A typical school at the beginning of the century was a public elementary all-age school recruiting pupils at 5 or under and keeping them to the statutory leaving age. As may be seen from Table 6.1, which shows the percentage enrolment of various age groups, full-time attendance often stopped at 12 when children were permitted to work half-time. But the statutory age was raised generally to 14 in 1921 and to 15 in 1947. Table 6.1 is not based on a complete enumeration.[2] It clearly shows, however, a rising proportionate enrolment among children in the pre-school years and, more dramatically, among those aged 15 to 18.

The 1902 Education Act inaugurated a national system of secondary schools though, at that time, this was conceived as an education for the minority. Secondary schools were linked to the universities rather than to 'elementary' or primary schools. After 1902 the endowed grammar schools of earlier foundation received grants of public money and many new maintained secondary schools were built. Children entered these schools at age 7 or 8 and usually stayed till age 15 or over. Fees were charged. Thus in the early years of the century the elementary and secondary systems were parallel rather than integrated. An important link was established in 1907 when grants to secondary schools were made dependent on the establishment of 25 per cent of free places for pupils recruited from public elementary schools. This is the origin of the 'scholarship' or '11-plus' examination. Higher grade schools had been set up by some of the School Boards established under the 1870 Education Act, thus putting secondary education 'end-on' to primary education. The emphasis in these schools was on science and technology or crafts. Under the 1902 Act, counties and county boroughs became the responsible educational authorities instead of the School Boards with

[1] See Table 2.4.   [2] See Notes to Table 6.1.

some lower-level authorities retaining responsibility for elementary schools (these are the 'Part III' authorities, the reference being to the part of the Act which made provision for them). After 1902 the higher grade schools, in the main, did not survive but were assimilated into secondary education.

Two basic divisions have to be made between types of school: public and private, and elementary and secondary. The division between public and private is not simple. Administratively it is the distinction between maintained and independent schools. But the direct grant grammar schools are a hybrid, relying partly on private funds and fee-paying and partly on direct grants from the central government. Within the independent sector there is a wide range of schools including the famous so-called 'Public Schools'[1] and a wider group of independent schools recognised as efficient by the state.

Table 6.2 shows the gradual increase of public and the decline of private provision in the twentieth century. The following quotation from the Plowden Report summarises the position with regard to the definition of types of school and the trends in numbers of children attending private schools:

> The Department of Education have shown an interest in independent education since the beginning of the century, although before the 1944 Act the Department's powers were minimal; and proprietors of a school not in receipt of grant were simply required to supply a brief description of the school in a prescribed form. Under Part III of the 1944 Act – which was not brought into force until 1957 – all independent schools must be registered. In the first instance, provisional registration was accorded to all existing independent schools: this still happens when a new school is opened. A visit of inspection follows provisional registration and if HMI is satisfied, registration is made substantive; if not, he reports to that effect to the Secretary of State, who may either allow a longer period of provisional registration in order that the school may improve or he may issue a Notice of Complaint on one of four grounds:
>
> 1. Unsuitability of the premises.
> 2. Deficiencies of accommodation, having regard to the number, ages and sex of the children.
> 3. Deficiencies of the instruction.
> 4. Unsuitability of the head teacher or staff to be in charge of children.

[1] There is no clear definition of a Public School in this sense. The status involves membership of the Headmasters' Conference, the Governing Bodies Association or the Governing Bodies of Girls Schools Association – a club which is self-perpetuating.

The Secretary of State can, subject to the opportunity of an appeal to a Tribunal, close the school if his requirements are not met.

In addition to registration a school may also seek to be 'recognised as efficient'. Recognition, which has existed since 1906, is granted only after full inspection by HMI. Recognised schools are automatically deemed to be registered. Their higher status makes it easier for them to recruit staff, particularly as they are entitled, unlike the staff of other independent schools, to belong to the national superannuation scheme. Recognised schools which fall below the high standard required may lose recognition, or their recognition may be made provisional for a stated period. The Incorporated Association of Preparatory Schools makes possession of recognition a condition of membership. A list of recognised schools (List 70) is published by the Department. In January 1965 it showed that of the total of 2762 independent primary and primary and secondary schools in England 1188 were recognised or provisionally recognised as efficient.

The number of independent schools has decreased progressively over the years. In 1861 the Newcastle Commission estimated that there were 860,000 pupils (of the whole school age range including secondary) in 'private venture' schools. In 1931 it was estimated that there were approximately 10,000 private schools containing 400,000 pupils. In January 1965 there were 256,000 children under the age of 12 (about five per cent. of the whole primary age group) in 2762 primary and primary and secondary independent schools in England.[1]

Table 6.2 shows that by 1968 there were 302,000 children in independent 'recognised' schools, 128,000 in other independent schools and 129,000 in direct grant schools. All three categories together made up 6·9 per cent of the total population of school children but 15·3 per cent of those staying beyond the statutory leaving age. The total proportion of pupils in independent schools is small and declining. In 1947 it was 9 per cent, in 1957 7 per cent and in 1967 5·5 per cent. But as more private schools have received recognition as efficient the proportion attending these schools, which include the 'public' schools, has risen from 2·9 per cent in 1947 to 3·9 per cent in 1967.[2]

Within the state sector the school system is historically a fusion of religious and secular foundations.[3] Table 6.3 shows the declining

[1] *Children and their Primary Schools*. A report of the Central Advisory Council for Education (England), vol. 1 (HMSO 1966) pp. 380-1.

[2] Further information on the public and direct grant schools may be found in the first and second reports of the Public Schools Commission (HMSO 1968 and 1970).

[3] See M. Cruikshank, *Church and State in English Education* (Macmillan 1963).

importance of the denominational schools over the course of the century and Table 6.4 shows the status of voluntary schools (aided, controlled or special agreement) in 1960 and 1968.

The main division of schools at the beginning of the century was between elementary and secondary. Reform has been in the direction of replacing this distinction by a division between primary and secondary schools. After 1907 there was a gradual increase in the secondary proportion of 12 to 14 year olds (from 7·5 per cent in 1911 to 20·6 per cent in 1938). Then the 1944 Act abolished the elementary schools and made state secondary schools end-on to primary schools. Hence the figures for 1951 look very different. Only 20·5 per cent of the 11 to 14 year old group remained in LEA primary all-age and special schools with 18·8 per cent in LEA grammar and technical and 53·9 per cent in secondary modern and comprehensive schools. The remainder were in direct grant (2·4 per cent) and independent schools recognised as efficient (4·4 per cent). By 1968 the process was nearly complete – only 8·8 per cent of 11 to 14 year olds were in primary all-age and special schools with 67·3 per cent in moderns and comprehensives and a reduced proportion in grammar and technical schools (16·1 per cent).

Thus for those aged 11 the secondary replaced the primary school. But there are divisions within secondary education. Some secondary schools are selective. A table showing the proportion of 13-year-olds in such selective schools is included as Table 6.5. The proportion rises from 1911 (4·7 per cent) to 1951 (22·6 per cent). The figures for 1961 and 1968 show a trend in the opposite direction with the rise of the comprehensive school.

EXPENDITURE AND RESOURCES

Allocation of resources is the responsibility of local education authorities, but throughout the century there has been a trend towards increasing centralisation of policy-making and administration. Under the Education Act of 1918 the responsibility for developing a national system of public education was placed on the local authorities, and it was not until the 1944 Act that this duty was formally transferred to the Minister of Education acting through local education authorities. From the passing of the 1918 Act, specific percentage grants were made by the Board of Education in respect of approved expenditure by education authorities and in this way financial support was given automatically to local initiative which fell within the provisions of the Act and the grant regulations. This left the way open to a good deal of regional and local variations in educational development and expenditure which is illustrated in Table 6.6 for 1967–8.

Since 1920 there has been a marked growth of monetary and of real expenditure on education. Table 6.7 summarises this trend. A comparison of the indices in columns (ii) and (iv) shows that real expenditure has not risen as fast as monetary expenditure, i.e. that prices of goods and services used in education have in general risen. This has especially been the case in the post-second world war years, i.e. from 1948 to 1965, when with expenditure in 1948 at 100, the index of money expenditure was in 1965 at 518, while that of real expenditure was only 210. Thus in this period, more than half the increase in expenditure on education was swallowed up by rising prices. This is important to note, and it has a bearing on the presentation of much of the subsequent analysis. Purely monetary statistics of expenditure of unit costs are in these circumstances almost meaningless.

The overall growth in expenditure was accompanied by large structural changes. These were partly a direct result of legislation and of the changing financial and organisational framework of public education in the present century. For instance, the advent of 'free'[1] secondary education stemming from the Acts of 1907 and 1944 undoubtedly was an important reason for the increasing weight of secondary schools in the total (as was the movement of elementary school pupils aged about 11 into secondary schools). But the long-term and pervasive nature of some of the trends in Table 6.8 (which covers England and Wales) suggests that deeper social forces were at work. Educational change would appear to be self-sustaining: as more achieve certain levels of education they transmit awareness of the value of education to their contemporaries and to their children. Also, the development of the economy and the increasing demand for more specialised and more complex skills have made the demand for education all the greater. Thus between 1940 and 1967 there has been a steady rise in the shares of secondary, and further and adult, education in total spending. The rise in the university share occurs for the entire 1920–67 period, as does the very substantial fall in the share of primary education (from 57·4 per cent of total current expenditure in 1920 to 27·5 per cent in 1967). Of course, diminishing *shares* of total expenditure were generally accompanied by increases in the *absolute* magnitude of real expenditure, as the overall growth in the provision of educational resources was so large.

Of greatest interest are the sectors of the educational system which provide compulsory education for a large majority of the school-age population, and for an increasing proportion of voluntary enrolment in each age-group beyond the school-leaving age. These are the maintained primary and secondary schools.

[1] i.e. free of direct costs to parents or pupils. Education from a social or economic point of view is hardly ever a free good in the proper sense of the term.

In the inter-war years, public expenditure on maintained primary[1] schools rose by 40·1 per cent in money terms, from £28·7 million in 1920 to £40·2 million in 1938. In real terms the rise was 51·9 per cent over the same period,[1] i.e. prices fell, so real expenditure increased somewhat faster than monetary expenditure. During this period enrolments decreased by about 15 per cent,[2] so the gain in per pupil expenditure was considerable – almost certainly 65 per cent in the 1920–38 period. In maintained secondary schools these trends were even more pronounced: real expenditure per pupil almost certainly doubled. These trends all occurred with rates of increase in monetary expenditure which, by post-war standards, were very modest. They were due to two favourable factors, conspicuously absent from the post-war scene: (i) static or declining enrolments; and (ii) a static or falling price level.

Much more detail is available for the post-war years, and especially for the 1955–67 period. Unlike the pre-war years enrolments increased rapidly, and the general price level rose continuously throughout the period. Table 6.9 shows current annual expenditure per pupil in maintained primary schools. Total current expenditure on maintained primary schools rose from £134 million in 1955 to over £350 million in 1967 (including indirect expenditures such as on administration).

The constant-price figures given in Table 6.9 have been obtained by deflating each item of expenditure by an appropriate price index. Thus if the various categories of expenditure correspond to inputs into the educational process, the constant price figures give a time-series of *real inputs* into education. It is not the absolute values which are of interest, but their trend over time. When the major item of expenditure – teachers' salaries – is compared with non-teacher items and with total expenditure, some significant trends are apparent. In money terms, as the first half of the table shows, teacher items rose more or less in line with total spending (i.e. an increase of 7·4 per cent per annum compared to 7·8 per cent, between 1955 and 1967). But in *real* terms, as the second half of the table shows, expenditure on teachers' salaries rose by only 0·87 per cent per annum compared to 4·3 per cent for non-teacher items and 2·1 per cent for the total.

While non-teacher monetary expenditure grew at a fairly similar rate to teacher monetary expenditure, the real rates of growth, or rather the rates of growth of real expenditure diverged widely. This of course implies a divergence in price trends of the various inputs. On the whole the unit price of teachers rose faster than that of the other (largely goods

[1] Vaizey and Sheehan, *op. cit.*, Table XII, Appendix B.

[2] *Ibid.*, Table XXXIII. The figures for enrolments refer to all *aided* primary schools, but maintained schools were by far the largest group of these and would have followed fairly similar trends.

and services) items. This trend is also found for secondary education, as is shown in Table 6.10.

In the secondary schools also, money expenditure increased more rapidly than real expenditure, and the major components of money expenditure increased fairly uniformly: by 8·43 per cent per annum for teachers and by 8·08 per cent for all other items. The real expenditure items showed wide divergence in their rates of growth, as in the case of primary schools: 0·93 per cent and 3·92 per cent per annum respectively for the teacher and other items. The implications for unit price trends are similar to those for primary schools.

These trends can be discerned for the entire 1944–68 period, no matter what year is used as a base.[1] However, they are not so obvious for the pre-war period. Their significance is that they provide one important reason for the growth of educational expenditure and for the expectation of further growth. On a broader scale they point to a reason for the growth of public expenditure as a whole.

The reason is the labour-intensive nature of the educational process. This can be measured by the high proportion which teachers' salaries bears to total current expenditure (between 60 per cent and 70 per cent – or even more if one adds non-teachers' salaries). It happens that the prices of non-personnel current expenditure items rose at more or less the same rate in the post-war period as prices of goods and services generally. Wages and salaries rose in terms of goods and services in the post-war period, i.e. real income per head rose steadily. Thus if teachers' incomes correspond to other incomes, if non-personnel items (goods and services) used in education follow price trends which are in general similar to overall price movements and if income per head rises, then two things follow:

(i) prices of personnel (i.e. teacher) inputs rise relatively to other inputs;
(ii) the more labour-intensive the industry, the greater the impact of rising income, or the price of labour, on overall costs.

One thing which could offset this is sufficiently rapid technical change. However, it does not seem, from casual observation, that significant cost-reducing innovations have been incorporated into education,[2] in the same sense that they have been in much of manufacturing industry.

[1] Vaizey (*Costs of Education*) shows that similar trends in real and monetary expenditure occurred in the 1948–55 period.

[2] The use of television for teaching, or other innovations, may be cost-reducing in the long run. However, they have not yet had any significant impact on overall trends.

The labour-intensive nature of education, and the absence of significant cost-reducing technical change would appear to lead to fairly large increases in unit costs over time, given the general economic trends and the assumptions which we have noted above. It happens that much current government expenditure is, like education, labour-intensive. Also, it can be argued that, again like education, technical change has not been very significant in reducing costs. This may be an important reason for the increasing share of government expenditure in national income in many countries, i.e. not so much that the demand for these services has increased, or that political pressures influenced trends, but that the relative price of some government services increased (as in the case of education), thus contributing to an increased level of expenditure in monetary terms.

Pupil/teacher ratios by type of school are given in Table 6.11 and class sizes in Table 6.12. Note the slow and steady amelioration in public elementary schools between 1901 and 1938. But this of course disguises variations between particular schools. Note also the better teacher/pupil ratios in secondary schools and especially those in the private sector.

Quality and turnover of teachers is also important. We seem to have no statistics on class of degree among graduate teachers. The trend of formal qualifications is shown in Table 6.13. There was a steady rise in certification among teachers in public elementary schools up to 1938 and a slowly rising proportion of graduate teachers in grant-aided secondary schools.

Table 6.14 shows for 1967 the regional variations in the percentage of graduate teachers in different types of school. Note the relatively poor conditions in the North and relatively good conditions in London and the South-East.

SOCIAL CLASS, LENGTH OF SCHOOLING AND EDUCATIONAL ATTAINMENT

Leaving age varies with the type of school attended (Table 6.15). Figures for the inter-war period show the growing tendency for both boys and girls to stay in the grant-aided secondary schools until they were at least 16. After the war, when secondary education of some kind became universally available, the variation in leaving age between different types of school becomes clear. Direct grant and independent schools have the highest proportion staying on until 18 or more, followed by the grammar schools, though the difference between the different types of institution has lessened since the war while the leaving age for all children has risen. In 1951 a fifth of boys in grammar schools left before they were 16, but only 6.3 per cent did so in 1967. The proportion who stayed on until they were 18 or over rose during the same period from a fifth to a half. Table 6.16 shows the regional variations in leaving age, children tending to stay longer at school in the South and in Wales. Associated with this is the fact that a substantially higher proportion of children in Wales than in England have in the past been to grammar schools (Table 6.17) though the figures for 1968 show a marked shift to comprehensive schools which absorbed many of the grammar schools of the earlier period.

Table 6.18 shows the proportion of children from secondary schools going on to further full-time education at different dates during the first half of the century. The proportion remained fairly constant, with a consistently higher percentage of girls than of boys proceeding to some kind of further education. Some regional variations for 1925–6 are shown in Table 6.19. After the war the proportion going on from the grammar schools increased (Table 6.20) though the differential between boys and girls remained, as did that between England and Wales.

The association between educational attainment and social class is well established. A higher proportion of children from the professional and managerial classes have a grammar school and university education than of children from the manual worker classes, and the difference is most marked at the extremes. Comparing children of different generations, it may be seen that substantially more of those born in the later 1930s than of those born before 1910 had a grammar school education, though the differential chances of the different social classes remained much the same (Table 6.21). A more detailed analysis of the group of children born in the late nineteen-thirties shows the proportion of children from different social classes in grammar schools at different ages and illustrates class differences well (Table 6.22). Over 40 per cent of children from professional and managerial families were still in grammar schools when they were 17 compared with 10 per cent. of all children and 1½ per cent only of those from unskilled worker backgrounds.

Looking at it the other way round, and considering all children leaving school at 17 in 1960–1, the proportion with at least two A-level passes – the minimum requirement for university entry – diminishes with social class and is smaller among girls than among boys for all classes (Table 6.23). If the qualifications of school leavers are analysed by both parental occupation and type of school attended, the relation between social background and achievement may be seen in more detail, and it also becomes clear that the direct grant and independent schools have a very much better record than the maintained schools (Table 6.24). An examination of the social composition of boys in public schools shows the non-manual classes to be heavily over-represented while the manual classes are barely represented at all

(Table 6.25). Furthermore, children in public schools do significantly better in their O- and A-level exams than children in maintained grammar schools, while the proportion awarded a university place is three times as great among the public schools pupils. Perhaps most striking is the success of these schools with children who had failed their 11 + exams (Table 6.26). Only 8 per cent of such children failed to gain any O-levels compared with 92 per cent in maintained secondary modern schools. 35 per cent obtained one or more A-level passes and 15 per cent were awarded a university place, but no children from the secondary modern schools achieved either of these distinctions. Class background may also be seen at work among children in maintained grammar schools (Table 6.27). Those from social classes I and II have a much better chance of gaining at least two O-levels even after poor 11 + results than children from the manual classes.

Similar influences govern the chances of entry to universities. Although a higher proportion of children from all social backgrounds now have a university education, the chances of those from unskilled backgrounds as compared with those from the professional classes have actually worsened (Table 6.28). It is the middle classes who have most effectively used the growing opportunities to gain university places. Table 6.29 indicates the correlation of social background with educational attainment for children of similar measured intelligence. Of the most intelligent children – those with an I.Q. of over 130 – twice as many from the non-manual as from the manual classes took a university degree. For the less clever children the differences were even more pronounced.

It is possible to look at the situation the other way round. In Table 6.30 the social background of university entrants in 1955–6 is compared with that of the adult male population. All the non-manual groups – particularly class I – are over-represented among university entrants, and all the manual classes – particularly class V – are under-represented. The percentage of undergraduates drawn from the manual classes has barely changed since the nineteen-thirties (Table 6.31). What change there is is due to a higher proportion of women coming from this kind of background. The proportion among male undergraduates actually fell slightly in 1961.

TABLE 6.1

Children in all Listed(a) Schools as a Proportion of the Total Population in Certain Age Groups, 1901–1968, England and Wales (percentages)

Year	Age 2–4 incl.		Age 5–11 incl.	Age 12–14 incl.	Age 15–18 incl.	Age 2–18 incl.
1901	2·8		89·3	41·5	0·3	49·6
1911		67·2		57·5	1·5	51·0
1921		67·3		65·8	3·2	52·4(b)
1931	8·8		91·7	73·0	6·0	54·1(b)
1938	10·0		92·4	74·5	6·6	53·7

	2–4 incl.		5–10 incl.	11–14 incl.	15–18 incl.	2–18 incl.
1951	7·7		97·2	93·1	12·5	58·3
1961	10·8		99·9	99·9	19·6	66·0(c)
1968	10·7		99·3	101·1(d)	30·0	66·4(c)

Notes:
(a) 'Listed schools': 1901 public elementary schools; 1911, 1921, 1931, 1938 public elementary schools, grant-aided secondary schools, and 'recognised efficient' independent schools; 1951 L.E.A. maintained schools, Direct Grant and 'recognised schools'; 1961 and 1968 the same schools as in 1951 with the addition of 'other independent schools'.
(b) Not including estimated numbers in independent schools in 1921 and 1932.
(c) A small number of 19-year-olds are shown in the *Statistics of Education* and not included here.
(d) Rather more children recorded on school registers than given in the Registrar General's mid-year estimates.
Sources: 1901 and 1911 figures from *Statistics of Public Education* 1900–1, and 1910–11; 1921, 1931, 1938, and 1951 figures from *Education in* (given year), Annual Reports and Statistics of Education of the Board (Ministry) of Education. 1961 and 1968 from *Statistics of Education*, pt 1, 1961, and *Statistics of Education*, vol. 1, 1968.

TABLE 6.2

Numbers and Proportions of Children in different types(a) of Schools in Certain Age Groups, 1901–1968, England and Wales
(Numbers in thousands)

	Age 2–4		Age 5–11		Age 12–14		Age 15–18		Age 2–18	
	no.	%	no.	%	no.	%	no.	%	no.	%
1901										
Public elementary and special	618		4316		836		8		5778	
1911										
Public elementary and special	351	100	4613	99·2	1096	92·5	7	17·4	6067	97·4
Grant-aided secondary	neg	n.a.	38	0·8	89	7·5	33	82·6	161	2·6
Total	351	n.a.	4651	100	1185	100	40	100	6228	100
1921										
Public elementary	177	100	4421	99·2	1258	87·2	8	8·8	5865	94·2
Grant-aided secondary	neg	—	94	0·8	186	12·9	82	91·2	362	5·8
Total	177	—	4515	100	1444	100	90	100	6227	100
1931(b)										
Public elementary	159	100	4382	98·3	1024	83·9	29	17·6	5594	93·2
Grant-aided secondary	neg	—	75	1·7	200	16·1	136	82·4	411	6·8
Total	159	—	4457	100	1224	100	165	100	6005	100
1938(b)										
Public elementary and special	166	100	3734	98·0	1190	79·4	33	18·5	5123	91·6
Grant-aided secondary	neg	—	76	2·0	248	20·6	145	81·5	470	8·4
Total	166	—	3810	100	1438	100	178	100	5593	100

Notes:

(a) Detailed age-group breakdowns are not given for 'Independent Recognised' schools before 1951. No figures are given in the *Statistics of Education* for other independent schools before 1961 except for the 1921 estimated figures.

(b) In 1931 and 1938 the number of children in age groups 2–4 and 15–18 were estimated by dividing the age groups given in the statistics into equal years.

Table 6.2 continued

	Age 2–4		Age 5–10		Age 11–14		Age 15–18		Age 2–18	
1951										
LEA primary, all-age and special	177	97·4	3454	97·2	431	20·5	4	1·5	4067	66·5
LEA grammar and technical	neg	—	2	—	396	18·8	176	63·7	574	9·4
LEA modern comprehensive & other secondary	—	—	3	—	1132	53·9	24	8·6	1159	19·0
Direct grant	2	0·8	19	0·5	51	2·4	24	8·8	96	1·5
Independent 'recognised'	3	1·8	77	2·2	92	4·4	48	17·4	220	3·6
Total	182	100	3555	100	2102	100	276	100	6115	100
1961										
LEA primary, all-age and special	203	89·4	3683	94·3	320	10·6	5	1·0	4211	55·0
LEA grammar and technical	—	—	—	—	536	17·7	274	54·4	811	10·6
LEA modern comprehensive & other secondary	—	—	—	—	1914	63·4	104	20·7	2018	26·4
Direct grant	1	0·6	20	0·5	63	2·1	38	7·4	122	1·6
Independent 'recognised'	5	2·4	100	2·6	128	4·3	67	13·2	300	3·9
Other independent	17	7·6	102	2·6	59	1·9	16	3·2	195	2·5
Total	226	100	3906	100	3019	100	504	100	7658	100
1968										
LEA primary, all-age and special	244	90·5	4267	95·5	233	8·8	9	1·1	4752	57·9
LEA grammar and technical	—	—	—	neg	426	16·1	291	35·5	718	8·7
LEA modern comprehensive & other secondary	—	—	—	neg	1782	67·3	396	48·1	2178	26·5
Direct grant	1	0·5	19	0·4	63	2·2	45	5·3	129	1·6
Independent 'recognised'	7	2·5	103	2·3	118	4·5	73	8·9	302	3·7
Other independent	18	6·5	76	1·7	25	0·9	9	1·1	128	1·6
Total	269	100	4466	100	2647	100	823	100	8205	100

Sources: 1901 and 1911 figures from *Statistics of Public Education* 1900–1, and 1910–11; 1921, 1931, 1938 and 1951 figures from *Education in* (given year), Annual Reports and Statistics of Education of the Board (Ministry) of Education. 1961 and 1968 from *Statistics of Education*, pt 1, 1961, and *Statistics of Education*, vol. 1, 1968.

TABLE 6.3

**Type of school – County(a) and Voluntary(b) 1900–1968
England and Wales (percentages)**

	1900	1930	1938	1950	1960	1968
Primary and all age(c) schools or departments(d)						
County	34·4	52·6	55·8	54·8	59·5	62·5
Church of England	52·7	39·7	36·4	37·0	32·3	28·4
Roman Catholic	5·7	6·1	6·5	7·1	7·4	8·3
Other	7·2	1·6	1·2	1·1	0·8	0·7
All primary schools or departments	100·0	100·0	100·0	100·0	100·0	100·0
	(31,313)	(30,429)	(29,224)	(23,133)	(23,488)	(22,932)
Secondary(e) schools or departments(d)						
County	—	51·8	55·3	83·8	85·3	82·2
Church of England	—	—	—	5·6	4·3	3·9
Roman Catholic	—	6·4	6·6	3·9	5·8	9·5
Others	—	41·9	38·1	6·6	4·5	4·3
All secondary	—	100·0	100·0	100·0	100·0	100·0
		(1354)	(1398)	(4765)	(5801)	(5576)

Notes:
(a) Buildings provided and schools wholly maintained by the local education authority. County schools were previously known as council or board schools.
(b) Schools maintained by the local education authority but buildings provided by a voluntary organisation. For details see p. 148.
(c) In 1900, 1930 and 1938 public elementary schools and, subsequently, maintained primary schools.
(d) Departments with a separate head teacher.
(e) In 1930 and 1938 secondary schools on the grant list, subsequently maintained secondary schools.
Source: Statistics of Education.

TABLE 6.4

Status of Voluntary Schools, 1960–1968, England and Wales (maintained only)

| | *1960* | | *1968* | |
	Primary and all-age schools and departments	*Secondary schools and departments*	*Primary and all-age schools and departments*	*Secondary schools and departments*
Church of England				
aided	3174	139	2709	115
controlled	4393	83	3811	73
special agreement				
and not determined	18	27	2	31
Roman Catholic				
aided	1725	254	1907	408
controlled	1	1	1	—
special agreement	1	90	1	121
Others				
aided	57	93	44	86
controlled	139	165	121	155
special agreement	—	1	—	1
All voluntary schools				
aided	4956	486	4660	609
controlled	4533	249	3933	228
special agreement				
and not determined	19	118	3	153
Total	9508	853	8596	990

Note: See p. 148 for definition of voluntary schools.
Source: Statistics of Education.

TABLE 6.5

Proportion of all 13-year-olds in Selective Schools 1911–1968 England and Wales (percentages)

	Boys	*Girls*	*Total*
1911	5·5	4·0	4·7
1931	12·8	11·5	12·1
1938	13·8	12·7	13·2
1951	23·4	21·9	22·6
1961	20·8	20·8	20·8
1968	19·6	20·9	20·2

Note: Selective schools are: 1911–38 secondary schools on grant list; 1951–68 grammar, technical and direct grant grammar schools.
Sources: 1901 and 1911 figures from *Statistics of Public Education* 1900–1, and 1910–11; 1921, 1931, 1938, and 1951 figures from *Education in* (given year), Annual Reports and Statistics of Education of the Board (Ministry) of Education. 1961 and 1968 from *Statistics of Education*, pt 1, 1961, and *Statistics of Education*, vol. 1, 1968.

TABLE 6.6

Regional Variations in Net Current and Capital Expenditure on Services other than Meals and Milk, 1967–1968, England and Wales

Region	Total expenditure from revenue (excluding loans) £000's		Expenditure per pupil £s	
	Primary	Secondary	Primary	Secondary
North	28,704	33,617	82·2	157·7
Yorks. & Humberside	38,741	46,443	79·4	153·3
East Midlands	26,848	32,140	79·4	155·3
East Anglia	13,073	14,772	88·9	166·0
Greater London	55,067	76,168	86·4	168·5
Other South East	73,022	90,666	84·2	167·3
South West	28,569	35,248	83·5	160·9
West Midlands	41,752	50,026	81·7	156·8
North West	32,771	63,721	76·1	160·9
Wales	25,441	27,717	89·9	153·1

Source: Statistics of Education, vol. 5, 1968.

TABLE 6.7

Current Net Public Educational Expenditure in the United Kingdom 1920–1965

Year	(i) Expenditure at Current prices (£m.)	(ii) Index (1948 = 100)	(iii) Expenditure at 1948 prices (£m.)	(iv) Index (1948 = 100)	(v) Current exp. as percentage of National Income
1920	65·1	30	100·2	47	1·2
1925	84·1	39	141·3	66	2·1
1930	92·8	43	152·9	71	2·3
1935	92·7	43	158·4	74	2·4
1940	107·5	50	154·9	72	2·0
1945	143·9	67	144·6	67	1·7
1948	215·3	100	215·3	100	2·5
1950	272·0	126	263·0	122	2·7
1955	410·6	191	300·0	141	2·8
1965	1114·9	518	451·4	210	4·1

Notes: The National Income measurement used is Net National Product at Factor Cost. The current educational expenditures relate to all publicly provided educational services (including Further and Higher Education) by the Central Government and Local Education Authorities. In accordance with national accounting procedures, transfer items, such as aid to students and superannuation, are excluded. These exclusions (and the exclusion of capital spending) make the figures lower than those sometimes quoted, e.g. in estimates of public expenditure for budgetary purposes.

Source: J. Vaizey and J. Sheehan, Resources for Education (London 1968), Tables VIII and X.

TABLE 6.8

**Composition of Public Education Expenditures by Sector,
England and Wales 1920–1967 (percentages)**

	1920	1930	1940	1950	1955	1965	1967
Primary	57·4	56·4	54·8	37·3	38·9	28·1	27·5
Secondary	20·0	19·4	19·1	27·4	28·3	32·2	31·7
Teacher training	0·9	0·8	0·6	2·0	1·7	3·4	3·9
Further and Adult	5·0	4·9	4·9	7·5	7·9	12·2	12·5
Universities	5·2	5·9	6·7	8·0	8·2	9·9	10·5
Special Schools	2·3	2·5	2·7	1·5	1·9	2·0	2·0
Meals	0·4	0·5	1·1	7·2	6·2	5·9	6·0
Health Service	1·8	2·8	3·4	3·5	2·1	1·8	1·7
Administration and Inspection	7·1	7·0	6·8	5·7	4·9	4·5	4·4
TOTAL	100·0	100·0	100·0	100·0	100·0	100·0	100·0

Sources: 1920–1965: J. Vaizey and J. Sheehan, *op. cit.*
    1967: *Statistics of Education*, vol. 5, 1967.

TABLE 6.9

**Current Annual Expenditure per Pupil in Maintained Primary Schools,
England and Wales 1955–1967 (£s)**

Year	(i) Administration	(ii) Teachers' salaries	(iii) Non-teachers' salaries	(iv) Teaching, materials, Books, classroom supplies etc.	(v) Heating, lighting, cleaning, maintenance	(vi) Other	(vii) Total
AT CURRENT PRICES							
1955	1·29	21·25	0·39	0·99	6·12	0·39	30·44
1960	2·30	31·05	2·38	1·57	8·87	0·61	46·78
1965	3·73	42·50	4·95	1·86	8·85	0·84	62·72
1967	4·18	50·01	5·95	2·69	10·66	1·22	74·71
AT CONSTANT (1955) PRICES							
1955	1·29	21·25	0·39	0·99	6·12	0·39	30·44
1960	1·78	22·64	1·84	1·32	7·44	0·51	35·53
1965	2·22	23·24	2·95	1·34	6·38	0·61	36·74
1967	2·25	23·62	3·20	1·81	7·16	0·82	38·86

Sources: Statistics of Education, 1965 and 1967.
    J. Vaizey and J. Sheehan *op. cit.*
    D.E.S, and Ministry of Education Reports 1955, 1960, 1965 and 1967.

TABLE 6.10

Current Annual Expenditure per Pupil in Maintained Secondary Schools England and Wales 1955–1967 (£s)

Year	(i) Administration	(ii) Teachers' salaries	(iii) Non-teachers' salaries	(iv) Teaching, materials, books, classroom supplies etc.	(v) Heating, lighting, cleaning, maintenance	(vi) Other	(viii) Total
AT CURRENT PRICES							
1955	3·13	33·24	0·75	3·46	9·59	2·89	53·08
1960	4·40	47·29	4·05	4·78	11·03	2·65	74·19
1965	6·28	72·75	7·91	7·61	15·66	3·51	113·71
1967	7·77	87·77	9·94	9·15	19·58	3·92	138·14
AT CONSTANT (1955) PRICES							
1955	3·13	33·24	0·75	3·46	9·59	2·89	53·08
1960	3·39	32·59	3·13	4·01	9·25	2·22	54·59
1965	3·74	36·06	4·71	5·49	11·29	2·53	63·82
1967	4·18	37·13	5·34	6·15	13·15	2·64	68·59

Source: As in Table 6.9.

TABLE 6.11

Pupil to Teacher Ratios by Type of School 1901–1968 England and Wales

	Public Elementary	Grant-aided secondary
1901	48·5	n.a.
1911	37·4	16·0
1921	35·5	16·6
1931	33·1	19·0
1938	30·9	18·8

	All primary	Secondary modern	Grammar	Comprehensive	Total secondary	Direct grant grammar	Independent recognised efficient	Other independent
1951	30·0	22·4	18·1	19·7	20·6	19·0	13·7	—
1961	28·6	21·7	18·3	18·9	20·4	17·8	13·2	18·3(a)
1968	27·9	19·1	16·6	17·9	18·1	16·7	12·8	14·2

Notes: 'Teachers' includes all adult teachers qualified or unqualified but excludes student teachers, pupil teachers and probationer teachers. From 1951–68 part-time teachers are taken into account as two part-time equivalent to one full-time teacher.

(a) Part-time teachers not taken into account.

Source: Statistics on Public Education, 1901, 1911. *Annual Report of Board of Education* 1920–21 and 1930–31. *Education in 1931* and *Statistics of Public Education. Statistics of Education*, pt 1, 1961, *Statistics of Education*, vol. 1, 1968.

TABLE 6.12

**Percentage Distribution of Classes by Size 1910–1968,
England and Wales (percentages)**

	1910	1930	1938	1950	1961	1968
PRIMARY(a)						
Up to 20 pupils	—	9·2	10·0	10·2	10·0	7·5
21–30 ,,	—	20·0	22·0	22·8	27·0	24·3
31–40 ,,	—	30·8	37·3	38·2	48·7	57·4
41–50 ,,	—	33·3	29·2	27·5	14·2	10·7
51 and over	—	6·6	1·4	1·3	0·1	—
41 and over	—	39·9	30·6	28·8	14·3	10·8
SECONDARY(b)						
Up to 15 pupils	34·2	19·0⎫	26·4	4·2	4·2	5·8
16–20 ,,	18·6	13·4⎭		6·7	7·4	10·0
21–25 ,,	19·4	19·9	17·4	13·2	12·8	16·9
26–30 ,,	21·9	26·7	32·6	23·6	23·3	30·9
31–35 ,,	5·8	20·6	23·3	28·1	32·5	28·3
36–40 ,,	⎫	⎫	⎫	17·1	16·7	7·2
41–50 ,,	0·1	0·4	0·3	6·9	2·9	0·8
Over 50 ,,	⎭	⎭	⎭	0·1	0·1	0·1
31 and over	5·9	21·0	23·6	52·2	52·2	36·4

Notes:
(a) Public elementary schools in 1930 and 1938, maintained primary schools in 1950, 1961 and 1968.
(b) Secondary schools on the grant list in 1910, 1930 and 1938, maintained secondary schools in 1950, 1961 and 1968.
Source: Statistics of Education.

TABLE 6.13

Teachers' Qualifications in Different Types of School 1901–1967, England and Wales (percentages of total teachers)

	Public elementary		Grant-aided secondary	
	Certificated	Uncertificated and supplementary	Graduate	Non-graduate
1901	55·7	44·3	—	—
1911	62·7	37·3	57·4	42·6
1921	70·3	29·7	63·5	36·5
1931	74·7	25·3	74·1	25·9
1938	79·2	20·8	78·4	21·6

	Percentage of graduate teachers in different types of school			
	Primary	Modern	Grammar	Direct grant grammar
1951	3·2	14·0	76·8	67·4
1961	3·8	17·3	78·2	70·0
1967	4·4	15·7	73·9	61·3

Note: Based on full-time teachers. 1951 onwards no figures given for unqualified teachers.

Source: Statistics of Public Education 1900–1, 1910–11; *Annual Report of Board of Education* 1920–1. *Statistics of Education,* pt 1, 1961. *Statistics of Education,* vol. 4, 1967.

TABLE 6.14

Distribution of Graduate Teachers by Region and Type of School, 1967 England and Wales (percentages)

	Primary	Modern	Grammar	Comprehensive	Direct grant grammar	Maintained primary and secondary
North	3·1	12·5	73·5	36·9	60·9	17·5
Yorks. and Humberside	4·1	13·9	72·6	37·1	64·9	19·7
East Midlands	3·6	13·2	74·2	37·9	59·7	19·3
East Anglia	3·4	14·7	74·1	40·7	58·4	17·0
Greater London	6·1	19·0	74·6	36·3	56·2	24·3
Other South East	4·7	16·8	75·0	36·8	61·8	20·1
South West	4·0	15·4	73·3	40·0	62·4	20·2
West Midlands	4·2	14·8	72·6	40·1	65·3	19·0
North West	4·4	14·5	71·7	32·5	61·7	18·5
Wales	4·5	24·7	78·5	51·8	59·8	25·2
England and Wales	4·4	15·7	73·9	39·7	61·3	20·3

Note: Based on full-time teachers.
Source: Statistics of Education, vol. 4, 1967.

TABLE 6.15

Proportion of Children Leaving School at different ages by Type of School 1920–1967, England and Wales (percentages)

Date Type of school	14 and under 16		16 and under 18		18 and over		Total	
	Boys	Girls	Boys	Girls	Boys	Girls	Boys	Girls
1920								
grant-aided secondary	55·1	45·9	44·9	54·1	—	—	100	100
1931								
grant-aided secondary	27·7	28·9	58·1	53·8	14·2	17·3	100 (35,299)	100 (32,377)
1938								
grant-aided secondary	25·0	26·9	62·5	59·8	12·6	13·4	100 (43,288)	100 (38,168)
1951								
grammar	20·1	23·8	60·2	60·2	19·7	16·0	100 (45,453)	100 (45,164)
technical	61·1	52·8	38·3	46·4	0·5	0·8	100 (16,215)	100 (8567)
bilateral, multilateral and comprehensive	69·7	68·9	25·7	26·9	4·6	4·3	100 (3599)	100 (3439)
all-age and modern	98·3	98·0	1·7	1·8	neg	0·2	100 (178,188)	100 (175,802)
direct grant	10·4	14·1	60·3	63·4	29·4	22·4	100 (5120)	100 (5536)
1961								
grammar	8·2	12·6	56·4	60·7	35·2	26·7	100 (52,713)	100 (54,505)
technical	27·5	27·3	64·6	65·6	7·9	7·2	100 (11,917)	100 (6857)
bilateral, multilateral and comprehensive	65·6	63·0	29·2	31·5	5·2	5·5	100 (17,062)	100 (16,286)
other maintained secondary(a)	73·7	71·9	24·6	26·6	1·8	1·5	100 (13,890)	100 (15,034)
direct grant	4·4	7·2	46·3	55·2	49·2	37·7	100 (7040)	100 (6751)

Table 6.15 continued

Date	Type of school	14 and under 16		16 and under 18		18 and over		Total	
		Boys	Girls	Boys	Girls	Boys	Girls	Boys	Girls
	independent recognised efficient	5·7	12·8	49·2	68·6	45·1	18·5	100 (14,326)	100 (13,431)
1967	grammar	6·3	7·2	43·7	50·9	50·0	41·9	100 (55,740)	100 (55,480)
	technical	12·8	13·3	59·6	68·1	27·6	18·6	100 (7170)	100 (4890)
	compre-hensive	56·7	56·8	31·7	33·9	11·7	9·6	100 (40,000)	100 (36,730)
	other maintained secondary	58·2	58·0	35·0	37·5	6·8	4·6	100 (19,670)	100 (19,220)
	modern and all-age	75·3	76·2	24·1	23·4	0·5	0·4	100 (160,990)	100 (152,330)
	direct grant	4·9	2·8	38·2	41·4	56·9	55·7	100 (7960)	100 (6890)
	independent recognised efficient	3·7	8·1	43·7	63·4	52·5	28·5	100 (15,270)	100 (13,270)

Note: (a) excluding leavers from secondary modern and all-age schools for which information is not available.

Source: Annual Report of Board of Education 1920. *Annual Report and Statistics of Education,* 1931, 1938, 1951. *Statistics of Education,* pt 2, 1961. *Statistics of Education,* vol. 2, 1967.

TABLE 6.16

Percentage of Pupils Remaining at School until Age 16 and 18 by Region Maintained Schools (excluding Special Schools) only, 1950, 1961, 1965, England and Wales (percentages)

		1950		1961		1965	
		Boys	*Girls*	*Boys*	*Girls*	*Boys*	*Girls*
North	until 16	8·5	9·0	16·0	14·3	23·1	21·7
	until 18	2·0	1·4	4·1	2·7	—	—
Yorkshire and Humberside	until 16	10·9	10·5	20·0	17·0	27·0	25·2
	until 18	2·3	1·3	4·4	3·0	—	—
East Midlands	until 16	10·5	9·5	19·0	16·1	25·3	22·7
	until 18	2·3	1·3	4·5	2·9	—	—
East Anglia	until 16	8·7	8·6	16·4	15·4	24·0	23·4
	until 18	2·1	1·0	4·0	2·4	—	—
South East	until 16	13·9	13·9	27·6	24·2	36·2	34·7
	until 18	2·8	1·6	5·8	3·5	—	—
South West	until 16	12·6	12·1	22·3	19·6	30·5	28·7
	until 18	2·2	1·7	5·2	2·9	—	—
West Midlands	until 16	9·3	9·2	19·3	17·0	26·6	24·5
	until 18	1·9	1·0	4·2	2·8	—	—
North West	until 16	9·8	9·7	19·3	17·0	24·5	24·0
	until 18	2·1	1·3	3·9	2·9	—	—
Wales	until 16	17·4	18·6	26·0	26·3	31·2	34·2
	until 18	5·1	3·1	8·2	5·1	—	—
England and Wales	until 16	11·7	11·7	22·3	19·8	29·6	28·3
	until 18	2·5	1·5	5·1	3·2	—	—

Note: The percentages are calculated by expressing the numbers in schools aged 16 and 18 as percentages of the pupils aged 13 in the schools 3 and 5 years earlier. The percentages are somewhat overstated if there has been a net inward migration, and understated if there has been a net outward migration, to or from the areas shown.

Source: Statistics of Education, vol. 1, 1968.

TABLE 6.17

Proportion of 13-year-old Pupils for whom the LEA was Financially Responsible in Schools and Streams of Various Types 1956, 1961, 1968, England and Wales Regions (percentages)

Area	Primary and all-age			Modern			Grammar (maintained, assisted and d.g.)			Independent (mainly grammar)			Technical		
	Boys	Girls	Total	Boys	Girls	Total	Boys	Girls	Total	Boys	Girls	Total	Boys	Girls	Total
1956(a)															
ENGLAND															
Counties	9.5	9.4	9.4	64.6	64.7	64.7	20.1	21.4	20.7	0.6	0.5	0.6	4.3	2.7	3.5
County Boroughs	9.6	10.5	10.1	64.6	67.7	66.1	17.1	17.3	17.2	0.5	0.1	0.3	7.2	3.7	5.5
Total	9.5	9.7	9.6	64.6	65.7	65.1	19.1	20.0	19.6	0.6	0.4	0.5	5.2	3.0	4.2
WALES															
Counties	7.4	7.1	7.2	54.9	55.8	55.3	30.1	33.8	31.9	neg	neg	neg	4.4	—	2.3
County Boroughs	8.2	9.1	8.6	59.3	58.6	59.0	26.9	29.9	28.4	neg	neg	neg	5.6	2.4	4.0
Total	7.6	7.5	7.5	55.8	56.4	56.1	29.4	33.0	31.2	neg	neg	neg	4.7	0.5	2.6
ENGLAND AND WALES															
Counties	9.3	9.2	9.3	63.9	64.1	64.0	20.8	22.3	21.5	0.6	0.5	0.6	4.3	2.5	3.4
County Boroughs	9.6	10.5	10.0	64.4	67.3	65.9	17.5	17.8	17.7	0.4	0.1	0.3	7.1	3.6	5.4
Total	9.4	9.6	9.5	64.0	65.1	64.5	19.8	20.9	20.3	0.5	0.4	0.5	5.2	2.9	4.1

Note (a): There were also small numbers in comprehensive schools in this year.

Table 6.17 continued

Area	Modern and all-age	Technical	Comprehensive	Other secondary	Grammar	Direct grant	Independent
1961							
ENGLAND							
Counties	67·7	2·3	5·2	5·4	17·8	1·0	0·5
County Boroughs	69·6	4·5	2·6	3·8	15·3	1·9	0·3
Total	67·4	3·0	4·4	5·5	17·0	1·3	0·5
WALES							
Counties	61·3	0·6	12·1	0·4	25·3	0·3	—
County Boroughs	69·5	1·9	3·1	—	25·1	0·2	0·2
Total	63·2	0·9	10·0	0·3	25·3	0·3	0·1
ENGLAND AND WALES							
Counties	67·3	2·2	5·6	5·1	18·3	1·0	0·5
County Boroughs	69·6	4·3	2·7	5·5	15·7	1·9	0·3
Total	68·1	2·9	4·7	5·2	17·5	1·3	0·4
1968							
North	51·2	1·5	17·4	11·0	16·9	1·3	0·7
Yorks. and Humberside	49·3	2·2	23·7	6·4	16·6	1·7	0·2
E. Midlands	49·9	1·2	21·7	8·2	17·8	1·0	0·2
E. Anglia	76·3	0·6	2·9	0·6	18·1	1·0	0·4
Gr. London	36·5	2·4	30·7	11·1	17·6	1·0	0·7

Table 6.17 continued

Area	Modern and all-age	Technical	Comprehensive	Other secondary	Grammar	Direct grant	Independent
Other							
South-East	54·9	2·6	12·6	11·1	17·1	0·8	1·0
South-West	55·2	1·0	22·9	1·3	18·2	0·9	0·5
W. Midlands	59·7	1·8	12·7	7·2	17·4	0·9	0·3
North-West	57·0	1·7	17·4	1·2	17·2	4·6	0·9
Wales	34·1	0·2	43·6	3·4	18·4	0·2	0·1
England and Wales	51·4	1·8	20·4	7·0	17·4	1·5	0·6
ENGLAND							
Counties	59·3	1·2	12·5	6·1	18·8	1·4	0·7
County Boroughs	48·3	2·9	24·3	7·4	14·5	2·2	0·5
Total	52·5	1·9	18·9	7·2	17·3	1·6	0·6
WALES							
Counties	40·7	0·1	33·0	4·4	21·5	0·2	0·1
County Boroughs	12·5	0·5	78·4	0·2	8·1	0·2	—
Total	34·1	0·2	43·6	3·4	18·4	0·2	0·1
ENGLAND AND WALES							
Counties	57·8	1·1	14·2	5·9	19·1	1·3	0·6
County Boroughs	46·6	2·8	26·8	7·0	14·2	2·1	0·5
Total	51·4	1·8	20·4	7·0	17·4	1·5	0·6

Source: List 69: Secondary Education in England and Wales. For 1968, Statistics of Education, vol. 1, 1968.

TABLE 6.18

**Proportion of School Leavers continuing Full-time Further Education
for Selected Years, England and Wales (percentages)**

Year	School	Boys	Girls
1897(a)	Higher grade schools	11·9	33·6
	Grant aided secondary schools	29·0	
1925–6(b)	Grant aided secondary schools	16·2	32·4
1932–3(b)	,,	16·3	28·2
1937–8(c)	,,	15·6	32·8
1946–7(c)	,,	15·0	29·3

Notes:
(a) Figures for this year include leavers of all ages and so include those going to other secondary schools.
(b) Figures refer to leavers over 12 and exclude those going to other secondary schools.
(c) Figures refer to leavers of 14 and exclude those going to other secondary schools.
Source: Olive Banks, *Parity and Prestige in English Secondary Education* (Routledge 1955) pp. 170, 171, 191.

TABLE 6.19

**Proportion of School Leavers(a) continuing Full-time Further Education
in 1924–1925 in Different Districts (percentages)**

Area	Boys	Girls
Leeds secondary schools	12	28
Derbyshire secondary schools	23	39·6
London secondary schools(b)	21	44

Notes:
(a) Includes those leaving to go to other secondary schools.
(b) Figures are for the year 1925–6.
Source: Olive Banks, *op. cit.*, pp. 174, 175, 177.

TABLE 6.20

**Destination of School Leavers, 1952, 1961, 1967, England and Wales
(percentages of Total Leavers in the Academic Years)**

	To attend university, technical college and other further education		To take up employment or other reasons	
	Boys	Girls	Boys	Girls
1952				
LEA grammar schools				
England	17	27	83	73
Wales	23	34	77	66
Direct grant grammar				
England	30	42	70	58
Wales	43	54	57	46
Other LEA secondary				
England	3	3	97	97
Wales	1	5	99	95
All LEA and direct grant schools				
England	4	8	96	92
Wales	8	14	92	86
1961				
LEA grammar and technical				
England	26	34	74	66
Wales	32	38	68	62
Direct grant grammar				
England	47	54	53	46
Wales(a)	64	72	36	29
Independent recognised efficient				
England	50	62	50	38
Wales(a)	21	63	79	37
Other LEA secondary schools				
England	5	7	95	93
Wales	7	13	93	87
All listed schools				
England	12	16	88	84
Wales	14	21	86	80

Table 6.20 continued

	To attend university, technical college and other further education		To take up employment for other reasons(b)	
	Boys	Girls	Boys	Girls
1966-7				
LEA grammar				
England and Wales	47	49	53	51
England	47	46	53	54
Wales	47	52	53	48
Direct grant grammar				
England and Wales	58	66	42	34
England	59	67	41	33
Wales	23	50	77	50
Independent recognised efficient				
England and Wales	53	59	47	41
England	53	55	47	45
Wales	33	54	67	46
Secondary modern and all age				
England and Wales	6	9	94	91
England	6	9	94	91
Wales	11	18	89	82
Comprehensive				
England and Wales	10	12	90	88
England	9	11	91	89
Wales	19	19	81	81
Other maintained secondary				
England and Wales	15	12	85	88
England	15	12	85	88
Wales	16	24	84	76
All listed schools				
England and Wales	19	21	81	79
England	19	21	81	79
Wales	22	28	78	72

Notes:
(a) Small numbers in direct grant and independent schools in Wales.
(b) Including small numbers taking temporary employment before going on to further education.
Source: D. C. Marsh, *op. cit. Statistics of Education*, pt 2, 1961. *Statistics of Education*, vol. 2, 1967.

TABLE 6.21

Proportion in Different Classes obtaining Education of a Grammar School Type, among Children of Different Generations, England and Wales

Sex and father's occupational group		Percent obtaining secondary education in grammar and independent schools			
Pre-war generations (Hall-Jones groups)	Post-war generations (Crowther groups)	Born pre-1910	Born 1910–19	Born 1920–29	Born late-1930s
BOYS					
1–3	Professional/managerial	37	44	54	62
4–5	Other non-manual and skilled manual	7	13	15	20
6–7	Semi- and unskilled	2	4	9	10
All boys		12	16	19	23
GIRLS					
1–3	Professional/managerial	37	50	50	62
4–5	Other non-manual and skilled manual	7	13	16	20
6–7	Semi- and unskilled	1	3	5	10
All girls		11	16	17	23
BOYS AND GIRLS					
1–3	Professional/managerial	37	47	52	62
4–5	Other non-manual and skilled manual	7	13	16	20
6–7	Semi- and unskilled	1	4	7	10
All children		12	16	18	23

Notes: For pre-war generations (born before 1930) Jean Floud, 'The Educational Experience of England and Wales', Chap. V of D. V. Glass, *Social Mobility in Britain* (Routledge 1954).

For post-war generations (born late-1930s) same source as for Table 6.19.

Figures for children born late 30s include only independent schools recognised as efficient and therefore slightly understate the chances of a selective education mainly for middle-class children.

Source: A. Little and J. Westergaard, 'Trend of Class Differentials in Educational Opportunity in England and Wales', *Brit. J. Sociol.*, December 1964, 309.

TABLE 6.22

Proportions obtaining Education of a Grammar School Type and in Universities, among Children of Different Classes born in the Late 1930s, England and Wales

Sex and father's occupation	Percent in Grammar Schools and equivalent ages 11–13			Percent still in Grammar Schools and equivalent age 17			Percentage entering universities
	In maintained and direct grant schools	In independent efficient schools	Total both types	In maintained and direct grant schools	In independent efficient schools	Total both types	
BOYS							
Professional and managerial	40	22	62	24	19	43 }	16½
Other non-manual	30	4	34	13	3	16)	2½
Skilled manual	17	0	17	5	0	5	1½
Semi-skilled	12	0	12	3	0	3	½
Unskilled	7	0	7	1½	0	1½	½
All boys	20	3½	23½	8	3	11	5½
GIRLS							
Professional and managerial	42	20	62	25	14	39)	8
Other non-manual	31	3	34	14	1½	15)	1
Skilled manual	17	0	17	5	0	5	½
Semi-skilled	12	0	12	3	0	3	½
Unskilled	7	0	7	1	0	1	0
All girls	20	3	23	8	2	10	2½
BOYS AND GIRLS							
Professional and managerial	41	21	62	24½	17	41½)	12
Other non-manual	30½	3½	34	13½	2	16)	1½
Skilled manual	17	0	17	5	0	5	1
Semi-skilled	12	0	12	3	0	3	½
Unskilled	7	0	7	1½	0	1½	½
All children	20	3	23	8	2½	10½	4

Note: The table is based on *Early Leaving* (Ministry of Education, Central Advisory Council 1954); *The Crowther Report, 15 to 18* (Ministry of Education, Central Advisory Council 1959–60); R. K. Kelsall, *Report on an Enquiry into Applications for Admissions to Universities*, 1957. All contain information on children born in the late 1930s and use very similar social class classifications. Adjusted to cover England and Wales.

Source: A. Little and J. Westergaard, *loc. cit.*, p. 304.

TABLE 6.23

Children of Different Classes Leaving School at age 17 or more in 1960–1961 with at Least two A-level Passes i.e. Minimum Requirement for University Entry (percentages)

Father's occupation	Boys	Girls	All
Professional and managerial	53	41	48
Clerical	50	39	45
Skilled manual	51	33	43
Semi-skilled and unskilled	39	24	32
Unknown	41	29	35
All	50	36	44

Note: Calculated from the Ministry of Education *Statistics of Education* 1961, Supplement to pt 2, Table 12. Data do not include small numbers of children aged 17 and over leaving from secondary modern schools or independent schools not recognised as efficient.

Source: A. Little and J. Westergaard, *loc. cit.*, p. 305.

TABLE 6.24

Proportion of Leavers Gaining 4 or Less 'O' Levels and Proportion of those Gaining 2 or more 'A' Levels from Different Types of School by Social Class of Father, 1960–1961, England and Wales (percentages)

	with 4 or less 'O' levels		with 2 or more 'A' levels	
	Boys	*Girls*	*Boys*	*Girls*
MAINTAINED AND DIRECT GRANT GRAMMAR				
Professional and managerial	23·4	30·3	48·3	32·9
Clerical	38·1	37·6	31·8	22·4
Skilled manual	44·0	45·8	28·9	16·3
Semi- and unskilled	59·5	66·3	14·9	7·2
Total (including Father's occupation unknown)	43·3	44·7	31·3	20·0
OTHER MAINTAINED SECONDARY(a)				
Professional and managerial	64·4	72·9	7·9	7·7
Clerical	77·0	87·1	6·0	1·5
Skilled manual	86·9	87·5	3·4	2·0
Semi- and unskilled	88·3	94·3	2·4	0·9
Total (including Father's occupation unknown)	86·7	88·3	3·0	1·5
INDEPENDENT RECOGNISED EFFICIENT				
Professional and managerial	27·3	39·5	40·6	17·0
Clerical	34·4	54·7	42·2	7·4
Skilled manual	50·0	64·0	23·0	11·6
Semi- and unskilled(b)	83·3	75·0	—	1·0
Total (including Father's occupation unknown)	31·8	45·7	36·5	13·7

Notes:
(a) Including bilateral, multilateral and comprehensive but excluding secondary modern schools.
(b) Percentages based on very small numbers.
Source: Based on Table 12 in supplement to pt 2 of *Statistics of Education*, 1961.

TABLE 6.25

Entrants to Headmaster's Conference Schools by Social Class of Father 1964, England and Wales (percentages)

Social class of father (RG's classification)	Independent schools				Direct grant schools			Male population of England and Wales
	Day	Mixed		Boarding	Day	Mixed		
		Day	Boarding			Day	Boarding	
Classes								
I	29	35	37	32	25	27	27	4
II	47	50	56	60	44	45	61	15
III (a) non-manual	13	9	4	5	14	14	8}	51
(b) manual	7	5	2	2	13	11	4}	
IV semi-skilled	2	1	1	1	3	3	—	21
V unskilled	1	—	—	—	—	—	—	9
Total	100	100	100	100	100	100	100	100

Source: G. Kalton: *The Public Schools* (Longmans 1966) p. 35.

TABLE 6.26

Achievements of Leavers from Headmasters' Conference School and Maintained Schools known to have Passed or Failed the 11 + Examination, England and Wales (percentages)

	Headmasters' Conference schools		Maintained schools (boys only)	
	Passed 11+	Failed 11+	Grammar	Secondary Modern
O-LEVEL PASSES				
None(a)	2	8	11	92
4 or more	92	72	67	3
8 or more	47	20	20	—
A-LEVEL PASSES				
1 or more	74	35	38	—
2 or more	67	27	33	—
AWARDED A UNIVERSITY PLACE	50	15	17	—
Number of boys	4923	913	58,290	218,890

Note: (a) includes none attempted.
Source: G. Kalton, *op. cit.*, p. 102.

TABLE 6.27

11 + Grading and GCE Achievements of Leavers of all ages from Maintained Grammar Schools 1960–1961, by Social Class of Father, England and Wales (percentages)

Leavers	Top		Middle		Bottom		Total	
	Boys	Girls	Boys	Girls	Boys	Girls	Boys	Girls
PROFESSIONAL AND MANAGERIAL								
with no 'A' levels and								
0–4 'O' levels and	8·4	10·4	26·6	37·0	38·6	52·1	24·3	31·0
5 or more 'O' levels	20·4	28·3	24·9	24·0	34·6	24·2	23·9	28·3
with 1 'A' level	7·7	10·4	8·3	12·6	9·4	11·4	7·1	10·4
2 or more 'A' levels	63·6	50·9	40·2	26·4	17·3	12·3	44·7	30·3
Total	100	100	100	100	100	100	100	100
CLERICAL								
with no 'A' levels								
and 0–4 'O' levels	13·8	27·5	46·8	32·9	57·7	48·9	40·8	38·1
and 5 'O' levels	23·6	32·7	27·3	37·1	23·2	27·1	22·8	34·2
with 1 'A' level	7·3	5·2	6·5	13·3	5·6	6·0	6·5	6·4
2 or more 'A' levels	55·3	34·6	19·5	16·8	13·4	18·0	29·9	21·4
Total	100	100	100	100	100	100	100	100
SKILLED								
with no 'A' levels and								
0–4 'O' levels and	20·4	25·8	43·3	47·5	68·1	67·0	44·9	46·0
5 or more 'O' levels	24·4	42·8	26·6	32·5	14·1	22·0	21·9	33·1
with 1 'A' level	6·0	4·5	6·1·	7·7	4·8	4·6	5·4	5·2
2 or more 'A' levels	49·1	26·9	24·0	12·3	13·0	6·4	27·8	15·6
Total	100	100	100	100	100	100	100	100
SEMI- AND UNSKILLED								
with no 'A' levels and								
0–4 'O' levels and	52·3	48·5	49·7	57·2	73·9	81·3	59·9	66·2
5 or more 'O' levels	24·3	33·7	33·1	28·8	16·1	16·7	23·0	22·9
with 1 'A' level	—	—	3·4	7·4	2·0	1·0	2·5	3·8
2 or more 'A' levels	23·4	17·8	13·7	6·5	8·0	1·0	14·6	7·1
Total	100	100	100	100	100	100	100	100

Source: Based on Table 13 in supplement to *Statistics of Education*, pt 2, 1961, omitting those with Father's occupation unknown and those whose 11+ grading was unknown.

TABLE 6.28

Proportion in Different Classes Entering Universities among Children of Different Generations, England and Wales (percentages)

Social class of father(a)		Period of birth		
Hall-Jones groups	Registrar-General's social classes	Before 1910	1910–1929	late 1930s
BOYS				
1–4	I and II professional/managerial, intermediate	$4\frac{1}{2}$	$8\frac{1}{2}$	$19(15)(b)$
5	III skilled manual and other non-manual	1	$1\frac{1}{2}$	$3\frac{1}{2}(3)(b)$
6–7	IV and V semi- and unskilled	$\frac{1}{2}$	1	1
All boys		2	$3\frac{1}{2}$	$5\frac{1}{2}$
GIRLS				
1–4	I and II professional/managerial, intermediate	2	4	$9\frac{1}{2}(7)(b)$
5	III skilled manual and other non-manual	—	—	$1(1)(b)$
6–7	IV and V semi- and unskilled	—	—	$\frac{1}{2}$
All girls		$\frac{1}{2}$	$1\frac{1}{2}$	$2\frac{1}{2}$
BOYS AND GIRLS				
1–4	I and II professional/managerial, intermediate	3	6	$14\frac{1}{2}(11)(b)$
5	III skilled manual and other non-manual	$\frac{1}{2}$	1	$2\frac{1}{2}(2)(b)$
6–7	IV and V semi- and unskilled	—	$\frac{1}{2}$	$\frac{1}{2}$
All children		$1\frac{1}{2}$	$2\frac{1}{2}$	4

Notes: — indicates a percentage of less than 0·3.

(a) The Registrar-General's social classes I–V are used for post-war entrants and the Hall-Jones groups 1–7 for children born pre-war.

(b) Hall-Jones group 5 may include a somewhat smaller segment of lower-grade non-manual workers than Registrar-General's class III. Figures in brackets show the position if all non-manual workers in social class III were allocated to the top rather than to the middle group.

Source: A. Little and J. Westergaard, *loc. cit.*, p. 310, based on Floud (see note to Table 6.19) and Kelsall (see note to Table 6.19) except that parental class distribution of the age group born in the late 1930s has been assumed to correspond to that of all males aged 20–64 in 1951; if this assumption had been modified to take account of class differentials in fertility and mortality, social inequalities in post-war access to universities would be slightly greater than they appear here.

TABLE 6.29

Highest Course of Education by Children born in 1940–1941 from Maintained Grammar Schools (and Senior Secondary Schools in Scotland): by IQ at 11 + and Father's Occupation, Great Britain

| IQ | Father's occupation | Higher education | | | 'A' level or S.L.C.(a) | Other post school course or 'O' level/ S.L.C.(a) | All children |
| | | Full-time | | Part-time | | | |
		Degree level	Other				
130 and over	Non-manual	37	4	10	7	—	100
	Manual	18	12	10	14	1	100
115–129	Non-manual	17	17	4	17	3	100
	Manual	8	7	9	10	13	100
100–114	Non-manual	6	11	8	7	4	100
	Manual	2	4	7	6	31	100

Note: From a survey of 21-year-olds undertaken for the Committee on Higher Education.

(a) Scottish school-leaving certificate subjects may be taken either at ordinary grade or higher grade.

Source: Higher Education, Appendix 1, p. 42 of Report of Committee on Higher Education (Lord Robbins), Cmnd 2154–1.

TABLE 6·30

Social Origins of University Entrants of 1955–1956 whose Father's Occupations were known, Compared with Occupations of Adult Male Population in 1951 Census (percentages)

| R.G. social class | | University entrants | | Males 20–64 1951 census |
		Male	Female	
ENGLAND				
	I	21·6	27·0	3·4
	II	41·2	45·4	15·0
non-manual	III	11·1	9·0	9·6
manual	III	21·7	16·1	43·6
	IV	3·5	1·9	15·6
	V	0·9	0·6	12·8
WALES				
	I	13·5	17·2	2·7
	II	37·6	46·3	15·3
non-manual	III	10·4	10·9	6·6
manual	III	27·1	19·6	41·0
	IV	9·1	5·1	20·4
	V	2·3	0·9	14·0

Source: R. K. Kelsall, *Report on an Enquiry into Applications for Admissions to Universities 1955–56.*

TABLE 6.31

Proportion of Undergraduates with Fathers in Manual Occupations, Selected Dates (percentages)

	Men	Women	Men and women
1928–47	27	13	23
1955	27	19	25
1961	26	23	25

Note:

1928–47: J. Floud in *Social Mobility in Britain* (ed. D. V. Glass).

1955: R. K. Kelsall: *Applications for Admission to Universities.*

1961: Survey undertaken for the Robbins Committee on Higher Education.

1928–47: Figures relate to England and Wales.

1955 and 1961: Figures relate to Great Britain.

1928–47: Figures relate to those aged 18 in those years who at any time attended a University. Data for 1955 are for entrants in that year. Data for 1961 relate to all undergraduates in that year.

Source: Higher Education, Appendix 2 (B), Cmnd 2154 11–1.

7 Higher Education

A. H. HALSEY

Education beyond primary and secondary schools is dealt with in this chapter. There are four main sections: (1) The growth of higher education up to the publication of the Robbins Report in 1963.[1] (2) Developments since the Robbins Report. (3) Development of the universities since 1900. (4) Students in higher education.

GROWTH OF HIGHER EDUCATION 1900–63

The Robbins Report on Higher Education, which appeared in 1963, is a landmark in the definition of education beyond school. Various phrases are used in the literature to describe different kinds of post-school education including higher education, further education, and adult education. There are no absolute clear dividing lines between institutions, and this chapter refers mainly to statistics on the universities,[2] but also more briefly to statistics on further and adult education. Statistics on universities for Great Britain and Northern Ireland are published in a convenient form from 1966 (Volume VI, *Statistics of Education*). This form of publication took the place of the University Grants Committee's *Returns from Universities and University Colleges* which were previously published in command paper form up to and including the statistics for 1965–6 (Cmnd 3586).

The Robbins Committee defined higher education for their purposes as follows: 'In the main we have concentrated on the universities in Great Britain and those colleges, within the purview of the Ministry of Education and the Scottish Education Department, that provide courses for the education and training of teachers or systematic courses of further education beyond the advanced level of the General Certificate of Education (in Scotland, beyond the higher grade of the Scottish Certificate of Education) or beyond the Ordinary National Certificate or its equivalent.'[3]

---

[1] This Report, together with its five appendices constitutes a comprehensive description of higher education in Great Britain in 1963. See *Higher Education*, Report and Appendices, Cmnd 2154. The Committee was appointed by the Prime Minister under the Chairmanship of Lord Robbins 1961–3.

[2] i.e. those institutions (now 44) whose charters empower them to grant degrees.

[3] *Higher Education*, Report, chap. 1, para. 6.

The definition is further elucidated by a consideration of further education which embraces 'in addition to the colleges of advanced technology, the advanced work undertaken at a great number of technical and commercial colleges and schools of art; but it excludes the initial stages of much professional and other education provided in such colleges'.[1]

An indication of the growth of higher education is provided in the Robbins Report (Table 53, p. 199). Using the definition referred to above and including part-time as well as full-time study, the outlays of central and local government (in respect of teaching and other services, rent and maintenance of buildings, apparatus and materials, student grants and building development) on higher education in Great Britain rose from (at 1962–3 prices) £26m in 1937–8 to £90m in 1954–5 and to £219m in 1962–3. The percentage of seventeen-year-olds receiving full-time education in Great Britain had risen from 1 per cent in 1870 to 2 per cent in 1902 to 4 per cent in 1938 and to 15 per cent by 1962.

The pattern of higher education as described by Robbins in 1962 and using his definitions may be summarised as follows. At the turn of the century nearly all full-time higher education had been provided by universities: the courses then given in teacher-training colleges and colleges of education involved only two years of study and the standard of instruction was correspondingly restricted. The training colleges had grown substantially in the years before the Robbins Committee, both because of rising standards of entry and, in England and Wales, because of the introduction of three-year courses in 1960. The stature of some colleges engaged in further education had also grown dramatically in the 1950s. While the number of university students had slightly more than doubled since before the war, the number in training colleges and colleges of education had increased just over fourfold. But even more striking had been the marked increase in the number of full-time students in advanced courses in further education. This group had been negligible at the beginning of the century but by 1962 constituted a fifth of all full-time students in higher education. Most part-time higher education was provided in institutions of further education. In 1962/3 there were 54,000 advanced students attending these institutions for at least one day a week (compared with 29,000 in 1954/5): most of them were released by their employers for the purpose. Another 54,000 advanced students attended only in the evening. In the universities the number of part-time students was 9000 (over two-thirds of them at postgraduate level) compared with 6000 before the war. Students in training colleges and colleges of education were almost always full-time. The trends are presented in Table 7.1.

[1] *Ibid.*, para. 7.

These trends may also be presented in terms of percentages of the age group.[1] For those entering full-time higher education courses they are given in Table 7.2.

HIGHER EDUCATION SINCE 1963

Since the Robbins Report in 1963 higher education has grown continuously. In 1962 there were 31 British universities, 10 colleges of advanced technology, 150 teacher-training colleges and upwards of 600 technical colleges and other institutions of further education in which about 33,000 students were enrolled on courses of higher education standard. The total number of higher education students was 216,000 (Table 7.1). Robbins set targets for 1973 of 219,000 university students, 122,000 teachers trainees in (renamed) colleges of education and 51,000 in technical colleges. These targets were reached by 1970 and surpassed by over 40,000 in the case of the technical colleges. Between 1963 and 1970 the total student population in full-time higher education doubled to 435,000.

In this period the colleges of advanced technology were given university charters, seven new universities were founded in England and one in Scotland, where in addition two others were formed from leading technical institutions. The colleges of education have doubled their student places and have been drawn closer to the universities by the creation of joint Bachelor of Education degrees.

But the most rapid expansion has taken place in further education in the technical colleges – the number of advanced students rising from 33,000 in 1963 to 90,000 in 1970. Some 30 of the leading technical colleges, commercial colleges and art colleges were in process of development as polytechnics – offering part-time as well as full-time courses at all levels of higher education. A Council for National Academic Awards (C.N.A.A.) has been created by Royal charter with powers to award degrees to students in the polytechnics and other institutions of further education who have completed courses of a satisfactory standard.

Finally the inauguration of the Open University should be mentioned; it began in 1970, teaching partly by radio and television, partly by correspondence courses and partly by tutorial and summer school groups. There are no formal qualifications for entry.

The emergence of a 'system' of higher education has its most recent expression in the proposal of a select committee of the House of Commons that a Higher Education Commission be set up with statutory

[1] Entrants in any given year are of various ages. The method used in the Robbins report was to express the number of each age as a percentage of the total number of that age and then to sum the percentages. This gives a weighted percentage of a composite age group.

powers to coordinate the organisation, research and teaching of all such institutions.

THE UNIVERSITIES, 1900–70[1]

The British universities developed slowly in the nineteenth century and entered the twentieth century as a restricted and élite group of institutions. In England, Oxford and Cambridge stood at the centre, the University of London had emerged as a federation of heterogeneous colleges in the capital, and university charters were being granted to colleges in the major provincial cities. Scotland, meanwhile, had four well-established universities. The system as a whole mustered only 20,000 students out of a population of forty million.

In the twentieth century there has been more substantial growth from this tiny base. The number of students has risen from twenty-five thousand before the first war to twice as many between the wars and nearly eight times as many at the present time so that in 1966–7 there were nearly one hundred and ninety thousand university students on full-time or 'sandwich' courses.

The two wars stimulated this growth; partly because they created climates of opinion favourable to reform in general and to educational reform in particular and thus increased the effective demands for university places, and partly also because they dramatised the utility of university research for military and industrial efficiency. Also underlying these accelerating forces of war, there has been the steady pressure from beneath, made possible by the increase in the number of grammar schools which followed the creation of a national system of secondary schooling in 1902.[2] At the same time the demands for graduates has strengthened slowly as the managerial and professional occupations have expanded in government, in industry and in the educational system itself.[3] The universities form a larger market for graduate teachers. During the course of the century they have also increased their ratio of staff to students, as they have become centres of every kind of research in the sciences and the arts.

Although the growth of the universities has been continuous throughout the century, and although the two wars accelerated the trends, it is clear that social and economic developments since the second war have surpassed all previous pressures towards expansion and will continue

---

[1] For an account of the evolution of the universities and the academic professions in Britain, see A. H. Halsey and M. Trow, *The British Academics* (Faber 1970).

[2] The percentage of seventeen-year-olds in full-time education doubled from 2 per cent. to 4 per cent. between 1902 and 1938 and rose further to 15 per cent. by 1962 and 20 per cent. by 1970.

[3] For the growth of the professional occupations see Table 4.1.

to do so. The change in opinion about the scale of provision of university and other forms of higher education since the mid-1950s is quite unprecedented.

Moreover, the older class conceptions of education have been eroded rapidly in the post-war years. Statistics of inequality of educational opportunity have become popular knowledge and have turned access to the universities into an almost commonplace criterion of distributive justice. This motif has been strengthened by the economic aim of eliminating waste of potential talent in the work force, and particularly by the insistent attack on the assumption of a restricted 'pool of ability' which has come to be seen increasingly as a rationalisation for preserving class privileges. In this process the ideological defence of an élite system of universities has been seriously undermined, and policy for the development of higher education has come to be seen more in terms of economic feasibility.

The course of expansion has had three phases. The first began around the turn of the century with the foundation of the civic universities and continued after the First World War until the depression years of the 1930s. The second, which was more rapid, occurred after the Second World War. Unlike its predecessor it did not fade out, but instead has formed the basis for the third phase in the 1960s and 1970s. At the beginning of the first period Oxford and Cambridge were numerically, as well as academically and socially, preponderant. By the end of it, just before the second war, they had been surpassed in numbers of students and staff by the major redbrick universities, and overtaken by London. Within the first decade of the century Birmingham, Bristol, Leeds,[1] Manchester[2] and Sheffield[3] all gained charters as independent universities: together with the nineteenth-century foundation at Durham and its Newcastle constituent, they began to lead the expansion of of British university system and have continued to do so ever since.

The second period of growth after the second war included the granting of independent charters to the former provincial university colleges at Nottingham, Southampton, Hull, Exeter and Leicester.[4] The last-named became independent in 1957 bringing the total number of British universities to twenty-one. Meantime the establishment of the University College of North Staffordshire at Keele[5] without tutelage

[1] A. H. Shimmin, *The University of Leeds* (C.U.P. 1945).

[2] H. B. Charlton, *Portrait of a University 1851–1951* (Manchester U.P. 1951).

[3] A. D. Chapman, *The Story of a Modern University: A History of the University of Sheffield* (O.U.P. 1955).

[4] J. Simmonds, *New University* (Leicester U.P. 1958).

[5] W. B. Gillie, *A New University: A. D. Lindsay and the Keele Experiment* (Chatto & Windus 1960).

from London was the precursor of a much publicised movement at the end of the 1950s to found new universities with independence *ab initio*. The first of these, Sussex,[1] admitted its first students in 1961. Subsequently East Anglia, York, Essex,[2] Kent, Warwick and Lancaster have received charters and four new Scottish universities have been formed, one at Strathclyde (out of the Royal College of Science at Glasgow), one at Stirling, Heriot Watt in Edinburgh and one at Dundee. No doubt these new foundations will contribute greatly to the third phase of expansion. But in the second phase they counted for little. The bulk of the expansion between 1947 and 1964 was borne by the established universities in the industrial provincial cities, by London, by Wales and by the ancient universities in England and Scotland.

THE FORMER CATS

Numerically a more important addition has been the translation of nine English colleges of advanced technology (CATs) to university status.[3] Their incorporation into the university system during the three or four years after the Robbins Report has produced a group which is larger than either the new English universities, the ancient English colleges or the University of Wales.

The CATs were designated in 1957 (except for Bristol, which was elevated in 1960, and Brunel, in 1962) and were taken from the control of the local education authorities, who had nurtured them from their nineteenth-century origins, to be given independent status under the direct control of the Ministry of Education in 1962. Robbins' recommendation that they be upgraded to university status was accepted (though not the linked proposal for the creation of five Special Institutions for Scientific and Technological Education and Research) and all except Chelsea, which has been absorbed into the University of London, now have an independent charter. Only two of them have retained the technological label in their titles – Loughborough University of Technology and Bath University of Technology. The Bradford Institute of Technology has become the University of Bradford; Northampton College of Advanced Technology has become the City University; Battersea College of Technology has become the University of Surrey and has moved to Guildford; Brunel College has moved ten miles away from Acton to a larger site near Uxbridge as Brunel University.

---

[1] Sir John Fulton, *Experiment in Higher Education*, Tavistock Pamphlet No. 8, 1964; and David Daiches (ed.), *The Idea of a New University: An Experiment in Sussex* (André Deutsch 1964).

[2] A. E. Sloman, *A University in the Making* (British Broadcasting Corporation 1964).

[3] These are Aston, Bath, Bradford, Brunel, Chelsea, City, Loughborough, Salford and Surrey.

UNIVERSITY FINANCE

The growth of reliance on the state for financial support expresses itself dramatically in Table 7.3 which shows the income of universities from 1920–69 distributed by its source.

There are two essential features of the statistics. First, the rate of growth in the 1960s, associated of course with the Robbins enquiry and the re-definition of higher education which has increased the number of universities from twenty-four to forty-four in the last ten years, dwarfs all previous experience. Second, an increasing proportion of university income is provided by the state. Direct parliamentary grants alone account for 82·7 per cent.

Since the creation of the University Grants Committee the total income of the universities on the grant list has risen from just over £3 million in 1920–1 to over £216 million in 1968: and these figures do not include non-recurrent grants by parliament for new building and equipment which in 1966–7 amounted to a further £77·4 million[1] bringing total expenditure in that year to something near £270 million.

UNIVERSITY STAFF

There were 31,476 full-time academic members of the staff of British universities in 1968/9 including all teaching and research staff irrespective of the source of finance.

The academic professions, like the institutions in which they serve, have evolved in response to the changing structure of society, having developed from the pre-industrial traditions of Oxford and Cambridge, where they constituted a tiny group oriented to the customs and demands of the clerical and aristocratic classes to which, at least by the seventeenth century, they largely owed their existence. The academic career began to change in the second half of the nineteenth century with the development of professionalism, specialisation and expansion. The nineteenth-century developments were of small numerical importance. At the end of the century there were about eight hundred Oxford and Cambridge dons, five hundred teachers in the provincial redbrick universities, a similar number in Scotland and less than two hundred and fifty in London. Figs 7.1 and 7.2 and Tables 7.4 to 7.7 give a numerical outline of the distribution of university teachers between different types of university, different grades or academic ranks, and different faculties or subjects. They demonstrate the shift away from traditional conceptions, the elongation of the professions and their increasing specialisation.

As may be seen from Fig 7.1 the number of university teachers in

[1] The total capital expenditure on buildings and equipment from public and private sources has risen from less than £30 millions in the 1952–7 quinquennium to £99 millions in 1957–62 and to £295 millions in 1962–7.

Britain has grown from rather under two thousand at the beginning of the century to over thirty thousand at the present day. The statistics, however, are unusually imperfect because of changes in administrative habits during the course of the century and especially because of the vagaries of Oxford and Cambridge records. The main source from 1919 is the U.G.C. in its Annual and Quinquennial Returns. Only for 1965–6 (Cmnd 3586) is it possible, for the first time, to discover an exact count of the number of university teachers irrespective of the source of funds for their employment. The effect in Fig. 7.1 is to produce a jump in the numbers at this point through the inclusion for the first time of staff paid from other than general university funds. They numbered 3429 out of the total of 25,294 in 1965–6.

The growth has been continuous but it accelerated sharply in the nineteen-sixties following acceptance of the Robbins Report. The latest estimate (1970) for the numbers of university students in 1980 is over 400,000 which, given a continuation of the present staff/student ratios, means that there will be fifty thousand university teachers in this country at the end of the seventies. The figures for December 1968 showing the number of staff in each university institution according to academic rank and source of financial support are reproduced in Table 7.4. We have further divided the universities into eight groups, each group differing according to its character, age and location.

In 1968 the largest group, employing more than a quarter of all university teachers, was made up of the major redbrick universities in the larger provincial industrial cities.[1] The second largest group, with a fifth of the university teachers, was formed by the constituent colleges of the University of London.[2] Third in order, and accounting for 15·5 per cent of all university teachers, were the seven Scottish institutions.[3] Fourth came the minor redbrick universities[4] which between them

[1] These were Birmingham, Bristol, Durham, Leeds, Liverpool, Manchester (including the school of Business Studies and the Institute of Technology), Newcastle and Sheffield, most of which received their charters within a few years of the turn of the nineteenth and twentieth centuries.

[2] London received its charter in 1836, mainly on the basis of the recently formed University and King's colleges; in 1968 it was composed of 31 self-governing schools and 14 institutes directly controlled by the university. We also include the Graduate School of Business Studies.

[3] Aberdeen, Edinburgh, Glasgow, Heriot-Watt, St Andrews, Strathclyde and Stirling. St Andrews, founded in 1410, was the oldest of these, with an additional college at Dundee founded in 1881. Aberdeen, Edinburgh, and Glasgow were fifteenth- and sixteenth-century foundations. The Royal College of Science and Technology at Glasgow goes back to 1796 but received a charter as the University of Strathclyde in 1964. Stirling was new, admitting its first (107) students in 1967.

[4] Exeter, Hull, Leicester, Nottingham, Reading and Southampton. With the exception of Reading all were at one time provincial colleges preparing students for

employed 9·7 per cent of all university teachers. Oxford and Cambridge came next with 8·1 per cent and they were closely followed by the former English colleges of advanced technology.[1] The new English universities occupied the seventh place[2] with 6·8 per cent of all academic staff and last came the University of Wales[3] accounting for 5·9 per cent of university teachers.

The distribution of university teachers among these groups in 1968 is set out, again in order of numerical importance, in Table 7.5 and is compared with the situation for earlier years. The group of universities which were formerly colleges of advanced technology is, by definition, excluded from the earlier figures; but in the years after the Robbins Report, the institutional pattern shows a shift away from Oxford, Cambridge, London and the Victorian foundations to the new technological universities.

The pattern of growth from 1910 in each of the seven university groups in existence before 1963 is plotted in Fig. 7.2. Though they have changed their relative numerical positions, every group has increased its numbers. The exact number of dons at Oxford and Cambridge at the beginning of the century is not known, but there were probably about eight hundred including all university teachers and college fellows. There were 471 resident M.A.s at Oxford in 1900 and 3446 undergraduates. Oxford's total academic staff in 1922 was 357 rising to 1127 in 1964–5 with 9450 students. At Cambridge the number of dons primarily engaged in teaching and research, with or without college fellowships, rose from 458 in 1928 to 1001 in 1959 when there were 8997 students. The Scottish full-time academic staff numbered 498 in 1920 and 2600 in 1963–4.

Oxford and Cambridge, numerically the strongest group in the early nineteen hundreds, gradually lost their lead. Our estimate is that academic staff at Oxford and Cambridge increased from eight hundred at the beginning of the century to something like one thousand in the nineteen thirties. In the major redbrick universities the increase was from 626 in 1910 to 1349 in 1938–9 and in London from 202 to 1057.

the examinations of the University of London. They received their charters between 1948 and 1957. Reading was founded in 1926.

[1] Aston, Bath, Bradford, Brunel, Chelsea, City, Loughborough, Salford and Surrey.

[2] East Anglia, Keele, Sussex, York, Lancaster, Kent, Essex and Warwick.

[3] It received its charter in 1893 though several of its constituent colleges dated from earlier in the nineteenth century. Aberystwyth was founded in 1859, Bangor in 1885, Cardiff in 1885 and Swansea in the 1920s. St David's College, Lampeter, also received grants from the University Grants Committee under a scheme agreed in 1961 through the University College of South Wales, Cardiff.

The elongation of the university professions

By 1968 the academic staff of the British universities, taken as a whole, formed a hierarchy headed by a professoriate of only 10 per cent. The shape of the hierarchy, which is shown in Table 7.6, developed historically from the collegiate guilds of masters in the Oxford and Cambridge colleges, and the established professorial system of the Scottish universities.

The academic hierarchy has been elaborated and regularised during the twentieth century and its changing shape is shown in Table 7.6. The sharpest drop in the proportion of professors took place during the nineteen twenties (from nearly a third to little more than a fifth), though the fall has been continuous throughout the period for all the groups included in the statistics.

Before 1920, the ranks below the professorship were neither equivalent from one university to another, nor distinguished in the Board of Education statistics. Many of them carried low status and low pay, but, as may be seen in the table, the proportion in the main career grade – the lectureship – has risen. Thus there have been two rather conflicting processes at work. On the one hand the hierarchy has been lengthened with the creation of a non-professorial staff and a corresponding decrease in the proportion of professorial chairs; and on the other, within the non-professorial ranks there has been a tendency towards up-grading with a corresponding decrease in the proportion of assistant lecturers. In recent years there has been renewed pressure to increase the proportion of senior posts. In 1967 the U.G.C. announced that, in any given university, senior posts (including professorships, senior lectureships and readerships), could be filled to a maximum of 35 per cent of the total academic staff.[1]

Moving down the ranks, the numerical proportions for all universities in 1968 were, professors 10·1 per cent, readers and senior lecturers 17·6 per cent, lecturers 53·2 per cent and assistant lecturers 13·2 per cent, leaving 5·8 per cent in posts of various kinds outside the main hierarchy.

These figures include Oxford and Cambridge whose staffs are classified in the same terms as those for other universities. This means that the great bulk are classified as lecturers (988 out of 1345 in Oxford and 738 out of 1153 in Cambridge) which is misleading in that many college teaching fellows have a salary and status superior to that of

[1] 'The ratio is to be applied to the total numbers of full time academic staff wholly paid from general university funds. . . . The ratio is calculated for each university 'across the board'. . . . The actual distribution of the number of senior posts within each university between the different faculties and departments is entirely a matter for the university itself to decide.' U.G.C., *University Development 1962–67*, para. 77.

lecturers elsewhere. Moreover, the fact that Oxford and Cambridge have no senior lectureships is of no significance in the context of the collegiate staff structure. The proportion of professors and readers is relatively low, partly because some college dons have equivalent positions.

London has a higher proportion of professors and readers, partly because of the strength of the medical faculty, while the new English universities have a high proportion of professors as 'founder members'. Scotland and Wales have relatively few readerships though the former has a compensating high proportion of senior lectureships. The minor redbricks have fewer staff of senior rank than the major redbricks. Apart from London, the differences in the proportion of senior staff among the several types of university institution are quite small. It is very close to 26 per cent or 27 per cent for all universities except London, Oxford and Cambridge. However, the figures for 1965–6 show that the ex-CATs were exceptional in their low proportion of professors; they had only 4·3 per cent. in that year. This reflected the recent promotion of these institutions from the ranks of the technical colleges where professorships do not exist and where staffing is different in both nomenclature and structure.[1] The distribution of ranks in the former colleges of advanced technology had moved much closer to those in the other types of university by 1968 (Table 7.6).

Specialisation and the changing balance of studies
University studies in the twentieth century have widened in scope, and the balance between the faculties has also shifted. The first change, however, has been continuous while the second has fluctuated. Widening the scope of studies has meant that university teachers have specialised increasingly in their academic interests, choosing between research and teaching, and between undergraduate and graduate supervision. One crude but dramatic illustration of the widening range of specialisms may be derived from the U.G.C's statistics on the branches of study pursued by advanced students. In 1928, 123 subjects were distinguished: a quarter of a century later there were 382. In the meantime, economics had been divided into economics, industrial economics, econometrics and economic history; the number of branches of engineering had risen from 7 to 22 and such subjects as Ethiopic studies, fruit nutrition, immunology, personnel management, medical jurisprudence and space science had appeared.

The changing balance of studies since the First World War is shown

[1] For a detailed comparison of academic salaries and ranks in the various institutions of higher education see Eric E. Robinson and David Jaynes, 'Pay and the Academics', *Higher Education Review*, Autumn 1968.

in Table 7.7. After the war the arts faculties expanded, especially at the expense of medicine and the applied sciences. In the nineteen-thirties, the trend was reversed and the arts faculties have been in relative decline ever since. By the end of the nineteen-twenties they constituted half of the academic staff, they now account for only one-sixth.[1] The social studies have expanded much more rapidly than the other faculties in the nineteen-sixties. Between 1961/2 and 1966/7 social studies teachers increased by 155 per cent compared with 46·5 per cent for university staff as a whole. The pure science faculties declined during the inter-war period, but have risen steadily since the Second World War to become the largest faculty group in 1968. Medicine has declined relatively throughout the period, sharply in the nineteen-twenties with a recovery at the end of the nineteen-thirties, and with a further decline since the Second World War. The applied sciences and technology were proportionately more significant after the First World War than at any subsequent point until 1950, and even with the incoporation of the former CATs these subjects still accounted for less than a fifth of all academic staff in 1966–7.[2]

Nonetheless, it is clear from the figures for 1968 that the traditional stereotype of the academic as an arts don is seriously inaccurate: and this was already so at the time of the Robbins Report. In 1968 the arts faculties made up only one-sixth of the total. The largest single faculty was pure science (29 per cent), the remainder in descending order of size, were arts, medicine and dentistry, applied science, social studies, education and last agriculture, forestry and veterinary science. Thus even assuming that half the social scientists were 'pure', nearly 50 per cent of academics worked in some kind of natural or social science based technology. The technologist, thus broadly defined, has the most plausible claim to be thought of as the typical university teacher.

STUDENTS IN HIGHER EDUCATION

We have already referred to the increase in the number and proportion of students in full-time higher education since 1900. Here we look more closely at sex and social class, at the type of institution attended and the type of course pursued.

In 1920, women constituted well under one-third of all full-time university students; in 1939 they made up less than a quarter and in

---

[1] It should be noticed, however, that the decline was not as marked after 1950 as may appear from Table 7.7 since before 1959 the social studies were included with arts subjects.

[2] The figures in Table 7.7 up to 1950 are based on the distribution of students and therefore in comparing the relative importance of subjects over time we have implicitly assumed that staff/student ratios were equal between faculties.

1968 rather more than a quarter (Table 7.8). In other words they formed a slightly smaller proportion of the total than they did in 1920; a woman's chances of getting into a university relative to a man's are now rather poorer than they were fifty years ago. By contrast, a rather higher proportion of part-time students were women in 1968 than in 1920. Oxford and Cambridge have a specially small proportion of women. Table 7.9 suggests that children of manual workers are scarcely better represented among undergraduates than they were during the period 1928–47. Indeed there were proportionately fewer men from this kind of social background in 1961 than during the earlier period. On the other hand women from the same social class considerably improved their position making up 13 per cent of all women students between 1928 and 1947 and 23 per cent in 1961. The true significance of these proportions is evident from Table 7.10 which compares the proportion of students from different backgrounds with the proportion of male adults in the population in the Registrar-General's five social classes. For England and Wales 63 per cent of all students came from social classes 1 and 2 which made up only 18 per cent of the population. The 26 per cent of students with manual backgrounds came from classes 3, 4 and 5 which make up 72 per cent of the total population. These figures are from England; in Scotland the distribution of the population is rather different with classes 1 and 2 forming a smaller and the manual workers a larger proportion of the total and this is reflected in the slighly higher percentage of students from manual backgrounds and slightly lower proportion from classes 1 and 2. But in Wales the pattern is very considerably different with the manual worker class much better represented among students. For all three countries there is a marked difference in the social backgrounds of men and women, a higher relative proportion of women than of men coming from classes 1 and 2 in each case.

If we look at the proportion of students coming from outside the United Kingdom we see that it has increased considerably since 1921 and that the great majority of students from the Commonwealth and from foreign countries are men (Table 7.11).

Roughly two-thirds of undergraduates come from maintained[1] schools and a larger proportion of women than of men (Table 7.12).

Table 7.13 shows the changing balance of courses and in particular the increasing proportion of graduate students. The relative numerical importance of different faculties has also changed substantially since 1920 (Table 7.14). Pure science is now the most popular subject for men, followed by technology and the social studies, while in 1920 medicine was the largest faculty followed by the arts and then tech-

[1] For definition see Chap. 6, p. 148.

nology. For women the pattern is slightly different; the arts faculty has presently the largest number of students, followed by social studies and then pure science; and it was arts subjects that were also most popular among women in 1920, with medicine coming next but attracting only half as many.

University students may live at home or in halls of residence or in lodgings; Table 7.15 shows the extent of the move away from living at home. It is now most usual for students to live in lodgings though the number and proportion in halls of residence or colleges has increased very substantially since 1920.

Student teachers
The number of student teachers has multiplied by almost twenty since the beginning of the century, but since 1921 has shown a similar rate of increase to full-time university students (Table 7.16). Unlike the universities, however, the colleges of education have always been mainly attended by women. Two-thirds of those in training in 1910 were women and a slightly higher proportion in 1967. There continues to be only a very small proportion of student teachers who are graduates.

Further education
The number of students having some type of further education has increased sixfold since 1910 and the balance of the sexes has changed; in 1967 rather more women than men were involved, whereas the reverse was true in 1910 (Table 7.17). The majority of students go to evening classes only and this is the only group that has a preponderance of women. Part-time day attendance is the next most popular type of course and only just over 200,000 out of three million students are full-time (Table 7.18).

TABLE 7.1

Students in Full-time Higher Education 1900/1–1962/3, Great Britain

	University	Teacher training	Further education	All full-time higher education
1900–1	20,000	5000	—	25,000
1924–5	42,000	16,000	3000	61,000
1938–9	50,000	13,000	6000	69,000
1954–5	82,000	28,000	12,000	122,000
1962–3	118,000	55,000	43,000	216,000

Notes: Figures for further education in 1924–5 and 1938–9 are approximate.

The table does not include full-time advanced students in the colleges of music and other colleges mentioned in paragraph 8 of Chapter 1.

Part of the large increase in teacher training between 1954–5 and 1962–3 was due to the lengthening of the Training College course in England and Wales.

Source: Higher Education, p. 15, Table 3.

TABLE 7.2

Percentage of Age Group* entering Full-time Higher Education 1900–1962, Great Britain

	University	Teacher training	Further education	All full-time higher education
1900	0·8	0·4	—	1·2
1924	1·5	1·0	0·2	2·7
1938	1·7	0·7	0·3	2·7
1954	3·2	2·0	0·6	5·8
1955	3·4	2·0	0·7	6·1
1956	3·5	2·1	0·8	6·4
1957	3·9	2·2	0·9	7·0
1958	4·1	2·4	1·2	7·7
1959	4·2	2·8	1·3	8·3
1960	4·1	2·7	1·5	8·3
1961	4·1	2·5	1·7	8·3
1962	4·0	2·5	2·0	8·5

* See footnote 1, p. 194.

Source: Higher Education Report Table 4. p. 16.

TABLE 7.3

Sources of University Income 1920–1968, United Kingdom: Sources as Percentage of Total Income

Year	Total income of Universities £	Parlia-mentary grants	Grants from L.A.s	Fees	Endow-ments	Donations and subscriptions	Other sources (a)
1920–1	3,020,499	33·6	9·3	33·0	11·2	2·7	10·2
1923–4	3,587,366	35·5	12·0	33·6	11·6	2·5	4·8
1928–9	5,174,510	35·9	10·1	27·8	13·9	2·4	9·9
1933–4	5,593,320	35·1	9·2	32·8	13·7	2·4	6·8
1938–9	6,712,067	35·8	9·0	29·8	15·4	2·6	7·4
1946–7	13,043,541	52·7	5·6	23·2	9·3	2·2	7·0
1949–50	22,009,735	63·9	4·6	17·7	5·7	1·7	6·4
1953–4	31,112,024	70·5	3·6	12·0	4·3	1·6	8·0
1955–6	38,894,000	72·7	3·1	10·8	3·8	0·9	8·7
1961–2	74,113,000	76·5	2·1	9·0	2·7	0·9	8·9
1964–5	124,161,715	79·9	1·4	8·1	1·9	0·6	8·1
1967–8	216,204,321	72·9(b)	0·9	7·4		1·7	17·1(b)

Notes: (a) Includes payment for research contracts from 1955–6.

(b) The amount of parliamentary grant shows an apparent drop in 1967–8 because for that year only grants from the Exchequer are distinguished in the statistics. Grants and payments for research from other government departments are included in 'other sources'. Previously all parliamentary grants had been grouped together.

Source: U.G.C. Returns.

TABLE 7.4

University Staff by Rank and Source of Finance 1968, Great Britain

Ref. nos	Universities	Professors			Readers and senior lecturers		
		Wholly financed	Partly financed	Not financed	Wholly financed	Partly financed	Not financed
1	Aston	30	—	1	71	—	—
2	Bath	19	—	—	50	—	—
3	Birmingham	117	—	1	196	9	9
4	Bradford	29	—	—	63	—	—
5	Bristol	75	1	4	123	6	20
6	Brunel	13	—	2	33	—	1
7	Cambridge	120	4	2	85	1	—
8	City	18	—	—	60	—	—
9	Durham	41	2	—	54	1	—
10	East Anglia	29	—	—	29	—	1
11	Essex	23	—	2	22	—	3
12	Exeter	36	1	1	54	1	1
13	Hull	35	—	—	78	—	—
14	Keele	21	—	—	33	—	1
15	Kent	27	—	—	30	—	1
16	Lancaster	25	1	—	29	3	1
17	Leeds	101	3	1	205	8	7
18	Leicester	42	—	1	53	—	—
19	Liverpool	87	—	—	183	—	1
20	London Grad. Sch. of Business Studies	6	—	—	8	—	1
21	London University	743	10	29	1255	17	111
22	Loughborough	20	—	—	45	—	1
23	Manchester Sch. of Business Studies	4	—	—	9	—	4
24	Manchester University	124	1	1	189	8	11
25	Manchester Inst. Science & Tech.	28	—	1	70	—	—
26	Newcastle	85	4	—	138	8	5
27	Nottingham	58	1	2	95	1	4
28	Oxford	114	—	3	17	—	2
29	Reading	52	1	15	72	—	29
30	Salford	21	—	—	67	—	—
31	Sheffield	84	—	—	142	—	—
32	Southampton	53	1	1	75	—	3
33	Surrey	20	2	—	53	1	—
34	Sussex	48	1	5	57	3	16
35	Warwick	19	4	—	30	1	—
36	York	22	—	1	34	—	3
37	TOTAL ENGLAND	2389	37	73	3867	68	236
38	Aberystwyth University Coll.	28	1	1	53	6	—
39	Bangor University College	33	—	1	52	—	1
40	Cardiff University College	40	—	—	71	—	2
41	St David's, Lampeter	6	—	—	3	—	—
42	Swansea University College	34	1	—	58	3	1
43	Welsh Nat. Sch. of Medicine	13	—	—	35	—	—
44	Univ. Wales Inst. Science & Tech.	14	—	—	31	—	—
45	TOTAL WALES	168	2	2	303	9	4
46	TOTAL ENGLAND AND WALES	2557	39	75	4170	77	240
47	Aberdeen	52	2	—	95	—	5
48	Dundee	36	—	—	78	—	—
49	Edinburgh	118	5	3	240	2	19
50	Glasgow	114	—	—	226	4	7
51	Heriot-Watt	16	—	—	32	—	—
52	St Andrews	32	—	—	57	—	—
53	Stirling	14	—	—	10	—	—
54	Strathclyde	45	1	1	151	—	—
55	TOTAL SCOTLAND	427	8	4	889	6	31
56	TOTAL GREAT BRITAIN	2984	47	79	5059	53	271

Table 7.4 continued

Ref. nos	Lecturers			Assistant lecturers			Others		
	Wholly financed	Partly financed	Not financed	Wholly financed	Partly financed	Not financed	Wholly financed	Partly financed	Not financed
1	245	—	15	12	—	9	—	—	—
2	169	—	5	5	—	4	—	—	—
3	526	20	99	64	1	33	39	2	84
4	263	—	3	19	—	—	—	—	—
5	383	12	74	85	1	27	10	—	—
6	125	—	8	12	—	7	—	—	—
7	640	60	38	180	14	9	—	—	—
8	193	—	—	24	—	—	—	—	—
9	201	6	6	32	—	8	9	—	43
10	107	—	7	48	—	20	7	—	5
11	95	—	22	23	—	—	4	2	1
12	177	5	14	43	—	10	22	—	—
13	226	1	3	74	—	21	5	—	—
14	115	1	19	28	—	3	36	—	11
15	126	1	1	32	2	15	7	—	8
16	94	7	16	40	2	10	3	—	3
17	502	36	58	83	7	48	73	7	79
18	184	—	17	39	—	—	—	—	—
19	426	2	35	90	1	27	19	1	32
20	9	—	4	3	—	1	2	—	3
21	2226	32	533	470	5	98	107	—	202
22	153	1	17	10	—	—	—	—	—
23	9	—	6	7	—	0	—	—	—
24	573	15	55	178	3	43	70	—	31
25	253	—	—	22	—	—	73	—	—
26	355	13	83	65	10	57	25	3	49
27	290	8	35	41	1	34	33	—	39
28	862	—	126	53	1	64	15	—	28
29	276	—	71	52	—	70	39	—	31
30	298	—	4	29	—	8	6	—	—
31	365	—	—	80	—	—	41	—	—
32	295	5	10	28	—	2	8	—	—
33	181	—	—	8	—	—	—	—	—
34	216	2	40	35	1	38	—	—	9
35	54	2	8	22	—	26	3	—	—
36	112	2	14	15	—	18	3	—	9
37	11,354	231	1446	2051	49	1020	659	15	667
38	147	7	—	35	1	—	29	—	—
39	179	—	13	28	—	10	18	1	13
40	184	—	13	40	1	14	17	—	11
41	18	—	—	11	—	—	2	—	—
42	184	5	15	44	—	25	30	—	27
43	23	—	—	2	—	—	—	—	—
44	152	—	2	21	—	1	1	—	—
45	887	12	43	181	2	50	97	1	51
46	12,241	243	1489	2232	51	1070	756	16	718
47	301	—	26	67	—	30	23	—	25
48	177	—	13	35	—	9	8	—	21
49	544	2	118	57	1	59	48	1	71
50	471	2	72	244	1	51	32	—	45
51	99	1	—	21	—	—	1	—	—
52	142	1	3	38	—	—	7	—	—
53	34	—	1	17	—	8	4	—	1
54	359	2	25	57	—	27	9	—	5
55	2127	8	258	536	2	184	132	1	168
56	14,368	251	1747	2768	53	1254	888	17	886

Table 7.4 continued

Universities	Total Staffs				Ref. Nos
	Wholly financed	Partly financed	Not financed	Total	
Aston	358	—	25	383	1
Bath	243	—	9	252	2
Birmingham	942	32	226	1200	3
Bradford	374	—	3	377	4
Bristol	676	20	125	821	5
Brunel	183	—	18	201	6
Cambridge	1025	79	49	1153	7
City	295	—	—	295	8
Durham	337	9	57	403	9
East Anglia	220	—	33	253	10
Essex	167	2	28	197	11
Exeter	332	7	26	365	12
Hull	418	1	24	443	13
Keele	233	1	34	268	14
Kent	222	3	25	250	15
Lancaster	191	13	30	234	16
Leeds	964	61	193	1218	17
Leicester	318	—	18	336	18
Liverpool	805	4	95	904	19
London Grad. Sch. of Business Stud.	28	—	9	37	20
London University	4801	64	1273	6138	21
Loughborough	228	1	18	247	22
Manchester Sch. of Business Stud.	29	—	20	49	23
Manchester University	1134	27	141	1302	24
Manchester Inst. of Science & Tech.	446	—	1	447	25
Newcastle	668	38	194	900	26
Nottingham	517	11	114	642	27
Oxford	1121	1	223	1345	28
Reading	491	1	216	708	29
Salford	421	—	12	433	30
Sheffield	712	—	—	712	31
Southampton	459	6	16	481	32
Surrey	262	3	—	265	33
Sussex	356	7	108	471	34
Warwick	158	7	34	199	35
York	186	2	45	233	36
TOTAL ENGLAND	20,320	400	3442	24,162	37
Aberystwyth University Coll.	292	15	1	308	38
Bangor University College	310	1	38	349	39
Cardiff University College	352	1	40	393	40
St David's, Lampeter	40	—	—	40	41
Swansea University College	350	9	68	427	42
Welsh Nat. Sch. of Medicine	73	—	—	73	43
Univ. Wales Inst. Science & Tech.	219	—	3	222	44
TOTAL WALES	1636	26	150	1812	45
TOTAL ENGLAND AND WALES	21,956	426	3592	25,974	46
Aberdeen	538	2	86	626	47
Dundee	334	—	43	377	48
Edinburgh	1007	11	270	1255	49
Glasgow	1087	7	175	1269	50
Heriot-Watt	169	1	—	170	51
St Andrews	276	1	3	280	52
Stirling	79	—	10	89	53
Strathclyde	621	3	58	682	54
TOTAL SCOTLAND	4111	25	645	4781	55
TOTAL GREAT BRITAIN	26,067	451	4237	30,755	56

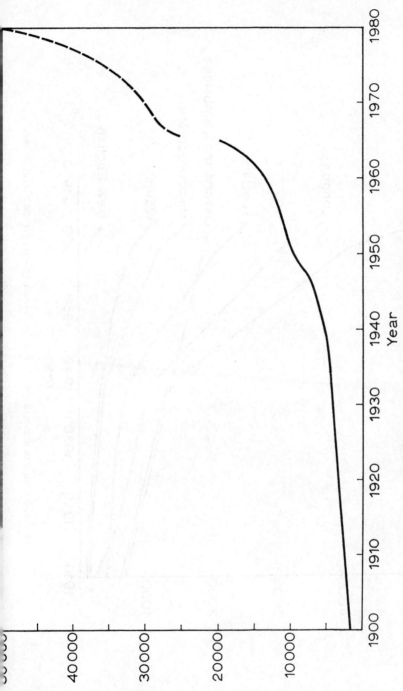

FIG. 7.1. Number of university teachers 1900–80, Great Britain.

Note: The figures from 1938/9 and 1962/3 are taken from the Robbins Report, Appendix 3, Table 1, p. 4. Those for 1965/6 and 1966/7 are from the U.G.C. Returns and include all staff in all universities irrespective of their sources of financial support. The figures for 1971/2 and for 1980 are estimates which assume that the present official target for the former year of 225,000 student places in universities will be met and that a new estimate of 400,000 for 1980 will also be met and that both will be subject to present staff/student ratios.

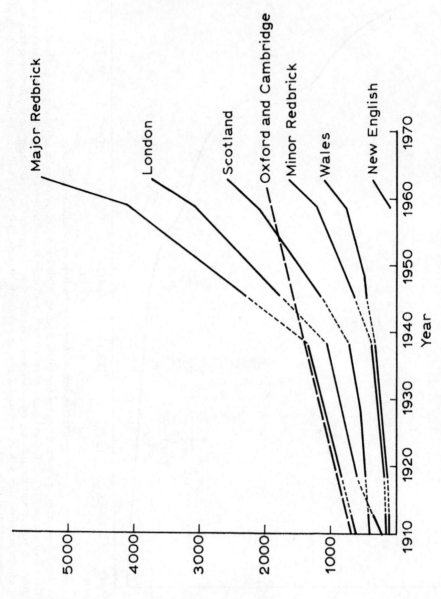

FIG. 7.2. Number of university teachers by university group 1910–64, Great Britain.

TABLE 7.5

Distribution of Full-time Staff among University Groups 1961–1968, Great Britain (percentages)

University Group	Full-time staff		
	1961–2	*1964–5*	*December 1968*
Major redbrick	32·4	32·7	25·9
London	23·6	21·7	20·1
Scotland	15·5	16·2	15·5
Minor redbrick	10·2	10·6	9·7
Oxford and Cambridge	10·4	8·6	8·1
Ex-CATs	—	—	8·0
New English	1·0	3·2	6·8
Wales	6·9	6·9	5·9
Total Great Britain	100	100	100
Grand Total	14,276	18,352	30,755

Source: Calculated from U.G.C. Returns and information from the U.G.C. The two earlier years include staff at Oxford and Cambridge who were paid only partly from university funds since they also did college work. The 1968 figures include those not financed at all from university funds – 223 at Oxford and 49 at Cambridge.

TABLE 7.6

Full-time Academic Staff by University Group and Rank 1910–1968, Great Britain (percentages)

	1910–11(a)	1919–20(b)	1929–30	1938–39	1949–50	1959–60	1963–64	1965–66	Dec. 1968
A. MAJOR REDBRICK									
Professors	30	28	21	18	13	11	10	10	10
Readers \									
Asst. Prof. }	—	—	6	6	5	4	5\	17	18
Indep. Lects. /									
Senior Lects.	70	72	—	—	9	12	12/		
Lecturers	—	—	41	48	42	52	48	50	51
Asst. Lects.	—	—	22	18	18	9	8	17	12
Others	—	—	9	10	13	12	17	6	9
TOTAL	(626)	(849)	(1081)	(1349)	(2743)	(4148)	(5456)	(6754)	(7956)
B. LONDON									
Professors	31	31	21	19	14	13	14	13	13
Readers \									
Asst. Profs. }	—	—	16	16	12	15	14\	24	23
Indep. Lects. /									
Senior Lects.	69	69	—	—	10	11	12/		
Lecturers	—	—	29	31	34	42	40	42	45
Asst. Lects.	—	—	27	26	21	12	11	17	14
Others	—	—	7	8	9	7	9	5	5
TOTAL	(202)	(601)	(856)	(1057)	(2146)	(3072)	(3750)	(5205)	(6175)
C. MINOR REDBRICK									
Professors	27	31	21	16	12	11	11	10	10
Readers \									
Asst. Profs. }	—	—	10	8	4	2	4\	16	16
Indep. Lects /									
Senior Lects.	73	69	—	—	3	6	10/		
Lecturers	—	—	43	39	43	54	48	50	54
Asst. Lects.	—	—	18	20	22	10	11	17	14
Others	—	—	9	17	16	16	16	7	6
TOTAL	(104)	(151)	(258)	(324)	(842)	(1236)	(1669)	(2344)	(2975)
D. WALES									
Professors	42	37	24	23	17	14	12	9	9
Readers \									
Asst. Profs. }	—	—	6	12	8	0	2\	16	17
Indep. Lects. /									
Senior Lects.	58	63	—	—	14	14	13/		
Lecturers	—	—	26	35	39	47	47	51	52
Asst. Lects.	—	—	29	23	21	13	10	14	13
Others	—	—	15	16	7	12	15	10	8
TOTAL	(143)	(178)	(301)	(371)	(512)	(799)	(1121)	(1649)	(1812)
E. SCOTLAND(c)									
Professors	32	35	23	22	13	11	10	9	9
Readers \									
Asst. Profs. }	—	—	8	7	5	3	3\	20	19
Indep. Lects. /									
Senior Lects.	68	65	—	—	10	17	18/		
Lecturers	—	—	41	44	46	50	49	47	50
Asst. Lects.	—	—	27	25	19	16	15	20	15
Others	—	—	1	2	7	4	5	5	6
TOTAL	(403)	(498)	(553)	(718)	(1439)	(2120)	(2600)	(3759)	(4781)

Table 7.6 continued

	1910–1	1919–20	1929–30	1938–39	1949–50	1959–60	1963–64	1965–66	Dec. 1968
F. ENGLISH NEW UNIVERSITIES									
Professors	—	—	—	—	—	14	14	13	11
Readers ⎫ / Asst. Profs. ⎬ / Indep. Lects. ⎭	—	—	—	—	—	1	3⎱	14	14
Senior Lects.	—	—	—	—	—	3	10⎰	43	52
Lecturers	—	—	—	—	—	56	42	21	18
Asst. Lect.	—	—	—	—	—	24	18	8	5
Others	—	—	—	—	—	3	13		
TOTAL	—	—	—	—	—	(108)	(331)	(1107)	(2105)
G. OXFORD AND CAMBRIDGE									
Professors	—	—	—	—	—	—	—	9	10
Readers & Sen. Lects.	—	—	—	—	—	—	—	8	7
								66	69
Lecturers	—	—	—	—	—	—	—	17	13
Asst. Lects.	—	—	—	—	—	—	—	—	2
Others	—	—	—	—	—	—	—		
TOTAL	—	—	—	—	—	—	—	(2287)	(2498)
H. EX CATS									
Professors	—	—	—	—	—	—	—	4	7
Readers & Sen. Lects.	—	—	—	—	—	—	—	15	18
								65	69
Lecturers	—	—	—	—	—	—	—	11	6
Asst. Lects.	—	—	—	—	—	—	—	5	0
Others	—	—	—	—	—	—	—		
TOTAL	—	—	—	—	—	—	—	(2189)	(2453)
ALL UNIVERSITIES IN GREAT BRITAIN EXCEPT OXFORD AND CAMBRIDGE(d)									
Professors	31	31	22	20	13	12	12	10	10
Readers ⎫ / Asst. Profs. ⎬ / Indep. Lects. ⎭	—	—	10	9	6	6	7⎱	17	18
Senior Lects.	69	69	—	—	10	12	12⎰		
Lecturers	—	—	36	40	40	49	46	50	53
Asst. Lects.	—	—	25	22	20	12	11	17	13
Others	—	—	8	9	11	10	13	6	6
GRAND TOTALS	(1478)	(2277)	(3049)	(3819)	(7682)	(11,483)	(14,927)	(25,294)	(30,755)

Notes: (a) Figures in Group A for these years include the staff of the Merchant Venturers' Technical College, formed as part of Bristol University 'to afford preparation for an industrial or commercial career'.

(b) For 1919–20 Heads of Departments are counted as Professors. The numbers may then include some non-professorial Heads of Departments.

(c) The Board of Education Report for 1910–11 gives only staff numbers at Dundee University College. Staff numbers for Scotland have been calculated from the calendars of the Scottish Universities for 1910–11.

(d) 1965–6 and 1968 include Oxford, Cambridge and ex-CATs and are based on all teaching and research staff irrespective of source of financial support.

Source: U.G.C. Returns, information from the U.G.C. and *Statistics of Education.*

TABLE 7.7

Academic Staff or Students, by Faculty 1919–1968, Great Britain (percentages)

	1919–20 (a)	1928–9	1938–9	1949–50	1961–2	1964–5	December 1968
Arts(b) ⎱ Social Studies ⎰	38·7	53·3	44·8	43·6	⎰25·5 ⎱ 8·4	25·5 10·5	16·7 14·6
Pure Science	18·3	16·7	15·5	19·8	26·3	28·3	28·9
Applied Science ⎫ Technology Agriculture ⎬ Forestry ⎭	16·4	11·1	12·6	16·0	19·5	17·0 ⎫	
Medicine ⎫ Dentistry ⎬ Veterinary Science ⎭	26·6	18·9	27·1	20·6	20·2	18·6 ⎭	39·8
Total Numbers	(43018)	(44309)	(50246)	(85421)	(13104)	(17117)	(30755)

Notes: Student numbers are given for the years 1919–20, 1928–9, 1938–9 and 1949–50 and *include* Oxford and Cambridge. Staff numbers are given for the years 1961–2 and 1964–5 and *exclude* Oxford and Cambridge Lecturers and below. For 1968 all staff are included who were wholly paid from general university funds including Oxford and Cambridge.

(a) Oxford and Cambridge student numbers were not included in U.G.C. Returns for 1919–20. These numbers were taken from the Returns for 1922–3, the first year they were included, and added to the numbers for other universities given in the 1919–20 Returns.

(b) Including Education.

Source: U.G.C. Returns.

TABLE 7.8

Proportion of Male and Female, Full-time and Part-time Students by Type of Institution, and Full-time Students as a percentage of the Age Group(a) 1919-1968, Great Britain (percentages)

	Full-time		Part-time		Men and Women	
	Men	Women	Men	Women	Full-time	Part-time
1919–1920						
Oxford & Cambridge	—	—	—	—	—	—
London	67·6	32·4	64·2	35·8	53·5	46·5
Major redbrick	76·6	23·4	83·5	16·5	74·6	25·4
Minor redbrick	65·8	34·2	87·6	12·4	67·0	33·0
Wales	72·6	27·4	51·2	48·8	93·9	6·1
Scotland	72·0	28·0	79·2	20·8	96·9	3·1
Colleges of Technology	98·4	1·6	97·5	2·5	26·0	74·0
Total Great Britain	73·0	27·0	77·2	22·8	69·4	30·6
	(24,768)	(9183)	(11,585)	(3419)	(33,951)	(15,004)
Totals as percent of those aged 18, 19 and 20	2·2	0·8	—	—	1·5	—
1929–1930						
Oxford & Cambridge	87·5	12·5	—	—	100	0
London	66·3	33·7	70·3	29·7	57·4	42·6
Major redbrick	69·9	30·1	77·1	22·9	84·6	15·4
Minor redbrick	53·7	46·3	83·4	16·6	61·6	38·4
Wales	64·1	35·9	67·5	32·5	93·1	6·9
Scotland	66·8	33·2	87·6	12·5	89·8	10·2
Colleges of Technology	94·9	5·1	97·5	2·5	22·2	77·8
Total Great Britain	71·7	28·3	78·4	21·6	76·7	23·3
	(32,682)	(12,921)	(10,879)	(2992)	(45,603)	(13,871)
Totals as percent of those aged 18, 19 and 20	2·8	1·1	—	—	1·9	—
1938–1939						
Oxford & Cambridge	87·4	12·6	—	—	100	0
London	73·6	26·4	73·8	26·2	67·7	32·3
Major redbrick	75·1	24·9	77·1	22·9	81·3	18·7
Minor redbrick	67·1	32·9	79·6	20·4	74·6	25·4
Wales	73·4	26·6	75·3	24·7	88·3	11·7
Scotland	71·9	28·1	89·2	10·8	90·3	9·7
Colleges of Technology	96·1	3·9	98·6	1·4	24·9	75·1
Total Great Britain	76·7	23·3	80·7	19·3	78·8	21·2
	(38,368)	(11,636)	(10,834)	(2584)	(50,004)	(13,418)
Totals as percent of those aged 18, 19 and 20	3·9	1·0	—	—	2·3	—

Table 7.8 continued

	Full-time		Part-time		Men and Women	
	Men	Women	Men	Women	Full-time	Part-time
1950–1951						
Oxford & Cambridge	88·1	11·9	—	—	100	0
London	73·4	26·6	74·8	25·2	70·1	29·9
Major redbrick	77·8	22·2(b)	80·4	19·6	90·2	9·8
Minor redbrick	65·8	34·2	82·3	17·7	94·8	5·2
Wales	74·5	25·5	49·8	50·2	94·0	6·0
Scotland	73·6	26·4	85·0	15·0	88·0	12·0
Colleges of Technology	94·8	5·2	97·0	3·0	35·7	64·3
Total Great Britain	77·2	22·8	81·4	18·6	86·3	13·7
	(65,831)	(19,483)	(13,591)	(3107)	(85,314)	(16,698)
Totals as percent of those aged 18, 19 and 20	7·6	2·0	—	—	4·6	—
1960–1961						
Oxford & Cambridge	88·1	11·9	0	0	100	0
London	71·7	28·3	79·0	21·0	71·8	28·2
Major redbrick	75·7	24·3	84·9	15·1	93·2	6·8
Minor redbrick	65·8	34·2	80·7	19·3	94·5	5·5
Wales	70·3	29·7	63·8	36·2	96·7	3·3
Scotland	70·7	29·3	84·3	15·7	89·9	10·1
Colleges of Technology	94·1	5·9	97·9	2·1	46·4	53·6
Total Great Britain	75·5	24·5	84·7	15·3	85·8	14·2
	(81,330)	(26,369)	(15,093)	(2,738)	(107,699)	(17,831)
Total as percent of those aged 18, 19 and 20	8·8	2·8	—	—	5·8	—
1967–1968						
Oxford & Cambridge	85·2	14·8	0	0	100	0
London	71·4	28·6	75·3	24·7	81·2	18·8
Major redbrick	71·7	28·3	79·9	20·1	95·1	4·9
Minor redbrick	65·6	34·4	76·9	23·1	91·6	8·4
New English	63·5	36·5	84·4	15·6	96·6	3·4
Ex-Colleges of Technology	89·4	10·6	93·9	6·1	89·1	10·9
Wales	67·0	33·0	80·1	19·9	97·7	2·3
Scotland	68·7	31·3	83·3	16·7	90·7	9·3
Total Great Britain	72·6	27·4	80·2	19·8	91·8	8·2
	(145,277)	(54,844)	(14,398)	(3,559)	(200,121)	(17,957)
Total as percent of those aged 18, 19 and 20	10·5	4·2	—	—	7·6	—

Notes: (a) Census 1921, 1931 and 1951 figures. 1938 estimated from age groups in National Register in U.K. 1939. 1960 and 1967 R.G. estimates.

(b) Including those in two-year teacher training.

Source: University Grants Committee: Returns from universities and university colleges.

TABLE 7.9

**Undergraduates with Fathers in Manual Occupations 1928–1961
(percentages)**

	Men	Women	Men and Women
1928–47	27	13	23
1955	27	19	25
1961	26	23	25

Note: 1928–47 figures from J. Floud in *Social Mobility in Britain* (ed. D. V. Glass 1954). 1955 R. K. Kelsall *Applications for Admissions to Universities* (Association of Universities of the British Commonwealth 1957). 1961 U.G. Survey.

Data for 1928–47 relate to England and Wales, for 1955 and 1961 to Great Britain. Data for 1928–47 relate to those aged 18 in these years who at any time attended a university; data for 1955 to entrants in that year; data for 1961 to all undergraduates in that year.

Source: Higher Education, Appendix 2 (B), Table 6.

TABLE 7.10

Social Class of Fathers of Student Admissions with Addresses in England, Scotland and Wales compared with Adult Male Population of 1951 Census: 1955, Great Britain (percentages)

Registrar-General's Social class	English addresses		Males aged 20-64 in England	Scottish addresses		Males aged 20-64 in Scotland	Welsh addresses		Males aged 20-64 in Wales
	Males	Females		Males	Females		Males	Females	
1	21·6	27·0	3·4	18·9	24·2	3·2	13·5	17·2	2·7
2	41·2	45·4	15·0	40·5	45·3	13·2	37·6	46·3	15·3
3 (non manual)	11·1	9·0	9·6	12·0	9·9	8·7	10·4	10·9	6·6
3 (manual)	21·7	16·1	43·6	21·9	16·1	42·5	27·1	19·6	41·0
4	3·5	1·9	15·6	5·3	3·9	18·0	9·1	5·1	20·4
5	0·9	0·6	12·8	1·4	0·6	14·4	2·3	0·9	14·0
Total	100·0 (11,595)	100·0 (4601)	100·0	100·0 (1470)	100·0 (694)	100·0	100·0 (912)	100·0 (449)	100·0

Source: R. K. Kelsall, *Applications for Admissions to Universities* (Association of Universities of the British Commonwealth 1957).

TABLE 7.11

Home Residence of Full-time Students in Universities 1920-1968, Great Britain (percentages)

Year	From United Kingdom			From outside United Kingdom						Total		
				British Commonwealth			Foreign countries					
	Men	Women	Total	Men	Women	Total	Men	Women	Total	Men	Women	Total
1920-1(a)			94·1			4·0			1·9			100(33,951)
1929-30			90·0			6·2			3·8			100(45,603)
1938-9			89·5			5·7			4·7			100(50,002)
1950-1			92·3			4·3			3·4			100(83,314)
1960-1			89·2			6·4			4·3			100(107,699)
1967-8	91·2	95·5	92·4	4·6	2·1	3·9	4·2	2·5	3·7	100(145,277)	100(54,844)	100(200,121)

Note: (a) Excluding students at Oxford and Cambridge.
Source: University Grants Committee, Returns from universities and university colleges in receipt of Treasury grant.

TABLE 7.12

**Secondary School of Undergraduates 1961–1962, Great Britain
(percentages)**

	Maintained Grammar and senior secondary	Other	Direct grant		Independent	
			HMC(a)	Other	HMC(a)	Other
Men	59	2	10	4	22	3
Women	65	1	—	16	—	18
Men and women	61	2	16		18	

Note: (a) Headmasters' Conference schools.
Source: Higher Education, Appendix 2 (B), U.G. Survey.

**Proportion of Children in Different Types of School in Age
Groups 11–14 and 15–19, 1961, England and Wales (percentages)**

Ages	Maintained	Direct grant	Independent
11–14	91·7	2·1	6·2
15–19	76·1	7·4	16·4

Source: Table 6.2 of this volume.

TABLE 7.13

Students by Type of Course 1919–1968, Great Britain (percentages)

	1919–20(a)		1929–30		1938–9		1950–1		1960–1		1967–8(c)	
	Men	Women	Men	Women	Men	Women	Men	Women	Men	Women	Men	Women
Full-time												
research	0·9	1·3	3·6	2·2	5·8 }	2·8 }	11·3 }	10·4 }	14·8 }	12·1 }	17·2	12·9
post-graduate	0·7	1·6	0·5	0·1								
first degree	49·6	55·9	59·5	63·6	61·2	64·1	65·8	68·6	65·8	74·2	72·5	78·8
diploma(b)	16·9	14·1	11·5	15·3	11·3	15·0	5·8	7·2	3·1	3·5	0·7	1·5
others	—	—	—	—	—	—	—	—	0·7	0·8	0·6	0·7
total full-time	68·1	72·9	75·0	81·2	78·0	81·8	82·9	86·2	84·3	90·6	91·0	93·9
Part-time												
research	1·1	1·3	2·1	1·8	3·4 }	2·3 }	4·3 }	3·4 }	5·4 }	3·6 }	7·4	3·5
post-graduate	2·3	1·5	1·0	0·3								
first degree	1·7	1·9	3·0	2·5	2·8	2·4	1·9	2·4	1·1	1·2	0·7	1·0
diploma(b)	4·5	3·7	5·3	3·5	3·8	3·1	2·3	1·3	0·8	0·5	0·3	0·1
occasional	22·4	18·7	13·6	10·7	11·9	10·4	8·7	6·5	8·3	4·1	0·6	1·4
total part-time	31·9	27·1	25·0	18·8	22·0	18·2	17·1	13·8	15·7	9·4	9·0	6·1
Grand Total	100·0	100·0	100·0	100·0	100·0	100·0	100·0	100·0	100·0	100·0	100·0	100·0
	(36,373)	(12,602)	(43,561)	(15,913)	(49,202)	(14,218)	(79,422)	(22,590)	(96,423)	(29,107)	(159,354)	(58,275)

Notes:
(a) excluding Oxford and Cambridge.
(b) 1950 onwards fourth-year teacher diploma students are excluded.
(c) excluding 449 students on courses *not* of university standard.
Source: University Grants Committee, *Returns from Universities and University Colleges.*

Full-time Students by Type of Faculty 1919–1968, Great Britain (percentages)

	1919–20(a)		1929–30		1938–9		1950–1		1960–1		1967–8(c)	
	Men	Women	Men	Women	Men	Women	Men	Women	Men	Women	Men	Women
Arts (including theology, fine art, music, economics and education)	23·8	54·6	44·8	74·7	38·7	64·7	37·2(b)	63·0(b)	25·4	52·7	16·5	42·4
Social studies (including social administrative and business studies)	—	—	—	—	—	—	—	—	11·5	9·4	18·8	23·1
Pure Science	19·4	15·2	17·1	15·0	15·2	15·9	21·1	17·0	25·5	21·7	28·1	21·7
Medicine (including health and dentistry)	33·4	28·6	23·3	8·8	30·3	17·3	21·0	16·6	14·5	13·6	10·5	9·6
Technology (including engineering, applied chemistry, architecture etcetera)	21·3	0·5	12·5	0·5	13·6	0·8	15·8	1·1	19·5	1·3	23·8	2·0
Agriculture (including forestry, horticulture and veterinary science)	2·0	1·1	2·2	0·9	2·3	1·3	4·9	2·4	3·6	1·3	2·3	1·2
Total	100·0	100·0	100·0	100·0	100·0	100·0	100·0	100·0	100·0	100·0	100·0	100·0
	(24,768)	(9183)	(32,682)	(12,921)	(38,368)	(11,634)	(65,831)	(19,483)	(81,330)	(26,369)	(144,956)	(54,716)

Notes: (a) excluding Oxford and Cambridge. (b) Birmingham figures include two-year teacher-training figures. (c) Excluding 449 students on courses not of university standard.
Source: University Grants Committee, *Returns from Universities and University Colleges.*

TABLE 7.15

Term-time Residence of Full-time Students 1920–1968, Great Britain (percentages)

	In colleges or halls of residence			In lodgings			At home			Men	Women	Total
	Men	Women	Total	Men	Women	Total	Men	Women	Total			
1920–1(a)	4·2	27·9	10·2	43·0	22·4	37·5	52·8	49·7	52·0	100·0 (23,939)	100·0 (8687)	100·0(b) (32,626)
1929–30	20·6	35·9	24·9	39·4	16·5	32·9	40·0	47·6	42·1	100·0 (32,682)	100·0 (12,921)	100·0 (45,603)
1938–9	21·4	37·3	25·1	37·5	19·2	33·2	41·1	43·5	41·7	100·0 (38,368)	100·0 (11,634)	100·0 (50,002)
1950–1	20·0	38·9	24·3	42·3	28·4	39·1	37·7	32·7	36·6	100·0 (65,831)	100·0 (19,483)	100·0 (85,314)
1960–1	23·5	39·3	27·4	54·3	39·7	50·7	22·2	21·0	21·9	100·0 (81,330)	100·0 (26,369)	100·0 (107,699)
1967–8	34·0	40·6	35·8	48·9	44·1	47·5	17·1	15·3	16·6	100·0 (142,276)(c)	100·0 (54,508)(c)	100·0 (196,784)(c)

Notes:
(a) excluding Oxford and Cambridge students.
(b) This total differs slightly from that shown in Table 7.11 from the same source.
(c) These figures do not include sandwich course students undertaking the industrial part of their training away from a university and some other students studying abroad for one year.

Source: University Grants Committee: Returns from Universities and University Colleges.

TABLE 7.16

Student Teachers 1900–1967, England and Wales

Year	Postgraduate		Others		Total		Men and Women
	Men	Women	Men	Women	Men	Women	
1900	—	—	—	—	—	—	5692
1910	30	133	4240	7871	4270	8004	12,274
1920	78	180	16,305		—	—	16,563
1930	273	561	6484	12,166	6757	12,727	19,484
1938	1016	794	2342	7589	3358	8383	11,741
1950	1750	1136	4612	17,274	6362	18,410	24,772
1960	2058	1437	12,103	24,636	14,161	26,073	40,234
1967	2448	2733	29,272	69,362	31,720	72,095	103,815

Note: In 1910 and 1920 teachers in training for secondary schools have been taken to be postgraduates and those training for elementary schools together with domestic science students form the 'others' category. Figures include students in university departments of education, numbering 6207 in England and Wales in 1967, who are also included in Tables 7.8–7.15.

Source: Statistics of Education.

TABLE 7.17

Further Education Students 1900–1967, England and Wales (thousands)

Year	Men	Women	Total
1900	—	—	546
1910	849	590	1439
1920	—	—	1030
1930	—	—	1044
1938	—	—	1343
1950(a)	1165	1220	2385
1960	1324	1173	2497
1967	1588	1623	3211

Note: Not including teacher training, universities, adult education provided by responsible bodies, independent establishments not recognised as efficient and residential colleges of adult education.

(a) Students who attended at any time during year.

Source: Statistics of Education.

TABLE 7.18

Further Education Students 1900–1967, England and Wales

Year	Full-time		Sandwich		Part-time day		Evening only		All students
	Men	Women	Men	Women	Men	Women	Men	Women	
1900	—	—	—	—	—		—	—	546,405
1910	23,361	22,022	—	—	7456	7525	818,155	560,383	1,438,902
1930	89,739		—	—	48,475		905,786		1,044,000
1938	103,885		—	—	60,317		1,178,863		1,343,065
1950	31,295	22,508	—		235,859	96,871	898,328	1,100,809	2,385,670
1960	75,510	58,377	9,862	176	418,694	134,238	820,416	980,406	2,497,679
1967	121,569	88,691	23,707	1086	572,959	171,801	869,405	1,361,638	3,210,856

Note: For 1900 the figure is that for scholars at evening continuation schools. For 1911, 1930 and 1938 this classification is approximate. Junior Technical, Junior Art, Senior Full-time Technical and Senior Art schools have been taken to be full-time. Day Technical classes, Day continuation classes and Art classes have been taken to be part-time day; Evening schools and classes to be evening only. Up to 1960 figures cover establishments maintained and assisted by local authorities and direct grant establishments. 1960 and 1968 figures include independent establishments recognised as efficient. All figures exclude residential colleges of adult education, independent establishments not recognised as efficient and adult education provided by responsible bodies.

Source: Statistics of Education.

8 Electors and Elected

DAVID BUTLER

This chapter covers some of the most readily defined or quantifiable aspects of the political process in Britain – the legal and social composition of the electorate, the votes recorded at parliamentary elections and the social and party composition of the House of Commons and the Cabinet. It is important to stress that quantifiable statements about political institutions are far from representing the whole truth about them.

All sorts of considerations that are relevant to balanced discussion of the evolution or the efficacy of the central instruments of British government are left untouched in this chapter, simply because they cannot be reduced to tables or other irrefutable statement of fact. The bibliographical references do, however, include some general evaluative and analytical writing.

ELECTORAL FRANCHISE

Parliamentary
In 1900, there were 6,731,000 names on the parliamentary electoral roll (approximately 58 per cent of the male population over 21). In 1970 the number was 39,615,000 (98 per cent of the total population over 18). In 1900, only men were entitled to vote and the franchise qualifications – under the Representation of the People Acts of 1867 and 1885 and the Registration Act of 1885 – limited the number, mainly by requiring 12 months' residence and occupancy of premises worth £10 a year; on the other hand some people could vote in more than one constituency, through having business premises or university qualifications or a second residence. By the Representation of the People Act of 1918, the qualifications were simplified and the vote was extended to almost all women over 30; by the Representation of the People Act of 1928, women were placed on a virtually equal footing with men. By 1931 the electorate was equal to 94 per cent of the adult population – although, since there were 137,000 university electors (0·5 per cent of the total) and 365,000 business electors (1·4 per cent), and since there were some inaccuracies in the register, the proportion of the adult population able to vote cannot have exceeded 90 per cent.

The Representation of the People Act of 1945 – and special wartime factors – greatly curtailed the business qualification and there were only 49,000 business electors entitled to vote in 1945; on the other hand, graduates on the lists for the twelve University constituencies now numbered 217,000.

By the Representation of the People Acts of 1948 and 1949, all plural voting was abolished. The 1950 register was equivalent to 99 per cent of the adult population (although a 1950 study by the Government Social Survey[1] suggested that about 4 per cent of the names were there in error; a 1967 study found a similar rate of inaccuracy).

By the Representation of the People Act of 1969, the voting age was lowered to 18 – although it was estimated that less than 70 per cent of the population between 18 and 21 were inscribed in the first register which came into force on 15th February 1970.

Local government

From 1889 to 1945 the local government franchise was confined to householders or occupiers of business premises, and from 1918 onwards, their wives (until 1928, only if over 30). By the Representation of the People Act of 1945, the parliamentary and local government franchises were assimilated. The business vote, although eliminated for parliamentary purposes in 1948, continued for local government purposes until the Representation of the People Act of 1969 when, except for the City of London, it was abolished.[2]

ELECTORAL ADMINISTRATION

General

From 1900 to 1918 electoral arrangements were governed primarily by the Representation of the People Act, 1867, as modified by the Ballot Act, 1872, the Corrupt Practices Act, 1883, the Franchise Act, 1884, the Registration Act, 1885, and the Redistribution of Seats Act, 1885. The Representation of the People Act, 1918, the Equal Franchise Act, 1928, the Representation of the People Act, 1948 (consolidated in

[1] See P. Gray and T. Corlett, *The Electoral Register as a Sampling Frame* (Central Office of Information 1950), and P. Gray and F. A. Gee, *Electoral Registration for Parliamentary Elections* (HMSO 1967).

[2] For details on changes in franchise qualifications see the successive editions of Parker's *Election Agent and Returning Officer* (Knight). See also B. Keith-Lucas, *The English Local Government Franchise* (Blackwell 1953), D. E. Butler, *The British Electoral System since 1918* (Oxford 1962), and the Representation of the People Acts of 1883, 1918, 1928, 1945, 1948, 1949 and 1969. A convenient summary of franchise qualifications at any given time is to be found in *Whitaker's Almanack* or (up to 1939) in *The Constitutional Year Book*.

1949), and the Representation of the People Act, 1969, constitute the only major legislation in the century.[1]

Redistribution

The Redistribution of Seats Act, 1885, left the House of Commons with 670 members. The 1885 Act, while removing the worst anomalies, specifically rejected the principle that constituencies should be approximately equal in size. This principle was, however, substantially accepted in the Representation of the People Act, 1918, on the recommendation of the Speaker's Conference of 1917, although Wales, Scotland and Ireland were allowed to retain disproportionate numbers of seats. The 1918 Act increased the size of the House of Commons to 707, but this fell to 615 in 1922 on the creation of the Irish Free State. Population movements produced substantial anomalies in representation and the Redistribution of Seats Act, 1944, authorised the immediate subdivision of constituencies with more than 100,000 electors, which led to 25 new seats being created at the 1945 election and raised the number of M.P.s to 640. It also provided for the establishment of Permanent Boundary Commissioners to report every three to seven years. The Boundary Commissioners' first recommendations were enacted in the Representation of the People Act, 1948 (with the controversial addition by the Government of 17 extra seats as well as the abolition of the 12 University seats), and the 1950 Parliament had 625 members. The next reports of the Boundary Commissioners, given effect by resolutions of the House in December 1954 and January 1955, increased the number of constituencies to 630. The controversy caused by these changes led to the Redistribution of Seats Act, 1958, which modified the rules governing the Boundary Commissioners' decisions and asked them to report only every 10 to 15 years. The Boundary Commissioners started their revision in 1965; when their recommendations came before Parliament in 1969, the Labour Government insisted upon their rejection. The Conservative Government gave effect to them in October 1970.[2]

[1] There have been five major inquiries into electoral questions:

1908–10 Royal Commission on Electoral Systems.
1917   Speaker's Conference on Electoral Reform.
1930   Ullswater Conference on Electoral Reform.
1943–4 Speaker's Conference on Electoral Reform.
1965–8 Speaker's Conference on Electoral Law.

[2] The problems of electoral administration are dealt with in the reports of the Speaker's Conferences on Electoral Reform of 1917, 1943–4 and 1965–8, and the Ullswater Conference of 1930. (See Cd 8463/1917; Cmd 3636/1930; Cmd 6534/1944; and Cmd 6543/1944, Cmnd 2917 and 2932/1966; Cmnd 3202 and 3275/1967 and Cmnd 3550/1968.)

See also the reports of the Boundary Commissioners (Cmd 7260, 7274, 7270, 7231 of 1947, Cmd 9311–14 of 1954, and Cmnd 4084, 4085, 4086, and 4087 of 1969. See also

ELECTION RESULTS: SOURCES

The only official record of election results is to be found in Parliamentary Papers on election expenses published six to twelve months after each election. Since these make no acknowledgement of parties, they are of limited analytic use. However results are in a number of other sources.

The official returns, listing candidates' votes and expenses, issued as Parliamentary Papers after every General Election, except 1918 are: 1901 (352) lix, 145; 1906 (302) xcvi, 19; 1910 (259) lxxiii, 705; 1911 (272) lxii, 701; 1924 (2) xviii, 681; 1924–5 (151) xviii, 775; 1926 (I) xxii, 523; 1929–30 (114) xxiv, 755; 1931–2 (109) xx, I; 1935–6 (150) xx, 217; 1945–6 (128) xix, 539; 1950 (146) xviii, 311; 1951–2 (210) xxi, 841; 1955 (141) xxxii, 913; 1959–60 (173) xxiv, 1031; 1964–5 (220) xxv, 587; 1966–7 (162) iv, 1; 1970–1 (305).

The Times House of Commons (published after every election since 1880 except for 1906, 1922, 1923 and 1924.)

The Constitutional Year Book (published annually 1885–1939. Until 1919 it gave every result since 1885; after 1919 it only gave post-1918 results and after 1931 only results since 1923 or 1924.)

British Parliamentary Election Statistics 1918–70 by F. W. S. Craig (Political Reference Publications 1971). (This gives national totals, together with much else.)

British Parliamentary Election Results 1918–49 by F. W. S. Craig (Political Reference Publications 1969). *British Parliamentary Election Results 1950–70* by F. W. S. Craig (Political Reference Publications 1971). (These volumes record all constituency results with percentages. They constitute easily the most authoritative and convenient source of electoral data.)

British Parliamentary Election Results 1950–64 by B. R. Mitchell and Klaus Boehm (C.U.P. 1966). (This gives all constituency results fully percentaged.)

British Political Facts 1900–1968 by D. E. Butler and Jennie Freeman (Macmillan 1969). (This gives national totals and other electoral data.)

The British Voter 1885–1966 by M. Kinnear (Batsford 1968).

From 1945, the results of each election have been analysed in statistical appendices to the Nuffield College series of studies, *The British General Election of 1945* (O.U.P. 1947) by R. B. McCallum and Alison Readman, *The British General Election of 1950* (Macmillan 1951) by H. G. Nicholas, *The British General Election of 1951* (Macmillan 1952) by D. E. Butler, *The British General Election of 1955* (Macmillan 1955) by D. E. Butler, *The British General Election of 1959* (Macmillan 1960) by D. E.

H. L. Morris, *Parliamentary Franchise Reform in England from 1885 to 1918* (New York 1921), and D. E. Butler, 'The Redistribution of Seats', *Public Administration*, Summer 1955, 125–47. See also R. L. Leonard, *Elections in Britain* (Van Nostrand 1968).

Butler and Richard Rose, *The British General Election of 1964* (Macmillan 1965) by D. E. Butler and Anthony King, *The British General Election of 1966* (Macmillan 1966) by D. E. Butler and Anthony King, and *The British General Election of 1970* (Macmillan 1971) by D. E. Butler and M. Pinto-Duschinsky.

A valuable source on pre-1914 election statistics is *Social Geography of British Elections 1885–1910* by H. Pelling (Macmillan 1967).

A general bibliography on British electoral statistics and psephological studies is to be found in the chapter by D. E. Butler and James Cornford in S. Rokkan and J. Meyriat (eds), *International Guide to Election Statistics* (Mouton 1969).

ELECTION RESULTS: STATISTICS

Tables 8.1 to 8.3 are taken from *British Political Facts 1900–1968*, because they provide a simple series compiled on the same basis for the whole century.

It is, however, impossible to present election statistics in any finally authoritative way. British law makes no acknowledgement of the existence of political parties, and in most general elections the precise allegiance of at least a few of the candidates is in doubt. This, far more than arithmetic error, explains the discrepancies between the figures provided in various works of reference.

Such discrepancies, however, are seldom on a serious scale (except, perhaps, for 1918). Election figures suffer much more from being inherently confusing than from being inaccurately reported. The complications that arise from unopposed returns, from plural voting, from two-member seats, and, above all, from variations in the number of candidates put up by each party are the really serious hazards in psephological interpretation.

In Table 8.1 an attempt is made to allow for these factors by a column which shows the average vote won by each opposed candidate (with the vote in two-member seats halved, and with university seats excluded). This still gives a distorted picture, especially when, as in 1900 or 1931, there were many unopposed candidates or when, as in 1929, 1931, or 1950 there was a sharp change in the number of Liberals standing; in 1918 the situation was so complicated that any such statistics are omitted, as they are likely to confuse more than to clarify; for other elections they should be regarded as corrective supplements to the cruder percentages in the previous column rather than as substitutes for them.

The turn-out percentages are modified to allow for the distorting effect of the two-member seats which existed up to 1950.

To simplify classification, some arbitrary decisions have been made. Before 1918 candidates have been classified as Conservative, Liberal, or Irish Nationalist, even if their designation had a prefix such as Tariff Reform, or Independent, but only officially sponsored candidates are classed as Labour. From 1918 onwards, candidates not officially recognised by their party have been classified with 'Others' (except that in 1935 Ind. Lib. are placed with Lib.). Liberal Unionists have been listed as Conservatives throughout. Liberal National, National Labour, and National candidates are listed with Conservatives except in 1931.

SOCIAL BASES OF PARTY STRENGTH

Since the advent of opinion polls a large amount of data about the background of voters have become available. Table 8.4 based on National Opinion Polls 1966 findings illustrates the broad picture which has only changed a little during the twenty years that such data have been available.

Data of this sort are discussed in the local studies of voting conducted since 1950, notably:

M. Benney, R. H. Pear and A. P. Gray, *How People Vote* (Routledge & Kegan Paul 1956).

R. S. Milne and H. C. Mackenzie, *Straight Fight* (Hansard Society 1955).

R. S. Milne and H. C. Mackenzie, *Marginal Seat* (Hansard Society 1958).

On a national scale the Gallup Poll have published their findings in a monthly Bulletin since 1960. NOP have done the same since 1963. Summaries of opinion poll findings are to be found in:

R. R. Alford, *Party and Society* (John Murray 1964).

J. Blondel, *Voters, Parties and Leaders* (Penguin 1963).

J. Bonham, *The Middle Class Vote* (Faber 1954).

R. L. Leonard, *Elections in Britain* (van Nostrand 1968).

P. G. J. Pulzer, *Political Representation and Elections* (Allen & Unwin 1967).

R. Rose, *Politics in England* (Faber 1965).

There is the special treatment of working-class voting using specially collected survey material in:

R. T. McKenzie and A. Silver, *Angels in Marble* (Heinemann 1968).

E. A. Nordlinger, *The Working Class Tories* (McGibbon & Kee 1967).

J. H. Goldthorpe, D. Lockwood, F. Bechhofer and J. Platt, *The Affluent Worker* (Vol. II *Political Attitudes*) (C.U.P. 1968).

A comprehensive academic study of voting behaviour, involving nationwide sample surveys, is provided in:

D. E. Butler and D. E. Stokes, *Political Change in Britain* (Macmillan 1969).

MEMBERS OF PARLIAMENT

There are considerable difficulties in drawing up tables about the backgrounds of M.P.s. Some are very reticent about themselves and a few are actively misleading. The classification of education and occupation eaves many borderline dilemmas. These problems are discussed at various points in the main sources on the subject.

W. L. Guttsman, *The British Political Élite* (McGibbon & Kee 1963).

J. F. S. Ross, *Parliamentary Representation* (Eyre & Spottiswoode, 2nd ed. 1944); *Elections and Electors* (Eyre & Spottiswoode 1955).

The Nuffield Studies of each election since 1945.

J. A. Thomas, *The House of Commons 1837–1901* (Univ. of Wales 1939); *The House of Commons 1900–1911* (Univ. of Wales 1958).

Age

The average age of members has been very constant. At the beginning of every Parliament from 1918 to 1970 it has lain between $48\frac{1}{2}$ and 52. The average age of Labour members has always been slightly higher than the rest.

Occupation

Details of the interests represented by members of the pre-1914 parliaments are provided by J. A. Thomas. Table 8.4 is based on W. L. Guttsman's adaptation of Thomas's figures. [1]

For the interwar and immediate post-1945 period J. F. S. Ross offers a summary of occupations (Table 8.5) while since 1951 the Nuffield studies reach results using a slightly different definition of occupation (Table 8.7).

Education

The educational background of Conservative and Labour members of Parliament is shown in Table 8.8.

Sex

Women's candidature for and membership of the House of Commons since 1918 are shown in Table 8.9.

THE CABINET

Table 8.10 shows the social and educational background of the Cabinet formed by each new Prime Minister on coming to office (except that

---

[1] *The British Political Élite,* p. 104.

Asquith's is not given for 1908 but for 1 August 1914; new wartime governments are omitted in 1915, 1916 and 1940; so is Baldwin's in 1923; MacDonald's National Government is given for its termination in 1935, not its inception in 1931; and Wilson's Government is reassessed as it existed on 31 May 1970).

The class composition of governments is largely drawn from the table on p. 78 of W. L. Guttsman, *The British Political Élite*. Aristocrats are those who had among their grandparents the holder of a hereditary title. Working class are those whose fathers appear to have had a manual occupation while they were growing up.

Schools are classified as Public Schools if they are members of the Headmaster's Conference.

The Oxbridge column includes three Oxford men to every Cambridge one: there is not much difference between parties in this although Mr Wilson's 1964 Cabinet was the only one in this century to contain no Cambridge men.[1]

[1] Other sources of value in this area are:

Richard Rose, *Class and Party Divisions*, University of Strathclyde Occasional Paper No. 1 (1969).

F. M. G. Willson, 'The Routes of Entry of New Members of the British Cabinet 1868–1958', *Political Studies* VII (Oct. 1959) 222–32.

Leon Epstein, 'British Class Consciousness and the Labour Party', *J. British Studies* II (1962).

TABLE 8.1

General Election Results 1900–1970, United Kingdom

	Total Votes	M.P.s Elected	Candidates	Un-opposed Returns	% Share of Total Vote	Average % Vote per Opposed Candidate
1900. 28 Sep–24 Oct						
Conservative	1,797,444	402	579	163	51·1	52·5
Liberal	1,568,141	184	406	22	44·6	48·2
Labour	63,304	2	15	—	1·8	26·6
Irish Nationalist	90,076	82	100	58	2·5	80·0
Others	544	—	2	—	0·0	2·2
Elec. 6,730,935	3,519,509	670	1102	243	100·0	—
Turnout 74·6%						
1906. 12 Jan–7 Feb						
Conservative	2,451,454	157	574	13	43·6	44·1
Liberal	2,757,883	400	539	27	49·0	52·6
Labour	329,748	30	51	—	5·9	39·9
Irish Nationalist	35,031	83	87	74	0·6	63·1
Others	52,387	—	22	—	0·9	18·8
Elec. 7,264,608	5,626,503	670	1273	114	100·0	—
Turnout 82·6%						
1910. 14 Jan–9 Feb						
Conservative	3,127,887	273	600	19	46·9	47·5
Liberal	2,880,581	275	516	1	43·2	49·2
Labour	505,657	40	78	—	7·6	38·4
Irish Nationalist	124,586	82	104	55	1·9	77·7
Others	28,693	—	17	—	0·4	15·4
Elec. 7,694,741	6,667,404	670	1315	75	100·0	—
Turnout 86·6%						
1910. 2–19 Dec						
Conservative	2,420,566	272	550	72	46·3	47·9
Liberal	2,295,888	272	467	35	43·9	49·5
Labour	371,772	42	56	3	7·1	42·8
Irish Nationalist	131,375	84	106	53	2·5	81·9
Others	8768	—	11	—	0·2	9·1
Elec. 7,709,981	5,228,369	670	1191	163	100·0	—
Turnout 81·1%						

Table 8.1 continued

	Total Votes	M.P.s Elected	Candidates	Unopposed Returns	% Share of Total Vote	Average % Vote per Opposed Candidate
1918. Sat., 14 Dec (Result announced 28 Dec 1918)						
Coalition Unionist	3,504,198	335	374	42	32·6	
Coalition Liberal	1,455,640	133	158	27	13·5	
Coalition Labour	161,521	10	18	—	1·5	
(Coalition)	(5,121,359)	(478)	(550)	(69)	(47·6)	
Conservative	370,375	23	37	—	3·4	
Irish Unionist	292,722	25	38	—	2·7	
Liberal	1,298,808	28	253	—	12·1	
Labour	2,385,472	63	388	12	22·2	
Irish Nationalist	238,477	7	60	1	2·2	
Sinn Fein	486,867	73	102	25	4·5	
Others	572,503	10	197	—	5·3	
Elec. 21,392,322 Turnout 58·9%	10,766,583	707	1625	107	100·0	
1922. Wed., 15 Nov						
Conservative	5,500,382	345	483	42	38·2	48·6
National Liberal	1,673,240	62	162	5	11·6	39·3
Liberal	2,516,287	54	328	5	17·5	30·9
Labour	4,241,383	142	411	4	29·5	40·0
Others	462,340	12	59	1	3·2	28·3
Elec. 21,127,663 Turnout 71·3%	14,393,632	615	1443	57	100·0	—
1923. Thu., 6 Dec						
Conservative	5,538,824	258	540	35	38·1	42·6
Liberal	4,311,147	159	453	11	29·6	37·8
Labour	4,438,508	191	422	3	30·5	41·0
Others	260,042	7	31	1	1·8	27·6
Elec. 21,281,232 Turnout 70·8%	14,548,521	615	1446	50	100·0	—
1924. Wed., 29 Oct						
Conservative	8,039,598	419	552	16	48·3	51·9
Liberal	2,928,747	40	340	6	17·6	30·9
Labour	5,489,077	151	512	9	33·0	38·2
Communist	55,346	1	8	—	0·3	25·0
Others	126,511	4	16	1	0·8	29·1
Elec. 21,731,320 Turnout 76·6%	16,639,279	615	1428	32	100·0	—

Table 8.1 continued

	Total Votes	M.P.s Elected	Candidates	Unopposed Returns	% Share of Total Vote	Average % Vote per Opposed Candidate
1929. Thu., 30 May						
Conservative	8,656,473	260	590	4	38·2	39·4
Liberal	5,308,510	59	513	—	23·4	27·7
Labour	8,389,512	288	571	—	37·1	39·3
Communist	50,614	—	25	—	0·3	5·3
Others	243,266	8	31	3	1·0	21·2
Elec. 28,850,870 Turnout 76·1%	22,648,375	615	1730	7	100·0	—
1931. Tue., 27 Oct						
Conservative	11,978,745	473	523	56	55·2⎫	
National Labour	341,370	13	20	—	1·6⎬	62·9
Liberal National	809,302	35	41	—	3·7⎭	
Liberal	1,403,102	33	112	5	6·5	28·8
(National Government)	(14,532,519)	(554)	(696)	(61)	(67·0)	—
Independent Liberal	106,106	4	7	—	0·5	35·8
Labour	6,649,630	52	515	6	30·6	33·0
Communist	74,824	—	26	—	0·3	7·5
New Party	36,377	—	24	—	0·2	3·9
Others	256,917	5	24	—	1·2	21·9
Elec. 29,960,071 Turnout 76·3%	21,656,373	615	1292	67	100·0	—
1935. Thu., 14 Nov						
Conservative	11,810,158	431	585	26	53·7	54·8
Liberal	1,422,116	21	161	—	6·4	23·9
Labour	8,325,491	154	552	13	37·9	40·3
Independent Labour Party	139,577	4	17	—	0·7	22·2
Communist	27,117	1	2	—	0·1	38·0
Others	272,595	4	31	1	1·2	21·3
Elec. 31,379,050 Turnout 71·2%	21,997,054	615	1348	40	100·0	—
1945. Thu., 5 July (Result announced 26 July 1945)						
Conservative	9,988,306	213	624	1	39·8	40·1
Liberal	2,248,226	12	306	—	9·0	18·6
Labour	11,995,152	393	604	2	47·8	50·4
Communist	102,780	2	21	—	0·4	12·7
Common Wealth	110,634	1	23	—	0·4	12·6
Others	640,880	19	104	—	2·0	15·4
Elec. 33,240,391 Turnout 72·7%	25,085,978	640	1682	3	100·0	—

Table 8.1 continued

	Total Votes	M.P.s Elected	Candi- dates	Un- opposed Returns	% Share of Total Vote	Average % Vote per Opposed Candidate
1950. Thu., 23 Feb						
Conservative	12,502,567	298	620	2	43·5	43·7
Liberal	2,621,548	9	475	—	9·1	11·8
Labour	13,266,592	315	617	—	46·1	46·7
Communist	91,746	—	100	—	0·3	2·0
Others	290,218	3	56	—	1·0	12·6
Elec. 33,269,770 Turnout 84·0%	28,772,671	625	1868	2	100·0	—
1951. Thu. 25 Oct						
Conservative	13,717,538	321	617	4	48·0	48·6
Liberal	730,556	6	109	—	2·5	14·7
Labour	13,948,605	295	617	—	48·8	49·2
Communist	21,640	—	10	—	0·1	4·4
Others	177,329	3	23	—	0·6	16·8
Elec. 34,645,573 Turnout 82·5%	28,595,668	625	1376	4	100·0	—
1955. Thu., 26 May						
Conservative	13,286,569	344	623	—	49·7	50·2
Liberal	722,405	6	110	—	2·7	15·1
Labour	12,404,970	277	620	—	46·4	47·3
Communist	33,144	—	17	—	0·1	4·2
Others	313,410	3	39	—	1·1	20·8
Elec. 34,858,263 Turnout 76·7%	26,760,498	630	1409	—	100·0	—
1959. Thu., 8 Oct						
Conservative	13,749,830	365	625	—	49·4	49·6
Liberal	1,638,571	6	216	—	5·9	16·9
Labour	12,215,538	258	621	—	43·8	44·5
Communist	30,897	—	18	—	0·1	4·1
Others	224,405	1	56	—	0·8	10·0
Elec. 35,397,080 Turnout 78·8%	27,859,241	630	1536	—	100·0	—
1964. Thu., 15 Oct						
Conservative	12,001,396	304	630	—	43·4	43·4
Liberal	3,098,878	9	365	—	11·2	18·5
Labour	12,205,814	317	628	—	44·1	44·1
Communist	45,932	—	36	—	0·2	3·4
Others	302,982	—	98	—	1·1	7·9
Elec. 35,892,572 Turnout 77·1%	27,655,002	630	1757	—	100·0	—

Table 8.1 continued

	Total Votes	M.P.s Elected	Candidates	Unopposed Returns	% Share of Total Vote	Average % Vote per Opposed Candidate
1966. Thu., 31 Mar						
Conservative	11,418,433	253	629	—	41·9	41·8
Liberal	2,327,533	12	311	—	8·5	16·1
Labour	13,064,951	363	621	—	47·9	48·7
Communist	62,112	—	57	—	0·2	3·0
Others	390,577	2	89	—	1·5	8·6
Elec. 35,964,684 Turnout 75·8%	27,263,606	630	1707	—	100·0	—
1970. Thu., 18 June						
Conservative	13,145,123	330	628	—	46·4	46·5
Liberal	2,117,035	6	332	—	7·5	13·5
Labour	12,179,341	287	624	—	43·0	43·5
Communist	37,970	—	58	—	0·1	1·1
Others	865,329	7	195	—	3·0	7·9
Elec. 39,342,013 Turnout 72·0%	28,344,798	630	1837	—	100·0	—

Source: D. E. Butler and Jennie Freeman, *British Political Facts, 1900–68.*

	Total Votes	M.P.s Elected	Candidates	Unopposed Returns	% Share of Total Vote	Average % Vote per Opposed Candidate
1974. Thu., 28 February						
Conservative	11,868,906	297	623	—	37·9	38·8
Liberal	6,063,470	14	517	—	19·3	23·3
Labour	11,639,243	301	623	—	37·1	38·0
Communist	32,741	—	44	—	0·1	1·7
Plaid Cymru	171,364	2	36	—	0·6	10·7
Scottish Nat. P.	632,032	7	70	—	2·0	21·9
Others G.B.	207,884	2	174	—	0·7	2·4
Others (N.I.)[1]	717,986	12	48	—	2·3	25·0
Turnout	31,333,626	635	2,135	—	—	—

[1] In 1974 only all N.I. candidates are treated separately, even if they have some G.B. party links.
Sources: D. E. Butler and Anne Sloman, *British Political Facts 1900–75.*

TABLE 8.2

General Election Results by Regions 1900–1970(a), United Kingdom

	1900	1906	Jan. 1910	Dec. 1910	1918 (b)	1922	1923	1924	1929	1931	1935	1945	1950	1951	1955	1959	1964	1966	1970
County of London																			
Conservative	51	19	33	30	Coal. 53	43	29	39	24	53	39	12	12	14	15	18	10	6	9
Liberal	8	38	25	26		9	11	3	2	4	1								
Labour		2	1	3	Op. 9	9	22	19	36	5	22	48	31	29	27	24	32	36	33
Others						1		1				2							
Rest of S. England																			
Conservative	123	45	107	103	Coal. 149	130	89	150	111	156	147	88	144	153	163	171	157	134	169
Liberal	32	107	46	49		23	48	5	18	4	3	3	1			1	3	4	2
Labour		3	2	2	Op. 16	9	27	10	35	5	15	91	54	46	42	34	46	67	34
Others				1		3			1			3			1			1	1
Midlands																			
Conservative	60	27	49	50	Coal. 67	53	45	64	35	80	67	24	35	35	39	49	42	35	51
Liberal	27	59	31	30		17	17	2	5	3	1								
Labour	1	2	8	8	Op. 20	17	25	21	47	4	19	64	59	59	57	47	54	61	45
Others												2							
Northern England																			
Conservative	98	31	45	50	Coal. 121	82	57	101	51	146	106	43	61	69	75	77	53	44	63
Liberal	55	102	86	82		27	48	9	10	9	5	2	1	2	2	2	2	2	
Labour		20	22	21	Op. 50	60	64	59	108	15	60	128	107	99	90	88	114	121	104
Others	1	1	1	1		2	2	2	2				1						
Wales																			
Conservative	6		2	3	Coal. 20	6	4	9	1	11	11	4	4	6	6	7	6	3	7
Liberal	27	33	27	26		10	12	10	9	8	6	6	5	3	3	2	2	1	1
Labour	1	1	5	5	Op. 15	18	19	16	25	16	18	25	27	27	27	27	28	32	27
Others						1													1

(b)

	1900	1906	Jan. 1910	Dec. 1910	1918	1922	1923	1924	1929	1931	1935	1945	1950	1951	1955	1959	1964	1966	1970
Scotland																			
Conservative	36	10	9	9	Coal. 54	13	14	36	20	57	43	29	32	35	36	31	24	20	23
Liberal	34	58	59	58	Op. 17	27	22	8	13	7	3	—	2	1	1	1	4	5	3
Labour	—	2	2	3		29	34	26	37	7	20	37	37	35	34	38	43	46	44
Others	—	—	—	—		2	1	1	1	—	5	5	—	—	—	1	—	—	1
Ireland																			
Conservative	19	16	19	17	Coal. 1	10	10	12	10	10	10	9	10	9	10	12	12	11	8
Liberal	1	3	1	1		—	—	—	—	—	—	—	—	—	—	—	—	—	—
Labour	—	—	—	—		—	—	—	—	—	—	—	—	—	—	—	—	—	—
Others	81	82	81	83	Op. 100	2	2	—	2	2	2	3	2	3	2	—	—	1	4
Universities																			
Conservative	9	9	9	9	Coal. 13	8	9	8	8	8	9	4	—	—	—	—	—	—	—
Liberal	—	—	—	—	Op. 2	2	2	2	2	2	1	1	—	—	—	—	—	—	—
Labour	—	—	—	—		—	—	—	—	—	—	—	—	—	—	—	—	—	—
Others	—	—	—	—		2	1	2	2	2	2	7	—	—	—	—	—	—	—
Totals																			
Conservative	402	157	273	272	Coal. 478	345	258	419	260	521	432	213	298	321	344	365	304	253	330
Liberal	184	400	275	272	Op. 229	116	159	40	59	37	20	12	9	6	6	6	9	12	6
Labour	2	30	40	42		142	191	151	288	52	154	393	315	295	277	258	317	363	287
Others	82	83	82	84		12	7	5	8	5	9	22	3	3	3	1	—	2	7
Total seats	670	670	670	670	707	615	615	615	615	615	615	640	625	625	630	630	630	630	630

Notes:

(a) The vertical lines indicate redistribution of seats.

Northern England includes Cheshire, Lancashire, Yorkshire, and all counties to their north.

Midlands includes Hereford, Worcs., Warwickshire, Northants, Lincs., Notts., Leics., Staffs, Salop, Derbyshire.

Southern England includes the rest of England, except for the County of London.

(b) In 1918 all Coalition and all non-Coalition candidates are listed together. In fact a substantial number of the 48 Conservatives who were elected without the Coupon worked with the Government. Virtually no Coupons were issued to Irish candidates but 23 of the 101 non-University seats in Ireland went to Unionists.

Source: As for Table 8.1.

TABLE 8.3

By-Elections 1900–1970, United Kingdom

	Total (a) By-elections	Changes	Con. +	Con. −	Lib. +	Lib. −	Lab. +	Lab. −	Others +	Others −
1900–5	113	30	2	26	20	4	5	—	5	—
1906–9	101	20	12	—	—	18	5	—	3	2
1910	20	—	—	—	—	—	—	—	—	—
1911–18	245	31	16	4	4	16	2	4	10	8
1918–22	108	27	4	13	5(b)	11(b)	14	1	4	2
1922–3	16	6	1	4	3	1	2	—	—	1
1923–4	10	3	2	1	—	1	1	1	—	—
1924–9	63	20	1	16	6	3	13	1	—	—
1929–31	36	7	4	1	—	1	2	4	1	1
1931–5	62	10	—	9	—	1	10	—	—	—
1935–45	219	30	—	29	—	—	13	1	17	—
1945–50	52	3	3	—	—	—	—	—	—	3
1950–1	16	—	—	—	—	—	—	—	—	—
1951–5	48	1	1	—	—	—	—	1	—	—
1955–9	52	6	1	4	1	1	4	—	—	1
1959–64	62	9	2	7	1	—	6	2	—	—
1964–6	13	2	1	1	1	—	—	1	—	—
1966–70	38	16	12	1	1	—	—	15	3	—

Notes:
(a) Up to 1918, and to a lesser extent to 1926, the number of by-elections is inflated by the necessity for Ministers to stand for re-election on appointment. In 53 such cases the returns were unopposed.
(b) In 1918–22 Opposition Liberals won 5 seats and lost 2. Coalition Liberals lost 9.
Source: As for Table 8.1.

TABLE 8.4

Party Support by Sex, Age and Social Class 1966 (percentages)

	All	Men	Women	Age					
				21–24	*25–34*	*35–44*	*45–54*	*55–64*	*65+*
Con.	41·4	37·7	44·7	40·6	37·1	37·9	41·8	44·8	47·4
Lab.	48·7	52·4	45·4	51·2	54·6	51·2	47·0	45·9	43·2
Lib.	8·6	8·3	8·9	8·2	7·3	9·6	9·8	8·2	7·8
Other	1·3	1·6	1·0	—	1·0	1·4	1·4	1·2	1·6

		Social Class			
		Middle class AB (12%)	*Lower middle C1 (22%)*	*Skilled Working C2 (37%)*	*Unskilled 'very poor' DE (29%)*
	All				
Con.	41·4	72·2	58·4	32·4	26·3
Lab.	48·7	15·5	29·9	58·5	65·2
Lib.	8·6	11·4	10·7	8·0	6·6
Other	1·3	0·9	1·0	1·0	1·8

Source: National Opinion Polls 1966.

TABLE 8.5

Interests Represented by Conservative and Liberal M.P.s 1900–1910 Percentages of all Interests Represented (some members representing several interests) (percentages)

	Landowners	Commerce and Industry	Legal and Professional	Others	
	Con.	Con.	Con.	Con.	
1900	20	52	18	10	100
1906	17	64	11	8	100
1910 Jan.	26	53	12	9	100
	Lib.	Lib.	Lib.	Lib.	
1900	9	58	29	4	100
1906	8	65	23	4	100
1910 Jan.	7	66	23	4	100

Source: J. A. Thomas, *The House of Commons 1900–11* (1958).

TABLE 8.6

Main Occupations of Members of Parliament 1918–1951 (percentages)

	Conservative				Labour			
	1918–35 Average	1945	1950	1951	1918–35 Average	1945	1950	1951
Employers and Managers	32	32½	30½	32½	4	9½	9½	9
Rank and File workers	4	3	3	4½	72	41	43	45
Professional workers	52	61	62	57½	24	48½	46½	45½
Unpaid domestic workers	—	½	—	—	—	1	1	½
Unoccupied	12	3	4½	5½	—	—	—	—
	100	100	100	100	100	100	100	100

Source: J. F. S. Ross, Electors and Elected, p. 440.

TABLE 8.7

Main Occupations of M.P.s 1951–1970 (percentages)

	Conservative						Labour					
	1951	1955	1959	1964	1966	1970	1951	1955	1959	1964	1966	1970
Professional	41	46	46	48	46	45	35	36	38	41	43	40
Business	37	30	30	26	29	30	9	12	10	11	9	10
Miscellaneous	22	24	23	25	23	24	19	17	17	16	18	16
Workers	—	—	1	1	1	1	37	35	35	32	30	26
	100	100	100	100	100	100	100	100	100	100	100	100

Source: The British General Election of 1951, pp. 40–3, of 1955, pp. 42–4, of 1959, pp. 126–7, of 1964, pp. 234–5, of 1966, pp. 208–11, and of 1970, pp. 302–3.

TABLE 8.8

Education of Conservative and Labour M.P.s 1906–1970 (percentages)

	Conservatives		Labour	
	Public School	University Educated	Public School	University Educated
1906	67	57	0	0
1910 J.	74	58	0	0
1910 D.	76	59	0	0
1918	81	49	3	5
1922	78	48	9	15
1923	79	50	8	14
1924	78	52	7	14
1929	79	54	12	19
1931	77	55	8	17
1935	81	57	10	19
1945	85	58	23	32
1950	85	62	22	41
1951	75	65	23	41
1955	76	64	22	40
1959	72	60	18	39
1964	75	63	18	46
1966	80	67	18	51
1970	74	64	17	53

Source: Data for 1906 and 1910 are based on J. A. Thomas (1958), pp. 38–9. From 1918 to 1950 J. F. S. Ross provides the data on university education (*Elections and Electors*, p. 424) and public school education for Conservatives (*ibid.*, p. 413). The figures for Labour public schoolboys up to 1935 have been calculated afresh for this table. All figures from 1951 onwards are taken from the Nuffield studies.

TABLE 8.9

Women Candidates and M.P.s 1918–1970

	Conservative		Labour		Liberal		Other		Total	
	Cands.	M.P.s	Cands.	M.P.s	Cands.	M.P.s	Cands.	M.P.s	Cands.	M.P.s
1918	1	—	4	—	4	—	8	1	17	1
1922	5	1	10	—	16	1	2	—	33	2
1923	7	3	14	3	12	2	1	—	34	8
1924	12	3	22	1	6	—	1	—	41	4
1929	10	3	30	9	25	1	4	1	69	14
1931	16	13	36	—	5	1	5	1	62	15
1935	19	6	33	1	11	1	4	1	67	9
1945	14	1	41	21	20	1	12	1	87	24
1950	29	6	42	14	45	1	11	—	127	21
1951	25	6	41	11	11	—	—	—	77	17
1955	33	10	43	14	14	—	2	—	92	24
1959	28	12	36	13	16	—	1	—	81	25
1964	24	11	33	18	24	—	9	—	90	29
1966	21	7	30	19	20	—	10	—	81	26
1970	26	15	29	10	23	—	21	1	99	26

Source: F. W. S. Craig, *British Parliamentary Election Statistics 1918–70*, p. 79.

TABLE 8.10

Size and Social and Educational Composition of British Cabinets 1895–1974

Date	Party	P.M.	Cabinet Size	Aristocrats	Middle Class	Working Class	Public School		University educated	
							All	Eton	All	Oxbridge
Aug. 1895	Con.	Salisbury	19	8	11	—	16	7	15	14
Jul. 1902	Con.	Balfour	19	9	10	—	16	9	14	13
Dec. 1905	Lib.	Campbell-Bannerman	19	7	11	1	11	3	14	12
Jul. 1914	Lib.	Asquith	19	6	12	1	11	3	15	13
Jan. 1919	Coal.	Lloyd George	21	3	17	1	12	2	13	8
Nov. 1922	Con.	Bonar Law	16	8	8	—	14	8	13	13
Jan. 1924	Lab.	MacDonald	19	3	5	11	8	—	6	6
Nov. 1924	Con.	Baldwin	21	9	12	—	21	7	16	16
Jan. 1929	Lab.	MacDonald	18	2	4	12	5	—	6	3
May 1931	Nat.	MacDonald	20	8	10	2	13	6	11	10
Jun. 1935	Con.	Baldwin	22	9	11	2	14	9	11	10
May 1937	Con.	Chamberlain	21	8	13	—	17	8	16	13
May 1945	Con.	Churchill	16	6	9	1	14	7	11	9
Aug. 1945	Lab.	Attlee	20	—	8	12	5	2	10	5
Oct. 1951	Con.	Churchill	16	5	11	—	14	7	11	9
Apr. 1955	Con.	Eden	18	5	13	—	18	10	16	14
Jan. 1957	Con.	Macmillan	18	4	14	—	17	8	16	15
Oct. 1963	Con.	Home	24	5	19	—	21	11	17	17
Oct. 1964	Lab.	Wilson	23	1	14	8	8	1	13	11
Jun. 1970	Con.	Heath	18	4	14	—	15	4	15	15
Mar. 1974	Lab.	Wilson	21	1	16	4	7	—	16	11
Average 21 Cabinets			19½	5	11½	3	13	5	13	11
12 Con. Cabinets			19	7	12	—	16½	7½	14	13
5 Lab. Cabinets			20	1	9½	9½	7	½	10	5
2 Lib. Cabinets			19	6	11½	1	11	3	14½	12½

Source: see pp. 233–4

9 Urbanisation and Local Government

BRUCE WOOD

The twin Local Government Acts of 1888 and 1894 saw the con-
solidation of the Victorian local government structure into very
much the form which still exists today. The underlying basis of both
Acts was the recognition of the town unit – whether designated as
borough or urban district – and the provision of separate municipal
institutions for this unit. Hence the immediate link between urbanisation and the local government structure, a link which had its
roots far earlier in the nineteenth century (with the Borough reforms of 1835 and the sanitary legislation of the 1840s and later);
and which can be traced further back into history with the granting
of charters and parliamentary representation to the ancient
towns.

The local government structure, broadly speaking, recognises
the town in terms of its built-up area. It is true that numerous
examples of boroughs and urban districts which include open country within their boundaries can be cited. Nevertheless the 'bricks-
and-mortar' definition of the urban form, as represented by the
local government units, is reasonably realistic. A first definition of
urbanisation may thus be constructed as one based on the built-up
area of a town, and measured by analysing the areas of local
authorities.

Such a definition alone is no longer satisfactory. In 1888 personal mobility, certainly at the daily level, was extremely restricted.
Workers tended to live close to the factories and other places of
employment, shopping was a local activity, and journeys of any
length to seek entertainment were a rarity. Only a few of the more
wealthy had the resources, of time as well as money, which enabled
them to be regularly mobile. At the beginning of this period, therefore, this first concept of urbanisation was a useful one in that it
matched the general patterns of life.

Nowadays the bricks-and-mortar definition of urbanisation
needs to be supplemented by a second concept based more on
personal habits than physical factors. This second definition involves recognition of the growing interdependence of town and

country during the twentieth century by measuring change in such habits as the journey to work, shops, entertainment centres, and so on. In these and other respects, most towns no longer cater simply for the inhabitants of the immediate built-up area. Urban prosperity is dependent to a considerable extent on the 'rural' tracts around the town.

The aim of this chapter is to take these two definitions of urbanisation in turn, and to indicate developments in the twentieth century in relation to each of them. The data available do not always allow of a full exposition, particularly in the case of the second (or 'socio-geographic') concept, which at the beginning of the period was virtually unrecognised. The first data problem is thus one which cannot be overcome: the absence of particular statistics over the whole of the period under review.

A second major problem in compiling statistical evidence concerns the areas for which data are normally available, and its existence in fact helps to link the three main sections of this chapter. For many years the Census Office and most other government departments have collected information on the basis of whole local government areas. Two important and closely related drawbacks result from this practice:

(1) Local government boundaries have not remained unchanged since the turn of the century. Birmingham in 1970, for example, is far different from the Birmingham of 1888 in terms of its geographical limits, as is to be expected given that municipal boundaries seek, under the principles of local government legislation, to approximate to the built-up limits of towns. The final section of this chapter is devoted entirely to an exploration of the many boundary alterations which have taken place: for the time being, the important point to note is that the changes in boundaries are at one and the same time a help (as they give a broad indication of the physical development of towns) and a hindrance (as the different bases on which data have been collected mean that time-series can only be constructed, and trends analysed, with extreme caution).

(2) The nature of the boundary changes have unfortunately only rarely matched exactly the pattern of urban development. For one thing, such changes tend inevitably to occur after the physical developments have taken place. In addition, for the last four decades, there has been a policy of only urgent and limited piecemeal reforms to local boundaries, precisely at the time when suburbs have been growing outwards at a more rapid rate than ever before. (See below on Local Government Reform for details of this

embargo and its effects on municipal boundaries.) Municipal boundaries, therefore, no longer reflect the true urban limits in the case of many towns, and their apparent updating does not mean that the first definition of urbanisation (the 'bricks-and-mortar' one) can be measured with any great confidence or precision. Furthermore, measurement by the second definition is made extremely hazardous, particularly when taking the movement of people across boundaries. For example, the Halewood factory of the Ford Motor Company lies in a rural district outside Liverpool. Incautious use of the census journey-to-work statistics could cause one to conclude that the rural district involved is a major employment centre, whereas this is true of one very small corner of that rural district which ought realistically to be included in the neighbouring urban unit of local administration. A reverse illustration is when the census figures give a tremendously high rate of journeying to work into a town from a neighbouring rural district due largely to the building of large housing estates just over the boundary (the case of Slough and Eton R.D.C. being one of many examples).

These two major difficulties, which must be faced when interpreting the type of data being used in this chapter, are mentioned here in general terms. In later sections they will be re-emphasised where they are specifically relevant, and other lesser problems in handling statistics will also be mentioned.

URBANISATION – THE BRICKS-AND-MORTAR APPROACH
URBAN AREA
Visually, it is clear that virtually all towns have grown in area in the last three or four decades. Thus on the first definition of urbanisation, towns are today more important than they were at the turn of the century. Indeed, in several places – notably the six 'official' conurbations, a number of formerly separate towns have completely coalesced into one large urban area.[1]

Such developments are best illustrated statistically in figures found in the decennial census reports which refer to whole local authority areas, or whole boroughs and urban districts in the case of the data presented here. Bearing in mind the problem that, particularly since the late 1920s, local authority boundaries have tended not to keep pace with physical developments, Table 9.1 (which thus somewhat underestimates the 'true' rate of change) indicates that the urban area has increased by around 40 per cent since 1901, until today it accounts for about one-seventh of England and Wales.

[1] See pp. 252-3.

POPULATION IN GENERAL

Towns may only cover one-seventh of the area of England and Wales, but in terms of population they are, of course, far more dominant. In Table 9.2 parallel data are given to illustrate this, and it can be seen that between 1901-69 the proportion of the population classed as town dwellers under the terms of our first concept of urbanisation, rose only from 77 per cent to 79 per cent and, indeed, has declined from a peak of 81 per cent in 1951.

Such a rise is, of course, marginal. Given that the urban area has increased quite markedly, one is tempted to seek answers to the problem of why the urban population has been relatively static. Two reasons seem likely: (1) There is again the problem of the areas for which data is given. It has already been mentioned that municipal boundaries have failed to keep pace with the outward growth of residential areas in recent decades, and it is likely that the urban proportion of the population would be a little higher in 1961 and 1969 if the boundaries of a number of large cities were brought up to date for that time. (2) Whilst suburbs have been built, so too have the inner areas of many cities been progressively depopulated, partly by redevelopment for commercial and industrial use, and partly by rehousing at lower densities. For example, in 1901 no less than 4,536,541 people lived in the county of London. By 1961 only 3,200,484 were enumerated in the same area. In the provinces Salford declined from 220,957 to 155,090 during the same period. In both these cases the areas involved remained stable between 1901-61 but for most other towns boundary changes since 1901 make it virtually impossible to give truly comparable figures for these two dates.

So far, then, we have seen that the number of town dwellers, as classified from the official census returns, has risen in absolute terms by nearly 12 million this century. The proportionate increase is, however, on a very much smaller scale. The urban population in 1961 lived in an area some 40 per cent larger than in 1901, but still only in a small proportion (14·3 per cent) of the total land surface of England and Wales.

Within this framework it is interesting to take a closer look in the next three sections at some of the ways in which changes have taken place in the more detailed distribution of the urban population.

THE SIZE OF TOWNS

Boundary changes make it exceedingly difficult to obtain fully comparable data on the numbers of towns in different population categories at intervals since 1900. This problem can be illustrated by considering the figures presented in Table 9.3. The table gives the impression at first sight that something like 150 towns have 'disappeared' since 1931, but this reflects merely the success of the County Reviews held under the 1929 Local Government Act. Under these reviews, many small urban districts were either merged together or taken into larger towns of which they formed part of the suburbs. Only 42 towns actually 'disappeared' in the sense that they became parishes in rural districts, and all were under 7500 population.[1]

The figures for 1901 and 1931 are, of course, far more comparable in that there was little change in the total number of towns between these dates. With the urban population rising by nearly seven million in this period, it is not surprising to find rather fewer small towns in 1931. Table 9.4 indicates that the average medium-sized town of 50,000–200,000 was tending to grow fairly steadily during these three decades, whilst all other population categories retained a fairly stationary proportion of the total urban population (with the exception of the smallest towns, which had declined in number). These trends continued after 1931 even more markedly, and the lower percentage of population living in the large (200,000) towns in 1961 amply illustrates the point made earlier about population decline in urban centres.

CONURBATIONS

Government statisticians did not officially recognise the existence of these until the 1951 Census Special Report on 'Greater London and Five Other Conurbations'. The rather ugly word 'conurbation' appears to have been invented by Patrick Geddes much earlier in the century, and academic geographers had taken a considerable interest in the densely populated urban conglomerations several decades before the 1951 report was published.

Two interesting points for discussion emerge from a study of the Census Report. First, the boundaries of the conurbations were drawn extremely narrowly. Only whole local authority areas were included, and the boundaries were deliberately delimited to include, as nearly as possible, the built-up areas alone. In the context of the present study, this is particularly convenient as it coincides exactly with our first definition of 'urbanisation', but many observers have criticised the census definition as being too restrictive. Secondly, the census only recognised six conurbations in England and Wales, and a number of other potential candidates for inclusion were ignored (Tees-side and South Hampshire, for example). These six undoubtedly stand on their own in terms of population size and importance, but it has been suggested that, again, the line was drawn rather narrowly. Freeman, by

[1] See pp. 271–2.

contrast, was extremely liberal in his definition of conurbation, including as many as ninety-five areas in his later study.[1]

It is ironical that the conurbations were not recognised in official statistics until they were beginning to decline in importance – in terms of population, at any rate. In Table 9.5 the trend is traced from 1871 in order to show that by the beginning of the present century the period of relative growth of the six official conurbations was already over.[2] At that time the six, covering a mere 3½ per cent of the land area of England and Wales, accounted for no less than 41 per cent of the population. Since 1931 this 41 per cent has steadily declined to the 1961 figure of 37 per cent. As a proportion of the urban population alone, the conurbations have been losing importance since at least 1901, when they accounted for 54 per cent as against 46 per cent in 1961. Unfortunately, accurate comparable figures for the total urban population in 1871 are not obtainable, as at that time local government was still unreformed. However, the rapid absolute growth of five million between 1871 and 1901 makes it likely that the conurbation proportion of the urban population rose throughout this thirty-year period.

A further trend has become increasingly noticeable since the Second World War. In some of the conurbations the population decline has become absolute as well as relative. This was first apparent in the Greater Manchester (or SELNEC)[3] area, where the population declined marginally between 1931 and 1951. The 1961 Census revealed a very slight increase in population in the SELNEC conurbation as compared with 1951, but also indicated that Greater London was losing population and that Merseyside had become almost static. Later returns in the 1966 Census show further changes, and between 1961–6 no fewer than four of the six conurbations (London, SELNEC, Merseyside and Tyneside) lost population, whilst a fifth (West Yorkshire) remained almost unchanged. Only the prosperous West Midlands conurbation continues to grow at an appreciable rate. Thus the increased degree of urbanisation of the population of England and Wales since 1901 has been achieved in spite of, rather than as a result of, the presence of the conurbations. The opposite conclusion would almost certainly result from a parallel study of the nineteenth century, for it was then that the conurbations (apart, possibly, from London) were rapidly developed alongside the industrial revolution.

[1] T. W. Freeman, *The Conurbations of Great Britain* (Manchester U.P. 1959).

[2] There have been some slight boundary changes in the case of all six since 1901 which make the figures for the earlier dates not fully comparable. The 1951 Census described the effect as 'comparatively small'.

[3] SELNEC being an abbreviation for 'South-East Lancashire and North-East Cheshire'.

PLANNED URBANISATION—THE NEW TOWNS AND TOWN
DEVELOPMENT

The genesis of the 'new town' idea of planned new settlements can be
traced at least as far back as 1816, when Robert Owen built the town of
New Lanark. Sir Titus Salt's Saltaire (1853) and Sir George Cadbury's
Bourneville (1879) were other nineteenth-century pioneer developments,
whilst Ebenezer Howard's 'Garden City Association' paved the way for
the new towns of Letchworth, Hampstead Garden Suburb and Welwyn.
The first signs of local authority activity in this field were probably in
the inter-war period at Becontree (L.C.C.) and Wythenshawe (Manchester C.B.).

Following the recommendations of the Reith Committee,[1] the New
Towns Act, 1946, placed the responsibility for the planning and construction of new towns upon separate development corporations, appointed by the Minister. These were given extensive powers to acquire
and develop land and to provide certain public utility services, although
the county council remained the planning authority for the area, and
the provider of schools, health and other personal social services.

New towns were seen by the post-war government as a means of
dispersing both population and jobs from the conurbations which were
under severe pressure at that time – notably Greater London and Tyneside. The progress of new towns is summarised in Table 9.6 and it can
be seen from the year of designation that the new town movement has
been in two waves. During the years 1946–50 twelve new towns were
designated by the Minister, no less than eight of them specifically to
relieve London. No further designations took place until 1961, since
when a further nine development corporations have been created. This
second burst of activity has been aimed more at relieving the provincial
conurbations.

However, the 1946 Act has not relieved local authorities of all their
powers to deal with overspill. The Town Development Act 1952 was
designed to supplement the work of the New Towns Act by allowing for
help to be given to small towns chosen for planned population expansion.
Under the Act, 'exporting' authorities assist the 'importing' area in the
planning of developments and provision of the necessary services,
without an *ad hoc* development corporation being established.

By mid-1968, 66 agreed schemes were in operation in England,
involving the provision of 160,000 homes. At this time over one-third of
these had been completed.[2] The Greater London Council and its pre-

[1] Ministry of Town and Country Planning, New Towns Committee, *Interim Report*,
Cmd 6759 (HMSO 1946), para. 8.
[2] Ministry of Housing and Local Government, *Report for 1967 and 1968*, Cmnd 4009
(HMSO 1969), p. 72.

decessors have been particularly active, and no less than 31 schemes are designed to take London overspill. Geographically, the areas involved in agreements with London range from Bodmin to Burnley, though the vast majority are within 75 miles of London. The other main 'exporting' areas are Newcastle (2 schemes), Liverpool (4), Manchester-Salford (4), Birmingham (15), Wolverhampton (4), and Bristol (4).

Before the Second World War, the progress of urbanisation was largely dependent on market forces, and can therefore be described as spontaneous in character. The last quarter-century has seen a new approach, with the development of positive, or planned, urbanisation taking place alongside the former pattern. By 1968 something like half-a-million people had been moved to new towns or other planned developments designed to take overspilling populations, and this figure will be doubled, trebled and more during the next decade.

It should, of course, be realised that the effect of this new approach on the data relating to urbanisation and presented earlier in this section is very limited. The main effect is clearly on the urban area (new towns alone cover well over 50,000 acres) and not on the total urban population, as the vast majority of inhabitants of new towns and town development areas came originally from other urban areas. Furthermore, there is often a considerable time-lag between the designation of a new town and this affecting the total urban area, as it may be some years before a new town area is given borough or urban district status. Hatfield and Bracknell, for example, are still rural parishes in a rural district, despite their obvious 'urban' character.

THE 'URBANNESS' OF URBAN LOCAL AUTHORITIES
This first definition of 'urbanisation' has had to rely completely on the legal classification of local authorities into urban and rural. At the outset it was mentioned that, because of the nature of English and Welsh local authorities and the pattern of boundary changes (to be discussed later), this is a rough and ready index of the built-up areas of towns and cities. As Freeman comments, 'Nothing could be more misleading than to regard the local government map as effectively representing the limit on the ground of a rural or an urban landscape'.[1]

Given this somewhat makeshift or arbitrary nature of the data, it is useful to consider a special study of the urban–rural population, undertaken by the G.R.O. as part of the 1951 Census. This is, of course, a once-and-for-all study with data for this particular year only, and it therefore cannot help to illustrate trends.

The 1951 Census General Report justified this special study by commenting that 'For some time it has been felt that the customary analysis

[1] T. W. Freeman, *Geography and Regional Administration* (Hutchinson 1968), p. 21.

of the population by types of Administrative Area may not give an accurate picture of urban development'.[1] A special analysis was therefor made, using a different definition of 'urban'. This was based on the current (1951) Ministry of Housing and Local Government density categories. Categories 1 and 2 (a density of more than ten per acre) were classed as urban, and the areas used were whole wards or parishes. Inevitably, some slight blurring results from the use of these rather than even smaller areas, but the result is likely to be far more realistic than that using whole local authorities and accepting their status (urban or rural) as proof of the type of area.

This survey indicated that in 1951 only 31½ million people were living in urban areas on this special definition, whereas (see Table 9.2) 35⅓ million people lived in urban administrative areas at that time, or almost four million more. The urban proportion of the population under the density definition was therefore only 72 per cent as against 80 per cent using administrative areas alone.

The refined 1951 study also showed that something like one person in fifteen residing in a rural district was in fact living in a parish with an 'urban-type' density. At the same time four and a half million borough and urban district inhabitants lived in the more sparsely populated wards. As well as including whole local authorities like the anomalous Lakes U.D.C., these wards would also cover a number of semi-rural outskirts of far larger cities. Interestingly, in two regions of England (the North-West and the East and West Ridings) more 'nonurban' populations were living in urban authorities than in rural districts.

Not surprisingly, the Census Report concluded that 'the customary analysis . . . produces a more 'urban' picture than this more rigorous treatment'.[2] Nevertheless, even at ten persons per acre almost three-quarters of the population was deemed to be urbanised, and the definition used in the 1951 report could be argued to be too rigorous, given the lower densities at which suburban housing is being constructed in areas where land is not at a prohibitive price.

URBANISATION – THE SOCIO-GEOGRAPHICAL APPROACH
During the latter part of the nineteenth century, town and country were certainly not growing any less self-contained. Indeed, in 1885 G. C. Broderick was able to conclude that 'No readjustment of (local government) boundaries can be satisfactory which ignores the manifold and increasing differences between urban and rural districts.'[3] The first

---

[1] G.R.O., *Census 1951 – General Report* (HMSO 1958), p. 83.   [2] *Ibid.*, p. 83.
[3] Quoted in V. D. Lipman, *Local Government Areas, 1834–1945* (Blackwell, Oxford 1949), p. 133.

concept of urbanisation, discussed above, relying as it does on the boundaries of urban and rural authorities, may thus be considered to be useful in the light of conditions at or just before the turn of the century.

The frontier between town and country is, however, no longer as clearly defined. Table 9.2 indicates that the proportion of the total population living in rural areas has changed little since 1901. Yet at the same time the proportion of the economically active population engaged in agriculture – the traditional and most obvious rural occupation – has fallen by more than half, from 9 per cent to a mere 4 per cent. This change is illustrated in Table 9.7.

Because of improved efficiency in the collection of employment statistics, the table in fact underestimates the rate of decline of the agricultural industry (as measured in terms of the numbers employed). The total numbers employed in farming actually began to decline in 1851, and the increases recorded in 1911 and 1921 reflect a superior system of classifying 'labourers' rather than an expansion of the industry. By 1911 and 1921 census questionnaires were seeking a more exact definition of occupation than the single word 'labourer', and this led to many labourers being reclassified as agricultural workers.[1]

Although the numbers engaged in agriculture have fallen both absolutely and relatively at a fairly steady rate, it was earlier seen (Table 9.2) that the population living in rural districts has increased absolutely at a considerable rate and declined relatively only by about 3 per cent in sixty years. The two sets of data, placed together in Table 9.8, offer a first indication of the unsuitability of the 'bricks-and-mortar' definition of urbanisation as a measure of social change. The implication of the table is that there is, and has been, a growing interdependence between town and country. Fifty or a hundred years ago it may have been substantially correct to equate the word 'rural' with agricultural, whereas today 'rural' may still signify habitation at low densities, but it no longer indicates a peculiar or particular way of life.

If any one factor has caused this change, it can only be the growth in personal mobility caused by the invention and spread of mechanised transport facilities. Even in the nineteenth century this was having its effect through the provision of railways, and early in the present century trams and buses increased rapidly in numbers. More recently the motor-car has become a means of mass mobility, and the combined effect of all these developments has been to break down the barriers between town and country. Some indication of these changes appears in Table 9.9, which gives the number of motor vehicles at various dates from 1904 (the first year that licences were compulsory).

It should be noted that figures for Scotland are included in this table,

[1] See Census 1911, *Occupation Tables*, p. xlv.

though with only 1,065,260 vehicles licensed there in 1968,[1] this is unlikely to make any significant difference to the overall trends. The totals for public transport vehicles exclude tramcars, and this probably helps to underestimate their decline since the 1920s, for at that time there were several thousand tramcars as opposed to a mere handful (if any) by 1968.

The two crucial points to emerge are, first, that the means to mobility have increased rapidly and steadily throughout this period, and more particularly at an extremely rapid rate since the Second World War. Indeed, the last twenty years are clearly those of the growth of mass transportation, with $10\frac{3}{4}$ million private cars on the road in 1968 as against under two million in 1948. Second, public transport has remained fairly static in terms of numbers of vehicles, and thus most of the vast increase in total numbers is of personally owned vehicles. It can be seen then, that the means of transportation have both increased and become more flexible in scope.

Of more relevance to this section would be a series of tables indicating the precise effects on the town-country dichotomy of this increase in the means of mobility. Ideally, one would like data indicating changes in shopping, entertainment, leisure and working habits so that the growing links between town and country could be measured with precision. However, because mass transportation is largely a post-war phenomenon, this type of material is almost completely unavailable for the early part of the century, with the single exception of journey-to-work statistics, which were first collected on a national basis as part of the 1921 Census. For the rest, all that can be done is to give some indication of the present extent to which the traditional boundaries of town and country mask individual shopping and leisure habits. The marked lack of interest in, for example, shopping and entertainment habits shown by social geographers in the early part of the century is probably in itself sufficient indication of their relative unimportance at the time.

JOURNEY TO WORK

The very wealthy had been 'commuting' for many decades before the 1921 Census first collected in a systematic fashion data on the movement of the employed population to and from work. Mass movement, however, has a far shorter history, and it is for this reason that earlier census reports had not dealt with the growing phenomenon of large-scale commuting. In the words of the Census Report: 'At the present time in many parts of the country masses of population move in tides of daily ebb and flow.'[2]

[1] Ministry of Transport, *Highway Statistics, 1968* (HMSO 1969), Table 10.
[2] Census 1921, *Workplaces*, p. iv.

From 1921 onwards trends in journeying to work may be mapped and calculated on a comprehensive national scale. In Table 9.10 an analysis of the 1921 and 1966 figures is presented to indicate the rapid growth of commuting from rural to urban areas, but before the results are considered, a few words of warning in the use of these data are appropriate.

First, the 1921 Census was delayed for administrative reasons until mid-June (instead of the 'normal' April date). By then, of course, the holiday season was under way. As the census recorded journey to work on the basis of 'enumerated population' rather than 'usual residence' (much more satisfactory, and used in later census reports), the 1921 figures somewhat exaggerate the level of movement in certain areas. For example, a Bolton mill-worker enumerated on holiday in Blackpool would appear in the report as a commuter from Blackpool to Bolton. This could not happen in the case of the 1966 Census, because the use of 'usual residence' as a basis for the workplace tables means that our mill-worker would be excluded from the Blackpool figures and placed back in his 'home' town. Thus the 1921 figures are, at the outset, a little on the high side, and the Census Report estimated that in over 50 rural districts the 'enumerated' population was over 3 per cent. more than the 'normal' population due primarily to the presence of holiday-makers at the time of enumeration.

Secondly, figures for *both* years are slightly low because of the form in which the data are analysed in the Workplace Volumes. For each of the two years the numbers travelling into towns have been abstracted for each individual rural district. In 1921, only movements of 25 or more persons to a town were included in the tables, and in 1966 the figure was 50 or more (or, rather, 5 or more as in the latter year a 10 per cent sample was used). The correct figures for both years should, therefore, be somewhat higher – slightly more so in the case of 1966 than 1921.

A third reservation (by now familiar) concerns the nature of urban and rural boundaries in the two years. It will later be seen that in 1921 urban district boundaries were a far better reflection of the limits of built-up areas than was the case in 1966, as up to 1921 boundary changes took place frequently, whereas from 1945 there has been a comparative 'freeze' on such changes. Consequently the 1966 boundaries do not fully reflect the outward growth of towns since the war, and some journeys to work from 'rural' to urban areas in this year will be short ones from housing estates just outside the towns' limits.

Finally, mention must be made of the particularly large non-response to this question in 1921, when in some areas more than 15 per cent. did not record their place of work. As the response rate in 1966 was far higher, this problem has been overcome by including in both years only those respondents who gave a classifiable answer. The total numbers of economically active in rural districts in 1921 given in the table is thus somewhat reduced, but at least the data for the two years are more truly comparable as a result.

Bearing these points in mind (and, if anything, they roughly cancel each other out when making a comparison between the two years), Table 9.10 gives a clear indication of the growing extent to which the inhabitants of rural districts rely on towns for their employment. In view of the decline in numbers employed in the traditional rural occupation of agriculture, seen earlier in Tables 9.7 and 9.8, this trend is to be expected. However, the extent of the present dependence on towns for work is, perhaps, surprising. About two in five working rural dwellers travel daily into urban areas to their job, or, proportionately, more than two and a half times as many as in 1921. In that year, one rural district in eleven recorded a daily flow into towns of over 30 per cent. of its economically active population for employment purposes. By 1966 this was happening in 250 of the 472 districts, and in 30 of these over 60 per cent of workers were travelling into towns. At the other end of the scale only a handful of areas (42 out of the 472) recorded a flow of less than 10 per cent, whereas more than half of districts fell in this category at the earlier date.

The main reasons for the considerable increase in journeying across local authority boundaries to work are not difficult to find. A recent study concludes that two opposed sets of forces are the root cause: the growing concentration of jobs at a relatively few geographical points, and the over-spilling of population from the crowded centres, this latter only rarely (as in the case of some of the new towns, for example) being paralleled by a dispersal of jobs.[1] It is relevant to note here that the voluntary migration of city-dwellers to the surrounding countryside is having a considerable effect on the social balance of many towns and villages, as it is normally the younger and more 'prosperous' families which make this type of move. Thus a study of migration between fourteen major English provincial towns and their hinterlands, based on 1966 Census data, found that the movements in the year 1965–6 of professional and managerial classes and of the 25–44 working age group were 'proportionately something like twice as large as those of the population generally between these same areas'.[2]

That this type of voluntary migration to rural areas has been taking place for some years seems clear from another recent survey undertaken

[1] See R. Lawton, 'The Journey to Work in Britain: Some Trends and Problems', *Regional Studies*, **2** (1), Sept. 1968.

[2] For details see Royal Commission on Local Government in England, *Report*, Cmnd 4040, Vol. 3, Appendix 3 (HMSO 1969).

for the Royal Commission on Local Government in England by Research Services Limited. Respondents to the 'Community Attitudes Survey', were asked for the location of their workplace, and, overall, some 33 per cent were found to be employed outside the local authority in which they resided. Table 9.11, a simplified version of one found in the published survey report, shows that journeying into another local authority to work is far more common among people living in rural areas, respondents in the highest social class, those with a good educational background, and also among the inhabitants of areas undergoing a rapid expansion of population – this latter point reinforcing the evidence of migration to rural areas, though this survey, of course, covers urban as well as rural authorities.

The rather higher figure for journey to work for rural dwellers given in this table as opposed to Table 9.10 (43 per cent as against 37 per cent) is because the earlier figures included only those travelling into towns, and then only where the movement was of more than fifty persons. The 43 per cent. includes all movements, whether from rural area to town or merely from one rural area to another. Wales was not included in the Community Attitudes Survey, but there seems no reason to suppose that this omission seriously distorts the figures in any way – particularly as the Welsh population accounts for only a small proportion of that of England and Wales combined.

SHOPPING AND LEISURE

Information on shopping, leisure and entertainment habits is not available for the early part of the century, and even the recent data is somewhat piecemeal and difficult to obtain. Statistical evidence of historical trends cannot, therefore, be presented. All that can be done is to give some indication of people's habits today, in order to try to give an insight into the links between town and country.

Figures produced in the Census of Distribution are one fruitful source of information on shopping, as they include data on turnover in urban areas. An analysis of the data for 1961 for three large towns (Bedford, Cambridge and Norwich) revealed that in all three, between 53–56 per cent of sales of consumer durables and clothes could be attributed to non-resident shoppers (on the assumption that the town residents spent no more than the regional average per head on such items). For groceries and other more regular purchases only some 11–13 per cent of turnover appeared to result from non-residents journeying into these centres.[1] Cambridge and Norwich, in particular, are largely surrounded by rural areas which clearly depend on the urban centres for their more

[1] See H. Bliss, 'Local Changes in Shopping Potential: Difficulties Encountered in Interpreting Census of Distribution Data', *J. Town Planning Inst.*, **51** (1965), p. 334.

sophisticated needs. Studies of other areas confirm the dominant role of the towns in the distributive trades – for example 40 per cent of Berkshire turnover takes place in Reading (24 per cent of population live there), and so on.[1]

Some 59 per cent of respondents in the Community Attitudes Survey, used above in connection with movement to work, stated that for food and household goods they or their families have at least one family large shopping 'expedition' each week, the proportion varying only from 58 to 62 per cent according to the type of area in which they lived. Forty-four per cent. of all respondents undertook this 'expedition' without leaving their local authority, but in the case of rural district inhabitants this was true of only 22 per cent (as against 54 per cent for county boroughs and 50 per cent for urban districts and municipal boroughs).[2] This again indicates the mobility of those residing in rural areas, though in this case no details are given of where they go to shop. The earlier data for three East Anglian towns indicates, as one would suspect, that most go into towns rather than into a neighbouring rural area.

The national statistics on shopping do not allow catchment areas to be drawn around the towns, but a number of local studies of shopping habits do indicate the areas over which particular towns attract shoppers. Two particular studies – one of Kent and one of Guildford – were analysed for the Royal Commision on Local Government in England by the Greater London Group.[3] Data were extracted from the two studies and applied to the rest of the South-East in order to arrive at a shopping 'map' for the region. Two of the conclusions which emerged are particularly noteworthy: first, catchment areas for shopping appeared to be rather smaller than those for journeying to work, and, secondly, the shopping centres had changed little in relative importance between 1950–61 (apart from the development of the new towns). If anything, the shopping centres in 1961 were receiving a little more of their trade from out-of-town shoppers than in 1950.

The Community Attitudes Survey posed 'a battery of questions' on the frequency of visiting certain types of public entertainments, and their location. Of the results, the most significant for this study is that 52 per cent of rural inhabitants do not pursue *any* of the twelve types of entertainment listed (cinema, theatre, football, dance-halls, etc.) within their local authority area. This reply was given by only 17 per cent and 27 per cent of respondents in the case of county boroughs and of urban districts/municipal boroughs respectively.[4]

[1] For details see Board of Trade, *Report on the Census of Distribution and Other Services, 1961*, Part II, Table 3. Summary figures are given here for each local authority area.
[2] *Research Studies* 9, Table 80, p. 72.   [3] *Research Studies* 1, pp. 537–57.
[4] *Research Studies* 9, Table 61, p. 59.

Most of the data presented so far have emphasised the dependence of rural areas on urban centres – for work, leisure, shopping and so on. In one instance, however, it is the urban dweller who is reliant for the pursuit of his interests on rural areas. Of the twelve types of entertainment used in the questionnaire, only two could be considered from the replies to be 'frequently-indulged pastimes'. As many as 58 per cent of respondents claimed to go 'into the countryside' for pleasure or recreation at least once a month; 36 per cent used public parks or gardens this often, but of the other ten items listed only three (cinema, bingo and soccer, rugby or cricket matches) attracted a response rate of more than 10 per cent for frequent participation (soccer, etc., recording 17 per cent, bingo 12 per cent, cinema 10 per cent).[1] Thus the major source of entertainment of the English population appears to be the drive or walk into the countryside, and it is primarily this (plus the provision of foodstuffs by the agricultural industry, and the fact that trade from rural areas increases the prosperity of the towns) which justifies the phrase 'inter-dependence of town and country'.

To sum up, trend data to give a full analysis of the socio-geographic definition of urbanisation are simply not available in the case of many of the social habits which one would like to investigate. However, most, if not all, of these habits rely to a large extent on the growth of mobility, and licensing statistics for motor vehicles are available to illustrate the post-1945 growth of mass-mobility as well as the steady inter-war development of the motor industry. Trend statistics for the employment structure and, in a slightly more limited fashion, for journeying to work, amply illustrate this second concept of urbanisation, based on patterns of living rather than patterns of development. More recent evidence on such factors as shopping and leisure provides additional, but not unexpected, support for the theory that urban and rural areas have, during this century, had steadily growing links. Although a figure cannot be given, it is safe to say that the vast majority of the population live under the influence of the town, and that this majority includes a large number living in areas officially designated for local governmental purposes as 'rural'.

LOCAL GOVERNMENT REFORM

The twin Local Government Acts of 1888 and 1894, the culmination of a series of enactments relating to municipal administration from 1834 onwards, established the system of local government which, in essence, remains in existence today, some eighty years later. The two great principles which underlay these acts were, first, the democratisation of all local authorities, and, secondly, the recognition of an urban–rural

[1] Ibid., Table 58, p. 57.

dichotomy in local administration. It is this latter feature which will be further explored in this section. Thus the 1888 Act created counties and county boroughs as separate authorities, and the 1894 Act organised the county areas on a parallel basis by retaining the separate urban and rural districts which had first been fully recognised two decades earlier in the 1872 Public Health Act. Since then there have been a host of changes in the detailed blueprint of boundaries, as will be seen later, but few, if any, of these subsequent alterations have dented the original principle of the division between urban and rural units of government.

It would be wrong to pretend that the 'original' (i.e. 1888 and 1894 boundaries 'were an accurate reflection of the urban geography of England and Wales at that time. Some boroughs and urban districts contained considerable rural tracts, while others were already over-spilling their limits, as was evidenced by a number of requests for boundary extensions in the early years after 1888. Borough and urban district limits are only a rough approximation of the extent of the built-up area of a town; but, as a measure of this, data for these areas are the best available (apart from the special study in 1951, referred to earlier). Furthermore, subsequent changes are a more satisfactory guide to urban development in that no borough was likely to obtain a boundary extension bringing in to its area sizeable tracts of rural land. If anything, changes since 1888 have failed to keep pace with urban development, and the use of municipal aggregates as a measure of the growth of urbanisation tends to underestimate rather than exaggerate the growth of towns. The reason is largely to be found in the varying procedures for obtaining boundary changes, and these will be referred to when appropriate.

COUNTY BOROUGHS

Because of the contemporary political and parliamentary situation, the final 1888 Act bore rather less resemblance than usual to the original Bill. A major part, relating to the establishment of district and parish councils, had to be dropped completely due to the shortage of time. In twenty-two night sittings at the Committee State, clauses relating to the proposed decentralisation of parliamentary and Local Government Board functions were whittled away, as also were controversial sections on licensing.[1] In all some 1900 amendments to the original Bill were proposed.[2]

Other effective amendments related to the creation of county boroughs as entirely autonomous units of government. The Bill listed only ten, all

---

[1] J. Redlich and F. W. Hirst, *The History of Local Government in England*, vol. I, p. 201.
[2] Local Government Board, *Eighteenth Report (1883–89)*, p. 17.

with a population in excess of 150,000; but even at the first reading debate, the government speaker (Ritchie, President of the Local Government Board) forecast that 'many attempts will be made by Hon. Members who represent boroughs other than those I have named to have their boroughs also included in the Schedule'. He was right, and during the passage of the Bill, the government gave way to pressure by reducing the qualifying limit to 100,000, then to 50,000 (and almost to as low as 25,000!). The Parliamentary Secretary to the Board at that time said later that 'we came to the 50,000 line for a reason which very often obtains in the House of Commons – because we could not help ourselves'.[1]

The result of this political infighting was the creation of 61, instead of ten, county boroughs. The Act also recognised that subsequent demographic changes would necessitate the revision of boundaries from time to time, and a flexible system was established whereby a county borough could obtain a boundary extension, either by promoting a Local Act, or through the making of a Provisional Order – following a public inquiry held by a Departmental Inspector – by the Minister responsible (a provisional order had later to be approved in a compendious Act of Parliament). New county boroughs could be created in similar fashion, provided that the population qualification of 50,000 had been obtained.

The 61 original county boroughs covered an area of 308,000 acres in 1888, but within a year of the passing of the Act, both the numbers and extent of county boroughs began to be increased. In 1889, one new county borough (Oxford) was established, and the addition of 839 acres to Swansea marked the opening of a period of regular and frequent change,[2] a period which ended in the mid-nineteen-twenties with new legislation following recommendations of the Onslow Commission. By then 20 other towns had joined with Oxford as new creations, and these had taken out of county council control some 100,000 acres and 1·3 million population.[3]

Even more important was the rate of county borough extensions. From 1889–1922 there were no less than 109, covering arou d 250,000 acres and 1·7 million population.[4] The total effect on counties by these changes was thus the loss of more than one-third of a million acres and three million population. Particularly hard-hit were Lancashire (minus 667,000 population), Staffordshire and the West Riding (both losing

[1] Royal Commission on Local Government 1923–9, Evidence of Long, Q.8786 (hereinafter referred to as the Onslow Commission).

[2] By 1891 nearly 40,000 acres had been added through three new creations and several extensions (see Table 9.12).

[3] Onslow Commission, *1st Report*, Cmd 2506, para. 373.

[4] *Ibid.*, para. 374.

around 400,000). In all, however, 27 of the 61 counties outside London were affected.[1]

During this period the extension of the county borough system of government was effected without too much difficulty, and demographic changes were matched fairly closely by administrative reforms. Exactly two-thirds of the requests for county borough status or boundary extensions were granted by Parliament,[2] but county council opposition to such changes grew as time went by. Counties felt they were being robbed of their most important areas, and pressure from them helped cause the Government to establish the Onslow Commission to look into these and other municipal problems in 1923. As far as this study is concerned, one crucial outcome[3] of the deliberations of a Royal Commission consisting mainly of representatives of the various local authority associations, was the passing of the 1926 Local Government (County Boroughs and Adjustments) Act. This raised the qualifying population for new county boroughs to 75,000 and abolished the more popular Provisional Order method[4] of change (except in cases where all authorities affected agreed to the alteration). The aim was to curtail the rate of boundary reform.

As far as new creations were concerned, the 1926 Act was completely successful. Only Doncaster (1927) was made a county borough between 1926 and the establishment of the 1958 Local Government Commission (and this town was fortunate in that its Private Bill was passed just before the 1926 Act came into force). Doncaster increased the total number of County Boroughs to 83 from the original 61 in 1888. The rate of boundary extensions was also severely curtailed after 1926, in terms of their effect on the counties though not in terms of the number of alterations. Between 1927–58 some 229,000 acres of territory were included in county boroughs, an estimated 325,000 population being involved.[5] The actual number of extensions remained high, largely due to the initiation of County Reviews by the 1929 Act. Thus from 1929–37 there were no fewer than 154 extensions (and 26 small diminutions) of the areas of 47 of the 83 county boroughs, or rather more than in the whole of the period 1888–1922.[6]

From 1958 onwards a third phase in the history of county boroughs has been in progress. In both of the periods from 1888–1958, changes in

---

[1] *Ibid.*, para. 377.   [2] *Ibid.*, Table on p. 164.

[3] A second result was the Local Government Act 1929, which, *inter alia*, established County Reviews (see pp. 271–4).

[4] Onslow Commission, *op. cit.*, p. 164. The table shows that 133 of 198 proposals were made by this method.

[5] Royal Commission on Local Government in England, *Report*, Cmnd 4040, 1969, Vol. 3, Appendix 1, para. 15. Figures adjusted to take into account extensions to Cardiff and Newport in Wales.

[6] Census 1931, *General Report*, pp. 67–9.

status and area came only on the initiative of the authorities involved. From 1958–66 the initiative passed to two government-sponsored committees – the twin Local Government Commissions for England and Wales.

One reason for the reduction in the spate of county borough creations and extensions after 1926, apart from the more difficult legislative process involved, was the attitude of the government. This was particularly the case after the Second World War, when for more than a dozen years the future of the local governmental system was under review by successive governments. From 1945–58 only those local bills which were relatively non-controversial were supported by the government – others, such as the attempts of Ealing, and other large boroughs in Middlesex and Essex, to obtain county borough status, failed due to government opposition to piecemeal changes at a time when the whole structure of local government was under review.

The results of this lengthy review were seen in the establishment in 1957 and 1958 of the two Local Government Commissions and of the Royal Commission on London's local government. None of the three could themselves alter the pattern of local authorities: all were limited to recommending changes to the government. In the case of the first two, restrictive terms of reference limited the scope of potential recommendations to the minimum in any case. The existing structure was, in provincial England and Wales, taken for granted – only details could be changed (apart from within the five conurbations). In London, the Herbert Commission had a freer hand.

Governmental reception of the proposals of these three bodies varied considerably. The London blueprint was in many ways accepted – though the 1963 London Government Act was a considerably amended version of the 1960 Herbert Report.[1] In Wales, little happened as a result of the Commission's report. In provincial England a number of piecemeal alterations have taken place, notably in the Black Country or West Midlands conurbation.[2]

Despite the problems of restricted terms of reference, the effects of changes since 1958 on county boroughs has been not inconsiderable. Three have disappeared into the area now covered by the Greater London Council – Croydon, West Ham and East Ham. Three new ones – Luton, Solihull and Torbay – have been created. Thus the total number remains as before at 83 (though with a net population loss of

[1] For an excellent account of the work of the Herbert Commission and the outcome of its recommendations see Gerald Rhodes, *The Government of London: The Struggle for Reform* (Weidenfeld 1970).
[2] For details see W. A. Robson, *Local Government in Crisis*, 2nd ed. (Allen & Unwin 1968), pp. 122–35.

150,000). Had the reports of the Local Government Commissions been fully accepted, there would in fact have been a considerable net reduction in the number of county boroughs. However, Burton-on-Trent, Barnsley, Merthyr Tydfil and others escaped demotion for one reason or another.

A number of boundary extensions to existing county boroughs have also taken place since 1958. Only nine reports were produced by the Local Government Commission for England, and five other areas (broadly the North-West and South-East) were not finally studied. Nevertheless thirty English and Welsh county boroughs obtained boundary extensions (out of about forty in areas where government action on proposals took place), and as a result something like 1·3 million population was transferred from county to county borough administration, or rather more than four times as many people as in the whole of the period from the mid-1920s to 1958.

The history of county boroughs since 1888 is, therefore, one of a stream of new creations and boundary extensions. Indeed, only three of eighty-odd county boroughs have remained unchanged in area since their creation (apart from those established only in the very recent past). In all, territorial changes since 1888 have involved the transfer to county boroughs of approximately 4·5 million people, and the area of county boroughs has more than trebled from the original 308,000 to over one million acres. Despite this, and despite the fact that rather more people live in urban areas than was the case in 1888 (Table 9.2), the proportion of the total population who live in the county boroughs has, in fact, changed little in eighty years, and has fallen quite sharply from a peak in the 1920s. This is clearly shown in Table 9.12, which summarises much of the material discussed above, and the table provides further evidence of the population decline in urban centres, the outward growth of towns, and voluntary movement out to suburbs, quasi-suburbs and rural areas.

With the publication of the Redcliffe-Maud Report in June 1969, the whole future of the local government structure is again under scrutiny. Whether the Report is accepted, amended or rejected, it seems likely that the 'island' system of local government – typified by the county-county borough division – is likely to remain under strong pressure and to be a strong candidate for reform.[1] It may be that in the years to come it will no longer be possible to measure the degree of urbanisation simply by reference to data for local government units.

[1] See Cmnd 4040, 1969, op. cit., para. 85 – where this is described as 'the most fatal defect of the present structure'. (The Government plans to abolish county boroughs in its forthcoming legislation, though its proposals are less radical than those of the Redcliffe-Maud Commission (see Department of the Environment, Local Government in England – Government Proposals for Reorganisation, Cmnd 4584 (HMSO 1971)).

COUNTY COUNCILS AND LONDON

The detailed pattern of county government, in contrast to that of the county boroughs, has remained much more stable. Amalgamations, new creations and even minor boundary changes remain comparatively few and far between, although there has always been legal provision for such alterations as these. As a result, the main changes to county boundaries since the 1888 Act stem from the expansion of the county borough form of government, already explored in detail. The creation of a new county borough, or extension of an existing one, normally adversely affects a neighbouring county council, and it has already been seen that by this process more than 4·5 million people and around 700,000 acres have at one time or another been transferred from the counties to the county boroughs.

Sixty-one administrative counties were named in the 1888 Act, under which a number of geographical counties were divided into two or three separate administrative ones. Such divisions (e.g. of Yorkshire and Lincolnshire into three, of Sussex, Northamptonshire and others into two) normally reflected the previous holding of separate quarter sessions – for county councils were the successors to quarter session government by the county's justices – though one of the more bizarre amendments proposed to the Bill in the House of Lords sought the creation of a county (in several detached parts) of the Kent Cinque Ports. This was only narrowly defeated.[1]

The Act also established the county of London, based on the boundaries of its immediate predecessor, the Metropolitan Board of Works. This county was unique in that it was the only one carved out from a number of ancient counties, consisting as it did of parts of Kent, Surrey and Middlesex.

As with county boroughs, the 1888 Act made additional provision for the subsequent division or amalgamation of counties, as well as for more minor boundary changes. In the event, little attempt was made to use these, the only new county created after 1888 being the result of the separation of the Isle of Wight from the county of Southampton (only officially called Hampshire in 1959) in 1890. One or two other tentative suggestions were mooted (e.g. for a new county in South Wales), but no other definite applications were ever submitted to the Local Government Board.[2]

[1] By 35 votes to 32. *Hansard* (*H. of L.*), 3rd Series, vol. 329, cols. 1669–74.
[2] Onslow Commission, Evidence of Gibbon (Ministry of Health), pp. 82–3. The Isles of Scilly could be argued to be another case. Since 1890 successive statutory instruments have given its council the powers of a county, though it continues to have close links with Cornwall County Council – see Local Government Commission for England, *Report* No. 4, paras 259–301 (HMSO 1963).

From 1890 until the mid-1960s the number of county councils remained stable, at 62. The general reviews of local government boundaries initiated in 1957 and 1958 changed this, though alterations took place only in the East Midlands and in Greater London. In the latter area two counties, London and Middlesex, were abolished and replaced by the Greater London Council. If this new body is classed as a county (though in terms particularly of its range of functions this is a somewhat misleading classification, for it is unqiue among English and Welsh authorities), then these changes led to a net reduction of one in the number of county councils. At about the same time the government also accepted and implemented a report from the Local Government Commission for England, which recommended a reduction of two in the number of counties in the East Midlands. Thus Cambridgeshire was united with the Isle of Ely (the two had been created as separate counties under the 1888 Act), and Huntingdonshire with the Soke of Peterborough (separated from Northamptonshire in 1888). Including Greater London there are, therefore, now 59 counties instead of 62, and had other proposals from the two Local Government Commissions been accepted (e.g. for Rutland, Lincolnshire, Wales), the number would have been further reduced to only fifty or thereabouts.[1]

Although it was well known that county boundaries were in many areas in need of revision in 1888, the original Act did not contain any provision for a general review. Some improvements were made in a few areas in the years following the establishment of county councils, but it was not until the 1929 Act (following the Onslow Reports) set up statutory county reviews, that substantial progress was made. The 1931 Census reported that in the decade following the Act there were several hundred changes which affected some 14,800 acres and 20,300 people. In all, 22 counties were involved.[2]

The latest general review of boundaries (in the nineteen-sixties) made further proposals for hundreds of new changes to inter-county boundaries. The government implemented only a handful before the Local Government Commission for England was replaced by the Royal Commission on Local Government in England in 1966, and local government in Wales has remained under review ever since its Local Government Commission reported in 1962. The most important of the recent changes were in the Greater London area, under the London Government Act 1963. The new GLC absorbed between 28 per cent. and 46 per cent. of the populations of Essex, Kent and Surrey, and

[1] See Robson, *op. cit.*, pp. 122–35.
[2] Census 1931, *General Report*, pp. 66–7. For an interesting map of perhaps the most anomalous area see T. W. Freeman, *Geography and Regional Administration* (Hutchinson 1968), p. 85.

some 4 per cent. of Hertfordshire,[1] as well as the whole of the London and Middlesex County Council areas.[2]

Some of the statistical information referred to above is summarised in Table 9.13. The object of the table is to indicate that, despite the heavy population losses caused by the creation and extension of county boroughs (see above), the counties of England and Wales have continued to grow substantially, in terms of population, throughout the century. Indeed a very similar proportion of the population now lives in counties as at the turn of the century, and from 1901–61 the population of the counties increased absolutely by some nine million, despite the LCC area being depopulated to the extent of one and a half million. The growth rate (LCC area excepted) has been by no means universal, and several other counties (notably in Wales) have suffered from a declining population.

COUNTY DISTRICTS AND PARISHES

With as many as 1500 districts and 10,000 parishes involved, a detailed analysis of the changes which have taken place this century would fill at least a volume itself. All that can be attempted here is a brief summary, indicating the more important events and their results.

The period 1888–1969 can, broadly speaking, be divided into four convenient sections. From 1888–1929 there was a period best described as a 'free-for-all', where structural change depended very much on local initiative, and took place in piecemeal fashion. The 1929 Act, by making all county councils undertake a County Review of district (excluding municipal borough) and parish boundaries, heralded a decade of more comprehensive reform. Then came the post-war period of a comparative embargo on alterations, due to the general consideration being given to the question of local government reform. Finally, the last decade has seen a further attempt at a comprehensive overhaul of the system – although the creation of the Redcliffe-Maud Commission caused this to be abandoned in 1966, before much of it had got under way.

In essence, this is the history of district and parish reform since the 1888 and 1894 Acts – the latter establishing urban and rural district, and parish councils. In terms of the number of authorities at different dates, the bare bones are given in Table 9.14, with dates chosen as far as possible to indicate the pattern of events during the four periods outlined above.

[1] Royal Commission on Local Government in England, *Report*, Cmnd 4040, 1969, Vol. 3, Appendix 1, para. 30.
[2] Provincial changes included the abolition of Broadwoodwidger RDC (Devon) and its division between Devon and Cornwall, and the amalgamation of Linslade UDC (Bucks) and Leighton Buzzard UDC (Beds) into Leighton-Linslade UDC (Beds).

From the table it can be seen that it was during the 1930s that the most dramatic changes took place – a direct result of the round of County Reviews initiated in 1929 on the recommendation of the Onslow Commission. But the relatively static numbers of county districts in the period up to 1929 masks a high level of activity – it is just that amalgamations, creations, absorptions and so on tended to cancel each other out at that time. This was revealed in evidence to the Onslow Commission by the Ministry of Health, whose main witness produced figures to show that 55 new municipal boroughs had been given charters between 1889–1927, while 27 had disappeared (three into neighbouring county boroughs, and 24 had themselves become county boroughs). During this same period, 270 new urban districts were formed, but this number was largely cancelled out by 193 reductions in numbers (caused by 58 urban districts obtaining borough charters, 66 being swallowed by county borough, and 27 by municipal borough, extensions; 38 being amalgamated with neighbouring urban districts; three being transferred to rural districts, and one to a metropolitan borough). Finally, all but three of the 118 new rural districts were a direct result of the provisions of the 1894 Act, whereby any rural sanitary authority crossing a county boundary was divided into two rural districts. Thirty-eight rural districts had been absorbed into boroughs, urban districts or neighbouring rural areas.[1]

Despite this considerable volume of change, to which should be added more than 400 other orders (up to 1922) relating to alterations to district boundaries,[2] the Onslow Commission still saw an urgent need for a general review of district and parish boundaries. With no fewer than 66 boroughs, 302 urban districts, and 126 rural districts having a population of less than 5000, such a recommendation was not particularly radical or surprising.[3] The 1929 Act ordered all counties to undertake such a Review, though municipal boroughs managed somehow to obtain their exclusion from these provisions.

Table 9.14 clearly shows the results of the Reviews, amounting to a reduction in numbers of 326 county districts and almost 2000 civil parishes. Many of the smallest districts were merged, though a recent study indicates that the Reviews were far more successful in some areas than in others, depending on the attitude taken by the county council concerned.[4] Overall, the proportion of boroughs and urban districts containing fewer than 5000 population fell from 35 per cent. to 25 per

[1] Onslow Commission, Evidence of Robinson, paras 12, 19, 27, 278–80.
[2] Onslow Commission, Evidence of Gibbon (Ministry of Health), p. 81.
[3] Onslow Commission, Second Report, Cmd 3213, 1928, para. 19.
[4] P. G. Richards, 'Local Government Reform – the Smaller Towns and the Countryside', Urban Studies, 2 (2), Nov. 1965.

cent. As far as parishes were concerned the results were equally patchy, for as many as 118 detached parts remained even after these County Reviews (instead of 868 before then). Twenty-nine counties continued to contain at least one parish which was in two pieces, though 66 of the 118 divided parishes were in Essex and Northumberland alone.[1]

Following the Second World War, a period of relative stability took place, with the few alterations that took place being, for the most part, the result of voluntary agreement. Two or three small urban districts voluntarily merged with neighbouring rural authorities,[2] and a roughly similar number of new ones were created due to the rise of the new towns.[3] In comparison with the hectic decade before 1939, however, peace reigned supreme in the field of local government boundaries.

Despite numerous official reports, scarcely more has happened in the final period since 1958. Although, as the table indicates, a further hundred reductions in the number of districts has taken place, the vast bulk of this is accounted for by three sets of reforms – those in Greater London, the West Midlands conurbation and Shropshire. The net reduction in authorities in these three areas was about 50, 30 and 20 respectively.

The 1958 Act also instigated a second round of County Reviews, but in the event only Shropshire's was completed, and only five other counties got even as far as producing reports, before the 1966 clampdown on changes following the establishment of the Redcliffe-Maud Commission. The only real effect of the few reviews that got off the ground was the creation of a new type of authority. The rural borough is the name given to a municipal borough which is merged into a rural district, and the rural borough, although to all intents and purposes a mere parish council, retains its mayor and town clerk. With so few County Reviews being completed, there are at present only seven rural boroughs – five in Shropshire and one each in Cornwall and Devon.

If the Government had pressed ahead with changes which were in the pipeline in 1966, there is no doubt that an entirely new pattern of district councils would have emerged, with a reduction in numbers of several hundred. In Wales, the proposal was for a reduction to 36 districts (from 160)[4] and in provincial England, and three hundred districts of below 10,000 faced extinction following the demotion of Oswestry (11,000) under the Salop Review Order. Had such changes taken place, not only would this final section of the chapter have been very different, but in addition the continued use of municipal data to

[1] Census 1931, *General Report*, pp. 73–4 and Table 36.
[2] e.g. Axminster (Devon).
[3] e.g. Crawley (West Sussex).
[4] Welsh Office, *Local Government in Wales*, Cmnd 3340 (HMSO 1967).

measure urbanisation would have been far more difficult: for the principle of separate government for town and country would have received a severe denting with the mass extinction (as urban administrative units) of the smaller towns. Just such a change is likely to take place in the next decade, following the recent Royal Commission Report. For although the political process to be gone through will ensure that amendments will inevitably be made to any Commission's proposals before legislation is enacted, it seems clear that the government is highly likely to accept the need for a merger of authorities to reflect the trend charted earlier – the growing inter-dependence of town and country.

SOURCES OF DATA

1. *Official Documents* (published by HMSO)

Board of Trade, *Report on the Census of Distribution and Other Services*, Part II (1964).

Department of the Environment, *Local Government in England – Government Proposals for Reorganisation*, Cmnd 4584 (1971).

General Register Office, *Census Reports 1891–1966*. Particularly useful are:

(1) *General Report* 1931 and 1951.

(2) *Greater London and Five Other Conurbations*, 1951.

(3) *Workplace Tables*, 1921, 1951, 1961 and 1966.

General Register Office, *Registrar-General's Annual Estimates of the Population of England and Wales and of Local Authority Areas* (annual).

Local Government Board, *Annual Reports*. Particularly useful are:

(1) *18th Report*, 1888–9.

(2) *23rd Report*, 1893–4.

(3) *24th Report*, 1894–5.

Local Government Commission for England, *Reports* 1–9 (1961–5).

Local Government Commission for Wales, *Report and Proposals* (1962).

Ministry of Housing and Local Government, *Report for 1967 and 1968*, Cmnd 4009 (1969).

Ministry of Transport, *Highway Statistics* (annual).

New Towns Act 1965, *Reports of the Development Corporations* (annual – published as House of Commons Papers).

New Towns Act 1965, *Report of the Commission for the New Towns* (annual – published as House of Commons Papers).

Royal Commission on Local Government 1923–9, *First Report*, Cmd 2506 (1925); *Second Report*, Cmd 3213 (1928); *Minutes of Evidence* (1923–9).

Royal Commission on Local Government in England 1966–9, *Report*, Cmnd 4040 (1969) – especially: Vol. 3, Appendices 1–3; *Research*

Studies 1, 'Local Government in South East England' (1968); Research Studies 9, 'Community Attitudes Survey: England' (1969).
Royal Commission on Local Government in Greater London 1957–1960, *Report*, Cmnd 1164 (1960).
Welsh Office, *Local Government in Wales*, Cmnd 3340 (1967).

2. *Acts of Parliament*
Local Government Act 1888.
Local Government Act 1894.
Local Government (County Boroughs and Adjustments) Act 1926.
Local Government Act 1929.
New Towns Act 1946.
Town Development Act 1952.
Local Government Act 1958.
London Government Act 1963.
Local Government (Termination of Reviews) Act 1967.

3. *Books and Articles*
Heather Bliss, 'Local Changes in Shopping Potential: Difficulties Encountered in Interpreting Census of Distribution Data', *J. Town Planning Inst.*, **51** (8), 1965.
T. W. Freeman, *The Conurbations of Great Britain* (Manchester U.P. 1959).
T. W. Freeman, *Geography and Regional Administration* (Hutchinson 1968).
R. Lawton, 'The Journey to Work in Britain: Some Trends and Problems', *Regional Studies*, **2** (1), 1968.
V. D. Lipman, *Local Government Areas 1834–1945* (Blackwell, Oxford 1949).
D. C. Marsh, *The Changing Social Structure of England and Wales 1871–1951* (Routledge 1958).
Municipal Year Book (annual)
F. J. Osborn and A. Whittick, *The New Towns*, 2nd ed. (Leonard Hill 1969).
J. Redlich and F. W. Hirst, *The History of Local Government in England* (Macmillan 1958; reissued 1970).
G. Rhodes, *The Government of London: The Struggle for Reform* (Weidenfeld 1970).
P. G. Richards, 'Local Government Reform: the Smaller Towns and the Countryside', *Urban Studies*, **2** (2), 1965.
W. A. Robson, *Local Government in Crisis*, 2nd ed. (Allen & Unwin 1968).

TABLE 9.1

Urban Area 1901–1961, England and Wales

Year	Urban Area (acres)
1901	3,748,987
1911	4,015,701
1921	4,164,580
1931	4,504,928
1951	5,273,917
1961	5,323,656

Note: England and Wales total area = 37,342,460 acres (1961).
Source: Census Reports.

TABLE 9.2

Urban Population 1901–1969, England and Wales

Year	Total Pop. ('000)	Urban Pop. ('000)	Urban %
1901	32,528	25,058	77·0
1911	36,070	28,163	78·1
1921	37,887	30,035	79·3
1931	39,952	31,952	80·0
1951	43,758	35,336	80·8
1961	46,105	36,872	80·0
1969	48,827	38,390	78·6

Sources: (1) Census Reports.
(2) General Register Office, the Registrar General's Annual Estimates of the Population of England and Wales and of Local Authority Areas, 1969.

TABLE 9.3

Towns by Population Size 1901–1961, England and Wales

	Total Number of towns	Number with population of				
		under 10,000	10,000– 50,000	50,000– 200,000	200,000– 1 million	over 1 million
1901	1122	686	361	61	13	1
1931	1120	591	416	94	17	2
1961	965	333	450	162	18	2

Note: In this table the L.C.C. is taken as one town, and the Metropolitan Boroughs are not included individually.
Source: Census Reports, 1901, 1931, 1961.

TABLE 9.4

Proportion of Urban Population Living in Towns of Various Sizes 1901–1961, England and Wales (percentages)

	Total number of towns	Percentage of urban pop. living in towns of				
		under 10,000	10,000– 50,000	50,000– 200,000	200,000– 1 million	over 1 million
1901	1122	12·4	29·7	21·6	18·2	18·1
1931	1120	8·5	28·1	27·3	19·2	16·9
1961	965	4·7	28·9	37·9	16·9	11·7

Note and Source: See Table 9.3.

TABLE 9.5

The Conurbations–Population 1871–1961, England and Wales

	Population (thousands)					Area '000 acres
	1871	1901	1931	1951	1961	1961
Greater London	3889·5	6586·3	8215·7	8348·0	8182·6	462·9
SELNEC	1385·9	2116·8	2426·9	2422·7	2427·9	242·9
West Midlands	968·9	1482·8	1933·0	2237·1	2346·6	172·0
West Yorkshire	1064·3	1523·8	1655·4	1692·7	1703·7	310·1
Merseyside	690·2	1030·2	1346·7	1382·4	1384·2	96·0
Tyneside	346·1	677·9	827·1	835·5	855·3	57·7
Conurbation Totals	8344·9	13,417·8	16,404·8	16,918·4	16,900·2	1341·6
Conurbation % of Urban Totals(a)	—	54	51	48	46	25·2
Conurbation % of Eng. & Wales Totals(a)	37	41	41	39	37	3·6

Note: (a) Taken from Table 9.2.
Sources:
(1) Census 1951 and 1961
(2) D. C. Marsh, *The Changing Social Structure of England and Wales 1871–1951* (Routledge 1958), p. 94.

TABLE 9.6

Progress of New Towns to 31 March 1969(a), England and Wales

Name	Year designated	Area designated (acres)	Population		
			Original	Proposed(b)	At March 1969 (Est.)
1 LONDON RING					
Basildon	1949	7818	25,000	133,400	77,000
Bracknell	1949	3285	5140	60,000	33,300
Crawley	1947	6047	9000	120,000	67,500
Harlow	1947	6395	4500	90,000	76,000
Hatfield	1948	2340	8500	29,000	25,400
Hemel Hempstead	1947	5910	21,200	80,000	69,000
Stevenage	1946	6256	6700	80,000	61,500
Welwyn	1948	4317	18,500	50,000	42,500
2 OTHERS					
Aycliffe	1947	2508	60	45,000	21,600
Corby	1950	4296	15,700	80,000	48,550
Cwmbran	1949	3160	12,000	55,000	44,500
Peterlee	1948	2470	200	30,000	21,750
Redditch	1964	7200	29,000	90,000	34,000
Runcorn	1964	7250	30,000	90,000	32,000
Skelmersdale	1961	4029	10,870	80,000	18,450
Telford (Dawley)	1963	9168(c)	21,000	222,000	23,000
Washington	1964	5300	20,000	80,000	21,000
Totals		87,749	237,370	1,414,400	717,050

Notes:

(a) During 1968 and 1969 four further Development Corporations were established for Milton Keynes, Northampton, Peterborough and mid-Wales (Newtown). At March 1969 they had not made any substantial progress towards the implementation of their plans.

(b) Proposed population is the ultimate population to be reached (including natural increase) after in-migration of people and jobs has stopped.

(c) Area increased to 19,311 acres during 1968–9.

Main Sources:

(1) F. J. Osborn and A. Whittick, *The New Towns*, 2nd ed. (Leonard Hill 1969), p. 417.

(2) New Towns Act 1965, *Reports of the Development Corporations, 31st March 1969* (H.C. Paper 398, Session 1968–9).

(3) New Towns Act 1965, *Report of the Commission for the New Towns, 31st March 1969* (H.C. Paper 399, Session 1968–9).

URBANISATION AND LOCAL GOVERNMENT 279

TABLE 9.7

Employment Structure 1901–1961, England and Wales

Employed population engaged in

	Agric. & Fishing		Mining etc.		Manufacturing		Services		Total Employed
	No.	%	No.	%	No.	%	No.	%	
1901	1,221,814	9	805,185	6	5,354,692	37	6,947,037	48	14,328,727
1911	1,260,476	8	1,044,594	6	6,272,897	39	7,706,432	47	16,284,399
1921	1,283,324	7	1,065,113	6	5,295,108	31	9,534,605	56	17,178,150
1931	1,199,281	6	968,771	5	4,834,712	26	11,850,612	63	18,853,376
1951	1,074,061	5	591,030	3	6,517,332	32	12,153,995	60	20,336,418
1961	832,610	4	457,900	2	5,681,320	26	14,722,640	68	21,694,470

Note: 1901, 1911 includes persons aged 10 or over
1921 ,, ,, 12 ,, ,,
1931 ,, ,, 14 ,, ,,
1951, 1961 ,, ,, 15 ,, ,,

Source: Census Reports, *Occupation Tables.*

TABLE 9.8

Rural and Agricultural Populations 1901–1961, England and Wales

	Percentage of Population	
	Living in Rural Areas	Employed in Agriculture
1901	23	9
1911	22	8
1921	21	7
1931	20	6
1951	19	5
1961	20	4

Notes and Sources: See Tables 9.2 and 9.7.

TABLE 9.9

Motor Vehicles Licensed 1904–1968, Great Britain

	Private cars & vans	Motor cycles scooters & mopeds	Public transport vehicles	All vehicles
1904	8465	—	5345	17,810
1914	132,015	123,678	51,167	388,860
1924	482,356	504,367	97,479	1,316,314
1934	1,308,425	548,461	85,129	2,403,856
1948	1,960,510	559,313	127,625	3,728,432
1958	4,548,530	1,519,935	95,680	7,959,725
1968	10,816,100	1,324,400	99,300	14,446,500

Source: Ministry of Transport, *Highway Statistics, 1968* (HMSO 1969), Table 2.

TABLE 9.10

Rural to Urban Workplace Movements 1921 and 1966, England and Wales

	Economically Active: All RD's	Of these, Work in Urban Areas		No. of RD's	No. with Proportions Travelling into Urban Areas of						
		No.	%		0-10%	10-20%	20-30%	30-40%	40-50%	50-60%	Over 60%
1921	3,045,900	425,200	14·0	663	363	158	81	38	14	6	3
1966	4,315,700	1,600,300	37·1	472	42	75	105	89	75	56	30

Source: Table based on Table 6, Appendix 2, Vol. 3 of Report of Royal Commission on Local Government in England, Cmnd 4040 (1969). Figures for Welsh rural districts added from 1921 and 1966 Census Workplace Tables.

TABLE 9.11

Proportions Working Outside Their Local Authority Area 1967, England (percentages)

Employed outside L.A. Area of Residence	All Respondents	Social Class I	With Higher Education	With Secondary Education	Live in RDC Area	Live in Area of Population Growth(a)
	33	62	54	40	43	44
Base Number	(1313)	(77)	(81)	(271)	(295)	(441)

Note: (a) Growth of more than 1 per cent. per annum.
Source: Royal Commission on Local Government in England, Research Studies 9: Community Attitudes Survey: England (HMSO 1969), Table 49, p. 50.

TABLE 9.12

County Boroughs 1888–1969, England and Wales

Year	Number of C.Bs	Area		Population	
		Total (acres)	% of E & W(a)	Total ('000)	% of E & W(b)
1888	61	308,000	0·8	—	—
1891	64	347,889	0·9	7,588·5	26·2
1901	67	420,006	1·1	9,141·3	28·1
1931	83	760,007	2·0	13,308·5	33·3
1961	83	907,267	2·4	13,651·0	29·6
1969	83	1,058,700	2·8	14,288·3	29·3

Notes:
(a) England and Wales total taken from Table 9.1.
(b) England and Wales totals taken from Table 9.2.
Sources:
(1) Census Reports, 1891–1961.
(2) See Table 9.2.

TABLE 9.13

County Councils 1891–1969, England and Wales

Year	Number(a)	Population		Number with Population of			
		Total ('000)	% of E & W(b)	0– 50,000	50– 200,000	200,000– 1m	over 1m
1891	62	21,414·0	73·8	4	27	28	3
1901	62	23,386·6	71·9	4	25	30	3
1931	62	26,643·9	66·7	5	19	32	6
1961	62	32,454·0	70·4	4	18	33	7
1969	59	34,538·5	70·7	4	15	33	7

Notes:
(a) LCC and GLC are included as counties in the Table.
(b) England and Wales totals taken from Table 9.2.
Source: See Table 9.2.

TABLE 9.14

County Districts and Rural Parishes 1891–1969, England and Wales

	Municipal boroughs(a)	Urban districts	Rural districts (b)	Total districts	Parishes
1891(c)	238	709	575	1522	—
1929	256	781	647	1634	14,259
1940	278	602	478	1358	12,350
1961	317	564	474	1355	10,890
1969	259	522	469	1250	—

Notes:
(a) Figures for Metropolitan Boroughs (1929–61) and London Boroughs (1969) are not included.
(b) The Council of the Isles of Scilly is included in the table as a Rural District.
(c) 1891 was the nearest date to 1894 for which figures were available. As the number of Urban Sanitary Districts was rising steadily at the time, the total of 709 for that year underestimates the number existing when the 1894 Act was passed. The number of Rural Sanitary Districts in 1891 includes over 100 which crossed county boundaries and were made into two or more separate Rural Districts under the provision of the 1894 Act (see page 272).

Sources:
(1) Census Reports: *1891 Area, Houses and Population Tables,* Vol. I, Tables 3, 6 and Vol. II, Tables 2, 3. *1931 General Report,* pp. 69–71, and Table 34. *1961 Age, Marital Condition and General Tables,* Table 6.
(2) *Municipal Year Book, 1970.*

10 Housing

CONSTANCE ROLLETT

Trends in housing are divided into four main sections: (1) The size of the housing stock at successive points in time and its relation to the population – for example its density of occupation in terms of persons per room. (2) The age, structural condition, tenure and available amenities of dwellings at successive points in time. (3) The rate of building. (4) Aspects of housing finance.

There are three main types of statistics: census data, survey data, and housing returns and other records made by local authorities and government departments. Census reports for 1901, 1911, 1921, 1931, 1951, 1961 and the Sample Census for 1966 have a record for those particular dates of the number of houses available (occupied and vacant), the size of the population and the size of the household in relation to the size of the dwelling. Information about various aspects of housing and its relationship to households has become more varied and elaborate with each successive census.[1] From 1931 separate housing reports have been issued.

There is a lack of survey data covering the whole of England and Wales for the period up to 1947. Since then, however, the Government Social Survey, established during the war, has conducted a number of surveys – in 1947 of Great Britain, in 1960 and 1964 of England and Wales, in 1965 of Scotland with the Scottish Development Department, and in 1967 the house condition survey of England and Wales with the Ministry of Housing and Local Government. The Joseph Rowntree Memorial Trust has supported three national housing surveys and four local studies, and also enquiries into the ownership and management of rented houses. The first survey was undertaken in 1958. We have not made use of their information because the general data are similar to that obtained from the census reports and government surveys and often the analyses are too detailed for our purposes. Local authority returns and other records give details of the number of houses built and are fairly complete since 1919.

How satisfactory are the figures available?

[1] See Chap. 2, p. 22.

SIZE OF HOUSEHOLD STOCK AND DENSITY OF OCCUPATION

Size

Although figures do cover the whole·of our period beginning with the Census of 1901, and show the broad trends, there are discontinuities between the figures for 1901 and those for subsequent census dates. The 1901 Census did not distinguish between private families (subsequently called households since all members do not need to be related), and institutional or non-private households, so that it is not possible to say what proportion of the total population was living in private households. Also each separate building was counted as a house, so that the excess of households over dwellings (in the sense of self-contained dwellings, either house or flat), and the number of households sharing dwellings, is not known. The number of structurally separate dwellings was first distinguished in 1921, but an estimate of the number of such dwellings in 1911 was given in the housing report of the 1931 Census, so that figures for the number of dwellings and number of private households are on the same basis from 1911 to 1966.

Density of occupation

Again the figures are not very satisfactory before the 1921 Census. The number of persons per room was thought of chiefly as a rough guide to overcrowding, and households living at densities of more than two to a room were regarded as overcrowded. In 1901 only the density of occupation of households living in one to four rooms is given and the percentage of these households living at more than two people to a room. This understates the true figure as there were probably some over-crowded households living in more than four rooms. A similar difficulty occurs in 1911 where the percentage of families with more than two people to a room given is based on those living in one to nine rooms. Neither report gives the proportion of the population living at densities of more than two per room. From 1921 onwards figures show the average density of occupation of families of different sizes and the proportion of households living at varying densities. In order to get comparable figures from 1911 we have taken in our table 'over $1\frac{1}{2}$ persons per room' as the highest measure of density since the 1961 and 1966 census reports do not give the proportions of families living at higher densities than this. In 1966 there was however a change in the definitions of rooms to be counted which will have exaggerated the reduction in the numbers living at high densities;[1] the kitchen was always counted as a room,

[1] The extent of the reduction was also exaggerated by errors in enumeration, see *Social Trends*, Central Statistical Office 1970, App. B, p. 167.

whereas in previous census reports it was only counted as a room if it was used for eating meals. Another measure of overcrowding was proposed in 1931 relating the number of bedrooms available to the type of family, in terms of age, marital status and sex, occupying them. This was not applied to data covering the whole of England and Wales however until the Social Survey report *The Housing Situation in England and Wales in 1960* so that we have not used it in this chapter. A measure of some psychological if not necessarily physical overcrowding is the number of households sharing dwellings. Figures go back to 1921 and an estimate was made in 1931 of the approximate number of households sharing in 1911. Nevertheless the census definition of a household, as a single person catering for himself or a group sharing housekeeping, is in some ways inadequate. It means for instance that a young married couple living with parents and eating with them would not be counted as a separate sharing household, in spite of the fact that they would probably regard themselves as sharing.

Census figures also include analysis of the data by major regions, urban and rural areas, conurbations, counties and county boroughs. Unfortunately the major regions listed have been differently defined at different dates throughout the period with which we are dealing. Nevertheless we have re-grouped the regions to cover approximately the same areas as in 1931 to give some idea of regional variation in density of occupation. Figures for major conurbations have also been used to illustrate variation in the proportion of sharing households.

AGE, STRUCTURAL CONDITION AND AMENITIES OF DWELLINGS

Age

None of the census reports have included this information, and no comprehensive figures on the age of the total stock of dwellings at any one time seem to exist, though a rough division into pre-1919 and post-1919 houses could be made by adding the number of new houses built and subtracting those pulled down, as figures exist for new houses built and old ones pulled down from that date. The first of the Government Social Survey housing studies, *The British Household*, made an estimate of pre-1919 and post-1919 houses for a sample covering Great Britain. Unfortunately their published tabulations do not give a regional analysis of the age figures, so that we could not get figures for England and Wales to compare with later available figures. However a Social Survey study of Scottish housing and a house condition survey of England and Wales in 1967 by the Ministry of Housing and Local Government, do allow us to illustrate the broad trend.

Structural condition

The Ministry of Housing and Local Government reports in its quarterly publication *Housing Statistics of Great Britain*, No. 9, April 1968, that the house condition survey of England and Wales of 1967 was the first comprehensive survey designed to assess the structural fitness of houses. Previous estimates of 'unfit' houses were made by totalling local authority returns on numbers of 'unfit' houses. These were unreliable because not uniformly based and often referred only to houses on current slum clearance programmes.

Amenities

The Census of 1951 was the first to seek information about the amenities available to households. The 1947 survey also covered certain amenities, but as the tabulations refer to Great Britain as a whole, and as the amenities dealt with do not correspond exactly with those of the census reports, we have not included them in our tables. Although the area covered (England and Wales) is the same for the censuses 1961 and 1966, the amenities referred to in their schedules differ from those referred to in 1951, so that we have selected for comparison items which appear in all three lists. To give a regional comparison we have again amalgamated the standard regions of the 1951 and 1966 censuses into approximate conformity with those of 1931.

Tenure

This is an important aspect of the housing situation since different types of tenure represent differences in security and potential capital assets. In the nineteen-twenties and nineteen-thirties, the growth of the building society movement resulted in a considerable increase in the number of owner-occupiers, and the building of local authority houses resulted in substantial numbers of local authority tenancies, but there are no comprehensive tenure figures until the Government Social Survey report in 1947. Here tenure figures were tabulated by regions, so that we can extract figures for England and Wales to correspond approximately with those in the census reports for 1961 (the first census for which tenure figures were obtained) and for 1966. A regional comparison has been made by grouping 1961 and 1966 regions to correspond approximately with the regions used in the 1947 survey. Comparisons made in 1961 and 1966 between tenures for numbers of shared dwellings, density of occupation and amenities available, are also used.

Tenure, rather than the social class of the householder (based on type of occupation), has been used by the census reports since 1951 as a dimension of analysis. But the 1947 Social Survey report analyses data by economic group, using the weekly wage rate of the chief wage earner to form five groups. There is, however, no way of making these groups correspond to the five social classes of the Registrar General, which are based on type of occupation rather than actual wages, and which were used in census analysis for the first time in the 1966 housing report.

BUILDING

On the whole figures are reasonably complete since 1919. Local authorities have been obliged to make returns on their actions to the government; and records of the number of new houses built by private builders are also good from 1919, as the post-war government was aware of the importance of the whole house building programme. We have tried to present all the figures in totals for the same five-year periods. However this has not always been possible where a new type of policy (for example 'improvement grants') began in the middle of one of our periods or where the records we have been able to discover do not make this breakdown.

COSTS

The overall amounts of government and local authority expenditure on housing are documented, but it is more difficult to get a clear picture of amounts of the total spent on individual items. A complete record of government contributions for the improvement and conversion of older houses exists, but the housing statistics published by the government do not give local authority contributions in respect of this item before 1961, probably because they were small.

Costs of housing to occupiers have not been documented in a form which makes it possible to construct tables to show the trend over our period. It would be desirable, for instance, to relate the average weekly rent actually paid, preferably by both local authority and private tenants, and the average weekly mortgage payment, to the average weekly wage of the groups concerned at several points over our period. Reports on surveys of family expenditure conducted by the Board of Trade and the Ministry of Labour appeared in 1904, 1912, 1918, 1937/8, 1953/4 and 1967, but it is not possible to construct a table showing the proportion of income spent on housing over the period. The 1904 and 1912 surveys cover towns in England and Wales, the 1937/8 survey the United Kingdom and the other surveys Great Britain. More importantly the 1904 and 1912 surveys give a range of rents, according to size of property and not average rents, and a range of incomes according to type of employment without relating the two. The 1918, 1937/8 and the 1953/4 surveys give average rents but not average incomes of the sample concerned. It is possible to relate rents to the figures for average weekly wages, but these may not have been the average weekly wage of the people in the sample, and the figures obtained seem to be too much subject to error to be put in tabular form. The pre-war surveys dealt only with working class expenditure and therefore ignored the cost of mortgage payments. All these surveys gave rents including rates. The figures derived from the 1967 survey are the most satisfactory, as they give rents and mortgage payments as a proportion of the total household income, and of the income of the head of the household of the groups concerned. But rates are not included so the figures are not strictly comparable with the earlier ones. The Ministry of Labour Family Expenditure Survey 1964/5 allows some regional comparisons for that year.

The total amount of money loaned and the total number of mortgages granted by building societies are available over our period, though only since 1960 are the number of new mortgages for house purchase in the year separated from total mortgages in the year, which normally included a few re-mortgages on existing mortgages. Figures for local authority loans for house purchase are available from 1959 and for insurance companies only from 1966.

NOTES ON TABLES
Housing Stock and Density of Occupation
Tables 10.1 and 10.2 show the increases in dwellings, households, total population and population in private households. The percentage of the population in private households (Table 10.2) has not changed much over the period, remaining between 95 and 96 per cent. Table 10.3 summarises changes in the size of dwellings and of families, in the density of occupation and in the proportion of families and population living at high densities. The size of dwellings has not changed much over the period 1921 to 1966 in spite of a considerable drop in the average family size. The density of occupation declined with each successive census, though at a somewhat uneven rate, dropping eight percentage points in the years 1921 to 1931, only nine points in the following twenty years which include the virtual standstill of building during the second war, eight points from 1951 to 1961 and nine points in only five years from 1961 to 1966. The proportion of families living at high densities increased between 1901 and 1921. This was probably because of the lack of building during the war from 1914–18, though the 1901 figures and to a lesser extent those of 1911 are somewhat unreliable as they are not based on all dwellings. Since 1921 the proportion of families and population living at high densities has dropped sharply. In 1966 only 1·2 per cent of households were living at a density of more than one and a half persons per room compared with 16·3 per cent in 1921 and the number living at less than half a person per room

had multiplied by three (Table 10.4). Interestingly the proportion of households living at a density from half to one person per room, the biggest group, remained comparatively constant. Table 10.5 simply documents the well known fact that larger families tend to live at higher densities than smaller families. There is however considerable geographical variation in households living at high densities (Table 10.6); the Greater London conurbation and the Eastern Region retain their respective positions with the largest and smallest number of overcrowded households, Greater London having four times as many households living at more than one and a half persons per room as the Eastern Region in 1966, whereas it had under three times as many in 1931. Other areas have made slight shifts in relative positions, the North becoming slightly less crowded compared, for example, with the South-East.

Although the number of persons in relation to habitable rooms is not an entirely satisfactory way of measuring overcrowding, yet the marked reduction in density of occupation suggests a considerable improvement in the standard of housing as far as simple overcrowding is concerned. Even Greater London has only 2·4 per cent of overcrowded households by this standard. However, measured by our other standard of overcrowding, the sharing of dwellings, improvements have been less marked (Tables 10.7 and 10.8). The position worsened between 1911 and 1921 and did not recover noticeably until after 1931. Even in 1966, 7·3 per cent of all households were sharing a dwelling. Comparing the conurbations, Greater London has a much greater proportion of sharing households than any other; in 1966 24·2 per cent of all households were sharing, the next highest proportion being 7·2 per cent in Merseyside. West Yorkshire in contrast had only 1·9 per cent. Greater London was also the only area in which the situation deteriorated seriously between 1961 and 1966.

The condition of dwellings

We have little information about the structural condition of dwellings but Table 10.9 suggests three things: (1) The conservative nature of the estimates of unfit houses derived from slum-clearance programmes, which seem to have been based to a large extent on what the local authorities felt that they could achieve with the resources at their disposal. (2) Rising standards for determining fit dwellings. (3) The deterioration of old property which may have been structurally sound at the beginning of the period, but with which slum demolition and repair programmes have not kept pace. It is, of course, not possible to deduce from these figures what proportion of property was omitted from slum-clearance programmes although it would have been classified as unfit by the standards of the public health inspectors in 1967, and what proportion was originally fit and has subsequently deteriorated.

No figures were obtained giving an estimate for England and Wales of the proportion of older houses – say more than thirty years old – in the total stock in the nineteen-thirties. Since the nineteen-thirties saw considerable building activity, it is likely that the rate of building was higher than that in the eighteen-nineties, so that the proportion of older houses would be declining. However, Table 10.10 shows that in 1947, according to a sample survey, 68.3 per cent of houses in Great Britain were built before 1919, and this proportion had certainly increased since 1939 owing to the virtual building standstill during the war. By 1965 the proportion of pre-1919 houses had dropped to 40·5 per cent in Scotland and by 1967 to 38·4 per cent in England and Wales. It seems to have been accepted that 1919 marked a change of building style so that up to now the pre- and post-1919 distinction has tended to be the only one made. Since, however, the nineteen-fifties' house building rate was higher than the rate during the nineteen-twenties, the proportion of houses more than thirty years old must also have been dropping. Table 10.11 shows the proportion of the three main tenure groups with pre-1919 and post-1919 houses based on the same data. Owner occupiers had only 22 per cent of the older houses in 1947, but by 1967 they had 50·5 per cent in England and Wales. This reflects the fact that in the nineteen-thirties societies lent money almost exclusively for new houses; older houses were predominantly privately rented and not sold, because rent control imposed in 1919 made it difficult to evict sitting tenants and impossible to charge more rent. Since the war building societies have been encouraged to lend more money on older houses, and the decontrolling of some rents in 1957 has made it possible for people to buy the older cheaper houses. The small proportion of local authority pre-1919 houses remains more or less constant, unsurprisingly, as very few local authority houses have been sold and very few were built before 1919. Their share of post-1919 houses does not seem to have changed much either, and it appears likely that the Scottish situation, which differs markedly from that of England and Wales in this respect (86·5 per cent of post-1919 housing is local authority housing and only 10·2 per cent owner-occupied), slightly reduced the 1947 Great Britain figure. (The Scottish housing stock is only approximately one-tenth of the Great Britain total.) Other tenures (mostly privately rented housing) had 76 per cent of the pre-1919 housing in 1947 in Great Britain and 44·7 per cent in 1967 in England and Wales, 28 per cent of post-1919 housing in 1947 declining to 8·2 per cent in 1967. This reflects the declining share of privately rented houses in the total housing stock.

The next three tables are all derived from the 1967 house condition survey in England and Wales. Table 10.12 is a more detailed breakdown of housing stock by age and tenure group. Table 10.13 illustrates the fact that the local authorities have few unfit dwellings compared with their share of the total stock; owner-occupiers have 50·8 per cent of the total stock and 30·2 per cent of the unfit dwellings, whereas 'other tenures' have 21·4 per cent of the stock and 60·9 per cent of unfit dwellings. Table 10.14 shows that the South-East remains a comparatively favoured area with only 18·4 per cent of the unfit dwellings, and only 6·4 per cent of its total stock unfit, whereas the North has 41·5 per cent of the unfit dwellings and 15·1 per cent of its stock unfit. Tables 10.15, 16 and 17 show the availability of certain amenities during the period 1951 to 1966 to all households and to all households who share dwellings. In spite of substantial improvement over the period, 25·5 per cent of households who share dwellings had no hot water and 21·9 per cent had no fixed bath in 1966. Of all dwellings, 25·1 per cent lacked one or more of the four amenities listed in 1967 (Table 10.18). The rank order of the regions with regard to amenities (Table 10.19) seems somewhat different to that with regard to unfit houses (Table 10.14), though the latter is less detailed. The North was slightly better off for amenities than London and the South-East in 1951 though it had fallen slightly behind by 1966 when there was less overall variation. Wales was considerably below the national average in 1951 and in 1966 was still the lowest of the regions but slightly above the conurbation of Greater London.

Tenure

Tenure has generally been taken to be a more relevant way of analysing housing figures than social class or income group. It has important implications of security for owner-occupiers, and to a considerable extent also for local authority tenants. Private tenants of rent controlled houses had considerable protection from eviction, but this has lessened as many houses have been decontrolled since the Rent Act of 1957, and it has never extended to those renting furnished dwellings. Subsequently the Labour government tried to restore some protection to private tenants (1965). However, in many cases considerable psychological insecurity remains, particularly among those who cannot afford to rent alternative houses or buy their own home. This has tended to discourage mobility among those in rent controlled premises; prospective and sitting local authority tenants have also tended to be immobile, as local housing authorities operate only within their own area. Another aspect of housing which varies with tenure group, is the repair and maintenance of dwellings. While the local authorities have the lowest proportion of unfit houses, and undoubtedly look after their housing stock efficiently, their houses are newer and so raise fewer maintenance problems. It is on the whole the owner-occupiers who have bought old property who have contributed most to the rehabilitation and improvement of structurally sound but old fashioned houses (figures on this aspect will be given in the next section), though some local authorities have recently started campaigning to encourage the improvement of all houses within certain areas.

The tables on tenure (Tables 10.20 to 10.23) show the growth of owner occupancy, the slightly lesser growth of local authority tenancy, the considerable decline in private tenancies, and also the considerable regional differences within these general trends. The growth of owner-occupancy and local authority tenancy has, for instance, been considerably less in London than elsewhere. Average density of occupation also varies by tenure. In 1961 local authority property was the most densely occupied, except for shared dwellings rented furnished, which had an average density of 1·11 persons a room. By 1966 densities for all categories had dropped, but owner-occupied dwellings remained the least densely occupied and shared furnished dwellings the most. Figures for 1966 show local authority dwellings to be the best provided with amenities, closely followed by owner-occupied dwellings, with privately rented dwellings well behind. This is, of course, not surprising in view of the relative age of properties in the various tenure groups.

Building rates
Tables 10.24 to 10.31 document housing performance in both the public and private sector from 1919 to 1968. Figure 10.1 based on data from Table 10.24 shows how the overall rate of building fluctuated between the five year periods because of economic factors, and the local authority and private building rates fluctuated independently of each other at times, chiefly because of political factors. From 1919 to 1939 there was an increasing rate of local authority building, but it started at a lower rate and did not catch up with the rate of private building, so that by 1939 more than twice as many private as local authority houses had been built. Subsidies were available at varying rates for local authority houses during the period but it must be remembered that 431,669 of the 2,969,050 privately built houses also benefited from subsidies. The post-war Labour government of 1945 was convinced that the most equitable and efficient way of coping with the backlog in buildings after the virtual standstill during the war, was for local authorities to make the chief use of the available manpower and resources of the building industry, which had shrunk considerably in size during the war. The result was that during the five years 1945–9 local authorities built 432,098 houses and

private builders only 126,616. Altogether only half a million houses were built during the period, whereas from 1935 to 1939 over one and a half million were produced. Since the nineteen-fifties, when many of the controls on private building were removed, the building industry has expanded greatly, producing almost one and a half million houses in the five-year period up to the end of 1964. This was 200,000 less than the number produced in the 1935-9 period. However, 1,431,285 houses were built in the four years 1965-8, so that by the end of 1969 the number should have topped the 1935-9 figure for the first time. The rate of private building was still less than a third that of local authority building in the 1950-54 period, but by 1955-9 it had almost caught up. From 1960 the private building rate has been higher than the local authority rate.

Table 10.25 shows action under the local authority slum clearance programmes. They did not really get under way until 1934 but from then until 1939, demolitions were running at about 50,000 a year with about 200,000 people moved each year. During the war, slum clearance ceased entirely and was restarted afterwards much later than the house building programme. It was not until the late nineteen-fifties that it again reached the 1934-9 rate. Since 1961, the rate has been over 60,000 per year and most recently, in 1967 and 1968, over 70,000. Tables 10.26 and 10.27 are companion tables to Table 10.9 (number of unfit dwellings) and show how action has failed to keep up with slum clearance plans and estimates of unfit dwellings.

Table 10.28 shows the quite considerable amount of repair work done on older houses; first emergency work on war damaged houses; secondly the volume of repair work carried out on houses at the instigation of local authorities – over a million houses during the five-year period from 1951 to 1964, though the rate seems to have fallen off considerably in the last four years.

Over a million houses have been improved with the help of improvement grants financed by the government (Table 10.29). At first owners were slow to take advantage of the help offered and efforts were made to arouse public interest. Since 1960, grants have been taken up at the rate of over 100,000 a year, about a half of the total going to owner-occupiers, a quarter to local authorities and a quarter to housing associations and other private landlords. The grants do not seem to have fulfilled the government's hope of encouraging owners of old rented houses to improve their property, probably because, as surveys have shown, many of them are elderly, owning only one or two houses and unable to find the necessary half-cost.

There has been a slight fall in the proportion of one-bedroomed dwellings built during the nineteen-sixties, a considerable drop in two-bedroomed dwellings, and a rise in dwellings with three or more bedrooms (Table 10.30). Local authorities provide almost all the one-bedroomed dwellings; the proportion has risen compared with before 1960, but remained almost stationary in the five-year period since then. The proportion of two-bedroomed local authority dwellings has shown a slight rise and fall but the proportion of privately built two-bedroomed dwellings has declined. The proportion of local authority three-bedroomed dwellings dropped after 1960 and subsequently remained stationary, whereas the proportion of three-bedroomed privately built dwellings increased. The proportion of local authority four-bedroomed houses has remained almost stationary, while that of private four-bedroomed dwellings has doubled – though remaining only 7 per cent of the total.

Demographic and census data show a rise both in the number of one person households and recently a slight rise in the number of larger families,[1] but house building does not seem to have been adjusted to needs. It is true that there has been an increase in the number of larger houses, which may have been limited by the fact that families were unable to pay for the larger houses they would have liked on space considerations alone. However, there has been a continuing shortage of one-bedroomed accommodation as local authorities have tended to build directly for the people with young children on their waiting lists, rather than attempting the more difficult course of moving elderly people into new smaller dwellings and using the three-bedroomed dwellings vacated for their waiting list families.

Housing costs
Tables 10.31 and 10.32 and 10.33 show the growth of government and local authority contributions to permanent housing since 1919 through direct subsidies. The direct subsidies do not, however, represent the total cost of public funds. The government foregoes tax revenue by allowing income tax relief on mortgage payments made by owner-occupiers for instance, which, as will be seen in the footnote to Table 10.31, amounted in 1967/8 to more than the government subsidy, and probably to only slightly less than the government and rate funded contributions combined.

Table 10.34 documents the rapid growth of building societies, who were lending money on about a quarter of a million new houses in 1938 and on nearly half a million in 1966. Their growth allowed the growth in home ownership already discussed. Figures for loans for house purchase from insurance societies are only available from 1966, and from local authorities from 1959 (Tables 10.35 and 10.36), but the number of

[1] See Tables 2.32 and 2.41.

loans and amount lent from both sources are considerably less than the building society figures and have probably only been significant since 1960.

Perhaps the most difficult area to document in housing cost is that of the variation in rents during the century, and between different areas. Owing to the inflation of currency, the most satisfactory way of seeing trends in rent would be to show them as a proportion of household income. This has not been possible for the reasons given in the discussion on sources. However, some tentative information was obtained from the sources studied. From the 1905 survey it seems likely that approximately 13 per cent to 15 per cent of the head of household's income was spent on rent (including rates), and in the 1937/8 survey it was still approximately 15 per cent (using the 1938 average manual worker's weekly earnings given in the Ministry of Labour Gazette). However, Wendt[1] quotes the Political and Economic Planning Committee's unpublished housing report as estimating that, before the war, a working class family spent approximately 12 per cent of its total income (that is including income of other family members) on rent, and this declined to 8 per cent or 9 per cent by 1950. It is not stated whether rates are included.

Table 10.37 shows the more detailed figures derived from the latest family expenditure survey – mean and median rents (minus rates) as a proportion of head of household and total household incomes. The proportion of mean rent to total household income seems to have remained stationary since early 1950, with privately rented unfurnished dwellings taking about the same proportion of incomes as local authority dwellings, and mortgage repayments a slightly higher proportion (of a generally higher income it should be remembered).

Table 10.38 shows some regional variations in incomes and rents by tenure group. Incomes of those renting accommodation show rather less variation between regions than incomes of those buying with a mortgage. Rents, however, vary much more than income, though in the same order – the North lowest, the Midlands in the middle and East Anglia and the South East highest. To take the privately rented dwellings sector only, incomes in the North are 90 per cent of the national average, but rents only 70 per cent, Midlands' incomes are 106 per cent of the average and rents 93 per cent, whereas East Anglia and the South-East have incomes 107 per cent of the national average and rent 143 per cent. In absolute terms, however, national average local authority rents are considerably higher than private rents, and mortgage payments are again considerably higher than local authority rents.

[1] P. F. Wendt, *Housing Policy – the Search for Solutions* (University of California Press 1962), p. 20.

BIBLIOGRAPHY

Board of Trade	Enquiry by the Board of Trade into working class rents, Cd 3864, 1908.
Bowley, Marion	*Housing and the State* (Allen & Unwin 1945).
Central Statistical Office	*Social Trends*, no. 1, 1970.
Cullingworth, J. B.	*English Housing Trends*, Occasional Papers on Social Administration, no. 13 (Bell 1965).
Cullingworth, J. B.	*Housing and Local Government* (Allen & Unwin 1966).
General Register Office	Census reports of England and Wales:
	General Report, England and Wales, 1901.
	Housing Report, England and Wales, 1931.
	Housing Report, England and Wales, 1951.
	Housing Report, England and Wales, 1961.
	Sample Census *Housing Report*, England and Wales, 1966.
Government Social Survey (earlier published by Central Office of Information)	*The British Household* by P. G. Gray, unnumbered, 1947.
	The Housing Situation in 1960, ss. 319, 1960.
	The Housing Situation in England and Wales 1964, ss. 372, 1964.
	Scottish Housing 1965, by J. B. Cullingworth, ss. 375, 1967, undertaken for the Scottish Development Department.
Ministry of Health	*Annual Reports*, Part I, 1919 to 1952 inclusive.
Ministry of Housing and Local Government	*Report* for 1950–4; *Annual Reports* 1955 to 1964.
	Report for 1965–6.
	Handbook of Housing Statistics, 1965, 1966.
	Housing Returns for England and Wales, from 1946 monthly until 1948, then quarterly until 1966.
jointly with the Scottish Development Department and the Welsh Office	*Housing Statistics: Great Britain*, quarterly from 1966.
Ministry of Labour	*Labour Gazette*, issue for December 1940.
Ministry of Reconstruction	*Housing*, Cmd 6609, 1945.
Registry of Friendly	*Annual Reports* of the Chief Registrar (Great

Societies   Britain), Part 5: *Building Societies*, 1952–5.
                             Statistical Summary: Building Societies, 1920–
                             1952.
Wendt, P. F.   *Housing Policy – the Search for Solutions* (University of California Press 1962).

TABLE 10.1

Stock of Dwellings, number of Households and Population 1901–1966, England and Wales (thousands)

Census year	Buildings used as habitations (occupied and vacant) (a)	Dwellings for private families (or households) occupied and vacant	Occupied habitations or dwellings	Families or separate occupiers (b)	Private families (or households)	Population	
						Total	In private families (or households)
1901	6710	—	6449	7037	—	32,528	—
1911	7550	7691 (approx.)	—	8005	7943	36,070	34,776
1921	7798	7979	—	—	8739	37,887	36,180
1931	—	9400	9123	—	10,233	39,952	38,042
1951	—	12,389	12,080	—	13,118	43,758	41,840
1961	—	14,646	14,332	—	14,890	46,166	44,543
1966	—	15,449	14,977	—	15,694	48,075	45,750

Notes:

(a) In the Censuses of 1901 and 1911 all separate buildings were counted as 'houses', so that a block of flats was counted as one house. In 1921 the term 'structurally separate dwelling' was introduced and subsequently used as the unit counted. It means a dwelling occupied by a private household with independent access to the street or to a public hall. The figure given for 1911 is an estimate given in the 1931 Census housing report.

(b) The 1901 report counted those filling in the schedule as 'occupiers' and did not distinguish between private and non-private establishments. From 1911 onward a 'private family or household' is a group of persons, whether related or not, who live together and benefit from common housekeeping, or any person living alone who is responsible for his own needs.

Sources: Census of England and Wales, 1951 and 1961 and Sample Census 1966, *Housing Reports.*

TABLE 10.2

Proportion of the Population in Private Households 1911–1966, England and Wales

	Population in private households	Population in non-private households	Total population	Percent. of total population
1911	34,776,402	1,294,090	36,070,492	96·4
1921	36,179,946	1,706,753	37,886,699	95·5
1931	38,042,464	1,909,913	39,952,377	95·2
1951	41,840,000	1,918,000	43,758,000	95·6
1961	44,542,828	1,623,172	46,166,000	96·5
1966	45,749,590	2,325,700	48,075,300	95·2

Source: Census of England and Wales, 1931, 1951 and 1961 and Sample Census 1966, *Housing Reports.*

TABLE 10.3

Average Size of Dwellings and Density of Occupation 1901–1966, England and Wales

Census year	Average size of dwelling (occupied rooms) (b)	Private families per dwelling (a)	Average size of families	Average density (persons per room)	Percentage of families at more than 2 per room	Percentage of population at more than 2 per room
1901	—	1·1	4·6	—	5·6(c)	—
1911	—	1·0 (approx.)	4·4	—	5·6(d)	—
1921	5·1	1·1	4·1	0·9	5·7	9·6
1931	5·1	1·1	3·7	0·8	3·9	6·9
1951	4·7	1·1	3·2	0·7	1·2	2·2
					more than 1½ per room	more than 1½ per room
1961	4·8	1·0	3·0	0·7	2·8(e)	5·3
1966	4·9	1·0	3·0	0·6	1·2	2·5

Notes:

(a) In 1901 the unit counted was 'separate occupiers', not private families. See notes to Table 10.1.

(b) Rooms were defined in 1931, 1951 and 1961 as usual living rooms including bedrooms, and kitchens if used for eating, but excluded sculleries, landings, lobbies, closets, bathrooms, store rooms, offices, shops. In 1966 the kitchen always counted as a room, even if not used for meals; other conditions were the same.

(c) Understated because based on occupancies of 1–4 rooms only.

(d) Based on 1–9 room occupancies, so slightly understated.

(e) In 1961 and 1966 figures for numbers living at a density of more than two per room were no longer given.

Source: Census Reports of England and Wales, *General Report* 1901, *Housing Reports* 1931, 1951, 1961 and Sample Census 1966, *Housing Report.*

TABLE 10.4

Density of Occupation: Proportion of Households Living at Different Densities of Persons to a Room(a), 1911–1966 England and Wales

	1911(b)	1921	1931	1951	1961	1966
over 1½	16·9	16·3	11·4	5·1	2·8	1·2
1 up to and including 1½	18·5	17·6	14·6	10·9	7·5	4·2
½ up to and including 1	53·4	53·5	58·7⎫	84·0	64·1	59·2
less than ½	11·2	12·6	15·3⎭		25·6	35·4
	100·0	100·0	100·0	100·0	100·0	100·0

Notes:

(a) See notes to Table 10.3 for definition of 'room'.

(b) Based on occupancies of 1–9 rooms only.

Source: Census of England and Wales, *Housing Reports* 1931, 1951, 1961 and Sample Census 1966, *Housing Report.*

TABLE 10.5

Average Density of Occupation of Families of Different Sizes 1921–1966, England and Wales

Persons in family	Persons per room				
	1921	1931	1951	1961	1966
1	0·34	0·33	0·30	0·28	0·24
2	0·50	0·48	0·49	0·49	0·40
3	0·68	0·67	0·69	0·70	0·56
4	0·85	0·85	0·87	0·88	0·72
5	1·02	1·03	1·03	1·05	0·86
6	1·20	1·20	1·20	1·22	1·00
7	1·37	1·38	1·36	1·40	1·15
8	1·53	1·53	1·52	1·56	1·29
9	1·67	1·67	1·66	1·75	1·42
10	1·77	1·76	1·81		
11	1·81	1·79	1·94	1·98	
12	1·77	1·72	2·03		
13	1·68	1·54			1·65
14	1·50	1·24	2·05		
15 and over	1·01	0·78			
All families	0·91	0·83	0·74	0·66	0·57

Sources: Census of England and Wales, *Housing Reports* 1931, 1951, 1961 and Sample Census 1966, *Housing Report*.

TABLE 10.6

Density of Occupation by Region(a) 1931–1966: Proportion of Households Living at More than 1½ Persons per Room, England and Wales

	1931	1951	1961	1966
England and Wales	11·5	5·1	2·8	1·2
Greater London	15·0	5·8	4·4	2·4
London and South East	11·5	4·6	3·1	1·5
North	14·3	6·5	3·0	1·3
Midlands	9·7	4·9	2·6	1·1
East	5·7	3·2	1·9	0·5
South West	6·5	3·6	2·0	0·7
Wales	10·1	5·0	2·3	0·8

Note: (a) The composition of the standard regions was changed at each successive census. For this table regions have been combined to give approximately the same areas covered as the six regions used in 1931. Greater London conurbation is not one of the standard regions and remains more nearly the same area throughout. It is included in the South East region.

Sources: Census of England and Wales, *Housing Reports* 1931, 1951, 1961 and Sample Census 1966, *Housing Report*.

TABLE 10.7

Number and Percentage of Shared Dwellings: Number and Percentage of Sharing Households 1911–1966, England and Wales

Year	Shared dwellings	Percent of all dwellings	Number of sharing households	Percent of all households	Average density (persons per room) of sharing households
1911(a)	—	—	1,250,000	15·7	—
1921(b)	753,000	—	1,732,000	19·8	—
1931	838,695	9·2	1,948,555	19·0	2·7
1951	798,694	6·6	1,871,923	14·3	0·9
1961	349,521	2·4	885,778	6·1	0·9
1966	442,350	3·0	1,116,038	7·3	0·7

Notes:
(a) The figure for 1911 is an estimate given in the 1931 *Housing Report*.
(b) The 1931 *Housing Report* considers that the 1921 figure was somewhat understated.
Sources: Census of England and Wales, *Housing Reports* 1931, 1951, 1961 and Sample Census 1966, *Housing Report*.

TABLE 10.8

Percentage of Households Sharing a Dwelling: England and Wales and Conurbations 1951–1966

	1951	1961	1966
England and Wales	14·3	6·1	7·3
Tyneside conurbation	7·9	2·3	2·3
W. Yorkshire conurbation	3·8	1·3	1·9
S.E. Lancashire conurbation	6·4	2·3	3·1
Merseyside conurbation	7·4	7·4	7·2
W. Midlands conurbation	12·1	5·0	5·3
Greater London conurbation	34·2	20·0	24·2

Source: Census of England and Wales, *Housing Reports* 1951, 1961 and Sample Census 1966, *Housing Report*.

TABLE 10.9

Numbers of Unfit Dwellings 1934–1967, England and Wales

1934	266,851 ⎫	
1937	377,930 ⎬	based on slum clearance programmes
1939	472,000 ⎭	
1960	622,000 ⎫	based on local authority returns
1965	820,000 ⎬	often linked to current slum clearance
	⎭	programmes
1967	1,836,000	based on survey estimate made by public health inspectors

Sources: M. Bowley; *Housing and the State* (Allen & Unwin 1945). *Housing Statistics* no. 9. *The Housing Situation in 1960*, Government Social Survey, ss. 319.

TABLE 10.10

Age of Dwellings 1947, 1965, 1967: Great Britain, Scotland, and England and Wales (percentages)

Year	Pre 1919	Post 1919
1947 (Great Britain)	68·3	31·7
1965 (Scotland)	40·5	59·5
1967 (England and Wales)	38·4	61·6

Source: 1947 based on sample data from P. G. Gray, *The British Household*, Government Social Survey, 1947. 1965 sample data from J. B. Cullingworth, *Scottish Housing in 1965*, Government Social Survey, ss. 375, 1967. 1967 sample data from the House Condition Survey of England and Wales, *Housing Statistics* no. 10, 1968.

TABLE 10.11

Age and Tenure of Dwellings 1947, 1965, 1967: Great Britain, Scotland, and England and Wales (percentages)

Tenure group	1947 (Great Britain)		1965 (Scotland)		1967 (England and Wales)	
	Pre 1919	1919 & after	Pre 1919	1919 & after	Pre 1919	1919 & after
Owner-occupied	22	37	34·1	10·2	50·5	50·9
Rented from local authority or new town corporation	2	35	6·5	86·5	4·8	40·9
Other tenures	76	28	59·4	3·3	44·7	8·2
Total	100·0	100·0	100·0	100·0	100·0	100·0

Source: as above

TABLE 10.12

**Stock of Dwellings by Tenure and Age, February 1967
England and Wales**

Tenure	Age of dwelling							
	Pre 1919		1919–44		Post 1944		All dwellings	
	'000s	%	'000s	%	'000s	%	'000s	%
Owner occupied	3045	50·5	2472	58·1	2454	45·3	7971	50·8
Rented from local authority or new town corporation	291	4·8	1241	29·2	2716	50·2	4248	27·1
Other tenures	2598	43·1	536	12·6	234	4·3	3368	21·4
Closed*	95	1·6	6	0·1	12	0·2	113	0·7
All tenures	6029	100·0	4255	100·0	5416	100·0	15,700	100·0

*Dwellings closed under Housing or Planning Acts.
Note: See note to Table 10.13.
Source: Housing Statistics no. 10, 1968.

TABLE 10.13

**Stock of Dwellings by Tenure and Condition, Estimated February 1967,
England and Wales**

Tenure	All unfit dwellings		All dwellings	
	'000s	%	'000s	%
Owner-occupied	556	30·3	7971	50·8
Rented from local authority or new town corporation	72	3·9	4248	27·1
Other tenures	1118	60·9	3368	21·4
Closed*	90	4·9	113	0·7
Total	1836	100·0	15,700	100·0

*Closed under Housing or Planning Acts.
Note: from *Housing Statistics* no. 9. Estimates in these tables are based on the house condition survey carried out in February and March 1967 by the Ministry of Housing and Local Government. This was the first large-scale survey of its kind. Details are given in *Economic Trends* for May 1968. Previous national estimates of the number of unfit dwellings were made by adding the returns made by local authorities, but these were not uniformly based and unsatisfactory. Returns from local authorities in 1965 totalled 820,000 whereas the survey indicated about 1,800,000 unfit dwellings in 1967.
Source: Housing Statistics, no. 9, 1968.

TABLE 10.14

TABLE 10.14

Stock of Unfit Dwellings by Regions, Estimated February 1967, England and Wales

Region	Unfit dwellings '000s			Percentage of all unfit dwellings	Unfit dwellings as a percentage of total stock of permanent dwellings in the area
	In or adjoining clearance areas	Not in potential clearance areas	All		
Northern, Yorks. & Humberside & North West	578	184	762	41·5	15·1
South East	139	199	338	18·4	6·4
Rest of England & Wales	382	354	736	40·1	13·7
England & Wales	1099	737	1836	100·0	11·7

Note: See note to Table 10.13.
Source: Housing Statistics no. 9, 1968.

TABLE 10.15

Proportion of all Households Who Share the Use of or Lack the Use of Certain Amenities 1951–1966, England and Wales (percentages)

Type of amenity	1951		1961		1966	
	Share the amenity	Lack	Share	Lack	Share	Lack
Hot water tap	n.a.	n.a.	1·8	21·9	2·1	12·5
Fixed bath	8	37	4·6	22·0	4·3	14·9
W.C.	13	8	5·8	6·9	6·0	1·8

Source: Census 1951 and 1961 and Sample Census 1966, *Housing Reports.*

TABLE 10.16

Proportion of Households Who Share Dwellings Who Share the Use of or Lack the Use of Certain Amenities 1951–1966, England and Wales (percentages)

Type of amenity	1951		1961		1966	
	Share	Lack	Share	Lack	Share	Lack
Hot water tap	—	—	25·4	37·9	24·5	25·5
Fixed bath	57	28	55·0	30·1	52·9	21·9
W.C.	77	2	69·9	1·4	60·3	0·5

Source: See Table 10.15.

TABLE 10.17

**All Households and Households Who Share Dwellings
Who Have the Exclusive Use of Listed(a) Amenities 1951–1966,
England and Wales (percentages)**

Household type	1951	1961	1966
All households	52	69·3	72·4
Sharing households	11	10·7	19·1

Note: (a) The three census report lists vary. The 1951 list is: piped water, cooking stove, water closet and fixed bath; the 1961 list: cold water tap, hot water tap, fixed bath and W.C.; the 1966 list: hot water tap, fixed bath and inside W.C.
Source: See Table 10.15.

TABLE 10.18

**Permanent Dwellings Without Exclusive Use of Basic Amenities,
Estimated February 1967, England and Wales**

Amenities lacked	Dwellings 000's	Percentage of all permanent dwellings
Internal W.C.	2919	18·6
Fixed bath	2106	13·4
Wash basin	3040	19·4
Hot & cold water at three points	3400	21·7
One or more of the amenities	3943	25·1

Note: See note to Table 10.13.
Source: Housing Statistics no. 6, 1967.

TABLE 10.19

Proportion of Households with Certain (*a*) Amenities by Region (*b*) 1951, 1966 (percentages)

	1951	*1966*
England & Wales	52·0	72·4
Northern	54·1	72·7
Midlands	51·2	72·1
London & South East	53·2	73·8
South West	49·0	76·8
East	50·0	69·8
Wales	40·0	66·3
Greater London	51·0	65·6

Notes:
(*a*) Listed amenities as in note to Table 10.17.
(*b*) Regions as in Table 10.6.
Source: Census of England and Wales 1951 and Sample Census 1966, *Housing Reports.*

TABLE 10.20

Housing Stock by Tenure 1947–1966, England and Wales (percentages)

	1947	*1961*	*1966*
Owner-occupied	27	42·3	46·7
Rented from a local authority or new town corporation	12	23·7	25·7
Rented from a private landlord	58	27·8	22·5
(*a*) Other tenures	3	6·2	5·1
All tenures	100·0	100·0	100·0

Note: (*a*) In 1947 data in this category is described as 'Tenancy, part of wages', in 1961 'held by virtue of employment' and 'rented together with farm or business premises', and in 1966 'other tenures' covers 'held by virtue of employment', 'rented together with farm or business premises' and 'not stated'. (Consequently the 'other tenure' category is somewhat understated in 1947 and the 'rented from a private landlord' overstated, compared with the figures for 1961 and 1966.)
Sources: 1947 figures are from P. G. Gray, *The British Household*, Government Social Survey, 1947, and are based on sample data.
1961 figures from the 1961 Census *Housing Report*, and 1966 figures from the 1966 Sample Census *Housing Report*.

TABLE 10.21

Regional(*b*) **Comparison of Households by Tenure 1947, 1961 and 1966**
(percentages)

		All tenures	Owner occupiers	Renting from local authority or new town corporation	Renting from private person	Other tenures (*a*)
England & Wales	*1947*	100	27·0	12·0	58·0	3·0
	1961	100	42·3	23·7	27·8	6·2
	1966	100	46·7	25·7	22·5	5·1
North	*1947*	100	26·0	13·0	55·0	6·0
	1961	100	40·9	25·8	27·6	5·7
	1966	100	45·6	28·2	21·7	4·5
Midlands &	*1947*	100	32·0	11·0	55·0	2·0
Wales	*1961*	100	42·9	26·8	23·4	6·9
	1966	100	47·3	28·8..	18·5	5·4
South & East	*1947*	100	29·0	11·0	56·0	4·0
(excl. Greater	*1961*	100	43·6	28·3	20·5	7·6
London)	*1966*	100	51·9	23·0	18·2	6·9
London	*1947*	100	23·0	13·0	63·0	1·0
	1961	100	36·6	18·3	42·0	3·1
	1966	100	38·3	21·6	37·1	2·8

Notes:

(*a*) For notes on the content of this category see note to Table 10.20.

(*b*) Figures for 1961 and 1966 have been combined so that they refer to areas approximately equivalent to those used in the *British Household* study of 1947 – see below.

For 1961 North = Northern, East and West Ridings, and North West regions.
      Midlands & Wales = North Midlands, Midlands, and Wales regions.
      South and East = Eastern, Remainder of London and South East, Southern, and South West regions.
      London = Greater London conurbation.

For 1966 North = Northern, Yorkshire and Humberside, North West regions.
      Midlands & Wales = East and West Midlands, and Wales regions.
      South & East = East Anglia, Remainder of South East, South West regions.
      London = Greater London conurbation.

Source: As for Table 10.20.

TABLE 10.22

Density of Occupation, Persons per Room, by Type of Tenure in all Dwellings and Shared Dwellings 1961 and 1966, England and Wales

Tenure	1961		1966	
	All dwellings	Shared dwellings	All dwellings	Shared dwellings
Owner-occupied	0·59	0·69	0·52	0·56
Rented from local authority	0·83	0·93	0·70	0·75
Rented unfurnished	0·64	0·83	0·53	0·68
Rented furnished	0·82	1·11	0·74	0·89

Note: The categories 'rented together with farm or business premises' and 'held by virtue of employment' are omitted in 1961 and the category 'other tenures and not stated' in 1966.
Source: Census 1961 and Sample Census 1966, *Housing Reports.*

TABLE 10.23

Proportion of Households with Certain Amenities by Tenure 1966, England and Wales (percentages)

Amenities	All tenures	Owner occupied	Rented from local authority or new town corporation	Rented from a private person	Other and not stated
With shared hot tap	2·1	1·0	0·6	6·3	0·9
With *no* hot tap	12·5	6·9	4·6	34·2	8·1
With shared fixed bath	4·3	1·9	1·0	12·7	1·4
With *no* fixed bath	14·9	9·6	3·2	40·3	11·1
With shared inside WC	4·1	1·4	0·9	14·1	1·4
With outside WC only:					
exclusive use	6·4	12·4	7·9	33·9	12·2
shared	1·9	1·0	0·6	5·7	0·5
With *no* WC	1·8	1·5	0·5	3·1	4·3
With exclusive use of hot water, fixed bath and inside WC	72·4	81·1	87·8	35·3	79·3

Source: Sample Census 1966 *Housing Report.*

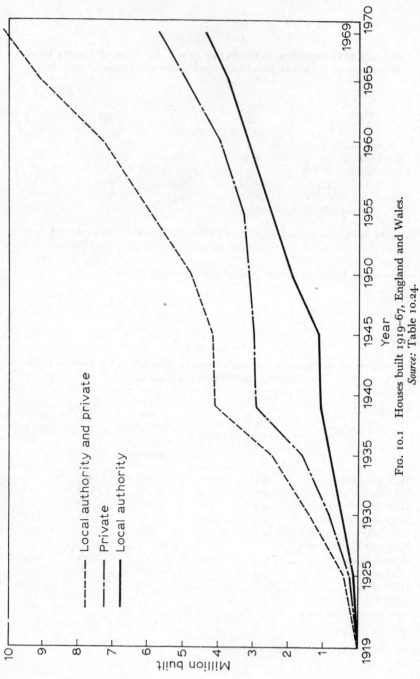

FIG. 10.1   Houses built 1919–67, England and Wales.
Source: Table 10.24.

TABLE 10.24

Permanent Houses Built in Five-Year Periods 1919–1968, England and Wales

Years ending 30th September	Local authority	Private builders (a)	Total
1919–24	176,914	221,543	398,457
1925–9	326,353	673,344	999,697
1930–4	286,350	804,251	1,090,601
1935–9	346,840	1,269,912	1,616,752
(Total 1919–39	1,136,457	2,969,050	4,105,507)
1940–4	—	—	151,000(b)
1945–9	432,098(c)	126,317	588,415
1950–4	912,805	228,616	1,141,421
1955–9	688,585	623,024	1,311,609
1960–4	545,729	878,756	1,424,485
1965–8 (d)	621,324	809,961	1,431,285

Notes:
(a) Including 431, 669 built between 1919 and 1939 with the aid of a subsidy.
(b) This figure is for the period September 1939 to March 1944. The Ministry of Health *Reports* give no figure for completed permanent houses for the rest of 1944. There was an embargo on the building of new houses during the period.
(c) From 1945 onward figures in this column include houses built by New Town Development Corporations and by Housing Associations and Government Departments, but exclude temporary houses built by local authorities.
(d) These figures are for four years only.
Sources: J. B. Cullingworth, *Housing and Local Government in England and Wales* (Allen & Unwin 1966). *Housing Statistics* no. 12, 1969. Ministry of Health *Report*, Cmnd 6562, for year ended 31.3.44. Ministry of Health *Report*, Cmnd 6744, for year ended 31.3.45.

TABLE 10.25

Slum Clearance 1930–1968, England and Wales: Houses(a) and parts of Buildings Closed

Period	Total houses demolished or closed	Parts of buildings closed	Persons moved
Up to March 1934 (b)	27,564	—	91,109
April 1934 to March 1939	245,272	—	1,001,417
1940–4(c)	nil	—	—
1945–9(d)	29,350	3850	98,950
1950–4	60,532	5913	211,090
1955–9	213,402	8571	682,228
1960–4	303,621	5514	833,746
1965–8(e)	270,186	3369	722,905

Notes:

(a) Houses for this purpose mean whole buildings, not structurally separate dwellings within a building. Where only some of the dwellings within a building were closed this is listed under 'parts of buildings closed'.

(b) Including approximately 11,000 houses demolished and 17,000 people moved up to 1930 (Ministry of Health *Annual Report*, 1931–2).

(c) Authorities were asked to postpone all slum clearance plans during the war (Ministry of Health *Summary Report*, 1939 to 1941).

(d) Based on estimates given in *Housing Statistics* no. 6. See Notes and Definitions no. 7.

(e) These figures are for four years only.

Sources: M. Bowley, *op. cit. Housing Statistics* no. 12 and no. 6.

TABLE 10.26

Slum Clearance Programmes and Progress 1934–1939, England and Wales

Date of programme	Number of houses to be closed or demolished	Number of persons to be rehoused
Jan. 1934	266,851	1,240,182
March 1937	377,930	—
March 1939	472,000	—

Period	Number of houses closed or demolished	Number of persons removed
1930 to March 1934	27,564	91,109
April 1934 to March 1939	245,272	1,001,417
Total 1930–9	272,836	1,092,526

Source: M. Bowley, op. cit. p. 153.

TABLE 10.27

Estimates of Numbers of Unfit Houses 1960, 1965 and 1968, and Numbers of Houses Demolished and Persons Moved 1945–1960 and 1960–1967, England and Wales

Date	Number of unfit dwellings	Numbers of persons to be rehoused
1960	622,000	—
1965	820,000	—
1967	1,836,000	—

Period	Numbers of dwellings closed or demolished	Numbers moved
1945–59 inc.	321,618	992,265
1960–4 incl.	309,135	833,746
1965–8	273,555	722,905

Note: 1960 and 1965 estimates were derived by asking about local authorities' clearance plans, 1967 estimate was made by public health inspectors.
Source: The Housing Situation in 1960, Government Social Survey, SS 319, for 1960 estimate. Housing Statistics no. 9, 1968, for 1965 and 1967 estimates.

TABLE 10.28

Houses(a) made Fit(b) 1945-1968, England and Wales

Period	Number of houses
1945-9	883,591 (occupied and unoccupied war damaged dwellings)
1945 to March 1951	510,301
March 1951 to end 1954	1,197,930
1955-9	1,247,895
1960-4	1,096,618
1965-8	394,125

Notes:
(a) Houses for this purpose means whole buildings, not the separate dwellings within them.
(b) 'Made fit' – for figures 1945-9 of war damaged houses this means simply making weathertight and habitable.
    Other figures refer to houses made fit under powers given by Housing Acts 1936, 1957 and 1961, either by owner or by local authority in default of owner after the houses had been declared unfit by the local authority.
Source: Ministry of Health *Report* for year ended 31st March 1949. Ministry of Housing and Local Government *Reports*. *Housing Statistics*, no. 12, 1969.

TABLE 10.29

**Improvement Grants(a) Approved 1949-1968, England and Wales.
Number of Dwellings**

Period	Local Authority dwellings	Owner occupiers	Housing association and other private owners	Total
1949-58 (incl.)	9846	150,023		159,869
1959	16,213	62,783		78,996
1960-4	180,054	301,487	129,237	610,778
1965-8 (b)	127,828	220,468	109,775	458,071
Total since Housing Act 1949	333,941	973,773		1,307,714

Notes:
(a) Includes standard and discretionary grants for the conversion and improvement of existing houses. Local Authorities are obliged to pay standard grants (introduced in 1959) if certain conditions apply. They are half the cost (up to a specified maximum) of installing five standard amenities. Discretionary grants to private persons (introduced in 1949) are payable at the discretion of Local Authorities for the conversion or improvement of dwellings which must then reach specified standards and be capable of providing accommodation for at least 15 years. Similar grants are available at the discretion of the Ministry for local authority dwellings.
(b) Four-year period.
Source: Housing Statistics no. 12, 1969.

TABLE 10.30

Houses and Flats Completed: by Numbers of Bedrooms 1945–1968, England and Wales (percentages)

Years	Local authorities and new towns				Private owners				Local authorities, new towns and private owners			
	1	2	3	4 or more	1	2	3	4 or more	1	2	3	4 or more
1945–60	10·0	29·6	58·0	2·4	—	—	—	—	—	—	—	—
1961	26·1	32·0	39·9	2·0	1·8	35·1	59·6	3·5	4·2	29·7	62·6	3·5
1962	27·5	32·3	38·3	1·9	2·1	34·5	59·7	3·7	4·5	28·1	63·6	3·8
1963	27·9	32·3	37·7	2·1	2·4	32·1	61·7	3·8	3·9	26·6	65·4	4·1
1964	27·6	34·6	35·8	2·0	2·2	29·5	64·2	4·1	3·8	25·0	67·0	4·2
1965	27·3	35·9	34·8	2·0	1·9	27·0	66·3	4·8	3·3	23·7	68·2	4·8
1966	26·5	34·7	36·6	2·2	2·0	25·0	67·3	5·7	3·1	21·9	69·6	5·5
1967	25·8	32·4	39·1	2·7	1·8	22·8	69·0	6·4	3·3	20·3	70·2	6·2
1968	26·4	31·8	39·0	2·8	1·7	21·2	70·1	7·0	3·0	19·3	71·0	6·7

Source: Housing Statistics no. 12, 1969.

TABLE 10.31

Cost of Housing Subsidies(a) 1919–1967, England and Wales (£ millions)

Date	Exchequer contributions to permanent housing	Local authority rate funded contributions
1919–20	0·2	0·5
1930–1	11·9	3·0
1938–9	15·0	3·8 (for 1936–7)
1945–6	14·1	—
1949–50	24·6	8·3
1953–4	35·5	14·7
1958–9	59·3	17·3
1963–4	75·2	21·0
1966–7	92·4	37·0

Notes: (a) Contributions includes contributions to new housing and grants for improvement and conversion of existing dwellings.

Housing subsidies to local authorities do not represent the only costs to the government in the field of housing. For example, for Great Britain as a whole in 1967–1968 the average benefit of government subsidies to council house tenants was £23 and the average amount of income tax relief on mortgage payments received by those buying their own houses was £42. The cost for the whole of Great Britain for 1967–8 of subsidies to local authorities was £117m and of mortgage interest relief £137m (*Housing Statistics* no. 12, p. 81).

Sources: Annual Report of Ministry of Health, 1938–39.

Ministry of Housing and Local Government *Report* for 1956.

Housing Statistics nos. 10 and 12, 1968 and 1969.

TABLE 10.32

Improvement Grants for Private Owners and Housing Associations 1959–1968, England and Wales

Number of dwellings; discretionary grants approved and standard grants paid in respect of the dwellings by local authorities

Year or period	Number of dwellings	Amount approved or paid £ooo's
1959	43,277	8654
1960–4	385,753	64,514
1965–8	298,591	55,097

Source: Housing Statistics no. 12, 1969.

TABLE 10.33

Improvement Grants in Selected Years, England and Wales
(£ thousands)

| | Government contributions | | Local authority grants for private owners (b) | |
	Local authority dwellings	Private owners	Discretionary grants approved (a)	Standard grants paid
1951–2	1	1	—	—
1955–6	33	182	—	—
1960–1	345	2478	1961 8824	4107
1965–6	1428	7232	1966 7353	5760

Notes:
(a) See note (a) to Table 10.29 about standard and discretionary grants The cost of standard grants is not known until after the work has been completed so that figures for grants paid are given. For discretionary grants the amount payable is stated at the time of approval.
(b) Including Exchequer contributions for private owners.
Source: Housing Statistics no. 12, 1969.

TABLE 10.34

Building Societies: Number of Mortgages and Amount Advanced
Annually, 1910–1966, Great Britain

Year	Total advanced during year £000's	Total number of advances on mortgages during year	Total advanced on new mortgages £000's	Number of new mortgages
1910	9292	—	—	—
1920	29,095	—	—	—
1930	88,767	159,348	—	—
1938	137,020	232,294	—	—
1941	9950	22,406	—	—
1950	269,717	302,145	—	—
1960	559,398	387,406	544,686	326,125
1966	1,244,750	535,512	1,204,200	444,170

Source: Annual Reports of Chief Registrar of Friendly Societies, pt 5: Building Societies. Chief Registrar of Friendly Societies, Statistical Summary of Building Societies.

TABLE 10.35

**Loans for House Purchase by Insurance Societies 1966–1968,
United Kingdom**

Year	Number of dwellings	£millions
1966	—	147
1967	33,950	124
1968 *	42,000	167

* Provisional.
Source: Housing Statistics no. 12, Feb. 1969.

TABLE 10.36

Housing Loans by Local Authorities 1959–1968, England and Wales

Year	For house purchase		Other housing loans	
	Number of dwellings	£millions	Number of loans	£thousands
1959	44,699	55	4,946	1910
1960	47,864	67	10,928	3288
1961	62,318	99	12,085	3717
1962	53,385	85	11,556	3561
1963	57,617	104	12,115	4521
1964	77,217	166	17,877	6744
1965	87,112	220	18,584	7965
1966	46,229	109	18,791	9865
1967	56,598	144	14,689	11,433
1968	38,792	86	15,606	15,024

Source: Housing Statistics no. 12.

TABLE 10.37

Rents(a) or Mortgage Payments as a Proportion of Head of Household Income(b) and of Total Household Income 1967, Great Britain (percentages)

	As percentage of head of household income		As percentage of total household income	
	Mean	Median	Mean	Median
Local authority rents	11·9	10·3	8·2	7·2
Private rents	11·4	9·1	8·6	6·8
Mortgage payments	13·1	11·8	10·8	9·7

Notes:
(a) Rents are exclusive of rates and service charges but water charges are included. Sums received from subletting have been deducted. Rents in private sector are for both controlled and uncontrolled tenancies.
(b) Incomes are gross. Incomes of owner occupied includes an amount equal to the rateable value of the dwelling.
Source: Housing Statistics no. 12, from data collected by the Family Expenditure Survey.

TABLE 10.38

Household Income, Rent and Mortgage Payments of Main Tenure Groups 1964 and 1965 England and Wales and Major Regions

	Median household income				Median rent			
	North	Midlands	East Anglia and South East	England and Wales	North	Midlands	East Anglia and South East	England and Wales
Privately rented, unfurnished								
£s p.a.	869	1019	1033	962	38	50	77	54
% of England and Wales	90	106	107	100	70	93	143	100
Rented from local authority								
£s p.a.	1068	1204	1227	1144	67	72	93	76
% of England and Wales	93	105	107	100	88	95	122	100
Owner occupied, with mortgage					*Median mortgage payment*			
£s p.a.	1266	1450	1537	1395	97	119	152	122
% of England and Wales	91	104	110	100	80	98	125	100
Owner occupied, owned outright								
£s p.a.	1009	1122	1061	1025	—	—	—	—
% of England and Wales	98	109	104	100	—	—	—	—

Note: The figures are based on a small sample and subject to considerable sampling error. Rents are exclusive of rates and services. Water charges are included. Sums received from subletting have been ignored. Rents in private sector relate to controlled and decontrolled tenancies. Incomes are gross before tax deductions. Income of owner occupied includes an amount equivalent to the rateable value of the dwelling.

Source: Housing Statistics no. 6, data from Ministry of Labour Family Expenditure Survey.

11 Health

JULIA PARKER AND CONSTANCE ROLLETT AND KATHLEEN JONES[1]

I: PHYSICAL HEALTH

To trace trends in physical health and the medical care of the physically ill, we concentrate in this section on three kinds of statistics: mortality rates and measures of prevalence of certain diseases; the supply of medical services in terms of institutions, doctors and nurses; and costs.

MORTALITY RATES

Total deaths and rates for different age groups are easily obtainable. It is more difficult to analyse death rates by cause of death, because definitions of diseases have changed and at different times different diseases have been classified in different ways. The Registrar General used the International List of Causes (revised in 1909 and subsequently), but for some time also gave tables using a short list of causes adopted in 1911 by his office and the Local Government Board. We have therefore been selective, and show death rates for particular diseases where definitions have not changed and which are, or were, important causes of death.

We have not been able to show the distribution of death rates by region or town, because boundary changes since 1900 make it very difficult to get consistent geographical areas for different dates. Geographical variations at any one time can however be demonstrated.

Death rates for different social classes and for different occupations are also available for certain periods.

MORBIDITY RATES

These are fragmentary compared with the mortality statistics and particularly so for the years before 1940. There are notification figures for some diseases, and some areas, from 1900 but notification of particular specified diseases only became compulsory for the whole of England and Wales in 1911. Notification figures are in any case an unreliable

---

[1] This chapter is in two sections dealing with physical and mental health respectively. Section I and Tables 11.1 to 11.41 are by Julia Parker and Constance Rollett; Section II and Tables 11.42 to 11.52 by Kathleen Jones.

measure of the prevalence of disease. The limits are indicated in *Studies in Medical and Population Subjects no. 2 – Sickness in the population of England and Wales 1944–47*, where it was suggested that only two-thirds of measles cases, a quarter to a third of pneumonia cases and a fifth to a quarter of whooping-cough cases, for instance, were in fact notified.

Alternative measures of sickness are hard to find. Before 1940 there were some local surveys but none concerned with the whole population. Records of friendly societies and approved societies refer only to the insured[1] population. The analysis of the illnesses of insured persons consulting their doctors between 1916 and 1933 is some indication of the incidence of different kinds of ill health, though the insured population would be relatively free from incapacitating sickness, and it might be expected that more minor illnesses would be treated in later years as the medical services connected with health insurance became more familiar.

In the post-war period, the sickness survey is an important source. It covers the years 1947–51 and is based on a national stratified sample of persons over 16. The results are reported in *Studies in Medical and Population Subjects nos 2 and 12*. Apart from the figures we reproduce, prevalence, sickness, incapacity and consultation rates are analysed by age, cause, income and occupation, and there are also maps showing the geographical distribution. The survey method has limitations; respondents were asked to report any illness during the preceding month, but memories may be inexact and illness wrongly labelled.

A second important source is the analysis of G.P. records made between 1951 and 1956, the results of which are reported in *Studies in Medical and Population Subjects nos 7, 9 and 14*. The figures are entirely based on medical consultations and on doctors' records; thus they may partly reflect the provision of G.P. services within a given area, or their availability to certain occupational groups or social classes. Nevertheless, the information obtained is probably more exact than that collected by the survey method, as G.P.s kept notes at the time of the consultations.

A survey of hospital in-patients, *The Hospital In-Patient Inquiry*, was started in 1958, and in England and Wales publications are issued jointly by the General Register Office and the Ministry of Health. The survey classifies patients by type of illness, length of stay, morbidity and so on.

No further studies of the prevalence of sickness in the whole population have been published by the GRO since 1962, when *Studies in Medical and Population Subjects no. 14 Vol. 3* was published.

---

[1] Persons statutorily insured under the National Insurance Act 1911 and subsequent legislation.

PROVISION OF HEALTH SERVICES

Information about provision is reasonably satisfactory and consistent since the inception of the National Health Service in 1948, but for earlier years it is fragmentary for two main reasons. First, there had been rapid developments in medicine and consequently in types of medical care leading to increasing specialisation of treatment and professional skill. Second, the administrative and financial responsibilities have been divided. Before the war there were four main types of public provision separately organised: (1) G.P. services provided by 'panel' doctors as part of the national health insurance scheme; (2) Poor Law medical services, which were the responsibility of the Poor Law authorities until they were taken over by the counties and county councils in 1929; (3) a range of medical services, in particular isolation hospitals, general hospitals and maternity and child welfare services run by local health authorities; (4) voluntary hospitals and clinics which were independently administered, and financed in a variety of ways – e.g. by endowments, voluntary gifts, patients' payments and contributory schemes.

Hospital provision
The only series we have been able to construct to cover the whole period are those for the number of beds provided for the physically ill, and the total numbers   of doctors and nurses.

Hospital provision for the physically ill before the war has been well documented by Robert Pinker in *English Hospital Statistics 1861–1938*. After 1948, when all health services were brought under the control of the Ministry of Health, records became simpler. Almost all the statistics were published by the Ministry of Health, mostly in annual reports. Figures since 1949 are fairly satisfactory for bed provision, type of specialty, the number of hospital staff and their qualifications. We have simplified the Ministry's figures in our tables in some cases by grouping categories.

Figures showing the number and size of hospitals are not published in the annual reports, but can be found in the *Health Service Accounts*, which are published annually as a House of Commons paper. Statistics showing the regional distribution of hospitals are not so easy to obtain. The Ministry published figures showing the distribution of hospital beds by hospital regions in 1949, but subsequently stopped. The *Abstract of Regional Statistics*, nos 1 and 2, give the number of hospital beds by hospital regions for 1961–5, but later issues give hospital beds by standard regions instead.

The number of medical staff and their qualifications must be some measure of the quality of hospital care. Figures for the years since 1948 are fairly complete, but difficult to calculate for the earlier period. Before 1948, the distinction between G.P.s and specialists was far less clear and only began to be made in the 1930s. We have not been able to find any very reliable estimates.

The position with regard to nurses' qualifications is similar. The central departments have published figures since 1949. Professor Abel-Smith[1] has a table to show the total number of nurses before 1949 based on census data, but there is no breakdown by type of qualification.

G.P. services

We have figures for the number of fully qualified doctors from 1901, but they include those who are retired and do not distinguish between G.P.s and specialists. A P.E.P. Report[2] gives the number of doctors practising in England and Wales in 1936 as 29,300. This includes those engaged in research and administration, and distinguishes between retired and practising doctors but not between G.P.s and specialists. The Report gives the number of panel doctors in England and Wales in 1935 as 16,000, but there were also an unknown number of G.P.s who were not panel doctors. The number of insured persons is given as 15,299,000, so that the average list size of panel patients was 922. However, most panel doctors would also be likely to treat other members of the insured person's family, and some would have private patients, so this does not represent the average number of patients per G.P.

Figures for the years since 1948 are reasonably satisfactory. The distribution of G.P.s has been analysed since 1952, showing the proportion working in under-doctored areas and the average list size. We also have figures for the number of G.P.s and consultants in the different hospital regions for one sample year.

COSTS

It has only been possible to draw up cost and expenditure tables for the years since the war. There are no comparable statistics for earlier years, when the administration of hospitals, domiciliary services and G.P. services was split among several statutory and voluntary bodies.

NOTES ON TABLES

Mortality rates

The decline in the death rate since the beginning of the century is shown in Table 11.1, and it also appears that the difference between the rates for men and women has lessened since the nineteen fifties. Analysis

[1] Brian Abel-Smith, *A History of the Nursing Profession* (Heinemann 1960).
[2] P.E.P., *Report on The British Health Services* (P.E.P. 1937).

of the rates for different age groups shows that people under 45 have made the greatest proportionate gain, as would be expected (Table 11.2), but it is notable that the rates for older men – i.e. over 55 – have decreased far less than those for older women. The fall in the infant mortality rate has been the most dramatic of all (Table 11.3).

The changing importance of different diseases as causes of death may be seen from Table 11.4. Infectious illnesses are now very insignificant compared with 1900, while pneumonia, diseases of the heart, and cancer are all as important, or more important, than in the earlier years of the century. Infant mortality from infectious diseases and T.B. has now been almost eliminated while congenital, developmental and wasting diseases have become relatively more important and now account for two-thirds of all deaths (Table 11.5).

Class differences in mortality are shown in Table 11.6. It is notable that males in the highest class have the lowest mortality rate up to 1932, but the third highest in the years 1949–53. During this later period Class II had the most favourable rate and Class V the worst – a position it has held consistently. The divergence from the norm for Class V was, however, less than half what it had been in 1910–12, though rather more than the difference in 1930–2. The figures for women are more limited, but suggest a worsening in the relative position of married and an improvement in that of single women in Class I. Women in Class V have the highest mortality rates apart from those described as un-occupied. Single unoccupied women were particularly vulnerable from 1949–53 (Table 11.7).

Analysis of cause of death shows Class V to suffer particularly from bronchitis and T.B. and relatively less from cancer, though the rate of deaths from this cause is still the highest of all the social classes (Table 11.8). The drop in infant mortality for all the classes is apparent from Table 11.9, but in spite of a decrease of 50 per cent or more, the rate for Class V in 1949–53 was still higher than it was for Class I in 1921–3. And the position of Class V in relation to the average, worsened between 1921 and 1953. The decline in stillbirths and neo-natal deaths was proportionately greater for Classes I and II between 1945 and 1964 (Table 11.10).

Morbidity

Tables 11.11 and 11.12 give some idea of the drop in the prevalence and seriousness of certain diseases since 1900. The trends are probably stronger than the figures suggest, since notification has become more comprehensive and more efficient in recent years. The analysis of reasons for which patients consult their doctors shows the most usual cases to have been bronchitis, tonsillitis and colds, or digestive disorders, for the period 1916–33 and there are no very marked changes in the consultation pattern – though pneumonia seems to have become less important at the end of the period (Table 11.13). In 1955–6 respiratory diseases remained the most important single cause for consulting the doctor (Table 11.14). Tables 11.15 and 11.16 show self-reported sickness and consultation with doctors increasing slightly between 1947 and 1951, but the consultation rate dropping after 1951.

Analysis by social class shows Class I with the lowest consultation rate in 1956 (Table 11.17). Class V had the highest consultation rates for bronchitis and cancer, but considerably lower rates relative to the other social classes for coronary diseases and T.B. (Table 11.18). The death rate for Class V for the listed diseases was relatively very high indeed, except for coronary diseases where the rate was much higher for Class I.

The supply of medical services
The ratio of hospital beds to population appears to have increased through the century until the end of the 1930s, and since declined (Table 11.19). The distribution of beds among different kinds of institution is shown in Tables 11.20 and 11.21 which, of course, relate only to the period before the war and before the National Health Service Act. It is notable that in 1921 over 50 per cent of all beds were provided by the Poor Law and well under a third of them were in the sick wards of the workhouses. By 1938 substantial numbers of the Poor Law hospitals had passed to municipal control, though it is not clear how far the administrative change also brought higher standards. The geographical distribution for the years before the war emphasises the concentration of hospital services in the metropolis.

The figures showing the distribution of beds among the different specialties are unsatisfactory; classification systems have changed so that it is impossible to produce comparable statistics for the whole period (Tables 11.22 and 11.23). The analysis of out-patient statistics for the post-war years, however, shows a substantial growth in the volume of work and suggests a relative increase in this branch of the hospital service (Table 11.24).

Some measure of the quality of hospital care is the ratio of staff to beds or to the population, and here there is evidence of clear improvement since the war (Tables 11.25, 11.26, 11.27). The number of hospital nurses has nearly doubled, though in 1966 there were proportionately rather fewer who were fully qualified (Table 11.28).

The geographical distribution of hospital beds seems to have improved slightly since 1948, though Sheffield stands out as one of the worst served regions in 1948 which had barely improved its position by

1965 (Table 11.29). The distribution of doctors in the different regions is markedly uneven (Tables 11.30 and 11.31) and has changed little since the early 1950s (Table 11.25). If hospital doctors and G.P.s are considered together, the inequalities remain: there is no clear tendency for areas badly served by the one to be particularly generously supplied with the other (Table 11.30).

Tables 11.31 and 11.33 show the distribution of consultants and hospitals among different specialties. The lack of correlation in the proportion of beds and of doctors is notable in some cases. The figures in Tables 11.32 and 11.33 are not strictly comparable, since they refer to different years and the classification of consultants and beds is not consistent. Nevertheless the most recent figures show 2 per cent of all beds as maternity beds and 16 per cent of all consultants as gynaecologists or obstetricians; and 40 per cent of all beds for psychiatric or subnormal patients and 11 per cent of all consultants as psychiatrists.

Taking all doctors, including G.P.s, there has been a fairly steady increase during the century both absolutely and in relation to the rest of the population (Table 11.34), and the same is true of nurses (Table 11.35). By contrast there has been a drop in recent years in the number of doctors in general practice and a consequent increase in the average size of G.P. lists (Table 11.36). The distribution of doctors has also worsened; the proportion of the population living in under-doctored areas dropped from over 50 per cent in 1952 to 17 per cent in 1961, but had risen to nearly 34 per cent by 1967. And the average size of G.P. lists in those areas where they had decreased slightly in the late 1950s, was again approaching the 1952 figure (Table 11.39).

Costs

The increase in expenditure on the National Health Service and local authority welfare services, and the sources of finance, may be seen from Tables 11.38 and 11.39. Local authority expenditure has risen proportionately more than central government expenditure, though within the latter, pharmaceutical and hospital costs have risen most steeply. Taxes and rates are still the overwhelmingly important source of finance, though contributions to charges now play a substantially larger part than in 1950.

The comparative figures showing the costs per patient for different types of hospital and distinguishing the teaching hospitals, speak for themselves[1] (Table 11.40). Perhaps most remarkable is that a bed in one of the three mental hospitals run by boards of governors costs four times

---

[1] Though see K. Jones and R. Sidebotham, *Mental Hospitals at Work* (Routledge 1962), on the difficulties of assessing in-patient costs.

as much as a bed in a non-teaching mental hospital. Table 11.41 shows expenditure on different types of hospital according to specialty. The distribution has not changed very much between 1950 and 1968, except for a decline in spending on isolation hospitals and in the proportion spent on T.B. sanatoria, and an increase in the amount going to 'other', that is specialised, institutions.

II: MENTAL HEALTH

The main sources of statistical information about the Mental Health Services are the *Annual Reports* of the Board of Control (1914–59); *Annual Reports* of the Ministry of Health (1948–67) and of its successor, the Department of Health and Social Security (1968 to date); the General Register Office *Supplements on Mental Health* (1952–3, 1954–6, 1957–8, 1959 and 1960) and *Studies in Medical and Population Subjects*, no. 16 and no. 18; and the Department of Health and Social Security *Statistical Report Series* nos 3–7 inclusive.

The procedures for the collection and analysis of statistical material changed radically as a consequence of the recommendations of the Royal Commission on the Law Relating to Mental Illness and Mental Deficiency (1954–7). In its report, the Commission drew attention to the complexity of existing procedures. 'Board of Control statistics' related to patients in hospitals and homes covered by the Lunacy and Mental Treatment Acts and the Mental Deficiency Acts, but gave no information on other forms of treatment.[1] Ministry of Health statistics, contained in Part I of their *Annual Reports*, were collected on a different basis. They included out-patients and some in-patients not covered by the relevant Acts of Parliament (e.g. those in 'de-designated' beds or in teaching hospitals), but excluded certain categories of care, such as the special hospitals. The GRO, under a scheme started in 1949, collected very full and detailed statistics, including information otherwise unobtainable about diagnosis and length of stay, but only for very limited categories of patients. The three sets of statistics were in many respects not comparable, and the Royal Commission, in its own calculations, had to work on approximate figures and leave many gaps. They recommended a review of procedures and the institution of a single system for 'whatever special mental health statistics are considered necessary, either from the administrative or the medical point of view'. These should be collected for all mentally disordered patients, irrespective of

[1] The Lunacy Commission (1845–1913) and its successor, the Board of Control (1914–59), were responsible for the collection of data on the lines indicated; but by the mid-1950s the work of the Board had so far been assimilated into the Ministry of Health that the distinction was largely nominal.

the designation of the hospitals to which they were admitted or the use of particular admission procedures.[1]

Under the provisions of the Mental Health Act 1959, which closely followed the recommendations of the Commission, the Board of Control was abolished. The Ministry of Health and the GRO discussed the collection of statistics, and concluded in 1960 that two sets were necessary: the Ministry figures were needed for 'general planning and administrative purposes', while the GRO figures were 'designed primarily to contribute to medical knowledge and to help medical research workers'.[2] However, this decision was rescinded three years later, when it was agreed that:

> . . . in practice, the mental health statistics collected by [the GRO] have proved of considerable value for planning purposes, and since the existence of the two schemes resulted in some duplication, it was decided in 1963 to amalgamate them and bring the statistical work under the control of the Ministry of Health as the main user.[3]

From 1963, therefore, the Ministry's Statistics and Research Division became responsible, and its work is published either in the *Annual Reports* or in the special publications of the Statistical Report Series.

The recommendations of the Royal Commission, as embodied in the Mental Health Act, affected the statistical material available in another and more fundamental way. The special designation of mental hospitals and mental deficiency hospitals was abolished; the terminology was changed, 'mental disorder' now covering the previous categories of mental illness and mental deficiency, with four sub-categories: mental illness, psychopathic disorder, subnormality, and severe subnormality; admission procedures were changed, with a strong emphasis on informal admission; and a considerable expansion in community care was envisaged. Not only were the categories for the collection of statistics altered, but the whole shape of the Mental Health Services changed, so that it is virtually impossible to make comparisons of the work before and after 1959. (It should be noted that earlier Acts, notably the Lunacy Act of 1890, the Mental Deficiency Act of 1913, the Mental Treatment Act of 1930 and the National Health Service Act of 1946, had a somewhat similar effect in changing the shape of the services – mental health statistics can only usefully be studied in comparatively short runs between major pieces of legislation.)

[1] Report of the Royal Commission on the Law Relating to Mental Illness and Mental Deficiency, Cmnd 169, 1957, Appendix IV, pp. 307–13.

[2] *Annual Report* of the Ministry of Health, 1960, pt I, p. 18.

[3] *Annual Report* of the Ministry of Health, 1963, p. 40.

While these changes were in progress, statistics were necessarily somewhat patchy. The *Annual Report* of the Ministry of Health for 1960 gave only very brief tables. In the following year, more figures were available, but only for a limited period – 1 November to 30 April. Full statistics in the new form were given from 1962, but in the first few years of operation, these were often subject to subsequent revision. We have at present only a run of five or six years' figures from which to deduce current trends.

In the late fifties and early sixties, the re-planning of the Mental Health Services generated a variety of statistical material. Outstanding among the forecasts published is the work of Tooth and Brooke,[1] which formed the basis of the Ministry policy, expressed in Circular HM(61) 25, of running down beds for mental illness in England and Wales from about 3·4 per thousand population to about 1·8 per thousand population in 1975. The same policy underlay the calculations in the *Hospital Plan* (1962) and *Health and Welfare: the Development of Community Care* (1963). The quantitative forecasts involved were described as 'of the most rudimentary kind' by Rehin and Martin[2] and contested by Gore, Jones, Taylor and Ward.[3]

Miss Brooke's *Cohort Study of Patients first admitted to Mental Hospitals in 1954 and 1955* provided a valuable study of patterns of utilisation in the Mental Health Services in terms of age, sex, diagnosis and area of origin of patients, but was limited to a two-year follow-up period. This was the first serious attempt in an official enquiry to obtain records of what happened to patients as individuals. More recently, the Statistical Report Series has provided detailed information on the activities of psychiatric hospitals by region (nos 3 and 6); a useful pilot study of the work of day hospitals (no. 7); and the first results of the on-going Mental Health Enquiry (in-patient statistics for 1964, 1965 and 1966, published in no. 4, and for 1967, published in no. 5). All these publications refer to particular points in time, and do not give comparisons over time.

There is thus a good deal of material available, but it has a number of limitations. First, apart from the Brooke cohort study, it is a record of events and not of persons. It records admission, discharge, registration on the books of a local authority or an out-patient clinic, but not what sequence of events individual patients go through. Second, the means of

[1] I. G. Tooth and E. M. Brooke, 'Trends in the Mental Hospital Population and Their Effect on Future Planning', *Lancet*, 1st April 1961.

[2] G. F. Rehin and F. M. Martin, *Psychiatric Services in 1975* (P.E.P.), vol. XXIX, no. 468, 1963.

[3] G. P. Gore, K. Jones, W. Taylor and B. Ward, 'Needs and Beds: A Regional Census of Psychiatric Patients', *Lancet*, 29th August 1964.

care are now so diversified that it is almost impossible to get a picture of the work of the Mental Health Services as a whole – statistics for hospitals, local authority work and out-patient work are collected in different forms, and cannot be consolidated for analysis. Third, the Royal Commission made a strong recommendation that the Mental Health Services should be regarded as 'an integral part of the national health and welfare services',[1] and that 'no-one should be excluded from benefiting from any of the general social services simply because his need arises from mental disorder'.[2] This means that mental health statistics *per se* give only a very partial picture, and do not reflect the totality of care and treatment.

The evidence we have suggests that the Mental Health Services have expanded their scope very rapidly in the sixties, and that the principles of the Mental Health Act are in fact being put into operation. Direct admissions to hospitals and units for mental illness have risen steadily, and in 1968 were nearly 80 per cent above the 1959 figures (Table 11.42). The proportion of first admissions has risen slightly, and is now more than half of all admissions (Table 11.43) which goes some way to disproving the contention that the open door is no more than a revolving door. The resident population appeared to rise immediately after the 1959 Act, probably because of the change in criteria, but has since fallen steadily, the drop from 1961 to 1968 being of the order of 14 per cent (Table 11.44). Taken in conjunction with admission figures, this indicates a considerable increase in turnover. Following the review of patients' legal status at the time of the 1959 Act, the proportion of patients with informal status has remained at well over 90 per cent and the number admitted informally is over 80 per cent (Table 11.45). Of about 12,000 patients now subject to compulsory detention, less than a thousand appeal to Mental Health Review Tribunals annually, and discharge is directed in only about one case in seven (Table 11.46).

The reduction of about 20,000 beds for mental illness between 1961 and 1968 was matched by an increase in out-patient attendances and local authority work. There were 48,000 more new out-patients registered in 1968 than in 1961, and about a quarter of a million more out-patient attendances in all, though we do not know to how many patients this latter figure refers (Table 11.47). The number of patients on the books of local authority Mental Health Services has nearly doubled in the same period, and now stands at over 94,000, though we have no indication of how many of these patients receive intensive case-work services as opposed to routine visits (Table 11.49). However, the increased employment of trained social workers (Table 11.51) suggests

[1] *Op. cit.*, p. 45. [2] *Op. cit.*, p. 245.

an improvement in the quality of care. Rehin and Martin[1] have provided a detailed picture of community services in three areas (Oldham, East Middlesex, and Worthing and District).

Work with subnormal and severely subnormal patients appears to have been comparatively static. The number of hospital beds available increased slightly in the sixties (Table 11.48), and local authorities began to develop more residential places for patients in these groups, though the total number of places is still comparatively small (Table 11.50).

Table 11.52 deals with in-patient costs. On a patient-week basis, the cost of treatment for mental illness or subnormality (including severe subnormality) in Health Service hospitals is still very low in comparison with costs in general medicine. The Department of Health and Social Security issues cost-per-case figures for some types of hospital treatment, but not for psychiatric treatment. The limitations of in-patient week costs, and the methodological difficulties of cost-per-case calculations for mental illness have been described by Jones and Sidebotham.[2]

Major needs in research at the present time include further cohort studies, to trace how patients utilise the diversified services now available over periods of time, and intensive local studies of how resources are being deployed to meet needs in particular areas. A good introduction to the interpretation of mental health statistics is given in a paper by Professor Reid[3] for the World Health Organisation.

BIBLIOGRAPHY

I. PHYSICAL HEALTH

Abel-Smith, Brian, *A History of the Nursing Profession* (Heinemann 1960).
Board of Control, *Annual Reports*, 1914–59 as relevant.
British Medical Association, *British Medical Journal*, Supplement to 1964.
Central Statistical Office, *Abstract of Regional Statistics*, 1965 to date.
Department of Health and Social Security, *Annual Reports*, 1968 to date.
General Medical Council, *Medical Register*, 1900 to date as relevant.
General Register Office:
   Census Reports for England and Wales, 1901 to date.
   Decennial Supplements to the Registrar-General's *Statistical Review*, published 1921, 1931 and 1951.

[1] G. F. Rehin and F. M. Martin, *Patterns of Performance in Community Care* (O.U.P. 1968).
[2] K. Jones and R. Sidebotham, *Mental Hospitals at Work* (Routledge 1962).
[3] D. D. Reid, *Epidemiological Methods in the Study of Mental Disorders*, Public Health Papers, no. 2, World Health Organisation, 1960.

The Registrar-General's *Annual Reports for England and Wales*, 1900–1920 as relevant.

The Registrar-General's *Statistical Review for England and Wales*, *1921* to date as relevant.

Studies on Medical and Population Subjects:

  no. 2, P. Stocks, *Sickness in the Population of England and Wales 1944–47*, 1949.

  no. 7, W. P. D. Logan, *General Practitioners' Records, April 1951 to March 1952*, 1953.

  no. 9, W. P. D. Logan, *General Practitioners' Records, April 1952 to March 1954*.

  no. 14, W. P. D. Logan and A. A. Cushion, *Morbidity Statistics from General Practice*, vol. I (General), 1958.

  no. 14, W. P. D. Logan, *Morbidity Statistics from General Practice*, vol. II (Occupational), 1960.

  no. 19, C. C. Spicer and L. Lipworth, *Regional and Social Factors in Infant Mortality*, 1966.

P.E.P. (Political and Economic Planning), *Report on the British Health Services* (P.E.P. 1937).

Pinker, Robert, *English Hospital Statistics 1861–1938* (Heinemann 1966).

Stevens, Rosemary, *Medical Practice in Modern England* (Yale University Press 1966).

Ministry of Health, *Annual Reports 1919–1967* as relevant. Part I covers health and welfare services; from 1919 to 1948 it also covered national health insurance and contributory pensions; from 1919 to 1951 it included housing, local government services, local government finance and civil defence. Part II is the Report on the State of the Public Health by the Chief Medical Officer.

National Health Service Accounts, 1948 to date, as relevant.

2 MENTAL HEALTH

Board of Control, *Annual Reports*, 1914–59.

Department of Health and Social Security:

  Annual Reports, 1968 to date.

  Statistical Report Series no. 3: *The Activities of Psychiatric Hospitals: A Regional Comparison* (*Mental Hospitals and Units, 1964*), published 1968.

  Statistical Report Series no. 4: *Psychiatric Hospitals and Units in England and Wales*; in-patient statistics from the Mental Health Enquiry for the years 1964, 1965 and 1966, published 1969.

  Statistical Report Series no. 5: *Psychiatric Hospitals and Units in England and Wales*; in-patient statistics from the Mental Health Enquiry, 1967, published 1969.

Statistical Report Series no. 6: *Facilities and Services for Psychiatric Hospitals in England and Wales, 1966*, published 1969.

Statistical Report Series no. 7: *Pilot Survey of Patients Attending Day Hospitals, 1967*, published 1969.

General Register Office:

Studies on Medical and Population Subjects no. 16: *Area of Residence of Mental Hospital Patients*; Admissions to Mental Hospitals in England and Wales in 1957 according to Area of Residence, Diagnosis, Sex and Age, published 1962.

Studies on Medical and Population Subjects no. 18: *A Cohort Study of Patients first admitted to Mental Hospitals in 1954 and 1955*, by E. M. Brooke, published 1963.

Registrar-General's *Statistical Review*: Supplements on Mental Health, 1952–3, 1954–6, 1957–8, 1959 and 1960.

Gore, C. P., Jones, K., Taylor, W., and Ward, B., 'Needs and Beds: A Regional Census of Psychiatric Patients', *Lancet*, 29 August 1964, pp. 457–60. Reprinted in Freeman, H. and Farndale, W. A. J. (eds), *New Aspects of the Mental Health Services* (Pergamon Press 1967).

Jones, K., and Sidebotham, R., *Mental Hospitals at Work*, International Library of Sociology (Routledge 1962).

Mental Health Act, 1959.

Ministry of Health:

Annual Reports, part I, 1948–67.

Health and Welfare: The Development of Community Care, Cmnd 1973 (HMSO 1963) and subsequent revisions.

A Hospital Plan for England and Wales, Cmnd 1604 (HMSO 1962).

Report of Public Health and Medical Subjects no. 116: *A Census of Patients in Psychiatric Beds, 1963*, published 1967.

Rehin, G. F., and Martin F. M., *Patterns of Performance in Community Care* (Nuffield Provincial Hospitals Trust/O.U.P. 1968). *Psychiatric Services in 1975*, P.E.P., vol. XXIX, no. 468, 1963.

Reid, D. D., *Epidemiological Methods in the Study of Mental Disorders*, Public Health Papers no. 2, World Health Organisation, 1960.

Royal Commission on the Law Relating to Mental Illness and Mental Deficiency, *Report*, Cmnd 169 (HMSO 1957).

Tooth, I. G., and Brooke, E. M., 'Trends in the Mental Hospital Population and their Effect on Future Planning', *Lancet*, 1 April 1961, republished in Freeman, H., and Farndale, W. A. J. (eds), *Trends in the Mental Health Service* (Pergamon Press 1963).

TABLE 11.1

**Deaths, Death Rates and Mortality Comparisons 1901–1968,
England and Wales**

Period	Deaths			Crude rates per 1,000 living			Standardised (a) mortality ratios (1950-2=100)		
	Persons	*Males*	*Females*	*Persons*	*Males*	*Females*	*Persons*	*Males*	*Females*
1901–10	5,248,774	2,706,356	2,542,418	15·4	16·4	14·4	235	221	248
1911–20									
(b)	5,188,052	2,684,511	2,503,541	14·4	15·9	13·0	197	187	207
1921–30	4,722,991	2,407,475	2,315,516	12·1	12·9	11·4	151	142	159
1931–40									
(b)	4,992,208	2,551,612	2,440,596	12·3	13·1	11·5	131	125	136
1941–50									
(b)	4,997,653	2,586,188	2,411,465	12·4	14·1	11·0	106	104	107
1951–60	5,188,116	2,669,747	2,518,369	11·6	12·4	10·9	94	96	92
1961–5	2,766,372	1,415,447	1,350,925	11·8	12·4	11·2	91	95	87
1966	563,624	288,622	275,002	11·7	12·3	11·1	89	94	85
1967	542,516	277,178	265,338	11·2	11·8	10·7	84	88	80
1968	576,754	293,213	283,541	11·9	12·4	11·4	89	93	85

Notes:

(a) The standardised mortality ratio shows the number of deaths registered in the year of experience as a percentage of those which would have been expected in that year had the sex/age mortality of a standard period (1950–2) operated on the sex/age population of the year of experience.

(b) For the years 1915–20 and from 3rd September 1939 to 31st December 1949 for males, and from 1st June 1941 to 31st December 1949 for females, the mortality rates are based upon civilians only but, as in other years, the number of deaths include those of non-civilians registered in England and Wales.

Source: The Registrar-General's *Statistical Review for England and Wales for 1968*, Part I: *Medical Tables*.

Death Rates per 1000 living b

	Period	1–4	5–9	10–14	15–19	2
P	1901–10		3·56	2·11	2·99	3
E	1911–20 (a)		3·60	2·28	3·32	4
R	1921–30		2·42	1·64	2·55	3
S	1931–40 (a)	5·65	2·01	1·31	2·17	2
O	1941–50 (a)	2·55	1·13	0·85	1·58	2
N	1951–60	1·02	0·44	0·37	0·65	0
S	1961–5	0·86	0·40	0·33	0·67	0
	1966	0·84	0·37	0·34	0·74	0
	1967	0·77	0·37	0·35	0·69	0
	1968	0·80	0·37	0·33	0·63	0
M	1901–10		3·50	2·05	3·09	4
A	1911–20 (a)		3·61	2·23	3·44	4
L	1921–30		2·52	1·65	2·62	3
E	1931–40 (a)	5·96	2·13	1·36	2·30	3
S	1941–50 (a)	2·72	1·28	0·95	1·79	2
	1951–60	1·11	0·52	0·44	0·87	1
	1961–5	0·94	0·47	0·41	0·94	1
	1966	0·92	0·44	0·42	1·06	1
	1967	0·83	0·44	0·42	0·97	0
	1968	0·87	0·44	0·39	0·89	0
F	1901–10		3·61	2·17	2·89	3
E	1911–20		3·59	2·34	3·21	3
M	1921–30		2·33	1·63	2·48	3
A	1931–40	5·34	1·90	1·26	2·04	2
L	1941–50 (a)	2·36	0·97	0·76	1·40	1
E	1951–60	0·93	0·36	0·30	0·43	0
S	1961–5	0·78	0·32	0·25	0·38	0
	1966	0·75	0·29	0·25	0·40	0
	1967	0·70	0·29	0·27	0·41	0
	1968	0·73	0·30	0·26	0·37	0

Note: (a) Civilian mortality only in 1915–20 and from 3 September 1939 to 31 D
Source: The Registrar-General's *Statistical Review for England and Wales for 1968,*

s, 1901–1968, England and Wales

34	35–44	45–54	55–64	65–74	75–84	85 & over
	8.31	14·3	28·1	58·8	127·2	260·8
	7·41	12·6	25·0	55·8	125·5	254·2
	5·54	10·0	21·3	50·8	120·9	260·2
	4·58	9·26	20·2	48·8	119·5	259·8
	3·38	7·44	17·6	42·4	104·0	216·5
	2·27	6·11	16·2	41·0	102·5	227·5
	2·11	5·86	15·9	39·5	97·5	220·2
	2·07	5·81	15·6	38·8	94·5	219·1
	1·99	5·53	15·0	37·0	87·8	204·8
	1·99	5·62	15·5	38·7	94·5	228·4
	9·15	16·2	31·8	64·8	137·7	279·2
	8·61	14·5	29·0	63·5	139·3	274·5
	6·34	11·6	24·6	58·2	135·4	285·8
	5·17	11·1	24·3	56·8	137·5	282·9
	3·93	9·16	22·7	51·6	120·2	234·7
	2·58	7·63	22·2	54·2	124·7	251·0
	2·44	7·37	21·8	54·2	122·6	253·2
	2·43	7·26	21·4	53·6	120·8	258·2
	2·30	6·87	20·6	51·1	112·4	238·6
	2·33	7·01	21·1	53·7	123·2	267·4
	7·53	12·5	24·8	53·9	119·8	250·3
	6·42	10·9	21·5	49·6	116·3	243·6
	4·85	8·61	18·3	44·9	111·6	248·2
	4·07	7·71	16·7	42·3	107·9	249·1
	2·91	5·96	13·4	35·2	93·3	207·9
	1·97	4·67	11·4	31·8	89·2	216·8
	1·78	4·42	10·6	29·6	84·2	206·6
	1·70	4·42	10·3	28·6	81·1	204·0
	1·67	4·23	10·0	27·1	75·3	192·1
	1·65	4·28	10·4	28·2	80·2	214·1

9 for males, and from 1 June 1941 to 31 December 1949 for females.
Tables.

TABLE 11.3

Infant Mortality 1900–1968, England and Wales

Year	Total live births	Deaths under 1 year	Rate per 1000 live births	Deaths under 4 weeks	Deaths under 1 week	Number of * still births	Perinatal death rate
1900	257,480	142,912	154	—	—	—	—
1910	267,721	94,579	105	—	—	—	—
1920	379,982	76,552	80	33,694	20,979	—	—
1930	648,811	38,908	60	20,060	14,267	27,577	62
1940	607,029	33,892	56	17,503	12,611	22,731	58
1950	697,097	20,817	30	12,917	10,606	16,084	38
1960	785,005	17,118	22	12,191	10,475	15,819	31
1968	819,272	14,982	18	10,125	8,682	11,848	25

* Stillbirths not published until 1927.

Notes: Infant mortality rates are the number of deaths under one year per 1000 live births occurring in the year, except in the years 1931–56 when they were based on the related live births, i.e. combined live births of the associated and preceding year to which they relate. Perinatal mortality rates are the number of deaths under one week plus stillbirths, per 1000 live and stillbirths.

Source: The Registrar-General's *Annual Report* and the Registrar-General's *Statistical Review for England and Wales*, Part I; *Medical Tables*, for the relevant years.

Principal Epidemic and General Diseases 1901–1967, England and Wales

Standardised mortality ratios (base years 1950–2 taken as 100)

Period	Tuberculosis (all forms)	Syphilis	Typhoid and paratyphoid fevers	Meningococcal infections	Cancer	Diabetes mellitus	Diseases of the heart	Influenza	Pneumonia (all forms)	Peptic ulcer
1901–10	649		23,581	246		156		254		90
1911–20(a)	541		8926	157		162		605		99
1921–30	362		2729	343	97	154		345		110
1931–9(a)	245		1180	355	98	176	91	222	125	102
1940–9(a)	196	150	387	82	101	129	94	90	105	93
1950–9	60	80	59	40	103	88	90	69	130	72
1960–4	21	53	23	34	104	92	87	38	128	63
1965	16	51	44	32	105	98	86	9		64
1966	16	50	5			99		42	144	
1967	14	50	5	24	105	95	82	10	129	60

Death rates per million population at ages under 15 years

Period	Scarlet fever	Diphtheria	Whooping cough	Poliomyelitis	Measles
1901–10	271	571	815	—	915
1911–20(a)	123	437	554	13	838
1921–30	64	298	405	11	389
1931–9(a)	46	290	197	11	217
1940–9(a)	7	112	111	11	62
1950–9	neg	1	17	9	13
1960–4	neg	neg	3	1	7
1965	neg	—	2	2	11
1966	—	neg	2	neg	6
1967	—	—	2	neg	8

Notes: Changes in cause assignment are allowed for throughout as far as possible.
(a) Civilian mortality only in 1915–20 and from 3 September 1939 to 31 December 1949 for males, and from 1 June 1941 to 31 December 1949 for females.
Source: The Registrar-General's *Statistical Review for England and Wales for 1967*, Part I: *Medical Tables.*

TABLE 11.5

Death Rate Under 1 Year per 1000 Live Births from Various Causes 1891–1966, England and Wales

Cause of death	1891–1900	1910	1920	1930	1940	1950	1960	1966
All causes	153·33	105·44	79·93	59·97	55·83	29·99	21·80	19·00
Common infectious diseases (a)	10·0	7·22	4·20	3·13	2·76	0·48	0·04	0·5
Tuberculous diseases (b)	7·92	3·91	1·47	0·90	0·59	0·17	0·01	0·006
Diarrhoea and enteritis (c)	27·05	12·64	7·98	5·43	4·37	1·65	0·44	0·45
Congenital, developmental and wasting diseases (d)	44·44	40·46	32·45	28·31	24·99	16·04	14·72	12·6
All other categories (e)	63·89	41·21	33·83	22·21	23·11	11·75	6·55	6·3

Notes:

(a) Smallpox, chicken-pox, measles, scarlet fever, diphtheria, croup, whooping cough.

(b) Tuberculosis – all forms.

(c) All forms of diarrhoea, enteritis and gastritis.

(d) Prematurity, congenital defects, starvation, debility, birth injury.

(e) Remainder – including erysipelas, syphilis, meningitis, bronchitis, pneumonia, accidents and lack of care. See p. cxi of supplement to the 65th *Annual Report* of the Registrar-General, Part I, 1891–1900 for list of causes in each category. For 1950 onwards we have grouped causes according to the above categories.

Source: The Registrar-General's *Annual Reports*, and the Registrar-General's *Statistical Review for England and Wales*, Part I; *Medical Tables*, for the relevant years.

TABLE 11.6

Mortality by Social Class: Standardised Mortality Ratios(a) for Men Aged 20–64 from all Causes 1910–1912 to 1949–1953, England and Wales (percentages)

	1910–12 (b)	*1921–3*	*1930–2*	*1949–53*
All occupied and retired (c)	100	100	100	100
Class I	88	82	90	98
Class II	94	94	94	86
Class III	96	95	97	101
Class IV	93	101	102	94
Class V	142	125	111	118
Unoccupied	—	—	135	124

Notes: The table excludes non-civilians.

(a) Standardised mortality ratio can be defined as the number of deaths registered in a standard period within a given social class grouping ages 20–64, as a percentage of the number that would have occurred if the death rates in each separate age group in the social class groupings had been the same as in a standard population consisting of all males in England and Wales.

(b) In 1910–12 for ages 25–65 inclusive, other years for ages 20–64 inclusive.

(c) In 1910–12 miners, textile and agricultural workers were not included in the social class groupings. In 1930–32 minor changes were made in the classification of occupations into social class groupings. For the period 1949–53 there were some further changes in assignments of occupations to the social class groupings. The following table shows the 1949–53 figures grouped according to the classification of 1951 used in the preceding table and the 1931 classifications.

	Standardised mortality ratio (1951) *1949–53*	*Standardised mortality ratio (1931)* *1949–53*
Class I	98	100
Class II	86	90
Class III	101	101
Class IV	94	104
Class V	118	118

Source: Decennial Supplement to the Registrar-General's *Statistical Review for England and Wales*, Part II, vol. 1, *Occupational Mortality*.

TABLE 11.7

Standardised Mortality Ratio for Women(a) from all Causes from 1930–1932 to 1949–1953, England and Wales (percentages)

	1930–32		1949–53	
	Married	Single	Married	Single
All occupied and retired	100	100	100	100
Class I	81	100	96	82
Class II	89	64	88	73
Class III	99	95	101	89
Class IV	103	102	104	89
Class V	113	112	110	92
Unoccupied	134	122	95	142

Note: (a) For ages 20–64 inclusive, calculated in a manner similar to that for Table 11.6, married women classified according to their husband's social class.
Source: Decennial Supplement to the Registrar-General's *Statistical Review for England and Wales*, Part II, vol. 1: *Occupational Mortality.*

TABLE 11.8

Standardised Mortality Ratios for Certain Diseases for Males Aged 20–64 Inclusive 1910–1953 (1910–1912 Aged 25–64 Inclusive) England and Wales

		Social class				
Cause of death	Period	I	II	III	IV	V
All causes	1910–12	88	94	96	93	142
	1921–3	82	94	95	101	125
	1930–2	90	94	97	102	111
	1949–53	98	86	101	94	118
Respiratory T.B.	1910–12	86	87	109	92	152
	1921–3	49	84	98	100	140
	1930–2	61	67	100	104	125
	1949–53	58	63	102	95	143
Cancer	1910–12	99	91	101	96	131
	1921–3	80	92	99	96	123
	1930–2	83	92	99	102	115
	1949–53	94	86	104	95	113
Bronchitis	1910–12	41	68	95	98	184
	1921–3	27	55	94	120	176
	1930–2	31	56*	92*	135*	156
	1949–53	34	53	98	101	171

* These figures were read from a diagram and are therefore approximate.
Notes: Standardised mortality ratio calculated in a manner similar to that for Table 11.6. Changes in classification of occupations are the same as in Table 11.6.
Source: Decennial Supplement to the Registrar-General's *Statistical Review for England and Wales*; 1921, part II, *Occupational mortality, fertility and infant mortality*; 1931, part II (a), *Occupational mortality*; 1951, *Occupational mortality*, part II, vol. 1, commentary and vol. 2, tables.

TABLE 11.9

Infant Mortality Rate (Legitimate) by Social Class of Father 1921–1965, England and Wales

Social class	Rate per 1000 legitimate live births				Standardised mortality ratio			
	1921–3	1930–2	1949–53	1964–5	1921–3	1930–2	1949–53	1964–5
I	38	33	19⎱		48	53	63⎱	
II	55	45	22⎰	12·7	70	73	73⎰	72·6
III	77	58	29	17·2	97	94	97	98·3
IV	89	67	34⎱		113	108	115⎱	
V	97	77	41⎰	20·8	123	125	138⎰	118·9
All classes, including unemployed	79	62	30	17·5	100	100	100	100
Unoccupied	103	107	—	—	130	174	—	—

Note: Changes in classification of occupations as in previous tables.
Source: Decennial Supplement to the Registrar-General's *Statistical Review for England and Wales*, 1921, 1931, 1951 (see source to Table 11.8); *Studies on Medical and Population Subjects*, no. 19.

TABLE 11.10

The Fall in Stillbirths and Infant Mortality Rates Between 1949 and 1964 Expressed as a Percentage of 1949 Values

Social class	Stillbirths	Neonatal deaths (up to 4 weeks)	Postneonatal deaths (4 weeks to 1 year)
I and II	41	38	52
III	26	30	54
IV and V	23	30	56

Source: Studies on Medical and Population Subjects, no. 19, C. C. Spicer and L. Lipworth, *Regional and Social Factors in Infant Mortality.*

TABLE 11.11

Notification Rate for Certain Diseases per 1,000,000 Living During Stated Years 1900-1967, England and Wales

Disease	1900(a)	1909(a)	1920	1930	1940	1950	1960	1967
Smallpox	37	—	7	297	0·03	0·2	0·03	0·04
Scarlet fever	4428	4597	3178	2790	1637	1613	703	399
Diphtheria	2313	1538	1848	1858	1160	22	2	0·1
Typhoid and para-typhoid fever	1292	400	827	742	710	114	72	48
Puerperal fever and pyrexia	—	—	771	207	191	94	194	86
Erysipelas	—	—	427	460	329	174	65	29
Cerebro-spinal fever (meningococcal)	—	—	16	17	320	26	14	6
Polio (paralytic and non-paralytic)	—	—	9	15	27	177	8	0·4
T.B.—respiratory	—	—	1640	1271	906	968	457	228
—non-respiratory	—	—	422	422	261	158	64	45
Whooping cough	—	—	—	—	1344	3599	1278	693
Measles	—	—	—	—	10,266	8385	3482	9514
Dysentery	—	—	360	135	716	394	946	456
Food poisoning	—	—	—	—	—	171	169	104
Ophthalmic neonatorum	—	—	274	—	110	44	23	13
Encephalitis	—	—	24	18	5	6	6	5
Pneumonia	—	—	1034	1279	1200	699	318	123

Note: (a) The population covered in 1900 was 13,244,000 and in 1909 was 19,422,000; subsequently it was the total population.
Source: Annual Reports of the Ministry of Health, Part II: *On the State of Public Health*, the annual reports of the Chief Medical Officer, for relevant years.

TABLE 11.12

Notification Rate and Death Rate for Selected Diseases from 1920–1967, England and Wales
(N = Notification Rate per Million Living; and D = Death Rate per Million Living)

Disease	1920 N	1920 D	1930 N	1930 D	1940 N	1940 D	1950 N	1950 D	1960 N	1960 D	1967 N	1967 D
Diphtheria	1848	150	1858	88	1160	62	22	1	2	0·1	0·1	0
Measles	—	191	—	105	10,266	21	8385	5	3482	0·7	9514	2
Pneumonia	1034	991	1279	696	1200	734	699	421	318	548	123	675
T.B. – all forms	2062	1131	1568	898	1167	699	1149	470	516	75	273	42

Note: Notifications do not necessarily represent all the cases of a particular disease. This is particularly obvious in the case of pneumonia where the notification rate has continued to drop but the death rate has risen again since 1950 so that in 1967 it was considerably higher than the notification rate.

Source: Annual Reports of the Ministry of Health, Part II: *On the State of Public Health,* the report of the Chief Medical Officer.
The Registrar-General's *Statistical Review for England and Wales for 1967,* Part I: *Medical Tables.*

TABLE 11.13

Analysis of a Representative Sample of Insured Patients Consulting their Doctor 1916–1933, by Type of Illness, Great Britain

Type of illness	Urban male and female 1916	Urban and rural male		Urban and rural female	
		1924	1933	1924	1933
Bronchitis, tonsilitis, colds, etc.	181·3	201·1	235·1	181·9	238·4
Influenza	76·1	137·3	126·0	115·9	106·9
Pneumonia	67·2	19·5	15·9	12·0	9·9
Debility, neuralgia, headache	56·0	36·1	35·1	77·5	70·3
Digestive	143·1	115·9	116·4	124·5	101·8
Septic condition	49·1	79·3	76·1	69·3	60·3
Lumbago, rheumatism, etc.	66·3	103·0	98·0	74·0	77·6
Organic heart	22·1	14·0	13·3	12·5	11·6
Anaemia	39·8	1·9	2·2	59·8	29·0
Genito-urinary system	28·4	15·7	17·3	45·1	51·9
Skin	47·1	33·3	44·4	43·6	55·4
Nerves and senses	67·0	42·9	55·8	50·3	59·8
T.B.	12·0	10·9	7·0	12·0	7·5
Cancer	—	2·1	2·0	1·6	1·4
Injuries and accidents	60·7	134·8	106·6	43·9	53·2
Others	81·6	52·2	50·8	76·1	65·0
Total	1000·0	1000·0	1000·0	1000·0	1000·0

Note: Analysis covers only insured people, who would have been relatively free from chronic illness. It is probable that services became increasingly fully used so that more minor complaints were treated.

Source: P.E.P. *Report on the British Health Services,* 1937.

TABLE 11.14

Patients Consulting a G.P. in 1955–1956: Resulting Diagnosis, England and Wales (percentages)

Diagnosis	Patients
Respiratory disease	23·1
Circulatory	5·3
Locomotor	6·7
'Symptoms'	7·5
Accidents	8·2
Skin troubles	8·4
Digestive troubles	8·6
Nervous troubles	9·5
Other	22·7
All	100·00

Note: This was a survey of National Health practices widely distributed throughout England and Wales and to a fair degree representative.

Source: General Register Office, *Studies on Medical and Population Subjects,* no. 14, vol. I: *Morbidity Statistics in General Practice.*

TABLE 11.15

Mean Monthly Sickness, Prevalence, Incapacity and Medical Consultation Rates per 100 Persons Interviewed, all Ages 16 and over, Males and Females, 1947–1951, England and Wales

Period	Sickness		Prevalence		Incapacity		Consultations	
	M	F	M	F	M	F	M	F
1947	61	71	114	160	106	100	39	42
1948	61	71	116	163	102	102	39	44
1949	63	74	121	171	104	107	41	49
1950	63	74	120	166	101	95	43	49
1951	67	75	127	170	119	111	47	51

Note: Sickness rate = number of people per 100 interviewed reporting some illness or injury in a month, regardless of when they became ill.

Prevalence rate = number of illnesses reported in a month per 100 interveiwed (this can exceed 100 because some reported several illnesses).

Incapacity rate = number of days away from work during month or for people not usually employed the number of days confined to the house, per 100 interviewed.

Medical consultation rate = number of visits in the month made by or to a medical practitioner per 100 interviewed. (Includes visits to medically qualified ophthalmic or other specialists but excludes visits to dentists and attention received while a hospital in-patient.)

The figures are taken from a representative survey of the whole population over 16.

Source: General Register Office, *Studies on Population and Medical Subjects*, no. 12.

TABLE 11.16

Consultations and Patients Consulting per 100 on G.P. lists during Yearly Periods 1951–1956, all Ages, England and Wales

Period		Males	Females	Persons
1951–2	Consultations	336	420	383
	Patients consulting	67	74	70·9
1952–3	Consultations	344	411	381
	Patients consulting	66·3	72·2	69·5
1953–4	Consultations	310	394	356
	Patients consulting	63·2	71·3	67·6
1955–6	Consultations	339	408	—
	Patients consulting	63	70	—

Note: Consultations = number of visits in the period to or by a medical practitioner per 100 interviewed irrespective of when the illness began.

Source: General Register Office, *Studies on Medical and Population Subjects*, nos. 9 and 14 (Vol. I).

TABLE 11.17

Standardised(a) Patient Consulting Rates by Social Class for Males 15–64, 1955–1956, England and Wales

Social class	Consulting rates
I	93
II	96
III	103
IV	99
V	99

Note: (a) The standardised patient consulting rate represents the number of men aged 15–64 who consulted their doctor per cent of the number 'expected' to have consulted on the basis of the patient consulting rates at corresponding ages of men of all social classes.

Source: General Register Office, *Studies on Medical and Population Subjects,* no. 14, Vol. II: *Occupational.*

TABLE 11.18

Standardised(a) Patient Consulting Rates for Males Aged 15–60 from May 1955 to April 1956 and Standardised Mortality Ratios for Males Aged 20–64 from 1949 to 1953; by Illness and Social Class, England and Wales

Illness	Standardised patient consulting rates					Standardised mortality ratios				
	I	II	III	IV	V	I	II	III	IV	V
Respiratory T.B.	102	85	105	102	91	58	63	102	95	143
Malignant neoplasms	75	91	94	91	111	94	86	104	95	113
Coronary disease and angina	89	108	102	89	93	147	110	105	79	89
Bronchitis	49	70	99	118	146	34	53	98	101	171

Note: (a) See note (a) to Table 11.17.

Source: General Register Office, *Studies on Medical and Population Subjects,* no. 14, Vol. II: *Occupational.* General Practitioner survey.

TABLE 11.19

Hospital Beds for the Physically Ill 1891–1966: Beds per 1000 Population and Percentage Bed Occupancy, England and Wales

Year	Number of beds (a)	Number per 1000 of total population	Percentage bed occupancy
1891	112,750	3·89	73·16
1911	197,494	5.48	77·00
1921	228,556	6.03	80·17
1938	263,103	6.41	77·25
1949	276,705	6·32	74·3
1961	266,882	5·06	78·7
1966	264,979	5·51	79·2

Note: (a) 1949–66 figures cover all staffed beds including those temporarily unavailable (because of redecorating, quarantine or illness of staff).
Sources: Robert Pinker, *English Hospital Statistics 1861–1938* (Heinemann 1966). Ministry of Health *Annual Reports*.

TABLE 11.20

Number of Beds for the Physically Ill and Percentage Distribution in Voluntary, Poor Law and Municipal Hospitals 1891–1938, England and Wales

Hospital type	1891		1911		1921		1938	
	number	per cent	number	per cent	number	per cent	number	per cent
Voluntary	29,520	26·2	43,221	21·9	56,550	24·7	87,235	33·2
Poor law –								
infirmaries (a)	12,133	10·6	40,901	20·7	36,547	16·1	7,909	3·0
sick wards (b)	60,778	53·9	80,260	40·6	83,731	36·6	44,556	16·9
Municipal	10,319	9·2	33,112	16·8	51,728	22·6	123,403	46·9
Total	112,750	100·0	197,494	100·0	228,556	100·0	263,103	100·0

Notes: (a) separate institutions (b) in workhouses.
Source: Robert Pinker, *op. cit.*

TABLE 11.21

Number of Beds for the Physically Ill per 1000 Population, London and Provinces from 1891–1938, England and Wales

Type of hospital	1891	1911	1921	1938
Voluntary – London	1·71	1·73	1·85	2·38
– provinces	0·85	1·06	1·40	2·04
Poor law – London	0·76	2·64	2·53	—
– provinces	0·34	0·75	0·58	0·24
Municipal – London	—	—	0·03	0·24
– provinces	—	—	0·04	0·74

Source: Robert Pinker, *op. cit.*

TABLE 11.22

Number of Beds by Specialty in Voluntary and Municipal Hospitals 1891–1938, England and Wales

Type of hospital	1891	1911	1921	1938
Teaching	7228	8284	9584	12,610
General	15,189	21,677	28,736	90,462 (a)
Infectious diseases	10,757	31,946	41,593	39,451
T.B.	1075	5500	13,546	23,457
Maternity	210	311	2925	10,029
Other special	4701	6495	9547 (b)	20,686
Chronic and unclassified	679	2120	2347	13,943
Total	39,839	76,333	108,278	210,638

Notes:

(a) Municipal general hospitals also include an unknown number of chronic sick.

(b) The number of beds in other special municipal hospitals in 1921 is probably understated.

Source: Robert Pinker, *op. cit.* No breakdown by specialty is given for Poor Law beds for the physically ill.

TABLE 11.23

In-patient Beds by Specialty 1949–1966, England and Wales

Speciality	1949 Beds allocated(a)	1949 Waiting list	1961 Beds allocated(a)	1961 Waiting list	1966 Beds allocated(a)	1966 Waiting list
All departments (excluding psychiatric beds)	276,705	491,511	266,882	465,393	264,979	532,490
Medical departments	96,794	29,259	72,190	12,404	67,038	12,863
Geriatrics and chronic sick	54,587	7712	58,723	8199	59,186	8424
Surgical departments	57,507	375,200	72,290	367,435	74,137	413,550
Gynaecology, obstetrics and special baby care	24,705	59,066	28,421	63,795	39,627	83,569
Other specialist units	6768	4647	4295	2265	3572	2161
Pre-convalescent and convalescent	6664	326	8035	38	7464	4
General practitioner units	7864	7670	11,027	9705	11,456	7947
Staff ward and unclassified	15,169	6106	6308	—	6007	28
Private pay beds	6647	1525	5593	1552	5492	1944
Psychiatric(b)	198,713	6145	211,478	8988	203,316	5957
TOTAL (including psychiatric)	475,418	497,656	478,360	474,381	468,295	536,447

Notes:

(a) See note (a), Table 11.19.

(b) Includes abnormal, mentally ill and chronic sick under psychiatric care.
The psychiatric figures for 1961 and 1966 in this table do not correspond with those in Table 11.33 nor with the sum of the figures in Tables 11.44 and 11.48. This is because the calculations are on a different basis or the figures have been obtained at different stages of revision. In this table the reference is to allocated beds; in Table 11.33 it is to available beds, and in Tables 11.44 and 11.48 to the resident population.

Source: Ministry of Health *Annual Reports* for relevant years.

TABLE 11.24

Out-patients 1949–1966, England and Wales (thousands)

Department	1949 New outpatients	1949 Total attendances	1961 New outpatients	1961 Total attendances	1966 New outpatients	1966 Total attendances
All departments	6148	36,112	13,346	42,398	14,899	45,247
Medical departments(a)	1612	7595	2033	8865	2004	8942
Geriatrics and chronic sick(b)	—	—	14	64	19	100
Surgical departments	3334	11,989	3853	14,581	4014	15,692
Gynaecology, obstetrics and general baby care	629	2668	1077	4198	1292	4974
Psychiatry – subnormality, mental illness, chronic sick under psychiatric supervision	97	466	172	1274	212	1460
Other specialities and unclassified	476	3286	67	335	56	191
G.P. out-patients	—	—	135	403	157	478
Accident and emergency	—	10,108	5995	12,678	7145	13,410

Notes:
(a) Figures for neurology and neurosurgery are given together and included in medical departments.
(b) Geriatrics and chronic sick are included in appropriate specialities in 1949. In 1966 chronic sick are included in appropriate specialities.

Source: Ministry of Health Annual Reports for relevant years.

TABLE 11.25

Whole-time, Part-time and Honorary Consultants by Hospital Region per 100,000 Population 1954–1967, England and Wales

Region	1954	1957	1962	1964	1967 (target)
All regions	11·1	11·8	12·9	13·4	18·5
Newcastle	12·4	13·3	13·6	14·9	22·8
Leeds	8·7	9·2	10·6	11·1	16·2
Sheffield	7·5	8·2	9·1	9·6	13·7
East Anglia	9·3	10·4	11·6	12·3	16·8
Metropolitan and					
Wessex	14·2	14·7	16·0	16·5	21·3
Oxford	11·8	12·9	12·9	13·1	19·0
South Western	10·3	10·7	11·3	12·0	16·2
Wales	10·1	10·2	11·8	12·0	19·3
Birmingham	9·9	10·6	11·5	12·3	16·5
Manchester	7·6	8·8	9·8	10·2	14·9
Liverpool	10·9	11·9	13·8	14·5	21·9

Note: The populations do not necessarily represent the exact 'catchment areas' of each region. But this factor alone would not explain the difference between regions. Figures include staff of both teaching and non-teaching hospitals.

Source: Rosemary Stevens, *Medical Practice in Modern England* (Yale U.P. 1966), p. 236.

TABLE 11.26

Hospital Medical and Dental Staff and Beds Occupied 1949–1966, England and Wales

	1949	1961	1966
Medical and dental staff (whole-time equivalents)	11,940	17,052	19,556
Number of beds occupied	397,570	404,390	392,563
Number of occupied beds for each member of the medical and dental staff	33·3	23·7	20·1

Source: Ministry of Health *Annual Reports* for relevant years.

TABLE 11.27

Hospital Nursing and Midwifery Staff and Beds Occupied 1949–1966, England and Wales

	1949	1961	1966
Nursing and midwifery staff (whole-time equivalents)	137,282(a)	187,780(a)	231,542
Number of occupied beds	397,570	404,390	392,563
Number of occupied beds for each nurse or midwife	2·9	2·2	1·7

Note: (a) Two part-time counted as one whole-time.
Source; Ministry of Health *Annual Reports* for relevant years.

TABLE 11.28

Qualifications of Nursing and Midwifery Hospital Staff and Percentage of Total Staff 1949, 1961 and 1966, England and Wales

Staff	1949 (a)		1961 (a)		1966	
	Number	Per cent	Number	Per cent	Number	Per cent
Total	137,282	100	187,780	100	231,542	100
Registered nurses	44,460	32·4	62,291	33·2	72,104	31·1
Student nurses	46,182	33·6	53,696	28·6	56,064	24·2
Enrolled nurses	14,369	10·5	13,428	7·2	29,147	12·6
Pupil nurses	1658	1·2	6085	3·2	14,373	6·2
Other nursing staff	21,792	15·9	40,889	21·8	46,036	19·9
State certified midwives	5219	3·8	6751	3·6	8810	3·8
Pupil midwives	3602	2·6	4640	2·5	5008	2·2

Note: (a) Two part-time counted as one full-time.
Source: Ministry of Health *Annual Reports* for relevant years.

TABLE 11.29

Regional Distribution of all Hospital Beds 1948-1965, England and Wales

Region	1948		1961		1965	
	Number of beds (00's)	Number per 1000 population	Number of beds (00's)	Number per 1000 population	Number of beds (00's)	Number per 1000 population
Newcastle	19·1	6·7	23·4	7·8	23·5	7·7
Leeds	20·1	6·6	28·9	9·3	28·4	8·9
Sheffield	26·8	6·6	30·4	6·9	30·5	6·7
East Anglia	10·8	7·7	12·2	7·9	12·1	7·4
Oxford	11·0	8·1	12·8	7·8	12·6	7·1
South Western	29·4	11·0	28·8	10·0	28·2	9·4
Welsh	19·6	7·7	22·7	8·6	22·6	8·4
Birmingham	34·1	7·9	37·6	7·9	37·2	7·5
Manchester	35·6	8·2	37·3	8·4	35·5	7·8
Liverpool	18·1	8·8	20·4	9·4	20·6	9·2
Wessex	—	—	15·0	8·6	15·0	7·9
North West Metropolitan	27·9	7·3	29·9	7·3	29·4	
North East Metropolitan	26·0	8·8	25·7	8·0	25·6	
South East Metropolitan	27·0	8·7	27·8	8·4	26·2	9·2
South West Metropolitan	51·9	11·7	38·5	12·1	35·8	
London teaching hospital	10·5	—	12·8	—	14·0	
Provincial teaching hospital	8·3	—	—		—	
England and Wales	376·7	8·65	404·2	8·76	397·2	8·32

Notes: 1948 figures are for beds occupied on 31st December 1948. 1961 and 1965 figures are the daily average occupied in the year. For 1948 Wessex figures are included in the South West Metropolitan region. For 1961 and 1965 provincial teaching hospital figures are included in the appropriate region.

Source: Ministry of Health *Annual Report 1949. Abstract of Regional Statistics,* Nos. 1 and 2.

TABLE 11.30

Hospital Doctors and General Practioners by Regional Hospital Area 1963, England and Wales

Region	1963 home population in thousands	Doctors per 100,000 population	
		General practice	Hospital doctors
All regions	47,023	47·2	39·2
Newcastle	3054	43·8	37·7
Leeds	3148	44·9	32·2
Sheffield	4477	43·7	27·1
East Anglia	1585	46·6	31·7
Metropolitan	14,036	50·5	52·9
Oxford	1712	46·6	37·5
South Western	2932	53·2	33·1
Wales	2662	50·8	34·9
Birmingham	4893	43·1	31·0
Manchester	4493	43·9	33·5
Liverpool	2212	45·3	44·8
Wessex	1818	48·4	30·7

Note: According to Rosemary Stevens, figures are not strictly comparable owing to lack of generally accessible statistical information.

Source: Rosemary Stevens, *op. cit.*, p. 238.

TABLE 11.31

Distribution of Consultants by Selected Specialty and Region 1964, England and Wales (Whole-time equivalents: staffed beds per 1000 population)(a)

Region	All specialities	General medicine and geriatrics	General surgery	Anaesthetics	Pathology	Psychiatry	Other	Beds	
								Non-psychiatric	Psychiatric
Newcastle	14·9	1·3	1·6	2·1	1·3	1·4	7·1	5·4	3·8
Leeds	11·1	1·2	1·2	1·2	1·1	1·2	5·2	6·1	4·6
Sheffield	9·6	0·9	1·0	1·0	0·9	1·3	4·5	4·6	3·3
East Anglia	12·3	1·3	1·1	1·3	1·0	1·7	5·9	4·9	4·0
Metropolitan	17·0	1·9	1·6	2·0	1·9	1·8	7·7	6·0	5·1
Oxford	13·1	1·4	1·1	1·6	1·2	1·4	6·5	5·2	3·5
South Western	12·0	1·3	1·4	1·3	1·1	1·3	5·6	5·8	5·6
Wales	12·0	1·4	1·5	1·4	1·1	1·2	5·5	6·1	4·3
Birmingham	12·3	1·4	1·6	1·4	1·3	1·5	5·2	5·0	3·9
Manchester	10·2	1·2	1·0	1·0	1·1	0·8	5·1	5·4	4·1
Liverpool	14·5	1·8	1·5	1·8	1·2	1·7	6·5	7·3	4·0
Wessex	12·3	1·3	1·2	1·6	1·1	1·5	5·5	5·0	4·6
All regions	13·4	1·5	1·4	1·6	1·4	1·5	6·2	5·6	4·4
Total number	6372	693	662	739	649	692	2937	264,615	207,487

Note: (a) At 31 December 1963. Both consultants and beds include the appropriate teaching hospitals. Basic data supplied by Ministry of Health.

Source: Rosemary Stevens, *op. cit.*

TABLE 11.32

Distribution of Consultants by Specialty 1938–1967, England and Wales

Speciality	1938–9		1949		1959		1967	
	Number	Per cent	Number	Per cent	Number	Per cent	Number	Per cent
Total	1620	100	5316	100	7031	100	9341	100
General Surgery and related specialities	375	23·1	1126	21·2	1308	18·6	1522	16·3
Gynaecology and Obstetrics	137	8·5	370	7·0	439	6·2	537	5·7
Ear, nose and throat	156	9·6	276	5·2	304	4·3	306	3·3
Ophthalmology	244	15·1	295	5·5	299	4·3	335	3·6
Orthopaedics	67	4·1	227	4·3	329	4·7	467	5·0
Anaesthesiology	76	4·7	459	8·6	791	11·3	1117	12·0
General Medicine and related specialities	291	18·0	1217	22·9	1577	22·4	2102	22·5
Dermatology	51	3·1	114	2·1	140	2·0	160	1·7
Psychiatry	38	2·3	405	7·6	637	9·1	1019	10·9
Pathology	64	4·0	454	8·5	629	8·9	1030	11·0
Radiology and Radiotherapy	121	7·5	373	7·0	578	8·2	746	8·0

Note: The 1938–9 data are drawn from a retrospective study of incomes made by Bradford Hill for the *Spens Report* on consultants and specialists. They do not include all specialities practising in 1938–9, merely those who were alive and who replied to a questionnaire in 1947. The data relate to Great Britain. The 1949–67 figures refer to the number of consultants under the National Health Service. 'General Surgery and related specialities' include urology, neurosurgery, plastic and thoracic surgery, hospital dentistry and orthodontics. 'General Medicine and related specialities' include chest diseases, neurology, cardiology, paediatrics, geriatrics, venereaology, and social medicine. Comparable percentages for these subgroups are not available for 1938–9.

Source: Report of Interdepartmental Committee on Remuneration of Consultants and Specialists (*Spens Report*), pp. 22 and 25; and *Annual Reports* of the Ministry of Health for the relevant years.

TABLE 11.33

Number and Size of Hospitals by Specialty 1949–1968, England and Wales

Speciality	1949				1961				1968			
	Number of hospitals	Number of available staffed beds	Per cent. of all beds	Average number of available staffed beds per hospital	Number of hospitals	Number of available staffed beds	Per cent. of all beds	Average number of available staffed beds per hospital	Number of hospitals	Number of available staffed beds	Per cent. of all beds	Average number of available staffed beds per hospital
General	1175	180,957	39·8	159	920	157,939	33·3	172	932	168,110	36·2	180
Isolation	315	13,512	3·0	43	38	1283	0·3	34	25	838	0·2	34
Maternity	268	7329	1·6	27	244	7618	1·6	31	248	9153	2·0	37
T.B. sanatoria	233	20,475	4·5	88	149	17,467	3·7	117	82	8643	1·9	105
Convalescent homes	93	4339	1·0	47	139	6070	1·3	44	115	5119	1·1	45
Mental hospitals	136	145,918	32·1	1073	150	144,018	30·4	960	173	129,119	27·8	746
Mental subnormality institutions	138	47,676	10·4	345	212	57,771	12·2	273	211	59,487	12·8	282
Other institutions	516	34,851	7·6	68	787	81,471	17·2	103	787	83,485	18·0	106
All hospitals	2874	455,057	100·0	158	2639	473,637	100·0	179	2573	463,954	100·0	180

Notes:

For the years 1961 and 1968 the types of hospital listed have been put into categories corresponding to those listed for 1949 in accordance with information from the Department of Health and Social Security. 'General' includes all types of acute hospital. 'Other institutions' includes rehabilitation, orthopaedic, children's eye, chronic, long-stay and 'other' hospitals.

See note (*b*) to Table 11.23.

Source: National Health Service Accounts for relevant years.

TABLE 11.34

Number of Fully Registered Medical Practitioners 1901–1968 and Number of Registered Practitioners per 10,000 Population, England and Wales

Year	Number of fully registered medical practitioners	Number of registered practitioners per 10,000 population
1901	20,804	6·4
1911	22,241	6·2
1921	22,469	5·9
1931	26,469	6·6
1941	31,340	7·5
1951	38,850	8·9
1961	45,952	9·9
1968	52,346	10·8

Note: England and Wales refers to place of registration and therefore reflects place of qualification and not place where the doctor is practising. Twelve months' service is required as a resident House Officer before full registration. Removal from the register occurs on death or evidence of malpractices, etc.

Source: Medical Register (England and Wales) for relevant years.

TABLE 11.35

Number of Nurses (Male and Female) and Total Population 1901–1961, England and Wales

Year	Total population (000's)	Nurses (full-time equivalent)	Number of nurses per 1000 of total population
1901	32,538	69,200(a)	2·13
1921	37,887	122,804	3·24
1931	39,952	153,843	3·85
1951	43,745	207,771(b)	4·75
1961	46,205	267,320(b)	5·79

Notes:

(a) 1901 figures are Burdett's estimate. Other figures are from Census data. Categories taken from 1921 and 1931 censuses are 'midwives', 'sick nurses' and 'mental attendants'; from 1951 census 'trained nurses and midwives', 'assistant nurses' and 'student nurses and probationer assistant nurses'. Health visitors and T.B. visitors are included in these 1951 categories and 'mental attendants' is dropped as an obsolete description. The 1961 census has only one category – 'nurses'. Nurses here are those described as such in the census returns – not necessarily state registered nurses.

(b) Two part-time counted as one full-time. No adjustment was made for earlier years but probably there were few part-timers.

Source: Brian Abel-Smith, *A History of the Nursing Profession* (Heinemann 1966). Census 1951, and 1961, England and Wales, *Occupational Report.*

TABLE 11.36

Average Number of Patients per G.P. Principal Providing Unrestricted Services(a) 1952–1967, England and Wales

Year	Number of G.P.s	Annual Increase	Average number (b) of patients per G.P. principal
1952	17,272		2436
1953	18,044	772	2324
1954	18513	469	2293
1955	18,817	304	2283
1956	19,180	363	2272
1957	19,437	257	2273
1958	19,685	248	2267
1959	19,745	60	2282
1960	19,928	183	2287
1961	20,188	260	2292
1962	20,325	137	2304
1963	20,349	24	2326
1964	20,246	− 103	2362
1965	20,027	− 219	2412
1966	19,844	− 180	2453
1967	19,849	+5	2473

Notes:

(a) Unrestricted practice means that the G.P. does not restrict his work to staff of a hospital or institution, provide G.P. maternity services only, or restrict his work for other reasons.

(b) Some double counting is evident here. In 1967 the mid-year estimate of the population was nearly three-quarters of a million below the figure that would have been inferred from the average size of lists and the number of G.P.s.

Source: Ministry of Health *Annual Reports* for relevant years.

TABLE 11.37

Distribution of N.H.S. Patients by Medical Practices Committee Classification 1952–1967, England and Wales

Year	Percentage of patients in areas			Average number of patients per principal in areas		
	Designated	Open and Intermediate	Restricted	Designated	Open and Intermediate	Restricted
1952	51·5	44·1	4·4	2851	2184	1581
1953	38·9	56·4	4·5	2726	2183	1594
1954	27·3	67·5	5·2	2741	2228	1546
1955	23·4	72·0	4·6	2736	2229	1554
1956	21·7	73·4	4·9	2711	2234	1548
1957	19·4	75·6	5·1	2659	2264	1517
1958	18·6	76·4	5·0	2672	2247	1594
1959	19·9	74·9	5·2	2745	2251	1575
1960	20·1	74·5	5·4	2737	2257	1603
1961	17·1	78·3	4·6	2742	2272	1563
1962	17·6	76·4	6·0	2744	2297	1608
1963	19·2	74·6	6·2	2748	2313	1652
1964	20·9	70·6	8·5	2768	2359	1747
1965	24·7	66·9	8·6	2826	2263	1758
1966	29·8	62·2	8·1	2845	2324	1807
1967	33·7	57·9	8·3	2840	2338	1837

Note: 'Designated' areas are areas short of doctors where an initial practice allowance is payable. In 'open' areas admission is automatic but initial practice allowance is not payable. In 'intermediate' areas application may be refused. In 'restricted' areas no new practices are normally allowed.

1952 classification: 'designated' – over 2500 patients per practice, 'intermediate' – between 1500 and 2500, 'restricted' – under 1500. 1962: the intermediate category was divided into 'intermediate' and 'open'. 1964 classification: 'designated' – over 2500, 'open' – between 2100 and 2500, 'intermediate' – 1800 to 2100, 'restricted' – under 1800. (*B.M.J. Supp.*, 1964, 126.)

Source: Ministry of Health *Annual Reports* for relevant years; Rosemary Stevens, *op. cit.*, p. 266.

TABLE 11.38

Expenditure on Health and Welfare Services 1949–1950, 1960–1961 and 1967–1968, England and Wales (£ million)

	1949–50	1960–1	1967–8
Central administration	3	4	8
Hospitals – current	196	438	739
capital	9	26	97
Administration of executive council			
services	2	5	9
General medical	42	90	113
Pharmaceutical	31	84	155
General dental	43	53	73
Supplementary ophthalmic	22	16	21
Welfare foods	—	25	43
Other central government services	15	14	16
Total cost of central government			
services	363	755	1274(a)
Local authority health services	30	71	138
Local authority welfare service	13	34	78
Grand Total	406	860	1490

Note: (a) Payments by patients of £20 million are included in this total.
Source: Ministry of Health *Annual Report* for 1960–1. Information from Department of Health and Social Security for 1949–50 and 1967–8.

TABLE 11.39

The Financing of Health and Welfare Services 1949–1950 to 1967–1968, England and Wales (£ million)

Sources of finance	1949–50	1960–1	1967–8
CENTRAL GOVERNMENT			
Exchequer	318	617	1099
N.H.S. contributions	35	102	141
Charges to recipients	3	34	58
Miscellaneous	7	2	—
All central government sources	363	755	1298
LOCAL HEALTH AND WELFARE SERVICES			
Rates and exchequer grants	42	91	189
Charges to recipients	1	14	3
All local government sources	43	105	192
All sources	406	860	1490

Source: Ministry of Health *Annual Report* for 1960–1. Information from Department of Health and Social Security for 1949–50 and 1967–9.

TABLE 11.40

Average Weekly Cost of Maintaining Patients in Certain Types of Hospital Administered by Hospital Management Committees and Boards of Governors 1950–1951 to 1966–1967, England and Wales (£ s d)

Type of hospital	Governing body(b)	1950–1(a)	1959–60	1966–7
Acute	Hospital management committee	11. 12. 5	25. 16. 7	43. 2. 8
	Board of governors	18. 11. 9	33. 9. 3	58. 11. 10
Maternity	Hospital management committee	12. 19. 3	27. 3. 5	44. 13. 2
	Board of governors	18. 18. 7	34. 12. 5	55. 6. 5
Mental illness	Hospital management committee	3. 14. 2	7. 12. 8	13. 11. 1
	Board of governors	—	28. 15. 0	50. 17. 7
Mental subnormality	Hospital management committee	3. 9. 2	7. 0. 0	11. 11. 7
	Board of governors	—	—	—

Notes:

(a) The figures for 1950–1 are not exactly comparable with those for the later dates. They do not refer to all hospitals. The classification in use at the time gives a figure for 'wholly general' hospitals which is here used for 'acute'. The figure is taken from column C in the National Health Service Accounts for 1950–1, p. 4, and is adjusted to allow for out-patient expenditure and expenditure on vacant beds. The system of hospital accounting was changed in 1957 and subsequent figures are adjusted for out-patient and central administrative costs and refer to all hospitals.

(b) Hospital management committees are responsible to the regional hospital boards. Boards of governors are responsible directly to the Department of Health and Social Security and administer teaching hospitals.

Source: National Health Service Accounts. (House of Commons Paper) for 1950–1. Ministry of Health *Annual Reports* 1960 and 1967.

TABLE 11.41

**Hospital Expenditure by Specialty and Expenditure by Specialty as a
Percentage of all Hospital Expenditure 1949-1950 to 1967-1968,
England and Wales**

Type of hospital	1949-50		1960-1		1967-8	
	Gross expenditure £000's	Percentage of total expenditure	Gross expenditure £000's	Percentage of total expenditure	Gross expenditure £000's	Percentage of total expenditure
General	109,186	59·1	216,280	53·0	368,525	56·2
Isolation	5863	3·2	831	0·2	965	0·1
Maternity	5393	2·9	10,466	2·6	18,691	2·9
T.B. sanatoria	8899	4·8	15,446	3·8	12,791	2·0
Convalescent	1187	0·6	3532	0·9	4494	0·7
Mental illness	29,235	15·8	62,737	15·4	91,277	13·9
Mental sub-normality	9173	5·0	22,242	5·5	36,147	5·5
Other institutions	15,741	8·5	76,563	18·8	122,768	18.7
Total	184,677	100	408,097	100	655,658	100

Note: For the years 1960-1 and 1967-8 the types of hospital listed have been put into
categories corresponding to those listed for 1949-50 in accordance with information
from the Department of Health and Social Security. 'General' include all types of
acute hospital. 'Other institutions' include rehabilitation, orthopaedic, children's,
eye, chronic, long-stay and 'other' hospitals.

Source: National Health Service Accounts for relevant years.

TABLE 11.42

Mental Illness: Direct Admissions to Hospital Care 1955–1968, England and Wales

1955	78,586
1956	83,994
1957	88,943
1958	91,558
1959	95,344
1960	—
1961	138,716
1962	146,458
1963	160,405
1964	155,017
1965	155,554
1966	160,523
1967	165,095
1968	170,527

Notes: No figures given for 1960. The figure for 1961 (69,358 for the period 1st November 1960 to 30th April 1961) has been doubled here for the purpose of comparison.

Figures up to and including 1959 are for admission to designated beds in mental hospitals and units. The Royal Commission stated in 1957 (*Report*, p. 308) that patients receiving treatment outside the purview of the Lunacy and Mental Treatment Acts constituted 'a considerable proportion of the total receiving inpatient psychiatric treatment every year'.

In 1958, a revised figure of 94,083 was issued to include informal patients. See Registrar General's *Statistical Review* for the year 1959, Supplement on Mental Health, p. 2, Table M1 (*a*).

TABLE 11.43

Mental Illness: First Admissions to Hospital Care 1964–1968, England and Wales

	First admissions	*All admissions*	% *First admissions*
1964	76,628	155,017	49·4
1965	81,369	155,554	52·3
1966	83,699	160,523	52·1
1967	87,308	165,095	52·9
1968	90,699	170,527	53·2

Notes: Separate figures for first admissions, i.e. 'patients who have not previously received in-patient treatment in a psychiatric hospital or a psychiatric unit' were first given in 1964.

Published figures for 1964 were revised in 1965.
     ,,   ,,   ,, 1965 and 6 were revised in 1967.
     ,,   ,,   ,, 1967 were revised in 1968.

HEALTH 367

TABLE 11.44

Mental Illness: Resident Population: Patients in Hospital Beds as at 31 December 1959–1968, England and Wales

1959	133,154
1960	—
1961	135,381
1962	133,754
1963	127,583
1964	126,539
1965	123,576
1966	121,610
1967	118,996
1968	116,406

Notes: Figures for 1959 refer to 'hospitals vested in the Minister of Health – mental hospitals' and exclude about 3,000 patients separately listed as in teaching hospitals, Broadmoor, registered hospitals, licensed houses, and under single care. Figures from 1961 include all patients under psychiatric care in the National Health Service, i.e., they include patients in teaching hospitals; from this date, patients in the other categories listed above are no longer included in returns.

No figures are available for 1960.

Figures for 1964 were revised in 1965. Figures for 1965 and 1966 were revised in 1967, and those for 1967 were revised in 1968.

The totals in this table and Table 11.48 for 1961 and 1966 do not correspond with those in Tables 11.23 and 11.33. See note (*b*), Table 11.23.

TABLE 11.45

Mental Illness: Patients Under In-patient Care with Informal Status 1961–1968, England and Wales

	% informal admissions during year	% residents having informal status December 31st
1961	79·0	92·2
1962	79·3	92·4
1963	79·2	92·9
1964	79·4	92·6
1965	80·0	93·1
1966	80·5	92·8
1967	82·1	93·3
1968	82·3	93·4

Note: Figures for 1961 refer to half-year 1 November 1960 to 30 April 1961.

TABLE 11.46

**Mental Health Review Tribunals: Outcome of Hearings
1961–1968, England and Wales**

	Applications determined	Discharges directed	% Discharge directed
1961	710	86	12·1
1962	692	71	10·3
1963	1157	161	13·9
1964	960	122	12·7
1965	933	122	13·1
1966	913	122	13·4
1967	942	132	14·0
1968	826	117	14·2

Notes: Figures for 1961 refer to the half-year 1 November 1960 to 30 April 1961
(six months only).

The grouping of 'discharges directed' figures for 1964, 1965 and 1966 appears
to be fortuitous.

TABLE 11.47

Mental Illness: Out-patients 1961–1968, England and Wales (thousands)

	Annual no. of clinic sessions	New Out-patients	Total Attendance
1961	115	145	1078
1962	125	159	1189
1963	133	166	1227
1964	138	168	1240
1965	140	175	1250
1966	142	180	1261
1967	137	191	1312
1968	138	193	1329

Note: Figures refer to adult patients and mental illness only. They exclude child
psychiatry, subnormality and severe subnormality, and the chronic sick under
psychiatric supervision. Figures for all groups in 1968 were as follows:

	Annual no. of clinic sessions (ooo's)	New Out-Patients (ooo's)	Total Attendance (ooo's)
Mental Illness (adult)	138	193	1329
Child Psychiatry	62	33	201
Subnormal and Severely Subnormal	3	3	7
Chronic Sick under Psychiatric Provision	—	—	3

TABLE 11.48

**Subnormality and Severe Subnormality: Resident Population:
Patients in Hospital Beds as at 31 December 1959–1968,
England and Wales**

	Subnormal	Severely Subnormal	Total
1959	—	—	63,893
1960	—	—	—
1961	14,103	47,061	61,164
1962	13,804	47,667	61,471
1963	16,339	48,283	64,622
1964	14,165	45,643	59,808
1965	14,029	46,299	60,328
1966	13,938	46,586	60,524
1967	13,791	46,921	60,712
1968	13,522	46,978	60,500

Notes: Figures for 1959 refer to patients received under the Mental Deficiency Acts
1913–38 and patients outside the provisions of the Mental Deficiency Acts 1913–38
and patients outside the provisions of the Mental Deficiency Acts. The distinction
between subnormal and severely subnormal dates from the 1959 Mental Health
Act.

No figures are given for 1960.

Figures for 1964–7 inclusive were given as estimates and revised in subsequent
reports. The revised figures are quoted here.

The totals in this table and Table 11.44 for 1961 and 1966 do not correspond
with those in Tables 11.23 and 11.33. See note (*b*), Table 11.23.

TABLE 11.49

**Persons Receiving Mental Health Services Provided by Local Health
Authorities as at 31 December 1962–1968, England and Wales**

	Mentally Ill or Psychopathic	Subnormal or Severely Subnormal	Total
1962	51,032	83,984	135,016
1963	55,734	85,628	141,362
1964	64,884	87,743	152,627
1965	71,379	90,384	161,763
1966	80,818	93,486	174,304
1967	87,279	97,476	184,755
1968	94,158	99,820	193,978

Notes: These figures were provided for the first time in the 1963 Report, when statistics
for the two years 1962 and 1963 were quoted. Figures for 1964 were revised in 1965.
Includes persons in local authority residential care (see Table 11.50).

TABLE 11.50

Mental Disordered Persons Receiving Residential Care from Local Health Authorities as at 31 December 1962–1968, England and Wales

	Mentally ill or Psychopathic	Subnormal or Severely Subnormal	Total
1962	968	1435	2403
1963	1200	1957	3157
1964	1568	2707	4275
1965	2044	3526	5570
1966	2572	4254	6826
1967	2846	4818	7664
1968	3366	5645	9011

Note: Figures for 1964 were corrected in 1965

TABLE 11.51

Social Workers in Mental Health Employed by Local Health Authorities as at 31 December 1962–1968, England and Wales

	PSW	CSW	Other	Total
1962	—	—	—	1247
1963	105	—	1255	1360
1964	109	55	1234	1398
1965	139	135	1297	1571
1966	156	160	1365	1681
1967	179	231	1384	1794
1968	213	297	1362	1872

Notes: Part-time staff are included as whole-time equivalents. Welfare assistants are not included.

'PSW' means a member of staff with a Psychiatric Social Work training or the equivalent, i.e. a University Applied Social Studies course. 'CSW' means a training for the Certificate in Social Work or the equivalent.

A break-down by training was first given in the Annual Report for 1964.

TABLE 11.52

Average Cost of Maintaining In-patients in Certain Types of Hospital 1959–1960 to 1967–1968, England and Wales

	In-Patient Cost Per Week ($£$)			
	Mental Illness	Mental Subnormality	Chronic	Acute
1959/60	7. 12. 8.	7. 0. 0.	10. 18. 7.	25. 16. 7.
1960/61	8. 7. 5.	7. 9. 6.	11. 14. 3.	27. 16. 11.
1961/62	9. 2. 10.	8. 2. 0.	12. 17. 4.	30. 1. 3.
1962/63	9. 15. 5.	8. 12. 8.	13. 14. 9.	31. 8. 5.
1963/64	10. 9. 5.	9. 1. 8.	14. 9. 5.	33. 6. 4.
1964/65	11. 5. 11.	9. 17. 6.	15. 9. 5.	35. 14. 5.
1965/66	12. 12. 3.	10. 17. 8.	17. 6. 5.	39. 11. 9.
1966/67	13. 11. 1.	11. 11. 7.	18. 6. 2.	43. 2. 8.
1967/68	14. 7. 5.	12. 5. 7.	19. 1. 2.	45. 11. 1.

Notes: The financial year operates from 5 April.

Figures refer to all Health Service hospitals administered by Regional Hospital Boards and Hospital Management Committees, i.e. excluding Teaching Hospitals. The average in-patient cost per week for a London Teaching Hospital bed in 1967/68 was £67. 2. 10.

Sources of Tables 11.42–11.52 inclusive: *Annual Reports* of the Ministry of Health, 1959–67.

Annual Report of the Department of Health and Social Security, 1968.

Note: All figures have been checked with the Research Division of the Department of Health and Social Security and in some cases recent statistical revisions have been incorporated.

12 Welfare

JULIA PARKER

We have examined the character and extent of the public welfare services in the following ways. First, we have tried to collect statistics for institutions, excluding hospitals. Second, we have tried to trace the development of domiciliary welfare services. Third, we have gathered together figures relating to different kinds of cash grants; and fourth, we have attempted some overall assessment of the costs of the welfare services as we have defined them.

It proved extremely difficult to assemble the required statistics, and in many cases the tables are very incomplete. For the most part we deal with statutory services, since there are no comprehensive statistics for voluntary services. Even for the statutory services, however, no single department of central government has been responsible for welfare and attempts to trace developments, even in the same service, often entail searching through the records of several government departments.

The national statistics are unsatisfactory in several ways. Much social legislation has been permissive in its early stages, and the records are often either inadequate or non-existent for these periods because local authorities have not been required to make regular returns. Also there have been changes in the kind of information collected and in methods of recording it. At certain times and for certain purposes, for instance, the old and the chronic sick, or the old and the handicapped, form a single category; but at other times and for other purposes they are distinguished. Further, the geographical areas for which figures are collected have changed frequently, so that it may be difficult to present statistics which accurately reflect developments. Minor problems also arise through changes in the form of publication. There are no uniform series which contain all the figures for the whole period; parliamentary papers change to departmental papers, or the same report may appear partly as a departmental and partly as a parliamentary publication.

INSTITUTIONS

In 1900 social care and welfare services hardly existed, The Poor Law provided support only for the destitute and then under deterrent conditions, though the situation of paupers varied in the different Poor Law unions.[1] The Poor Law provided institutional care or out-door relief in the form of cash grants. Institutions housed a wide range of persons with a wide variety of needs – children, the old, the sick, the mentally defective, single women with dependent children, the unemployed and so on. By 1900, however, some degree of specialisation was developing within the Poor Law system. In some unions, notably in London, separate hospitals had developed which sometimes maintained very high standards of medical care; children might be placed in 'barrack schools', in cottage homes or even boarded out with foster parents; and in some cases old people had separate accommodation where they had more privacy, freedom and amenities.

Figures for the population in public institutions come from the annual returns on persons receiving poor relief, the annual reports of the Local Government Board, the Ministry of Health, the Home Office and the Ministry of Education. It is not possible to give precise figures for the population of institutions for the years before the second world war. Inmates were differently classified in different years and sometimes categories overlap – the old with non-able-bodied and able-bodied adults for instance. In the early years, sick children are not distinguished from healthy ones and sick old people are not always distinguished from other sick adults. Therefore it is not possible to construct tables showing the numbers in particular age groups in institutions at different times. Nor is it always possible to distinguish the type of accommodation provided; there are no consistent figures showing the proportion of the sick in infirmaries or special sick wards, nor the number of old people in special institutions separated from the general mixed workhouse. In 1948 the Poor Law was formally abolished, and the inmates of Poor Law institutions were dispersed into various kinds of accommodation run by different departments of local government, and by the hospital authorities. It is not possible to get an exact picture of trends in the proportion of people having residential care by comparing the number of children, and old and handicapped people, in local authority homes after the war with those in Poor Law institutions before the war, since the pre-war figures sometimes include an unstated proportion of hospital patients who would later appear in the hospital statistics. Thus an apparent drop in the numbers in residential homes represents to some extent a transfer of responsibility away from local government to the hospital authorities. The figures since the second war are much less complicated, and it is generally possible to show the fluctuations in the

[1] The areas of local administration for the Poor Law, formed increasingly after 1834 by 'unions' of parishes.

number of old people and children in different kinds of public accommodation since 1948.

DOMICILIARY WELFARE SERVICES

In some cases government departments have published statistics which
indicate the development in domiciliary services since the 1900s or
1930s for different groups, such as the blind or the mentally ill; but
generally the figures are incomplete. In other cases it is possible to get
some idea of the growth of particular services (health visiting, home
nursing and domestic help, for example), even though it may not be
possible to say how far the service has benefited special groups of people;
in the health visiting statistics, visits to old people are not distinguished,
while figures for the domestic help service relate to different categories
in different years, so that groups distinguished in one year may be
included in a single classification in another. Some services, such as
welfare clinics and occupation centres for the mentally handicapped,
were started by voluntary organisations and at first supplemented by
local authorities under permissive legislation; and then in some cases
taken over entirely by the local authorities as legislation became
obligatory. Consequently figures sometimes distinguish voluntary organisation workers or clinics at first and later drop the distinction. Furthermore, statistics may relate to visits in one year and cases served in
another, as with the home nursing service. At best, and even if they are
consistent, the statistics give only a rough guide. They do not reveal the
amount of attention given to each case in relation to need, so there is
nothing to show how adequately individuals have been served.

DOMICILIARY CASH GRANTS

The number of persons having assistance and insurance payments
under the legislation of 1911 and later insurance acts can, for the
most part, he discovered for the years before the second war as well as
for the later period. The total figures are for Great Britain, but for the
earlier years it has been necessary, in some cases, to use the England
and Wales figures for particular groups since the Scottish statistics were
not presented in the same way. Further, the early figures distinguish
only persons entitled to sickness benefit, not those actually receiving it.

THE COST OF SERVICES AND BENEFITS

The cost of selected cash benefits has been analysed for Great Britain, as
this was the easiest geographical unit to use for the whole period (with
the exception of the figures for workmen's compensation which from
1900 to 1938 are for the United Kingdom). The tables for welfare

services relate to England and Wales, but we return to the UK for comparisons between welfare services, education and health.

Institutions

The population in public institutions or supported in institutions by public authorities may be seen from Table 12.1. The numbers dropped through the first half of the century but have been rising again since 1950. A higher proportion of the total population is now in institutions than in any of the years we examined since 1910. The difficulty of distinguishing between the healthy and the sick may be seen by comparing Tables 12.2 and 12.3. The former table shows the total number of persons in special institutions or wards for the sick or infirm, and the latter distinguishes sick and infirm according to the state of their health but not by institution. The number of sick and infirm tends to be greater when the distinction is by health rather than by institution, particularly for 1910, the earliest year when comparison is possible. Further, Table 12.3 refers only to adults, while Table 12.2 includes children, so that the real difference between those described as sick or bodily or mentally infirm, and those in special accommodation, must be greater than the figures suggest.

The number of old people in public residential accommodation has increased nearly fourfold since 1900 (Table 12.4), though they now represent a smaller proportion of the age group than at the beginning of the century. There seems to have been a substantial increase in the number of old people in residential homes after 1950, though the real increase is obscured since the 1950 figures exclude old people who were also disabled. It is notable that the proportion of old people in institutions is now the same as it was in 1920.

It is less easy to trace the changing nature of the institutions inhabited by old people. In 1910 there were 1070 old people, or just under 4 per cent of those in Poor Law institutions, in separate homes for the aged rather than in the notorious general mixed workhouses. Figures for the separate homes are not given for the later years of the Poor Law administration, and it is only possible to distinguish different types of institution again after 1948. Since that date there has been some movement towards smaller homes for less than 35 people, though this seems to have slackened off in most recent years. There has been a much more marked trend towards providing homes taking from 35 to 70 people, and nearly two-thirds of all local authority residents now live in institutions of this size. At the same time, a sixth still lived in institutions for over 70 persons in 1968.

Table 12.5 shows the number of younger handicapped[1] people in local authority care since the war. It is not possible to distinguish this group in the earlier Poor Law statistics. The table is not very informative. There appears to have been a slight increase during the 1960s, but comparison with 1950 is impossible since the statistics for that year include unknown proportions of elderly people who were excluded in the later years.

The number of adults and children in local authority accommodation as a result of homelessness has risen dramatically since 1950 (Table 12.6). The total more than trebled between 1950 and 1968, and in the later year included 12,000 children – an increase from under 3000 in 1950.

In 1900 there were over 75,000 children in public care, 57,000 were supported by the Poor Law – between a third and a half of them in general mixed workhouses, rather more in special institutions of different kinds and 13 per cent boarded out (Table 12.7). The number and proportion of children in public care dropped markedly after 1920, though the proportion boarded out rose. In 1938 there were still over 2000 children in the general mixed workhouses. After the Children Act of 1948 the terminology changed and public care of children became rather more humane. Perhaps because of the higher quality service and the greater readiness to take children into care temporarily, and because of the substitution of social for financial need as a criterion of eligibility, the number of children in public care rose both in absolute terms and as a proportion of the age group. A far higher percentage – nearly half of those in local authority care – were boarded out, and those in residential homes were all in special institutions for children. The general mixed workhouse had gone, though a number of the buildings were still being used, housing presumably some of the children in 'other local authority accommodation'. Over a quarter of all those in institutions were in homes taking not more than 12 children. It is notable that the number of children in public care – including those in reformatory or approved schools – has remained a fairly constant proportion of the age group at risk throughout the century. The proportion in 1968 was less than one per cent lower than in 1900 and the total numbers were much the same at both dates.

Domiciliary services
Statistics for the domiciliary welfare services are sketchy. For the old and the handicapped, the major developments in the statutory services

---

[1] Local authorities usually take into their institutions only persons so handicapped as to be unable to look after themselves and who have no relatives or friends who can support them.

have come since the last war. Table 12.8 shows the expansion in the home nursing service since the 1930s with a very great rise in the number of cases dealt with in 1950. In 1968 over half the cases were people over 65, but it is not possible to distinguish old people in the earlier years. Figures for the domestic help service are available only since the war: again the expansion is marked and the majority of recipients are old people, but it is not possible to see precisely how the service has been distributed among different groups (Table 12.9). Again, single bedroom dwellings have been built largely though not exclusively for old people and the increasing proportion can be seen from Table 12.10. The same table also contains estimates of the number of old people receiving a range of different services: unfortunately the 1963 figures, based on a national survey, are not available for earlier years. However the table does demonstrate how very small a proportion of old people benefit from domiciliary care.

The growth of community care for the mentally ill and the mentally subnormal may be seen from Table 12.11. Since 1930 the number of persons under local authority supervision has quadrupled. Over 42,000 people of all ages attended training centres in 1968 compared with 4000 before the war. Hostels, which have only developed since 1959, provided places for over 3000 mentally subnormal people in 1968, and for 2000 who were mentally ill. In addition 2000 of the former and 1000 of the latter were either in voluntary homes or boarded out in private households. The most dramatic increase in services has been for the mentally ill, and this developed after the 1959 Mental Health Act in the early 1960s.

Compared with services for the mentally ill, those for the blind were fairly well established in the 1930s (Table 12.12). Since 1930, the number of blind persons registered with local authorities has doubled, but the great majority of blind people are old and the increase in numbers largely represents the growing proportion of old people in the population. Slightly more children under five were registered as blind in 1967 than in 1920, though the earlier figure probably reflects incomplete registration rather than a smaller prevalence of blindness among young children at that time. (Local authorities keep registers of blind persons and of those with other types of physical handicap. Such registers may give some indication of the level of services needed, though they are very incomplete. Persons able to work may also register as a Disabled Person at the local employment exchanges, the object being to get extra help in finding a job. In all cases, registration is voluntary.) Community services seem to have maintained a fairly even level. The number of blind persons employed in workshops, or in their own homes, has dropped slightly and there are rather more in outside employment – a result probably of the deliberate policy of encouraging handicapped people to be as independent as possible. The number of home teachers has risen as the number of blind people on the register has risen, though in 1967 the ratio of home teachers to blind persons was slightly higher than for earlier years. The increase in the register of the partially sighted may be seen from Table 12.13, but we have no statistics to indicate the extent of the services they receive.

Statistics for other types of physical handicap are scarce. Table 12.14 shows the numbers on the registers of handicapped persons maintained by local authorities – though these registers are notoriously incomplete. Some indication of the recent growth in the social work staff of the local authority welfare departments concerned with old people and the physically and mentally handicapped may be gained from Table 12.15.

The development of domiciliary care for children may be seen both in the increasing number of children lacking normal family care who are boarded out with foster parents by the public authorities, rather than maintained in institutions (Table 12.7), and also in the growth of a variety of welfare services, often linked to health and education, available for all children.

The increase in boarding out, which has been particularly marked since the war, means that there are now more than four times as many children in public care in foster homes as there were in 1900. Meanwhile, welfare services for all children have been developing outside the Poor Law – particularly in connection with education. There has been a dramatic increase in the number of children having school meals and milk – particularly in the first half of the century (Table 12.16). After 1950 the increase was much slower. School meals and milk began as a measure to improve the physical health of the children as did the school medical service.[1] Medical inspections were arranged for children first starting school and at intervals subsequently, and the number of routine inspections rose steadily with the school population until the 1950s when local authorities began to be more selective (Table 12.17). The growing provision for treatment may also be seen from the table. In the post-war period it is noticeable that, although the number of minor defects treated in the school clinics dropped very sharply, presumably as a result of the National Health Service, eye treatment increased and so did dental inspection. Speech therapy, child guidance, E.N.T. and orthopaedic cases have all increased substantially since 1950.

The educational needs of handicapped children have also been increasingly distinguished and provided for. In 1900 special schooling

[1] Bentley B. Gilbert, *The Evolution of National Insurance in Great Britain: The Origins of the Welfare State* (Michael Joseph 1966), chapter 3.

was limited to the blind and the deaf, and to the mentally defective and epileptic, but by 1966 the kinds of handicap separately provided for had multiplied to more than a dozen types (Table 12.18). There were just over 9000 children having special education in 1900; less than half the school boards made special arrangements at that time for handicapped children. By 1967 nearly 76,000 children were having special schooling – one per cent of all children under 16 compared with 0·1 per cent at the beginning of the century. Fewer blind children received special education in 1960 than in 1910, but there were slightly more children in schools for the deaf. The really dramatic increase, however, occurred for the mentally defectives; less than 4000 were having special education in 1900, and over 46,000 in 1967. By the latter date, too, other types of child were being distinguished for special attention. Numerically the most important were the physically handicapped, the delicate, whose numbers had however dropped by a half since the late 1930s and the maladjusted whose numbers had been rising since 1950. Overall, by far the greater part of special provision in education is now for the mentally ill rather than the physically handicapped; a reversal of the position in 1900.

The development of health visiting may be noted here as a service involving advice and information for families with young children. By 1930, 50 per cent of all children under one year were visited, and this proportion had increased to 100 per cent by 1968 (Table 12.19). The number of clinics also increased, and so did the number of health visitors employed. The ratio of health visitors to the population improved, but the figures for 1960 and 1967 include women who were employed solely as T.B. visitors.

Cash grants
The number of persons receiving assistance or insurance grants is shown in Table 12.20. Perhaps the most remarkable thing is that, in spite of the development of insurance benefits of all kinds, the number of people receiving public assistance payments increased from just over half a million in 1900 to nearly 4 million in 1967 – a rate of increase which far exceeded the rate of population growth. The majority of assistance and insurance payments are made to the old, and this tendency has become more marked as the proportion of old people in the population has grown. The other notable feature of the distribution of cash payments is the substantial drop in benefits to the unemployed since the depression years of the 1930s; a reflection of the generally high rate of employment since the second world war.[1]

[1] For details of trends in unemployment see Chap. 4, especially Table 4.8.

The cost of services and benefits

The increasing expenditure on cash benefits is shown in Table 12.21. Poor Law relief, pretty well the only form of statutory benefit in 1900, fell dramatically to represent only 3·6 per cent of all cash payments in 1920, but since that date assistance grants have accounted for an increasing proportion of the total. Otherwise, insurance benefits and pensions have fluctuated with unemployment, war and population structure. Old age or retirement pensions are the most costly of all benefits, and expenditure has risen as the number of old people in the population has increased, and as contributory pension schemes have matured and have been extended to the whole population.

The total expenditure on cash payments represented an increasing proportion of G.N.P. from the beginning of the century until the 1930s; although the absolute level of expenditure then continued to rise, it represented a smaller proportion of the G.N.P. in the late 1930s, and did not recover its position until 1960. Since then the proportion has increased.

Table 12.22 shows the changing costs of selected welfare services, with the expenditure on particular items expressed as a proportion of the cost of the whole for different years. There has, of course, been a general shift from institutional provision to domiciliary services, institutional Poor Law relief representing 100 per cent of the cost of welfare services in 1900, while the most significant forms of institutional welfare provision remaining in 1967 accounted only for a third or so of the total.

Finally we look at the movement in expenditure on a range of welfare services since the war, to compare the shares of some of the local welfare services with those of health, education and housing. It is clear (Table 12.23) that housing and education have both improved their relative position, while the share of the Health Service has diminished. The cost of the local welfare services, and of child care, seems to have remained at much the same proportion of total expenditure on the listed services.

BIBLIOGRAPHY

Board of Control: *Annual Reports* 1900–49.
Board of Education: *Annual Reports, part I,* 1900–38.
  Annual Reports, part II, the Report of the Chief Medical Officer of the Board of Education from 1921 to 1965 published under the title *Health of the School Child.*
  Statistics of Public Education, annually 1900–18.
  Report on Schools for the Blind and Deaf for the two years ending 31 August 1900, Cd 600, 1901.

Report on the Working of the Education (Provision of Meals) Act, Cd 5724, 1906.

Central Statistical Office: *Annual Abstract of Statistics* (formerly the Statistical Abstract of the United Kingdom), 1946 to date.

Social Trends no. 1 1970.

Statistical Abstract of the United Kingdom, annually 1900–39.

Department of Education and Science (before 1964 Ministry of Education): *Statistics of Education*, annually to date.

Department of Employment and Productivity: *Employment and Productivity Gazette* (formerly *Labour Gazette*), monthly, 1966 to date.

Department of Health for Scotland (before 1929 Scottish Board of Health): *Annual Reports*, 1929–61.

Home Office: *Annual Reports of the Inspector of Reformatory and Industrial Schools*, 1900–15.

Fifth Report on the work of the children's branch, 1938.

Reports on the work of the children's department, 1951, 1955 and 1961, 1961–3 and 1964–6.

Annual Returns on Children in the care of Local Authorities in England and Wales, 1952 to date.

Local Government Board: *Annual Reports*, 1900–19.

Poor Relief (Annual Returns), 1900–20.

Local Government Board for Scotland: *Annual Reports*, 1900–19.

Ministry of Education (formerly Board of Education): *Annual Reports and Statistics of Education*, 1947 to 1960.

Ministry of Health (took over the duties of the Local Government Board in 1919): *Annual Reports, part I*, 1919–67.

Annual Reports of the Advisory Committee on the Welfare of the Blind, 1919–36.

Health and Welfare: The Development of Community Care, Cmnd 1973, 1963; revision to 1975–6, Cmnd 3022, 1966.

Poor Relief (Annual Returns), 1921–39, 1946–7, 1947–8 and 1948.

Register of the Blind – unpublished material.

(jointly with the Department of Health for Scotland) *Younghusband Report*, Report of the working party on social workers in local authority health and welfare services, 1959.

Department of Health and Social Security: *Annual Reports, parts I and II*, 1968 to date.

Ministry of Labour: *Annual Abstract of Labour Statistics of the United Kingdom*, 1900–36.

Annual Reports, 1923–60.

Labour Gazette, monthly, 1900–66.

Report of a Working Party on Workshops for the Blind, 1962.

Ministry of National Insurance: *Annual Reports*, 1944–53.

Ministry of Pensions: *Annual Reports*, 1918–52.
Ministry of Pensions and National Insurance: *Annual Reports*, 1953–65.
Ministry of Social Security: *Annual Reports*, 1966 and 1967.
National Assistance Board: *Annual Reports*, 1948–65.
Scottish Board of Health: *Annual Reports*, 1919–28.
Scottish Home and Health Department (formerly Department of Health for Scotland): *Annual Reports*, 1962 to date.
Townsend, Peter and Wedderburn, Dorothy: *The Aged in the Welfare State*, Occasional Papers in Social Administration no. 14 (Bell 1965).
Treasury: *Returns of Expenditure on Public Social Services*, annually, 1922–38.
Unemployment Assistance Board: *Annual Reports*, 1935–9.

TABLE 12.1

Persons Supported by Local Authorities in Institutions(a) 1900–1968, England and Wales

Year	Men	Women	All adults	Children(b)	Total in institutions	Total excluding persons in infirmaries and Poor Law sick wards	Total excluding persons in infirmaries and Poor Law sick wards, per 1000 of total population
1900(c)	97,217	61,781	158,998	50,095	209,093	—(d)	—
1910	134,627	75,668	210,295	70,409	280,704	171,347	48
1920	69,671	62,202	131,873	58,443	190,316	110,819	29
1930	103,959	72,340	176,299	55,991	232,290	123,070	31
1938	84,425	56,493	140,918	33,580	174,498	101,491	25
1950	29,789(e)	25,646	55,435	40,257	95,692	—	22
1960	36,408(e)	51,886	88,294	34,471	122,765	—	27
1968	41,348(e)	76,820	118,168	42,489	160,657	—	33

Notes:
(a) Institutions include Poor Law infirmaries, mixed workhouses, homes for the handicapped and children's homes and schools up to 1948. Small numbers were also supported in non-Poor Law institutions. Reformatory and industrial schools and asylums for the insane are not included. From 1950 institutions mean local authority welfare accommodation for the old and handicapped, children's homes, temporary accommodation and National Assistance Board Reception Centres. Persons supported by local authorities in voluntary homes are also included. Those in hospitals managed by hospital boards and Home Office approved schools do not appear in the figures for institutions.

(b) Children are defined as under 16 up to and including 1938; 1950 onwards they are under 18. Figures do not include children boarded out, in lodgings, residential employment or local authority hostels.

(c) Vagrants are included with males as the male/female breakdown was not given in 1900.

(d) Persons in sick wards and infirmaries were not distinguished in 1900.

(e) National Assistance Board figures (nightly averages) were included with males. 1966 figures are included in the 1968 male total as the latest available.

Sources: Local Government Board: *Poor Relief (Annual Returns)* 1900–20; Ministry of Health: *Poor Relief (Annual Returns)* 1921–39; Ministry of Health Annual Reports 1930–60; Department of Health and Social Security *Annual Report* 1968; *Annual Returns on Children in the care of Local Authorities in England and Wales*, 1952, 1960 and 1968.

TABLE 12.2

Persons Supported by the Poor Law in Special Institutions and Wards in General Institutions for the Sick and Mentally or Physically Handicapped (excluding Asylums for the Insane) 1910–1938, England and Wales

Year	Separate Poor Law infirmaries	Separate Poor-Law institutions for the mentally infirm	Sick wards in general Poor Law institutions	Non Poor-Law institutions for mentally and physically handicapped	Total
1910	58,732	9896	37,241	3487	109,356
1920	23,288	7711	43,053	5445	79,497
1930	32,437	9187	61,591	6005	109,220
1938	9034	6097	50,773	7103	73,007

Source: Local Government Board, *Poor Relief (Annual Returns)* 1900–20. Ministry of Health, *Poor Relief (Annual Returns)* 1921–39.

TABLE 12.3

Adults in Poor Law Institutions and Supported by the Poor Law in other Institutions 1900–1938, England and Wales

Year	'Healthy'	'Sick and bodily infirm'	'Mentally infirm' (a)	Total (b)
1900	16,307	132,968		149,275
1910	24,916	175,423		200,339
1930	58,718	79,217	27,009	164,944
1938	54,792	51,193	24,712	130,697

Notes:

(a) Not certified patients in mental institutions

(b) This total is less than the total figures for men and women given in Table 12.1 because it does not include vagrants who were not classified in this way. Vagrants totalled 9723 in 1900; 10,249 in 1910; 11,418 in 1930; 10,235 in 1938, and included a small number of children.

Sources: Local Government Board, *Poor Relief (Annual Returns)* 1900–20; Ministry of Health, *Poor Relief (Annual Returns)* 1921–39.

TABLE 12.4

Old People(a) Resident in Institutions(b) 1900–1968, England and Wales

Year	Poor Law institutions		Local authority homes			Joint user premises shared with hospital boards	Voluntary homes and hospitals (d)	Total persons in public care	Total in age group. (over 70 1900–20; 1930 & on over 65) (000's)	Total in public care per 1000 of the age group
	General mixed workhouses	Homes for the aged poor	Less than 35 beds	35–70 beds	Over 70 beds(c)					
1900	25,024	—					168	25,192	888·08	28
1910	28,535	1070					116	29,721	1071·7	28
1920	20,643	—					91	20,734	1313·04	16
1930	29,081	—					187	29,268	2963·1	10
1938	24,998	—					1427	26,425	3720	7
1950(a)	11,818	—	15,189	19,222		13,057	5980	50,077	—	—(e)
1960			11,554	20,846	21,592	6887	9367	73,881	5458	14
1968				55,227	14,696	5392	11,888	98,757	6135	16

Notes:

(a) Old people are people over 70, up to and including 1920. After 1920 they are people over 65, except for 1950 when it is not possible to separate younger handicapped from old and handicapped. A very approximate estimate of numbers of younger handicapped might be 7000. In all years figures include those who were both old and handicapped.

(b) Institutions include Poor Law mixed workhouses, voluntary homes for the handicapped and local authority welfare residential accommodation, but exclude Poor Law infirmaries and sick wards and institutions managed by hospital boards.

(c) 1960 and 1968. These large homes include former mixed workhouses.

(d) Figures are for people paid for by the Poor Law or local authorities. Totals in voluntary and private homes are not known until after the 1948 Registration Act.

(e) Proportion of old in public care not given in this year because of inclusion of younger handicapped.

Source: Local Government Board: *Poor Relief (Annual Returns)* 1900–20; Ministry of Health; *Poor Relief (Annual Returns)* 1921–39; Ministry of Health and Department of Health and Social Security *Annual Reports*; Registrar-General's population estimates.

TABLE 12.5

Younger(a) Handicapped People in Welfare Accommodation 1950–1968, England and Wales

Year	Local authority homes			former mixed workhouses	Premises shared with hospital boards	Voluntary (c) homes and hospitals	Total in public care
	less than 35 beds	35–70 beds	over 70 beds (b)				
1950(d)		9219		5973	6331	3571	25,094
1960	785	1428	3671	—	1623	3168	10,675
1968	726	3427	1844	—	936	4389	11,322

Notes:

(a) Under 65 years of age except for 1950, see note (d). Figures may include a few children under 18. The Ministry only analyses figures into an under 30 years age group in 1960 and 1968.

(b) In 1960 and 1968 these large homes include former mixed workhouse premises.

(c) People paid for by local authorities in voluntary accommodation.

(d) 1950 figures include disabled over 65, as analysis of figures for people in welfare accommodation does not allow us to distinguish in this year. Also included are 49 children accommodated with people over 16.

Sources: Ministry of Health *Annual Reports* for 1950 and 1960; Department of Health and Social Security *Annual Report* 1968.

TABLE 12.6

Persons in Temporary Accommodation 1950–1968, England and Wales

Year	Total	Men		Women		Children		Approximate ratio of men to women
		evicted	not evicted	evicted	not evicted	evicted	not evicted	
1950	5820	311	804	771	1082	1791	1061	3:5
1960	6462	278	461	805	793	2450	1675	1:2
1967	16,174(a)	2357		3884		9933		3:5
1968	18,849(b)	2912		3997		11,960		3:4

Notes:
(a) Including 686 persons in local authority communal accommodation.
(b) Including 512 persons in local authority communal accommodation.
Sources: Ministry of Health *Annual Reports*, 1950, 1960, 1967; Department of Health and Social Security *Annual Report* 1968.

T

Children(a) in Public

Children su

Year	Poor Law establishments					Non-Poor La establishment	
	Workhouses	*Grouped cottage homes*	*Scattered homes*	*Other schools and children's homes*	*Homes and hospitals for the mentally or physically handicapped*	*Voluntary(b) homes for the sick and handicapped*	*Training and*
1900(f)	23,478		19,395		—	237	69
1910	15,834	11,640	7366	13,607	3067	1322	91
1920	6016	11,742	7619	11,198	7429	2162	74
1930	4703	9484	7398	10,270	1286	1486	67
1938	2284	8573	6257	5251	17	1081	52

Children in t

Year	*Residential nurseries*	*Reception centres*	*Grouped cottage homes*	*Family group homes*	*Other local authority accommodation*	*Schools and homes for handicapped*	*In voluntary homes(b)*	*Total in institutions*
1952(g)	5035	1167	7213	4218	11,176	1998	6549	37,356
			Homes for not more than 12 children					
1960	3543	1586	5064		14,053	2243	3857	30,346
1968	2797	2104	7990		10,262	2243	5133	30,529

Notes:

(a) Children defined as under 16 up to and including 1938; after 1938 as und

(b) Totals of children in private and voluntary homes are not known befor Children's Act 1948. Figures given are only for children in voluntary h supported by the Poor Law and local authorities. In 1949 28,760 children wholly in the care of voluntary bodies and in 1967 10,839.

(c) Not including a small number of 'care and protection' cases who were boarde after the 1933 Children's Act.

(d) After the 1933 Children's Act these were all known as Approved Schools.

(e) Estimates of the population age groups are approximate as the Registrar-Ger published figures are for five-yearly groups for some of the years shown.

(f) Including children in Poor Law infirmaries and sick wards who have excluded in subsequent years. Numbers of those in voluntary homes for sic handicapped have been retained because the sick and handicapped are not

1968, England and Wales

Poor Law

institutions	Boarded out (c)	Total supported by Poor Law	Children boarded out as a percentage of all children supported by the Poor Law	Children in reformatory and industrial schools	Total number of children in public care	Children in public care per 1,000 of the age group under 16 (e)
)95	7358	57,453	12·8	17,995	75,448	6·7
)75	8813	70,788	12·4	16,307	87,095	7·4
'31	9354	62,985	14·9	14,467	77,452	6·9
.o6	8186	49,592	16·5	5946	55,538	5·5
)93	6031	34,724	17·4	8764	43,488	4·6

authorities

employment	In care of friend or relative	Boarded out	Total in local authority care	Percentage in local authority care boarded out	Children in approved schools	Total in public care	Children in public care per 1,000 of the age group under 18 (e)
	—	26,277	64,682	40·6	9079	73,761	6·5
6	—	28,684	61,729	46·4	7770	69,499	5·8
2	5077	30,968	69,358	44·6	7994(h)	77,352	5·8

ted in the published Poor Law figures and it was considered that the majority
these establishments would have been handicapped rather than acutely sick.
e latter we have excluded where possible.
tailed figures are not available for 1950 because of changes following the
ildren's Act of 1948.
test available figure for 1966.
:
Government Board: *Poor Relief (Annual Returns)* 1900–1920; Ministry of Health:
Relief (Annual Returns) 1921–1939; Home Office: *Annual Reports of Inspector of
atory and Industrial Schools* 1900, 1910; *Fifth Report* on the work of the Children's
h, 1938: *Reports* on the work of the Children's Department 1955, 1961, 1961–63
964–66; *Annual Returns on Children in the Care of Local Authorities in England and
1952, 1960, 1968: Central Statistical Office: *Annual Abstracts of Statistics* for the
nt years.

TABLE 12.8

The Expansion of the Home Nursing Service 1930–1968, England and Wales

Year	Number of nurses employed			Type of case						Total cases during the year	Total population (000's)	Total cases as percentage of total population
	Local authority	Voluntary organisation	Total	Medical	Surgical	Maternal complications	Infectious diseases	T.B.	Other			
1930	37	1990	2027							72,487	39,801	0·18
1938	55	2599	2654							66,560	41,215	0·16
1950	5811	2587	8398			mostly chronic sick				1,001,670	45,020	2·3
1960	8634	1688	10,322	643,261	173,838	10,561	3235	13,811	52,913	897,619	45,775	2·0
				14,331,968 visits to patients over 65								
1967	not distinguished		10,840 (equivalent to 8572 full-time)			468,867 cases over 65				867,369	48,075	1·8
1968			10,962 (8803 full-time equivalent)			502,611 cases over 65				908,447	48,669	1·9

Sources: Ministry of Health Annual Reports for relevant years; Registrar-General's population mid-year estimates from Annual Abstracts of Statistics.

TABLE 12.9

The Expansion of the Home Help Service 1950–1968, England and Wales

| Year | Number of home helps employed | | | | Type of case | | | | | Total cases during the year | Total population (000's) | Total cases as percentage of total population |
	Full-time	Part-time	Total	Maternity	T.B.	Chronic sick	Old	Mentally disordered	Other			
1950	3659	19,716	23,375	41,660	6935	{113,810}				162,405	44,020	3·6
1960	2528	46,786	49,314	36,027	3410	{233,365}		{39,211}		312,013	45,775	6·8
1967	2981	64,767 (29,008)	67,748 (31,989)	24,174		32,193	338,238	1819	27,338	423,762	48,075	8·7
1968	2966	65,129 (28,984)	68,095 (31,950)	19,104		31,830	353,933	1879	26,058	432,804	48,669	8·9

Note: Full-time equivalents are given below in brackets.
Sources: Ministry of Health *Annual Reports* for relevant years; Registrar-General's population mid-year estimates from *Annual Abstracts of Statistics.*

TABLE 12.10

Domiciliary Services for Old People 1963–1968, England and Wales

Year	No. of 1 bed houses and flats completed by L.A.'s from 1945 to beginning of year	Old people resident in sheltered housing	Old people receiving:				Total population 65 and over
			Home help	Nursing	Meals	Chiropody	
1963	255,612	35,894(a)	258,000(a)	46,000(a)(f)	66,000(a)	423,000(a)	5,617,600
1968	430,780	63,541(b)	353,933(c)	502,611(c)	101,817(d)	807,425(e)	6,135,900

Notes:

(a) Numbers receiving this service on a particular day in the year.
(b) 1965 figure the latest available.
(c) Refers to the number of cases over 65 in a year.
(d) Refers to average number of persons served in a week.
(e) Number of old people treated in the year.
(f) Belfast only.

Sources: Peter Townsend and Dorothy Wedderburn, *The Aged in the Welfare State* (Bell 1965); Department of Health and Social Security *Annual Report* 1968; *Health and Welfare: The Development of Community Care*, Cmnd 3022 (1966); Registrar-General's population estimate in *Annual Abstracts of Statistics*.

TABLE 12.11

Domiciliary Services for the Mentally Defective and (after 1959 Mental Health Act) Mentally Ill 1930–1968, England and Wales

Local Authority services for the mentally subnormal	1930	1939	1950	1961	1968
Cases under LA supervision:					
Statutory	24,710	43,531	51,716	81,800	99,820
Voluntary	21,999	26,006	18,646		
Occupation centres & clubs:					
Local authority	10	69	166	626(a)	—
Voluntary	161	122			
No. attending occupation centres	—	4244	5340	22,000	42,316(b)
No. of areas with home training schemes	3	22	—	—	622(c)
No. in LA residential care:					
In LA homes				500	3492
In other homes and households					2153
Local authority services for the mentally ill					
No. under LA supervision				40,200	94,158
No. attending training centres				400	2400
No. in LA residential care:					
In LA homes				700	2098
In other homes & households					1268
No. of LA mental health workers				1247(a)	1872

Notes:
(a) of which 281 adult and 345 junior. Figures are given for 1962, as detailed figures for 1961 are not available owing to the change over after the 1959 Mental Health Act.
(b) Of which 22321 were 16 and over, 19995 under 16.
(c) This is the number receiving home training.
Sources: Annual Reports of the Board of Control and the Ministry of Health: *Health and Welfare: The Development of Community Care*, 1966; *Social Trends*, no. 1, 1970, Central Statistical Office.

TABLE 12.12

Domiciliary Services for the Blind 1920-1968, England and Wales

Year	Numbers of registered blind					Blind persons employed			Home teachers§	Workshops
	0-4	5-15	16-64	65 and over and age unknown	total	in workshops	in homeworkers' schemes	elsewhere		
1920	248	2366	28,094 (brace)		30,708		7589		40	
1930					56,853	2956	1573	5025	441	59
1936	206	1855	27,090	30,983	60,134	3812	1828	3146	400	58*
1950	356	1364	32,877	46,723	81,320	3185	1465	4985	591	
1960	322	1950	30,456	64,741	97,469	2958	1112	6237	777	62
1967	396	1775	28,600	71,826	102,597	2421	840	6526	903	
1968	386	1747	28,464	72,133	102,730	2304	774	6534	903†	

* Estimated figure.   † 1967 figure   § Equivalent full time.

Sources: Ministry of Health *Annual Reports*; Advisory Committee on the Welfare of the Blind *Annual Reports*; Ministry of Labour, *Report of the Working Party on Workshops for the Blind*, 1962; Ministry of Labour *Annual Reports*; *Register of the Blind* (unpublished, issued by Ministry of Health).

TABLE 12.13

Persons Registered as Partially Sighted 1950–1968, England and Wales

Year	Persons on register by age				Total
	0–4	5–15	16–65	65 and over and age unknown	
1952(a)	80	1665	3632	5849	11,226
1960	113	2176	7613	14,337	24,239
1968	144	2414	10,430	22,013	35,001

Note: (a) 1952 was the first year that figures were given.
Sources: Ministry of Health *Annual Reports* and Department of Health and Social Security *Report*, 1968.

TABLE 12.14

Persons Registered as Handicapped (Deaf, Deaf without Speech and Hard of Hearing and General Classes(a) 1955–1968, England and Wales

	Under 16		16 to 64 inclusive		65 and over		
	Deaf and deaf without speech and hard of hearing	General classes	Deaf and deaf without speech and hard of hearing	General classes	Deaf and deaf without speech and hard of hearing	General classes	Total
1955(b)	2849	4509	16,597	35,121	5262	5931	74,052(c)
1960	3462	5405	22,592	66,319	9427	21,641	128,846
1968	4997	5602	22,647	104,634	14,343	93,837	246,060

Notes:
(a) Physical handicaps excluding blind or deaf.
(b) The first year the register appeared in Ministry of Health Annual Reports.
(c) Including some for whom age is not given.
Sources: Ministry of Health *Annual Reports* and Department of Health and Social Security *Annual Report*, 1968.

TABLE 12.15

Social Workers(a) in Local Authority Health and Welfare Departments 1956–1968, England and Wales

Year	Total
1956	2493
1962	2943
1968	5335

Note: (a) Social workers exclude health visitors, home helps, home nurses – they may not be precisely the same type of worker in the different years.

Source: Social Workers in Local Authority Health and Welfare Service (Younghusband Report), 1959. Health and Welfare: The Development of Community Care, 1963. Department of Health and Social Security Annual Report, 1968.

TABLE 12.16

Provision of School Meals and Milk 1910–1966, England and Wales

Year	Number of main meals(a) in a year	Number of children served (b)	Population aged 5–16 inclusive	Percentage of population 5–16 served (b)	Number of milk meals in a year	Percentage of population 5–16 receiving milk(b)
1910	327,246	114,925	8,539,424	1·3	—	—
1920	11,867,934	148,082	8,613,179	1·7	—	—
1930	16,327,120	295,121	7,874,101	3·8	22,737,459	—
1938	26,819,108	687,855	7,263,100	9·5	114,961,182	—
		Number served on a particular day			Number served on a particular day	
1950	—	2,408,000	7,071,524	34·1	4,377,600	62
1960	—	3,408,000	8,403,151	40·5	5,832,270	70
1966	—	4,846,500	8,253,600	58·7	5,969,671	72

Notes:

(a) From 1910 to 1938 main meals included breakfasts, dinners and teas; from 1950 onwards, dinners only.

(b) Numbers served refer only to children in local authority schools so that percentages do not allow for those receiving these services in non-local authority schools.

Sources: Board of Education and Ministry of Education, Annual Reports; Department of Education and Science, Statistics of Education; Report on the Working of the Education (Provision of Meals) Act 1906; population figures at census dates 1911, 1921, 1931, 1951, 1961, 1966, Registrar-General's census data, in Statistical Abstracts of United Kingdom and Annual Abstracts of Statistics (1938 figure estimated).

TABLE 12.17

The School Medical Service 1910–1966, England and Wales

Year	Number of routine medical inspections	Number (a) of children aged 5–16	Percentage inspected in a year	Number of school nurses employed	Number of local authorities providing different facilities		
					Clinics	Dental services	Eye services
1910	1,377,000	8,539,424	16	632	30	—	70
1920	1,829,658	8,613,179	21	2671	288	203	282
1930	1,770,779	7,874,101	22	5485	316	310	313
1938	1,677,008	—		5589			
1950	1,888,594	7,071,524	27	5208 (2312)(b)			
1960	2,139,000	8,403,151	25	6999 (2667)(b)			
1966	1,892,000	8,253,600	23	8499 (2929)(b)			

Different cases treated by Local authorities

Year	Minor defects	Dental inspections	Eye cases	ENT cases	Orthopaedic cases	Speech therapy cases	Child guidance cases
1938	1,072,204	3,225,376	275,999	—	—	—	—
1950	1,285,740	2,487,000	369,862	—	—	24,000	22,000
1960	605,000	3,595,000	560,000	150,000	129,000	56,000	36,000
1966	306,000	4,140,000	491,000	177,000	89,000	65,000	57,000

Notes:
(a) Population figures are for census dates.
(b) Full time equivalents.
Sources: Annual Reports of the Board of Education and the Ministry of Education *Statistics of Education.*

TABLE 12.18

Educational Provision for Handicapped Children by Type of Handicap: Children in Special Schools 1900–1967(a), England and Wales

Year	Blind Boarding	Blind Day(b)	Deaf Boarding	Deaf Day	Mentally defective(c) Boarding	Mentally defective(c) Day(b)	Epileptic Boarding	Epileptic Day(b)	Physically defective Boarding	Physically defective Day(b)	'Delicate' Boarding	'Delicate' Day(b)
1900	3330 (Blind or deaf Boarding)	2069 (Blind or deaf Day(b))			3751							
1910	2295		4183		509	11,094	464	—	331	4087		
1920	3161		4984		15,361		496	—	11,809			
1930	1872	2775	2784	1912	1984	14,552	609	—	5338	6010	2572	7702
1939	1891	2753	2669	1848	2770	14,115	609	—	7213	6412	4129	12,881
1950(d)	1761	981	2271	943	4888	13,134	772	—	1798	13,807	3173	5241
1960	2996	838	3334	2563	9363	23,284	696	—	2473	7961	3130	4363
1967	531	888	2572	2220	8729	37,618	609	5	1353	12,251	2562	2829

Year	With heart disease Boarding	With heart disease Day(b)	With Pulmonary T.B. Boarding	With Pulmonary T.B. Day(b)	With Ophthalmic defect Boarding	With Ophthalmic defect Day(b)	With speech defect Boarding	With speech defect Day(b)	Maladjusted Boarding	Maladjusted Day(b)	Total number in special schools	Total in age-group 5–15 inclusive (000's)	Percentage of age-group in special schools
1900											9150	7478	0·1
1910											22,963	7864	0·3
1920											35,811	7578	0·5
1930	196	—	1711	585	254	—					50,856	7190	0·7
1939	486	20	2475	—							60,271	6735	0·9
1950(d)							50		688	172	49,679	6486	0·8
1960							83		1347	256	62,687	7560	0·8
1967							85		2213	1244	75,709	7767	1·0

Notes: (a) 1900–1939 figures are number of places, 1950 onwards number on roll. (b) Day pupils at boarding schools are counted with day pupils. (c) Mentally defective children catered for by the local education authorities are now termed educationally subnormal. (d) From 1950, following the Ministry's classification, children at hospital schools are counted as day children.

Sources: Board of Education and Ministry of Education: Annual Reports pts I and II; Report on Schools for Blind and Deaf 1898–1909; Statistics of Public Education; Statistics of Education.

TABLE 12.19

The Expansion of the Health Visiting Service and Child Welfare Clinics 1920–1968, England and Wales

Year	Number of health visitors employed				Total population (000's)	Ratio of health visitors to population	Total number of visits	Numbers of children 0–1 visited	Percentage of children 0–1 visited	Number of clinics	
	Paid by local authority	Paid by voluntary organisations	Total	Full-time equivalent						Local authority	Voluntary organisation
1920	1879	1480	3359	1607	37,596	1:2300	—	—	—	1061	993
1930	3078	2279	5357	3508	39,801	1:1135	—	—	—	2113	822
1938	3672	2306	5978	3079	41,215	1:1340	8,694,489	—	66·2 Eng. 71·7 Wales	2752	1833
1950	5897	233	6130	4011	44020	1:1100	11,000,000	583,000	88·5	4565	235
1960 (a)	local authority and voluntary organisations no longer distinguished		7203	4826	45,775	1:950	12,207,000	613,000	71·1	5651	
1967 (a)			7854	5548	48,391	1:872	3,186,302 (number of cases)	646,398	77·0	6491	280
1968			8001	5645	48,669	1:862		841,277	100·0(b)		—(c)

Notes:
(a) 1960 and 1967 figures include those employed solely as T.B. visitors.
(b) In 1968 the number of births recorded was 819,272.
(c) In 1968 only the number of sessions are recorded.
Sources: Ministry of Health Annual Reports; Annual Abstracts of Statistics; Registrar-General's Census Data.

TABLE 12.20

The Number of Persons Receiving Assistance 1900–1967, Great Britain

Year	Outdoor relief(a) Total	Adults	Children	Old(b) also with pension	Old(b) Total	Sick	Unemployed	Non-contributory old age pensions
				(included in total in column 1)				
1900	584,311	(350,327)	(158,190)	—	(152,843)	(292,660)	—	—
1910	622,837	(355,032)	(184,171)	—	(138,223)	(282,939)	—	607,000
1920	368,792	(167,469)	(138,380)	(6284)	(8621)	(104,958)	—	785,833
1930	1,356,293	(866,475)	(338,942)	(99,231)	(143,376)	(271,351)	163,313(c)	1,373,331
1938	1,327,665	(835,442)	(270,552)	(226,756)	(225,130)	(439,746)	512,356(c)	1,789,207

Supplementary benefits (National Assistance)

Year	Total(d) persons benefiting from assistance	Total number of weekly allowances	Dependants Adults	Dependants Children	Old(e) With national insurance	Old(e) Without national insurance	Sick With national insurance	Sick Without national insurance	Unemployed With national insurance	Unemployed Without national insurance	Others With national insurance	Others Without national insurance	Non. contrib. pensions in payment without supplement
1950	2,289,030	1,350,000	271,850	351,180	677,000	106,000	114,000	102,000	38,000	39,000	96,000	178,000	316,000
1960	2,724,000	1,857,000	385,000	436,000	1,075,000	111,000	139,000	128,000	43,000	85,000	65,000	211,000	46,000
1967	3,848,000	2,559,000	591,000	698,000	1,557,000	183,000	160,000	149,000	229,000		120,000	161,000	—(f)

Notes. Figures refer to persons receiving payments on one day in the year.

(a) Figures in brackets are for England and Wales only as Scottish figures do not make this breakdown. The numbers in the categories do not add up to the numbers in the total column as they are not mutually exclusive. Nor do we give figures for other categories such as the mentally infirm where the method of classification changed during the period. Dependants are included, that is, where relief is given to the head of the family, the wife (if any) and children under 16 living with the head and dependent on him for support are counted. If outdoor relief is given exclusively to a wife or child, the head of the family is also counted as relieved, but other dependants are not. (b) The old are over 70 up to and including 1920; in 1930 and 1938 they are over 65. (c) Unemployed in England and Wales are added to the Scottish category 'Destitute and able bodied'; (d) Including those receiving non-contributory pensions; (e) Men over 65, women over 60; (f) No longer separately counted.

Sources: Poor Relief (*Annual Returns*) 1900–39; Scottish Local Government Board *Annual Reports*; Ministry of Health *Annual Reports*; National Assistance Board *Annual Reports*; Ministry of Social Security *Annual Report, 1967; Statistical Abstracts* of the United Kingdom.

TABLE 12.20A

The Number of Persons Receiving Insurance Grants 1900–1967, Great Britain

Insurance benefits

Year	Contributory old age pensions	Widows(a) orphans etc.	Entitled to(b) national health insurance benefits	Unemployment benefit including transitional benefit	Unemployment assistance	War pensions	Workmen's(c) compensation cases of disablement in the year
1900	—	—	—	—	—	—	21,174
1910	—	—	—	—	—	—	378,340
1920	—	—	15,278,600	226,477	—	3,083,500(d)	381,966
1930	632,234	873,292	18,144,200	1,282,274	—	1,187,000	461,794
1938	815,642	1,100,080	20,034,200	1,031,933	560,863	882,000(e)	425,676

Insurance benefits

Year	Retirement(f) pensions	Widows(a) orphans etc.	Average number(g) incapacitated by sickness and injury at one time during year	Disablement pensions	Maternity benefit		Un-employment(h) benefit	Children attracting family allowances	War pensions
					Maternity grants awarded during year	Maternity allowances awarded during year			
1950	4,152,000	474,000	971,000	59,000	757,000	124,000	226,000	4,756,000	1,047,423
1960	5,563,000	549,000	957,000	173,000	867,000	198,000	192,000	5,764,000	724,024
1967	6,770,000	574,000	1,020,000	203,000	901,000	249,000	333,000	6,638,000	577,240

Notes. Figures refer to persons receiving payments on one day in the year unless otherwise stated in the headings or notes. Dependants are not included. (a) Widow's benefit (excluding widow's allowances), orphan's pensions and individual children's allowances. (b) Numbers receiving benefit at any one time are not available. Benefits included sickness, disablement, maternity and medical benefit. (c) Workmen's compensation figures are for the United Kingdom. They do not include death benefit. The figure in the 1938 line is for 1935. (d) 1921 figures; (e) 1936 figures; (f) Men over 65, women over 60. (g) Not including death benefit. (h) Average number of claims current during the year.

Sources: Statistical Abstracts of the United Kingdom; Abstracts of Labour Statistics; Ministry of Labour Gazette; Return of Expenditure on Public Social Services; Ministry of Social Security Annual Report 1967.

TABLE 12.21

Expenditure on Income Maintenance: Cash Grants and Insurance Benefits in £000's and as Percentages of Total Yearly Expenditure 1900–1967, Great Britain

Year	Assistance			Insurance Benefits						
	Poor Law outdoor relief	Non-contributory old age pensions	Un-employment allowances	Sickness, disablement maternity	Un-employment	Old age contributory	Widows orphans and guardians	Workmen's accidents	Compensation industrial disease(a)	War pensions
1900	3166 (97·6%)							78 (2·4%)		
1910	4084 (30·0%)	7360 (54·1%)						2108 (15·5%)	54 (0·4%)	
1920	5416 (3·6%)	20,676 (13·7%)		10,089 (6·7%)	8752 (5·8%)			4857 (3·2%)	366 (0·2%)	100,949 (66·8%)
1930	15,616 (6·0%)	36,676 (14·0%)		19,303 (7·4%)	101,594 (38·9%)	16,363 (6·3%)	16,890 (6·5%)	5127 (3·2%)	583 (0·2%)	49,205 (18·7%)
1938	19,380 (7·3%)	44,154 (16·7%)	41,309 (15·6%)	18,599 (7·1%)	51,662 (19·5%)	21,130 (8·0%)	24,305 (9·2%)	4940(b) (1·9%)	546 (0·2%)	38,428 (14·5%)

Year	Supplementary Benefits (National Assistance)			Family allowances	Insurance Benefits						
	Weekly allowances	Non-contributory old age pensions	Single payments		Sickness and maternity	Un-employment	Old age contributory pension and death grant	Widows, orphans and guardians	Industrial injury(a)	Industrial disablement pension and supplementation	War pensions
1950	56,430 (9·4%)	25,230 (4·2%)	—	63,590 (10·6%)	74,032 (12·3%)	19,209 (3·2%)	250,534 (41·7%)	22,000 (3·6%)	9162 (1·5%)	2760 (0·5%)	78,084 (13·0%)
1960	166,200 (12·1%)	10,900 (0·8%)	4250 (0·3%)	130,000 (9·5%)	159,649 (11·0%)	41,911 (3·1%)	662,172 (48·4%)	61,930 (4·5%)	18,032 (1·3%)	27,567 (2·0%)	95,501 (7·0%)
1967	385,000 (15·1%)		—	162,000 (6·3%)	298,809 (11·7%)	78,322 (3·1%)	1,279,535 (50·1%)	141,555 (5·5%)	32,233 (1·3%)	54,038 (2·1%)	121,000 (4·7%)

TABLE 12.21A

Financial Summary (£ooo's)

	Total expenditure	Gross National Product of United Kingdom	Total expenditure as percentage of Gross National Product
1900	3244 (100%)	1,970,000	0·2
1910	13,606 (100%)	2,231,000	0·6
1920	151,105 (100%)	5,128,000 (c)	2·9
1930	261,357 (100%)	4,576,000	5·7
1938	264,453 (100%)	5,310,000	5·0
1950	601,031 (100%)	11,679,000	5·1
1960	1,369,112 (100%)	22,639,000	6·0
1967	2,552,492 (100%)	32,498,000	7·9

Notes:
(a) Workmen's compensation figures 1900–38 are for the United Kingdom. Workmen's compensation and industrial injury figures do not include death benefits.

(b) Figure for the year 1935–6.

(c) Figure for 1921. 1920 figure not available.

Sources: Statistical Abstracts of the United Kingdom; Annuals Abstracts of Labour Statistics; Annual Reports of the Local Government Board for England and Wales, the Scottish Local Government Board, the Ministry of Labour, the Ministry of Health, the Scottish Board of Health, the Ministry of Pensions, the Ministry of Pensions and National Insurance, the National Assistance Board, the Ministry of Social Security; British Economy: Key Statistics 1900–1964 (London and Cambridge Economic Services).

TABLE 12.22

Local Authority Expenditure on Certain Welfare Services (£000's) and the Cost of the Item as a Proportion of the Total Expenditure on these Items 1900–1967, England and Wales

Year	Poor Law indoor relief (a)	Maternity, child welfare, health visitors (f)	Welfare of the blind	School meals, milk and medical services	Educational provision for handicapped children
1900–1	2664 (100%)				
1910–11	3477 (91·0%)			340 (9·0%)	—
1920–1	5903 (48·5%)	3363(e) (27·6%)		1612 (13·2%)	1294 (10·6%)
1930–1	9899(d) (51·8%)	4415(e) (23·1%)	817 (4·3%)	2295 (12·0%)	1688 (8·8%)
1936–7	9297(d) (42·5%)	5725(e) (26·2%)	1526 (7·0%)	3076 (14·1%)	2228 (10·2%)

Year	Residential accommodation for old, handicapped and temporary accommodation	Children in care	Maternity, child welfare, health visitors	Welfare of the blind	Welfare services for physically handicapped and old	Domestic help	Home nursing	School meals and medical services	Educational provision for handicapped children
1950–1	9030 (11·3%)	12,120(c) (15·2%)	10,172 (12·7%)	2320 (2·9%)		2960 (3·7%)	4173 (5·2%)	35,504 (44·4%)	3635 (4·5%)
1960–1	21,070 (13·7%)	18,595 (12·1%)	13,784 (8·9%)	1482 (1·0%)	1209 (0·8%)	9494 (6·2%)	7883 (5·1%)	68,036 (44·1%)	12,725 (8·2%)
1967–8	44,823 (15·2%)	36,620 (12·4%)	25,617 (8·7%)	2955 (1·0%)	9426 (3·2%)	21,482 (7·2%)	14,424 (4·8%)	117,774(b) (39·8%)	22,695(b) (7·7%)

TABLE 12.22A

Financial Summary (£000's)

Year	A Total expenditure on services specified	B Public authorities current expenditure on goods and services	Column B as percentage of column A
1900–1	2664	185,000	1·4
1910–11	3817	171,000	2·2
1920–1	12,172	482,000	2·5
1930–1	19,114	448,000	4·3
1936–7	21,852	540,000	4·0

	Total	Public authorities current expenditure on goods and services	Column B as percentage of column A
1950–1	79,914	2,068,000	3·9
1960–1	154,278	4,172,000	3·7
1967–8	295,816	7,063,000	4·2

Notes:

(a) Poor Law indoor relief does not include cost of children boarded out. This was included in cost of outdoor relief and is not distinguished in the sources below. Cost of children boarded out is included in the expenditure on child care 1950–67.

(b) Provisional figures.

(c) Figure for 1951–2, first available year.

(d) Figures for cost of Poor Law general institutions and children's homes and schools, but now excludes costs of Poor Law hospitals and special institutions.

(e) Includes salaries of medical officers of health and sanitary officers as these are indistinguishable from health visitor figures in the Local Taxation Returns for these years.

(f) Maternity and child welfare figures 1920–38 include costs of midwifery as they are not separately distinguished. 1950–68 midwifery costs are excluded.

Sources: Annual Reports of the Ministry of Health, the Local Government Board of England and Wales, the Ministry of Education; Statistical Abstracts of the United Kingdom; Annual Abstract of Statistics; Returns on Children in the Care of Local Authorities; Statistics of Education 1968, Vol. 5; British Economy: Key Statistics 1900–1964 (L.C.E.S.).

TABLE 12.23

Consolidated Current and Capital Expenditure on Social Services and Housing by the Public Sector 1949–1950, 1960–1961 and 1967–1968, United Kingdom

	1949–50		1960–1		1967–8	
	£ million	Per cent	£ million	Per cent	£ million	Per cent
Education	288·0	19·1	926·8	23·3	1986·8	25·1
National Health Service	415·9	27·6	902·2	22·7	1564·0	19·7
Local welfare services	(a)	(a)	32·9	0·8	76·9	1·0
Child care	13·7	0·9	26·6	0·7	54·2	0·7
School meals and milk	63·9	4·2	67·5	1·7	112·5	1·4
Welfare foods			27·6	0·7	48·3	0·6
National Insurance and industrial injuries	415·1	27·6	1056·0	26·7	2247·7	28·3
War pensions	81·8	5·4	100·8	2·5	126·6	1·6
Non-contributory old age pensions	28·9	1·9	11·4	0·3	—	—
Supplementary benefits (b)	65·9	4·4	190·1	4·8	433·0	5·5
Family allowances	65·4	4·3	140·6	3·5	174·2	2·2
Housing	67·7	4·5	494·6	12·4	1106·7	13·9
Total	1506·3	100·0	3977·1	100·0	7930·9	100·0

Notes:
(a) Not separately distinguished.
(b) Formerly 'National Assistance'.
Source: Annual Abstract of Statistics.

13 Religion

ROBERT CURRIE AND
ALAN GILBERT*

The sociology and social history of religion in industrial Britain are still at a preliminary stage, where emphasis lies on collection rather than analysis of data, where description remains an important task, and where explanation is in part more or less informed guesswork. This chapter is largely confined to the area of indigenous Christianity, and makes few references to Judaism, and none to Christian or non-Christian religions introduced to the UK by recent immigration.

SOURCES OF INFORMATION

Three types of data are available for religious organisations in the twentieth century: (1) Irish censuses, alone, record the stated faith (not Church attendances) of inhabitants of all thirty-two counties at various intervals. (2) The Registrars General publish figures for civil and religious marriages (the latter broken down by rite). (3) The denominations themselves publish (in handbooks or in serials such as *Whitaker's Almanack*), or have kindly supplied, annual or other series of figures for various types of membership or attendance, clergy, ministers and lay preachers and church buildings. The major denominational series which could be obtained are printed in this chapter.

Denominational statistics are almost invariably collected locally and published centrally. Three main types of *membership* data can be distinguished: (1) The major nonconformist, and many other denominations, publish membership as evidenced by periodical revision of local records. (2) The Church of Scotland and other presbyterian churches publish figures for communicants as counted locally at various times. (3) The Catholic Church in Britain publishes locally estimated figures for the Catholic population. These figures are the most difficult types of church membership data to handle, as the notes to Table 13.13 show.

The reliability of membership statistics has been questioned from time to time, but we have not found the data materially less trustworthy in this respect than other types of social statistics. Errors in handling the

* The authors wish to acknowledge the assistance of Mrs Dorothy Coates; the support they have received from the Department of Social and Administrative Studies of Oxford University; and the co-operation of many denominations.

figures, the presence on membership rolls of persons whose active commitment has ceased, and the possibility of exaggeration in estimates,
must all be allowed for. But none of these factors seems to prevent the
general use of this material since, however important they may be, they
are not large enough to prevent the emergence of clear and characteristic patterns which repeat themselves from denomination to denomination, and which in the main seem to allow plausible explanations.

NOTES ON TABLES

The tables give the most detailed numerical presentation at present
available of the development of Christianity in Britain since 1901. Few
of the figures printed here have appeared elsewhere on a serial basis.
The authors are conscious of the gaps which remain and will be glad of
advice on any errors that may be detected.

Density

The density of a religious denomination (Tables 13.44 to 13.48) is here
defined as the membership of that denomination expressed as a percentage of the population from which it recruits. For the purposes of
this chapter, that population has been interpreted as the total population *aged 15 and over*, in the part of the British Isles to which available
denominational membership data refer. The available data on estimated Catholic population have not been used to generate a density
series, because of the difficulties of using these data. Figures for Roman
Catholic density are, however, given in Table 13.50.

Wherever possible the population data used have been taken from the
Annual Reports of the Registrars-General for England and Wales and
Scotland, but these *Reports* do not always contain information on the
age distribution of the population. The data for Scotland for 1901–21
have been taken from the 1901, 1911 and 1921 *Reports*, from which have
been extrapolated data for 1906, 1916 and 1926. The Registrar-
General's series on age distribution of the population of Wales is
incomplete for the years 1916–21, 1942–4 and 1946–9. The data for
1916, 1921 and 1946 have therefore been estimated.

Non-civilians are excluded from the Registrars-General annual estimates of the population of England and Wales for the period 1915–20,
but are included in the annual estimates of the population of Scotland
for that period. To this extent density figures for England, Wales and
Great Britain for 1916 are too high.

Patterns of increase and decrease of religious adherence

Adherence to organised religion has in general decreased since 1901.
Table 13.49 shows the steady increase of civil marriages over the first

six decades of the century, an increase concentrated, however, in the early years of this period, when the churches also were relatively successful in recruiting and retaining members. Yet the churches' own membership records confirm the evidence of the Registrars-General that twentieth-century Britain has seen an overall decline in religious activity in relation to population. Table 13.50 shows that membership of the major Protestant denominations has fallen by more than five per cent since 1901. This small decrease in absolute numbers represents a fall from twenty to twelve per cent of the population age fifteen and over, a highly important trend illustrated in some detail by the density tables. Only the two, part-established Protestant sectors, Episcopalianism and Presbyterianism have maintained their numbers. But even these groups have sharply decreased as a percentage of the population. The Catholics appear to have escaped this trend, perhaps because of an ability, in an apparently unfavourable cultural climate, to create and maintain a 'sub-culture' relatively impervious to external factors.

Probably the largest example of a sub-culture within the English-speaking community of the British Isles is that afforded by Ireland. Table 13.51 summarises data from the census of Ireland, of the Republic of Ireland and of Northern Ireland which show that, for census purposes at least, even in 1961 well over 97 per cent of the population claimed allegiance to a religious organisation. Of course such claims are defective evidence for *active* religious commitment: in 1961 three times as many persons claimed to be Presbyterian as received communion from the Presbyterian Church in Ireland. But both general political and social developments in present-day Northern Ireland, and the records of Protestant denominations in Ireland, point at least to a continuing enthusiasm for religion among Irish Protestants. While their British counterparts have all lost many members, Irish Presbyterians, Methodists and Baptists have all greatly increased their membership. In this respect, these Irish groups behave much more like newer denominations such as the Jehovah's Witnesses, or the Seventh Day Adventists, than like the older British nonconformity.

The measurement of active religious commitment among Irish *Catholics* is extremely difficult on the data available. Nor can the development of British Catholicism be assessed much more accurately. Catholic statistics tend to measure demographic trends rather than changes of attitude, and even Catholic demographic data seem somewhat obscure: Table 13.13 notes certain difficulties. What evidence of patterns of commitment can be found suggests that, despite the relative isolation of Catholicism from cultural trends in Britain, Catholics have experienced at least something of these movements. The number of secular and religious Catholic priests in Great Britain increased 29·8 per cent in 1931–41, 15·3 per cent in 1941–51, 11·0 per cent in 1951–61 and only 6·8 per cent in 1961–6. Since 1966 the number of priests has absolutely decreased. Although the estimated Catholic population increased nearly 75 per cent between 1931 and 1966, while the number of Episcopalian communicants has decreased by about 13 per cent, recruitment to the Catholic priesthood has steadily declined. Adult conversions to Catholicism (evidence on which is available for England and Wales only), show a pattern similar to that of Protestant denominations' membership since the 1930s. Between 1931 and 1941, while Protestant denominations declined rapidly, the number of conversions to Catholicism fell three to four per cent a year to 9,511 in 1941. Between 1941 and 1956, a period when almost all Protestant denominations increased their numbers, adult conversions rose by more than five per cent per annum to 14,077. Since 1957 adult conversions, like Protestant membership, have rapidly diminished, falling on average by over four per cent per annum to 9,121 in 1966.

If the growth of British Catholicism is not unlike that of British Protestantism, the increase and decrease of the membership of most individual Protestant denominations quite strongly suggest the following broad pattern (which may be modified by regional evidence). Rapid expansion of membership continued from the nineties until 1905–10, usually ceasing before the 1908–9 depression. From those years till about 1920, membership growth was either checked or turned into absolute decline. Growth was resumed or accelerated either before or during the sharp post-war slump of 1921, and continued until the late twenties, in most cases to a point between 1926 and 1929, but in some instances until 1930–2. The depression of the thirties saw a fall in membership of some denominations, but this was immediately followed by slight expansion in certain cases. Almost all denominations lost members rapidly during the Second World War, however. They began to grow again after 1945, and continued to increase their membership till the late fifties or early sixties, since when most groups have entered a period of severe decline.

The trend of the Episcopalian churches' membership was upward to a point between 1927 and 1938 and downward since then. But the movement of their membership also illustrates this cyclical pattern. Anglican and Scottish Episcopal communicants increased by about one and a half per cent per annum until the First World War, but either decreased or increased more slowly between 1913 and 1920. For most of the twenties Episcopalian communicants – unlike Nonconformist members – expanded about as quickly as they did before the First World War. From the late twenties until 1938–9, however, the Episcopalian churches either shrank or grew less rapidly, despite increases of communicants during the recovery years. The war period, 1939–47 marked a reversal for these organisations. On Easter Day 1946 the Church of England received only 77 per cent of the number of communicants on Easter Day 1936. Between 1946 and 1956 and, to a lesser degree, until 1961, Episcopalian churches recovered much, though not all, of the ground they had lost from the beginning of the Second World War. Yet the greater part of these post-war gains have disappeared since 1961. The Church of England had 1,899,000 Easter Day communicants in 1966, 153,000 more than in 1946, but 46,000 less than in 1900.

The Presbyterian churches have a somewhat better record: while Church of England Easter Day communicants reached a peak in 1927, Church of Scotland communicants were at a maximum in 1956. Perhaps because of the inherent characteristics of the two indices, the Church of Scotland seems to suffer from less severe fluctuations than those experienced by the Church of England, or indeed by the Presbyterian Church of England. The incomplete amalgamation of the Church of Scotland and the United Free Church of Scotland in 1929 had no more apparent affect on growth patterns than did the incomplete amalgamation of British Methodists in 1932. The number of Church of Scotland communicants rose quickly before 1911, and after the First World War, but quite slowly between 1911 and 1918. Between 1926 and 1936 membership was virtually stable. But from 1936 to 1946 the Church of Scotland lost some ground, though much less than the Church of England. In 1946, Church of Scotland communicants numbered 97·9 per cent of the figure for 1936. The Church then gained 58,000 communicants (4·6 per cent) between 1946 and 1956, and lost 97,551 communicants (7·4 per cent) between 1956 and 1967. These movements also were much slighter than contemporary changes in numbers of Church of England Easter Day communicants.

Some of the Church of Scotland's relative success may be due to its national appeal. The membership of the Presbyterian Church of England has decreased about 15 per cent. this century, while that of the Church of Scotland has slightly increased. During periods of expansion, such as 1901–16 and 1946–61, the English Presbyterians enjoyed more success than have the Scottish. But between 1926 and 1946 and after 1961 the English Presbyterians suffered much greater losses. Yet the appeal to a national community has not greatly helped the Presbyterian Church of Wales (the Calvinistic Methodists), which has had little success in retaining members. While the Presbyterian Church of England's membership increased, partly by migration from Celtic countries into England (it decreased only three per cent between 1946 and 1966), the membership of the Presbyterian Church of Wales fell thirty per cent. Like other churches in Wales, the Calvinistic

Methodists increased very rapidly till 1906, then lost members, enjoyed a slight increase till the late twenties and finally entered forty years of almost unbroken decline.

A great deal of this pattern can be seen in the history of the Methodist Church and of its constituents before 1932. These constituent denominations increased by nearly two per cent. per annum until 1906, but together lost over 50,000 members between 1906 and 1921. The revival of religious activity in the twenties gave the Primitive, United and Wesleyan Methodist Churches 98·4 per cent of their 1906 membership figure by 1926. But between 1926 and 1946 membership fell ten per cent. The Methodists gained little from the post-war recovery: between 1946 and 1956 their membership actually fell. Since 1956 their numbers have decreased a further ten per cent.

Baptist and Congregationalist membership figures confirm the evidence provided by Church of Scotland data, for the proposition that the denominations have been more successful in Scotland than in either England or Wales during the last seventy years. Between 1906 and 1926 English and Welsh Baptist and Congregationalist membership decreased by as much as five per cent. While English and Welsh membership fell sharply between 1926 and 1946, Congregationalists lost few members in Scotland during these years, and the Baptists still retained slightly more members than they had in 1906. Since 1946, conditions seem to have been less favourable in Scotland. But the Baptists and Congregationalists are still more successful there than anywhere else in Great Britain.

If Scottish churches, or Scottish sectors of churches, have been more fortunate than other areas of British Protestantism, the newer Protestant denominations have grown even faster than the Catholics. Evidence of trends in the membership of these new denominations is not easily obtainable. The Jehovah's Witnesses grew very quickly in the thirties, nearly doubling the number of their publishers[1] between 1931 and 1941. Like other denominations they were less successful in the war period, but even during 1941–6 publishers increased seventeen per cent. The Jehovah's Witnesses shared fully in the post-war revival. But while other groups added a few percentage points to their membership, the Witnesses nearly trebled their publishers between 1946 and 1956. Since 1956 the Witnesses, again like other churches, have been less fortunate, although the number of publishers has nearly doubled in a period when many denominations' membership fell by at least ten per cent. Certain other recently established denominations, such as the Seventh Day Adventists, present a similar picture on a smaller scale.

[1] See Table 13.28, note 2.

GENERAL REFERENCE WORKS
A bibliography on Christianity in the United Kingdom is outside the scope of this chapter. The denominational publications cited in the tables of denominational data often contain further series of membership, other indices of religious activity, some geographical breakdown of statistics, lists of churches, clergy or ministers, etc. The following publications are general works of reference:

F. L. Cross (ed.), *The Oxford Dictionary of the Christian Church* (London 1958).
The Free Church Directory.
Kenneth Grubb *et al.*, *World Christian Handbook* (various editions since 1947).
Johannes Grundler, *Lexikon der Christlichen Kirchen und Sekten* (Vienna 1961).
Franklin H. Littell and Hans Hermann, *Weltkirchen Lexikon* (Stuttgart 1960).

TABLE 13.1

Profession of Religion in Ireland (excluding the Six Counties of Northern Ireland) by Census Years 1901–1961

	Catholics	All other religious denominations	Church of Ireland	Other religious denominations				
				Presbyterians	Methodists	Jews	Baptists	Others
1901	2,878,271	343,552	264,264	46,714	17,872	3006	1590	10,106
1911	2,812,509	327,179	249,535	45,486	16,440	3805	1588	10,325
1926	2,751,269	220,723	164,215	32,429	10,663	3686	717	9013
1936	2,773,920	194,500	145,030	28,067	9649	3749	715	7290
1946	2,786,033	169,074	124,829	23,870	8355	3907	462	7651
1961	2,673,473	144,868	104,016	18,953	6676	3255	481	11,487

Source: Census data. See p. 407

TABLE 13.2

Profession of Religion in Northern Ireland by Census Years 1901–1961

	Catholics	All other religious denominations	Church of Ireland	Other religious denominations		
				Presbyterians	Methodists	Others
1901	430,390	806,562	316,825	396,562	44,134	49,041
1911	430,161	820,370	327,076	395,039	45,942	52,313
1926	420,428	836,133	338,724	393,374	49,554	54,481
1937	428,290	851,455	345,474	390,931	55,135	59,915
1951	471,460	899,461	353,245	410,215	66,639	69,362
1961	497,547	927,495	344,800	413,113	71,865	97,717

Source: See sources for Table 13.1

TABLE 13·3

Marriages by Manner of Solemnisation 1901–1967, England and Wales (Showing in parentheses the percentages represented of all marriages)

	All marriages	Religious marriages	%	Church of England and Church in Wales	%	Religious marriages by type of rite											
						Roman Catholics	%	Jews	%	Baptists	%	Congrega-tionalists	%	Methodists	%	Others	%
1901	259,400	218,333	(84·2)	172,769	(66·6)	10,624	(4·1)	1813	(0·7)					33,217	(12·8)		
1906	270,038	219,316	(81·2)	170,579	(63·2)	11,455	(4·2)	2139	(0·8)					35,183	(13·0)		
1911	274,943	217,508	(79·1)	167,925	(61·1)	12,002	(4·4)	1820	(0·7)					35,761	(13·0)		
1914	294,401	223,521	(75·9)	171,700	(58·3)	13,729	(4·7)	1973	(0·7)					36,119	(12·3)		
1919	369,411	284,081	(76·9)	220,557	(59·7)	19,078	(5·2)	1861	(0·5)	7176	(1·9)	8657	(2·3)	20,804	(5·6)	5948	(1·6)
1924	296,416	225,812	(76·2)	171,480	(57·8)	16,286	(5·5)	1972	(0·7)	5950	(2·0)	7335	(2·5)	17,757	(6·0)	5032	(1·7)
1929	313,316	232,841	(74·3)	171,113	(56·2)	18,711	(6·0)	2088	(0·6)	5801	(1·9)	7189	(2·3)	17,606	(5·6)	5333	(1·7)
1934	342,307	245,187	(71·6)	183,123	(53·5)	22,323	(6·5)	2233	(0·7)	6056	(1·8)	7276	(2·1)	17,979	(5·3)	6197	(1·8)
1952	349,308	242,531	(69·4)	173,282	(49·6)	33,050	(9·4)	1876	(0·5)	5277	(1·5)	6952	(2·0)	16,640	(4·8)	5454	(1·6)
1957	346,903	249,819	(72·0)	172,010	(49·6)	39,960	(11·5)	1713	(0·5)	5897	(1·7)	6632	(1·9)	17,182	(5·0)	6425	(1·9)
1962	347,732	244,630	(70·4)	164,707	(47·4)	42,788	(12·3)	1549	(0·4)	5991	(1·7)	6479	(1·9)	16,927	(4·9)	6189	(1·8)
1967	386,052	254,476	(65·9)	173,278	(44·9)	43,305	(11·2)	1557	(0·4)	5523	(1·4)	6632	(1·7)	17,468	(4·5)	6713	(1·7)

Notes:
1. The Registrar-General published an annual series for civil and religious marriages in England and Wales up to 1914. Since 1914 these figures have been published only at the intervals here indicated.
2. Before 1919 Baptist, Congregationalist, Methodist and Other marriages are included under the heading 'other denominations'. Church of England, Church in Wales and, to a lesser extent, Roman Catholic marriages include persons of other or of no religion.
3. Church of England, Church in Wales and, to a lesser extent, Roman Catholic marriages include persons of other or of no religion.

Source: *Annual Reports* of the Registrar General of Births, Deaths and Marriages in England and Wales.

TABLE 13·4

Marriages in Ireland by Manner of Solemnisation 1901–1919 (Showing in parentheses the percentages represented of all marriages)

Year	All marriages	Religious marriages	Roman Catholic	Church of Ireland	Presbyterian	Jewish	Others
1901	22,564	22,196 (98·4%)	15,603 (69·1%)	3542 (15·7%)	2480 (11·0%)	3 (neg.)	568 (2·5%)
1906	22,662	22,262 (98·2%)	15,818 (69·8%)	3604 (15·9%)	2330 (10·3%)	16 (neg.)	494 (2·2%)
1911	23,473	23,038 (98·1%)	16,729 (71·3%)	3627 (15·4%)	2211 (9·4%)	7 (neg.)	464 (2·0%)
1914	23,695	23,318 (98·4%)	17,014 (71·8%)	3601 (15·2%)	2252 (9·5%)	16 (neg.)	435 (1·8%)
1919	27,193	26,679 (98·1%)	18,756 (69·0%)	4247 (15·6%)	3008 (11·1%)	19 (neg.)	649 (2·4%)

Source: Annual Reports (published up to 1920) of the Registrar-General (Ireland) of the Marriages, Births and Deaths registered in Ireland.

TABLE 13·5

Marriages in Northern Ireland by Manner of Solemnisation 1924–1967 (Showing in parentheses the percentages represented of all marriages)

Year	All marriages	Religious marriages	Roman Catholic	Church of Ireland	Presbyterian	Methodist	Jewish	Others
1924	7514	7111 (94·6%)	1999 (26·6%)	2401 (32·0%)	2189 (29·1%)	(—)	3 (neg.)	519 (6·9%)
1929	7426	6947 (93·5%)	2126 (28·6%)	2201 (29·6%)	2084 (28·1%)	(—)	7 (0·01%)	529 (7·1%)
1934	8230	7649 (92·9%)	2375 (28·9%)	2390 (29·0%)	2281 (27·7%)	(—)	10 (0·01%)	593 (7·2%)
1952	9300	8624 (92·7%)	2731 (29·4%)	2244 (24·1%)	2845 (30·6%)	487 (5·2%)	3 (neg.)	314 (3·4%)
1957	9391	8852 (94·3%)	2811 (29·9%)	2377 (25·3%)	2809 (29·9%)	507 (5·4%)	2 (neg.)	346 (3·7%)
1962	9842	9361 (95·1%)	3249 (33·0%)	2285 (23·2%)	2987 (30·3%)	486 (4·9%)	(neg.)	354 (3·6%)
1967	10,924	10,455 (95·7%)	3913 (35·8%)	2328 (21·3%)	3204 (29·3%)	566 (5·2%)	(neg.)	444 (4·1%)

Note: Figures for 'other' religious marriages for 1924–34 include Methodist marriages.
Source: Government of Northern Ireland, *Annual Reports* of the Registrar General.

TABLE 13.6

Marriages in Scotland by Manner of Solemnisation 1901–1967 (Showing in parentheses the percentages represented of all marriages)

Year	All marriages	Religious marriages	Church of Scotland	United Free Church of Scotland	Roman Catholic	Scottish Episcopal Church	Others
1901	31,387	29,435 (93·8%)	14,167 (45·1%)	8669 (27·6%)	3184 (10·1%)	942 (3·0%)	2473 (7·9%)
1906	33,142	31,157 (94·0%)	14,983 (45·2%)	8634 (26·1%)	3644 (11·0%)	983 (3·0%)	2913 (8·8%)
1911	31,844	29,237 (91·8%)	14,032 (44·1%)	8083 (25·4%)	3404 (10·7%)	984 (3·1%)	2734 (8·6%)
1914	35,028	30,629 (87·4%)	14,644 (41·8%)	8260 (23·6%)	3951 (11·3%)	1032 (2·9%)	2742 (7·8%)
1919	44,060	35,709 (81·0%)	16,709 (37·9%)	9808 (22·3%)	4663 (10·6%)	1429 (3·2%)	3100 (7·0%)
1924	32,328	28,393 (87·8%)	13,488 (41·7%)	7657 (23·7%)	3849 (11·9%)	974 (3·0%)	2425 (7·5%)
1929	32,967	28,816 (87·4%)	15,503 (47·0%)	5849 (17·7%)	3925 (11·9%)	930 (2·8%)	2609 (7·9%)
1934	36,934	32,633 (88·4%)	23,476 (63·6%)		4888 (13·2%)	1040 (2·8%)	3229 (8·7%)
1952	41,154	33,687 (81·9%)	23,671 (57·5%)		6033 (14·7%)	1022 (2·5%)	2961 (7·2%)
1957	42,661	35,231 (82·6%)	24,325 (57·0%)		7093 (16·6%)	939 (2·2%)	2874 (6·7%)
1962	40,244	32,131 (79·8%)	21,843 (54·3%)		6858 (17·0%)	846 (2·1%)	2584 (6·4%)
1967	42,116	31,522 (74·8%)	21,284 (50·5%)		6940 (16·5%)	920 (2·2%)	2378 (5·6%)

Note: In 1929 the Church of Scotland and the United Free Church of Scotland united.
Source: Annual Reports of the Registrar-General of the Births, Deaths and Marriages in Scotland.

TABLE 13.7

Assemblies of God in Great Britain and Ireland 1951–1966

The Assemblies of God were founded in 1925.

	Members	Adherents	Pastors	Assemblies
1951	—	—	—	447
1961	20,000	60,000	—	534
1964	21,000	—	398	529
1966	28,000	65,972	561	534

Note: The figures for 1951, 1961 and 1966 are taken from the *World Christian Handbooks* of 1952, 1962 and 1967. The 1964 figures are taken from the *Free Church Directory.*
Sources: See Note.

TABLE 13.8

Baptist Union of Great Britain and Ireland 1901–1969

The Baptists originate in the seventeenth century. The Baptist General Union, formed in 1813, and later known as the Baptist Union of Great Britain and Ireland, has united General and Particular Baptists.

	Members	Young People and Juveniles	Sunday School Scholars	Pastors	Chapels and Churches
1901	372,998	—	532,219	2030	4012
1906	434,741	—	590,321	2134	4021
1911	418,608	—	575,830	2143	4169
1916	408,029	—	531,295	2070	4227
1921	402,688	—	517,969	2078	4180
1926	416,665	—	525,564	2069	4188
1931	406,216	—	479,193	2037	4174
1936	396,531	—	418,483	2067	4162
1941	382,337	—	377,316	2101	4215
1946	354,900	—	302,160	1928	4156
1951	335,640	—	320,898	1943	4091
1956	327,806	—	319,438	2023	3830
1961	313,885	54,961	234,453	2068	3294
1966	290,313	57,516	197,272	2105	3295
1969	274,871	54,768	199,793	2081	3264

Notes:
1. Wartime conditions precluded the collection of figures for 1941. The 1941 figures above are a repetition of the 1940 figures.
2. 'Sunday School Scholars' are classified as 'Juveniles' from 1961 onwards, and defined as being under 14. 'Young People', defined as aged 14–20, have been subtracted from 'Sunday School Scholars' for these years.
3. Baptists in Eire are included in these figures.
4. From 1961 the data under 'Chapels and Churches' relates to 'Churches' only.
Source: The Baptist Handbook.

TABLE 13.9
Baptists 1901–1969, England and Wales

	Members	Sunday School Scholars	Pastors	Lay Preachers	Chapels and Churches
1901	352,683	515,827	1883	5060	2588
1906	410,283	569,189	1982	5467	2898
1911	394,152	552,760	1975	5223	2900
1916	383,633	509,568	1905	4887	2958
1921	378,164	496,395	1934	4877	2872
1926	389,625	502,109	1911	5098	2924
1931	379,509	455,243	1875	5106	2971
1936	368,890	396,042	1892	5112	2983
1941	355,074	356,422	1932	4728	3044
1946	329,055	283,891	1753	4316	3060
1951	310,848	300,830	1776	4166	3121
1956	302,174	298,377	1855	4282	3043
1961	288,579	216,934	1893	4068	3055
1966	265,254	182,154	1932	4171	3052
1969	250,903	185,826	1890	4165	3029

Notes:
1. Wartime conditions precluded the collection of figures for 1941. The 1941 figures above are a repetition of the 1940 figures.
2. The figures for 'Sunday School Scholars' for 1961, 1966, 1968 refer to age group under 14 only.
Source: The Baptist Handbook.

TABLE 13.10
Baptists 1901–1969, Ireland

	Members	Sunday School Scholars	Pastors	Lay Preachers	Chapels and Churches
1901	2649	2094	25	86	31
1906	3013	3124	27	90	39
1911	2936	3178	30	103	41
1916	2680	2900	26	116	43
1921	2759	2917	23	118	41
1926	3430	4186	24	128	43
1931	3678	4779	31	160	56
1936	3802	4817	35	144	55
1941	3743	—	38	156	53
1946	4234	4405	37	168	60
1951	4644	5123	42	179	62
1956	5164	5673	39	57	65
1961	5661	5533	47	106	72
1966	6524	5677	46	88	77
1969	6922	6531	53	74	79

Notes:
1. Wartime conditions precluded the collection of figures for 1941. The 1941 figures above are a repetition of the 1940 figures.
2. The figures for 'Sunday School Scholars' for 1961, 1966, 1969 refer to age group under 14 only.
Source: The Baptist Handbook.

TABLE 13.11

Baptists 1901–1969, Scotland

	Members	Sunday School Scholars	Pastors	Lay Preachers	Chapels and Churches
1901	17,266	13,689	117	211	122
1906	20,962	17,412	120	152	138
1911	21,025	19,328	132	175	147
1916	21,268	18,369	133	166	152
1921	21,260	18,016	115	138	147
1926	23,097	18,713	128	130	149
1931	22,499	18,644	125	155	151
1936	23,298	17,126	134	131	156
1941	23,024	—	127	147	159
1946	21,106	13,402	134	114	155
1951	19,593	14,407	119	143	156
1956	20,146	14,990	124	116	157
1961	19,321	11,620	124	106	160
1966	18,230	9078	123	109	159
1969	16,716	7123	133	90	159

Notes:
1. Wartime conditions precluded the collection of figures for 1941. The 1941 figures above are a repetition of the 1940 figures.
2. The figures for 'Sunday School Scholars' for 1961, 1966, 1969 refer to age group under 14 only.

Source: The Baptist Handbook.

TABLE 13.12

Bible Christians 1901 and 1906, Great Britain

The Bible Christians were formed in 1815 and merged into the United Methodist Church in 1907.

	Members	On Trial Members	Juvenile Members	Sunday School Scholars	Ministers	Local Preachers	Chapels
1901	28,315	458	1260	43,401	168	1861	973
1906	32,317	683	2089	46,741	177	1534	644

Note: These figures cover Great Britain only.
Source: Minutes of the Bible Christian Conference.

TABLE 13.13

Catholic Church 1901–1969, England and Wales

Catholicism ceased to be the State religion of England and Wales, Scotland and Ireland in the sixteenth century. The continuity of the Catholic community in the British Isles has not been broken however.

	Estimated Catholic Population	Baptisms	Adult Conversions	Priests		Churches and Chapels
				Secular	Religious	
1901	—	—	—	2308	990	1536
1906	—	—	—	2580	1359	1640
1911	—	40,492	3609	2758	1544	1773
1916	1,885,655	62,046	8501	2475	1417	1891
1921	1,915,475	73,322	11,621	2490	1479	1932
1926	2,042,630	67,710	11,714	2644	1452	2003
1931	2,206,244	64,717	12,162	2897	1587	2228
1936	2,335,890	65,809	10,617	3389	1730	2388
1941	2,414,002	67,119	9511	3830	2009	2580
1946	2,415,428	85,024	10,363	4122	2135	2746
1951	2,808,596	88,953	11,360	4363	2365	2910
1956	3,169,700	100,438	14,077	4452	2590	3873
1961	3,553,500	129,469	14,174	4667	2699	4222
1966	4,000,695	131,890	9121	5096	2791	4642
1969	4,143,854	—	—	4962	2788	4770

Notes:

1. 'Churches and Chapels' includes private chapels used at least for celebration of weekly mass.
2. Data for baptisms, adult conversions and Catholic population are drawn from parish records.
3. 'Estimated Catholic Population' data are based upon the calculation of local clergy as to the number of catholics living in their parish. Introduction of standard parish register return forms since 1955 has modified these calculations in some respects and introduced some anomalies. The overall effect of this change has been to raise the estimate of Catholic population substantially.
4. A discussion of the difficulties of using estimated Catholic population figures may be found in the Catholic Education Council for England and Wales' handbook *Catholic Education* for 1967. This publication cites the following figures:

	1961	1962	1963	1964	1965	1966
Actual Mass Attendance	2,018,000	2,093,000	—	—	—	2,114,000
Est. Catholic Population'(a)	3,803,000	3,905,000	3,977,000	4,001,000	4,048,000	—
Est. Catholic Population'(b)	5,690,000	—	—	5,900,000	—	—

(a) Parish Priests' estimates.   (b) Estimates based on baptisms.

Source: The Catholic Directory.

TABLE 13.14

Catholic Church 1901–1967, Scotland

	Estimated Catholic Population	Baptisms	Con-firmations	Priests		Churches, Chapels, Stations etc.
				Secular	Religious	
1901	432,900	18,892	7493	394	82	351
1906	514,400	20,546	11,546	444	95	381
1911	518,969	19,717	4495	460	98	406
1916	548,000	18,309	14,793	489	98	432
1921	601,304	22,393	11,796	510	98	445
1926	600,000	19,066	28,484	523	94	440
1931	607,000	17,996	19,249	590	105	457
1936	614,205	17,461	23,854	628	126	471
1941	614,469	16,789	8468	723	162	481
1946	621,398	13,527	15,289	765	182	496
1951	748,463	19,809	—	803	220	—
1956	757,130	23,464	19,474	900	240	—
1961	799,180	25,825	23,287	983	258	—
1966	827,410	22,806	19,847	1021	284	—
1967	824,800	—	—	1015	279	—

Notes:

1. 'Estimated Catholic Population' is returned on a diocesan basis. Since some dioceses do not revise their estimates from year to year the figures are approximate only.
2. Some of the series are incomplete, and some, e.g. 'confirmations', appear to vary in character from year to year.

Source: The Catholic Directory for the Clergy and Laity in Scotland.

TABLE 13.15

Christian Brethren (Open) 1951–1967

Brethren churches were formed in Dublin, Plymouth and Bristol between 1825 and 1830. J. N. Darby was the outstanding early leader. In 1849 they divided into the Open and the Exclusive Brethren. They are also known as Plymouth Brethren.

	Members	Adherents	Full-time workers	Places of worship
1951	115,000	—	—	—
1956	146,300	—	—	1795
1961	—	246,000	—	—
1967	100,000	240,000	181	—

Notes:

1. These figures refer to the Open Brethren only.
2. The figure for 1951 refers to England and Wales and Scotland. The subsequent figures refer to the British Isles.
3. *Assemblies in Great Britain and Other Parts*, published by Open Brethren in 1959, records 1862 assemblies in the British Isles. The *Free Church Directory* for 1965–6 reports 1958 assemblies in the British Isles.

Sources: see Note 3.

TABLE 13.16

Church in Wales 1901–1966

The Anglican or Episcopalian Church was disestablished in Wales in 1920.

	Easter Communicants	Baptisms	Sunday School Scholars	Confirmations	Churches
1901	—	—	—	9165	—
1906	—	—	—	10,674	—
1911	—	—	—	—	—
1916	—	—	—	—	—
1921	157,614	25,454	143,963	11,579	1755
1926	184,568	22,427	135,432	14,913	1732
1931	185,484	19,548	122,172	13,633	1754
1936	195,494	18,862	109,163	15,342	—
1941	175,000	—	—	—	1766
1946	—	—	—	—	—
1951	—	—	—	—	—
1956	—	—	—	—	—
1961	183,000	—	—	—	1783
1966	165,000	—	—	—	1777

Notes:

1. No data are available for 1901. The above figure is from the statistics of 1902.
2. No data on 'Churches' are available for 1926. The 1928 figure has been cited.
3. The above figures for 1941, 1961 and 1966 were in each case collected in the previous year.
4. The figures for 'Easter Communicants' for 1941, 1961 and 1966 and for 'Churches' for 1920 are drawn from D. Butler and J. Freeman, *British Political Facts, 1900–1967*, which cites the Secretary of the Representative Body of the Church in Wales. These figures appear to diverge substantially from those published in the *Church of England Yearbook* for earlier years.

Sources: The Church of England Yearbook.
The Official Handbook of the Church in Wales; see Note.

TABLE 13.17

Church of England 1901–1966

The Crown was established as supreme head of the Church of England by Act o
Parliament of 1534.

	Easter Day Communicants (000s)	Sunday School Children (000s)	Clergymen
1901	1945	2333	23,670
1906	1988	2337	—
1911	2293	2433	23,193
1916	2097	2167	—
1921	2236	1994	22,579
1926	2397	1880	—
1931	2311	1798	21,309
1936	2264	1562	—
1941	2018	1434	—
1946	1746	—	—
1951	1867	—	18,196
1956	2168	1308	—
1961	2159	1039	18,749
1966	1899	—	20,008

Notes: The figures for 'Easter Day Communicants' and 'Sunday School Children' for
1941, 1946, 1951 and 1960 are those of either the preceding or the succeeding year.
Sources: Facts and Figures about the Church of England.
Church of England Yearbook.

TABLE 13.18

Church of Jesus Christ of the Latter-Day Saints 1951–1966

The Church of Jesus Christ of the Latter-Day Saints, also known as Mormons, was
established by Joseph Smith in 1830, and first entered the United Kingdom in 1837.

	Members	Adherents	Places of worship
1951	7386	—	76
1956	9460	—	93
1961	9460	—	—
1966	9460	11,400	93

Source: The above data were published in the *World Christian Handbooks* of 1952, 1957,
1962 and 1967.

TABLE 13.19

Church of Scotland 1901–1967

The Church of Scotland was established in 1560 and adopted presbyterian government by statute of 1690. Various secessions culminated in the Disruption of 1843 and
the formation of the Free Church of Scotland. The Church of Scotland and most of
the United Free Church of Scotland amalgamated in 1929.

	Communicants	Sunday School Scholars	Ministers	Parish Churches	Congregations
1901	661,629	—	1800	1371	—
1906	698,566	—	1800	1413	—
1911	714,915	—	1800	1440	—
1916	721,158	—	1800	1473	—
1921	745,783	—	1825	1457	—
1926	761,946	191,389	1800	1470	—
1931	1,280,620	369,115	—	—	2920
1936	1,288,571	325,397	—	—	2588
1941	1,268,839	231,226	—	—	2483
1946	1,261,646	256,424	—	—	2410
1951	1,273,027	291,259	—	—	2340
1956	1,319,574	325,200	—	—	2280
1961	1,290,617	297,192	—	—	2093
1966	1,233,808	—	—	—	2166
1967	1,222,023	—	?	—	2150

Notes:
1. Figures for 'Communicants' and 'Parish Churches' in 1901 are not available. The
   figures cited above are for 1900.
2. From 1931 the figures include that part of the United Free Church of Scotland
   which amalgamated with the Church of Scotland.
Source: The Church of Scotland Yearbook.

TABLE 13.20

Congregational Church of England and Wales 1901–1969

The Congregational Union of England and Wales was formed in 1832 from county Associations of congregations, some of which had their origins in the sixteenth century.

	Members	Sunday School Scholars	Ministers	Lay Preachers	Places of worship
1901	403,352	652,377	2887	5081	4667
1906	459,614	698,465	2950	5012	4671
1911	454,429	655,548	2917	5186	4723
1916	451,229	605,796	2883	4674	4701
1921	—	—	—	—	—
1926	317,148	432,321	2714	4100	3476
1931	311,625	406,503	2229	3480	3505
1936	297,267	337,401	2232	3598	3423
1941	283,207	290,774	2200	3465	3435
1946	246,246	205,264	1985	3122	3330
1951	227,002	225,126	1966	2998	3156
1956	218,671	227,426	1924	3192	3064
1961	206,830	169,733	1809	3037	2911
1966	196,171	147,302	1747	2735	2747
1969	181,101	117,872	1683	2216	2544

Notes:

1. No statistics were collected between 1917–26. The figures for 1926 (above) were collected in 1927.
2. No statistics were collected between 1940–4. The figures for 1941 (above) were collected in 1939.
3. The figures for 1901–26 include, while those since 1927 exclude, those churches which formed the Union of Welsh Independents.
4. No data on 'Sunday School Scholars' were published in 1969. The above figure is for 'Children in Churches'.

Source: Congregational Yearbook of England and Wales.

TABLE 13.21
Congregational Union of Ireland 1901–1956
The Congregational Union of Ireland was formed in 1829.

	Members	Sunday School Scholars	Ministers	Lay Preachers	Places of worship
1901	2298	3425	29	41	44
1906	2193	4630	22	62	41
1911	2300	4787	25	55	80
1916	2133	4213	19	55	67
1921	—	—	—	—	—
1926	2105	3125	—	30	—
1931	2231	3822	14	22	53
1936	2159	3907	18	22	127
1941	2078	3510	17	21	83
1946	1741	2536	19	29	83
1951	1752	2482	22	31	36
1956	1834	2529	19	44	30

Notes:
1. No statistics were collected between 1917–27. The figures for 1926 (above) were collected in 1928.
2. No statistics were collected between 1940–4. The figures for 1941 (above) were collected in 1939.
3. No statistics are available for the period since 1956.
Source: Congregational Yearbook of England and Wales.

TABLE 13.22

Congregational Union of Scotland 1901–1969

The Congregational Union of Scotland was formed in 1811. Some of the constituent chapels were built in the eighteenth century.

	Members	Sunday School Scholars	Ministers	Churches
1901	30,270	27,690	200	208
1906	36,785	34,738	200	219
1911	35,266	35,444	176	189
1916	35,336	29,709	168	185
1921	36,331	26,821	152	169
1926	37,610	30,097	149	168
1931	38,688	17,808	149	162
1936	39,351	17,552	147	163
1941	39,522	12,428	149	158
1946	35,680	12,601	135	156
1951	35,140	13,251	133	151
1956	35,190	14,143	133	150
1961	33,993	10,953	119	145
1966	29,521	10,311	105	131
1969	26,527	8829	92	120

Note: No data were collected for the years 1915–16 to 1919–20. The figure for 1916 (above) is the 1914–15 figure.

Sources: Congregational Yearbook of England and Wales; Yearbook of the Congregational Union of Scotland. Figures for 1911–26, unavailable in published sources, were supplied by the Congregational Union of Scotland.

TABLE 13.23

Elim Foursquare Gospel Alliance 1919–1967

The Elim Foursquare Gospel Alliance originated from George Jeffreys's Elim Evangelistic Band about 1915. Schism reduced the numbers of Alliance members and places of worship between 1939 and 1942.

	Communicants or Full Members	Adherents	Full-time workers	Places of worship
1919	—	—	17	—
1920	—	—	21	—
1939	—	—	—	280
1942	—	—	—	206
1952	16,000	—	—	240
1954	—	—	—	250
1957	19,000	—	—	268
1962	20,000	25,000	—	—
1967	20,000	44,800	467	308

Note: B. R. Wilson (see Sources) estimates that in 1939 less than 30,000 persons were in fellowship in Elim.

Sources: Bryan R. Wilson, *Sects and Society. A Sociological Study of Three Religious Groups in Britain* (Heinemann 1961). *World Christian Handbook.*

Table 13.24

Episcopal Church in Scotland 1901–1968

The Scottish Episcopalians have maintained continuity with the pre-1690 Scottish Church.

	Permanent Members	Communicants	Congregations
1901	127,093	46,922	361
1906	133,122	50,499	373
1911	142,464	54,751	397
1916	144,853	55,722	417
1921	147,518	59,246	418
1926	142,605	60,495	421
1931	133,752	59,977	414
1936	127,151	60,333	411
1941	119,508	59,130	402
1946	108,558	55,471	393
1951	103,598	56,121	387
1956	106,069	56,132	375
1961	97,508	56,460	361
1966	94,476	53,585	364
1968	94,332	51,919	364

Notes:
1. Figures for 1901 are taken from the *Scottish Episcopal Church Yearbook and Directory*.
2. Figures for 'Congregations' for 1921 and 1946 are taken from *Whitaker's Almanack*.
3. All other figures are from the *Annual Report of the Representative Church Council* of the Episcopal Church of Scotland.

Sources: See Notes.

TABLE 13.25

The First Church of Christ Scientist 1901–1969

The First Church of Christ Scientist was founded by Mrs Mary Baker Eddy in 1879. The Church was first established in Britain about 1900.

	Churches and Societies	Practitioners
1901	5	—
1906	—	—
1911	65	—
1916	—	—
1921	113	346
1926	169	585
1931	206	750
1936	289	—
1941	313	979
1946	323	—
1951	341	876
1956	349	746
1961	336	—
1966	330	—
1969	321	—

Notes:
1. With the exception of the figures for 1901 and 1911 (Great Britain only) and 1921 (England only), the data on 'Churches and Societies' refer to the United Kingdom.
2. The 1926 figure for 'Practitioners' refers to the United Kingdom; all other figures for 'Practitioners' refer to England only.
3. The 1926, 1936 and 1956 figures for 'Churches and Societies' are taken from the statistics of 1927, 1937 and 1957 respectively.
4. B. R. Wilson (see Sources) reports that about 8000 Christian Scientists served with British armed forces in the Second World War.

Sources: Bryan R. Wilson, *Sects and Society. A Sociological Study of Three Religious Groups in Britain* (London 1961). *Whitaker's Almanack.*

TABLE 13.26

Free Church of Scotland 1900–1964

The Free Church of Scotland, also known as the Wee Frees, was established in 1843. A minority of this Church did not enter the United Free Church of Scotland formed in 1900.

	Communicants	Adherents	Ministers	Places of worship
1900	20,000	—	100	—
1909	—	60,000	77	150
1957	—	25,000	—	—
1962	—	—	111	160
1964	21,779	—	103	—

Notes:
1. The figures for 1909 are from the *Encyclopaedia Britannica*, 1911.
2. The figures for 1957 and 1962 are from the *World Christian Handbook*.
3. The figure for 'Communicants' for 1964 is from the *Free Church Directory*, 1965–6; the figure for 'Ministers' for 1964 is from *Chambers's Encyclopaedia*, 1966.
Sources: See Notes.

TABLE 13.27

General Assembly of Unitarian and Free Christian Churches, 1923–1966

The General Assembly was formed in 1928 from the national conference of Unitarian churches founded in 1881 and the British and Foreign Unitarian Association of 1825. British Unitarianism was begun by Theophilus Lindsey in 1773–4.

	Ministers	Congregations
1923	333	356
1926	322	352
1931	291	348
1936	297	340
1941	305	340
1946	274	338
1951	239	334
1956	222	318
1961	229	313
1966	223	313

Notes:
1. All figures refer to the United Kingdom.
2. The *World Christian Handbook* reports that there were 28,000 full members of Unitarian churches in 1957.
3. The 1946 figures (above) are repetitions of the 1945 figures.
Source: General Assembly of Unitarian and Free Christian Churches.

TABLE 13.28

Jehovah's Witnesses 1926–1969

Charles Taze Russell founded the Watch Tower Bible and Tract Society in the U.S.A. in 1884. From this Society the Jehovah's Witnesses movement has developed. It was established in Britain about 1914.

	Publishers	Pioneers	Companies
1926	6000	278	400
1931	5033	314	365
1936	4067	284	364
1941	9741	1283	480
1946	11,395	877	602
1951	23,080	1161	695
1956	30,342	933	733
1961	44,974	1423	932
1966	49,073	896	2806
1969	55,876	883	4262

Notes:

1. The figures for 1926–66 cover Great Britain and Northern Ireland, the figures for 1969 cover Great Britain only. In 1967, as a result of this change in categories, the figures were reduced by approximately 500 publishers, 50 pioneers and 15 companies.
2. 'Publishers' distribute Jehovah's Witnesses' publications.
3. 'Companies' were originally known as 'classes' and are now referred to as 'Congregations'. The figures for 1926 include all registered companies, the figures thereafter active companies only. In 1928 there were 452 registered companies, 386 of which were active.
4. The figure for 1926 includes all registered 'Publishers', whether active or not. For 1931–69 the series refers to active publishers only.
5. The 1926 figures for 'Publishers' and 'Pioneers' are from the statistics of 1927 and 1928 respectively. The figures for 'Pioneers' and 'Companies' in 1951 are 1952 figures.

Sources: Yearbook of the International Bible Students' Association. Yearbook of the Jehovah's Witnesses.

TABLE 13.29

Methodist Church 1932–1968, Great Britain

The Methodist Church was formed in 1932 from an amalgamation of the Primitive Methodist, United Methodist and Wesleyan Methodist Churches.

	Members	Sunday School Scholars	Ministers	Local Preachers	Chapels
1932	838,019	1,297,953	4357	34,948	14,552
1936	818,480	1,138,795	4671	34,032	14,596
1941	778,712	929,942	4645	31,307	16,045
1946	746,757	739,470	4514	27,560	13,524
1951	741,596	805,659	4561	24,701	—
1956	742,444	742,592	4634	23,369	—
1961	723,529	557,839	4517	22,063	—
1966	678,776	476,436	4296	20,666	—
1968	651,139	—	4167	20,244	—

Notes:
1. All figures cover Great Britain only.
2. The figures for 1932–46 are taken in March of each year, those for 1951–67 are taken in December of each year.
3. The figure for 'Chapels' for 1946 is a 1947 figure which was reprinted annually until 1955. From 1953 it was described as 'Methodist Church Buildings – Statistical Summary, 1940' (Prior to war damage). This figure does not include 108 rented chapels.
4. Since 1962 the *Minutes* have contained the statement that 'The total estimated Methodist community in Great Britain is 2,100,000'.
5. No figures for 'Ministers', 'Local Preachers', 'Chapels' and 'Sunday school scholars' were published for 1932. The 1933 figures are cited above.
6. No figure for 'Local Preachers' was published for 1968. The 1967 figure is cited above.

Source: Minutes of the Methodist Conference.

TABLE 13.30

Methodist Church in Ireland 1901–1969

The Methodist Church in Ireland covers both Eire and Northern Ireland.

	Members and Probationers	Sunday School Scholars	Ministers	Local Preachers	Churches, Chapels etc.
1901	27,745	25,270	251	617	382
1906	28,511	26,046	259	686	426
1911	29,351	25,575	201	708	392
1916	27,795	23,801	252	699	—
1921	27,147	22,188	210	635	—
1926	29,062	23,011	231	693	—
1931	30,087	20,877	250	667	—
1936	30,757	19,713	253	633	—
1941	31,053	16,626	265	569	—
1946	31,193	13,232	269	546	—
1951	31,933	14,631	261	492	—
1956	32,724	15,886	261	548	—
1961	31,909	14,671	249	490	—
1966	30,996	13,542	240	456	—
1969	30,173	—	226	438	—

Notes:
1. The figure for 'Churches' for 1901 (above) is the 1900 figure.
2. Figures for 'Sunday School Scholars' have not been published since 1967.
Source: Minutes of the Methodist Church in Ireland.

TABLE 13.31

Methodist New Connexion 1901, 1906 and 1907, United Kingdom

The Methodist New Connexion separated from the Wesleyan Methodist Connexion in 1797 and merged into the United Methodist Church in 1907.

	Members	Sunday School Scholars	Ministers	Local Preachers	Chapels
1901	33,142	83,188	204	1089	457
1906	37,017	88,522	204	1123	455
1907	37,009	87,741	204	1123	457

Note: The figures refer to the United Kingdom.
Source: Minutes of the Methodist New Connexion.

TABLE 13.32

Presbyterian Church in Ireland 1901–1967

Presbyterianism was established in Ireland with the plantation of 1610.

	Communicants	Sunday School Scholars	Ministers	Congregations
1901	106,121	99,263	650	569
1906	106,516	97,119	650	567
1911	105,118	109,916	651	562
1916	103,760	101,163	640	562
1921	106,482	100,071	611	562
1926	109,748	101,409	604	560
1931	110,330	95,017	567	547
1936	113,697	95,053	571	548
1941	117,402	61,720	579	564
1946	119,582	61,118	585	567
1951	128,041	65,975	578	555
1956	134,446	67,008	562	557
1961	138,596	—	569	560
1966	144,284	—	571	569
1967	144,156	—	568	566

Note: No data were collected for 1951. The 1951 figures (above) are from the statistics of 1952.

Source: Whitaker's Almanack.

TABLE 13.33

Presbyterian Church of England 1901–1968

English Presbyterianism can be traced to the Wandsworth Presbytery of 1572. The Presbyterian Church of England was formed in 1876 from the United Presbyterian Church, established by Scots living in England in 1842, and English Presbyterian groups.

	Communicants	Sunday School Scholars	Elders	Congregations
1901	78,024	81,967	2303	326
1906	85,755	88,609	2605	345
1911	86,848	84,180	2900	354
1916	88,525	70,660	2938	355
1921	84,375	65,050	3178	352
1926	84,729	61,630	3376	350
1931	84,298	55,158	3580	352
1936	80,420	43,245	3693	345
1941	74,575	20,912	3463	333
1946	67,236	27,846	3541	334
1951	68,562	35,296	3925	333
1956	70,567	36,558	4272	326
1961	71,100	29,363	4572	318
1966	66,187	24,406	4872	312
1968	63,091	21,875	4878	307

Sources: Minutes of the Synod of the Presbyterian Church of England. Minutes of the General Assembly of the Presbyterian Church of England.

TABLE 13.34

Presbyterian Church of Wales (Calvinistic Methodists) 1901–1968

The Calvinistic Methodist Connexion, which has its origins in the eighteenth century, was formed in 1811. It adopted a Presbyterian confession of faith in 1824, and has since become known as the Presbyterian Church of Wales. It enjoys relations of mutual eligibility with the Church of Scotland.

	Adherents (including communicants)	Communicants	Sunday School Scholars	Ministers and Preachers	Churches
1901	323,951	160,332	180,278	1224	1374
1906	347,785	187,768	193,599	1239	1428
1911	337,096	183,647	185,643	1320	1471
1916	327,246	185,377	170,819	1216	1481
1921	319,484	187,260	163,512	1161	1485
1926	312,393	189,727	155,941	1165	1499
1931	288,503	185,239	142,970	1155	1491
1936	266,879	180,999	122,422	1116	1487
1941	243,593	175,036	94,783	1068	1477
1946	232,090	171,185	84,940	938	1463
1951	213,399	157,124	80,681	875	1440
1956	201,068	147,132	75,190	814	1435
1961	172,870	133,795	59,179	726	1410
1966	153,055	119,276	49,744	641	1351
1968	145,309	113,468	46,876	615	1329

Sources: Blwyddiadur, neu, Lyfr swyddogol y Methodistiaid Calfinaidd am y Flwyddir.

TABLE 13.35

Primitive Methodist Church 1901–1931

The Primitive Methodist Church was formed in 1819 and merged into the Methodist Church in 1932.

	Members	Sunday School Scholars	Ministers	Local Preachers	Chapels, etc.
1901	188,683	460,763	962	16,497	5413
1906	205,182	477,114	1079	15,963	4905
1911	205,086	466,848	1094	16,139	5129
1916	201,345	436,077	1116	15,335	4807
1921	198,806	419,245	1059	14,211	4663
1926	202,533	398,923	1089	13,636	4566
1931	200,816	361,307	1092	12,909	5175

Notes:
1. For the years 1901–21 the figures for 'Sunday School Scholars' include a small percentage of scholars resident outside Great Britain.
2. In all other cases the figures refer to Great Britain.

Source: Minutes of the Conference of the Primitive Methodist Church.

TABLE 13.36
Salvation Army 1904–1967
William Booth founded the Salvation Army in 1865.

	Bandsmen	Senior local officers	Officers and employees	Corps, outposts and societies
1904	12,633	13,313	2783	1399
1906	13,031	16,090	2868	1431
1911	14,724	17,351	2555	1316
1916	15,523	20,695	3049	1244
1921	16,950	25,487	3302	1221
1926	—	—	—	—
1931	—	—	—	—
1936	—	—	4076	—
1941	—	—	—	—
1946	—	—	—	—
1951	—	—	—	—
1956	—	33,811	3682	1216
1961	—	31,916	3466	1227
1966	—	—	3327	1181
1967	—	—	3302	1158

Notes:
1. 'Bandsmen' are members who seek to further the work by music.
2. 'Local officers' are part-time workers with local authority.
3. 'Officers and employees' are full-time workers.
4. 'Corps, outposts and societies' are centres of work.
5. All figures refer to Great Britain.
6. John Highet, 'Scottish Religious Adherence', *Brit. J. Sociol.*, June 1953, 148, estimates Salvation Army membership in Great Britain at approximately 123,000.
7. The 1911 figure for 'Officers and employees' (above) is the 1912 figure, and the 1936 figure is a repetition of the 1935 figure. The 1961 figure for 'Senior local officers' is a repetition of the 1960 figure.

Source: Salvation Army Year Book.

TABLE 13.37

Seventh Day Adventist Church 1903–1968

The Seventh Day Adventist Church was founded in 1844.

	Members	Full-time workers	Churches
1903	1160	—	—
1906	1727	—	—
1911	2045	—	—
1916	2874	—	—
1921	3622	—	—
1926	4450	—	67
1931	4743	—	72
1936	5525	—	88
1941	5955	—	—
1946	6268	—	98
1951	6797	273	106
1956	8081	353	108
1961	9561	345	112
1966	10,884	630	122
1968	11,666	583	130

Notes:
1. The 1926 figure for 'Churches' (above) is the 1927 figure.
2. From 1964 'Full-time workers' include employees in Seventh Day Adventist Church-owned businesses.

Source: The Secretary of the British Union Conference of the Seventh Day Adventist Church.

TABLE 13.38
Society of Friends 1901–1968

The Society of Friends, also known as the Quakers, has its origins in the Rule for the Management of Meetings drawn up by George Fox in 1668, but it did not adopt its present title until about 1800.

	Members	Recorded Ministers	Elders	Meetings
1901	17,476	408	—	406
1906	18,677	424	—	421
1911	19,612	381	—	438
1916	19,218	288	—	397
1921	19,071	232	818	384
1926	19,147	—	858	380
1931	19,151	—	980	395
1936	19,257	—	1050	403
1941	20,153	—	1080	414
1946	20,661	—	1111	419
1951	20,839	—	1213	428
1956	21,454	—	1283	436
1961	21,170	—	1420	446
1966	21,007	—	1404	444
1968	20,909	—	1438	440

Note: 'Meetings' are congregations of members.
Sources: Extracts from the *Minutes of the London Yearly Meeting of Friends.*
    Whitaker's Almanack.

TABLE 13.39

Union of Welsh Independents 1900–1968

Welsh-speaking congregationalists formed the Union of Welsh Independents within the Congregational Union of England and Wales in 1871.

	Members	Sunday School Scholars	Ministers	Lay Preachers	Places of worship
1900	126,265	118,024	483	251	843
1926	137,299	94,341	—	248	941
1931	136,389	86,703	465	249	1004
1936	135,096	81,655	461	288	991
1941	133,235	76,199	458	231	1022
1946	128,577	56,777	455	177	1030
1951	123,563	52,096	429	167	973
1956	117,981	51,265	406	165	974
1961	106,357	—	—	—	810
1966	94,925	—	—	—	803
1968	92,990	—	—	—	775

Notes:
1. Separate figures are available for the Union of Welsh Independents from 1927 only. The figures for 1900 show the strength of those churches which belonged to the Union.
2. The figures for 1926 (above) are the 1927 figures, and the 1941 figures (above) are a repetition of the 1939 figures.
3. The figures for 1961, 1966 and 1968 have been supplied by the Secretary of the Union of Welsh Independents.

Sources: Congregational Yearbook of England and Wales; see Notes.

TABLE 13.40

United Free Church of Scotland 1901–1967

The United Free Church of Scotland was formed in 1900 by amalgamation of the Free Church of Scotland and the United Presbyterian Church. In 1929 the great majority of the Church united with the Church of Scotland. A 'continuance' has remained separate.

	Communicants	Sunday School Scholars	Ministers	Congregations
1901	—	244,339	1764	1672
1906	—	244,513	—	1623
1911	504,672	235,929	—	1545
1916	518,747	211,031	—	1516
1921	531,849	197,817	—	1482
1926	536,409	187,545	—	1449
1929	13,791	4227	37	106
1931	18,531	7645	51	120
1936	21,826	8823	61	126
1941	23,375	6773	78	124
1946	24,164	8217	87	122
1951	24,528	8749	84	120
1956	24,783	8281	84	117
1961	22,815	6999	87	111
1966	20,396	5537	81	101
1967	19,752	5538	83	100

Notes:
1. The figures for 1929 refer to the 'Continuance' of the United Free Church which refused to unite with the Church of Scotland.
2. The figures for 1936 (above) are a repetition of the 1935 figures.
Sources: Handbook of the United Free Church of Scotland.
    Whitaker's Almanack.

TABLE 13.41

United Methodist Church 1907–1931

The United Methodist Church was formed in 1907 from the amalgamation of the Bible Christians, Methodist New Connexion and United Methodist Free Churches, and merged into the Methodist Church in 1932.

	Members	Sunday School Scholars	Ministers	Local Preachers	Chapels, etc.
1907	148,988	315,723	833	6217	2360
1911	144,888	305,335	845	6187	2325
1916	141,336	279,348	789	6095	2287
1921	138,110	262,595	715	5764	2223
1926	142,151	246,832	714	4708	2221
1931	140,458	222,430	691	5214	2167

Note: These figures cover Great Britain only.
Source: Minutes of the Conference of the United Methodist Church.

TABLE 13.42
United Methodist Free Churches 1901, 1906 and 1907

The United Methodist Free Churches was formed in 1857 from seceders from the Wesleyan Methodist Church and merged into the United Methodist Church in 1907.

	Members	Sunday School Scholars	Ministers	Local Preachers	Chapels, etc.
1901	72,568	185,448	356	3392	1604
1906	80,323	194,862	370	2979	1331
1907	79,948	189,168	377	2983	1324

Note: These figures cover Great Britain only.
Source: Minutes of the Assembly of the United Methodist Free Churches.

TABLE 13.43
Wesleyan Methodist Church 1901–1931

The Wesleyan Methodist Church, founded by John Wesley, merged into the Methodist Church in 1932.

	Members	Sunday School Scholars	Ministers	Local Preachers	Chapels, etc.
1901	454,982	965,057	2238	18,323	8508
1906	498,464	1,013,391	2399	19,519	8475
1911	485,535	976,752	2478	19,715	8668
1916	473,673	893,527	2603	19,211	8504
1921	464,945	850,871	2474	18,409	8539
1926	495,113	830,318	2451	18,850	8591
1931	500,010	759,968	2568	18,844	8662

Source: Minutes of the Methodist Conference.

TABLE 13.44

Density of Religious Denominations Recruiting in England
1901–1967

The membership of the following religious organisations expressed as a percentage of the English population aged 15 years and over.

	Church of England (a)	Presbyterian Church of England
1901	9·481	0·380
1906	8·993	0·381
1911	9·772	0·370
1916	9·856	0·412
1921	8·766	0·331
1926	8·864	0·313
1931	8·095	0·295
1936	7·579	0·269
1941	6·448	0·238
1946	—	0·208
1951	5·814	0·213
1956	6·672	0·217
1961	3·746	0·212
1966	5·435	0·189
1967	—	0·185

Note: (a) In the case of the Church of England density is calculated on the basis of Easter Day communicants.

TABLE 13.45

**Density of Religious Denominations Recruiting in England and Wales
1901–1967**

The membership of the following religious organisations expressed as a percentage of the English and Welsh population aged 15 years and over.

	Baptist Church	Congregational Church
1901	1·616	1·848
1906	1·742	1·951
1911	1·571	1·812
1916	1·653	1·945
1921	1·381	—
1926	1·344	1·083(b)
1931	1·246	1·023
1936	1·161	0·936
1941	1·070(a)	0·865(c)
1946	0·975	0·730
1951	0·911	0·665
1956	0·876	0·634
1961	0·810	0·581
1966	0·717	0·529
1967	0·699	—

Notes:

(a) Based on 1940 Baptist data.

(b) Congregational figures for 1901–16 include the Union of Welsh Independents. From 1927 the Union published its own statistics. Expressed as a density figure, the combined strength of the Union of Welsh Independents and the Congregational Union of England and Wales was 1·552 in 1927 and 0·813 in 1966.

(c) Based on 1939 data. The publication of Congregational statistics was suspended during the war years.

TABLE 13.46

Density of Religious Denominations Recruiting Chiefly or only in Scotland 1901–1967

The membership of the following religious organisations expressed as a percentage of the Scottish population aged 15 years and over.

	Church of Scotland	United Free Church of Scotland	Congregational Union of Scotland	Episcopal Church of Scotland	Baptist Union of Scotland
1901	22·443	—	1·014	4·259	0·579
1906	22·498	—	1·185	4·287	0·675
1911	22·244	15·709	1·097	4·433	0·654
1916	21·814	15·790	1·069	4·382	0·643
1921	21·667	15·574	1·055	4·285	0·617
1926	21·615	15·216	1·067	4·046	0·655
1931	36.196(a)	0·528(b)	1.093	3.780	0·636
1936	34·350	0·617	1·069	3·436	0·630
1941	32·440	0·598	1·010	3·055	0·600
1946	31.923	0.604	0·903	2.747	0·534
1951	33.112	0·639	0·914	2·695	0·510
1956	34·369	0·647	0·916	2·762	0·525
1961	33·505	0·601	0·881	2·532	0·502
1966	32·060	0·538	0·767	2·455	0·474
1967	31·855	0·532	0·743	2·460	0·472

Notes:

(a) In 1929 the United Free Church of Scotland merged with the Church of Scotland.

(b) The figures for 1931 refer to the 'Continuance' which rejected Union with the Church of Scotland in 1929.

TABLE 13.47
Density of Religious Denominations Recruiting Chiefly or only in Wales 1901–1968

The membership of the following religious organisations expressed as a percentage of the Welsh population aged 15 years and over.

	Church in Wales(a)	Presbyterian Church of Wales	Union of Welsh Independents
1901	—	12·193	—
1906	—	12.923	—
1911	—	11·336	—
1916	—	10·685	—
1921	8·52	10·122	—
1926	9·431	9·695	6·966
1931	9·747	9·734	7·167
1936	10·333	9·567	7·140
1941	9·245	9·121	6·979
1946	—	9·814	6·821
1951	—	7·821	6·500
1956	—	7·335	5·881
1961	9·050	6·620	5·214
1966	7·967	5·745	4·548
1968	—	5·429	4·449

Note: (a) In the case of the Church in Wales density is calculated on the basis of Easter Communicants.

TABLE 13.48

Density of Religious Denominations Recruiting in Great Britain

The membership of the following religious organisations expressed as a percentage of the population of Great Britain aged 15 years and over.

	Wesleyan Methodist Church	Primitive Methodist Church	United Methodist Church	Methodist Church	Jehovah's Witnesses
1901	1·834	0·760	—	—	—
1906	1·869	0·770	0·543(a)	—	—
1911	1·715	0·724	0·526	—	—
1916	1·787	0·760	0·533	—	—
1921	1·508	0·645	0·448	—	—
1926	1·522	0·623	0·437	—	0·018(b)
1931	1·471	0·591	0·413	—	0·015
1932	—	—	—	2·463	—
1936	—	—	—	2·308	0·011
1941	—	—	—	2·098	0·026
1946	—	—	—	1·981	0·030
1951	—	—	—	1·953	0·061
1956	—	—	—	1·936	0·079
1961	—	—	—	1·833	0·114
1966	—	—	—	1·661	0·120
1967	—	—	—	—	0·122

Notes: The Wesleyan, Primitive and United Methodist Churches formed the Methodist Church in 1932.
(a) The 1907 figure.
(b) Based on 1927 data.

TABLE 13.49

Civil and Religious Marriages in Great Britain 1900 and 1967
(percentages)

	Civil	Religious	All
1901	14·8	85·2	100·0
1967	32·7	67·3	100·0

Source: Tables 13.3 and 13.6.

TABLE 13.50

Membership and Density of Major Denominations in Great Britain
1901 and 1966

	Membership 1901	Membership 1966	Column (2) as a percentage of column (1)	Density 1901	Density 1966
Church of England	1,945,000	1,899,000			
Episcopal Church in Scotland	46,922	53,585	99·2	8·5	5·3
Church in Wales	142,000	165,000			
Church of Scotland					
United Free Church of Scotland	1,165,000	1,254,204			
Presbyterian Church of England	78,024	66,187	106·2	5·0	3·3
Presbyterian Church of Wales	160,333	119,276	74·4	0·6	0·3
Methodists	777,690	678,776	87·3	3·1	1·7
Baptists	369,949	283,484	76·6	1·5	0·7
Congregationalists	433,622	328,692	75·8	1·7	0·8
All	5,118,540	4,848,204	94·7	20·4	12·1
Catholics	2,165,900	4,834,360	223·2	5·9	9·2

Notes:
1. 'Membership' is here taken as Easter Day communicants for the Church of England; Easter communicants for the Church in Wales; communicants for the Episcopal Church in Scotland, Church of Scotland, United Free Church of Scotland and Presbyterian Church of England; members for Methodists, Baptists and Congregationalists; and estimated Catholic population for Catholics.
2. Membership has been expressed as a percentage of *total* population to derive Catholic density, and as a percentage of population *age 15 and over* to derive densities of other denominations.
3. Church in Wales Easter communicants for 1901 have been estimated on the basis of Church of England figures.
4. Church of Scotland and United Free Church of Scotland communicants for 1901 have been estimated at 665,000 and 500,000 respectively. In 1966 the Church of Scotland had 1,233,808 communicants and the United Free Church of Scotland 20,396 communicants.
5. The figure for Methodist membership for 1901 is the sum of the membership of all the Methodist churches which constituted the union of 1932.
6. Figures for Congregational membership include membership of the churches which form the Union of Welsh Independents, estimated at 103,000 in 1966.
7. England and Wales estimated Catholic population for 1901 has been calculated, on the basis of marriage figures, at 1,733,000.

Sources: Tables 13.6 to 13.48 *passim.*

TABLE 13.51

Population of Ireland by Claimed Religious Adherence, 1901 and 1961

	Catholics	Church of Ireland	Presby-terians	Methodists	Others
1901	74·2	13·0	9·9	1·4	1·5
1961	74·7	10·6	10·2	1·9	2·6

Note: Between 1901 and 1961 only the 'Methodist' and 'Others' categories in the censuses show absolute increases.

Sources: Tables 13.1 and 13.2.

14 Immigration

JULIET CHEETHAM

Immigrants to the United Kingdom can be divided into five major groups. Some are citizens of the U.K. and colonies or of the Commonwealth, Dependencies and Protectorates. Others are 'aliens', i.e. persons of foreign nationality. In this chapter an immigrant is taken to be anyone born outside the British Isles of whatever nationality and resident (i.e. not a visitor in the terms of the Census) in England and Wales.

At different times during this century different groups of immigrants have been the focus of interest. For example, in the Censuses of 1901 and 1911, special efforts were made to enumerate accurately the large number of foreign-born Jews who had emigrated to the U.K. during the last part of the nineteenth century because of political and economic pressure in their native countries. Census forms were printed in Yiddish and families visited by members of a 'Committee of Ladies and Gentlemen' whose task it was to explain the aim of the Census and how forms should be completed.

Since the early nineteen-sixties the immigrant group which has attracted most attention has been that from the 'new Commonwealth' (a phrase first used in the 1966 Sample Census), i.e. immigrants from India, Pakistan, the West Indies, Africa (excluding the Republic of South Africa), Malta and Cyprus. From about 1955 there was increasing concern about the number of coloured immigrants in the U.K. Not until the Commonwealth Immigrants Act 1962 are there any detailed and accurate statistics dealing with immigrants from the Commonwealth.[1] However, there are some fairly reliable estimates for the numbers from the new Commonwealth in the immediately preceding years.

The five immigrant groups to be discussed are:
(1) Immigrants from the old Commonwealth (e.g. Australia, New Zealand and Canada);
(2) Immigrants from the new Commonwealth (e.g. India, Pakistan and the West Indies);
(3) Immigrants from Ireland;

[1] *Commonwealth Immigrants Acts 1962 and 1968: Statistics* (HMSO 1962–).

(4) Jewish Immigrants;
(5) Alien Immigrants.
Most of the information regarding immigrants can be obtained from the National Census. Other useful sources are listed in footnotes throughout this chapter.

GENERAL TRENDS

The Registrar-General points out that exact comparison between the Census for different years is not possible because of the varying methods of classifying some information. For example, in 1911, 1921 and 1931 visitors to the U.K. were included in the figures for different countries of birth but not in 1951 and 1961. In 1931, if nationality or birthplace were not stated, they were assigned according to the other information in the Census return. This was not the practice in 1951 and in the following Census, when a separate category was kept for 'birthplace not stated'. However, given these and other reservations, the Registrar-General does not consider comparisons to be invalid as any discrepancies will be small.

Table 14.1 indicates that approximately 96 per cent of the total population were born in England and Wales in the years 1901–31. This proportion decreased to 94 per cent and 93 per cent in 1951 and 1961, and it should be noted that all children of immigrants, whether British subjects or aliens, are classified as British subjects if born in the U.K. No separate records are kept of these children in the Census except for the 1961 Census (Commonwealth Immigrants in Conurbations) and the 1966 10 per cent Sample Census which made a special study of the children of immigrants from the new Commonwealth. In the 1971 Census the birthplace of *all* parents was recorded. The number of immigrants born in the British Commonwealth, Colonies and Protectorates and Dependencies increased steadily from 418 per 100,000 in 1901 to 1489 in 1961 and 1999 in 1966. The number of alien immigrants fluctuates with the world political situation: the two world wars were particularly influential. The smallest number of aliens is recorded between the two wars (602 and 449 per 100,000, compared with 762 in 1901). However, this number rose sharply in 1951 and 1961 with a particularly large increase in the number of naturalised British subjects, 412 per 100,000 in 1951 compared with 161 per 100,000 in 1931. The number of immigrants from Ireland declined steadily between 1901 and 1931 but increased sharply in 1951 and 1961. The reasons for these fluctuations in different groups will be discussed in the appropriate sections.

1. IMMIGRATION FROM THE OLD COMMONWEALTH (PRIMARILY
    AUSTRALIA, NEW ZEALAND AND CANADA)

Until the 1961 census no distinction was made between the old and new
Commonwealth, and the words 'old' and 'new' were not used until the
1966 10 per cent Sample Census. This division was adopted to give
some indication of the numbers of Commonwealth citizens resident in
the U.K. who might reasonably be expected to be white and those who
might be coloured. The division into old and new Commonwealth does
not, of course, give exact numbers of white and coloured immigrants.
Because of British colonial interests it is reasonable to suppose that a
number of white people (i.e. citizens of the U.K. and colonies) will be
among those born in a new Commonwealth country who emigrate to
the U.K. However, with the passage of time this number (who may
represent, for example, staff of the Indian Army or British trading
interests) will decline (Table 14.3).

Table 14.2 shows a steady increase in the number of residents of
England and Wales born in Commonwealth countries, colonies, Dependencies and Protectorates. The early reports of the Registrar-General
attribute this increase to improved quick and cheap communications
between the Commonwealth countries and the mother country. The
very marked increase in 1951, 1961 and 1966 can be explained by

  (a) the return to the U.K. of people of British nationality when a
      number of Commonwealth countries attained independent status,
      e.g. India and Pakistan;
  (b) the demand for labour, skilled and unskilled in the U.K. and the
      coincidence of this with economic hardship in new Common-
      wealth countries;
  (c) the reunion between families and heads of households from the
      new Commonwealth who have settled in the U.K.

Both (b) and (c) will be discussed more fully in the next section.

It is fair to assume that between 1901 and 1951 the great majority
of those resident in England and Wales but born in the Commonwealth
were either heads of households who had returned to the mother country
after working abroad, or their dependants. The Census gives no information about the occupations of British subjects born abroad until 1961
and 1966, when the occupations of immigrants from the new Commonwealth in 1961 and both the old and new Commonwealth in 1966 were
recorded. Before then the socio-economic background of the old
Commonwealth immigrants is indicated only by their areas of settlement in the U.K. A large proportion are recorded as living in the
London boroughs of Kensington, Westminster and St. Marylebone.
Outside London many settled in the home counties, the seaside resorts

and watering-places, and the university city of Oxford. It is in these areas that large numbers of professional and retired professional people congregated.

From 1901 to 1961 by far the largest number of immigrants came from India. In 1901 and 1911 41 per cent. of all residents of England and Wales born in Commonwealth countries were born in India. Only after 1961 did the number of immigrants from the West Indies exceed those from India.

Until the early nineteen-fifties the vast majority of immigrants from the new Commonwealth were white, and before the mid-nineteen-fifties it is artificial to make any distinction between the old and new Commonwealth. Eversley and Sukdeo[1] have estimated that even from the new Commonwealth countries a large number of white persons were included in the enumerated population of Indian and Pakistani origin (Table 14.3). In 1951 approximately two-thirds of the population of Indian and Pakistani origin were white. In 1961 the proportion of white persons in the population of Indian and Pakistani origin was slightly more than half, and slightly less than one-quarter respectively, and in 1966 rather less than one-third of the population of Indian origin was white compared with a far smaller proportion of those of Pakistani origin (approximately seven per cent).

The Commonwealth Immigrants Acts of 1962 and 1968 provide for the control of immigration into the U.K. of Commonwealth citizens. After the passing of these acts it was possible for detailed statistics to be kept about the country of origin and status (e.g. head of household, dependant, Department of Employment and Productivity voucher holder, etc.) of Commonwealth immigrants. The Home Office *Commonwealth Immigrants Acts 1962 and 1968: Statistics*, published annually from 1962, provide information about the intentions of immigrants (e.g. whether they are visitors expecting to stay less than three months, or whether they hold work vouchers and intend to settle, at least temporarily, in the U.K.). These statistics, together with information from the 1966 Sample Census, give a clearer picture of numbers and occupations of Commonwealth immigrants than has existed before.

Briefly, under the acts entry is restricted to

(a) holders of current employment vouchers issued by the Department of Employment and Productivity. There are three types of voucher: (A) vouchers for those who have been offered definite jobs; (B) for those with certain defined skills (usually professional); and (C) for immigrant workers with no definite job and no special skills. From 1964 this last category was discontinued. In

[1] D. Eversley and F. Sukdeo, *The Dependants of the Coloured Population of England and Wales* (O.U.P. for Institute of Race Relations 1969).

1965 the issue of A and B vouchers was restricted to 8500 annually.

(b) students attending full-time or substantial part-time courses;
(c) entrants who can support themselves and their dependants without working in the U.K.;
(d) members of the armed forces serving in the U.K.;
(e) the wife of a Commonwealth citizen who has satisfied one of these conditions and their children if they accompany his wife or come to join both parents.[1]

The Home Office *Commonwealth Immigrants Acts 1962 and 1968: Statistics* indicate that the vast majority of citizens of the old Commonwealth countries whose entry to the U.K. is recorded at a port of entry are either visitors for three months or less, in transit to another country or returning home after a temporary absence abroad. Few hold Department of Employment and Productivity vouchers and those who do, like immigrants from the new Commonwealth, will either be coming to specific employment in the U.K. or possess certain professional skills, e.g. as doctors, teachers or engineers (Table 14.4).

The number of voucher holders amongst the immigrants from the old Commonwealth decreased by more than a half in 1966. No clear reason can be given for this apart from the fixing of the number of A and B vouchers in 1965. However, these vouchers are not all taken up. The number of dependants remained static until 1966 and 1967 when there were sharp increases. The numbers dropped again in 1968 and 1969. However, the number of immigrants from the old Commonwealth is a small proportion of the immigrants from the whole Commonwealth, the great majority of whom are dependants of voucher holders from the new Commonwealth.

Table 14.5 gives some indication of the socio-economic background of the old as opposed to the new Commonwealth immigrants. A large percentage of immigrants from the old Commonwealth occupy managerial and professional positions. This is partly because of the number of people with a professional background who returned to the U.K. after Commonwealth countries gained independence and partly because very few immigrants from the new as opposed to the old Commonwealth came to the U.K. with C vouchers (for people without defined skills and without any definite jobs arranged before their arrival). Although immigrant voucher holders from both the old and new Commonwealth

---

[1] The 1971 Immigration Bill proposes substantial alterations to these conditions. For example, Commonwealth citizens wishing to come to the U.K. will need a work permit for a specific job in a specific place for a fixed period; dependants will need entry certificates and will only be admitted if the head of the household is able to support them. Right of entry to the U.K. is restricted to 'patrials', i.e. to those who have direct personal or ancestral links with the U.K.

have nearly all been skilled or professional people since 1965, this is unlikely to affect the total picture greatly since their numbers are very small and very large numbers of unskilled workers from the new Commonwealth came to the U.K. before 1964.

2. IMMIGRATION FROM THE NEW COMMONWEALTH – BRITISH WEST INDIES, INDIA, PAKISTAN, BRITISH COMMONWEALTH IN AFRICA (EXCLUDING THE REPUBLIC OF SOUTH AFRICA), BRITISH COMMONWEALTH IN THE FAR EAST, MALTA AND CYPRUS

Until the late nineteen-fifties little attention had been given to the number of coloured immigrants from the new Commonwealth. Their numbers were largely unrecorded. Most of the studies of coloured communities concentrated on their settlement in large towns, particularly seaports, where the coloured immigrants were mainly traders and seamen. However, after World War II a number of coloured servicemen settled in the U.K. Estimates of numbers depended on local surveys and could give no accurate picture of overall numbers of coloured immigrants and their families resident in the U.K. The most accurate estimates were for the numbers of West Indians coming to the U.K. since records of their arrival were kept in some detail from 1956 by the Migrant Services Division of the Commission in the U.K. for the West Indies, British Guiana and British Honduras. Further difficulties confronted research workers in the nineteen-fifties and early nineteen-sixties in that few local authorities or welfare agencies kept records of their contacts with coloured people. There was active until very recently a belief that to count coloured people could be interpreted as discrimination against them. Although most local authorities do now keep some records of their work with coloured people, whether they are immigrants or not, the only government department bound to keep records, in this case of the ethnic origin of schoolchildren, is the Department of Education and Science.

In December 1958 the estimated coloured population from the Commonwealth was 210,000; West Indians 115,000, West Africans 25,000, Indians and Pakistanis 55,000, other coloured Commonwealth citizens 15,000.[1] Some writers have disagreed with these figures, giving estimates ranging from 169,000 to 250,000.[2] These estimates are based

[1] Figures given by Joint Under Secretary of State for Home Office in House of Commons, 5 December 1958. *Hansard*, Col. 1580-1.

[2] For a fuller discussion of numbers see:
  M. Banton, *White and Coloured* (O.U.P. 1959).
  J. A. G. Griffiths, *Coloured Immigrants in Britain* (O.U.P. 1960).
  R. Glass, *Newcomers – West Indians in London* (Allen & Unwin 1960).

on information gained from, amongst other sources, government departments, police, employment exchanges, officials and voluntary welfare societies and leaders of the immigrant communities. The Census gives the numbers of immigrants in the U.K. born in the new Commonwealth but as has already been indicated, a large number of these are white. Before 1961 no attempts were made via the Census to estimate the total coloured population in the U.K., i.e. both immigrants and their children, born in the British Isles. However, since 1961 immigration policies and public concern about them has led to detailed compilation of statistics relating to the coloured population.

The most important factor influencing immigration into the U.K. after World War II was the shortage of labour not, as widely believed, the poor conditions in the sending countries. Peach, in a detailed study of West Indian migration 1955–61, has demonstrated that the trends in migration were governed by factors external to the West Indies, notably the demand for labour in the U.K. A correlation was found between rises in labour demand in the U.K. and rises in the rate of migration. Adverse conditions in the West Indies should be considered as a necessary but not a sufficient factor in migration – 'they [adverse conditions] allow migration to take place, they do not cause it'.[1]

This pattern of migration from the new Commonwealth altered completely with the threat from 1960 of immigration control. In eighteen months the net inflow of immigrants from the Commonwealth was greater than that for the previous five years (Table 14.6).

Table 14.6 shows that immigration from the new Commonwealth reached a peak in 1961 because of the large numbers entering the U.K. before the restrictions on immigration imposed from 1st July 1962. Total numbers for 1963, 1964 and 1965 remained fairly static; as in the most recent years, the majority of immigrants during this period were dependants. The number of voucher holders dropped very significantly in 1964 and 1966 because of changes in the number of vouchers issued. In 1964 the issue of C vouchers (for immigrants with no definite skills and no definite job in the U.K.) ended and in 1965 a ceiling was imposed on the total number of work vouchers to be issued annually. The number was fixed at 8500 of which 1000 are reserved for immigrants from Malta. In 1966 there was a sharp decrease in the number of voucher holders entering the U.K. from the new Commonwealth and these numbers have continued to decrease steadily with only 3000 being

S. Patterson, *Dark Strangers* (Tavistock Publications 1963).

R. Desai, *Indian Immigrants in Britain* (O.U.P. for Institute of Race Relations 1963).

[1] G. C. K. Peach, *West Indian Migration to Britain* (O.U.P. for Institute of Race Relations 1968) p. 92.

admitted in 1970. At no stage have all the vouchers issued been taken up. However, the number of dependants entering the U.K. is relatively high and from 1966 the ratio of voucher holders to dependants is roughly 1 : 10. This ratio decreased to 1 : 7 in 1970.

The Census gives figures for those born in Commonwealth countries and resident in the U.K. However, these include large numbers of white people born in the Commonwealth (see Table 14.3 and previous section). Taking these figures into account, Eversley and Sukdeo[1] have estimated that the coloured immigrant population (including Cypriots and Maltese) of England and Wales increased fourfold between 1951 and 1961 from 103,100 to 414,700. There were further substantial increases between 1961 and 1966 (Table 14.7).

The tension that has surrounded some of the immigration of coloured people into the U.K. accounts for the interest in and estimation of the total coloured population, immigrant and British-born, in the U.K., rather than overall numbers of immigrants. E. J. B. Rose, formerly the Director of the Survey of Race Relations, calculated[2] that towards the end of 1965 there were approximately 850,000 coloured Commonwealth citizens in the U.K. including approximately 200,000 children up to school-leaving age. Of these about three-quarters were born in Britain and about 100,000 were under five. However, the most authoritative data are provided by the 1966 10 per cent Sample Census although there are certain problems in interpreting it. The General Register Office has said that the total national figures were underestimated by 1·8 per cent but under-enumeration in the conurbations, where two-thirds of Commonwealth immigrants live, was higher. Eversley and Sukdeo[3] have estimated that for the country as a whole under-enumeration was as follows: Jamaica 10·2 per cent. Rest of Caribbean 12·2 per cent India 4·6 per cent Pakistan 29·5 per cent. Taking into account Census under-enumeration the Institute of Race Relations Survey of Race Relations in Britain[4] has estimated that in England and Wales in mid-1966 Commonwealth immigrants and coloured British-born totalled 924,000, slightly less than 2 per cent of the total population of England and Wales (47,135,510). After estimating birth and net arrivals since then the suggested totals for mid-1968 and 1969 are 1,113,000 and 1,185,000 respectively. The main coloured groups in 1966 were

[1] D. Eversley and F. Sukdeo, op. cit., p. 9.
[2] Commonwealth Journal (Oct. 1965) p. 225.
[3] Eversley and Sukdeo, op. cit.
[4] E. J. B. Rose and associates, Colour and Citizenship: a Report on British Race Relations (O.U.P. for Institute of Race Relations 1969), summarised in Colour and Immigration in the U.K., Institute of Race Relations Facts Paper, 1969.

Caribbean   454,100
India   223,600
Pakistan   119,700

—————

797,400

(these figures exclude white people born in India and Pakistan). Since it is these three groups of immigrants which form the great majority of all immigrants from the new Commonwealth, most statistics given in this chapter will take into account these numbers and not those of other minority groups.

In a recent study of immigration to Bedford, Brown estimates that the under-enumeration of certain immigrant groups, notably Pakistanis, is very much greater than either the Registrar-General or Eversley and Sukdeo had anticipated. For example, Brown found that, although the 1966 Sample Census gave the number of Pakistanis in Bedford as 390, in the same year the Borough Public Health Department had registered 548 Pakistanis living in multi-occupation alone. From this Brown estimates that the probable number of Pakistanis in Bedford in 1966 was between 800 and 900. Overall Brown thinks that in 1966 Commonwealth immigrants made up nearly 7 per cent of the total population of Bedford or approximately 60 per cent more than the Registrar General's estimate of 4·6 per cent. However, it should be remembered that at the Census some immigrant groups are far more difficult to enumerate accurately than others. Single men living in houses given over to multi-occupation are sometimes unaware of the Census or not available to fill in questionnaires as they are engaged in night shift work. In addition some landlords and tenants may be reluctant to fill in Census forms as they fear that the information given may lead to enquiries or prosecutions relating to overcrowding. In 1966 a large number of Pakistanis who were separated from their families could have been included in this group. It is unlikely that similar difficulties over enumeration are found with those immigrants who are living in the U.K. with their families, and so the figures in the Census which relate to them will be more accurate. For a fuller discussion see J. Brown, *The Unmelting Pot* (Macmillan 1970), pp. 231–5.

The 1966 Sample Census shows that 2,478,060 immigrants lived in England and Wales or 5·26 per cent; 942,000 were born in the Commonwealth and of these 155,310 came from the old Commonwealth. There were also 837,150 foreign-born people resident in England and Wales and 698,600 born in Eire. Immigrants from the new Commonwealth, numbering 877,000, most of whom will be coloured, represented therefore in 1966 rather less than one-third of all immigrants.

AREAS OF SETTLEMENT

Coloured immigrants have clustered in the large conurbations, particularly in London and the South East, and in towns where there has been a demand for unskilled labour in the heavy or less attractive industries, e.g. to the metal manufacturing industries in the West Midlands and the textile industries in the North West. Peach has shown that West Indian migrants were 'drawn to those regions which, in spite of demand for labour, have not been able to attract much net population from other parts of the country. In towns they are proportionally twice as numerous in those that lost population between 1951 and 1961 as in those which increased. They have gone to the depopulating urban cores of expanding industrial regions.'[1] In other words, West Indian immigrants and others (of whom no such detailed study has been made) went in most cases to areas of expanding industry but falling population. (Table 14.8 illustrates the numbers and percentages of coloured immigrants (three main groups) in the U.K. in regions and conurbations.) The London borough with the highest percentage of immigrants from the new Commonwealth is Brent with 7·4, followed by Hackney with 7·1 and Lambeth 6·7. The boroughs with the lowest percentage are Havering (0·5), Barking (0·7) and Bromley (0·9). Several of the London boroughs have substantial numbers of immigrants from Cyprus, e.g. Islington with 10,300, Camden with 3690 and Southwark with 3410. In the West Midlands the towns having the highest percentage of immigrants are Wolverhampton (4·8), Leamington Spa (4·5) and Birmingham (4·2). In Yorkshire the towns with the highest percentages are Bradford (4·2) and Huddersfield (4·1). The town with the highest percentage of immigrants from the new Commonwealth is High Wycombe with 4·9.[2]

Some studies of the distribution of Commonwealth immigrants within boroughs at the 1961 Sample Census have been made,[3] but no work has been published on changes since 1961 and the under-enumeration of the 1966 Sample Census does not give a very reliable basis for analysis. Peach[4] suggests that in 1961 there were possibly a few enumeration districts in which coloured people – including immigrants and British-born – formed a majority and that since then they may have come to form a majority in a few other districts. He argues that West Indians

[1] G. C. K. Peach, *op. cit.*, p. 82.

[2] Details for many other towns can be found in Institute of Race Relations Facts Paper, 1969 and 1970–1.

[3] R. Glass and J. Westergaard, *London's Housing Needs: Statement of Evidence to the Committee on Housing in Greater London* (Centre for Urban Studies 1965). P. Jones, *The Segregation of Immigrant Communities in the City of Birmingham 1961* (University of Hull publications 1967).

[4] G. C. K. Peach, *op. cit.*

have become more and not less concentrated largely due to 'negative forces preventing dispersal', e.g. racial discrimination in the property market. However, Eversley[1] has argued that there is increasing dispersal from the original centres of immigration. For example, the proportion of all Jamaicans who lived in the six conurbations in 1961 declined by 10·8 per cent in 1966, and the proportion of Pakistanis by 8·4 per cent. It is not accurate to describe any district in the U.K. as a ghetto. A preliminary examination of 1966 Sample Census data for Greater London shows that in only eight of the 100 wards were 20 per cent. or more of the population born in the new Commonwealth: the highest single concentration was 30·8 per cent. Even allowing for under-enumeration and for children born in the U.K. it is unlikely that there was any ward in Greater London in 1966 with more than half its population coloured.

DEPENDANTS OF COMMONWEALTH IMMIGRANTS

Before 1962 the number of women and children among the total number of immigrants was not known. However, there are the records kept by the Migrant Services Division for immigrants from the Caribbean and these indicate that between 1955 and 1961 the numbers of men and of women and children together were fairly similar.[2] However, since 1964 the large majority of immigrants from the new Commonwealth are wives and children coming to join the head of a household already settled in the U.K., of whom many came to 'beat the ban' in 1962. It is reasonable to assume that many of these immigrants were heads of households who were determined to enter the U.K. before restriction on immigration but who were not able to bring their families with them at that stage. The Home Office has estimated that nearly half the dependants arriving in 1968 came to join men who settled in the U.K. before 1965. Sixteen per cent are joining men who settled in Britain before control was introduced in 1962.[3] Since the number of voucher holders entering the U.K. is now very small, if immigration policy does not alter, the number of dependants will fall as families are reunited or their children become too old (16+) to be eligible to join their parents in the U.K. The numbers for 1969 already show a very significant decrease (Table 14·4).

Of the total number of child dependents of immigrants from the new Commonwealth, a large and increasing number were born in the U.K. and are therefore not immigrants. They do however belong to the total

[1] See Institute of Race Relations Facts Paper, 1969, *op. cit.*, pp. 11–12, and D. Eversley and F. Sukdeo, *op. cit.*

[2] S. Patterson, *op. cit.*

[3] Statement by Mr Callaghan in Expiring Laws and Continuance Debate, *Hansard*, 13 Nov. 1968, col. 439.

coloured population in the U.K. and it is this group, rather than coloured immigrants, that is the focus of interest and concern.

The Survey of Race Relations has estimated that in 1966 there were about 200,000 coloured children born to parents from India, Pakistan, Ceylon, Jamaica, the rest of the Caribbean and British West Africa.[1] With the exception of the Pakistani group, the majority of children living in immigrant households were born in Britain (Table 14·9). Over 80 per cent of children in Jamaican households and over 66 per cent of children in Indian households were born in Britain.

Compared with the total population coloured immigrants are youthful. The Survey of Race Relations has estimated that in 1966 34 per cent of all coloured immigrants and their British-born children were under 15; 55 per cent were aged between 15 and 45 and only 11 per cent were over 45. The age distribution for the total population is 23 per cent under 15; 39 per cent 15–45 and 38 per cent over 45 (Table 14.10).

Some of the implications of a population group with this age structure are that a substantial number will be economically active and that there will be a relatively large number of children born to immigrant women since a large proportion in the U.K. are in the 15–44 age group.[2] This also means that immigrants and their dependants will make greater demands on maternity and child welfare services (including education) than they will on other social services.[3]

The Department of Education and Science defines an 'immigrant' pupil as a child born outside the British Isles who has come to the U.K. to join parents or guardians whose country of origin was abroad or as one who was born in the U.K. to parents whose countries of origin were abroad and who came to the U.K. up to 10 years before the date to which the figures apply. Children from the Republic of Ireland are excluded.[4] On this basis the Department of Education and Science

[1] E. J. B. Rose et al., op. cit.

[2] For a full discussion of the growth of the coloured population see D. Eversley and F. Sukdeo, op. cit., and E. J. B. Rose and associates, op. cit., chap. 30.

[3] See K. Jones, 'Immigrants and the Social Services', National Institute of Economic and Social Research, Economic Review, August 1964, and K. Jones and A. D. Smith, The Economic Import of Commonwealth Immigration (C.U.P. 1970).

[4] Brown has pointed out that, in Bedford at least, many teachers are unhappy with the definition, as they think it does not realistically take into account the difficulties experienced by children whose parents had been in the U.K. longer than 10 years. They believe that to abide strictly by it would mislead the public and give a false impression of the educational needs of those children whose parents have been in the U.K. more than 10 years. They also think that the collection of data in accordance with the official definition is cumbersome and time-consuming, if not impossible. Brown thinks that for these reasons many teachers use their own much more flexible definition of an 'immigrant' pupil when making their returns to the Department of

estimate that in 1967 immigrant pupils represented 2·5 per cent. of the total number of school children in England and Wales. However, since immigrants from the new Commonwealth are concentrated in certain areas, some schools have a much higher proportion. It is estimated that in those schools with 10 or more immigrant pupils, they represent 13·6 per cent of the total numbers. In 1967, 362 schools had 15–20 per cent of immigrant pupils and 861 had over 20 per cent. In 345 schools immigrants represented more than 33 per cent of all pupils. The age structure of the immigrant population (Tables 14·9 and 14·10) means that the largest number of immigrant pupils are in the younger age group (5–9) and that overall the numbers will increase significantly in the next decade.[1]

Estimates for the growth of the coloured population vary. The Economist Intelligence Unit made an estimate in August 1964 of 3·2 million coloured people in Britain in 2002 in a total population of 72·6 million, a proportion of 4·4 per cent. In June 1967 as a result of a Parliamentary question the Ministry of Health estimated a coloured population of 3·5 million in 1985. Both these estimates assume a birth-rate of 25 per 1000 and this high figure has been questioned by Eversley and Sukdeo, who also questioned the assumptions made in these two estimates of the continued high rate of immigration, particularly of dependants. E. J. B. Rose and associates, analysing material available from the 1966 Sample Census and other surveys, estimate a coloured population in 1986 of between 2 and 2¼ million.[2]

OCCUPATIONS

At the 1961 Census about two-thirds of all immigrants from the Commonwealth were economically active compared with less than half the total population. The age structure of the immigrants from the new Commonwealth allows for practically no retired people. In London,

Education and Science. It is possible, therefore, that the official statistics, while being inaccurate according to the official definition, do give a true impression of the number of children of all immigrant parents whether or not they come to the U.K. 10 or more years previously. However, as Brown points out, the uncertainty over the definition of an 'immigrant' pupil can lead to serious fluctuations in the returns made to the Department of Education and Science, as numbers will vary according to the way the teachers collecting the data interpret them. In 1970 the D.E.S. announced that the basis on which these statistics are collected would be changed in 1972. (J. Brown, *op. cit.*, pp. 232–5.)

[1] *Statistics of Education* (HMSO 1967) and Department of Education and Science: Evidence to Select Committee on Immigration and Race Relations 13 February 1969. The D.E.S. provisional estimates of the total number of immigrant pupils in 1969 was 249,664 or 3·2 per cent. of all pupils.

[2] E. J. B. Rose *et al.*, *op. cit.*, chap. 30, and Institute of Race Relations Facts Paper, 1969, pp. 36–7.

Davison[1] shows that, while 66 per cent of men and 39 per cent of women born in England and Wales were economically active, the figures for immigrants from the new Commonwealth were 88 per cent of men and 62 per cent of women born in Jamaica, 79 per cent of men and 48 per cent of women born in India and 76 per cent of men and 31 per cent of women born in Pakistan.

Special tabulations of the 1966 Sample Census show the occupations of workers from the Commonwealth in London and the Midlands. The largest proportions are found in the manufacturing industries, particularly engineering and allied trades, and in general labouring jobs. The next largest groups are transport workers.[2]

The great majority of immigrant voucher holders from the new Commonwealth since 1965 have been either skilled or professional people. Amongst the professions doctors form the largest single group, followed by teachers. Since September 1964 the only unskilled workers admitted have been coming to definite jobs in the U.K. However, before the imposition of controls in 1962 large numbers of those intending to work in the U.K. were unskilled, many of them coming from rural areas, especially those immigrants from India and Pakistan. Until their cessation in 1964 C vouchers for unskilled workers were by far the most frequently issued. For example, in 1962 and 1963 33,150 C vouchers were issued to Indians, Pakistanis and West Indians compared with 5560 A vouchers and 10,410 B vouchers.[3] Table 14·5 shows that, compared with the total population immigrants from the new Commonwealth, particularly males from Pakistan and the Caribbean, are over-represented in the unskilled manual category. Practically none have attained positions as foremen and supervisors, and only immigrants from India and Pakistan are significantly represented in the employer, manager and professional worker categories. However, since this table includes white immigrants born in the new Commonwealth, of whom large numbers came from India and Pakistan (Table 14.3), these figures do not give an entirely accurate picture of the employment status of coloured immigrants. Nonetheless, it is evident that immigrants from the new Commonwealth are distributed most unevenly in the different socio-economic groups with concentrations in the lowest groups and in certain categories, such as intermediate non-manual, which include nurses. It is interesting to compare this position with that of immigrants from Ireland, who, although being over-represented in certain groups, are also significantly represented in all of them. This wider distribution reflects a longer-established immigration

---

[1] R. B. Davison, *Black British* (O.U.P. for Institute of Race Relations 1966), chap. 4.
[2] Institute of Race Relations Facts Paper, 1969, *op. cit.*, pp. 21–4.
[3] Figures from *Commonwealth Immigrants Act, 1962, Statistics*.

from Ireland as well as the greater variety of jobs available to the Irish.

It is a familiar pattern for the newest immigrant group to a country to fill unskilled and unattractive jobs which are often poorly paid. The immigrants from the new Commonwealth are no exception. However, after some years in their adopted country it is usual for immigrants and certainly their children, as a result of promotion, education and increased familiarity with a new country, to be spread more widely among the occupations. It is not yet clear whether this will be the pattern in the U.K. for immigrants from the new Commonwealth and their dependants. The P.E.P. Report[1] draws attention to widespread discrimination against coloured immigrants in employment and housing (both letting and purchase) as well as other areas. Whether coloured people will achieve a normal distribution among the occupations will depend partly on the success of the Race Relations Acts 1965 and 1968, which prohibit discrimination on the grounds of colour, race, ethnic or national origins in the supply of goods, facilities and services, housing and employment. The pattern will become clearer in the next ten years and during that time public attention will be focused on the numbers and way of life of coloured immigrants and their dependants in the U.K. It is worth noting finally that, especially in political controversy, statistics of the coloured population are frequently misinterpreted.

3. IMMIGRATION FROM IRELAND

Emigration from Ireland has been heavy for the last two centuries. Early in the eighteenth century 3000–4000 people were annually leaving Ireland for America and the West Indies and between 1820 and 1910 nearly five million people left Ireland for destinations overseas, excluding the U.K. The decline in the standard of living in Ireland in the eighteenth and nineteenth centuries, reaching a peak with the famine of 1846 and 1847, the growth of the population and fears of religious and political persecution were the main factors prompting emigration and these coincided with huge demands for manpower in the U.S.A. and U.K. Jackson[2] notes that, at the height of the exodus in the 1880s, two-thirds of the persons born in Ireland were living outside the country. The great majority in the nineteenth century emigrated to the United States either directly or via the U.K. However, geographical proximity and easy travel between the countries as well as the constant demand for labour in her expanding industries made the U.K. an acceptable alternative either to those who could not afford the more

[1] P.E.P., *Racial Discrimination in Britain* (April 1967).
[2] J. A. Jackson, *The Irish in Britain* (Routledge 1963), p. 5.

expensive transatlantic fares or to those who saw their migration as less permanent and who wished to return to Ireland if their own prosperity, or the prosperity of their country, improved.

Irish migrants to the U.K. during the nineteenth century also included a substantial number who had hoped to make the United States their ultimate destination but who could not raise the fare. However, since the middle of this century the U.K. has become the main destination for Irish emigrants. Although emigration to the United States continues, the quota allowed to Irish citizens has not been filled for several years. Continued freedom of access to the U.K. adds to its attraction as a destination for Irish emigrants and while in 1890 the number of Irish-born in the U.K. was only one-third of the number in the U.S.A., there are now more Irish-born in the U.K. than in the United States.[1]

Much of Irish immigration to this country has been temporary in that it has always included large numbers of seasonal workers, navvies and harvesters. This migration is at its height during the spring and summer. Undoubtedly there are also many Irish who come to the U.K. as a 'migratory experiment' returning home after brief periods. Although most large towns have had Irish communities since the mid-nineteenth century, the composition of these communities may change quite rapidly with the to and fro movement between the U.K. and Ireland. One effect of this frequent contact with the homeland has been for Irish communities in the U.K. to maintain their identity as Irish over long periods. However, this does not mean that the majority of Irish immigrants have remained separate economically, socially or culturally from the population of the U.K.

A number of factors make it very difficult to estimate accurately the size of the Irish population in the U.K. Sources of information – for example, the Census and the records of passenger movement kept by the Authorities in the Republic of Ireland – can indicate trends but only within a wide margin of error. The transitory nature of much Irish migration makes Census records unreliable since they include numbers of Irish who are intending in the near future either to return to Ireland or to continue their migration to the United States or the new Commonwealth countries. Census records are also unreliable in that the children of Irish migrants, born in this country, will be classified as British even though they may spend a large part of their life in Eire and regard themselves in every important respect as Irish. As Jackson[2] points out, a decline in the size of the Irish community as recorded by the Census really represents a situation in which new arrivals are insufficient to make up the number of Irish-born who have died or left the U.K.

[1] Ibid., p. 21.   [2] Ibid., p. 10.

Records of passenger movement between Ireland and the U.K. are scanty and no records are kept of passengers travelling by air, a method of travel increasingly used by migrants. Citizens of the Republic of Ireland are not subject to immigration control either by the Aliens Restriction Acts 1919 or by the Commonwealth Immigrants Acts 1962–1968. Migration between the countries is therefore uncontrolled and largely unrecorded, a fact frequently regretted by the Overseas Migration Board, who, in their various reports state that 'there is no direct and accurate means of estimating flow of manpower from the Irish Republic to U.K . . . . and the magnitude of movement is so great that the question of migration statistics to cover it raises an almost insoluble technical and administrative problem'.[1]

The size of the economically active Irish population in the U.K. is recorded in the figures published since 1956 by the Ministry of Pensions and National Insurance and the Department of Health and Social Security (Table 14.13). However, these figures do not give an accurate indication of the total size of the Irish population as they only include persons over school-leaving age and do not include non-working dependants.

Estimates of the Irish population are likely therefore to be inaccurate either because there are no means to record necessary information such as number of children born in the U.K. of Irish-born parents and passenger movements between the U.K. and Ireland, or because the impermanent nature of some Irish immigration to the U.K. makes Census records unreliable. It is unlikely that more accurate information will be collected since there is at present little public concern about the size of the Irish community in the U.K. It is interesting to compare this state of affairs with the increasingly sophisticated attempts to collect detailed information about immigrants from the new Commonwealth and their dependants. While there was, and to some extent still is, hostility expressed towards Irish immigrants, particularly when they are the most recent arrivals in densely populated inner urban areas, a considerable degree of assimilation has taken place and Irish-born persons are to be found in all socio-economic groups living in areas and conditions which would normally be associated with this wide distribution.

The hostility of the host community towards immigrants is now mainly directed to those from the new Commonwealth who are far more easily identified than the Irish and whose social background and culture seem more unfamiliar. The 1966 Sample Census provides some

[1] See *Reports* of the Overseas Migration Board, 1956–64, Cmnd 9835. 1956, 336; 1957, 619; 1958, 979 and 1243, 1960; 1586, 1961; 1905, statistics for 1961; 2217, statistics for 1962; 2555, statistics for 1963; 2861, statistics for 1964.

information which makes it possible to compare the position of the Irish-born in the U.K. with that of more recent immigrants, particularly those from the new Commonwealth. It is these comparisons which provide some of the most interesting information about immigrants in the U.K.

Irish-born Population in England and Wales and Scotland

The Census of 1841 was the first to record the numbers of Irish-born in the U.K., a reflection of growing public concern about the numbers of Irish immigrants to the U.K. In 1841 the Irish-born formed 1·8 per cent of the total population of England and Wales and 4·8 per cent of the total population of Scotland which, until the last twenty years, has always attracted large numbers of Irish. The Irish-born population in Britain continued to rise throughout the peak years of emigration from Ireland and reached a climax in 1861 when they formed 3 per cent of the total population of England and Wales and 6·7 per cent of the population of Scotland. (The proportion in Scotland had been even higher in 1851, when it stood at 7·2 per cent.)

From 1861 until 1931 the number of Irish in the U.K. fell. Although the overall numbers increased slightly in 1931, the proportion of the Irish per 100,000 dropped considerably but increased sharply in 1951 and 1961 (Tables 14.11 and 14.12). However, although the actual numbers of Irish-born in the U.K. were greater in the period 1951–66 than in 1861–71 they did not form so great a proportion of the population.

As with immigration from the new Commonwealth, the pattern of immigration from Ireland to the U.K. reflects conditions in both countries. Unrest following the establishment of the Irish Free State combined with the tightening of immigration controls in the United States turned an increasing number of immigrants towards the U.K. This increase is reflected in the figures of the 1921 Census and this flow continued in spite of the depression in 1931 and 1932, until 1939.[1] Although restriction on immigration by citizens of the Republic of Ireland was imposed after the outbreak of war, large numbers of Irish workers were recruited by the Ministry of Labour for civilian work in Britain. The post-war rebuilding programme also provided opportunities for Irish immigrant labour. The 1951 Census reveals a substantial increase of 65 per cent. since 1931 in the number of Irish-born in the population. This trend continued during the period 1951–66 when the increase was 39·3 per cent and it appears that England and Wales is receiving a new wave of Irish immigration which the 1966 Sample Census shows to be still increasing (Table 14.12). Scotland, however,

[1] J. A. Jackson, op. cit., pp. 13–14.

has not shared this increase and there has been a steady decline in the number of Irish-born in Scotland since 1921. This reflects the lack of economic opportunity in Scotland.

Table 14.11 indicates that except for 1921 when the Irish political situation must have influenced the number of emigrants, the great majority of Irish-born in the U.K. are from Southern Ireland where opportunities for employment are less than in Northern Ireland.

It is difficult to estimate the annual net flow of Irish immigrant labour to the U.K. However, some indication is given by figures compiled by the Ministry of Pensions and National Insurance and the Department of Health and Social Security. These indicate that on the basis of new insurance cards issued, approximately 60,000 to 30,000 workers have entered Britain annually since 1954 (Table 14.13). It should be noted that these figures do not include any immigrants from Northern Ireland, or non-working dependants. The number of re-registrations also indicate a considerable two-way flow between the U.K. and Ireland.

The recent interest and concern about immigration from the new Commonwealth and the size of the coloured population in the U.K. has drawn attention away from Irish immigrants, who, until 1966, when they were overtaken by immigrants from the Commonwealth, represented the single largest minority group in Britain.

Areas of Irish Settlement

Irish immigrants have followed the usual pattern of migrant settlement in that they initially settled in large numbers in the ports where they landed and in the expanding industrial areas. Glasgow, Liverpool and Bristol (all ports used heavily by ships travelling between Ireland and the U.K.) had large Irish populations until declining economic opportunity in these areas confirmed the shift of Irish migrants to the South East and Midlands where there has been a continuous demand for labour. In 1901 there were 45,673 Irish-born in Liverpool, 6·7 per cent of her total population. Large numbers were also found in Manchester and Salford and two-fifths of all the Irish-born were resident in Lancashire and Cheshire. A further substantial proportion was resident in London and the South East. (In 1911 75 per cent of the Irish-born were resident in London and the Home Counties, Lancashire, Cheshire, Yorkshire and Durham.) However in 1931 the Census records a decrease of 11 per cent in the numbers of Irish-born in Lancashire and Cheshire and 29 per cent in the Northern Counties and an increase of 34 per cent in London and the Home Counties. The shift to the South East is again reflected in the 1951 Census when 34 per cent of Irish-born males and 42 per cent of females were living there. The Irish formed

3 per cent of the population of London in 1951 and 5·4 per cent in 1961. Substantial numbers (13 per cent of males and 10 per cent of females) were also resident in the Midlands. In 1951 the Irish-born formed 4 per cent of the population of Coventry and 3 per cent of Birmingham. In 1961 90,581 or 10·4 per cent of the total number of Irish-born in the U.K. were resident in Warwickshire. Table 14.14 gives the most recent distribution of the Irish-born in the U.K. and indicates the continued demand for labour in the Midlands and the South East.

Although the Irish-born are concentrated in the larger urban areas, the spread of light industry to smaller towns of up to 50,000 has been accompanied by a wider distribution of Irish labour and in 1951 and 1961 the Irish-born represented 1 per cent of the population outside the principal towns.

Within the large urban areas the Irish population is heavily concentrated mainly in areas which have always offered shelter for new immigrants and which are also often near the industries where there is a demand for immigrant labour. These are frequently the decaying inner cores of large towns or boroughs where there is a large amount of old property which can be divided up into flats or rooms for immigrant families. In the London boroughs of Paddington and Hammersmith the Irish formed over 10 per cent of the population in 1961 while in St. Pancras, Westminster, Kensington and Chelsea and Holborn they represented over 7 per cent of the total population. Figures for 1966 are not directly comparable because of changes in borough boundaries but the 10 per cent Sample Census indicates that the Irish-born formed 3·8 per cent of the total population of Greater London, and 8·4 per cent, 7·1 per cent and 6·4 per cent respectively of the total populations of Hammersmith, Islington and Kensington and Chelsea. It should be noted that these proportions may be somewhat higher since the Registrar-General estimates that overall the under-enumeration of immigrants in the 1966 Census was 10 per cent, but more in the conurbations.

Since Irish immigration to the U.K. has now been established for nearly 150 years it is reasonable to expect a fairly wide distribution of the Irish-born in the U.K. There is some evidence that this has been achieved and, as has already been described, Irish-born are resident not only in the conurbations but also in the smaller towns which have attracted light industry. In 1961 no London borough had less than 2 per cent of Irish-born amongst its population and Peach[1] found that the Irish were present in all residential districts of Birmingham whereas the West Indians were absent from half of them. It should be noted

[1] G. C. K. Peach, op. cit., p. 88.

that these figures relate to those who were actually born in Ireland and there is no accurate information about the geographical and social distribution of those who were themselves born in the U.K. and whose parents' birthplace was Ireland or the Commonwealth. It is this information which would provide a clearer picture of the assimilation of the families and dependants of immigrants from the new Commonwealth and Ireland. Since immigration from Ireland has been established so much longer, it is not always illuminating to compare it with that from the new Commonwealth, although such comparisons do give some indication of different living conditions which Irish and coloured immigrants might expect to find in the U.K.

Age and Family Structure

The 1911 Census was the last to record more males than females among the Irish-born in England and Wales and since then female immigrants have outnumbered males although males are still in the majority in Scotland. In addition, male immigrants from Northern Ireland have continued to predominate whereas there has been a majority of female immigrants from Southern Ireland. This reflects both the lack of economic opportunities for females in Southern Ireland and also the predominance of males in the population. The late age of marriage among men in the rural areas of Southern Ireland means that Irish girls come to the U.K. not only to find work but also to increase their chance of marriage. In some parts of the U.K., for example, some London boroughs, the ratio of Irish-born women to men is as much as 3:1. However, this reflects the demand for female labour in hospitals, hotels and domestic service and the overall ratio of Irish-born females to males is not so high. In 1951 49 per cent of the Irish-born were males and the 1961 and 1966 percentages of males were 49·9 per cent and 48·5 per cent respectively.

Like most migrant groups, the Irish-born are a predominantly young population. The various Census reports note repeatedly that the number of Irish in the 15–44 age group is proportionately higher than for the native population of the U.K. Jackson[1] states that in 1959 56 per cent of females and 48 per cent of males from Southern Ireland were aged between 20 and 39. The proportion of this age group from Northern Ireland was very similar. The late age of marriage among the Irish means that the Irish-born immigrants have typically been single men and women although the total numbers have undoubtedly included some whole families many of whom have only been reunited after a period of years.

Rose[2] has calculated the median ages for adult male and female

[1] J. A. Jackson, *op. cit.*, p. 19.   [2] E. J. B. Rose, *op. cit.*, p. 111.

immigrants for the London and Birmingham areas. All the coloured adult immigrant groups had median ages within the 14–32 range. However, the median age of the Irish was 41·5 and for the English 44 years. This difference of median age between the Irish and coloured immigrants probably reflects the very large number of immigrants from the new Commonwealth who came to the U.K. prior to the 1962 Commonwealth Immigrants Act who have recently been joined by their dependants. This difference is also a reflection of the longer-established Irish migration.

This age structure would naturally be associated with a high birthrate and the Irish birthrate is paralleled but not equalled by the birthrate for immigrants from the new Commonwealth where the great majority are also of childbearing age.

Rose[1] has calculated (Tables 14·15 and 14·16) that in 1966 in the London and Birmingham conurbations Irish fertility exceeded that of the total population by 77 per cent. A large percentage of Irish families have three or more children and the average number of children in Irish families is also higher than for any other immigrant group. Using the figures for the 1961 Sample Census Thompson's study of the relative fertility of groups of women marrying at ages 20–29 found that the highest rate for those in their second year of marriage was for Irish women.[2] This exceeded the England and Wales rate by 40 per cent whereas the rate for Indian, Pakistani and Caribbean women was about 20 per cent more than for women born in England and Wales. However, as marriage duration increased these differentials narrowed but did not disappear. It is not easy to explain this high fertility rate among the Irish-born in the U.K. compared with other immigrants, apart from pointing out that the great majority are Roman Catholic.

Socio-economic status of Irish immigrants

In the nineteenth century the Irish had become well established as labourers willing to undertake the heaviest and most unpleasant kinds of work. Irish navvies were responsible for much of the railway and canal building in the U.K. They were also relied on in some rural areas as seasonal harvesters. They were distinguished by their willingness to move around the country from job to job and to work for rates of pay

[1] E. J. B. Rose, *op. cit.* See pp. 112–18 for a full discussion of the comparison between immigrant and native groups in the London and Birmingham conurbations. Since English residents in the Inner London and Birmingham areas are considerably older than the immigrants, the differential between the two groups is greater than it would be if data were available which related to the whole population.

[2] J. Thompson, *Differential Fertility among Immigrants to England and Wales and some Implications for Population Predictions.* Paper delivered to Eugenics Society's Symposium 'The Biosocial Aspects of Race', Sept. 1968.

frequently lower than those demanded by English workers. The work undertaken by Irish labourers was mostly seasonal and large numbers returned to Ireland during the winter months. Jackson[1] has described the Irish workers of the nineteenth century as migrant labour rather than immigrants. However, gradually the Irish became established wage earners. Records for this period are scanty and unreliable, but while in the earlier part of the century the Irish had attracted the wrath and concern of the natives, who were, nonetheless dependent on their services, by the end of the century they figure far less in contemporary literature and records. Their place as the newest, poorest, and most unfamiliar immigrants had been taken by the increasingly large numbers of European Jews.

The Census of 1911 gives the occupations of the Irish-born in Scotland but not England. One-third of the females were occupied in domestic service whereas the great majority of men were engaged in the manufacturing industries and mining. Not until the 1951 Census is there any further official overall record of the occupations of the Irish-born. However, records of the occupational distribution of male and female emigrants from Ireland to all places show that, between 1901 and 1920, 10–12 per cent of male emigrants had professional, commercial or student status, 6–7 per cent were skilled workers and approximately 70 per cent labourers. Amongst the females 85–92 per cent were engaged in domestic service.[2] This would seem to indicate that in the early part of the twentieth century Irish workers were filling the jobs that normally fall to immigrant workers. However, the political difficulties of the 1920s led to some distrust of Irish labour and most of the unskilled were only acceptable in industries such as building where there was a long tradition of using Irish labour.

During the 1930s increasing numbers of Irish workers came to the U.K. and, in spite of a period of heavy unemployment, continued to find work mostly because of their willingness to work long hours in the heaviest, most unpleasant industries and to travel from job to job.

Fears for national security at the outbreak of World War II led to initial restrictions on Irish immigration. However, these were relaxed as the demand for labour on the land and in essential industries became more acute. Large numbers of Irish were recruited by the various Ministries and the initial reluctance to use Irish labour in anything other than the heaviest unskilled work disappeared because of the urgent need for labour in industries which had previously not employed Irish workers. Jackson[3] sees the war period as an important one for Irish

---

[1] J. A. Jackson, *op. cit.*, p. 79.
[2] *Annual Emigration Statistics of Ireland*, 1876–1920.
[3] J. A. Jackson, *op. cit.* For a full discussion of this period see pp. 96–105.

labour in that it provided opportunities of becoming established in work which was previously closed to them. Whereas before the war Irish were mostly employed in building, labouring and domestic service, opportunities now existed in various industrial occupations, transport and catering. Immediately after the war Irish were recruited for nursing, the mines, agriculture and metal manufacture and many firms, hotels and hospitals continue to advertise their vacancies in the Irish press.

Unfortunately, because of changes in classification, the occupational tables of the 1951 and 1961 Sample Census are not directly comparable. However, they provide fairly adequate information about the occupational distribution of the Irish-born and while the figures indicate that large numbers of Irish-born are employed as labourers or unskilled workers, they also show substantial minorities engaged in skilled and professional work. In 1951 13·7 per cent of Irish males were employed as unskilled labourers, 17·8 per cent in the building industry, 13·3 per cent in metal manufacture and 8·7 per cent in transport.

Tables 14·17 and 14·18 show that in 1961 compared with the total population Irish males, together with those from Pakistan and the Caribbean were over-represented as labourers. However, the percentage of those employed in professional and technical work compares quite favourably with the percentage for the total population. The position is similar in relation to the other occupations listed.

Irish-born females together with those from India, Pakistan and the Caribbean are over-represented as professional and technical workers partly because of the large numbers engaged in nursing.

Table 14·5 which gives percentages of some of the foreign-born relating to certain socio-economic groups shows that the Irish-born males, particularly those from the Irish Republic, are over-represented in the unskilled manual group compared with the total population. However, their position compares favourably with that of males from Pakistan and the British Caribbean. The percentage of males from the Irish Republic in the skilled manual group is only slightly less than for the total population and together with immigrants from India, the percentage of Irish men in the employers and managers group, while being less than the percentage for the total population, is still significant. They are also well represented in the professional workers' group. The percentages of Irish women in the intermediate non-manual group is much higher than that for the total population, no doubt because this group includes nurses.

While the Irish immigrants are significantly represented in all the socio-economic groups, it is not possible to say how far this has been achieved through immigration or whether it mainly represents the immigrants' socio-economic groups prior to departure from Ireland.

Although records have been kept of the professions, trades and skills of immigrants from the Commonwealth since 1962, no similar records exist for the Irish. It is known that a large number of doctors who qualified in Ireland have chosen to practise in the U.K. while the majority of Irish nurses in the U.K. are recruited untrained in Ireland. Large numbers of unskilled workers from Southern Ireland come from rural areas where they may have worked on small farms. Without information about the occupations of the children of the Irish-born it is only possible to speculate about their social mobility. However, it is interesting to note that the percentage of males from the Irish Republic in the foreman and supervisors group is higher than that for the total population and for any other immigrant group. This may be some indication that Irish workers are attaining positions of responsibility in the U.K.

The information available concerning socio-economic status shows that the Irish occupy an interesting position in British society. They are less well represented than the total population in the first three socio-economic groups, but far better represented than immigrants from Pakistan and the British Caribbean. Together with immigrants from India whose socio-economic groupings are similar, they occupy a middle position between the total population and the most recent immigrants.

4. JEWISH IMMIGRATION

For several reasons estimates of the Jewish population in the U.K. are extremely unreliable. Firstly it is uncertain who should be included in these estimates, as opinions differ about the definition of a Jew. Clearly, it is irrelevant to consider birthplace as a criterion and there are no particular racial or physical characteristics which can be attributed to Jews. At one time the most reliable method of identifying and counting Jews was by establishing whether they professed, however generally, the Jewish faith. Jewish religious practice involves some participation in social and cultural affairs and many Jews may be associated with these while not involving themselves in more formal aspects of religion. For example, large numbers of Jews belong to Jewish Friendly Societies and other organisations which protect and promote Jewish interests. Until the last 20 years it was almost possible for commentators on the Jewish population to make estimates based on the numbers who were buried in Jewish burial grounds as it was assumed that however detached from the Jewish community a Jew had been during his lifetime, he would choose, or his family would ensure, that the last rites were performed according to established Jewish tradition.

More writers now agree that since Jews, like the rest of the population, are increasingly less concerned with religious practice, estimates of the Jewish population which depend on data relating to religious institutions are most unreliable. The decline in religious practice has also meant that many Jews are moving away from the established centres of the Jewish community and some are gradually losing contact with Jews who would formerly have included them in the category of 'other Jews known but not affiliated to Jewish organisations' when estimates are made of the Jewish population. Loss of contact with the established Jewish community almost certainly leads to greater assimilation with the Gentile population.

When, then, can be identified as a Jew? Some commentators have defined Jews as being those of 'Jewish origin', i.e. born of a Jewish mother. However, this will certainly include a number of people who have completely severed connections, if any existed, with the religion of their ancestors and who would deny any feeling of solidarity with the Jewish community. These people might also quite accurately point out that they were not regarded as Jews by the Gentile community. Recent writers[1] have used a definition involving self-identification, i.e. those individuals who when asked would call themselves Jews should be counted as Jews and no one else. However, even if this definition is accepted, there are almost insuperable difficulties involved in collecting this kind of data since the Census of England, Wales and Scotland does not include questions about religious affiliation. Those interested in assessing the Jewish population in the U.K. have therefore to resort to the use of private surveys and selective use of existing demographic data such as the statistics included in the Jewish Year Book.[2]

If estimates of the total Jewish population are unreliable, estimates of the Jewish immigrant population are even more doubtful. While the Census gives information about the number of aliens in the U.K. and these figures are also published annually, there is no means of ascertaining how many of these alien immigrants are Jews. Estimates have to be based on a number of assumptions and guesses. For example, it is well known that during 1881–1914 large numbers of European immigrants entered the U.K., particularly from Russia and Russian Poland. Certainly great numbers of these Jews were escaping from the pogroms and persecution in Russia. Jewish charitable organisations kept detailed records of the large numbers of Russian and Polish Jews with whom they were in contact during this period and members of the Royal Commission on Alien Immigration realised that much of their deliberation concerned Jewish immigrants. It was known that there were large and growing communities of Jews, many of whom could not speak English,

[1] H. Neustatter, in M. Freedman (ed.), *A Minority in Britain: A Study of Anglo-Jewry* (Valentine Mitchell, 1955), p. 61.

[2] For a full discussion of these difficulties see H. Neustatter, *op. cit.*, pp. 63–8.

in the East End of London. So serious an obstacle was this considered to be in the collection of accurate information that in 1901 and 1911 Census forms were printed in Yiddish. However, a recognition that very large numbers of immigrants are Jewish does not make the collection of accurate information concerning their numbers any easier. Is it to be assumed that because of the persecution of Jews in Russia, Poland and Romania, all immigrants from these countries are Jews? Even if this is accepted, is it possible to differentiate between Jewish immigrants landing in the U.K. who intend to stay here and those *en route* to America and the Commonwealth? The Royal Commission on Alien Immigration 1903 concluded that figures gathered primarily from ships' manifests relating to alien immigrants gave little guide to the numbers who would remain in the U.K. The decennial Census is the most reliable guide but, as with all immigrant groups, gives no information about the numbers of children born in the country whose parents were immigrants. These numbers are important since the concentration, isolation and self-sufficiency of the Jewish immigrant community meant that in the first years of settlement it was particularly hard for any assimilation to take place and a foreign community was readily identifiable.

Similar difficulties exist in the estimation of the second wave of Jewish immigration into the U.K. between 1930 and 1940. Are all immigrants from Nazi Germany presumed to be Jews escaping from persecution? And how many immigrants from other European countries were also Jews fleeing from persecution? How many Jewish immigrants finding refuge in the U.K. before World War II settled in other countries after the end of the war?

There is no accurate method of answering these questions and bearing in mind all the difficulties and likely inaccuracies already outlined, the most reliable estimate must be based on evidence from the Census, the annual statistics of alien immigration and the estimates of the Jewish Year Book, not only as they stand but as they have been interpreted and corrected by various writers.

Jewish Immigration 1880–1914

Economic and political factors played complementary roles in prompting the exodus of large numbers of Jews from Russia, Russian Poland, Romania and Austria. The emigration began in earnest after the first pogrom in 1881 and the majority of the emigrants were either Jewish peasants who had been forced to leave the land after the promulgation of the May Laws or tradesmen following the few occupations that were open to Jews. The majority of these workers were tailors and shoemakers.

Table 14.19 indicates that from 1891 to 1911 each Census showed large increases in the numbers of immigrants from Russia and Russian Poland. The 1881 Census General Report records a 51·2 per cent increase in the number of Russians and Poles and the percentage increases for 1891, 1901 and 1911 are respectively 21·1 per cent, 83·8 per cent and 15·2 per cent.

The 1905 Aliens Immigration Act reduced the flow of immigrants from Russia and Poland and this is reflected in the much smaller percentage increase recorded between 1901 and 1911. It is likely too that since the persecution of the Jews in Russia had lessened, fewer wanted to emigrate. The outbreak of the 1914 war stopped immigration from Russia and Poland completely and the decrease in the number of immigrants from these countries recorded in 1921 reflects a situation in which decreases because of further emigration or death were not made up by new immigrants. It is likely, too, that some Russian and Polish immigrants returned to their native countries before the outbreak of the war.

During the peak years of this immigration, immigrants from Russia and Poland formed over 30 per cent of all foreigners in England and Wales.

Before 1906, statistics issued by the Board of Trade relating to immigrants from Europe are not broken down to give the country of origin of the immigrants and it is therefore impossible to tell how many came from Russia and Poland. However, the annual reports issued in connection with the 1905 Aliens Act show that in 1906 and 1907 over 4000 Russians and Poles arrived on immigrant ships. This dwindled to under 2000 in 1908 the last year records of the nationality of European immigrants were kept.

Estimates of the total numbers of Jewish immigrants to the U.K. during 1881–1914 are necessarily vague. V. D. Lipman[1] has calculated that up to 150,000 came to the U.K. during this period, approximately 100,000 of them between 1891 and 1905. Exactly how he arrives at this figure is not clear. 1905, before the passing of the Aliens Act, was one of the peak years for immigration and Lipman estimates that about 8000 of the 40,000 Russians, Poles, Austrians and Romanians who landed in the U.K. remained here. Basing his estimates partly on statistics issued by the Jewish Year Book, Lipman also thinks that between 1891 and 1904 about 6500 Jews settled in the U.K. annually. Finestein[2] and Lipman both agree that between 1905 and 1914 about 45,000 Jews settled in the U.K.

---

[1] V. D. Lipman, *Social History of the Jews in England, 1850–1950* (Watts & Co. 1954), chap. v.

[2] I. Finestein, in V. D. Lipman (ed.), *Three Centuries of Anglo-Jewish History* (Jewish Historical Society of England 1961), pp. 107–23.

The Jewish Year Book was first published in 1896 and each edition includes estimates of the number of Jews in the U.K. The statistics are not very reliable and estimates are liable to change from year to year according to the interpretations and calculations of the editors. However, an increase of 58·1 per cent is recorded between 1891. and 1901 and over 41 per cent between 1901 and 1905. This rate of increase drops considerably between 1905 and 1911 to 4·6 per cent. These figures included in Table 14.20 do not tally with Lipman's and Finestein's estimates that 45,000 Jewish immigrants settled in the U.K. between 1905 and 1914. By 1916 the Jewish population was more than two and a half times larger than in 1891 and this increase must be attributed entirely to immigration.

The Jewish immigrants during this period were Ashkenazis, many of whom came straight from the ghettos of Russia. Some were skilled workmen but many were not equipped to fend for themselves in a complicated urban economy. Partly for self-protection they settled together in large numbers, living in impossibly overcrowded conditions on the edge of poverty.

The vast majority of Russians and Poles settled in the East End of London, chiefly in Stepney, where in 1901, 40 per cent of the Russians and Russian Poles were resident. There were also large numbers in Holborn and St. Pancras. Almost without exception the Jewish immigrants settled in the large industrial centres and ports but in only thirteen towns did they represent more than 10 per 1000 of the total population. This pattern of settlement continued in 1911 and 1921 although by then some dispersal to other industrial centres had begun.

Members of the Royal Commission on Alien Immigration were appalled, as was the Jewish Board of Guardians, at the conditions endured if not created by the immigrants in London. There was public concern about the burden large numbers of pauper aliens would put on the rates. The Sephardic Jews, long established in the U.K., who had ceased to think of themselves as foreigners, viewed this immigration with ambivalence. While they were glad that their brethren could find refuge from persecution they were anxious about the demands these new immigrants made on their charity. Although Jewish organisations were extremely active in the relief of the poor, there is no evidence that these new immigrants were a charge on public funds. The Registrar General was at pains to point out in 1901 that whereas 15·2 per 1000 of the general population were in workhouses the proportion for European immigrants was 1·7 per 1000. A similar point was made by the Registrar-General in 1891.

The Russian and Polish immigrants quickly established themselves in work which was familiar to them and which, because it could be done in small units, often in the immigrants' own homes, protected them from contact with the unfamiliar native population. New immigrants were quickly drawn into these established trades and competition, under-cutting, and the desperate need for employment provided a fertile environment for sweated labour. Between 1901 and 1911 approximately 40 per cent of Russian and Polish men and 50 per cent of women were engaged in tailoring work. A further 12 per cent made boots and shoes and about 10 per cent were cabinet-makers.

Approximately 60 per cent of immigrants from Russia and Poland were men and most fell in the age range 15–45 with substantial numbers also in the 45–65 age bracket. At each Census the Registrar-General comments on the very small proportion of children amongst the immi-grants. However, the Census figures do not include the children born to immigrants in the U.K. as they would be classified as British citizens.

It is remarkable that such very large numbers of foreign immigrants could settle in the U.K. in a short space of time and establish themselves successfully in trade and although enduring considerable material hardship, begin a process of quite rapid assimilation with the native population. That they were able to do so can be attributed to their industry and competence but also to the efforts made by the established Jewish community to ease their entry to British society.[1]

However, there certainly was public concern about both the numbers of immigrants and the conditions in which they lived. This anxiety was expressed in the efforts made to introduce legislation to control immi-gration, and in 1905 the first Aliens Immigration Act was passed. This Act was considerably more liberal than some of the Bills which had preceded it. A clause forbidding aliens to live in certain areas already overcrowded with immigrants was not finally included and the main clauses of the 1905 Act forbade entry to all those who could not support themselves and their dependants, those whose infirmities were likely to lead them to be a charge on the rates, and some known criminals. The principle of political asylum was assured. The public debate surrounding the passing of this Act is interesting as it echoes all the arguments, fears and speculation which are familiar features of current controversy concerning immigration.

Jewish Immigration 1930–51

The increase in the Jewish population between 1914 and 1930 was not very substantial when compared with the preceding quarter-century and the process of assimilation and anglicisation of the foreign community was well established during these 16 years. The 1911 Census was the

[1] For a full account of Jewish settlement during this period see L. P. Gartner, *The Jewish Immigrant in England 1870–1940* (Allen & Unwin 1960).

last when forms were published in Yiddish, the assumption being that foreign-born Jews were now proficient in English. Although large numbers of Jews continued to live in London, some had dispersed to other centres of industry and to some seaside towns. The Jewish Year Book estimates that in 1916 2·15 per cent of the total population of London were Jews who also represented 5·38 per cent and 4·19 per cent respectively of the population of Leeds and Manchester. However, another wave of foreign Jewish immigrants began to arrive in the U.K. in the early 1930s. These immigrants were central Europeans, mainly from Germany, and they were fleeing from the violent persecution that accompanied Hitler's rise to power. Table 14.21 shows that between 1931 and 1951 the number of German nationals resident in the U.K. increased by more than 20,000. This is all the more remarkable since the hostilities between England and Germany would normally have led to a decrease in German nationals in the U.K. after the war. This was certainly the case after World War I. Undoubtedly a substantial proportion of these Germans were Jews who had sought refuge in England. Large numbers of Jews would also be included amongst those of Polish nationality and the increased numbers of British subjects by registration or naturalisation (Table 14.1). Neustatter[1] states that 60,000 Jews settled in the U.K. between 1933 and 1939. The Jewish Year Book estimates that of the 80,000 refugees from central Europe in 1933–9, the 70,000 Europeans who were admitted to the U.K. during the war years, and the 60,000 displaced persons who were admitted after the war at least 80 per cent. were Jews. However, it is also pointed out that many were only temporary residents. Table 14·20 indicates that between 1931 and 1946 the Jewish population increased by 88,000. There was a further increase of 65,000 between 1946 and 1951 since when the Jewish population has remained the same. It is extremely difficult to estimate how many of these Jews were permanent foreign immigrants. Neustatter's[1] survey (1950–2) suggests that they represent only a small proportion. She found that one in seven of her sample were of foreign birth and only 4 per cent were not of British nationality at the time of the enquiry.

The Jews who came to the U.K. between 1933 and 1939 were very different from those who arrived at the beginning of the century. Many had had close ties with the Gentile populations of their native countries and only loose connections with orthodox Judaism. They were a largely middle- and upper-middle-class group, well represented in the professions, and found it easy to assimilate with the English population.

However, the Jews who were admitted to the U.K. during and after the war were from rather different backgrounds. Unlike the Jews who,

[1] H. Neustatter, *op. cit.*, p. 110.　　　[2] *Ibid.*

by reason of wealth or professional status, had found emigration fairly easy, these most recent Jewish immigrants had not been able to leave their native countries and their means of livelihood before the outbreak of the war. A substantial number were skilled or semi-skilled manual workers. Their experiences during the war and political developments in their native countries made emigration inevitable for large numbers, some of whom initially found their settlement in the U.K. difficult. Fortunately the post-war expansion of the economy meant that employment was relatively easy as there was a demand for all types of labour. Statistics relating to immigration to the old Commonwealth after the war also suggest that large numbers of foreign nationals used the U.K. only as a temporary home.

These two periods of Jewish immigration enormously increased the size of the Jewish population in the U.K. Britain was the only European country whose Jewish population increased during the period 1939–48. However, although according to some sources the Jewish population has remained the same size since 1951, other writers claim that, partly depending on how the term 'Jewish' is used, the population is decreasing. Neustatter[1] thinks that the birthrate amongst Jews is not only declining like that of the general population, but is also lower. This may partly be accounted for by the relatively large numbers of middle-class Jews,[2] but can also be attributed to the diminishing influence of a religious tradition which fosters a high birthrate. This decline in religious interest is a factor in the increasing number of marriages between Jews and Gentiles which will inevitably affect the numbers of those who either regard themselves as Jews who are regarded by others as being Jewish.[3] For some years the editors of the Jewish Year Book have added 10 per cent to the total when estimating the size of the Jewish population to include those with no communal affiliation. How they arrive at the figure of 10 per cent. is not known.

It is impossible to estimate whether the foreign-born Jews are assimi-

[1] *Ibid.*, p. 68.

[2] Neustatter found from her survey, *op. cit.*, pp. 124–32, that three-quarters of those in trades worked on their own account. 22 per cent. of men were engaged in professional work as against 5 per cent. of the general population. It is interesting to note that foreign-born Jews and Jewesses in this sample represented 9 per cent. of those belonging to the professions.

[3] For a fuller account of the estimates of the size of the Anglo-Jewish population see H. Neustatter, *op. cit.*, and S. J. Prais and M. Schmool, 'The Size and Structure of the Anglo-Jewish Population 1960–1965', *Jewish J. Sociol.*, Vol. X, No. 1, June 1968; 'Synagogue Marriages in Great Britain 1966–1968', *Jewish J. Sociol.*, Vol. XII, No. 1, June 1970; 'Statistics of Milah and the Jewish Birth Rate in Britain', *Jewish J. Sociol.*, Vol. XII, No. 2, December 1970; S. J. Prais only, 'Synagogue Statistics and the Jewish Population of Great Britain 1900 to 1970', *Jewish J. Sociol.*, Vol. XIV, No. 2, December 1972.

lating with the general population of the U.K. at the same rate as the British-born Jews. However, it is interesting to observe that a minority group which contained very large numbers of foreign immigrants, particularly in the first 25 years of this century, has none the less, in the space of three or four generations, achieved a measure of assimilation with the general population which would be regarded as total by many observers.

5. ALIEN IMMIGRATION

Tables 14.19 and 14.21 show that between 1881 and 1961 the proportion of aliens per 100,000 of the population of England and Wales has almost doubled.[1] The increase was particularly sharp between 1881 and 1891 and the reasons for this have been described in the previous section. The increases were smaller between 1891 and 1911 and the 1921 and 1931 Census revealed a decrease in the proportion of aliens resident in the U.K. This proportion more than doubled during the intercensal period 1931–57 and the 1961 Census showed a further increase. The nationality tables for the 1966 Sample Census have not yet been published. The decrease between 1911 and 1921 can be attributed almost entirely to a very large reduction in the number of Germans resident in the U.K. as a result of World War I. During this period the proportion of Germans per 100,000 of the population dropped from 147 to 32. The passing of the Aliens Act in 1919 also had some influence on immigration to the U.K. The decrease in the number of aliens in 1931 can be accounted for partly by the reduction in the numbers of Russians and Poles. Large numbers who came to the U.K. between 1881 and 1905 were dead by 1931 and their children born in the U.K. were classified as British subjects. The depression also made the U.K. a less attractive prospect for immigrants.

The great majority (approximately 80 per cent) of alien immigrants to the U.K. have always been of European origin. Apart from those coming from Russia and Russian Poland, the largest numbers have been Germans, French and Italians. Many of these were employed in personal service or catering. The 1901 and 1911 Census notes that large numbers of Germans and Italians were waiters, domestic servants and

[1] Variations in the procedures for enumerating aliens at the different Censuses affect the comparability of these figures, but it is not possible to correct for these. For example, until 1901 no questions relating to nationality were asked although British subjects born abroad were asked to state this. Those who omitted to do this but who had British surnames were enumerated as British subjects. The procedure relating to surnames was repeated at each Census until 1921, when an attempt was made to correct alien returns. In 1931 the classification of aliens by birthplace was supplemented by statistics of the numbers of aliens born in particular countries whose nationality did not correspond to the country of birth. The 1951 Census was the first to record the birthplace and the nationality of all aliens.

cake-makers. Many teachers also came from Germany and France in answer to the demand for European tutors and governesses.

The occupations of many alien immigrants has not changed substantially during the century although fewer are now in private service and most are employed in the hotel and catering trade, particularly on a seasonal basis.

Since World War II some European workers have been recruited for the under-manned industries and the largest post-war increases in the alien populations are to be found amongst those of Russian and Polish nationality who came to the U.K. immediately after the war under the recruiting schemes for European Volunteer Workers or who were settled after their discharge from the armed forces by the Polish Resettlement Corps.

Between 1946 and 1950 the two major recruitment schemes for European workers, the Balt Cygnet and Westward Ho! schemes, were responsible for recruiting 74,511 workers for the essential and under-manned industries in the U.K. The total number of workers recruited by all schemes has been estimated as 100,875. These schemes had been prompted by an acute shortage of domestic workers in hospitals and sanatoria and recognition that Britain as well as the other Western Allies carried some responsibility for the large numbers of European refugees living in Displaced Persons camps. The Secretary for the Ministry of Labour at this period described the schemes as 'partly an act of charity and partly to suit ourselves'.

Volunteers were recruited directly from the refugee camps for work in hospitals, agriculture, coalmining, the textile and building industries. The largest national groups were the Lithuanians, Ukrainians, Poles, Latvians and Yugoslavs.

The immigration of the European Volunteer Workers was strictly controlled and all who applied to be considered for the scheme had to work as manual workers in work designated and selected by the Ministry of Labour. Initially work permits were issued only for 12 months although these could be extended if a person was still willing to work in a specified job. Restrictions on the choice of employment by the European Volunteer Workers were lifted in 1950. The rates of pay and conditions were identical to those for all British workers but promotion of European Volunteer Workers was severely restricted and preference given to native workers.

Until July 1947 European Volunteer Workers were allowed to bring their dependants to the U.K. but after this date concern about housing shortages led to recruitment being restricted to single persons. 3707 non-working dependants came to the U.K. in 1946 and 1947 as well as an unknown number of dependants who were recruited for employment similar to that of the heads of families.

The British Government undertook to transport the European Volunteer Workers to the U.K. and to arrange to pay for accommodation until they were settled in work. Some hostels were maintained for single European Volunteer Workers and those who could not find accommodation for themselves and certain welfare schemes were provided such as special English classes and resettlement programmes.

Tannahill[1] has described the balance that had to be found between economic, political and humanitarian interests in the settlement of the European Volunteer Workers. On the whole there was little overt hostility from the British public to the recruitment of foreign labour partly because of the tremendous shortage of manpower in many of the essential services and industries and partly because the rights of the European Volunteer Workers were severely restricted as a protection for native labour. In addition, the immigration of dependants, who might make demands on health and welfare services, was also restricted in 1947.

Tannahill's[2] survey in 1956 suggests that in spite of language problems, difficult living conditions, unfamiliarity with the U.K. and the traditional suspicions of the British towards foreigners, the settlement of the European Volunteer Workers was achieved with some success. However, by 1956 a large number, including 48 per cent of the Lithuanians, 44 per cent of the Estonians, 26 per cent of Ukrainians and 23 per cent of Latvians and Poles had emigrated to the U.S.A. and various Commonwealth countries. Of those remaining in the U.K. Tannahill estimates that about 40 per cent still maintained strong links with their fellow countrymen.

It is difficult to estimate how many European Volunteer Workers have changed their employment since labour restrictions were lifted in 1950. Tannahill[3] thinks that about a third of those originally employed in the textile and coalmining industries remained there in 1956. Approximately 80 per cent were employed in unskilled or semi-skilled work.

The largest group of Europeans resident in the U.K. after the war were the Poles. Zubrzycki[4] estimates that in 1949 there were 157,300 Poles in the U.K. including those who had enrolled in the Polish Resettlement Corps which arranged the settlement of 114,000 Poles in the U.K. or abroad. The number of Poles in the U.K. decreased to approximately 140,000 in July 1950 and 120,000 in December 1954.

[1] J. A. Tannahill, *European Volunteer Workers in Britain* (Manchester U.P. 1958).
[2] *Ibid.*   [3] *Ibid.*
[4] J. Zubrzycki, *Polish Immigrants in Britain* (Nijhoff, The Hague 1956).

The Poles have a long tradition of emigration and a strong wish to maintain their national identity. This was respected by the British Government, partly under pressure from the Poles themselves, but also as a recognition of the services of the many Poles who had been members of the armed forces. Undoubtedly, too, the fate of Poland after the war and the creation of the Polish Government in exile was influential in the provision of special facilities for Poles in the U.K. The 1947 Polish Resettlement Act recognised the need for special Polish hospitals and educational facilities and many voluntary Polish social and welfare organisations are still in existence. It will be interesting to see whether they will continue to be maintained by children who, although born of Polish parents, have lived all their lives in the U.K.

The European Volunteer Workers scheme and the work of the Polish Resettlement Corps are interesting in that they illustrate the only attempts by the British Government both to recruit and select immigrant workers and to provide some services and facilities for them on their arrival in the U.K. Strict control, particularly relating to employment, was exerted over these European workers and in many respects this immigration policy was the antithesis of the *laissez-faire* attitudes which have, until recently, characterised British policy towards all immigrants except aliens whose entry to the U.K. has been restricted since 1906 but for whom general services were only provided during the brief period between 1946 and 1950.

Easy travel between the U.K. and Europe, the close links between Britain and many European countries and the demand for special skills possessed by certain Europeans have ensured a continuous flow of immigration from Europe into the U.K. However, in 1905 the first Aliens Act was passed as a result of the public anxiety concerning the number of 'undesirable' aliens, e.g. those who could not support themselves, who were entering the U.K. This Act removed the automatic right of entry to the U.K. and empowered immigration officers to refuse entry to aliens who did not meet certain conditions (see previous section). This principle was continued in the Aliens Act 1919 and Aliens Orders 1920 and 1953 which also imposed further conditions on the entry of immigrants. Entry is now granted to those coming to approved employment, to businessmen and to those who are self-employed or of independent means. Work permits are issued by the Department of Employment and Productivity and there is no fixed limit to the number of workers to be admitted annually. Work permits are normally issued for a year and are tied to a particular job. The admission of dependants lies within the discretion of the Home Secretary and is normally allowed to spouses, dependent children under 18 and widowed parents over the age of 60. Table 14.22 shows the number of alien workers and dependants admitted to the U.K. between 1960 and 1969. In addition, 20,000 to 25,000 under-21-year-olds, including large numbers of *au pair* girls and students, have been admitted annually for twelve months or more.

After four years' residence aliens normally have their conditions cancelled and are free to stay in the U.K. indefinitely and to engage in any kind of employment. Between 1960 and 1968 approximately 15,000–20,500 aliens have been taken off conditions annually.

The 1919 Alien Immigration Acts and Aliens Orders make it possible not only for immigration to be very tightly controlled but for immigrant labour to be directed towards those industries where the need for additional labour is greatest. Increasing concern about unemployment and the integration of immigrants in the U.K. could result in similar policies affecting all immigration to the U.K.[1] Some people believe that the moderate degree of control over immigrants other than aliens does not promote the interests of the British-born or the immigrants. It is argued that immigration policy should involve strict control over recruitment, selection, employment and the admission of dependants together with the provision of special services to immigrants, designed to aid their settlement in the U.K. Only under the European Volunteer Worker schemes have such policies so far been operated by the British Government.

6. THE BALANCE OF EMIGRATION AND IMMIGRATION

Table 14.23 reveals an overall loss by migration between 1881 and 1931. During this period an average of 56,000 emigrants were leaving the U.K. annually for the U.S.A. and Commonwealth countries. Among the factors which influenced this migration was the need in the Commonwealth and Empire for young male workers, particularly for work on the land. Britain's growing industrialisation meant that numbers of young men were faced with the choice of migration to the expanding urban areas where already large numbers of Irish and Scottish immigrants were to be found, or to the Colonies and Dominions. The emigrants during this period also included numbers of trans-migrants who had never intended to make the U.K. a permanent home. The promise of assisted passages and grants of land in the Commonwealth countries was an attractive one and emigration from the U.K. was encouraged by successive governments who were vigorously pursuing British imperial policies. In 1917 the Dominions Royal Commission stated that 'the successful organisation of migration lies at the root of the problem of Empire development and largely upon it depends the

[1] The 1971 Immigration Bill contains proposals such that many Commonwealth immigrants would be treated in a similar way to aliens.

progress of the immense territories of the Dominions and the increase of power of the Empire as a whole'.

After World War I the Dominions became more selective in their demands for immigrants and wanted skilled and semi-skilled workers for their own expanding industries rather than agricultural labourers. However, there was no shortage of recruits and the experience of many young men in the war seems to have left them with an urge to emigrate. Between 1919 and 1930 more than two million people emigrated from the U.K.

The depression in the 1930s largely put a stop to immigration to the Commonwealth and U.S.A. at a time when large numbers of agricultural and industrial workers would have liked to leave the U.K. However, immigration to the U.K. did not stop during this period and between 1931 and 1939 the net inward balance was approximately 60,000 annually. In 1949 the Royal Commission on Population reported that since the rate of natural increase declined during this period, immigrants accounted for 30 per cent. of the growth of the population.[1]

The events of World War II again left a large number of people who wished to emigrate and between 1946 and 1950 720,260 left the U.K., mainly for the Commonwealth countries although a few went to the U.S.A. This migration was viewed with some ambivalence by Britain. The Royal Commission on Population, anxious about the decline in the young working population and the increasing numbers of old people, reported with relief that the number of people wishing to emigrate was decreasing and was likely to continue to do so. The Commission noted that young emigrants represented an economic loss to Britain if they departed before they had made an adequate contribution to the cost of their maintenance and education but added that continued emigration to the Commonwealth and Empire maintained its strength and solidarity with Britain. Although the final conclusion of the Commission was that it was in the long-term interests of Britain and the Commonwealth as a whole to maintain the flow of emigrants to the Commonwealth at as high a level as possible, they expressed some concern that during the following 10 years 170,000 young immigrants to the U.K. would be needed to prevent a decline in the population. They also endorsed the view of the Under Secretary of State for Commonwealth Relations that Britain should reserve the right to check too great a flow of certain types of skilled workers.

Isaac[2] has estimated that between 1946 and 1949, 16–26 per cent of male emigrants from the U.K. were professional people and 19–28 per

[1] *Royal Commission on Population*, Cmd 7695 (HMSO 1949), chap. 12.
[2] J. Isaac, *British Post-War Migration*, National Institute of Economic and Social Research (C.U.P. 1954).

cent were skilled workers. Officials and proprietors represented a further substantial proportion.[1]

The Commission recognised that the negative effects of emigration could be counteracted by the operation of a selective immigration policy, but they were pessimistic about its chances of success. They state that 'immigration on a large scale into a fully established society like ours could only be welcomed without reserve if the immigrants were of good human stock and were not prevented by their religion or race from inter-marrying with the host population and becoming merged in it . . . every increase of our needs, e.g. by more emigration from Great Britain or by a further fall in fertility, would tend to lower the standards of selection. All these considerations point to the conclusion that continuous large scale immigration would probably be impracticable and would certainly be undesirable.'[2]

That relatively large-scale immigration, described in previous sections, might take place without the encouragement of the British Government does not seem to have occurred to the Commission and Table 14.23 shows that whatever may have been its anxieties in 1949, the net inward balance of migration has been in Britain's favour during the intercensal periods 1931–51 and 1951–61. This table also shows the net gain since 1931 is far greater for England and Wales than for the U.K. as a whole. However, Table 14.23 does not show the fluctuations in the different years. These are shown in Table 14.24 for the period 1961–9 and the figures indicate that during the intercensal period 1961–71 it is likely that there will be a substantial overall net loss by migration, in spite of the heavy immigration from the Commonwealth and Ireland that has already been described.

7. BRITISH IMMIGRATION POLICY

Except for a brief period after World War II the British Government during this century has never actively encouraged immigration to the U.K.[3] It has, however, allowed the recruitment of immigrant labour by various industries[4] and has also permitted the U.K. to be used as a refuge by those fleeing from political or religious persecution.[5] Until the early 1960s apart from the control of alien immigration (Aliens Act 1909 and Aliens Orders 1920 and 1953), British immigration policy

[1] For a full account of British migration see N. H. Carrier and J. R. Jeffrey, *External Migration: a Study of the Available Statistics 1815–1950*, General Register Office, Medical and Population Study No. 6.
[2] *Royal Commission on Population*, Cmd 7695 (HMSO 1949), pp. 124–5.
[3] See the section on Alien immigration.
[4] See the sections dealing with Irish immigration and immigration from the new Commonwealth.
[5] See the section on Jewish immigration.

has been a passive one which has tolerated immigration because it has been seen both to be in Britain's economic interests and a natural result of Imperial and Commonwealth policy. This laissez-faire attitude has also characterised the treatment of immigrants in the U.K., the assumption being that their needs could be met by existing services and that their contribution to the national wealth would offset any claims made on welfare services.

However, twice during this century, in 1909 and 1962, public concern over immigration has been strong enough to influence the Government to control it.[1] The origins of this anxiety are to be found not so much in concern about over-population, but in the belief that large numbers of poor working-class immigrants, unfamiliar with the British way of life and sometimes possessing their own distinctive cultures, will not be integrated into British society and may come to represent a foreign and potentially hostile minority. This anxiety is also increased by a realisa-tion that although the age structure of emigrants and immigrants is very similar, those who emigrate are frequently more educated and skilled than those who immigrate. Whatever may be the actual demands for labour, skilled and unskilled, the fear that certain areas of the U.K. will be swamped by people who possess few skills and who are foreign to Britain is a powerful one. These anxieties were frequently expressed by those who gave evidence to the Royal Commision on Alien Immigration which reported in 1903.[2] They also appeared frequently in the debate which led to the control of Commonwealth Immigration in 1962 and 1968 and which still continues. Rose[3] has described how this second period of immigration control coincided with some resurgence of nationalism and some loss of confidence in the multi-racial Common-wealth particularly if this entailed a multi-racial Britain. It is ironic that even though the very strict control of immigration from the new Commonwealth now allows entry only to a small number of skilled and professional workers of whom Britain has a need, and the dependants of those already in the U.K., the demand for even stricter control con-tinues. It is accompanied by a less vociferous demand for special aid not just for immigrants but for the areas in which they have settled in large numbers as it is recognised that the problems experienced by immigrants are largely a reflection of the problems of the decaying centres of large urban areas. This call for a double-edged policy, which will both strictly control immigration and meet the needs of immigrants has its origin in the recognition that there is now in Britain a minority group

[1] The Immigration Bill and Act 1971 and its accompanying regulations are further evidence of this concern.
[2] *Royal Commission on Alien Immigration* (HMSO 1903).
[3] E. J. B. Rose *et al.*, *op. cit.*, pp. 3–7.

of immigrants and their descendants who, partly because of their skin colour, may not integrate with and be absorbed by British society as other immigrant minorities have done. The most recent immigration to the U.K. has led to questions being asked not only about British immigration policy, but also about the nature of the Commonwealth, the rights and needs of minorities in Britain and the adequacy of the services which exist to meet them.

TABLE 14.1

Birthplaces of the Population of England and Wales (selected countries): Proportion per 100,000 Persons 1901–1966

Year	1901	1911	1921	1931	1951	1961	1966
Total enumerated population	100,000	100,000	100,000	100,000	100,000	100,000	100,000
Born in England and Wales	96,131	94,462	96,055	96,345	93,972	92,834	92,227
Other parts	3869	3538	3945	3655	6028	7166	7773
Ireland	1311	1041	963(a)	954(a)	1433(a)	1889(a)	1863(a)
British Commonwealth Dependencies, Colonies and Protectorates	418	448	540	565	769	1489	1999
Foreign countries	1044	1036	867	769	1470	1644	1778
British subject by birth	239	185	136	159	191	636(b)	—
British subject by registration or naturalisation	43	61	126	161	412		
Alien	762	790	602	449	867	1008	—

Notes:
(a) These are the total number of Irish from Northern Ireland and the Irish Republic.
(b) Commonwealth citizens (including Irish).
Source: Census Reports 1901–66.

TABLE 14.2

Residents of England and Wales Born in British Commonwealth Colonies, Dependencies and Protectorates 1901–1966

Year	1901	1911	1921	1931	1951	1961	1966
Total persons enumerated	32,527,843	36,070,492	37,886,699	39,952,377	43,757,888	46,104,548	47,135,510
Total born in B.C. Colonies, Dependencies and Protectorates	136,092	161,502(a)	204,466(a)	225,684(a)	319,486	599,815	942,310
Born in							
Australia and	25,999	23,162	26,348	28,319	30,718	33,131	44,480
New Zealand		5966	7257	8621	11,406	12,280	15,460
Canada	18,829	20,039	29,475	32,001	45,833	44,475	52,620
Newfoundland			1145	864			—
Cape of Good Hope and other Colonies in Africa	12,706	17,819	—	—			
Union of South Africa			22,990	23,804	27,437	34,265	88,510
Other colonies(b) or interests in Africa			17,417	5232	13,638	21,758	
West Indies	8680	9189	9954	8595	15,301	73,739	267,850
Gibraltar	8518	4662	4997	5391	31,707	7795	40,650
Malta		5703	6736	8000		22,439	
India	55,362	62,974	74,219	86,963	110,767	146,953	232,210
Ceylon		3357	3880	4564	5816	8595	
Pakistan					11,117	27,600	73,130
Cyprus			334	1059	11,717	36,873	59,190
Far East Territories							

Notes:

(a) The numbers of visitors included in these totals are: 1911, 6032; 1921, 16,036; 1931, 9267. The numbers of visitors in other censuses were either not kept or were separately recorded.

(b) From 1961 this figure includes residents born in Nigeria, Ghana, Rhodesia, Nyasaland, territories in East Africa and other African territories.

Source: Census Reports, 1901–66.

TABLE 14.3

White Persons in the Enumerated Population of England and Wales of Indian and Pakistani Origin 1951–1966

	India(a)	Pakistan(b)	Total persons
1951	79,000	7000	86,000
1961	76,000	6000	82,000
1966	68,600	5000	73,600

Notes:

(a) Total number of immigrants born in India: 1951, 110,767; 1961, 146,953; 1966, 232,210.

(b) Total number of immigrants born in Pakistan: 1951, 11,117; 1961, 27,600; 1966, 73,130.

Sources: Survey of Race Relations in Britain. D. Eversley and F. Sukdeo, The Dependants of the Coloured Commonwealth Population in England and Wales (O.U.P. for Institute of Race Relations 1969), p. 10.

TABLE 14.4

Commonwealth Immigrants Entering United Kingdom from Australia, Canada and New Zealand (old Commonwealth) and new Commonwealth 1962–1969

Year	Old Commonwealth (Australia, New Zealand and Canada)			New Commonwealth		
	Voucher holders	Dependants	Others for settlement	Voucher holders	Dependants	Others for settlement
1962 (1 July–31 Dec.)	904	614	843	4217	8218	4018
1963	1447	1775	513	28,678	27,393	2934
1964	817	1722	521	13,888	38,952	3214
1965	755	1968	671	12,125	39,228	2297
1966	320	2896	647	5141	39,130	2331
1967	262	2730	737	4716	50,083	2849
1968	338	1843	728	4353	42,036	3771
1969	498	1470	647	3512	27,984	2446

Sources: Institute of Race Relations Facts Paper, Colour and Immigration in the U.K., 1969. Commonwealth Immigrants Acts, 1962 and 1968: Statistics, 1962 Cmnd 2159, 2379, 2658, 2979, 3258, 4029, 4327, 1962.

TABLE 14.5

Socio-economic Grouping for Males and Females Born in Northern Ireland, Irish Republic, India, Pakistan, British Caribbean and the old Commonwealth, Resident in Great Britain, 1966

	Total population		N. Ireland		Irish Republic		India		Pakistan		British Caribbean		Old Commonwealth	
	Males	Females	Males	Females	Males	Females	Males	Females	Males	Females	Males	Females	Males	Females
Total economically active	100	100	100	100	100	100	100	100	100	100	100	100	100	100
Certain socio-economic groups														
Employers and managers	9·3	3·9	6·5	3·7	5·2	3·4	6·8	4·3	2·3	0·3	0·8	0·3	15·4	5·4
Professional	4·9	0·8	5·4	1·5	3·1	1·9	10·7	2·8	3·3	5·8	1·3	0·1	14·5	2·9
Intermediate non-manual	4·5	9·6	4·1	16·2	2·6	17·6	4·9	18·9	1·1	14·1	1·9	20·9	9·5	23·6
Personal service	10·1	1·3	1·4	15·2	1·5	20·1	1·7	7·5	2·3	5·1	0·8	10·2	1·3	9·3
Foreman and supervisors (manual)	3·6	0·5	2·6	0·4	4·3	0·4	1·3	0·2	0·6	neg.	0·6	neg.	3·1	0·4
Skilled manual	31·5	7·2	4·0	6·0	27·4	4·6	24·2	4·3	18·9	4·3	39·4	9·1	19·3	3·3
Unskilled manual	8·3	7·5	11·7	8·2	19·6	9·5	11·6	3·9	30·6	4·3	21·5	8·1	3·6	3·0

Source: 1966 Census (10% Sample), Economic Activity Tables and Commonwealth Immigrant Tables.

TABLE 14.6

Commonwealth Immigrants entering the United Kingdom 1955–1970 (excluding Australia, Canada and New Zealand)

	Voucher holders	Dependants	Total
1955	—	—	42,700
1956	—	—	46,850
1957	—	—	42,400
1958	—	—	29,850
1959	—	—	21,600
1960	—	—	57,700
1961	—	—	136,400
1962 to 30 June		94,900⎫	
1962 (1 July–31 Dec.)	4217	8218	12,435⎭ 107,335
1963	28,678	27,393	56,071
1964	13,888	38,952	52,840
1965	12,125	39,228	51,353
1966	5141	39,130	44,271
1967	4716	50,083	54,799
1968	4353	42,036	46,389
1969	3512	27,984	31,496
1970	3052	21,334	24,384

Sources: Institute of Race Relations Facts Paper, *Colour and Immigration in the United Kingdom*, 1969. *Commonwealth Immigrants Acts 1962 and 1968: Statistics*, 1962–.

TABLE 14.7

Commonwealth Natives in England and Wales by Place of Birth from 1951–1966 (excluding White Persons Born in India and Pakistan(*a*)

Birthplace	1951	1961	1966	% increase 1961–6
India	30,000	81,400	158,200	93·4
Pakistan	5000	24,900	68,500	175·1
Jamaica	6400	100,100	151,800	51·6
Rest of Caribbean	8900	71,700	116,000	61·8
Commonwealth West Africa	5600	19,800	36,000	81·8
Commonwealth East Africa	3900	10,600	31,300	195·3
Cyprus and Malta	24,700	66,600	90,800	36·3
Ceylon	5800	9000	12,900	43·3
Hong Kong and Malay colonies	12,000	29,900	47,000	57·2
Estimate of Total Coloured	103,100	414,700	742,500	79·4
Commonwealth Total	336,100	659,800	942,300	40·0

Note: (*a*) See Table 14.3 for white persons of Indian and Pakistani origin.
Source: Census 1951, 1961, 1966; D. Eversley and F. Sukdeo, *op. cit.*, p. 9.

TABLE 14.8

**Regional Distribution of Population by Birthplace, Great Britain 1966
(the figures from the 1966 Census have been multiplied by 10 to
give totals for the whole population)**

Region(a)	Total population	Birthplace			W. Indies, India, Pakistan, as % of total popn.
		W. Indies	India	Pakistan	
England and Wales	47,135,510	267,850	232,210	73,130	1·2
N. Region	3,264,410	930	5030	1570	0·2
Yorkshire and Humberside region	4,669,200	12,510	14,890	15,010	0·9
N.W. Region	6,635,240	14,560	16,150	8550	0·6
E. Midland Region	3,262,290	12,700	14,290	2,590	1·2
W. Midland Region	4,909,350	41,900	38,780	17,290	0·9
East Anglia	1,539,960	5630	3310	760	0·6
S.E. Region	16,651,690	174,090	125,890	25,780	1·9
S.W. Region	3,559,930	7080	11,460	1490	0·6
Wales	2,663,440	1710	2460	690	0·2
Scotland	5,168,210	1480	8090	2030	0·2
CONURBATIONS					
Tyneside	832,230	280	1950	630	0·3
W. Yorkshire	1,708,260	8360	10,350	12,660	1·8
S.E. Lancashire	2,404,100	10,670	7730	5120	1·0
Merseyside	1,337,530	1710	2280	410	0·3
W. Midlands	2,374,070	35,800	26,930	14,110	3·3
Greater London	771,220	151,810	80,230	15,940	3·2
Central Clydeside	1,755,630	570	3470	1330	0·3

Note: (a) The regions refer to the Race Relations Board Conciliation areas.
Source: Quoted by Institute of Race Relations Facts Paper, 1969, *op. cit.*

TABLE 14.9

Children in Coloured Commonwealth Households Born in England and Wales(a) as a Proportion of all Children in those Households 1966

Type of household	Age group of children						Total children 0–14 in households	Children 0–14 years born in England & Wales	Percentage of all children in households
	0–4		5–9		10–14				
	Number	%	Number	%	Number	%			
India(b)	38,776	88·6	24,176	60·0	22,878	35·2	85,830	56,886	66·3
Pakistan(c)	7863	73·3	5186	32·5	4148	0·1	17,197	7427	43·2
Jamaica	47,775	98·1	26,999	80·2	13,032	20·7	87,806	71,218	81·1
Rest of Caribbean	34,686	96·7	17,704	66·0	9495	12·0	62,885	47,364	75·3
West Africa	6363	86·5	2342	33·4	993	25·4	9699	6632	68·4
Cyprus	11,894	93·5	10,391	62·9	7488	38·1	29,773	20,431	68·6
Total		100		100		100			100

Notes:
(a) These estimates do not include children who were under-enumerated.
(b) Children of white Indians are included.
(c) Children of white Pakistanis are included.
Sources: D. Eversley and F. Sukdeo, op. cit.

TABLE 14.10

A Comparison of the Age Structure of Immigrants from the New
Commonwealth and their Dependants and Total Population of
England and Wales 1961 and 1966 (percentages)

Age	1961		1966	
	All coloured groups	Total population	All coloured groups	Total population
Under 15 years	29	23	34	23
15–24 years	16	14	13	14
25–44 years	45	26	42	25
45+ years	10	37	11	38

Source: E. J. B. Rose and associates, op. cit., p. 111.

TABLE 14.11

Numbers of Irish-Born Resident in England and Wales 1901–1966 (Proportion per 100,000 persons)

Year	1901	1911	1921	1931	1951	1961	1966
Total enumerated population	100,000	100,000	100,000	100,000	100,000	100,000	100,000
Born in England and Wales	96,131	94,462	96,055	96,345	93,972	92,834	92,227
All Ireland	1311	1041	1705	954	1433	1889	1863
N. Ireland	—	190	963	175	308	407	381
Irish Republic	—	786	742	761	1079	1398	1431
Ireland (part not stated)	—	65	—	18	46	84	51

Source: Census Reports, 1901–66.

TABLE 14.12

Numbers of Irish-Born Resident in England and Wales and Scotland in Relation to total Population 1901–1966

Date	England and Wales		Scotland	
	Number of Irish-born	% of total population	Number of Irish-born	% of total population
1901	426,565	1·3	205,064	4·6
1911	375,325	1·0	174,715	3·7
1921	364,747	1·0	159,020	3·3
1931	381,089	0·9	124,296	2·6
1951	627,021	1·4	89,007	1·7
1961	870,445	1·8	80,533	1·6
1966	878,530	1·8	69,790	1·3

Source: Census Reports, 1901–66.

TABLE 14.13

Insurance Cards Issued to Citizens of Irish Republic 1958–1968, Great Britain

Year	1958	1960	1962	1964	1966	1968
Total number issued	58,316	72,962	52,362	56,020	61,380	44,280
Registering first time	47,869	57,798	38,367	39,100	44,319	30,929
Re-registering	10,447	15,164	13,995	16,920	17,061	13,351

Sources: Figures from the Ministry of Pensions and National Insurance and the Department of Health and Social Security.

TABLE 14.14

Areas of Settlement of Irish-Born in the United Kingdom 1961 and 1966

Region	1961	1966	% increase/decrease
England	847,484	857,260	+ 1·2
Wales	22,961	21,270	− 7·4
Scotland	80,533	69,790	− 13·3
East Midlands	41,126	43,090	+ 4·8
West Midlands	118,933	119,440	+ 0·4
South Eastern	436,125	442,630	+ 1·5
North Western	131,827	131,660	− 0·1
Northern	19,164	17,230	− 10·1

Source: Figures from 1961 and 1966 Census quoted by Irish Trade Journal and Statistical Bulletin, June 1968.

TABLE 14.15

Children under five per 1000 Women aged 15-44 years in the London and Birmingham Conurbations 1961 and 1966

Area of Origin	1961	1966
India(a)	830	771
Pakistan	1338	979
West Indies	576	821
British West Africa	572	510
Cyprus	740	604
Ireland	—	768
Total population	396	434

Note: (a) Excluding White Indians.
Source: E. J. B. Rose, *op. cit.*, p. 113.

TABLE 14.16

Family Structure of Major Immigrant Groups in London and Birmingham Conurbations 1961 and 1966

Area of Origin	% of all households without children		Average number of children in families		% of all families with 3+ children	
	1961	1966	1961	1966	1961	1966
India(a)	51	50	2·02	2·35	26	36
Pakistan	55	62	2·28	2·30	32	34
West Indies	56	36	1·97	2·43	25	35
British West Africa	53	69	1·79	1·87	20	22
Cyprus	36	34	2·12	2·13	30	30
Ireland(b)	—	46	—	2·52	—	42
England(b)	—	69	—	1·85	—	20

Notes:
(a) White Indians *not* excluded.
(b) Data refer to selected control zones only.
Source: E. J. B. Rose, *op. cit.*, p. 117.

TABLE 14.17

Occupational Distribution of Commonwealth and Irish Male Citizens Resident in England and Wales 1961 (percentages)

Certain occupations	All persons	Ireland(a)	India	Pakistan	Caribbean
Transport and communication workers	8·4	7·3	8·2	7·4	11·5
Clerical workers	7·1	5·2	12·7	5·3	3·1
Sales workers	8·0	3·5	6·6	4·3	0·8
Administrative and managers	3·8	1·9	4·7	2·2	0·4
Professional and technical workers	8·0	6·2	18·6	8·6	3·2
Labourers	7·5	20·0	6·7	25·6	24·3

Note: (a) Includes Northern Ireland and Irish Republic.
Source: 1961 Census (10% sample), *Occupation Tables*.

TABLE 14.18

Occupational Distribution of Commonwealth and Irish Female Citizens Resident in England and Wales 1961 (percentages)

Certain occupations	All persons	Ireland(a)	India	Pakistan	Caribbean
Clothing workers	5·1	2·5	2·7	0	11·8
Clerical workers	25·9	15·9	39·2	36·2	6·6
Sales workers	12·7	7·8	6·1	7·9	1·0
Professional and technical workers	10·0	20·1	22·3	36·2	22·6
Labourers	1·3	1·8	0·8	0·8	4·3

Note: (a) Includes Northern Ireland and Irish Republic.
Source: 1961 Census (10% sample), *Occupation Tables*.

TABLE 14.19

Birthplaces of Certain Groups of Alien Immigrants Resident in England and Wales 1881–1921

	1881	Number per 100,000	1891	Number per 100,000	1901	Number per 100,000	1911	Number per 100,000	1921	Number per 100,000
Total enumerated population	24,855,822	100,000	27,882,629	100,000	32,527,843	100,000	36,070,492	100,000	37,886,699	100,000
Foreign subjects	117,999	474	198,113	710	247,758	761	284,830	789	228,266	602
Born in:										
Germany	37,301	150	50,599	181	49,133	151	53,324	147	12,358	32
France	14,596	58	20,797	74	20,467	62	28,827	79	23,659	62
Russia and Russian Poland	14,468	58	45,074	161	82,844	254	95,541	264	84,896	224
Italy	6504	26	9909	35	20,332	62	20,389	96	19,098	50
Holland	5357	21	6350	22	6851	21	7643	21	7426	19
Switzerland	3226	12	6617	23	8357	25	10,267	28	8965	23
Belgium	2462	9	3917	14	4314	13	4657	12	9681	25
Austria and Hungary	2809	11	5673	20	9685	29	13,230	36	—	36
America	18,496	74	26,226	94	18,311	56	16,860	46	22,730	59

Source: Census Reports, 1881–1921.

TABLE 14.20

Numbers of Jews in the United Kingdom 1891–1970

Year	Number	Actual increase or decrease	% increase or decrease
1891	101,189	—	—
1901	160,000	+58,811	+58·1
1905	227,166	+67,166	+41·9
1911	237,760	+10,594	+ 4·6
1916	257,000	+19,240	+ 8·1
1921	300,000	+43,000	+16·7
1926	297,000	− 3000	− 1
1931	297,000	—	0
1936	333,000	+36,000	+12·1
1946	385,000	+52,000	+15·6
1951	450,000	+65,000	+16·9
1961	450,000	—	0
1966	450,000	—	0
1970	450,000	—	0

Source: Jewish Year Book, selected years.

TABLE 14.21

Birthplaces or Nationality of Certain Groups of Alien Immigrants Resident in England and Wales 1931–1961

	1931	Number per 100,000	1951(a)	Number per 100,000	1961(a)	Number per 100,000
Total enumerated population	39,952,377	100,000	43,757,888	100,000	46,104,548	100,000
Foreign subjects	183,794	460	360,358(b)	823	416,715	903
Born in:						
Russia (including Finland)	24,959	62	57,801	132	33,914	73
Poland	31,423	78	130,865	299	82,957	179
France	15,628	39	11,398	26	13,143	28
Italy	16,878	42	20,204	46	66,251	143
Germany	14,981	37	35,549	81	34,346	74
Switzerland	9762	24	8084	18	8565	18
United States	11,220	28	34,472	78	76,264	165

Notes:
(a) In 1951 and 1961 aliens are enumerated by their country of nationality, not their birthplace.
(b) This does not include 7815 stateless persons and 11,960 with nationalities not stated but born in foreign countries.
Source: Census Reports, 1931–61.

TABLE 14.22

**Alien Workers and Dependants Admitted to the United Kingdom
1960–1969**

| Year | For 12 months | | Less than 12 months |
	Workers	Dependants	Workers
1960	31,111(a)	1107	14,948
1961	21,303(a)	1943	17,119
1962	27,349	4033	16,941
1963	21,860	3337	17,803
1964	23,664	4098	18,920
1965	27,883	5689	20,991
1966	26,606	6434	22,031
1967	23,114	5647	22,753
1968	22,645	5436	22,497
1969	22,877	5266	24,975

Note: (a) Including adult dependants.
Source: Home Office, *Annual Statistics of Foreigners entering and leaving the U.K.*

TABLE 14.23

**Net Gain (+) or Loss (−) by Migration 1881–1961 U.K. and England
and Wales (thousands)**

| Year | Census population at beginning of period | | Net gain or loss by migration | |
	U.K.	England and Wales	U.K.	England and Wales
1881–1891	31,015	25,974	−960	−601
1891–1901	34,265	29,003	−190	−69
1901–1911	38,237	35,528	−820	−581
1911–1921	42,082	36,070	−919	−620
1921–1931	44,027	37,887	−672	−170
1931–1957	46,038	39,952	+465	+758
1951–1961	50,225	43,758	+12	+387

Source: Annual Abstract of Statistics, no. 105, 1968.

TABLE 14.24

Net Balance of Migration in the U.K. 1961–1968

Year	Net gain (+) or loss (−)	
1961	+130,000	
1962	+136,000	+316,000
1963	+10,000	
1964	−60,000	
1965	−78,000	
1966	−83,000	−361,000
1967	−84,000	
1968	−56,000	

Source: Registrar-General's Quarterly Return for England and Wales.

15 Crime and Penal Measures

NIGEL WALKER

This chapter deals with national, as distinct from local, trends in

(i) *Judicial Statistics for Criminal Proceedings:* i.e. appearances in criminal courts and their outcome, whether this takes the form of an acquittal or a sentence.

(ii) *Prison Statistics:* i.e. admissions to prisons, their populations and the lengths of prison sentences.

(iii) *Statistics of Recidivism:* i.e. of persons who are convicted more than once.

(iv) *Criminal Statistics Proper:* i.e. statistics of offences committed, in so far as these are officially known.

(v) *Clear-up Statistics:* i.e. statistics of officially known crimes which are 'cleared up'. 'Clearing up' means tracing the crime to an offender, even if the offender is not always convicted of it. This is the nearest equivalent – although in most ways superior – to the statistics of 'arrests' which are published in some other countries (e.g. the U.S.A.).

(vi) *Police and Probation Manpower Statistics:* i.e. the number of persons employed by police forces and probation and after-care committees.

The government department responsible for the collection of periodic national statistics of these kinds is the Home Office, through its Statistical Branch. Most of them are published annually in the form of 'The Criminal Statistics for England and Wales', which is usually on sale at Her Majesty's Stationery Office by the end of August in the following year; other official publications are listed at the end of this chapter. The Home Office relies on local police forces for the returns on which statistics of types (i), (iv), (v) and (vi) are based, and on local prisons for (ii).

There have been two major overhauls of the criminal and judicial statistics since they began to be collected and published in the middle of the nineteenth century. One took place in the eighteen-nineties, and so was completed before the period with which we are concerned; the other is taking place at present as the result of the Report of the two Departmental Committees on

Criminal Statistics.[1] When it is completed the British[2] Criminal Statistics (which are already more informative than those of most other countries) will be greatly improved both in content and in presentation. For the first seven decades of this century, however, the main criminal and judicial statistics have been compiled on much the same basis, although with minor changes in definition and accuracy, of which the most important examples are:

1. *Age of criminal liability.* The minimum age at which a child could be charged with any kind of offence was raised from the 7th to the 8th birthday from 1934; and from the 7th to the 10th birthday from February 1964.

2. *Age of juvenile court jurisdiction.* The maximum age at which a young person could be dealt with by a juvenile court was raised from 16 to 17 from 1934.

3. *Murder.* The creation of the new offence of 'infanticide' in 1922 excluded substantial numbers of homicides by women from both the recorded murders and the convicted murderers from 1923.

The creation of the new defence of 'diminished responsibility' in March 1957 excluded substantial numbers of homicides by men and women from both the criminal and judicial statistics for murder; these homicides were henceforth shown as 'manslaughter', although separately from other homicides in this category.

4. *Manslaughter.* In addition to the change just mentioned, the creation of the new offence of 'causing death by dangerous driving' from 1956 excluded substantial numbers from the judicial and criminal statistics for manslaughter.

5. *Homosexual offences.* These were redefined in 1967 so as to exclude (with minor exceptions) sexual acts in private between consenting men aged 21 or older.

6. *Acquisitive offences.* The Theft Act, 1967, revised the definitions of most acquisitive offences from 1968.

Again, in interpreting changes in courts' choices of sentence it is important to be sure of the extent to which choices were freely available. Thus the apparent caution with which courts began to use detention centre orders in the nineteen-fifties is explained by the slow increase in detention centre vacancies: it was many years before every court could make use of this measure.

[1] i.e. the Perks Committee (1967, Cmnd 3448), which was concerned with England and Wales, and the Thompson Committee (1968, Cmnd 3705), which was concerned with Scotland.

[2] Separate and roughly equivalent statistics for Scotland are published by the Scottish Home and Health Department. The statistics for England and Wales do not include Northern Ireland, Eire, the Isle of Man or the Channel Islands.

Nor should it be assumed that every penal statute came into operation as soon as it received the Royal Assent. Some do; but if a provision involves administrative changes it is likely that the statute will provide that it should not come into operation until such a date as the Home Secretary (or other Minister) may appoint by order (such orders being statutory instruments). Thus, for example, the sections of the Criminal Justice Act of 1967 which created the suspended prison sentence were brought into operation on 1st January 1968; but the parole provisions, which called for much preparation, were not brought into operation until three months later.

JUDICIAL STATISTICS

Statistics of trials and sentences (i.e. 'Criminal Judicial Statistics') have been published annually as parliamentary or departmental papers since 1834. At first they were confined to trials on indictment (i.e. before a jury at Assizes or Quarter Sessions), but in 1857 they were extended to summary trials in magistrates' courts. Judicial statistics are based on reports from local police forces, who send the Home Office's Statistical Branch a form for every person brought to trial. Being based, therefore, on reports of easily observed events by persons who are trained to understand what they are observing, they are not subject to large-scale inaccuracies of the kind which vitiate some other forms of statistics. It is important, however, to note their limitations. They do not count persons, but *appearances in criminal courts* by persons who in some cases appear more than once a year (e.g. for offences of drunkenness). They do not show all the offences of which a person was accused at his appearance, nor all the sentences which he received: only the most serious. Thus a person imprisoned for taking and driving away a motor-car, and fined for careless driving at the same time, would be shown only as imprisoned for the first of these offences.

Occasional inaccuracies arise from technicalities. Thus a decision to commit a mentally disordered offender to hospital is sometimes confused with one of 'unfit to plead', since both are rare and unfamiliar to police officers. But these are minor exceptions: on the whole the judicial statistics, within their self-imposed limitations, give an accurate picture of the reality which they represent.

In their modern published form the judicial statistics distinguish summary trials in magistrates' courts (Table I of the *Criminal Statistics*) from trials on indictment before juries at Assizes and Quarter Sessions (Table II). Within each category they distinguish certain age-groups, so that for example, Tables I(d) and (e) deal with children and young persons[1] tried in juvenile courts. The statistics for magistrates' courts also subdivide offences into three main groups: indictable (i.e. liable in certain circumstances to be tried at higher courts, with the possibility of more severe penalties), non-indictable (i.e. triable only by summary courts) and motoring (all but the most serious of these being non-indictable). The centuries-old distinction between 'felonies' and 'misdemeanours' is obsolete, and was replaced in 1967 by the distinction between 'arrestable' and 'non-arrestable' offences, which is not reflected in the published statistics.

Table 15.1 shows the numbers of persons dealt with in higher and summary courts in selected years of this century, together with the percentages who were found guilty (unfortunately the statistics do not make it possible to subdivide these into persons who pleaded guilty and persons who pleaded not guilty). It also shows the numbers of those found guilty who were sentenced in the various ways open to the courts.

INDICTABLE OFFENCES

Most of the indictable offences tried, whether by higher or by summary courts, are acquisitive offences of one sort or another, ranging from minor thefts to large-scale robberies or frauds. A substantial number of the minor thefts which reach the courts are by juveniles, especially boys in their mid-teens (girls nowadays show the same peak age, although the peak itself is much lower).

Less numerous, but causing more concern, are offences involving personal violence, sexual molestation or both. The peak age for personal violence seems to be the late teens and early twenties, at least so far as official statistics are concerned: but a great deal of schoolboy violence is unreported. Sexual molesters are more widely distributed in age.

It is important to realise that over the last hundred years there has been a tendency to 'demote' whole categories of offences which used to be triable only on indictment at higher courts so that they could be tried summarily by magistrates. The chief reason has been the increasing demands on the time of the higher courts. The result of such demotions is that the great majority of indictable offences – i.e. those which could be tried at higher courts if the accused or prosecution so requested or the magistrates thought fit – are now tried summarily; and in most of these cases the accused pleads guilty. The research worker who is following trends in judicial statistics must be on the alert for administrative changes of this sort. For example, the number[2] of shopbreaking cases dealt with by higher courts fell from 8848 in 1962 to 2803 in 1963;

---

[1] 'Children' in the criminal law means 'persons under the age of 14'. 'Young persons' are aged 14, 15 or 16.
[2] Ignoring juveniles in both years.

but in magistrates' courts the corresponding number rose from 5805 to 12,460: all that had happened was that the Criminal Justice Administration Act, 1962, had made it possible for most shopbreaking cases to be tried summarily.

NON-INDICTABLE OFFENCES

These are very miscellaneous. Some are acquisitive in nature: for example, evasion of revenue or travelling on public transport without paying. Other numerous groups are minor assaults, which do not result in serious injury; drunkenness; obstructing highways (usually by selling goods on pavements); offences by prostitutes; damage to property; and taking vehicles without the owner's consent. The last two are to a considerable extent offences of teenage males, and the offence of taking a vehicle without the owner's consent was created by the Road Traffic Act 1930, in order to secure the conviction of 'borrowers' and 'joyriders' who had no intention of permanently depriving the owner and could not therefore be convicted of larceny.

Prostitutes' offences usually consist of persistent soliciting by adult women in public places: prostitution itself is not prohibited by British law. Girls under 17 are not usually charged with soliciting, but instead are dealt with as in need of care and protection. Even adult women who are found soliciting are not usually charged with it on the first or second occasion, for the police are under instructions to caution them instead in these circumstances. Men are charged not with soliciting but with 'importuning', which need not be for mercenary purposes.

POLICE WARNINGS

It is particularly important to be aware of the practice known as the 'police warning' or 'caution' (not to be confused with the 'caution' which the police are required by Judges' Rules to administer when they are questioning suspects). English and Welsh police forces are allowed to use their discretion in prosecuting, and may substitute a 'caution' for prosecution even when the latter seems both justifiable and likely to succeed. Motoring offences are frequently dealt with in this way; and so are offences by juveniles. Statistics for police cautions were first published for the year 1954, and Table 15.2 shows the numbers of cautions administered for offences other than motoring offences (for which cautions are not recorded systematically) for that and subsequent years.

A comparison of Table 15.1 with Table 15.2 shows that on the whole being let off with a caution is more likely if the offender is a juvenile than if he is an adult, and more likely in the case of female than of male offenders.[1] It is interesting to note, too, that although the numbers of persons found guilty of non-indictable offences has increased over the period, the numbers cautioned for such offences has *decreased* (after a slight increase in the late nineteen-fifties for juveniles and women). This contrasts with the increasing percentage of *indictable* offenders who are allowed to escape prosecution in this way. Where juveniles are concerned this increase in leniency would have been even more evident if the Children and Young Persons Act, 1963, had not exempted children under 10 from both prosecution and cautioning, since children of 8 and 9 were benefiting most of all from the growing popularity of this practice.

The differing trends for indictable and non-indictable offences may be connected with the fact that whereas the decision to prosecute rests with the police[2] in the case of the great majority of indictable offences there are several quite numerous non-indictable offences which it is the responsibility of the Department concerned to prosecute. When a Department or private person decides not to prosecute they cannot substitute a police caution as an alternative. Consequently cautions are an index of increasing leniency in the matter of prosecution only so far as concerns offences prosecuted by the *police*.

MOTORING OFFENCES

Tables 15.1 and 15.2 do not show prosecutions for motoring offences, which are set out separately in Table 15.3 (Cautions for such offences can be found in the annual Home Office publication 'Offences relating to Motor Vehicles').

The Table emphasises the extent to which, as Lady Wootton has put it, 'the internal combustion engine has revolutionised the business of our criminal courts'. The volume of such prosecutions has forced them to adopt procedures, such as pleading guilty by post, which would not otherwise have been contemplated. More recently, it has even led to

---

[1] Except in the case of non-indictable offences by boys and girls aged 14–16, where the difference is negligible. The explanation probably lies in the nature of their offences, of which the great majority are either taking and driving away cars, cyclists' offences, damage to property, or offences on railways (mostly attempts to evade ticket-buying). The relatively small number of girls involved in such offences are probably in the company of boys, and are therefore dealt with by the police in the same way.

[2] The exceptions being the relatively small number of offences where the decision must be taken by the Director of Public Prosecutions or – even more rarely – the Attorney-General, either because the consequences of conviction are so serious (as in the case of murder) or because the evidential problems call for special expertise (as in the case of certain sexual offences). In Scotland – in theory at least – the decision to prosecute never lies with the police, but always with the Procurator-Fiscal, burgh fiscal or Government Department concerned.

the introduction of a system of fining without trial, known as the 'fixed penalty procedure', under which certain types of motoring offence can be penalised by means of a notice demanding a fixed payment (although the offender can choose summary trial if he prefers, he seldom does, since he risks a fine which would probably be higher). In 1961, immediately after this procedure was introduced, it was used in 101,780 cases, and its use has since increased tenfold: 1,046,358 notices were issued in 1968. Even so, although a motoring offence takes up on average less of the court's time than offences of other sorts, every prosecution, fixed penalty notice or caution makes unavoidable demands on the man-hours of police forces, and must affect their efficiency in dealing with other sorts of offence. (This does not imply that other offences are always more deserving of police attention. Bad driving, or neglected brakes or tyres and unlit vehicles probably cause larger numbers of serious injuries than intentional assaults.)

TRENDS IN SENTENCING
Some clear trends in sentencing policy are demonstrated in Table 15.1:
1. A decline in the use of imprisonment is obvious, and easily explained. Parliament has passed successive statutes limiting the circumstances in which imprisonment can be used. The Criminal Justice Administration Act, 1914, for example, was explicitly 'An Act to reduce the number of cases admitted to prison', and (with exceptions) prohibited summary courts from immediately imprisoning offenders who could not pay fines on the spot. The result was a drop in the number of prison sentences, which persisted even after the First World War. The imprisonment of young offenders has also been restricted by successive pieces of legislation in 1908, 1932, 1948 and 1961. The First Offenders Act, 1958, also made it more difficult for summary courts to impose prison sentences on adults who had not previously been convicted of indictable offences since their 17th birthdays. It seems, however, to have had little effect on the imprisonment-rate of summary courts, perhaps because it was already rare for them to imprison 'first offenders', perhaps too because in cases in which they wanted to imprison the Act did not make it impossible for them to do so.

Furthermore, even within the permissible limits sentencers have become increasingly inclined to reserve imprisonment for what they regard as dangerous, persistent or particularly culpable offenders. Consequently the trend has been more marked in summary than in higher courts, but even in the latter the percentage of offenders imprisoned has fallen from over 90 per cent to just under 54 per cent.

2. A similar decline can be seen in the use of custodial measures for

juveniles, which has however been much less marked, partly because such measures were used only for about 16 per cent at the beginning of the century, but partly also because modern custodial measures are regarded – rightly or wrongly – as being remedial rather than punitive, and as being in the interests of the juvenile as well as of society. A magistrate who regards imprisonment as a last resort for adults may not take the same view of approved schools for boys.

3. The measure which has increased most in popularity in the higher courts is probation. In juvenile courts, on the other hand, the heyday of probation was in the nineteen-thirties, when it was used for more than half of those found guilty. Nowadays, though still used very frequently for juveniles, it has to compete with attendance centres; and under the Children and Young Persons Act, 1969, probation proper – i.e. as distinct from 'supervision' by a social worker of the local authority – will eventually be replaced by 'supervision orders' so far as juveniles are concerned. Probation is gradually becoming a measure reserved for adults.

4. So far as adults in summary courts are concerned, the most important measure is the fine, for which the percentage has climbed from 22% early in the century to 56% in 1960. For traffic offences the percentage is nearly 99%. Even in higher courts, which have increasingly specialised in sentencing more serious cases, there has been a marked increase in the use of fines, especially since higher courts' power to fine – hitherto restricted to offences specified by statute – was extended in 1948 to all offences except murder and one or two very rare crimes.

5. Nominal measures – absolute or conditional discharges and recognizances – have always been popular for juveniles, about a third of whom on average seem to be dealt with thus. For adults, they reached their zenith in the nineteen-thirties, and now seem to be declining slowly in relative numbers. They tend to be used for offenders whom the courts regard as only technically guilty, or as guilty only of a trivial form of the offence, or as most unlikely to break the law again, or as mildly disordered in mind.

6. The introduction of the suspended sentence of imprisonment, however, at the beginning of 1968, had marked effects, not all of them intended. It was meant to reduce the number of persons who were actually sent to prison, especially for short periods; and summary courts were in fact obliged to suspend sentences of six months or less, although allowed to make quite a number of exceptions. In the event, the percentages of indictable offenders who were sent straight to prison – which had been increasing in higher courts, and falling only slightly in lower courts during the sixties – did show a definite fall. There was also, however, a fall in the percentages of those fined and those put on

probation, which could hardly be attributable to any other factor. (There were also decreases in the percentages dealt with by nominal measures; but these had been declining gradually even before 1968, so that it is hard to be sure whether any of the decrease was attributable to the suspended sentence.) It is too soon to say whether these observations indicate a lasting effect or merely the temporary attractions of a new addition to the courts' repertoire. It is also too soon to estimate what percentage of suspended sentences merely postpones, instead of averting, a prison sentence.

PRISON STATISTICS

Although fining is now by far the most frequent penalty, imprisonment is the most drastic. The annual reports of the Prison Commissioners[1] give numbers of prisoners received, daily average populations of the prisons and lengths of sentences. Table 15.4 shows two sets of statistics: prisoners received under sentence of imprisonment (i.e. excluding those awaiting trial, or sentence, or extradition or hanging); and the daily average prison population. The ratio between the two is a rough indication of the average length of sentence actually served[2] since the daily average population divided by the prisoners received shows the average fraction of a year which prisoners spent inside. Thus at the turn of the century the average sentence served was about one ninth of a year, or six weeks. Nowadays it is considerably *longer*, not because courts are more severe but because offenders who would formerly have received short sentences of imprisonment are now fined, put on probation or discharged (see 'Trends in Sentencing', para 1).

It is not usually realised that in addition to its punitive function the prison system has played an increasingly important part in providing sentencers with information about prisoners in order to assist them in their choice of sentence. An increasing percentage of the prison population consists of prisoners who have been found (or pleaded) guilty, and have been remanded for social or medical reports. The great majority of offenders who are entrusted to mental hospitals or out-patient clinics for treatment instead of being sentenced have been examined by prison

[1] From 1962 most of the statistical tables were published in a separate Command Paper. In 1963 the Prison Commissioners became 'The Prison Department of the Home Office'.

[2] As distinct from the nominal sentence, which in practice is shortened by remission for good conduct (except in the case of very short sentences). From 1899 until the middle of the Second World War remission for men (women were more generously treated) was one sixth of prison sentences, one quarter of penal servitude; since then it has been one third of all sentences. The introduction of parole in 1968 for sentences of 19 months or more further widened the gap between nominal and real duration for a substantial minority of prisoners.

medical officers, with or without the assistance of outside consultants. Table 15.5 shows the number of remands to prisons for psychiatric examination from 1920 (the earliest year from which regular annual figures are available, although there were several hundred psychiatric remands a year at the turn of the century). The figures show a slow but steady rise until the Second World War, after which they continued at a higher but fairly stable level, until they began to rise again, much more sharply, in the nineteen-sixties (no doubt because the Mental Health Act, 1959, had made committal to mental hospitals an easy and attractive way of dealing with disordered offenders).

RECIDIVISM

Trends in the prevalence of recidivism are usually regarded as one of the indications of a society's success or failure in preventing crime and dealing with criminals. Since it is impossible to be sure how many convicted offenders offend again without detection, a recidivist has to be defined for practical purposes as a person who is found guilty of at least one further offence committed after he had already been warned by the police or dealt with by a court for a previous offence. In England and Wales the limitations of central records mean that at present only recidivists with two or more successive[1] findings of guilt *in court* and for *indictable*[2] offences can be identified. Thus there are no national statistics to indicate the extent of recidivism amongst, for example, bad drivers, drunks, or soliciting prostitutes, although in all these cases it is suspected that it is very high.

In this restricted sense, recent trends in recidivism have been studied by McClintock and Avison, who were able from Home Office records to compare 1954–5 with 1962, and produced, *inter alia*, Tables 15.6 and 15.7.

Not only can it be seen from Table 15.6 that the percentage of offenders with clean records has declined in all age-groups, but it is also clear from Table 15.7 that amongst those with previous proved offences the percentages with large numbers of previous offences has increased.

To some extent the increase in the frequency of previous convictions is no doubt due to greater efficiency in linking offenders to their records. This is particularly likely in the case of juveniles; for provincial police forces tend to be selective in reporting their offences to the central record office. This could hardly, however, explain away entirely the

---

[1] A person who is found guilty of more than one offence, or has more than one offence taken into account, at a single court appearance is not counted as a recidivist.
[2] Together with a very few non-indictable ones which are sufficiently similar to indictable offences to be centrally recorded.

increased recidivism of adult males, and the figures appear to reflect a rather unsuccessful rearguard action against the advance of crime. Another possibility must nevertheless not be overlooked. This is that what the figures reflect is not so much an increasing frequency of criminal acts on the part of a given number of men (although this cannot be ruled out) as the tracing of a larger number of reported crimes to their perpetrators. This hypothesis is not inconsistent with a *decrease* in the clear-up *percentage*, so long as the actual *numbers* of cleared-up offences *increased:* (and in fact in the period covered by Tables 15.6 and 15.7 the numbers of cleared-up indictable offences rose from some 213,500 to some 393,600, although the clear-up rate fell from 49 per cent to 44 per cent). For an explanation of 'clear-up rates', see below.

CRIMINAL STATISTICS

To be carefully distinguished from the judicial and prison statistics are figures of 'crimes made known to the police', which were first included in the annual volumes for 1857. These are subject to several limitations, some of them deliberate, some of them inevitable:

(i) They are confined to offences which are regarded as sufficiently important to warrant the work involved in reporting them to the Home Office: these are referred to as 'Standard List Offences'.

(ii) Even where standard list offences are concerned they show only what local police forces record and report as 'made known to' them. Thus a member of the public may report that his dog has been stolen, but unless there is evidence to support this the police may, quite reasonably, treat it as a 'lost dog' case and not as a reported crime. In the early nineteen-thirties it was found that the Metropolitan Police were recording large numbers of reported thefts merely as 'lost property', and when this was corrected the statistics for recorded thefts rose sharply.

(iii) The police cannot of course be expected to record offences which do not come to their notice.

This last difficulty is the major limitation of all criminal statistics, and means that they reflect what actually occurs in a very distorted fashion. (It is not of course confined to criminal statistics, but occurs in most other attempts to record social facts, such as mental illness.) The 'dark figure' – that is, the unreported percentage – varies from one sort of crime to another. The reasons why a crime may not be reported are numerous:

1. All those involved may fail to realise that an offence has been committed. Children commit assaults and indecencies without being aware of their criminality.

2. All those involved may be willing participants. This is especially

frequent in the case of abortions, homosexual offences, incest, and carnal knowledge of girls under 16.

3. Even an unwilling victim may not wish to involve the offender in the consequences of prosecution. This happens not only with sexual offences such as indecent assaults; but also in minor cases of pilfering, embezzlement, or fraud.

4. The victim may himself be antagonistic to the police. Many assaults in certain districts of large cities are not reported because this would be regarded as handing the aggressor over to a common enemy.

5. The victim may regard the offence as too trivial to be worth the trouble of reporting. Many minor thefts are not reported for this reason.

6. The victim may be so pessimistic about the chances of bringing the offender to book that he does not bother to report the offence. This is more likely with minor offences.

7. The victim may be too embarrassed to report the offence. Women – especially the very young – are often inhibited in this way from reporting indecent exposure. Men may keep silent about homosexual importuning in case they are suspected of attracting such advances. Parents of child victims of sexual offences may wish to spare the child the experience of interrogation and appearance in court.

8. The offence may be observed only by someone who disapproves of the law. Poaching is often unreported for this reason.

9. The victim or observer may be intimidated by the offender's threats of violence or by blackmail.· Prostitutes' thefts from clients are seldom brought to the notice of the police.

10. The offence may be unknown to anyone but the offender, as must often happen in the case of speeding motorists.

Broadly speaking, it can probably be assumed that the more serious the harm caused by the offence the more likely it is to be reported, either because the harm is resented by the victim or the victim's family, or because help is needed to deal with it. Serious physical injury requires medical attention; large-scale thefts lead to insurance claims; serious sexual molestation causes shock and distress. In general, the more trivial the offence the larger the dark figure, although there may well be important exceptions, such as serious drug abuse. Public attitudes change, however, in this as in other respects, and readiness to report certain types of offence increases or decreases. Thus the considerable increase in recorded homosexual offences since 1900 (see Table 15.8) is probably due in part at least to a greater readiness to report such offences (and perhaps also in part to increasing activity on the part of the police, especially where public importuning by men is concerned). Consistent with this hypothesis is the fact that homosexual and heterosexual offences are the only groups which, after considerable long-term increases in their reported frequencies, have recently settled down to a stable level.

With these reservations, trends in recorded indictable offences during this century are set out in Table 15.8.[1] In order to show the extent of the increase for each group, its average annual frequency for the years 1901–5 has been taken as the 'base' (i.e., as 100 per cent.), and frequencies for selected subsequent years have been represented as a percentage of that base. Thus it can be seen that at one extreme the frequency of murder has apparently[2] changed very little (1963 = 98 per cent of 1901–5) while the frequency of attempts at burglaries and at other 'breaking and entering' crimes has increased forty-twofold (1963=4186 per cent of 1901–5).

These changes must, of course, be seen against the perspective of substantial increases both in population and affluence. Not only have the numbers of potential offenders risen, but so have the numbers of potential victims and the amounts of money and other portable goods which are the main targets of property offenders. It is usual to allow for population increases by representing frequencies of reported offences as rates per 100,000 of persons of all ages; but this can be misleading. It does not accurately reflect the number of potential victims, whose age-groups and economic groups differ widely according to the type of crime (for example, most victims of heterosexual offences are girls or young women in social classes IV and V, while most victims of theft and robbery are mature men in social classes I–III, or commercial organisations). Nor does it reflect the number of potential offenders, the great majority of whom are males between puberty and middle age. Probably the least inaccurate basis for a general comparison of reported offence-frequencies and potential offenders is the numbers of males between their 15th[3] and 50th birthdays, and the extent to which this has increased since the turn of the century is shown in the last line of Table 15.8. The increase is surprisingly small, until one realises that the increase in our total population is largely the result of increases in the older age-groups.

CLEARED-UP CRIMES

Since 1938 the annual Criminal Statistics have also shown the numbers of recorded standard list offences which are 'cleared up'. 'Clearing up'

[1] Based on a table compiled by F. H. McClintock *et al.*: see bibliography at the end of the chapter.

[2] Although changes in the definition of murder may have concealed an upward trend: see the article by A. J. Ashworth in *Criminal Law Review* (1969) 645 ff.

[3] Ideally, one would wish to include males in their 14th and 15th years, who have high rates for minor larcenies: but the Registrar-General's figures do not lend themselves to this.

usually means 'tracing and arresting (or summoning) the offender' (even if he is in fact acquitted); but it includes other eventualities: an offence is also counted as 'cleared up' if at least one of the perpetrators is identified and cautioned, or dies, or enters a mental hospital, or cannot be prosecuted for technical reasons, such as the death or recalcitrance of an essential witness. (See *Home Office Instructions for the Preparation of Statistics Relating to Crime*, obtainable by research workers from the Statistical Branch.) The clear-up percentage varies greatly from one type of crime to another. For murder and other serious crimes against the person it is high, partly because police take great trouble over such crimes, partly because the perpetrators are usually close acquaintances of their victims, and are easily identified either by the victims themselves or by their families. Many murderers who have killed spouses, lovers or children either commit suicide or give themselves up to the police. For minor thefts, on the other hand, the percentage is much lower, partly because the police can spare less time for them, partly because the offences themselves are easy to commit without much risk of detection.

Consequently, the tendency to regard overall clear-up rates as an index of police efficiency, and to use this to compare police forces in different areas or decades, is fallacious. It has had unfortunate effects on the recording of reported crime, since it discouraged police from recording minor crimes which they had little chance of tracing to their perpetrators. For these reasons only recent clear-up rates for fairly specific sub-divisions of indictable crimes are worth tabulating; and this is what has been done in Table 15.9. This shows that the clear-up rate for property offences is low and getting lower still, while for offences against the person it is high, but also declining.

POLICE MANPOWER

A factor which must have some considerable influence on clear-up rates is of course the size of police forces, although some organisations – such as British Railways – employ their own security staff. It is therefore interesting to compare trends in police manpower with the trends in reported offences and clear-up rates which have been described. Table 15.10 shows that while the numbers of men and women employed by police forces have more than doubled since 1900 (if civilians as well as officers are counted) the increase in the estimated man-hours actually worked – from some 114,000 to some 173,000 – is less impressive, being only about 52 per cent. Moreover, the estimated number of man-hours worked per 1000 of population has remained at more or less the same level throughout the century, if we disregard a temporary decrease during and after the Second World War.

No doubt the increasing use of motor-cycles, cars, helicopters, radio and other mechanical aids means that police man-hours are now more effectively used than they were. Even so, the absence of any close correspondence between trends in crime and trends in police man-hours is striking. Part of the reason is undoubtedly financial and other difficulties in increasing police establishments, which means that they are not free to expand as quickly as police authorities might wish to do. It may also, however, reflect the difficulty of attracting suitable recruits.

THE PROBATION AND AFTER-CARE SERVICE

The problem of recruiting suitable men and women is not confined, of course, to the police, but is general to the social services (even the selection and training of lay magistrates has become a matter of official concern in recent years). From the point of view of sentencers, however, by far the most important service is the probation and after-care service, which, beginning as a small body of Church 'missionaries' in London courts in the late nineteenth century, has grown into a secular profession of some 3000 men and women, three-quarters of them with formal training, organised into 79 local probation and after-care departments, many of substantial size. The service is responsible not only for the supervision of offenders put on probation by the courts, but for several other tasks of equal, if not greater, importance. Chief among these is the preparation of 'social inquiry reports' for the use of sentencers. Another is the welfare of inmates of prisons, borstals and detention centres and their families; and a third is the supervision of the growing numbers of these inmates who are 'on licence' for a period after release, and the after-care of ex-prisoners who voluntarily accept this although they are not 'on licence'. Matrimonial conciliation and the supervision of persons ordered by courts to pay fines or compensation are among its other duties. Some of these responsibilities – such as making social inquiries for courts – were acquired between the wars, although they have grown in scope since then. Institutional welfare and the after-care of ordinary prisoners, however, were not added until the middle of the sixties. These developments are reflected in the manpower figures in Table 15.11. During the second and third decades of the century the numbers of individual probation officers declined, but this was almost wholly attributable to the replacement of part-time by whole-time officers; for by 1951 only 10 per cent were part-timers, and since then the number of whole-time officers has nearly trebled. The numbers of men have increased more than the numbers of women, and the Children and Young Persons Act, 1969, which was intended to make the supervision of all delinquents under 14 (and of some in the

14–17 age-group) the responsibility of children's departments, may have diverted some recruits (especially women) in that direction. It is too early to say in what other ways the service will be affected by the Act, or by the recent reorganising of local authorities' social services involving families. The Seebohm Committee, which recommended this, did not deal with the probation and after-care service, which, not being a local authority service, was outside their terms of reference; and there seems to be no immediate prospect of the probation service being absorbed into local authorities' social work departments, although there is a body of opinion which holds that it cannot remain independent of local authority services without suffering in effectiveness and quality.

BIBLIOGRAPHY

The main sources of periodical criminal judicial and penal statistics (which unless otherwise indicated are compiled *annually*) are:

A. Published by H.M. Stationery Office:

The Criminal Statistics for England and Wales (which include judicial statistics for criminal but not civil courts, and statistics for care, protection and control proceedings, hospital and guardianship orders and the use of the royal prerogative of mercy) (from 1857).

Reports of the Prison Commissioners (or, from 1963, Prison Department of the Home Office. From 1962 the main statistical tables have been published in a separate volume.)

Reports of the Parole Board (from 1968).

Offences of Drunkenness (excluding those involving vehicles) (from 1950).

Offences relating to Motor Vehicles (from 1928).

Statistics relating to Approved Schools, Remand Homes and Attendance Centres in England and Wales (from 1962).

Reports on the Work of the Children's Department (of the Home Office) (nine have been published, at irregular intervals, from 1923).

Reports on the Work of the Probation and After-Care Department (of the Home Office) 1962–5, and 1966–8.

Home Office Studies in the Causes of Delinquency and the Treatment of Offenders (at irregular intervals) and especially:

No. 3 'Delinquent Generations'
No. 8 'Trends and Regional Comparisons in Probation'
No. 11 'Studies of Female Offenders'
No. 4 'Murder'.

Home Office Research Studies (at irregular intervals) and especially No. 3 'Murder, 1957 to 1968'.

Reports of H.M. Inspectors of Constabulary (from 1945).

B. Unpublished, but obtainable by research workers from the Home Office's Statistical Branch:

Supplementary Criminal Statistics (from 1949).

Approved School Statistics (from 1956 to 1968).

Approved School After-care Statistics (from 1956 to 1968).

Attendance Centre Index Statistics (from 1962).

Detention Centre Index Statistics (from 1961).

Borstal Index Statistics (from 1961).

C. Other Main Sources (including local sources):

Reports of the Metropolitan Police Commissioners (HMSO, from 1869).

Reports of local Chief Constables.

Reports of local Probation Committees.

Reports of local Children's Departments.

G. Rose *The Struggle for Penal Reform* (Stevens 1960), Appendix 1.

F. H. McClintock *et al.*, *Crime in England and Wales* (Heinemann 1968).

F. H. McClintock *et al.*, *Crimes of Violence* (Macmillan 1963).

F. H. McClintock *et al.*, *Robbery in London* (Macmillan 1961).

Cambridge Department of Criminal Science, *Sexual Offences* (Macmillan 1957).

TABLE 15.1
Judicial Statistics for Selected Years 1900–1968, England and Wales

1 ASSIZES(a) AND QUARTER SESSIONS: ALL AGES

Year	No. for trial Total	Male	Female	Nos. found guilty(b)	Death(l)	Custodial measure(c)	Probation	Fine	Nominal penalties(d)	Otherwise dealt with(e)
						Sentences as percentage of those found guilty				
1900	10,149*	8928	1219	7975	0·3	90·5	—	1·1	8·1	2(n)
1910	13,680*	12,522	1157	11,337	0·2	83·6	5·2	0·6	10·2	0·2
1920	9130	8141	989	7225	0·5	76·5	8·1	0·8	13·4	0·7
1930	8384*	7781	601	6921	0·2	71·4	11·3	1·6	15·0	0·5
1938	10,003	9322	681	8612	0·3	62·4	19·2	1·3	16·0	0·8
1950	18,935	17,990	945	17,149	0·2	62·6	17·2	6·6	13·2	0·2
1960	30,591	29,462	1129	27,830	8(n)	53·8	22·5	13·8	9·3	0·6
1968	32,347	30,690	1657	27,395	—	{50·7 / 16·3†}	14·6	12·8	5·0	1·2

* Including 1 or 2 limited companies.   † Suspended prison sentences.

2 SUMMARY COURTS. INDICTABLE OFFENCES: ADULTS(fg)

Year	Nos. proceeded against Total	Male	Female	Nos. found guilty or charge proved(b)	Custodial measure(c)	Suspended prison sentences	Probation	Fine	Whipping(k)	Nominal penalties	Otherwise dealt with(e)	Attendance centre(m)
					Sentences as a percentage of those found guilty							
1900(h)	43,479	Not		30,736	47·1	—	14·0	26·7	9·0	2·9	0·3	—
1910	40,434	dis-		36,094	47·5	—	11·3	22·1	0·2	18·1	0·8	—
1920	37,107	tin-		32,942	31·7	—	11·3	38·6	0·1	17·3	1·0	—
1930	43,464	guished		38,709	25·6	—	21·1	28·3	1(n)	23·4	1·6	—
1938	46,014			41,976	22·0	—	22·2	28·9	—	24·9	2·0	—
1950	61,701	49,980	11,721	57,102	18·5	—	11·9	48·8	—	16·7	4·1	—
1960	84,523	70,103	14,420	79,538	13·4	—	12·5	56·1	—	13·7	4·3	—
1968	209,498	179,510	29,988	166,512	7·8	11·0	10·0	53·2	—	11·8	6·1	0·1

Table 15.1 continued

3 SUMMARY COURTS(i): INDICTABLE OFFENCES: JUVENILES

Year	Nos. proceeded against — Total	Male	Female	Nos. found guilty or charge proved(b)	Sentences as a percentage of those found guilty — Custodial measure(c)	Probation	Fine	Whipping(k)	Nominal penalties(d)	Fit person order	Attendance centre(m)	Otherwise dealt with(e)
1910	12,275	Not distinguished		10,786	16·1	25·7	7·8	14·4	35·7	—	—	0·3
1920	14,380	Not distinguished		12,919	10·9	31·3	17·2	9·9	30·1	—	—	0·6
1930	12,198	Not distinguished		11,137	10·0	55·3	3·8	1·2	29·3	0·8	—	0·4
1938	29,388	Not distinguished		27,875	10·3	50·9	6·0	0·3	30·9	1·4	—	1·0
1950	43,823	40,434	3389	41,910	10·6	40·8	16·3	—	30·0	1·6	—	0·9
1960	58,350	53,253	5097	56,114	8·4	33·6	19·3	—	32·0	1·9	4·1	0·6
1968	68,220	60,672	7548	63,426	7·7	27·7	26·5	—	26·1	1·9	8·2	1·9

4 SUMMARY COURTS: NON-INDICTABLE OFFENCES OTHER THAN HIGHWAY OFFENCES(j): ADULTS(fg)

Year	Nos. proceeded against — Total	Male	Female	Nos. found guilty or charge proved(b)	Sentences as a percentage of those found guilty — Custodial measure(c)	Probation	Fine	Nominal penalties(d)	Attendance centre(m)	Otherwise dealt with(e)
1900	672,989(h)	Not distinguished		557,489	9·5	0·1	86·8	1·4	—	2·2
1910	551,395	Not distinguished		483,111	12·9	0·4	77·1	9·2	—	0·4
1920	427,556	Not distinguished		374,565	4·0	0·5	87·1	8·2	—	0·2
1930	317,231	Not distinguished		287,691	4·1	0·7	81·5	13·1	—	0·6
1938	236,752	Not distinguished		216,759	4·2	0·8	80·3	14·1	—	0·6
1950	220,188	181,458	38,730	202,286	3·0	1·0	86·7	9·1	—	0·2
1960	247,133	221,703	25,430	232,992	2·5	0·9	90·1	6·2	—	0·3
1968	327,657	292,887	34,769	295,783	{ 1·6 / 1·5†	1·3	89·5	5·4	59(n)	0·6

† Suspended sentence.

Table 15.1 continued

5 SUMMARY COURTS(i): NON-INDICTABLE OFFENCES OTHER THAN HIGHWAY OFFENCES(j): JUVENILES

Year	Nos. proceeded against			Nos. found guilty or charge proved(b)	Sentences as a percentage of those found guilty						
	Total	Male	Female		Custodial measure(c)	Probation	Fine	Nominal penalties(d)	Fit person order	Attendance centre(m)	Otherwise dealt with(e)
1910	18,059	Not dis- tin- guished		14,694	3.9	5.3	51.6	38.9	—	—	0.3
1920	16,953			14,956	1.6	4.3	67.4	26.4	—	—	0.3
1930	8842			7577	1.2	11.4	38.2	49.0	1(n)	—	0.2
1938	16,873			15,310	0.5	8.8	40.3	49.5	0.1	—	0.8
1950	19,810	18,868	942	18,410	0.9	6.4	56.9	35.4	13(n)	—	0.4
1960	28,025	26,521	1504	26,337	0.8	4.8	67.8	24.3	0.1	0.7	1.5
1968	21,314	19,551	1763	19,457	2.2	8.1	62.0	23.3	0.6	2.9	0.9

Notes on Table 15.1.

(a) Including the Central Criminal Court and the Crown Courts. (b) Excluding those found guilty but insane or (since 1964) acquitted by reason of insanity. (c) Including imprisonment, or committal to a reformatory, approved school, remand home or (since 1952) detention centre, or (in the case of Assizes and Quarter Sessions) borstal training. (d) Includes absolute and conditional discharge and binding over with recognisances. (e) Includes days in prison cells, admission to institutions for the mentally disordered, and other miscellaneous and numerically unimportant methods of disposal.

(f) Until 1932, persons aged 16 or older were tried and sentenced as adults (although in some cases sent to establishments reserved for younger offenders, e.g. borstals). From 1933, however, 'adult' means a person aged 17 or older.

(g) Includes small numbers of juveniles tried jointly with adults.

(h) The published tables for 1900 unfortunately do not distinguish adults from juveniles, although one table shows that those found guilty include 9450 persons under 16. Consequently the figures showing the disposal of adult offenders in 1900 include unknown numbers of juveniles. Almost certainly most of the 3218 who were whipped in 1900 were boys.

(i) From 1908 these were in effect 'juvenile courts', although lacking many special features which were introduced later.

(j) From 1900 to 1938 'highway offences' have been taken to include all offences under the Highway Acts together with offences against regulations etc. dealing with stage coaches, trams, trolley buses and so on. For 1950 they have been taken to include offences numbered 123–38, 173 and 180 in the Home Office code, and for 1960 and 1968 offences numbered 124, 130, 135–8, 173 and 180.

(k) Whipping, which had become very infrequent, was abolished by statute in 1948.

(l) The death penalty was, in practice, confined to murder throughout this period (except for war-time executions for treason or similar offences). 'Infanticides' were excluded from 'murder' from 1922, and from 1957 murders in certain circumstances became 'non-capital': the death penalty for murder was completely suspended from 1965. Some murderers who were sentenced to death were subsequently reprieved.

(m) Attendance centres and detention centres were introduced by the Criminal Justice Act, 1948, although it was not until a few years later that the first centres were opened. (n) Negligible numbers too small to be represented as percentages, i.e. total number of boys

TABLE 15.2

Police Cautions 1954-1968, England and Wales

Year	Indictable offences				Non-indictable (excluding motoring) offences			
	Juveniles		Adults		Juveniles		Adults	
	M	F	M	F	M	F	M	F
1954	6672	885	2023	987	12,425	851	33,608	7024
1955	8405	1133	2156	1044	13,611	905	33,848	6900
1956	10,372	1293	2341	1086	14,610	934	32,734	6697
1957	12,373	1516	2875	1185	16,151	1092	35,188	6753
1958	13,933	1903	2880	1251	17,036	1160	32,383	6546
1959	16,725	2107	3374	1429	16,725	1171	26,544	6052
1960	15,841	2548	4013	1470	15,517	1071	21,607	9636
1961	16,297	2861	3909	1495	15,491	1023	19,740	8905
1962	16,511	2981	4274	1542	15,642	1058	19,470	8879
1963	17,686	3207	4683	1896	14,281	856	18,118	8639
1964	17,008	3237	4902	2198	11,547	787	16,606	7715
1965	16,198	3892	5551	2331	10,069	662	14,782	6451
1966	17,681	4327	5520	2481	7984	596	13,465	6045
1967	18,210	3938	6049	2811	7435	574	13,237	6409
1968	19,056	4703	6168	2999	7424	530	14,341	6360

Source: Introduction to the Annual Criminal Statistics, Chap. 14.

TABLE 15.3

Traffic Offences(a) 1900–1968, England and Wales

Year	(1) Nos. of persons found guilty of traffic offences(b)	(2) Nos. found guilty of all offences(b)	Col. (1) as percentage of Col. (2)
1900	2548	629,197	0·4
1910	55,633	613,374	9·1
1920	157,875	601,858	24·9
1930	267,616	624,636	42·8
1938	475,124	787,482	60·3
1950	357,932(c)	688,650(c)	52·6
1960	622,551	1,035,212	60·1
1968	1,014,793	1,576,868	64·4

Notes:

(a) For the years 1900–38 these include offences against the Highway Acts by owners and drivers of carts, obstructions and nuisances, and offences involving heavy locomotives and bicycles as well as motor-cars. For later years they include only offences in Home Office groups 122–38.

(b) As usual, these include unknown numbers of occasions on which the same person was found guilty more than once in the same year.

(c) The temporary fall was no doubt due to war-time and post-war limitations on petrol supplies and the manufacture of vehicles.

TABLE 15.4

Prison Sentences and Populations in Selected Years 1901–1968, England and Wales

Year	Prisoners received under sentence (a)	Daily average prison population (b)		
		Male	Female	Total
1901	149,397	14,459	2976	17,435
1910	179,951	19,333	2685	22,018
1914	136,424	15,752	2484	18,236
1916	58,839	9244	2067	11,311
1919	26,050	7595	1604	9199
1920	35,439	8279	1404	9683
1930	38,832	10,561	785	11,346
1938	31,993	10,388	698	11,086
1940	24,870	8443	934	9377
1943	32,490	11,430	1360	12,790
1946	29,998	14,556	1233	15,789
1948	36,802	18,621	1144	19,765
1950	33,875	19,367	1107	20,474
1960	42,810	26,198	901	27,099
1965	56,315	29,580	841	30,421
1967	60,611	34,056	953	35,009
1968	49,258	31,656	805	32,461

Notes:

(a) This column excludes those sentenced by courts martial and those under sentence of death or recalled under licence; but includes sentences of penal servitude (which were abolished in 1948), borstal training and committals to Detention Centres from 1952 (boys) and 1962 (girls). Civil prisoners are not included as they are not 'under sentence'.

(b) Figures are for daily average population of penal establishments in prisons, borstals and (from 1952 for boys and 1962 for girls) detention centres.

Source: Annual Reports of the Prison Commissioners, later the Prison Department of the Home Office.

TABLE 15.5

Remands to Prison for Psychiatric Examination 1920–1967, England and Wales

Year	(1) Number of remands	(2) Column (1) as percentage of receptions under sentence
1920	1611	4·5
1930	2528	6·5
1938	2779	8·7
1950	5009	15·0
1960	5825	13·6
1967	10,919	18·0

Source: As for Table 15.4.

TABLES 15.6

First Offenders as percentages of all Persons Found Guilty of Indictable Offences 1954–1955 and 1962, England and Wales

	1954–55 (averaged)				*1962*		
		'First offenders'(a)				'First offenders'(a)	
Age groups	Total convicted	No.	Per cent		Total convicted	No.	Per cent
8 to 14	20,226	15,697	77·6		31,874	23,853	74·8
14 to 17	14,965	9792	65·4		34,318	22·301	65·0
17 to 21	12,509	7137	57·1		35,346	19,682	55·7
21 to 26	13,614	7015	51·5		30,021	14,295	47·6
26 to 39	26,575	14,085	53·0		43,340	21,427	49·4
40+	19,010	11,946	62·8		28,618	17,233	60·2
Total	106,899	65,672	61·4		203,517	118,791	58·4

Note: (a) i.e. persons without known previous convictions for centrally recorded offences: see text.
Source: As for Table 15.8.

TABLE 15.7

Recidivists in Four Age Groups 1955 and 1962, England and Wales

Number of previous proved offences	1955					1962				
	8–14	14–17	17–21	21+	All ages	8–14	14–17	17–21	21+	All ages
1	55·3	46·0	35·2	26·0	32·3	50·3	42·0	32·5	23·2	29·5
2–4	40·1	44·9	44·9	35·3	38·1	41·5	44·6	44·5	35·1	38·6
5–10	4·4	8·3	17·7	26·7	21·3	7·6	12·0	20·0	27·9	22·8
11–20	0·1	0·7	2·0	10·0	6·9	0·5	1·3	2·7	11·1	7·4
20 or more	0·1	0·1	0·2	2·0	1·4	0·1	0·1	0·3	2·7	1·7
5 or more	4·6	9·1	19·9	38·7	29·6	8·2	13·4	23·0	41·7	31·9
Total %	100·0	100·0	100·0	100·0	100·0	100·0	100·0	100·0	100·0	100·0
No. (000's)	3·2	4·1	4·7	23·2	35·2	5·4	8·0	12·4	41·8	68·5

Source: As for Table 15.8.

TABLE 15.8

Rates of Change for Different Classes of Offence in Selected Years from 1901 to 1963 (Rates: Annual Average 1901-1905 = 100)(a)
England and Wales

Classification of offences according to relative magnitude of percentage increase between 1901–5 and 1963. Annual average 1901–5 = 100	Rate of change: annual average 1901–5 = 100				
	1921	1938	1948	1961	1963
1. HIGH INCREASE (>1700)					
Malicious woundings	56	174	386	1520	1779
Homosexual offences	178	572	1405	2513	2437
Shopbreaking	206	556	1464	1990	2568
Attempted breakings	218	1088	2392	3213	4186
Larceny from dwelling house	140	767	2428	3068	3903
Forgery	138	396	1449	1688	2106
2. MEDIUM HIGH INCREASE (1300 < 1700)					
Housebreaking	141	377	710	1051	1427
Receiving	160	295	777	1184	1527
Malicious damage	108	113	737	1110	1373
3. AVERAGE INCREASE (900 < 1300)					
Heterosexual offences(b)	155	282	588	1218	1248
Robbery	86	117	449	959	1013
Simple and minor larcenies(c)	115	335	557	879	1053
Frauds and false pretences	187	420	506	1042	1204
4. MEDIUM LOW INCREASE (500 < 900)	nil	nil	nil	nil	nil
5. LOW INCREASE (<500) OR DECREASE					
Murder	88	74	110	94	98
Felonious woundings, etc.(d)	84	127	194	440	450
Larceny by servant and embezzlement	90	141	281	331	360
Larceny from the person	46	61	121	136	146
Total indictable crimes	118	323	597	921	1117
Males aged 15–49(e)	115	130	135	131	130

Notes:
(a) Based on figures extracted from relevant volumes of *Criminal Statistics, England and Wales*.
(b) Including Home Office Statistical Classes 19–23.
(c) Including Home Office Statistical Classes 44–9.
(d) Including Home Office Statistical Classes 2, 4 and 5.
(e) Not in McClintock and Avison's table.
Source: F. H. McClintock and N. H. Avison, *Crime in England and Wales* (Heinemann 1968): but see note (e) above.

TABLE 15.9

Clear-up Rates for Each of the Main Classes of Offence Shown for Selected Years from 1951 to 1965, England and Wales

Class of offence	Crimes cleared up as a percentage of the total recorded in each class				
	1951	*1955*	*1958*	*1961*	*1965*
OFFENCES AGAINST THE PERSON:					
1. Violence against the person	90·2	90·6	89·2	88·1	84·7
2. Sexual offences	79·9	82·6	81·4	81·7	75·8
Total	82·9	85·1	84·4	84·5	80·7
OFFENCES AGAINST PROPERTY:					
3. Breaking offences	39·9	38·9	39·3	38·9	33·3
4. Robbery	46·8	52·5	46·6	39·3	36·9
5. Thefts and frauds	44·7	46·1	42·7	42·0	37·1
6. Receiving	99·1	99·7	99·5	99·6	99·4
7. Malicious damage	69·6	63·5	60·0	56·5	44·2
Total	45·0	45·8	43·1	42·5	37·4
MISCELLANEOUS OFFENCES:					
8. Other offences(a)	96·2	95·5	96·3	95·0	87·9
All indictable offences	47·1	48·7	45·6	44·8	39·2

Note: (a) Including attempted suicide, which ceased to be an offence in 1961.
Sources: Based on data obtained from relevant volumes of *Criminal Statistics, England and Wales*; and a table in McClintock and Avison (see Bibliography).

TABLE 15.10

Police Service Man-hours(a) 1901–1965, England and Wales

Year (1)	Total no. of police officers (2)	No. of police officers (adjusted for sickness) (3)	Hours worked by police officers		Total no. of civilians (6)	No. of civilians (adjusted for sickness) (7)	Hours worked by police service (including civilians)	
			ooo's (4)	per 1000 population (5)			ooo's (8)	per 1000 population (9)
1901	43,463	42,138	114,278	3513	—	—	(as in col. 4)	(as in col. 5)
1911	51,203	50,000	135,200	3748	—	—	,,	,,
1921	60,709	58,693	140,863	3718	—	—	,,	,,
1931	60,492	58,577	140,585	3519	—	—	,,	,,
1938	63,800	62,098	149,035	3595	—	—	,,	,,
1949	60,418	57,763	133,086	3040	4774	4645	142,934	3264
1951	62,629	59,690	137,526	3144	6023	5860	149,949	3428
1961	75,798	73,367	169,038	3669	12,515	12,177	194,853	4229
1965	84,425	81,503	163,658	3426	19,093	18,577	197,394	4133
Adjusted for regular overtime in 1965								
1965	84,425	81,503	173,438	3631	19,093	18,577	207,174	4337

Notes:

(a) Man-hours in this table include hours worked by women.

Source: Adapted by permission from J. P. Martin and G. Wilson, *Police: a Study of Manpower* (Heinemann 1969).

TABLE 15.11

The Manpower of the Probation and After-care Service in Selected Years 1911–1968, England and Wales

Year	Men	Women	Total
1911	730	279	1009

Source: The first Register of Probation Officers published by the Home Office. Probably more than three-quarters of the officers were part-time. The Register also lists 1002 petty sessional divisions, of which 268 had appointed no officer.

Year	Men	Women	Total
1923	527	309	836

Source: The Home Office Register for 1923 (the series became annual in 1919), which says that 'about one fourth' were whole-time, and about 650 were paid. 259 were employees of Missions or Societies (155 by the Church of England Temperance Society, 29 by the Salvation Army, 22 by the Church Army, 19 by Discharged Prisoners Aid Societies, and 11 by the National Society for the Prevention of Cruelty to Children). There were 1029 petty sessional divisions, excluding Metropolitan Police and Juvenile Courts: but 189 had not appointed officers.

Year	Men	Women	Total
1930	480	289	769

Source: The Home Office Directory of Probation Officers, Probation Hostels and Homes and Borstal Institutions, which had replaced the annual Register. Of the total of 769 officers, 501 were part-time; of the 268 whole-time officers, 82 were women: 226 of the officers were employees of Missions or Societies, in much the same proportions as in 1923.

Year	Men	Women	Total
1938	612	392	1004

Source: The Home Office's annual Directory (see note for 1930), which says that 585 of the 1004 were part-time officers, and that 104 of the full-time officers were women, but gives no information about the numbers of paid officers or of those employed by Missions or Societies. By this date there were 1023 petty sessional divisions, 611 of which were combined into 44 areas, the rest being independent.

Table 15.11 continued

Year	Men	Women	Total
1950	656	350	1006
1955	801	412	1213
1960	1135	498	1633
1965	1687	632	2319
1968	2168	792	2960

Source: The Home Office report *The Work of the Probation and After-Care Service, 1962–1965,* Cmnd 3107, supplemented by Home Office figures for 1968. By the end of 1965 the process of combining petty sessional divisions had reduced the total of probation areas to 84, of which 5 covered Greater London, and 54 others were combined areas, most of them covering whole counties with all the urban areas in them. In 1968 there were only 57 part-time officers, and by the end of that year 72 per cent. of all officers had received a formal professional training in probation.

16 Leisure

A. H. HALSEY

The distinction between work and leisure and therefore the definition of leisure is controversial. Most sociologists would share the view of Joffra Dumazedier that 'leisure has certain traits that are characteristic only of the civilisation born from the industrial revolution.'[1] This is not to deny the existence of work and play in non-industrial societies but rather to stress their articulation through religion and communal ceremonial and, by contrast, their sharp separation in the organisation of modern industrial society. Modern leisure presupposes this separate organisation of work and also a high degree of individual freedom of choice among possible non-work activities.

Leisure occupies an increasingly large place in the sociological literature as in the life of the richer societies.[2] However, the statistics on leisure in Britain which we present in this chapter are disappointing. They reflect, what we have found in other chapters, a poor connection between sociological definitions and statistical compilations by official and other bodies. We have divided them under five headings: cinema, sport, reading, youth clubs and adult education.

SOURCES OF INFORMATION

Trend statistics on leisure activity generally and the relative popularity of different pursuits are almost impossible to obtain. There are surveys by different organisations at different dates but they approach the subject in different ways and do not provide comparable information, though each gives a picture of some aspect of the use of leisure time at different periods.

There are a number of useful reports of a general kind.

1. *Patterns of British Life* (1950) is based on the Hulton readership

---

[1] *International Encyclopedia of the Social Sciences* (Free Press: The Macmillan Co., N.Y. 1968), Vol. 9, p. 248.

[2] See the bibliography provided by Dumazedier in the article cited. See especially his *Towards a Society of Leisure* (Free Press: The Macmillan Co., N.Y. 1967) and H. Wilensky, 'Mass Society and Mass Culture: Interdependence or Independence?', *Amer. Sociol. Rev.*, **29** (1964), 173–97.

surveys of 1947, 1948 and 1949 and on official sources. Quota sampling was used for the surveys – involving, in 1949, 6979 women and 6003 men in Great Britain. Included in the 1950 report are tables showing the number of men and women taking holidays away from home, analysed by age and social class, the proportion owning cars and motor bikes and the percentages smoking and drinking and attending various kinds of sport or entertainment. There is also an analysis of reading habits. None of the tables, however, attempts to quantify the time spent on the various activities, nor to rate them in order of importance.

2. *Products and People* is a Reader's Digest publication based on the marketing survey of the European Common Market countries and Great Britain in 1963. The findings are the result of interviews with randomly selected samples of 2000 individuals in each of the countries except one, but including Britain. The report presents tables showing the frequency of different leisure activities analysed by social class, education, sex and age. The totals, however, do not give any indication of the amount of time spent on the different activities.

3. *The People's Activities*, published by the BBC in 1965, presents a statistical summary of what people do every half-hour of the day from 6 a.m. until midnight. The survey was based on a random sample of 2353 persons in Great Britain aged 15 and over who each kept a diary of their activities for seven days. The totals show the proportion of people doing particular things during each half-hour period and the analysis is by sex, age, education and social class. Activities are broadly divided into 'at home' and 'not at home'. There is thus a comprehensive picture of the most popular activities of particular groups in the population at given times, but again no estimate of the total amount of leisure time devoted to particular interests.

4. In 1967 the University of Keele published the pilot *National Recreation Survey* report no. 1, based on a random sample of the population aged 12 and above. There were 3167 respondents. A number of circumstances were investigated – the total of hours worked, the amount of annual paid holiday and the proportion of households with a car, for instance, as well as the actual leisure activities. This enquiry also attempted to demonstrate changes over time. It is, however, very difficult to say how far changes are a result of age or how far they reflect secular changes in popular tastes and habits.

5. *Planning for Leisure*, published by the Government Social Survey in 1969, gives information about the proportion of leisure time devoted to particular activities. The survey material is drawn from three random samples – a national sample of 2682 persons aged 15 and over from England and Wales, an inner London sample of 1321 persons and a new town sample of 1732 persons. We have been able to draw up tables

from this source showing the most popular leisure activities for men and women of different ages, marital status and social class and also the proportion belonging to different kinds of clubs. The totals are all based on the larger national sample. The report also contains a great deal of information about the frequency of different activities for different social categories, about expenditure and about attitudes and incentives; but we have not used these statistics.

We interpret leisure activities as those things that people voluntarily choose to do in their spare time when they are not working. This means that we have not attempted, for instance, to investigate smoking or drinking habits, as these are generally carried on in association with some other activity. Even so, we would have been interested in the figures for pub attendances had we been able to get them.

During this century working hours have dropped (Tables 4.9 and 16.1) and real incomes have risen (Table 3.1) and we would therefore expect to see more people spending more time and money on leisure. Wider opportunities for education and changes in family structure enabling women to lead more independent lives should also affect the pattern of leisure activities between different age groups and between the sexes. We have tried to assemble statistics reflecting leisure pursuits showing trends through time and, where possible and appropriate, distinguishing participation by different sexes, age groups and social classes.

The various statistics show the changing amount of leisure available for different groups in the population or for the average worker. The Ministry of Labour Gazette is particularly useful in indicating trends. Before 1914 manual workers did not usually have paid holidays but, by 1919, two million or so were covered by agreements specifying from three to twelve days annually. In 1938 three million workers were covered, most commonly for a week. By 1952 when agreements operated in practically all industries where conditions of work were regulated by collective bargaining (or statutory orders determined the length of paid holidays for industries governed by wage councils) two-thirds of those covered received twelve days or two weeks, and by 1969 two or three weeks was equally common.

The proportion of adults of different age and income groups spending holidays away from home in the late nineteen-forties may be seen from Tables 16.3 and 16.4. As would be expected more younger than older people went away and many more of the higher than of the lower social classes. Class also affected the length of holiday taken. Half of classes A and B had more than 11 days compared with 20 per cent. of classes D and E in 1947 (chart not reproduced). The variations between different age, income and educational groups persisted into the nineteen-sixties (Table 16.2). Slightly fewer younger than older people have no paid holiday or only one week though slightly fewer also have four weeks or more. Higher income brings longer holidays; only 6 per cent of those earning under £650 a year have three weeks or more paid leave compared with 44 per cent of those earning £1950 and over. The educational categories are no doubt associated with the income ones; 47 per cent of those who had a university education had three or more weeks' paid holiday compared with 10 per cent of those with only a secondary education. The actual hours worked by the different groups appear in Table 16.1. As would be expected manual workers work longer than 'other' workers, the relatively poor longer than the relatively rich, and those without a university education longer than graduates. The contrast is most marked for the occupational groups; 45 per cent of manual workers but only 17 per cent of 'others' worked more than 45 hours a week.

Statistics showing the number of persons travelling abroad are sparse. Figures for 1947 appear in Table 16.5 but different social classes are not distinguished. Statistics published by the British Travel Association suggest a substantial increase particularly in holidays taken abroad during the period 1950–67 (Table 16.6). The increasing number of people travelling abroad may also be seen from Table 16.7 though the figures relate to all foreign travel rather than to holidays only and are therefore not fully comparable with those in Table 16.5. Class differences are apparent though the most significant influence on whether or not people go abroad seems to be their education. A further indication of long-term trends in foreign travel may be obtained from Table 16.8 which shows the number of passports issued in given years since 1921.

Perhaps the most notable developments in leisure activities since the war have been associated with increasing car ownership and the development of television. The growth in the number of private vehicle licences – particularly since the 1940s – is clear from Table 9.9. There were less than 2 million private cars and vans in 1948: by 1968 the number was 10,816,100. The ownership pattern for 1949 appears in Table 16.9 where it may be seen that nearly half the men in classes A and B owned a car but only 6 per cent of those in classes D and E. The figures from the 1966 census (Table 16.10) show the changes since the war and allow rough comparison with 1949. Figures for 1965 produced by the University of Keele and the BTA analyse the distribution in more detail (Table 16.11).

Television has spread extremely rapidly since the war (Tables 16.12 and 16.13). In 1969 watching TV was easily the most popular leisure activity of both men and women, taking up a quarter of their leisure time (Table 16.14). The table shows the pattern of leisure activity in 1969 but there is no exactly comparable data for earlier years. Reference to the BBC survey of 1961, which analysed activities at different times during the day, might suggest some slackening of interest in television during the nineteen-sixties (Table 16.15). On the other hand figures from the BBC Research Department (Table 16.16) show a strong upward trend in evening viewing between 1952 and 1968.

Fragmentary and not strictly comparable information has been collected since the war by various surveys on the social patterns of television viewing according to social class, income, education and age. The typical distributions are illustrated in Table 16.17 which relates to 1960–1 and 1968. The two surveys are not strictly comparable but they show a similar pattern. In 1961 the most regular viewers were to be found among the skilled manual workers and among those aged between 25 and 44. There were no marked differences between the sexes though slightly more men were regular viewers and slightly fewer never watched. In 1968 the figures were analysed rather differently, but if 'heavy' and 'medium' can be taken to correspond to 'regular' in the earlier enquiry the later study shows a fall in intensive viewing for all social classes except D and E which now rival the skilled manual workers. 'Heavy' viewing was also concentrated in a rather higher age group, the 55–64s, in the later study.

Cinema

National statistics for the cinema industry exist, but only since the nineteen-thirties. Various kinds of data are available, including the number of cinemas in existence, the number of admissions and the amount of money taken. We have been able to use figures from various studies of the cinema, to which we refer in the notes to the tables, from the quarterly journals of the Board of Trade and from the readership surveys conducted by the Hulton Press and by the Institute of Practitioners in Advertising.

Table 16.18 shows the predominance of the cinema over other kinds of commercial entertainment, but the decline in the number of buildings used as cinemas, in their seating capacity, in the number of their patrons and in their receipts is evident from Tables 16.19 and 16.20. Gross takings are still higher than in the thirties in money terms but the number of admissions is only one-third of what it then was. Cinema-going declined among all social classes between 1950 and 1960 but most markedly in classes A and B, who have been, in any case, the least frequent attenders (Table 16.21). The decline continued in the sixties among all classes and all age groups and both sexes (Table 16.22). In 1968 the 16–24-year-olds were the most regular attenders and visits to the cinema were slightly more popular among men than women and among skilled manual workers than among other social groups.

Sport
Quantitative information on sporting activities is extremely incomplete. In most cases figures only go back ten or twenty years. Moreover data about clubs or individual membership are very uncertain guides to growth or decline. Where numbers appear to have increased this may represent greater efficiency in collecting statistics on the part of the central organisation. Many sports have a large proportion of casual participants and only very rough guesses are possible of the total number of people engaged in them. The figures in many cases refer only to those who follow a particular activity in the sense of joining some organisation. There must be many campers, walkers, tennis players and so forth who belong to no club or organised body. Thus the figures are only a very rough indication of trends even for those sports where there is a central body which has collected membership statistics. They tell us little or nothing about the total volume of sporting activity in the country and how it may have grown over the past years. We cannot tell how far individuals tend to participate in a number of different sports.

Nevertheless some points emerge from Table 16.23. In general the statistics representing *participation* in sports show an increase in activity over the period for which figures are available. Cycling is the exception where membership of the C.T.C. has declined since 1950 and there has also been a drop in the number of badminton and tennis clubs since 1960. On the other hand figures for *attendances* at sporting events show a very substantial decline since 1950.

Reading
Some idea of the amount of reading of books among the population may be obtained from statistics for public libraries which go back to the beginning of the century and the figures – much less complete – for book sales and for new books published. The reading of newspapers, weeklies and magazines is analysed by age, sex and social class in the Hulton Readership Survey for 1950 and in the I.P.A. National Readership Survey of 1967, both based on the population of Great Britain of 16 and over. The first used a quota sample of 15,796 selected by a mixture of methods. The technique of interviewing involved asking people what daily newspapers they had read the previous day, what Sunday newspapers the previous Sunday, what weeklies during the past 7 days, in order to make the responses as accurate as possible.

The statistics for the library service have to be interpreted cautiously as the notes to Table 16.24 imply. Nevertheless the figures give some idea of the growth of the service. Perhaps the most notable statistics are for books in stock; the number having increased from about five million at the beginning of the century to over 100 million in 1968. The figures for book sales are less helpful (Table 16.25). They cover only a relatively short period and do not distinguish between different kinds of books. Information about books published is also scanty though the increasing numbers appear in Table 16.26. The readership surveys, by contrast, give an exhaustive analysis of newspaper and periodical reading by age, sex and social class though not showing how much time is spent on such reading in relation to other leisure pursuits, nor what proportion of people see more than one publication.

Table 16.27 shows a decline in the proportion of all women reading the *News of the World* between 1950 and 1967 and an increase in those reading the more serious *Daily Telegraph, Sunday Times* and *Observer*. There was a substantial increase over the same period in the proportion reading the fashion magazines – *Vogue* and *Ideal Home*. Changes in men's reading habits show a similar kind of trend though the increased popularity of the serious papers is more pronounced. Both in 1950 and in 1967 a slightly higher proportion of men than of women read newspapers and periodicals though the order of their preference was similar. The most popular papers were most popular among the younger age groups for both sexes at both dates. For 1950 the reverse was true of the more serious papers which were preferred by older people. But in 1957 it was the younger age groups of both sexes who tended to have a higher proportion of readers of the *Observer, Sunday Times* and *Daily Telegraph*. The trend to smaller readership of the sensational *News of the World* and the greater popularity of the serious papers is reflected by both sexes and in all social classes. It is not possible to attach too much importance to these figures. Though perhaps the decline in the readership of the *News of the World* and the increasing popularity of the more solid papers – particularly among the young – reflects a longer period of education for all classes.

Youth clubs
There are no comprehensive statistics showing the membership of youth organisations. Since 1944 local authorities have played an increasing part in the youth service, but although individual authorities have collected details of youth groups in their own areas from time to time no national survey has been attempted. The statistics in Table 16.28 have been obtained from a selection of some of the major voluntary organisations. They are in many ways a very unsatisfactory guide to trends in the youth movement. First, they refer only to a handful of the

larger organisations; second, they are very incomplete, in many cases dating only from the nineteen-forties; third, we do not know the extent of multiple membership of different organisations; fourth, figures do not distinguish between active and nominal members. Thus the statistics do not give any indication of the proportion of all boys and girls who belong to youth groups – or how active they are in their membership. They show simply the varying strength of some of the more important bodies over very limited periods.

For what they are worth, the figures show a fairly steady increase in membership for most of the organisations, though in some cases there has been a drop over the past ten years or so. Naturally enough the service organisations reached a peak in the nineteen-forties and their membership has declined since the war. Table 16.29 shows the increase in local authority youth work since the end of the nineteen-fifties; during a ten-year period the number of centres maintained and assisted, the number of staff employed and the expenditure per head of the population have all more than doubled.

Adult education

The adult education movement is documented by statistics produced by the Department of Education and Science and its predecessors. Records of the number of classes, student attendance and amount of government grant go back to the beginning of the century, and details of curricula are obtainable since the nineteen-thirties. The number of students attending classes increased from 78 in 1908 to nearly a quarter of a million in 1967. Over the same period government grants to organising bodies rose to over £1 million (Table 16.30).

In the early nineteen-thirties men and women attended in roughly equal numbers, but by 1938 men outnumbered women. This trend reversed itself during and after the war until in 1967 women students in adult education classes outnumbered men by nearly 30,000. Women tend to be interested more in arts subjects and in music, while men prefer the social studies, though the pattern of interests has changed considerably through the years (Table 16.31).

The growth of residential courses is traced in Table 16.32 – a notable if relatively small sector of adult education.

Total expenditure on all public adult education has almost doubled during the nineteen-sixties (Table 16.33).

The trends in schools and higher education are dealt with in Chapters 6 and 7.

BIBLIOGRAPHY

Adams, W. G. S., *A Report on Library Provision and Policy* (Carnegie United Kingdom Trust 1915).

Belson, William, *The Impact of Television* (Crosby Lockwood 1967).

Board of Education, *Report* 1921–2; *Annual Reports* and *Statistics of Public Education*, 1931 and 1938.

Board of Trade, *Journals*, 1914–66.

British Broadcasting Corporation, *The People's Activities* (1965).

Browning, H. E. and Sorrell, A. A., 'Cinemas and Cinema-going in Great Britain', *J. Roy. Statist. Soc.*, series A (1954), 117.

Department of Education and Science, *Youth and Community Work in the 70s* (1969); *Statistics of Education*, 1961, pt. 2; *Statistics of Education*, 1967, vol. 3.

Government Social Survey, *Planning for Leisure* (1969).

Hulton Press, *Patterns of British Life* (1950); *The Hulton Readership Survey* (1950).

Institute of Municipal Treasurers and Accountants, *Public Library Statistics*.

Institute of Practioners in Advertising, *National Readership Surveys*, 1961, 1967 and 1968.

The Library Association, *A Century of Public Libraries 1850–1950*; *Statistics of Public Libraries in Great Britain and Northern Ireland*.

Ministry of Education, *The Organisation and Finance of Adult Education in England and Wales* (1954); *Report and Statistics of Education*, 1951.

P.E.P., *The British Film Industry* (1952); *The British Film Industry* (1958) (pamphlet).

The Reader's Digest, *Products and People* (1963).

The Sports Council, '*Trends in Sport*' (1969) (unpublished).

Spraos, John, *The Decline of the Cinema* (Allen & Unwin, 1962).

University of Keele and British Travel Association, *Pilot National Recreation Survey, Report* No. 1, 1967.

Rowntree, B. S. and Lavers, G. R., *English Life and Leisure: A Social Study* (Longmans 1951).

TABLE 16.1

Actual Hours Worked: by Sex, Occupational Group, Income and Education 1965, Great Britain (percentages)

Hours worked	All adults	Sex		Occ. group			Income		Education	
		Men	Women	Manual	Exec.	Other	£650–849	£1200–1949	Sec.	Univ.
Under 35	17	7	43	13	18	27	14	18	16	32
35–37	10	10	15	5	16	18	7	14	9	20
40	14	14	12	14	8	15	12	14	14	5
40–45	16	15	15	17	10	14	19	14	18	5
over 45	35	45	9	45	30	17	40	32	39	18
Average hours worked	42	46	34	44	41	37	43	42	43	36

Note: See notes to Table 16.2. Some respondents are not included as they were unable to estimate hours worked.
Source: University of Keele, *Pilot National Recreation Survey*, 1964.

TABLE 16.2

Length of Annual Paid Holiday for Adults: by Age, Income and Education 1965, Great Britain (percentages)

Annual paid holiday	All adults	Age			Income			Education	
		17–24	35–44	65+	£650	£850–1195	£1950+	Sec.	Univ.
One week	2	1	3	2	1	2	1	2	0
Two weeks	42	58	48	9	22	52	30	48	14
Three weeks	19	23	21	3	6	27	20	7	16
Four and over	8	7	9	1	0	7	22	3	31
None	24	8	12	80	67	10	12	25	30

Note: The survey is based on 3167 interviews in England, Wales and Scotland, randomly selected as representative of the population aged 12 and over. Of the total sample about 5 per cent are not included as they had holidays of varying length.
Source: University of Keele, *Pilot National Recreation Survey*, 1967.

TABLE 16.3

Proportion of Adults Spending Holidays Away from Home: by Sex, Age and Social Class(a) 1947, Great Britain (percentages)

	All ages	16–24	25–34	35–44	45–64	64+
MEN						
Class AB	76·1	66	80	62	76	71
C	64·9	58	69	71	65	54
DE	50·5	50	51	55	50	41
All men	55·8	53	55	61	57	46
WOMEN						
Class AB	74·9	83	83	85	73	60
C	70·1	81	74	71	69	59
DE	51·1	60	54	50	52	37
All women	57·0	65	59	58	58	43
Total men and women	56·4	60	57	59	59	44

Note: (a) The social class categories are here defined as
   A = Higher managerial or professional.
   B = Lower managerial or administrative.
   C = Lower non-manual workers and skilled manual workers.
   D = Unskilled manual workers.
   E = Residual, state pensioners.
   For a detailed discussion of social class classification see M. Kahan, D. Butler and D. Stokes, 'On the analytical division of social class', *Brit. J. Sociol.*, XVII, no. 2 (June 1966), pp. 122–32.
Source: Hulton Press, *Patterns of British Life* (1950).

TABLE 16.4

Proportion of Adults Spending Holidays Away from Home: by Sex and Social Class(a) 1948, Great Britain (Percentages)

	Men	Women	Total
Class AB	76·9	78·0	77·5
C	68·0	71·8	70·0
DE	53·5	53·3	53·4
Total	58·8	59·3	59·1

Note: (a) See Note to Table 16.3 on Classes.
Source: Hulton Press, *op. cit.*

TABLE 16.5

Proportion of the Population Spending Holidays Away from Home: by Sex and Domestic Status 1947, Great Britain (percentages)

	Total adult population	Men		Women	
		Head of household	Other	Housewives	Other
Holidays in Britain	53·0	54·1	49·2	51·0	60·7
Holidays abroad	3·3	2·4	4·8	3·0	4·9
No holidays	43·7	43·5	46·0	46·0	34·4

Note: Holiday is not defined.
Source: Hulton Press, *op. cit.*

TABLE 16.6

Estimated Number of Holidays in Given Years 1951–1967 by British Population (millions)

Years	In Britain	Abroad	Total
1951	25	1·5	26·5
1955	25	2·0	27
1961	30	4·0	34
1965	30	5·0	35
1967	30	5·0	35·5

Note: The information in the table is derived from regular sample surveys of British holidaymakers representing the adult population aged 16 and over. Holiday is defined as four nights or more spent away from home.
Source: British Travel Association, *Digest of Tourist Statistics* (1969).

TABLE 16.7

Proportion of Population Travelling Abroad from Great Britain: by Social Class, Education, Sex and Age 1963 (percentages)

	Ever	Within last 3 years
Social group(a) A	63	34
M	47	20
S	28	11
W	20	6
F	16	8
T.E.A. 15(b) or under	26	9
16–20	56	27
21 or over	87	49
Sex Male	37	15
Female	28	11
Age 21–29	43	23
30–39	34	11
40–54	28	11
55 and over	29	11

Notes:
(a) The social groups are here defined as follows (see also note to Table 16.3).
  A = Administrators and senior executives in business, industry and the professions.
  M = The broad middle class and self-employed artisans.
  S = Foremen and skilled workers.
  W = Other manual workers.
  F = Farmers and agricultural workers.
(b) Terminal education age.
Source: Reader's Digest, *Products and People* (1963).

TABLE 16.8

Number of New Passports Issued in Given Years 1921 to 1966, United Kingdom

Year	New passports issued
1921	255,539
1926	239,430
1931	206,891
1936	199,165
1940	5406
1946	428,117
1951	469,778
1956	581,455
1961	563,159
1966	980,799

Source: Passport Office.

TABLE 16.9

Proportion of Population with one or more Cars: by Sex and Social Class(a) 1949, Great Britain (percentages)

	All classes and ages	AB	C	DE
Men	13·1	46·8	21·2	5·6
Women	2·1	8·8	3·1	0·8
Total men and women	7·2	26·5	11·5	3·0

Note: (a) See note to Table 16.3 on Classes.
Source: Hulton Press, *op. cit.*

TABLE 16.10

Proportion of Households and Persons in Those Households Owning Cars: by Social Class 1966, England and Wales (percentages)

Social class	With no car		With 1 car or more	
	Households	Persons	Households	Persons
Professional, managerial and intermediate non-manual	25·0	20·8	75·0	79·3
Junior non-manual and personal service	57·3	50·2	42·7	49·9
Skilled manual	51·3	49·3	48·7	50·6
Semi-skilled and unskilled manual	73·5	70·2	26·5	29·8
All classes	50·8	46·9	49·2	53·1

Note: Categories 12–17 shown in the census table consisting of workers on own account, farmers, agricultural workers, members of Armed Forces and 'Indefinite' have been omitted. Professional, managerial and intermediate corresponds approx. with Reg.-Gen. Social Classes I and II; junior non-manual and personal service, and skilled manual with Class III; semi-skilled manual with Class IV and unskilled manual Class V. The table is restricted to households of which at least one member was present on the census night.
Source: Based on Table 16, Sample Census 1966, *Housing Report.*

TABLE 16.11

Proportion of Households Having Cars: by Occupation, Income and Education 1965, Great Britain (percentages)

No. of cars in household	Total adults	Occupation			Family income					Education		
		Manual	*Executive*	*Other*	*£650*	*£650– £849*	*£850– £1119*	*£1200– £1294*	*£1950+*	*Secondary*	*Grammar*	*College or University*
None	55	60	14	49	89	73	57	38	21	63	36	20
One	39	36	69	45	10	26	42	56	55	34	55	57
Two	4	4	13	5	0	1	1	5	19	2	7	18
Three+	1	1	4	2	0	1	0	1	5	1	2	6

Note: See note to Table 16.2.   *Source:* University of Keele, *op. cit.*

TABLE 16.12

Television Licences Issued 1950 to 1968, Great Britain (thousands)

Year	T.V. Licences
1950	382·3
1955	4,651·0
1960	10,554·2
1965	13,516
1968	15,506

TABLE 16.13

Growth of Television Reception 1947–1964, United Kingdom (percentages)

Year	Propn. of adult popn. with T.V. set in home
1947	0·2
1950	4·3
1955	39·8
1960	81·8
1964	90·8

Source: William A. Belson, *The Impact of Television* (Crosby Lockwood 1967), p. 213.

Sources: John Spraos, *The Decline of the Cinema* (Allen & Unwin 1962). Central Statistical Office, *Monthly Digest of Statistics* no. 293, May 1970.

TABLE 16.14

**Proportion of Leisure Time Spent on Different Activities 1969,
England and Wales (percentages)**

Activity	All males	All females
Television	23	23
Reading	5	9
Crafts and hobbies	4	17
Decorating and house maintenance	8	1
Gardening	12	7
Social activities	3	9
Drinking	3	1
Cinema and theatre	1	1
Non-physical games and misc. club activities	5	4
Physical recreation		
participants	11	4
spectators	3	1
Excursions	7	7
Parks, visits, walks	5	5
Anything else	7	7
No answer or don't know	3	4

Source: Government Social Survey, *Planning for Leisure* (HMSO 1969).

TABLE 16.15

Family or Home-Centred and Other Activities: the Proportion of the Population Engaged in Different Activities at 8.30–9 p.m.: by Sex, Age, Class, Education and Occupation 1961, Great Britain (percentages)

	Not at home				At home						
	At work	Friends, cinema, sports, classes	Other activs.	No informn.	Meals	H'sehold duties	Misc.(a)	No informn.	Radio	TV	In bed
All adults Sat	1	19	2	10	1	1	11	3	4	42	1
Sun	1	17	1	8	2	1	14	3	4	48	—
W'day	4	13	1	6	2	4	19	4	4	38	1
All men Sat	2	19	2	11	1	—	7	3	3	47	1
Sun	2	19	1	10	2	—	10	2	4	47	1
W'day	7	14	2	6	2	1	16	4	4	40	1
All women Sat	1	18	2	9	1	2	14	3	4	39	1
Sun	—	16	—	6	3	3	15	4	5	47	—
W'day	2	12	1	5	3	6	21	5	4	36	1
Age 15–24 Sat	1	40	2	13	1	1	5	2	2	26	—
Sun	1	33	1	9	2	1	15	3	1	34	1
W'day	3	27	2	9	2	2	11	3	3	30	1
Age 25–44 Sat	1	17	3	9	1	2	11	2	3	45	1
Sun	2	15	—	7	2	2	16	3	3	49	—
W'day	5	13	1	4	3	2	21	3	2	39	1
Age 45–64 Sat	2	5	1	10	1	2	9	5	3	46	1
Sun	1	13	1	8	2	1	11	4	5	52	—
W'day	4	11	1	6	2	3	18	6	4	40	1

Table 16.15 continued

		Not at home			At home						
	At work	Friends, cinema, sports, classes	Other activs.	No informn.	Meals	H'sehold duties	Misc.(a)	No informn.	Radio	TV	In bed
Age 65+ { Sat	1	10	1	8	2	1	13	6	10	41	2
Sun	—	10	—	5	6	2	14	5	8	46	2
W'day	1	9	—	5	3	2	17	7	11	39	1
U.M.	—	15	7	6	2	2	9	5	3	45	—
Sat(b) { L.M.	2	20	1	8	2	1	12	3	5	41	1
W.C.	1	18	2	11	1	2	9	3	3	43	1
Sat { T.E.A. 14	1	14	2	11	1	2	10	4	3	45	1
(c) { T.E.A. 17+	1	20	3	5	1	2	13	3	4	44	1
Prof.	1	21	4	6	1	1	12	3	5	41	—
Sat { skilled	1	19	1	10	1	1	11	4	4	42	1
Semi- and unskilled	1	18	2	12	2	2	8	3	2	42	1

Note:
(a) Reading, writing, sewing, knitting, looking after children, resting, entertaining, paid work at home, etc.
(b) Approximate classification: upper middle, lower middle, working classes.
(c) Terminal education age.
Source: BBC, *The People's Activities* (1965).

TABLE 16.16

Estimated Average TV(a) Audiences 1952 to 1968, Great Britain (percentages)

Year	Evening(b) audience (% population 16+)
1952	5.8
1955	13.7
	(% population 5+)
1960	28.7
1965	32.6
1968	32.9

Notes:

(a) Figures refer to ITV and BBC viewers.

(b) Before 1957 times of evening TV varied. After 1957 the period covered is 6 p.m. to 11 p.m.

Source: B.B.C. Audience Research Department.

TABLE 16.17

Frequency of ITV Viewing; by Age, Sex and Social Class 1960–1961 and 1968, Great Britain (percentages)

Frequency of ITV viewing	Total		Age										Social class(a)							
			16–24		25–34		35–44		45–64(b)		65+		AB		C1		C2		DE	
	1960–61	1968	1960–61	1968	1960–61	1968	1960–61	1968	1960–61	1968	1960–61	1968	1960–61	1968	1960–61	1968	1960–61	1968	1960–61	1968
Men																				
Regularly(c)	67	56	69	55	71	55	72	53	72	—	67	60	49	28	63	47	75	61	65	66
Occasionally(a)	22	36	25	39	23	37	23	41	19	—	21	22	35	60	26	43	17	33	21	24
Never	11	9	6	7	6	8	6	6	9	—	12	17	17	11	12	9	8	6	14	10
Women																				
Regularly	64	60	66	58	73	64	71	61	65	—	44	58	47	39	60	51	75	68	61	67
Occasionally	22	39	27	33	19	39	18	32	21	—	27	20	33	49	26	37	16	25	22	18
Never	14	11	7	9	8	8	11	6	14	—	29	23	19	12	14	12	9	5	17	4
All adults																				
Regularly	65	58	68	56	72	59	72	57	66	—	46	59	48	34	61	49	75	65	63	66
Occasionally	22	32	26	37	21	37	19	37	21	—	26	20	34	54	26	40	17	30	22	21
Never	13	10	7	8	7	6	10	6	13	—	29	21	18	12	13	11	8	6	16	12

Notes: In 1968 a fourfold classification of viewing habits was used – heavy, medium, light, and never. The heavy and medium figures have been combined to give groupings comparable with those used in 1961.

(a) For the definition of the social classes used in I.P.A. surveys see note to Table 16.27.
(b) Figures for this age group are not available for 1968.
(c) For 1961 'regularly' means 3 or more days a week.
Sources: As for Table 16.22.

TABLE 16.18

Estimated Admissions and Gross Takings for Taxable Entertainments 1952, Great Britain

Entertainment	Admissions (million)	Gross takings (£ million)
Cinema	1204	106·5
Theatres + music halls	83	18·7
Football	81	8·2
Cricket	4	0·4
Horse racing	6	3·4
Dog racing	25	2·9
Other racing sport	19	2·7
Other entertainment	36	4·0
All	1485	146.8

Source: H. E. Browning and A. A. Sorrell, 'Cinemas and Cinema-going in Great Britain', *J. Roy. Statist. Soc.*, series A (1954), 117.

TABLE 16.19

Number of Cinemas Open and Seating Capacity for Selected Years 1914–1966, Great Britain

Year	Cinemas open	Seating capacity (millions)
1914	3500	—
1926	3000	—
1934	4305	3·8
1939	4800	—
1941	4618	4·2
1951	4597	4·2
1956	4349	4·0
1958	3892	3·8
1960	3080	—
1962	2421	2·4
1964	2057	2·1(a)
1966	1847	1·8

Note: (a) Average capacity filled 20·4 per cent. Similar estimates are not available for other years.
Sources: Board of Trade *Journals*. P.E.P., *The British Film Industry* (1952) and *The British Film Industry* (1958). H. E. Browning and A. A. Sorrell, *loc. cit.*

TABLE 16.20

Cinema Admissions and Gross Door Takings for Selected Years 1934–1966, Great Britain

Year	Admissions (million)	Gross takings (£ million)	Net takings(a) (£ million)
1934	903	38·8	32·4
1938	987	41·5	36·0
1940	1027	44·9	38·2
1942	1494	87·2	64·0
1944	1575	111·8	72·0
1946	1635	118·3	75·9
1948	1514	108·8	70·0
1950	1396	105·2	68·0
1952	1312	109·9	68·9
1954	1276	110·0	71·4
1956	1101	104·2	67·6
1958	755	83·4	63·9
1960	515	64·3	58·2
1962	395	56·9	—
1964	343	57·5	35·1
1966	289	59·4	—

Note: (a) Gross takings less entertainment duty and payments to the British Film Production Fund.
Sources: H. E. Browning and A. A. Sorrell, *loc. cit.* (1934–52). Board of Trade *Journals* (1952–66).

TABLE 16.21

Sample Estimates of Frequency of Adult Cinema Going: by Social Class 1950–1960, Great Britain

Class	1950	1955(a)		1959/60			
	Visits per head of population per week			Regularly(b)	Occasionally(b)	Infrequently(b)	Never
				%	%	%	%
AB	0·42	0·25		7	12	39	42
			C₁	10	13	32	45
C	0·49	0·37	C₂	14	10	26	50
DE	0·56	0·54		16	7	19	58

Notes:
(a) Not comparable with earlier years because adjusted to compensate for under-estimate of cinema going which is evident in comparing Hulton Surveys with Board of Trade figures.
(b) 'Regularly' means once a week or more.
    'Occasionally' means less than once a week to once a month.
    'Infrequently' means less than once a month.
Source: John Spraos, *The Decline of the Cinema* (Allen & Unwin 1962), based on Hulton *Readership Survey* and I.P.A. *National Readership Survey.*

TABLE 16.22

Frequency of Cinema Attendance: by Age, Sex and Social Class 1960–1961 and 1968, Great Britain (percentages)

Frequency of attendance	Total		Age										Social class (c)							
			16–24		25–34		35–44		45–64		65+		AB		C$_1$		C$_2$		DE	
	1960–61	1968	1960–61	1968	1960–61	1968	1960–61	1968	1960–61	1968	1960–61	1968	1960–61	1968	1960–61	1968	1960–61	1968	1960–61	1968
ALL ADULTS																				
Regularly(a)	11	5	41	18	10	5	6	2	4	—	4	2	7	4	10	5	12	6	12	5
Occasionally(a)	10	12	25	38	14	16	7	9	5	—	2	2	13	16	12	15	10	12	7	9
Infrequently(a)	27	36	23	34	36	51	35	49	26	—	14	17	37	49	31	43	28	38	21	26
Never	52	46	10	10	39	27	53	41	64	—	79	80	43	31	48	37	50	43	60	59
MEN																				
Regularly	13	6	46	20	13	7	6	2	4	—	3	2	9	4	11	5	13	7	14	7
Occasionally	11	14	25	39	17	19	8	10	5	—	2	2	14	17	11	17	11	13	9	11
Infrequently	26	35	21	31	34	48	34	48	25	—	12	14	35	48	29	41	28	37	19	25
Never	51	45	8	9	35	27	51	40	66	—	83	82	42	31	49	37	49	44	58	56
WOMEN																				
Regularly	10	3	37	16	7	4	5	2	5	—	4	2	5	4	9	4	11	5	10	4
Occasionally	9	11	25	36	11	14	7	8	5	—	3	2	11	15	12	14	9	12	6	8
Infrequently	28	37	26	37	39	54	35	49	27	—	16	18	40	50	32	45	29	41	22	27
Never	53	47	12	11	43	28	54	41	63	—	77	79	44	32	47	37	51	43	61	62

Notes:
(a) 'Regularly' means once a week or more, 'occasionally' means once a month or more and 'infrequently' means less than once a month.
(b) Figures for this age group not available for 1968.
(c) For definition of social class used in I.P.A. surveys see note to Table 16.27.
Sources: Institute of Practitioners in Advertising, *National Readership Survey* (1961), Supplementary Tables. *National Readership Survey* (1968), vol. 3.

TABLE 16.23

Participation in Various Sporting Clubs and Activities, 1920–1967, Great Britain

	Angling Circn. of Angling Times	Angling Licences issued by all river auths.	Camping club members in G.B. and N. Ireland	Canoeing Clubs affiliated to British Canoe Union	Cricket Attendances Lords (000's)	Cricket Attendances County matches (000's)	Cycling Cyclist Touring Club Members	Fencing Members Amateur Fencing Assoc.
1940	—	—	—	—	—	—	(1939) 36,609	—
1945	—	—	—	—	—	—		—
1950	—	—	12,000	(1948) 12	317,783	1979	53,574	767
1955	90,445	661,000	21,437	28 (1961)	374,145	1640	40,752	1566
1960	136,382	977,000	51,800 (1968)	124	197,510 (1965)	1046	25,786 (1963)	2263 (1964)
1967	138,825	967,000	111,610	349	287,327	101	22,000	3408

Table 16.23 continued

	Association Football Attendance at League matches (England & Wales) (000's)	British Gliding Association Number of		Lawn Tennis Association Associated clubs	Table Tennis Estimated club members	Rambling Y.H.A.		
		Gliders	Flying hours			Members	Hostels	Beds
1920	—	—	—	(1922) 423	—	—	—	—
1925	—	—	—	—	—	—	—	—
1930				(1932) 2275	10,000	6439	(1931) 73	1562
1935	—	—	—	(1935) 2874				
1940	—	—	—	—	75,000	50,864	236	8267
1945	(1949)	(1946) 66	1667	—	—	—	—	—
1950	41,271 (1954)	121	7560	2741	130,000	210,142	303	13,971
1955	36,175 (1959)	(1954) 155	11,726	—	—	—	—	—
1960	33,611 (1966)	(1964) 389	33,121	(1968) 3730	(1966) 170,000	(1968) 181,958	(1968) 270	13,385
1967	27,200	(1968) 562	53,955	2991	200,000	217,842	263	13,320

Table 16.23 continued

	Rugby Union Clubs	Yachting Members Royal Yachting Association	Sailing & Boating on Broads Licences issued	Bowling Clubs	Bowling Entries for National Championships	Badminton Clubs
1920	—	—	—	—	—	—
1925	—	—	—	—	—	—
1930	—	—	—	966	(1929) 12,485	—
1935	909	—	—	—	—	—
1940	—	—	—	1815	(1930) 23,384	(1939) 1312
1945	—	(1946) 273	(1947) 3400	—	—	(1947) 1682
1950	(1951) 757	1387	—	2117	49,096	—
1955	—	10,543	(1957) 6318	—	—	—
1960	(1961) 959	—	7178	2470	59,521	1958(a) 3000
1965	(1968) 1634	(1968) 26,327	9701	2631	(1966) 67,152	(1968) 2600

Note: (a) Approximate figures.
Source: The Sports Council, 'Trends in Sport' (unpublished document).

TABLE 16.24

Public Library Service 1896–1968, Great Britain and Northern Ireland

Year	No. of library authorities	No. of source points	No. of (c) registered borrowers (000)	No. of books in stock (000)	No. of (c) book issues (000)	Total expenditure (£000)	Total book expenditure (£000)	Expenditure on books per head	Population served (million)
1896	—	480	823	4450	26,225	286	—	—	7 (1884)
1900	352	—	—	—	—	—	—	—	—
1911	—	920	—	10,874	54,256	805	—	—	25·7 (1914)
1920	551	—	9% of pop. served	—	—	—	—	—	—
1924	—	5730	2683	14,784	85,668	1398	—	—	—
1932	—	15,000	—	—	—	—	—	—	—
1935	—	—	7142	26,776(a)	207,982(a)	2,441	—	—	—
1939	—	18,000	8937	32,549(a)	247,335(a)	3178	—	—	—
1940	601	—	—	—	—	—	—	—	—
1947	545	—	—	56,056	285,007	5647	1305	6½d.	47·2
1953	—	30,902	—	—	359,700	11,183	2869	under 6d to over 2s	50·4
1957	597	32,160(d)	13,933	66,216	419,428	15,906	3863	1s 6d national average	51·2
1962	—	40,000(e)	28% of pop. served	77,200	460,504	24,431	6048	2s 3d national average	—
1968	454	—	—	101,072	—	45,477(b)	10,750	—	54·7

Notes: The figures in the table are not complete; they are based on questionnaires sent out by the Library Association and not all libraries responded or responded fully. Nor is it known exactly how many failed to reply for each year. The coverage of the library service was almost complete by the 1940s, though a few areas remained unserved until the 1960s. Before 1919 all provision was urban; no counties had library powers.   (a) These figures include an unstated number of reference issues. In later years reference issues were totalled separately; during 1956/7 there were roughly 9½ million, though the figures are not given for succeeding years.

(b) This figure excludes the cost of the public library service for schools which appears to be included in the total for the earlier years.

(c) These statistics are not being currently collected. The Library Association considers that duplication of use between different libraries and the different systems of record-keeping mean that such figures are unreliable criteria of the extent of the service.

(d) In addition there were 186 mobile libraries which were included in the total in earlier years.   (e) In addition 327 mobile libraries. W. G. S. Adams, *A Report on Library Provision and Policy* (Carnegie United Kingdom Trust 1915). Institute of Municipal Treasurers and Accountants, *Public Library Statistics*.

Sources: The Library Association, *A Century of Public Libraries 1850–1950* and *Statistics of Public Libraries in Great Britain and Northern Ireland.*

TABLE 16.25

Publishing Home Turnover (Sale of Books) for Selected Years 1939–1969 United Kingdom

Year	Book Sales
1939	7,167,059
1946	20,246,410
1950	25,764,432
1960	45,592,817
1964	55,263,571
1969	77,170,000

Note: Export turnover was in 1969 some £68 millions.
Source: Publishers Association.

TABLE 16.26

Books Published in Selective Years 1928 to 1969, United Kingdom

Year	Total including fiction	Fiction
1928	13,981	3503
1931	14,876	4259
1939	14,904	4222
1951	18,066	3871
1961	24,893	4485
1969	32,393	4405

Source: Whitaker's *Cumulative Book List* (J. Whitaker & Sons), first published 1924.

TABLE 16.27

Readership of Newspapers and Periodicals: by Sex, Age and Social Class 1950 and 1967, Great Britain (percentages)

Newspaper or periodical	Age										Social class							
	16-24		25-44	25-34	35-44	45-64	45-54	55-64	65+		AB		C	$C_1 C_2$	DE		All	
	1950	1967	1950	1967	1967	1950	1967	1967	1950	1967	1950	1967	1950	1967	1950	1967	1950	1967
WOMEN																		
Daily Mirror	39·3	45	33·1	38	36	21·8	36	30	12·8	22	11	9	20	24	32	40	28	34
Daily Express	23·4	20	24·5	20	24	26·3	28	27	21·9	24	26	26	28	29	23	21	25	24
Daily Telegraph	3·3	7	5·3	8	7	8·2	8	9	10·5	7	23	26	11	13	3	2	7	8
News of the World	53·1	45	52·2	37	37	45·7	38	39	34·6	33	23	13	37	24	55	47	48	38
Sunday Express	16·1	21	19·4	22	26	21·3	29	29	19·3	26	35	47	29	37	15	16	19	25
Sunday Times	2·0	10	4·1	12	12	5·1	11	8	7·1	5	20	30	6	14	2	3	5	9
Observer	2·7	6	3·8	7	8	4·7	6	5	4·9	3	9	19	5	10	3	2	4	6
Women's Own	38·4	47	23·5	39	34	17·3	35	32	12·5	26	20	31	24	36	22	32	22	35
Good Housekeeping	6·0	7	7·6	9	10	8·6	12	10	6·6	6	17	20	11	12	5	5	7	9
Ideal Home	5·1	11	4·8	10	11	3·6	8	8	2·0	5	9	19	5	10	3	5	4	9
Vogue	9·2	17	7·6	10	11	5·2	10	8	3·3	4	17	18	9	12	4	6	7	10
MEN																		
Daily Mirror	38	57	33	51	44	21	44	33	14	27	13	13	21	32	32	50	28	44
Daily Express	28	27	34	32	34	32	33	36	26	29	35	32	37	38	31	27	32	32
Daily Telegraph	3	9	6	10	11	7	10	7	9	8	23	33	10	14	3	3	6	9
News of the World	55	48	57	45	41	52	44	46	45	39	28	17	41	30	61	53	54	44
Sunday Express	20	26	23	24	30	23	28	30	21	27	43	50	30	38	17	17	22	27
Sunday Times	3	13	3	12	12	5	12	9	6	7	17	35	6	18	1	3	4	11
Observer	3	8	3	6	8	4	6	4	4	4	12	18	7	11	1	2	3	6

Note: The several class categories used were slightly different at the two periods. Each distinguishes 5 classes according to the occupation of the head of the household, but the IPA survey divides class C into two. Both surveys tend to group classes A & B and D & E together in their analyses and in fact the similarity of the groupings at the different dates seemed to permit the comparisons we have made.

TABLE 16.27 continued

The two systems of classification are as follows:

The Hulton Survey

Class	Status	Brief Definition
A	Well-to-do	Successful business or professional man, senior civil servant, considerable private means.
B	Middle class	Younger man who will probably move into A.
C	Lower middle class	Highly skilled workers, small tradespeople, high clerical grades.
D	Working class	Manual workers and clerical workers in less responsible positions.
E	The poor	Pensioners and those unable to reach higher grades through sickness, unemployment, or lack of opportunity.

The IPA Survey

Social Grade	Social Status	Occupation
A	Upper middle class	Higher managerial, administrative, professional.
B	Middle class	Intermediate managerial, administrative, professional.
C_1	Lower middle class	Supervisory, clerical and junior administrative, managerial and professional.
C_2	Skilled working class	Skilled manual workers.
D	Working class	Semi- and unskilled manual workers.
E	Those at lowest levels of subsistence	State pensioners or widows, casual or lowest grade workers.

Sources: Hulton Press, *Hulton Readership Survey* (1956). Institute of Practitioners in Advertising, *National Readership Surveys* (1967).

TABLE 16.28

Membership of Certain Youth Organisations 1900 to 1968

	Boys' Brigade(a)	Girls' Brigade(b)	Scouts(a)	Girl Guides(a)	Y.W.C.A.(c)	C. of E. Youth Groups(d)	Catholic Youth Service(b)	Methodist Assoc. of Youth Groups(b)	Baptist Youth Organisn.(c)
1900	41,096	— (1912)	—	—	—	—	—	—	—
1910	61,660	3414 (1922)	106,937	—	—	—	—	—	—
1920	57,582	15,710 (1931)	324,707	183,533	— (1933)	—	—	—	—
1930	121,424	38,084 (1939)	438,098	560,654 (1941)	34,636 (1944)	—	—	—	—
1940	112,531	35,985 (1949)	343,000	400,236	44,178 [19,954] (1954)	—	—	100,000	—
1950	144,993	63,965	471,467	434,459	28,287 [10,129] (1964)	—	—	100,000	—
1960	160,610	64,192	588,396	594,491	28,584 [17,790]	—	—	115,000 (1962)	52,979 (1962)
1968	148,112	59,334	530,919	694,507	29,485 [12,608]	394,340 (1967)	62,298	121,324 (1967)	52,848

Table 16.28 continued

	Army Cadet Force(a)	Combined Cadet Force(a)	A.T.C.	Sea Cadets	National Federation of 18+ Groups(b)	National Association of Youth Clubs (a)	Young Farmers Clubs
1930	—	—	—	—	—	(1934) 34,114	(1928) 500
1940	(1939) 50,000	—	144,000	(1939) 10,000	(1943) 350	(1942) 56,622	(1939) 15,000
1950	(1942) 205,000	(1948) 76,000	—	(1958) 17,109	(1949) 391	152,705	(1949) 67,200
1960	(1957) 52,600	—	31,300	14,299	(1961) 675	170,398	
1968	(1967) 42,123	(1967) 50,540	32,112	14,591	7334	281,996	(1967) 43,746

Notes:

(a) Figures for U.K.
(b) Figures for England and Wales.
(c) Figures for Great Britain.
(d) Figures for England.
[   ] numbers under 21 years of age.

Sources: The relevant voluntary organisations; G. P. Hirsh, *Young Farmers Clubs* (duplicated (N.F.Y.F.C. 1952)).

TABLE 16.29

L.E.A. Youth Work Activity 1957/8 and 1967/8, England and Wales

	Estimated population in Youth Service age range	Centres fully maintained by L.E.A.	Officers employed by L.E.A.				Officers aided by L.E.A.	No. youth groups assisted financially by L.E.A.	Expenditure per head of popn. in Youth Service age range
					Youth Leaders				
			Youth Officer Organiser		Full Time	Part Time			
1957/8	3,507,075	1220	351		221	4692	466	7828	0·74
1967/8	4,934,680	2028	662¾		932	10,107	707	16,609	2·03

Source: Department of Education and Science, *Youth and Community Work in the 70s* (HMSO 1969), Appendix 2.

TABLE 16.30

Growth of Adult Education(b) 1907 to 1967, England and Wales

Year (educational)	No. of classes	Registered students	Full-time tutors	Government grants to responsible bodies(a)			
				University extra-mural	W.E.A.	Other	Total
				£	£	£	£
1907–8	2	78	—	—	—	—	—
1911	72	1829	—	—	—	—	—
1913–14	219	—	—	—	—	—	3993
1921	599	17,477	—	—	—	—	—
1923	682	—	—	—	—	—	18,240
1930–1	2118	41,290	—	49,305	12,208	2212	63,725
1937–8	3004	56,712	33	69,485	15,577	3941	89,003
1945–6	5050	99,333	112	102,681	35,280	2193	140,154
1951	8090	162,850	258	258,340	63,580	4828	326,748
1961	8288	164,148	—	—	—	—	712,000
1967	10,615	236,330	—	—	—	—	1,071,000

Notes:
(a) Adult education was already established before 1907 on a voluntary basis by the University Extension Movement and others, including the YMCA. The Workers' Educational Association was founded in 1903. From 1890 some local authorities had begun to make grants towards adult education.
(b) Excluding vacation and residential courses.
Sources: Ministry of Education, *The Organisation and Finance of Adult Education in England and Wales* (HMSO 1954); *Statistics of Education*, 1961, pt 2; *Statistics of Education*, 1967, vol. 3: *Further Education*; *Report* of Board of Education, 1921–2; *Report* of Board of Education, 1938 and *Statistics of Public Education*; *Report* of Board of Education 1931 and *Statistics of Public Education*.

TABLE 16.31

Students Taking Courses of Adult Education Provided by Responsible Bodies(a) 1931 to 1967, Great Britain

Type of Course(b)	1931		1938		1951		1961		1967	
	Men	Women	Men	Women	Men	Women	Men	Women	Men	Women
Literature & languages	4600	8432	3548	6547	7277	13,526	6852	13,315	9799	19,233
History	1764	1552	5204	3722	11,829	14,183	9798	15,341	18,415	28,414
Geography	8705	4161	713	578	2022	1943	1318	1557	2199	2617
Social studies			12,077	6382	23,473	20,241	15,214	14,328	27,564	17,571
Natural sciences and maths.	1564	1325	2556	1999	7946	5626	8588	7522	14,437	11,849
Music and visual arts	1144	2032	1696	2634	9553	15,561	10,019	19,908	12,556	25,972
Philosophy and psychology	2846	3165	4382	4674	5811	8110	4425	5286	5240	8834
Other			—	—	8236	7513	13,369	17,308	14,735	16,895
Total	20,623	20,667	30,176	26,536	76,147	86,703	69,583	94,565	104,945	131,385

Notes:

(a) Responsible bodies include University Extra Mural Departments, The Workers' Educational Association and others.

(b) Figures exclude students on residential courses. Subjects have been grouped to correspond roughly with those used in 1938. Literature and language includes English, ancient, modern, and Welsh languages, literature and culture. History includes historical subjects and archaeology. Social studies includes political science, economics, industrial organisation, sociology. Natural Science includes physical and biological science and mathematics. Unclassified includes International and Commonwealth Affairs, Religion, Law and unclassified courses.

Sources: Board of Education Annual Reports and Statistics of Public Education for 1931 and 1938; Report of Ministry of Education and Statistics of Education, 1951; Statistics of Education, 1961, pt. 2, and Statistics of Education, 1967, vol. 3.

TABLE 16.32

Vacation and Residential Courses Held by 'Responsible Bodies' and L.E.A. and Direct Grant Colleges 1931 to 1967, England and Wales

Year	Vacation courses(a)				Residential colleges(b)			
		No. of students				No. of students		
	No.	Men	Women	Total	No.	Men	Women	Total
1931	12	870	484	1354	5	103	29	132
1937/8	13	955	637	1592	5	88	49	137
1951	38	1526	1043	2569	5	186	86	272
		Residential courses				Residential colleges and centres of adult education		
1961	528	8428	6822	15,250	34	22,729	23,824	46,553
1967/8	662	10,742	7724	18,466	34	30,323	29,058	59,381

Notes:

(a) Held by 'responsible bodies', i.e. university extra-mural departments, Workers' Educational Association and the Welsh National Council of the Y.M.C.A.

(b) Held in colleges and conference centres maintained by L.E.A.s and by organisations assisted by direct grant not including courses held by 'responsible bodies'.

Sources: Board of Education, *Annual Reports* and *Statistics of Public Education*. Ministry of Education, *Statistics of Education*.

TABLE 16.33

Adult Education – Income and Expenditure of Responsible Bodies 1960/1 and 1967/8, England and Wales (£ thousands)

	1960/61	*1967/68*
Total Expenditure	1332	2527
Total Income	1322	2511
Comprising:		
Students fees	85	181
Grants from Department of Education and Science	650	1145
Local Authorities	128	217
Universities	345	665
Workers Educational Association	28	67
Other sources	86	236

Source: Statistics of Education, 1968, vol. 5; *Finance and Awards*.

Index